Evaluation Guide for *Focus on Physical Science*

FOCUS ON PHYSICAL SCIENCE discusses modern principles and concepts of physical science in a language suited to the abilities of the student. To strengthen the presentation of textual material and to increase student understanding and interest in physical science, the authors have included many *special features*.

To examine selected examples of the format and outstanding features of FOCUS ON PHYSICAL SCIENCE, please turn to the following pages:

FOCUS ON
PHYSICAL SCIENCE
SECOND EDITION

TEACHER'S Annotated EDITION and Solutions Manual including Behavioral Objectives

Charles H. Heimler

California State University
Northridge, California

Jack Price

San Diego City Schools
San Diego, California

Behavioral Objectives revised from
BEHAVIORAL OBJECTIVES for FOCUS ON PHYSICAL SCIENCE

Arthur L. Costa and James A. Livingston

Sacramento State College
Sacramento, California

CHARLES E. MERRILL PUBLISHING CO.
A Bell & Howell Company
Columbus, Ohio

Introduction

Text Design

Focus on Physical Science is designed in seven units. The units are divided into 22 chapters with each chapter divided into numbered sections. The units organize the text into major areas of study. The chapters and sections subdivide the units into specific topics for study. These divisions and subdivisions serve in planning lessons and assigning classwork and homework. In addition, they provide for flexibility and adaption to local school and individual classroom needs.

The organization of each chapter into Sections, Problems, Experiments, Activities, Main Ideas, Study Questions, Investigations, and Interesting Reading makes the text particularly useful in situations where flexible scheduling and modules of instruction are employed.

Questions in the Margins

Questions in the margins help the student identify major principles and concepts. They also serve as a guide to reading and study. In assigning a section for study, you may wish to first read these questions to the class. Or, have students read them silently to clarify the nature and purpose of the assignment.

Questions in the margins provide motivation as well as an opportunity for the student to check his learning as he proceeds through the assignment. Oral review of the questions following each assignment makes an excellent summary and will help you identify points which may require additional explanation.

Vocabulary

Definitions of scientific words and terms are incorporated where they first occur. New scientific words and terms appear in boldface type or italic type. Phonetic pronunciations of new scientific words appear directly after the words are introduced. Definitions and pronunciations are repeated in the glossary.

Problems, Experiments, and Activities

Problems are inserted as a quick review of newly learned concepts. Students should solve each problem on an individual basis. Solutions may then be demonstrated and discussed. This will clarify concepts and guard against vague acceptance of statements without definite application of new ideas.

Experiments and activities are designed to introduce and clarify new concepts and to teach laboratory techniques. Many of the experiments provide

ISBN 0-675-07511-4

Published by
CHARLES E. MERRILL PUBLISHING CO.
A Bell & Howell Company
Columbus, Ohio 43216

for the use and development of prob-lem-solving skills. Experiments and activities are presented where they apply rather than in a separate laboratory manual.

By scanning the procedure for an experiment, you may easily determine the materials required. It is good practice to make note of needed new or replacement materials. Planning lessons in advance allows time for the collection of needed equipment and materials for experiments and demonstrations. Materials required are inexpensive and readily available. Lists of necessary equipment for individual chapters precede the discussion of each chapter in the Teacher's Guide. A complete list of equipment needed for all activities and experiments in the book appears on pp. 5-10.

Students should perform experiments and activities individually or in small groups. A few experiments are specially suited to demonstrations. These should be done by an able student unless otherwise directed in the text. Show students how to record experiments and demonstrations in their notebooks. One method is to organize the experiment under these headings: Problem, Procedure, Observations, Conclusions. When the experiment is carried out by the teacher or a few students at the lecture-demonstration table, you may wish to develop a statement of the problem through class discussion. The procedure for the experiment may be stated for the students. Allow each student to record his own observations and conclusions.

Emphasis should be placed on student participation and involvement. Although laboratory situations are desirable, they are not mandatory. Many of the experiments can be done in the classroom. Each experiment or activity teaches an important concept without elaborate equipment. The laboratory segments are effective without being overwhelming or time-consuming.

Safety

Demonstrate general safety procedures for laboratory work at the beginning of each semester. These procedures should be reviewed at frequent intervals. Require that all students wear safety glasses when conducting activities or experiments. Specific safety precautions necessary for individual experiments are given in the student's text and the teacher's annotations. Note these precautions and explain them to the students. Student laboratory work must always be supervised. Encourage the student to develop a serious attitude toward laboratory methods.

Figures and Tables

Photographs, drawings, graphs, and tables aid in clarifying scientific principles and concepts. Each activity and experiment is accompanied by an illustration of the procedure and equipment to be employed. Photographs and drawings help the student to visualize scientific principles and concepts. They also show practical applications of scientific principles. You may wish to review and analyze a figure and its caption as a means of introducing a new topic or stimulating class discussion. Graphs and tables show how data is organized in a meaningful way.

Chapter End Material

The five sections at the end of each chapter include: Main Ideas, Vocabulary, Study Questions, Investigations, and Interesting Reading. Main Ideas summarize major principles and concepts and serve as a quick review of material presented in the chapter. Discussion of the Main Ideas in class provides a good chapter summary. Ask the students to identify two or three examples or illustrations for each principle or concept listed under Main Ideas. Use the Vocabulary to emphasize concepts and to review students' use of new words. The Study Questions may be used for student self-study, review, or testing. Correcting wrong answers to the Study Questions is an effective learning technique.

Investigations and Interesting Readings gives an "open-ended" aspect to each chapter and further enhances the flexibility of *Focus on Physical Science.* Investigations extend beyond the textbook presentations and encourage the student to develop his knowledge and interest in science. Particular investigations are valuable as projects for science fairs. Interesting Readings include books and articles correlated with topics in the text. These supplementary readings offer opportunities for students having special interests to find suitable references in science topics.

Mathematics

Selected mathematics concepts from the junior high school curriculum are integrated into the text. This integration provides meaningful illustrations of practical applications of mathematics in science. It also makes mathematics more relevant and interesting for the student. Also, the use of selected mathematics concepts in science reinforces learning.

Calculations for working each kind of physical science problem are presented in step-by-step detail. To provide for individual differences, the problems following each explanation vary in difficulty. You may choose to use only easy problems with students who have less skill in mathematics.

All problems dealing with chemical composition and chemical change involve the concept of ratio or proportion. This topic is covered in the upper elementary and junior high school mathematics curriculum. In teaching quantitative chemical concepts, you may wish to review ratio and proportion. Point out to students the frequency with which this type of calculation is used in chemical change problems.

Plan for the Course

Focus on Physical Science may be used in a full-year course of two semesters covering the text material, experiments, problems, and chapter-end material. Through the selection of specific units, chapters, and sections which conform to the local course of study, this text may be used in a one-semester physical science course.

Focus on Physical Science lends itself to a variety of teaching methods—activity-centered demonstration, group reading of text material, lecture, reporting on an experiment, class discussion of a science current event, reviewing a homework assignment, viewing a film or filmstrip. Different methods serve to reinforce each other and, thereby, may increase student achievement.

Focus on Physical Science is a one-year course in the fundamentals of physical science. However, the text is designed so that the material may be delimited to meet the needs of individual teachers and classes. Some examples are given below.

One-Semester Course in Physical Science

Unit	Chapter	Sections	Title
One	1	all	Introduction to Physical Science
Two	2	all	Classification of Matter
Three	3	all	Atoms and Compounds

	8	all	Solutions
Four	9	9:1-9:4	Conservation of Mass
	10	10:1-10:6	Acids, Bases, and Salts
Five	11	all	Forces and Work
	12	all	Moving Bodies
Six	14	14:1-14:3	Heat Energy
	16	16:1-16:3	Waves
	17	17:1-17:4	Optics
	18	all	Electricity

Two-Semester, One-Year Course in Physical Science

Semester I: Units One through Four
Semester II: Unit One (review), Units Five through Seven

As an alternate plan, Units 5 through 7 may be used for the first semester and Units 2 through 4 for the second semester. Unit 1 is a good introduction for the first semester of either plan.

Three-Quarter, One-Year Course in Physical Science

Quarter	Unit	Chapter	Title
I	One	1	Introduction to Physical Science
	Two	2	Classification of Matter
	Three	3	Periodic Table
		4	Atoms and Compounds
		5	Families of Elements
		6	Carbon and Its Compounds
II	Four	7	Solids and Fluids

	8	Solutions
	9	Conservation of Mass
	10	Acids, Bases, and Salts
Five	11	Force and Work
	12	Moving Bodies
	13	Laws of Motion
III Six	14	Heat Energy
	15	Heat and Its Uses
	16	Waves
	17	Optics
	18	Electricity
	19	Electronics
Seven	20	Radiation
	21	Nuclear Reactions
	22	Nuclear Technology

Laboratory Equipment

This list is complete for the entire course for your convenience in ordering equipment for the entire school year. The experiments are designed so that very simple apparatus can be used. Use materials that are available locally whenever possible.

Laboratory Equipment
Required for One Demonstration
of Each Experiment

Item	Quantity
aluminum foil	1 box
aluminum sheet, 2 mm thick	0.2 m²
ammeter, D.C., 0-5 amp	1
asbestos pad	2
aspirator	1
balance, beam	1
pan	1

ball, hollow rubber	1	Crooke's tube and high	
large (basketball for		voltage source	1
model)	1	crucible and cover	1
Ping-Pong	several	cup, china	1
small metal	1	paper	12
small rubber	1	styrofoam	12
iron with ring	1	deflagrating spoon	1
styrofoam for models	several	diffraction grating	several
balloons, various sizes	several	diodes and triodes, used	several
bath, ice	1	dowel, ¼ in.	several
beakers, 400ml	2	distilling flask	2
250 ml	6	dry cell, used	several
150 ml	6	battery 6 v	3
bimetallic strip (with		battery 1.5 v	6
wooden handle)	1	dye, vegetable (ink)	5 types
bottles, pint (glass with		electric bell	1
screwcap)	4	electric drill (to make holes	
quart	1	in wooden top of home-	
Bunsen burner	1	made calorimeter)	1
buret, 25 ml	1	electric hot plate	1
buret clamp	1	electrolysis apparatus	
calorimeter, laboratory		(Hoffman)	1
(styrofoam cups)	1	electroscope	1
candles	several	electrostatic machine (van	
cans, #2½, #1	1	de Graff generator)	1
same size and makeup	several	evaporating dish	3
card, playing or index	5	file, triangular	1
cardboard	several pieces	filter paper	1 pkg
mailing tubes (that will		fingerbowl	2
slide in each other)	3	flashlight (any light source)	1
shoebox	2	flask, distilling	2
cathode-ray tube or tele-		Erlenmeyer 500 ml	1
vision	1	400 ml	3
cellophane, red and blue	several pieces	250 ml	4
cement, rubber	1 bottle	funnel, glass	1
chalk	several pieces	galvanometer	1
clamp, tubing	2	Geiger counter	1
flask	4	glass, 8 oz tumbler	2
clay, modeling	1 pkg	block of, 0.5 to	
clock (to dismantle)	1	1.5 cm thick	1
coin	several	plate, 5 cm × 5 cm	6
collection bottles	4	prism, 60° × 60° × 60°	1
condenser coil	1	45° × 45° × 90°	1
corks, assorted sizes	several	glass rod, static	2
cotton, absorbent	1 pkg	stirring	1

glass slides, microscope	1 box	needle, knitting (metal)	1
glass wool	1 pkg	paint, black (black shoe	
graduated cylinder, 10 ml	2	polish)	1 small can
25 ml	2	pan, flat clear glass	2
50 ml	2	oblong metal	1
250 ml	2	paper, white	several sheets
graph paper, centimeter		colored	several sheets
ruled	100 sheets	paper towels	2 pkg
hacksaw blade	1	paper clips	1 pkg
hammer	1	pencil	2
hanger, wire	2	pins, straight	1 pkg
hydrometer, straw	1	plastic bags, various sizes	several
knife	1	plastic static rods (ebonite	
labels	1 pkg	rods)	2
lead sinker (or other small,	several	pneumatic trough	1
dense object)		polarizing filters (old sun-	
lens — convex	several	glasses)	2
concave, different focal		projector, overhead	1
lengths	several	protractor	1
light meter (or camera with		pulley, movable, double	
light meter)	1	sheave	1
litmus, red and blue	1 vial each	single sheave	3
magnets, of varying		radiation source (watch	
strength	several	with radium dial)	1
magnifying glass	1	razor blades, single edge	1 pkg
marbles, various sizes	30	resonator box	1
masking tape	1 roll	refrigerator	1
medicine dropper	4	rheostat or resistance box	1
metal, pieces of Al, Fe, Cu		ring stand and ring	2
of same mass	3	ring-stand clamps, assorted	
metal rods (with ball end		sizes	several
for making electroscope	2	rubber bands	1 pkg
meter stick (with English		rubber sheeting, 5 cm ×	
units)	2	5 cm	2 pieces
metronome (if available)	1	ruler, foot and metric	2
microlamp (electric bulb		safety apron	several
that can be connected to		safety glasses	several
circuit)	3	sandpaper, sheets	several
microscope, binocular	1	scale, bathroom	1
mirror, plane, small	2	scissors	1 pr
curved, metal	1	screwdriver, small, large	2
magnifying	1	screw eyes	several
mortar and pestle	1	silk cloth	1 piece
mouse traps	8	silk thread	1 spool
nail, iron, assorted sizes	several	sink (large, deep container)	1

slinky coil spring	1	tuning forks, assorted	
shot (steel ball bearings)	25	frequencies	several
solder, liquid or cold	1 tube	same frequency as	
spatula	2	resonator box	1
splints, wooden	1 pkg	tweezers	1
spring balance, 250 g	4	universal pH paper	1 box
2000 g	4	vacuum bottle, pint size	1
25 lb	1	vacuum pump	1
spring	2	voltmeter, D.C., 0-10v	1
steam boiler	1	washer, metal	several
steel wool	1 pkg	watch glass (large)	several
stone, small (mineral		weights, for balance	1 set
samples)	several	whistles (inexpensive)	2
stoppers, rubber 2-hole,		wire, fine iron	1 m
1-hole, no-hole, assorted		copper	10 m
sizes	several	insulated bell	10 m
straws, soda	1 pkg	wire gauze	1
string, strong cord	1 ball	wood, blocks of various	
switch	2	sizes	several
table	1	stick, 1 m	1
tape measure	1	plywood board, 60 cm²	1
test tubes, various sizes,		smooth plank	1
some Pyrex	3 doz	board, 15 cm × 4 cm	2
test tube brush	1	circular piece (top for	
test tube clamp	3	calorimeter)	1
test tube rack	2	wool cloth	1 piece
textile samples	several	zinc plate, 5 cm × 5 cm	1
thermometer, Celsius	4		
thermostat (from old gas			
hot water heater)	1		

wood, blocks of various stick, 1 m plywood board, 60 cm^2; zinc plate 5 cm × 5 cm.

Chemicals

The approximate amounts needed for four classes of students. Most chemicals are more economical to buy in larger lots rather than in the smaller amounts listed.

Item	Quantity
acetic acid, 99.5%	0.5 l
alcohol,	
ethyl, 95%	1 l
isopropyl	0.5 l
alum	250 g
aluminum potassium	
sulfate	250 g
ammonium chloride	125 g

Additional items from the left column:

thimble (or other small common object)	1
thread spools (to make pulleys)	6
timer (watch with second hand)	1
tongs, metal	1
toothpicks (pipe cleaners)	1 pkg
towel	1
tube, glass 1 in. × 18 in.	1
thistle	1
U-shaped	1
tubing, glass, assorted diameters	several meters
tubing, rubber, flexible	several meters
thick-walled	1 meter

antimony (III) chloride	125 g	manganese dioxide	
aspirin	several	(MnO$_2$)	125 g
banana	1	mercury, metal	125 g
barium chloride	125 g	mica	several pieces
bread	several slices	milk	0.25 l
bromine water	0.5 l	mineral oil	0.5 l
cadmium nitrate	125 g	naphtha (lighter fluid)	1 can
calcium metal	125 g	nickel sulfate	125 g
calcium carbide	125 g	phenol	125 g
calcium chloride	125 g	phenolphthalein	125 g
calcium oxide	450 g	platinum or nichrome	
carbon tetrachloride	0.5 l	wire	1 small roll
carrot	1	potassium, metal	125 g
chlorine water	0.5 l	potassium bromide	125 g
copper, strip	12 strips	potassium chlorate	125 g
copper (II) sulfate,		potassium chloride	125 g
crystals	250 g	potassium iodide	125 g
corn kernels	100	potassium permanganate	125 g
cream of tartar	1 box	potassium sulfate	125 g
detergent, liquid	1 bottle	potato	1
dry ice	25 g	Rochelle salt crystals	450 g
Epsom salts		sand	1 kg
(MgSO$_4$·7 H$_2$O)	25 g	silver nitrate (AgNO$_3$)	125 g
ether	0.25 l	soda pop	1 bottle
ethylene glycol	0.25 l	sodium, metal	125 g
formalin (formaldehyde)	0.5 l	sodium acetate	125 g
graphite (pencil lead)	10 g	soda water	0.5 l
hydrochloric acid, 38%	1 l	sodium bicarbonate	1 box
hydrogen peroxide		sodium carbonate	125 g
(H$_2$O$_2$), 3%	0.5 l	sodium chloride (table	
hydrogen sulfide (H$_2$S)	125 g	salt, uniodized)	1 kg
ice		sodium dichromate	
iodine solution	125 g	dihydrate	125 g
iodine crystals	125 g	sodium hydrogen	
iron filings	450 g	carbonate (baking soda)	1 box
iron, steel wool	1 box	sodium hydroxide, pellets	450 g
iron sulfate, FeSO$_4$	125 g	sodium hypochlorite	
lead, strip	12 strips	(commercial bleaching	
thin sheet	.1 m^2	solution)	1 bottle
lemon juice	0.5 l	sodium nitrate	125 g
soda lime (CaO and		sodium sulfate	125 g
NaOH)	125 g	sodium thiosulfate	
lithium chloride	125 g	·5H$_2$O (hypo)	450 g
lithium carbonate	125 g	starch, liquid solution	0.5 l
magnesium, metal	50 g	strontium chloride	125 g
wire	0.5 m	sucrose, table sugar	1 kg

sulfur (roll)	450 g
sulfuric acid, concentrated 96%	1 l
vegetable oil	0.5 l
vinegar, white	0.5 l
water, tap distilled	
wax (paraffin)	1 box
zinc, strip	12 strips
mossy	450 g
zinc sulfate	125 g

Preparation of Solutions

This list gives directions for the preparation of various reagent solutions. Volumes are in milliters (ml), masses are in grams (g). Use distilled water for the preparation of solutions.

Acetic acid, 0.5M: 28.5 ml of 17M $HC_2H_3O_2$ per liter of solution

Ammonium hydroxide (dilute), 3M: 200 ml of concentrated NH_4OH per liter

Antimony (III) chloride, 0.167M: 38 g $SbCl_3$ per liter

Barium chloride, 0.1M: 24.4 g $BaCl_2 \cdot 2 H_2O$ per liter

Bromine water: Use commercial solution.

Cadmium nitrate, 0.25M: 77 g $Cd(NO_3)_2 \cdot 4 H_2O$ per liter

Calcium hydroxide, 0.02M: Make a saturated solution of CaO; use some excess, then filter. Protect the solution from air.

Chlorine water (saturated): Bubble Cl_2 (g) from a cylinder of compressed Cl_2 into distilled water. Or, to 150 ml of 5% NaClO (commercial bleaching solution), add water and about 35 ml of 6M HCl as needed to give the characteristic greenish-yellow color of chlorine, and dilute to 1 liter.

Copper sulfate, 0.5M: 124.8 g $CuSO_4 \cdot 5 H_2O$ per liter

Hydrochloric acid, 6M: Mix equal volumes of 12M (concentrated) HCl and water.

Hydrochloric acid (dilute), 3M: 258 ml concentrated HCl per liter

Hydrochloric acid, 0.1M: 8.55 ml concentrated HCl per liter

Hydrogen sulfide water: Generate H_2S gas by adding dilute HCl in a gas generation apparatus. Bubble the gas in distilled water for at least 5 minutes. Use a 250-ml wide mouth jar about half-filled with distilled water.

Iodine solution, 0.05M: Dissolve 12.7 g I_2 and 53 KI in 250 ml water. After complete solution, dilute to 1 liter

Iron (II) sulfate, 0.5M: Dissolve 139 g of $FeSO_4 \cdot 7 H_2O$ in water containing 10 ml of concentrated H_2SO_4. Dilute to 1 liter. Solution does not keep well.

Lead nitrate, 0.1M: 33.1 g $Pb(NO_3)_2$ per liter

Limewater (see Calcium hydroxide)

Mercury (II) chloride, 0.25M: 68 g $HgCl_2$ per liter

Nickel sulfate, 0.25M: 66 g $NiSO_4 \cdot 6 H_2O$ per liter

Nitric acid (dilute), 3M: 195 ml HNO_3 per liter

Phenolphthalein: 1 g phenolphthalein (solid) per 100 ml 50% ethanol

Potassium bromide, 0.5M: 60 g KBr per liter

Potassium iodide, 0.5M: 83 g KI per liter

Potassium permanganate, 0.02M: 3.16 g $KMnO_4$ per liter

Silver nitrate, 0.1M: 17.0 g $AgNO_3$ per liter

Sodium chloride, 0.1M: 5.85 g NaCl per liter

Sodium hydroxide (dilute), 3M: 126 g NaOH per liter

Sodium hydroxide 0.1M: 4 g NaOH per liter

Sodium hypochlorite, 5%: Use commercial 5% NaClO bleaching solution.

Sodium nitrate, 0.1M: 8.5 g $NaNO_3$ per liter

Sodium thiosulfate, 1M: 248 g $Na_2S_2O_3$ per liter

Starch solution: This starch solution will keep for long periods of time. Mix 250 ml saturated $NaCl$ solution (filtered), 40 ml glacial acetic acid, 10 ml water, 2 g starch. Bring slowly to a boil and boil for 2 minutes.

Sulfuric acid (dilute), 3M: 167 ml concentrated H_2SO_4 per liter

Sulfuric acid, 0.25M: 14.0 ml concentrated H_2SO_4 per liter

Zinc sulfate, 0.25M: 72 g $ZnSO_4 \cdot 7\,H_2O$ per liter

Chapter 1 Introduction

Equipment and Reagents for Experiments

cardboard box
balloons
glass tubing
2 flasks (600 ml)
hot plate
ice
meter stick, yard stick
metric-English ruler
test tubes (different sizes)
graduated cylinder, 25 and 50 ml
balance
soda straw
protractor
masking tape
string
metal washer
block of wood, rectangular
small stone

Page 6. PROBLEM

1. Answers will vary. Examples are:
   (a) Solar cells for heating and cooking by sun
   (b) Chemical precipitation to recycle wastes
   (c) Nuclear reactor to desalinate sea-water
   (d) Seismograph to find new sources of energy

Page 6. ACTIVITY

Place an interesting object in a box and seal it. Show the box to the students and give them three clues to its contents. Have the students ask questions that have a "yes" or "no" answer. Then have the students shake the box or manipulate it and make observations.

Page 9. PROBLEMS

2. Problem: Do pigeons use their ears to guide them home?
   Procedure: Cover the ears of pigeons, let them fly home.
   Observations: No pigeons arrived home
   Conclusion: Pigeons use their ears to guide them
3. Problem: Does air expand when it is heated?
   Procedure: Attach balloon to glass tubing, place tube and balloon in flask, heat flask. Put flask on ice.
   Observation: Balloon expands when flask on hot plate; contracts when flask on ice.
   Conclusion: Balloon in heated flask expands.

Page 9. EXPERIMENT

Before students proceed with the steps of the experiment, make sure they have recorded the "problem" and outlined the "procedure."

Page 9. PROBLEMS

4. The group not given the drug.
5. Answers will vary. Example: Mask the ears of half of the birds; leave half without ear masks.

Page 12. PROBLEM

6. $\dfrac{65\ km}{}\ \dfrac{1\ mi}{1.61\ km} = 40\ mi$

   40 mi/hr is less than speed limit

7. Volume = $10\,cm \times 10\,cm \times 5\,cm = 500\,cm^3$
   Water density = $1\ g/cm^3$

   $D = \dfrac{m}{V}$, m = DV

   $m = (1\ g/cm^3)(500\ cm^3) = 500\ g$

8. Answers will vary. Example:
   $5.3g + 10.4g + 6.5g + 19g + 25g =$

   $\dfrac{66.2\ g}{}\ \bigg|\ \dfrac{1\ kg}{1000\ g}$ = 0.066 kg

9. Answers will vary. Example:
   $\dfrac{120\ lb}{}\ \bigg|\ \dfrac{1\ kg}{2.2\ lb}$ = 54.5 kg

10. $32°\,F = 0°\,C$

   $\dfrac{(100°\,F - 32°\,F)}{}\ \bigg|\ \dfrac{5C°}{9F°}$ =

   $\dfrac{68F°}{}\ \bigg|\ \dfrac{5C°}{9F°}$ = 37.8°C

   $\dfrac{(40°\,F - 32°\,F)}{}\ \bigg|\ \dfrac{5C°}{9F°}$ =

   $\dfrac{8F°}{}\ \bigg|\ \dfrac{5C°}{9F°}$ = 4.4°C

   $\dfrac{(10°\,F - 32°\,F)}{}\ \bigg|\ \dfrac{5C°}{9F°}$ =

   $\dfrac{-22F°}{}\ \bigg|\ \dfrac{5C°}{9F°}$ = 12.2°C

   $\dfrac{(25°\,F - 32°\,F)}{}\ \bigg|\ \dfrac{5C°}{9F°}$ =

   $\dfrac{-7F°}{}\ \bigg|\ \dfrac{5C°}{9F°}$ = -3.9°C

11. $0°\,C = 32°\,F$
    $100°\,C = 212°\,F$

   $\dfrac{25°C}{}\ \bigg|\ \dfrac{9F°}{5C°}$ + 32°F = 77°F

   $\dfrac{50°C}{}\ \bigg|\ \dfrac{9F°}{5C°}$ + 32°F = 122°F

   $\dfrac{37°C}{}\ \bigg|\ \dfrac{9F°}{5C°}$ + 32°F = 98.6°F

Students will need much help with this activity. You might introduce it by dis-cussing scale drawings and maps. Sample scale drawing:

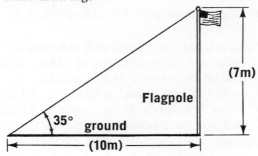

If the angle is taken from a ground position 10 meters from the pole, and the angle is 35°, the pole will be about 7 meters high.

12. Answers will vary. Examples:
    Aluminum, use in airplane construc-tion because of low density. Balsam wood, use in model airplanes be-cause of low density. Lead, fish sinkers, high density. Cast iron, engine blocks, high density. Styro-foam, packing material, low density.

13. Density of water is $1\ g/cm^3$

D. *How and Why*
1. Answers will vary. Examples are ruler, thermometer, graduated cylin-der, balance, sextant; centimeters, degrees, milliliters, grams, angles

2. Answers will vary. Examples are: physics, study of matter and energy; chemistry, study of changes in mat-ter; biology, study of living systems; geology, study of earth; astronomy, study of universe.

3. Answers will vary. Examples are: Ob-servation: carefully noting changes under controlled conditions; making and testing hypotheses: trying to test for all possible exceptions to hypo-thesis; stating theories that explain known facts.

4. Science includes the body of knowledge and the methods. Technology includes application of science to inventions and processes.

5. Answers will vary. Examples are: decimal system is easier to calculate; universal system for whole world.

6. $\dfrac{50 \text{ km} \mid 1 \text{ mi}}{\mid 1.61 \text{ km}}$ = 31 mi Speedometer reads 31 mi/hr

7. $\dfrac{250 \text{ ml} \mid 1 \text{ l}}{\mid 1000 \text{ ml}}$ = 0.25 l

    1000 ml = 1 l

    5000 ml = 5 l

8. Mass is measured on a beam balance, volume is measured either by linear measurement or in graduated cylinder.

9. Measure a known distance from object. Measure angle (vertical) to top of object. Make a scale drawing. Read height from drawing.

10. Answers will vary. Example: find the mass of a container, add a measured volume of oil, find the mass of the oil. D = $\dfrac{m}{V}$

Page 21. INVESTIGATIONS

1. This is a good way for students to practice finding volume by water displacement. Be sure that all of the mineral samples are insoluble in water.

2. Other objects may be substituted.

3. Some students might like to make a scale model of buildings in one city block using their measurements.

Chapter 2 Classification of Matter

Equipment and Reagents for Experiments

Equipment

asbestos pad
beaker (400-ml)
Bunsen burner
condensing tube
distilling flask
filter paper
flasks (400-ml)
funnel (glass)
glass tubing (10-cm)
hammer
magnet
milk bottle
plastic bag
ring stand and ring
rubber 2-hole stopper
   (to fit milk bottle)
rubber 1-hole stopper
   (to fit test tube)
   (to fit distilling flask)
rubber tube pinch clamp
rubber tubing (15-cm)
safety glasses
soft glass test tubes
test tubes
thermometer (Celsius)
towel
watch glass (large)

Reagents

alcohol (ethyl)
aluminum squares
hydrochloric acid (dilute)
ice cubes
iodine crystals
iron filings
mineral oil
sand
sugar
sulfur (powdered)
table salt
zinc (mossy)

Page 26. PROBLEMS

1. oxygen, carbon, magnesium, mercury, silver, sodium, chlorine, iron

2. (a) iron (b) carbon (c) mercury (d) oxygen (e) chlorine

Page 27. PROBLEMS

3. nitrogen, hydrogen — 1:3

4. N_2O

5. nitrogen, hydrogen
   carbon, hydrogen, oxygen
   iron, oxygen
   sodium, chlorine
   hydrogen, oxygen

Page 28. PROBLEM

6. magnet or dissolve salt in water

Page 30. PROBLEM

7. (a) coal and snow—color, melting point, density
   (b) strawberry ice cream and vanilla ice cream—color, taste
   (c) soda pop and water—taste, density
   (d) lead and aluminum—density
   (e) salt and sugar—taste
   (f) baseball and football—shape

Page 33. PROBLEMS

8. Chemical changes: (b) burning sulfur (d) baking a cake

9. Physical changes: (a) opening an envelope (c) paneling a room

Page 35. PROBLEMS

10. Separation of:
    (a) sulfur-sand; carbon disulfide (CS_2) or carbon tetrachloride (CCl_4)
    (b) iodine-iron; heat or magnet
    (c) salt-iodine; heat or alcohol
    (d) copper-nickel; magnet

11. A chemical change, electrolysis, separates water to H_2 and O_2.

12. Separations in the experiment were physical (distillation of liquid).

13. The water in the condenser cools the vapor so that it condenses.

14. CCl_4 and H_2O can be separated by distillation because of the difference in their boiling points. (CCl_4 and water are immiscible so this might not be necessary.)

15. Sulfur and iron react chemically when they are heated, so they could not be separated by vaporizing one of them. Iodine and iron could be separated by vaporization.

16. Sulfur and iron can be separated with a magnet or by dissolving sulfur in CS_2 or CCl_4.

Page 36. PROBLEMS

17. The HCl was evaporated to show that it did *not* produce the crystals.

18. Aluminum dissolves in HCl; a new compound is formed (white crystals); H_2 gas is formed; test tube becomes warm.

19. Aluminum chloride is formed:
    $$2\ Al + 6\ HCl \rightarrow 2\ AlCl_3 + 3\ H_2(g)$$

Pages 37-38. STUDY QUESTIONS

D. *How and Why*

1. Chemical properties of water: relatively stable, oxidizes metals, a product of a neutralization reaction, forms many crystal hydrates.
   Physical properties: density = $1 g/cm^3$, MP $0°C$, BP $100°C$, specific heat = 1 cal/g-C°, highly polar molecules, ice is less dense than water.

2. If a liquid turns blue while you are absent, it does not necessarily mean that a chemical change has taken place.

3. Physical—shape, color, taste, floats in water.
   Chemical—inside turns brown when exposed to air.

4. Physical (and chemical).

5. It can be demonstrated that helium will displace a liquid, therefore it has mass.

6. A mixture is not the same throughout, can be separated by physical means, and has no definite proportion of components. A compound is same composition throughout, is

decomposed by chemical means, and has definite proportion by weight.

7. Mixtures—air, soil, concrete, lemonade, etc.

   Compounds—water, sugar, salt, ammonia, etc.

8. Seat covers should have: strength, resilience, color, durability, little static producing ability.

9. Evaporate a small amount of the liquid. If a residue remains, it is salt water.

10. Use distilling flask and condenser. The liquid with the lower boiling point (if it is sufficiently different) will boil off first. See Experiment on page 35.

Pages 38-39. INVESTIGATIONS

1. Some properties that might be tested are density, hardness, color and luster.

2. Results will vary depending on the kind of oil and concentration of solutions. Be sure you have a thermometer with a wide enough range. The oil will become *very* hot (about $400°F$).

3. A Brinell test calculates the hardness of materials (especially metals) by forcing hardened steel balls against the sample at a specified pressure.

Chapter 3 Atoms and Compounds

Equipment and Reagents for Experiments

Bunsen burner
laboratory balance
potassium chlorate (powered)
safety glasses
test tube (Pyrex)
test tube clamp

Page 43. PROBLEM

1. Each additional proton increases the mass of an atom by one a.m.u.

Page 46. PROBLEMS

2. (a) HCl — 1 hydrogen, 1 chlorine
   (b) Na_2O — 2 sodium, 1 oxygen
   (c) KOH — 1 potassium, 1 oxygen, 1 hydrogen
   (d) H_2SO_4 — 2 hydrogen, 1 sulfur, 4 oxygen
   (e) F_2 — 2 fluorine
   (f) Fe_2S_3 — 2 iron (III), 3 sulfur
   (g) Br_2 — 2 bromine
   (h) NH_3 — 1 nitrogen (III), 3 hydrogen

3. Compounds: (a) HCl (b) Na_2O (c) KOH (d) H_2SO_4 (f) Fe_2S_3 (h) NH_3
   Elements: (e) F_2 (g) Br_2

Page 48. PROBLEMS

4. Chlorine gas Cl_2 :

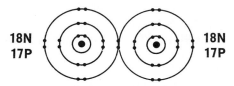

18N 17P   **18N 17P**

5. magnesium chloride $MgCl_2$

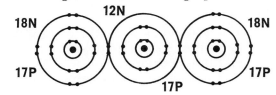

12N   **18N**   **18N**   **17P**   **17P**   **17P**

Page 49. PROBLEM

6. a. sodium bromide, $NaBr$
   b. potassium iodide, KI
   c. hydrogen bromide, HBr
   d. hydrogen sulfide, H_2S
   e. magnesium fluoride, MgF_2
   f. calcium chloride, $CaCl_2$
   g. lithium sulfide, Li_2S
   h. aluminum chloride, $AlCl_3$
   i. copper (II) sulfide, CuS

Page 50. PROBLEMS

7. a. $NaCl$, sodium chloride
   b. $CuBr$, copper (I) bromide
   c. BaS, barium sulfide

d. MgO, magnesium oxide

e. KI, potassium iodide

f. $MgBr_2$, magnesium bromide

g. CaS, calcium sulfide

h. CuO, copper (II) oxide

i. $FeCl_3$, iron (III) chloride

j. FeO, iron (II) oxide

8. a. calcium bromide, $CaBr_2$

b. potassium oxide, K_2O

c. aluminum chloride, $AlCl_3$

d. iron (III) iodide, FeI_3

e. copper (I) sulfide, Cu_2S

f. lithium fluoride, LiF

g. sodium bromide, NaBr

h. copper (II) chloride, $CuCl_2$

Page 53. PROBLEMS

9. a. sodium nitrate, $NaNO_3$

b. silver sulfate, Ag_2SO_4

c. iron (II) chloride, $FeCl_2$

d. potassium phosphate, K_3PO_4

e. copper (II) iodide, CuI_2

10. a. Na_2SO_4, sodium sulfate

b. $(NH_4)_3PO_4$, ammonium phosphate

c. FeO, iron (II) oxide

d. $AgNO_3$, silver nitrate

e. KBr, potassium bromide

11. In Problem 9:

a. 1 sodium, 1 nitrogen, 3 oxygen

b. 2 silver, 1 sulfur, 4 oxygen

c. 1 iron, 2 chlorine

d. 3 potassium 1 phosphorus, 4 oxygen

e. 1 copper, 2 iodine

In Problem 10:

a. 2 sodium, 1 sulfur, 4 oxygen

b. 3 nitrogen, 12 hydrogen, 1 phosphorus, 4 oxygen

c. 1 iron, 1 oxygen

d. 1 silver, 1 nitrogen, 3 oxygen

e. 1 potassium, 1 bromine

Page 53. EXPERIMENT

Before you start the experiment, have the students practice calculating the percentage of composition. Make sure that the students understand each step in the

data table and how it relates to the calculations.

Sample data table:

1. Mass of test tube with $KClO_3$ _____ g

2. Mass of empty test tube _____ g

3. Mass of $KClO_3$ (Step 1 − Step 2) _____ g

4. Mass of test tube + $KClO_3$ after heat _____ g

5. Mass of oxygen driven off (Step 3 − Step 4) _____ g

6. Percent of oxygen in $KClO_3$ _____ % $= \dfrac{\text{Step 5}}{\text{Step 3}} \Big| 100$

You can calculate the theoretical percentage of oxygen in $KClO_3$:

1 atom K @ 39 a.m.u. = 39 a.m.u.

1 atom Cl @ 35.5 a.m.u. = 35.5 a.m.u.

3 atoms 0 @ 16 a.m.u. = 48 a.m.u.

Total 122.5 a.m.u.

$$\% \text{ oxygen} = \frac{\text{a.m.u. oxygen}}{\text{a.m.u. compound}} \Big| 100\% =$$

$$\frac{48 \text{ a.m.u.}}{122.5 \text{ a.m.u.}} \Big| 100\% = 39\%$$

Calculate percent error:

$$\frac{\text{difference between theoretical value and experimental value}}{\text{theoretical value}} \Big| 100\%$$

If students have a large percentage of error, ask them to find some explanation for the large error.

You may also have the students find the percent of water in $CuSO_4 \cdot 5 H_2O$ or in $BaCl_2 \cdot 2 H_2O$. These compounds are a bit safer for the students to use than $KClO_3$. You can also use larger quantities without danger.

Pages 54-56. STUDY QUESTIONS

D. *How and Why*

1. In covalent bonding electrons are shared by atoms, in ionic bonding electrons are transferred and atoms are bonded electrostatically.

2. (a) NaCl, sodium chloride (b)

NH_4NO_3, ammonium nitrate (c) $Ca_3(PO_4)_2$, calcium phosphate

3. (a) potassium sulfate, K_2SO_4 (b) sulfur dioxide, SO_2 (c) mercury (I) sulfide, Hg_2S

4. Two electrons from the outer shell of Mg could be transferred to the outer shells of two bromine atoms. The resulting charged particles would bond together by electrostatic attraction.

5. Electrons have negligible mass, negative charge, and orbit nucleus. Protons are positive and have same mass as neutron. Neutrons have no charge. Protons and neutrons are found in nucleus.

6. Helium has 2 electrons in first shell. Oxygen has 2 in first, 6 in second shell.

7. (1) All matter is made of atoms. (2) Atoms cannot be divided. (3) All atoms of the same element are alike.
   The last two have been modified by experimentation. Atoms can be divided into subatomic particles. Isotopes point out that all atoms of the same element are not alike. All atoms of the same element have the same number of protons.

8. The element's valence should be +2. It would probably give up the two electrons in the outer shell to form compounds. It would probably exhibit ionic bonding.

9. Magnesium, 1 atom; nitrogen, 2; oxygen, 4.

Page 56. INVESTIGATIONS

1. Chemical formulas for some common substances are found in the *Handbook of Chemistry and Physics*. Examples are: Sodium bicarbonate, $NaHCO_3$; Vinegar, CH_3COOH; Aspirin, $CH_3COOC_6H_4COOH$; Borax, $Na_2B_4O_7$; Cream of Tartar, $KHC_4H_4O_6$; Epsom Salts, $MgSO_4$; Milk of Magnesia, $Mg(OH)_2$; Plaster of Paris, $CaSO_4$; Washing Soda, Na_2CO_3

2. Some students might be interested in reporting on the life of Lise Meitner, one of the early atomic physicists along with Bohr, Rutherford, and Fermi.

3.

	Shell 1	Shell 2		Total
H	1			1
He	2			2
Li	2	1		3
Be	2	2		4
B	2	2	1	5
C	2	2	2	6
N	2	2	3	7
O	2	2	4	8
F	2	2	5	9
Ne	2	2	6	10

5. Some examples are: H_2O, CO_2, SO_2, H_2S, $CaCO_3$, NH_4OH.

Chapter 4 The Periodic Table

Equipment and Reagents for Experiments

Equipment
balance
beaker
forceps
knife
marbles (about 20)
steel balls (about 20), ball bearings, or
   BB shot
test tubes
test tube rack

Reagents
bromine water
calcium metal
carbon tetrachloride (CCl_4)
chlorine water
iodine solution
magnesium metal
potassium bromide solution
potassium iodide solution
potassium metal
sodium chloride solution
sodium metal

1. Mass of breaker + bearings, marbles _____ g
2. Mass of empty beaker _____ g
3. Mass of ball bearings + marbles (Step 1-Step 2) _____ g
4. Mass of ball bearing + beaker _____ g
5. Mass of marbles (Step 1-Step 4) _____ g
6. Mass of ball bearings (Step 4-Step 2) _____ g

$$\frac{\text{mass bearings}}{\text{mass marbles}} = \frac{X}{1}$$

X will represent ratio of ball bearing mass to mass of marbles as 1.

Questions:

1. The lightest object is given a mass of 1 because if the heavier were given a mass of 1, the lighter would be less than 1. The experiment is, in effect, a way of using a binary compound XY to determine the mass of one element when the mass of the other is known.
2. If the ratio of marbles to ball bearings had been 2:1 rather than 1:1 (XY_2 rather than XY), an adjustment in the ratio would have had to be made.
3. The total mass of one element is of no value if the ratio of number of atoms is not known.

Page 61. TEXT QUESTIONS

1. A base of 10 might be used since other objects might have less mass than a marble. This would avoid fractional masses.
2. A comparison might be to CO (carbon monoxide). We could weigh a sample of the gas, remove the oxygen, weigh the remaining carbon. Assigning carbon a mass of 12 would allow us to find the relative mass of oxygen. Originally oxygen was used as the standard because so many elements combined with oxygen.

3. Knowing the ratio of the combining atoms would allow true determination of relative mass.

Page 62. EXPERIMENT

1. Sodium and potassium are stored in kerosene because they react with moisture in the air.
2. Family groups: Sodium, potassium; magnesium, calcium.
3.

	Chemical properties	Physical properties
Sodium and potassium	So reactive that it has little practical value in pure form. Combines violently with water.	Silvery white metal, soft
Magnesium and calcium	Less reactive than sodium and potassium. Combines readily with oxygen	Silvery white metal, soft

Page 66. PROBLEMS

1. The atomic number is the number of protons in the nucleus
2. 74

Page 68. PROBLEMS

3. Average atomic mass
$$= \frac{90 \ (20 \text{ a.m.u.}) + 10 \ (22 \text{ a.m.u.})}{100}$$
$$= \frac{2020 \text{ a.m.u.}}{100} = 20.2 \text{ a.m.u.}$$

4. Average atomic mass
$$= \frac{20(30\text{a.m.u.})+50(32\text{a.m.u.})+30(35\text{a.m.u.})}{100}$$
$$= \frac{3250 \text{ a.m.u.}}{100} = 32.5 \text{ a.m.u.}$$

5. If the atomic mass is not a whole number, it has isotopes.

6. Average atomic mass

$$= \frac{30\,(27\ \text{a.m.u.}) + 70\,(30\ \text{a.m.u.})}{100}$$

$$= \frac{2910\ \text{a.m.u.}}{100} = 29.1\ \text{a.m.u.}$$

7. Average atomic mass

$$= \frac{30(15) + 35(16) + 45(18)}{100}$$

$$= \frac{1670\ \text{a.m.u.}}{100} = 16.7\ \text{a.m.u.}$$

8. See Appendix D, International Atomic Masses, p. 470.

Element	Z	A
iron (Fe)	26	56
radon (Rn)	86	222
ytterbium (Yb)	70	173
vanadium (V)	23	51
copper (Cu)	29	64

Page 71. EXPERIMENT

1. After shaking KI solution with CCl_4, two layers form (CCl_4, and solution). After shaking with chlorine water, CCl_4 layer turns purple. Cl_2 replaces iodine which dissolves in CCl_4.

2. Bromine water added to KI solution and CCl_4 gives a purple layer. Bromine displaces iodine.

3. After shaking KBr solution with CCl_4, two layers form. When chlorine water is added, the CCl_4 layer becomes reddish-brown in color. Chlorine displaces bromine.

4. After adding iodine solution to KBr and CCl_4, there is no color change in either layer. Iodine does not replace bromine.

5. When iodine is added to NaCl solution and CCl_4, no color change results. Iodine does not replace chlorine.

Pages 73-74. STUDY QUESTIONS

D. *How and Why*

1. The outer shell of electrons is farther away from the nucleus in iodine than in fluorine. There is less chance for electrons to be attracted to the outer shell of the atom.

2. upper right—active nonmetals
   lower left—active metals

3. average atomic mass

$$= \frac{60\,(30\,\text{a.m.u.}) + 40\,(32\ \text{a.m.u.})}{100}$$

$$= \frac{3080\ \text{a.m.u.}}{100}$$

$$= 30.8\ \text{a.m.u.}$$

4.
                    Metals

   1-3 electrons in outer shell
   luster
   malleable or ductile
   conductor
                  Nonmetals
   4-8 electrons in outer shell
   no luster
   brittle
   nonconductor

5. Transition metals all add electrons in inner shells and in general have two electrons in the outer shell.

6. The element has 15 protons, 15 electrons; has isotopes; atomic mass number 33; electron structure, 2, 8, 5 ($1s^2\ 2s^2\ 2p^6\ 3s^2\ 3p^3$); probably a nonmetal.

7. All the differences of metals and nonmetals plus numbers of subatomic particles. Magnesium has +2 valence, chlorine —1.

8. Valences of A groups are the same as the Roman numeral.

Page 75. INVESTIGATIONS

1. Helium was discovered first in the spectrum of the sun. Its name is derived from the Greek word, *Helios*, sun. Helium was not actually isolated from earth's atmosphere until several years later.

2. The rare earth elements are very difficult to isolate. The element Lanthanum was named after the Greek word meaning hidden. Rare earth elements are hardly ever found in the

free state because they combine easily with other elements.

3. In 1863, John Newlands, an English chemist, found that, if he arranged the elements in order of their increasing atomic weights, there appeared to be a repetition of similar properties every eight elements.

One of the earliest attempts at classification of elements was by John Dobereiner, a German chemist, in 1817. Dobereiner observed that the properties of the three metals calcium, barium, and strontium were very similar and that the atomic weight of strontium was about midway between those of calcium and barium. He found other groups of three elements that reacted similarly.

MARS PERIODIC CHART INFORMATION

(Use this information to put elements in their proper positions on the periodic chart.)

Periodic Chart for Mars and Its 30 Known Elements

Can you place them in their proper place in the outline? Remember, natural laws are the same for the whole universe.

(Symbols and elements used are of course fictitious.)

	+1	+2	+3	+4	−3	−2	−1	
1	A							B
2	C	D	E	F	G	N	I	L
3	‡	Ƶ	Y	H	M	O	K	J
4	Q	⊠	R	T	S	U	V	W
5	X	P	♀	⊞	(Undiscovered at this time.)			

Elements List

A	K	U
B	L	V
C	M	W
D	N	X
E	O	Y
F	P	Ƶ
G	Q	⊠
H	R	♀
I	S	⊞
J	T	‡

*Material used with permission of the San Diego Unified School District, San Diego, Calif.

1. The most metallic element: x
2. The most nonmetallic element: I
3. Inert gases are B, L, W, J. B is lightest, W is the heaviest, L is in period 2.
4. Their lightest element of all is A
5. All the following elements have three shells and the number of electrons listed in the outermost shell—‡-1, Ƶ-2, Y-3, H-4, M-5, O-6, K-7
6. Element H has 14 protons
7. G has 7 electrons
8. C has an atomic weight of 5 and forms the compound CI

9. Q has only 1 electron in its outer shell but has 4 shells

10. The E family is made up of the elements E, Y, R, ♀ (in order of increasing weight)

11. ⊞ is the heaviest of all atoms and is radioactive

12. P is in period V and has a +2 oxidation state

13. D is in period II and has the formula DI_2 for a salt

14. F is like our element carbon and is in the same family as H, T and ⊞

15. Their solvent like our most important liquid has the formula A_2N

16. Here are a few compounds based on the Martian chart—AV, ▨I_2, DU, FA_4, ▨U, ▨$_3S_2$

17. Now every space should be filled. Can you give each element its proper atomic number?

(Symbols and elements used are, of course, fictitious.)

Chapter 5 Families of Elements

Equipment and Reagents for Experiments

Equipment
Bunsen burner
collection bottles
deflagrating spoon
flat pan
glass plates
graduated cylinder, 25 ml
labels
piece of cork
platinum (nichrome) wire
pneumatic trough
ring stand
rubber tubing
test tubes (glass and large, Pyrex)
test tube clamp
test tube rack
tongs
wing tip for Bunsen burner
wood splints

Reagents
alcohol (ethyl)
antimony (II) chloride solution
banana
barium chloride
bread
cadmium nitrate solution
calcium chloride
carbon tetrachloride
carrot
copper chloride
copper (II) sulfate solution
distilled water
hydrogen sulfide (H_2S) solution
iodine crystals
iodine solution
iron sulfate solution
liquid starch solution
lithium chloride
manganese dioxide
mineral oil
potato
potassium chlorate
potassium chloride
potassium nitrate
sodium chloride
sodium nitrate
steel wool
strontium chloride
sulfur
sulfuric acid (concentrated)
zinc sulfate solution

Page 77. PROBLEMS

1.

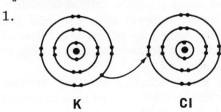

K   Cl

2.

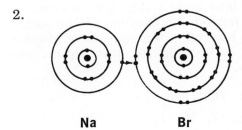

Na   Br

21

A demonstration of the relative activities of the halogens is their ability to bleach litmus paper. Place a piece of red litmus and blue litmus in a test tube. Add 5 ml of bromine water. Repeat the procedure separately with chlorine water and iodine solution. The chlorine bleaches readily; bromine, somewhat; iodine not at all.

Steel wool appears to "burn" in chlorine gas. This experiment should be done as demonstration under a hood. Prepare chlorine gas by adding one-half teaspoon of bleaching powder to a bottle. Add 2 ml of concentrated sulfuric acid. Cover with glass plate. Hold a small piece of steel wool with metal tongs and heat in a Bunsen burner flame until it glows red. Remove the cover from the bottle and quickly thrust the steel wool into the chlorine gas. The steel wool is rapidly oxidized forming $FeCl_3$.

Some of the properties of iodine are demonstrated in this experiment. Have the students set up the test tubes as described. Then have them make an identical set of test tubes filled with distilled water. Add a crystal of iodine to each of the test tubes (alcohol, carbon tetrachloride, water, mineral oil), but add the crystal to only one of the test tubes of distilled water. Iodine dissolves readily in alcohol and CCl_4.

Add starch solution to all of the test tubes. The starch will turn blue in any of the tubes in which the iodine dissolved. The blue color results from a complex ion formed by reaction of the starch with the iodine. Try some other solvents such as benzene, or other organic solvents.

3. F_2, Cl_2, Br_2, I_2

4.
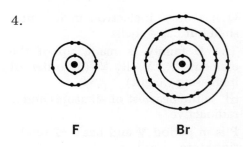

F   Br

5.   CaF2
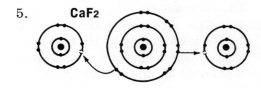

The steel wool will react more quickly with oxygen if it is rinsed in alcohol or vinegar to remove the rust-preventive coating and then dried.

The iron reacts with the oxygen forming rust.

$$4\,Fe + 3\,O_2 \rightarrow 2\,Fe_2O_3$$

The water level rises because the molecules of oxygen were removed from the atmosphere inside the graduated cylinder and reduced the pressure.

The decomposition of potassium chlorate ($KClO_3$) by heat with the catalyst manganese dioxide (MnO_2) results in the production of oxygen. Be sure that you do not mix the $KClO_3$ with anything except the MnO_2. Impurities may result in an explosion. Be sure to remove the delivery tube from the water as soon as you remove the heat. Otherwise the water will be siphoned back into the test tube and the rapid cooling will break it.

The glowing splint will burst into flame in the atmosphere of pure oxygen. The steel wool will oxidize very rapidly, and the sulfur will burn with a blue flame.

	cellulose
burning of wood	$(C_6H_{12}O_6)n + nO_2 \rightarrow$ $nCO_2 + nH_2O$
oxidation of iron	$4\,Fe + 3O_2 \rightarrow$ $2\,Fe_2O_3$
burning of sulfur	$S + O_2 \rightarrow SO_2$

Page 85. EXPERIMENT

One of the tests for metallic ions in qualitative analysis is the reaction of the metallic ions with hydrogen sulfide. The metallic sulfides have characteristic colors (Table 5-3, p. 85).

If students perform this experiment, have the reagents in dropper bottles to avoid spilling. Only a very small amount of each is needed for the reaction.

Ions		*Precipitate*		*Color*
$2\,Ag^+$	$+$	$S^=$ $\rightarrow$	Ag_2S	(black)
Cd^{++}	$+$	$S^=$ $\rightarrow$	CdS	(yellow)
Pb^{++}	$+$	$S^=$ $\rightarrow$	PbS	(black)
Zn^{++}	$+$	$S^=$ $\rightarrow$	ZnS	(white)
$2\,Sb^{+++}$	$+$	$3S^=$ $\rightarrow$	Sb_2S_3	(orange)
Cu^{++}	$+$	$S^=$ $\rightarrow$	CuS	(black)

Page 86. PROBLEMS

6.

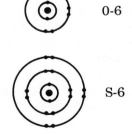

O-6

S-6

7. Six

Page 87. PROBLEM

8. All have the same numbers of electrons in their outer shell.

Page 88. EXPERIMENT

Test for nitrate ion. When Fe^{2+} and NO_3^- ions are in solution, they form a brown compound $(FeNO)^{2+}$ complex at the interface between the solution (upper layer in test tube) and concentrated sulfuric acid. If nitrate ions are not present, no brown ring (no iron complex) will form.

$3\,Fe^{2+} + NO_3^- + 4H^+ \rightarrow 3\,Fe^{3+} + NO$ $+ 2\,H_2O$
$Fe^{2+} + NO \rightarrow (FeNO)^{2+}$ brown

Page 91. PROBLEMS

9.

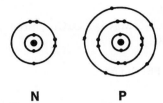

N   P

10. Five

11. covalent

Page 93. EXPERIMENT

The flame test is a common method of qualitative analysis. When heated to incandescence, elements give off characteristic spectra. The light occurs because electrons exicted by heat emit light of definite energies as they return to lower energy levels. If a pure solution of the compound is heated, the spectra can be used to identify component cations. Be sure to warn students to clean wire (and burner) between samples. Compare color of unknowns with knowns (or with photos on p. 94).

Page 93. PROBLEMS

12.

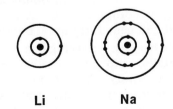

Li   Na

13. one

14. They combine very readily (explosively) with oxygen or water vapor in the air.

15. two

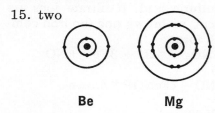

Be   Mg

16. two
17. $BeCl_2$, $MgCl_2$, $CaCl_2$, $SrCl_2$, $BaCl_2$, $RaCl_2$

18.

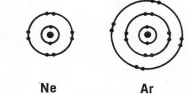

He   Ne   Ar

19. 8 (2 for helium)
20. First energy shell only has positions for two electrons.

Pages 99-100. STUDY QUESTIONS

D. *How and Why*

1. Those elements grouped in the same column in the periodic table are called a family. They exhibit similar properties—oxygen family.

2. ammonia, NH_3; urea, N_2H_4CO; nitric acid, HNO_3

3. Binary compounds of the nitrogen family form covalent bonds whereas binary compounds of alkali metals and halogens form ionic bonds.

4. You can distinguish between metallic and nonmetallic members of a family of elements by their properties. Generally the elements with the higher atomic numbers will be more metallic.

5. Sulfur and oxygen differ in atomic structure (number of protons, electrons, neutrons); physical state (solid versus gas); melting and boiling points; color; allotropic forms.

6. Law of Multiple Proportions: Two or more elements may unite to form more than one compound. The combining masses will be in the ratio of whole numbers. The law of definite proportions states that all compounds have a definite proportion by weight. Even though two elements may combine in two or more ways to form compounds, each of the compounds will always have the same proportions of elements.

7. Allotropes are different molecular forms of the same element whereas isotopes are forms of the same element which differ in the number of neutrons in the nucleus.

8. Noble gases do not combine easily with other elements. The first of the noble gases had been found as had the first of other families, thus giving a starting place. Answers will vary.

9. A diatomic gas is one in which the molecular form contains two atoms: Cl_2, chlorine; O_2, oxygen; N_2, nitrogen.

10. (a) (1) boron nitride (2) iron (III) oxide (3) magnesium chloride (4) carbon disulfide (5) lithium hydride

    (b) 1, 2, 4, 5 are covalent because of the number of electrons in the outer shell. They have a tendency to share rather than gain or lose electrons. 3 ionic—magnesium is likely to give up two electrons.

Page 101. INVESTIGATIONS

1. Pesticides: Chlorine, hydrocarbons
   Fertilizer: Phosphorus, nitrogen, potassium

2. Answers will vary depending on brands of products.

3. You might like to compare regular light bulbs with "long life" light bulbs of the same wattage.

4. Answers will vary. Chlorine is most common.

Chapter 6 Carbon and Its Compounds

Equipment and Reagents for Experiments

Equipment
beaker (250-ml)
Bunsen burner
collection bottles
filter paper
flask (250-ml)
glass plates (square)
glass tubing
medicine dropper
mortar and pestle
pipe cleaners (toothpicks)
pneumatic trough
ring stand and clamps
rubber stoppers (assorted)
rubber tubing
styrofoam balls
test tubes (small, glass; large, Pyrex)
water bath
wood splints

Reagents
acetic acid
alcohol (ethyl)
bromine water
calcium carbide
food coloring (various colors)
formalin (formaldehyde)
limewater (freshly made)
phenol
potassium permanganate solution
soda lime (CaO and NaOH mixture)
sodium acetate (solid)
sodium hydroxide (solid)
sulfuric acid (concentrated)

Page 107. ACTIVITY

The seven isomers of $C_5H_{11}Cl$ are:

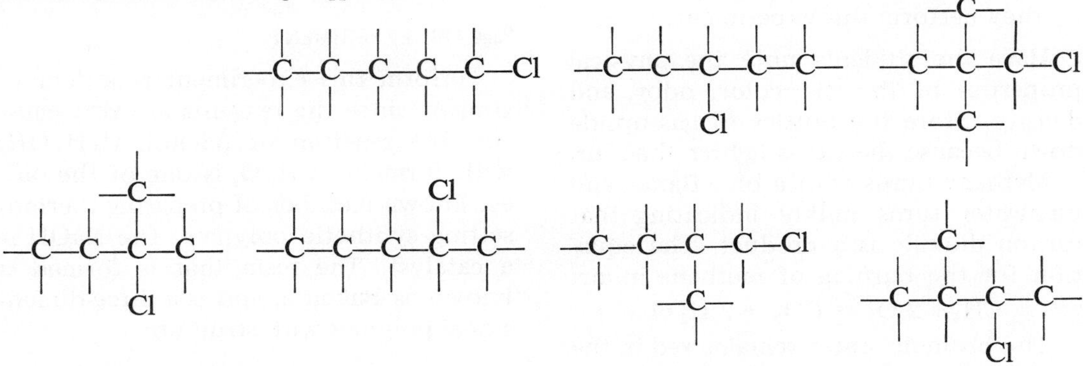

(The remaining bonds are filled by hydrogen atoms.)

Page 107. PROBLEM

1. The four isomers of C_4H_9Cl are:

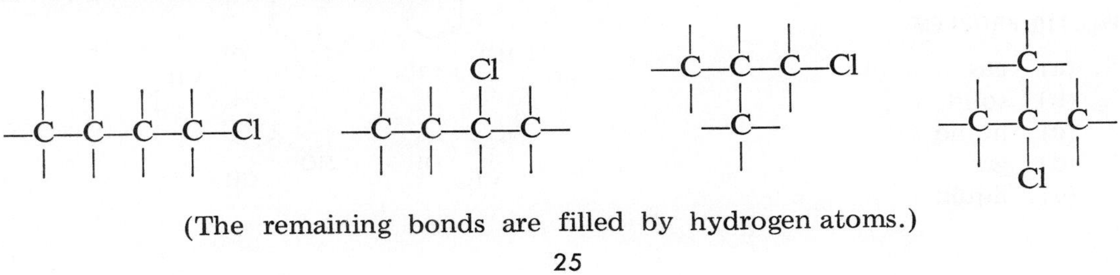

(The remaining bonds are filled by hydrogen atoms.)

25

2. A structural formula for $CH_3 CH_2 CHO$ is:

3. The simple molecular formula for the compound in Problem 2 is $C_3 H_6 O$.

Page 109. EXPERIMENT

This experiment is the preparation of methane gas. If the students perform the experiment, observe the following safety precautions:

1. Keep the gas collection bottles away from open flames.

2. Maintain proper ventilation or use the fume hood.

3. Have students wear goggles when they perform this experiment.

Have the students note the physical properties of the gas—color, odor, and density. Store the bottles of gas upside down because the gas is lighter than air.

Methane burns with a blue flame, and limewater turns milkly indicating that carbon dioxide is a product. The equation for the burning of methane in air:

$$CH_4 + 2 O_2 \rightarrow CO_2 + 2 H_2 O$$

The bromine water remains red in the presence of methane because methane is a saturated hydrocarbon and is therefore rather unreactive. Potassium permanganate is a strong oxidizing agent, but is not reduced by methane.

Page 110. PROBLEM

4. (a) gas
   (b) solid
   (c) liquid
   (d) gas
   (e) liquid

5.

Page 115. EXPERIMENT

Before performing this experiment, review the results of the experiment with methane. Observe the same safety precautions as with the preparation of methane—acetylene is more reactive than methane. Acetylene is an unsaturated hydrocarbon and is more reactive than the saturated methane. Acetylene bleaches red bromine water and reduces purple $KMnO_4$ solution. Be careful with the $KMnO_4$ solution as it can stain the hands and clothing.

Page 118. EXPERIMENT

Perform this experiment as a demonstration since the reagents are very caustic. The reaction of phenol, $C_6 H_5 OH$, with formalin, $CH_2 O$, is one of the oldest known methods of preparing thermosetting synthetic polymer. The NaOH is a catalyst. The resin that is formed is known as Bakelite, and is a three-dimensional polymer with structure:

6. The structural formula for cyclo-pentane is
The simple molecular formula is C_5H_{10}

7.

1, 2 dichlorobenzene
(ortho-)

1, 3 dichlorobenzene
(meta-)

Cl

1, 4 dichlorobenzene
(para-)

Page 121. ADDITIONAL EXPERIMENT

This experiment can be done readily by all students. Mix 3 ml of acetic acid and 2 ml of ethyl alcohol in a test tube. Add 3 drops of concentrated sulfuric acid. Heat gently. Do not sniff the odor directly but waft the vapor toward your nose with your hand. The organic compound you have prepared is called an ester. Repeat the procedure with amyl alcohol instead of ethyl alcohol. Esters are formed from organic acids and alcohols. The other product of the reaction is water. The esterification proceeds faster if the water is removed. This is the purpose of the concentrated H_2SO_4.

$$CH_3COOH + CH_3CH_2OH \xrightarrow[\text{H}_2\text{SO}_4]{\text{conc.}}$$
acetic acid   ethyl alcohol

$$CH_3COOCH_2CH_3 + H_2O$$
ethyl acetate   water

$$CH_3COOH + CH_3CH_2\underset{\overset{|}{OH}}{C}(CH_3)_2 \xrightarrow[\text{H}_2\text{SO}_4]{\text{conc.}}$$
acetic acid   amyl alcohol

$$CH_3COOC(CH_3)_2CH_2CH_3 + H_2O$$
amyl acetate   water

Ethyl acetate has the odor of apples, amyl acetate has the odor of bananas. Esters are known by their characteristic odors:

ethyl butanoate	peach
methyl butanoate	pineapple
octyl ethanoate	orange
pentyl butanoate	apricot
pentyl ethanoate	pear

Pages 123-124. STUDY QUESTIONS

D. *How and Why*

1.

$$H : \overset{\displaystyle \cdot\cdot}{\underset{\displaystyle \cdot\cdot}{C}} : H$$
H

2. Isomers are compounds with the same formulas but different structures. Isotopes are elements with the same number of protons but different numbers of neutrons.

3. Carbon bonds with other carbon atoms to form long chains, carbon atoms can form double bonds with other atoms, carbon can form ring compounds.

27

4. Benzene and cyclohexane are similar in that both have six carbon atoms formed into a ring. However, cyclohexane has the formula C_6H_{12}, whereas benzene is C_6H_6; benzene has three double bonds and cyclohexane is saturated.

5. Structural formulas for the isomers of C_4H_9Br:

6. (a) C_2H_6 (c) $NaBr$
   (b) HgI (d) $(NH_4)_3PO_4$

7.

$$C_5H_{10}$$

or

C_2H_5OH C_2H_3OH

8. Fractionation is a form of distillation in which many substances with different boiling points are separated in "fractions."

9. The name of the family describes the type of bonding: -*ane*, saturated; -*ene*, double bond; -*yne*, triple bond; -*diene*, two double bonds.

10. A "straight-chain" carbon compound does not occur in a straight line because the bond angle between two carbon-to-carbon bonds is $109°$. Since the four bonds occur at the vertices of a tetrahedron, there are actually no straight chains.

Pages 124-125. INVESTIGATIONS

1. Both chlorophyll and hemoglobin are large organic molecules containing carbon, hydrogen, and a metallic atom. Chlorophyll absorbs light energy. Hemoglobin transports oxygen.

Chlorophyll

Hemin (functional part of hemoglobin molecule)

2. Motor oil: lubricant, heat dissipator (does not break down under heat) Gasoline: different octane ratings for high and low compression engines. Should burn completely and evenly. Diesel fuel: kerosene-like fuel for diesel engines.

3. The local gas company can furnish some material. Various environmental publications will have information on shortages of natural gas.

4. Reports will vary depending on types of dyes chosen. Mordants used to "set" various kinds of dyes include: trivalent chromium complexes, metallic hydroxides, tannic acid.

Chapter 7 Solids and Fluids

Equipment and Reagents for Experiments

Equipment
beaker (250-ml)
Bunsen burner
clamp for thermometer

colored paper
filter paper
glass jar (covered)
glass slide (microscope)
glass tubing
glass U-tube
graduated cylinder (25-ml and 50-ml)
graph paper
hollow rubber ball
lamp (40-watt) and socket
marbles
microscope
magnifying glass
pins
ring stand and ring
rubber band
rubber sheeting
rubber tubing
sink
shot (ball bearings)
styrofoam balls
test tube
thermometers (2) Celsius
thistle tube
thread
toothpicks
wire gauze

Reagents

alcohol (ethyl or isopropyl)
alum
Epsom salts
ice cubes
lithium carbonate crystals
mercury metal
mica
nickel sulfate crystals
Rochelle salt crystals
sodium dichromate dihydrate
sodium dichromate
sodium hydroxide (solid)
sodium nitrate crystals
sugur
sulfur

Page 130. EXPERIMENT

Try to have several microscopes available so that each student has a chance to observe several types of crystal structure.

29

Compound	Formula	Structure
sodium chloride	NaCl	cubic
Rochelle salt (potassium sodium tartrate)	$KNaC_4H_4O_6 \cdot H_2O$	ortho-rhombic
alum (potassium ammonium sulfate)	KNH_4SO_4	cubic
nickel sulfate	$NiSO_4 \cdot 7H_2O$	ortho-rhombic
copper (II) sulfate	$CuSO_4 \cdot 5H_2O$	triclinic
sodium nitrate	$NaNO_3$	ortho-rhombic

Page 132. EXPERIMENT

This experiment illustrates the formation of a "double compound" (note that Rochelle salt is a "double compound"). Lithium trisodium chromate hexahydrate is formed by the reaction of sodium dichromate dihydrate with lithium carbonate and sodium hydroxide. The crystals of $LiNa_3(CrO_4)_2 \cdot 6H_2O$ are hexagonal and yellow in color.

If crystals fail to form spontaneously, evaporate few drops of the solution and use the residue as seed crystals.

Page 134. EXPERIMENT

This experiment demonstrates the crystallization of a metallic alloy. Mercury and sodium are crystallized together as an alloy.

Be careful as you handle mercury metal and sodium nitrate. Mercury vapor is very poisonous.

Some of the mercury goes into solution, replacing metallic sodium which combines with the rest of the mercury to form a crystalline, mercury-sodium alloy. The crystals are needle-shaped.

Page 136. EXPERIMENT

When extra salt is added, the solution becomes supersaturated. By suspending the crystal, crystallization is facilitated.

The crystal provides a natural surface for the formation of other crystals. Be sure the beaker is clean and unscratched.

Page 136. EXPERIMENT

The structure of sulfur crystals changes with temperature. At room temperature sulfur has rhombic crystals. Above room temperature but below the melting point, it has monoclinic crystals. If cooled very quickly, plastic sulfur can be formed.

Page 136. PROBLEMS

1. Both melting and dissolving involve increase in disorder of a substance. When a substance melts its molecules become less ordered and move about more because heat was applied. Energy is given off. When a substance dissolves, molecules of solvent interfere with its structure. Energy is usually absorbed.

2. Not really, the crystals in both cases resume original structure. In one case space between molecules decreases. In the other, solvent molecules no longer disrupt structure.

Page 139. PROBLEMS

3. The increased volume of gas inside the balloon exerts more pressure on the balloon, inflating it.

4. The volume of air inside decreases so the pressure on the inside of the tire wall decreases. The tire deflates.

Page 140. PROBLEM

5. The air forced into the balloon increases the internal pressure causing the balloon to expand.

Page 141. EXPERIMENT

Water will spray in all directions so do this experiment outside if possible. The liquid forced into the ball will not compress. The pressure exerted by the water is transmitted equally to all surfaces. Water flows at same speed from each hole.

D. How and Why

1. One atom in the molecule has a greater nuclear charge than another so it exerts more control over the shared electrons in the covalent compound.

2.

Type of bond	Physical properties	Melting point	Conductivity
ionic	hard, brittle	high	insulator
covalent	hard	high	insulator
van der Waals	soft	low	insulator
dipole-dipole	soft	low	insulator
metallic	malleable	middle	conductor

3. Electricity is conducted by movement of ions through the melt.

4. The new volume is 1 liter since the gas occupies a 1-liter container.

   2 (1 liter at 1 atm) = 2 atm

   1 (2 liters at 2 atm) = <u>2 atm</u>

                    4 atm

5. A macromolecule is a crystal of a substance which is not molecular. One piece is a "molecule."

6. The greater the number of electrons and protons, the greater the van der Waals attraction since it is dependent upon the attraction of electrons of one atom for the protons of another atom. However, the shielding effect of the electrons of heavier elements tends to lessen van der Waals forces somewhat.

7. In a hydraulic lift, force is exerted on a small area. This creates pressure in a confined liquid. The pressure is transmitted through the liquid undiminished to a larger surface. The pressure on the larger area provides more force than was exerted to produce the pressure.

8. The four carbon valence bonds are symmetric with respect to the nucleus.

9. (a) KBr = ionic, group IA and VIIA

   (b) diamond—covalent, three dimensional strong bond

   (c) graphite—covalent, van der Waals, two-dimensional strong bond

   (d) ethane—van der Waals, molecules joined together

   (e) hydrogen chloride—van der Waals, molecules joined together

Pages 150-151. INVESTIGATIONS

1. Synthetic diamonds are made by subjecting carbon (graphite) to great heat and pressure for extended lengths of time.

2. The major crystal types can be found in a geology book.

3. Compressor liquefies a gas. The liquid is carried to refrigeration unit where it expands, changing to gas. This change of state takes heat energy from surrounding unit.

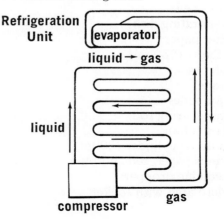

31

4. Hydraulic lift uses a reservoir of oil. Compressed air creates force on surface of reservoir. Pressure is transmitted through oil to piston which lifts car.

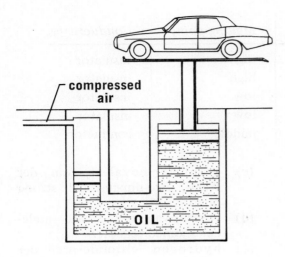

Chapter 8 Solutions

Equipment and Reagents for Experiments

Equipment
aspirator
balance
beaker (125-ml) (250-ml)
bell wire
Bunsen burner
cotton, absorbent
5 dropper bottles
2 dry cells
evaporating dish
filter paper
2 flasks (250-ml)
forceps
funnel
glass slides
glass stirring rod
glass tubing
graduate cylinder (50-ml)
litmus paper, red and blue
medicine droppers
microlamp with socket

microscope
ring stand and ring
rubber stoppers (to fit flasks)
rubber tubing—thick-walled
thermometer (Celsius)
test tubes
test tube rack
watch glasses
wire gauze
Reagents
alcohol, ethyl
ammonium chloride (solid)
calcium chloride
copper (II) sulfate (crystals)
distilled water
hydrochloric acid
ice cubes
liquid soap
mineral oil
naphtha
potassium sulfate
soda water (cold)
sodium carbonate
sodium chloride (solid)
sodium hydroxide (solid)
sodium nitrate (crystals)
sodium sulfate (crystals)
sodium thiosulfate (crystals)
sugar
vegetable oil
washing soda

Page 152. ACTIVITY

	water	*alcohol*
NaCl	soluble	insoluble
mineral oil	insoluble	insoluble
ethyl alcohol	soluble	soluble
sugar	soluble	soluble

Page 155. PROBLEMS

1. The sample with very small crystals will dissolve first because of the large surface area exposed.

2. In both chemical bonds are broken and reformed. Energy is given up or absorbed.

Page 155. EXPERIMENT

This experiment illustrates the energy change which takes place as a solid dissolves in a liquid. Ammonium chloride causes a decrease in temperature; sodium hydroxide causes a great increase in temperature. Be careful because beaker may become hot.

Page 156. PROBLEM

3. Since the solution becomes hot, the heat released is greater than the heat absorbed.

Page 157. EXPERIMENT

Do not agitate. Small crystals should dissolve more quickly. Be sure to check flasks periodically throughout the week.

Page 157. TEXT QUESTION

Dividing a cube to calculate the surface to volume ratio.

	Each Edge	Area of face	Number of faces	Number of cubes	Total Surface
First cube	20 cm	400 cm^2	$\times$ 6 $\times$	1 =	2400 cm^2
Second cube	10 cm	100 cm^2	$\times$ 6 $\times$	8 =	4800 cm^2
Third cube	1 cm	1 cm^2	$\times$ 6 $\times$	8,000 =	48,000 cm^2

Page 159. EXPERIMENT

Oil will not dissolve in water but will in naphtha. When liquid soap is added, vegetable oil forms a suspension in water.

Page 160. PROBLEM

4. Ionically bonded molecules dissociate in water. The molecules break up into ions each surrounded by water molecules. Molecular (covalently bonded) compounds ionize in water. Ions form but instantaneously react with the water molecules to form hydronium ions.
   Dissociation—potassium bromide
   Ionization—ammonia

Page 162. EXPERIMENT

This is a simple test for electrolytes. Pure water is a poor conductor of electricity. If the wires of the circuit are placed in water, little or no current should flow. The bulb will burn dimly or not at all. By adding an electrolyte (something that will dissociate or ionize in water) to the water, ions will form to carry the current.

NaCl is an electrolyte, alcohol is not. HCl and potassium sulfate are electrolytes, sugar will dissociate somewhat.

To make the bulb burn brighter, increase the concentration of the electrolyte or choose a substance that dissociates more completely.

Page 163. EXPERIMENT

Any convenient salt such as NaCl, NaNO$_3$, or KNO$_3$ will be very satisfactory for this experiment. To be sure that the volume of solution is as accurate as possible, measure the volume of the solution after it has been filtered. This can be done easily if the filtrate is collected in a graduated cylinder. Table for data:

1. Amount of solution _____ml
2. Mass of solution + dish _____g
3. Mass of dish + salt _____g

4. Mass of water (Step 2-Step 3) _____ g
5. Mass of dish _____ g
6. Mass of salt (Step 3-Step 5) _____ g

Calculate the mass of salt dissolved in 20 ml of water:

$$\frac{\text{Mass of salt (Step 6)}}{\text{Volume of water (Step 4)}} = \frac{x}{20 \text{ ml water}}$$

If the water is heated, more salt will dissolve. Repeat the experiment with the water at 70°-80°C.

Page 164. PROBLEMS

5. (a) Sodium nitrate is soluble.
   (b) Silver phosphate is not soluble.
   (c) Barium chloride is soluble.
   (d) Ammonium chloride is soluble.
   (e) Aluminum hydroxide is not soluble.
   (f) Magnesium carbonate is not soluble.

6. (a) Na^+, NO_3^-
   (c) Ba^{++}, Cl^-
   (d) NH_4^+, Cl^-

Page 164. EXPERIMENT

A straw hydrometer will give a relative (and very approximate) value of specific gravity. The specific gravities of the salt solutions will depend upon the concentration of each salt. Add enough salt to make the solution saturated but filter out undissolved crystals. Temperature can have a direct effect on solubility as shown in Figure 8-22. Adding heat may help more solute molecules overcome their mutual attraction and enable them to mix with the solvent.

Page 165. EXPERIMENT

Crystallization should occur as soon as the crystal is dropped in. The same experiment could be repeated and a crystal of sodium chloride added to the hypo solution. Because sodium chloride is not the right shape, crystallization would not take place. Sodium chloride is the wrong model for hypo crystallization.

Page 167. EXPERIMENT

Copper sulfate crystals lose their water of hydration at 100°C. The crystals will turn into white powder. Some crystals may form from the white powder by absorbing water.

Page 167. EXPERIMENT

$Na_2SO_4 \cdot 10 H_2O$ efflorescent (loses water of hydration at 100°C)
$CaCl_2$ deliquescent
$CuSO_4 \cdot 5 H_2O$ slowly efflorescent, white when dehydrated
(washing soda) $Na_2CO_3 \cdot 10 H_2O$ (loses water at M.P. 32.5-34.5°C) efflorescent at M.P. 32.5-34.5°C

Page 168. EXPERIMENT

Aspiration reduces vapor pressure above liquid and induces evaporation. Evaporation should reduce the temperature of the solution. Heat by increasing the kinetic energy of the liquid molecules allows more to escape. Heat and lower vapor pressure would increase evaporation. The solution never exceeds boiling temperature.

Page 169. PROBLEM

7. lower temperature since atmospheric pressure is less

Page 169. EXPERIMENT

The boiling point should be elevated due to presence of salt in the water. Boiling point elevation occurs because the vapor pressure of the solvent is lowered by the solute particles. Fewer overall solvent particles implies fewer escaping as vapor.

Page 170. PROBLEMS

8. No, salt water would boil at higher temperature than fresh water because of the increased concentration of dissolved salts in sea water.

9. Salt reduces the freezing temperature of water so it will melt the ice if temperatures are not too low.

D. How and Why

1. Change 50 ml to 0.05 liter.

$$\frac{50 \text{ g}}{1 \text{ liter}} = \frac{x}{0.05 \text{ liter}}$$

x = 2.5 g

2. Agitation, pulverization, and heat determine rate of solution.

3. At 20°C, 35 to 40 g dissolve. At 40°C 60 to 65 g dissolve. The solubility at 20° is about half the solubility at 40°.

4. Listed in order of the most soluble to the least soluble: (b) ammonium nitrate, (a) lead chloride, (d) calcium sulfate, (c) silver chloride.

5. If 100 ml of solution contains 50 g, then 60 ml of solution contains 30 g. Pour 60 ml of solution into a 100-ml graduate and fill the graduate with water.

6. The solution contains ions, and it is probably an inorganic solute in water.

7. Change 1 liter to 1000 ml.

$$\frac{50 \text{ g}}{300 \text{ ml}} = \frac{x}{1000 \text{ ml}} \quad x = 167 \text{ g}$$

8. Examples of household substances that dissolve in water: table salt, table sugar, baking soda, boric acid. Substances that dissolve in carbon tetrachloride: oil, grease, substances with oily base such as salad dressing or lipstick. Substances that dissolve in alcohol: iodine, colognes, perfume.

1. Silica gardens are made of "water glass," sodium silicates dissolved in water. Different colors are added and as crystals grow, a "garden" appears.

2. Fractional crystallization is a method for physically separating compounds. Most substances have a unique solubility in water at a given temperature. For example, at 70°C, potassium bromide is less soluble than potassium nitrate. If the water in a solution containing equal concentrations of these two compounds is evaporated at 70°C, the potassium bromide will crystallize first.

3. A hydrometer is used to find the specific gravity of the water-antifreeze mixture.

4. Sample graph:

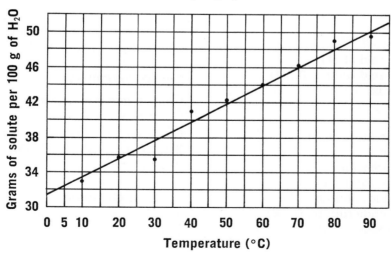

5. For variation, some students might try keeping some of the crystallization jars at different temperatures and noting day-to-day progress of each.

Chapter 9 Conservation of Mass

Equipment and Reagents for Experiments

Equipment
balance
beaker (250-ml)
bell wire
D.C. power supply
   (6-volt) or 4 dry cells
electrolysis apparatus (Hoffman)
filter paper
flasks (250-ml)
funnel
glass tubing
graduated cylinder (50-ml)
medicine dropper
microlamp
rubber stoppers (to fit flask, two-hole)
test tube
test tube (small enough to fit inside
   flask or use small pill bottle)
thistle tube
watch glass
wood splint

Reagents
barium chloride
calcium carbonate
calcium oxide
copper (II) sulfate (powdered)
copper wire
distilled water
hydrochloric acid (1 M)
hydrochloric acid (dilute, 0.3M)
hydrogen peroxide (3%)
lead metal strip
lime water
manganese dioxide (solid)
phenolphthalein
silver nitrate solution
sodium nitrate solution
sodium chloride solution
sodium hydroxide (dilute, 0.3M)
sodium hydroxide solution (0.1M)
sulfuric acid (concentrated)
zinc metal strip

Pages 180-181. PROBLEM

1. (a) $NaBr(aq) + AgNO_3(aq) \rightarrow AgBr(s) + NaNO_3(aq)$
   (b) $Ca(NO_3)_2(aq) + K_2SO_4(aq) \rightarrow CaSO_4(s) + 2KNO_3(aq)$
   (c) $2KCl(aq) + Pb(NO_3)_2(aq) \rightarrow 2KNO_3(aq) + PbCl_2(s)$
   (d) $AlCl_3(aq) + 3LiOH(aq) \rightarrow 3LiCl(aq) + Al(OH)_3(s)$
   (e) $3Ca(OH)_2(aq) + 2Fe(NO_3)_3(aq) \rightarrow 2Fe(OH)_3(s) + 3Ca(NO_3)_2(aq)$
   (f) $3MgSO_4(aq) + 2Na_3PO_4(aq) \rightarrow Mg_3(PO_4)_2(s) + 3Na_2SO_4$
   (g) hydrogen sulfide plus mercury (II) chloride in water yields 2 hydrogen chloride plus mercury (II) sulfide

Page 181. EXPERIMENT

A blue precipitate forms and the solution turns colorless if reaction goes to completion. Adding more sodium hydroxide and removing precipitates drives reaction further to the right.

$CuSO_4(aq) + 2NaOH(aq) \rightarrow Cu(OH)_2(s) + Na_2SO_4(aq)$

Page 181. EXPERIMENT

$Cu(s) + 2AgNO_3(aq) \rightarrow Cu(NO_3)_2(aq) + 2Ag(s)$

The silver plates out as a gray material on the wire. The solution turns blue due to the copper compound in solution.

Page 182. EXPERIMENT

Copper metal is deposited on zinc strip. Silver metal is deposited on lead
$CuSO_4(aq) + Zn(s) \rightarrow ZnSO_4(aq) + Cu(s)$
$2AgNO_3(aq) + Pb(s) \rightarrow Pb(NO_3)_2(aq) + 2Ag(s)$

Page 184. EXPERIMENT

$2H_2O_2 \rightarrow 2H_2O + O_2(g)$
MnO_2 acts as a catalyst to decomposition. A glowing splint bursts into flame in the presence of oxygen.

Pages 185-186. PROBLEM

2. (a) $Fe(s) + Cu(NO_3)_2 \text{ (aq)} \rightarrow Cu(s) + Fe(NO_3)_2 \text{ (aq)}$

(b) $2Mg(s) + O_2 \text{ (g)} \rightarrow 2MgO(s)$

(c) $2Hg_2O(s) \rightarrow 4Hg(s) + O_2 \text{ (g)}$

(d) $AgNO_3 \text{ (aq)} + KI(aq) \rightarrow AgI(s) + KNO_3$

(e) $CaI_2(aq) + Cl_2(g) \rightarrow CaCl_2(aq) + I_2 \text{ (g)}$

(f) $2H_2O(l) \xrightarrow{\text{elec.}} 2H_2 \text{ (g)} + O_2 \text{ (g)}$

Page 186. PROBLEM

3. $S(s) + O_2 \text{ (g)} \rightarrow SO_2 \text{ (g)}$ (a) yes (b) yes (c) solid (d) yields (e) synthesis (f) sulfur dioxide

Page 187. EXPERIMENT

Use care in putting thistle tube into the stopper. Lubricate tube before inserting and hold with towel to guard against cuts if breakage occurs.

Flask: $CaCO_3(s) + 2HCl \rightarrow CaCl_2(aq) + CO_2(g)$

Beaker: $CO_2(g) + Ca(OH)_2(aq) \rightarrow CaCO_3(s) + H_2O$

Heat is produced (exothermic reaction.) Ask students to give equations for reactions taking place. All three types of end reactions (gas, precipitate, and water) are present here.

Page 189. PROBLEM

4. (a) Na_2SO_4

Na	$2 \times 23 =$	46
S	$1 \times 32 =$	32
O	$4 \times 16 =$	64
		142

(b) $CaCO_3$

Ca	$1 \times 40 =$	40
C	$1 \times 12 =$	12
O	$3 \times 16 =$	48
		100

(c) NH_4NO_3

N	$2 \times 14 =$	28
H	$4 \times 1 =$	4
O	$3 \times 16 =$	48
		80

(d) $CuSO_4$

Cu	$1 \times 64 =$	64
S	$1 \times 32 =$	32
O	$4 \times 16 =$	64
		160

(e) $AgBr$

Ag	$1 \times 108 =$	108
Br	$1 \times 80 =$	80
		188

(f) K_3PO_4

K	$3 \times 39 =$	117
P	$1 \times 31 =$	31
O	$4 \times 16 =$	64
		212

Page 191. PROBLEM

5. (a) $C_2H_4 \text{ (g)}$ + $Br_2 \text{ (l)}$ $\rightarrow C_2H_4Br(l)$
1 formula unit + 1 formula unit → 1 formula unit
1 mole + 1 mole → 1 mole
28 g + 160 g → 188 g

(b) $3NaOH(aq)$ + $FeCl_3 \text{ (aq)}$ → $3NaCl(aq)$ + $Fe(OH)_3 \text{ (s)}$
3 moles + 1 mole → 3 moles + 1 mole
120 g + 161 g → 174 g + 107 g

(c) $2Na_3PO_4 \text{ (aq)}$ + $3MgSO_4 \text{ (aq)} \rightarrow Mg_3(PO_4)_2 \text{ (aq)}$ + $3Na_2SO_4 \text{ (s)}$
2 moles + 3 moles → 1 mole + 3 moles
328 g + 360 g → 262 g + 426 g

The NaOH solution should be about $0.1M$. The $1M$ HCl can be prepared by diluting the $6M$ standard reagent HCl by a ratio of 5 to 1 with distilled water. Phenolphthalein will be red in NaOH and colorless in neutral or acid solution. About 10 drops of HCl should be sufficient to neutralize the NaOH. If so, the following is a sample calculation:

0.5 ml HCl $\times$ $1\,M$ HCl $=$ 5 ml NaOH $\times$ x

$$x = \frac{0.5\ \text{ml}}{5\ \text{ml}} \Big|\, 1\,M$$

$$x = 0.1M \text{ NaOH}$$

Phenolphthalein is used as a indicator to show when neutralization has taken place.

Page 193. PROBLEMS

6. $BaCl_2$

Ba $\quad$ $1 \times 137 = 137$
Cl $\quad$ $2 \times 35 = \underline{70}$
$\qquad\qquad\qquad\quad 207$

$$\frac{0.5\ \text{moles}}{1\ \text{liter}} \Big|\, \frac{1\ \text{liter}}{} \Big|\, \frac{207g}{1\ \text{mole}} =$$
$$104g\ BaCl_2$$

7. $Na_2\,SO_4$

Na $\quad$ $2 \times 23 = 46$
S $\quad$ $1 \times 32 = 32$
O $\quad$ $4 \times 16 = \underline{64}$
$\qquad\qquad\qquad\quad 142$

$$\frac{0.3\ \text{moles}}{1\ \text{liter}} \Big|\, \frac{0.4\ \text{liter}}{} \Big|\, \frac{142g}{1\ \text{mole}} =$$
$$17g\ Na_2\,SO_4$$

8. $V_1 \times M_1 = V_2 \times M_2$

$$V_1 = \frac{V_2}{}\Big|\, \frac{M_2}{M_1}$$

$$V_1 = \frac{10\ \text{ml}}{}\Big|\, \frac{2M}{2M} = 10\ \text{ml}$$

$$V_1 = \frac{10\ \text{ml}}{}\Big|\, \frac{2M}{1M} = 20\ \text{ml}$$

$$V_1 = \frac{10\ \text{ml}}{}\Big|\, \frac{2M}{0.5M} = 40\ \text{ml}$$

$$V_1 = \frac{10\ \text{ml}}{}\Big|\, \frac{2M}{0.2M} = 100\ \text{ml}$$

D. *How and Why*

1. $\dfrac{28\ \text{g}}{56\ \text{g}} = \dfrac{x}{88g}$

$x = \dfrac{(28 \times 88)}{56}\,g$

$x = 44g$

2. gas, water, precipitate

3. $\dfrac{0.2\ \text{moles}}{1\ \text{liter}} \Big|\, \dfrac{0.3\ \text{liters}}{} \Big|\, \dfrac{74\ \text{g}}{1\ \text{mole}} = 4.4\,g$ KCl

4. KNO_3

K $\quad$ $1 \times 39 = 39$
N $\quad$ $1 \times 14 = 14$
O $\quad$ $3 \times 16 = \underline{48}$
$\qquad\qquad\qquad\quad 101$

1 mole KNO_3 = 101g

$\dfrac{20.2\ \text{g}}{101\ \text{g}} = \dfrac{x}{1\ \text{mole}}$

$x = 0.2$ mole

5. Endothermic reactions require the constant addition of heat for the reaction to be sustained; exothermic reactions give off heat as they proceed.

6. CO_2 $\qquad\qquad$ CS_2

C $\ 1 \times 12 = 12$ $\quad$ C $\ 1 \times 12 = 12$
O $\ 2 \times 16 = \underline{32}$ $\quad$ S $\ 2 \times 32 = \underline{64}$
$\qquad\qquad\quad 44$ $\qquad\qquad\qquad\ 76$

44 g CO_2 contain 12 g carbon
76 g CS_2 contain 12 g carbon
88 g CO_2 contain 24 g carbon

7. Br_2 $\ 2 \times 80 = 160$

$\dfrac{640\ \text{g}}{} \Big|\, \dfrac{1\ \text{mole}}{160\ \text{g}} = 4$ moles

8. (a) $Na_2 S(aq) + 2AgNO_3(aq) \rightarrow$
$\qquad 2NaNO_3(aq) + Ag_2 S(s)$

(b) $3H_2(g) + N_2(g) \rightarrow 2NH_3(g)$

(c) $2KClO_3(s) \rightarrow 2KCl(s) +$
$\qquad 3O_2(g)$

(d) $3CuSO_4(aq) + 2Al(s) \rightarrow$
$\qquad Al_2(SO_4)_3(aq) + 3Cu(s)$

(e) $2Na(s) + 2H_2 O(l) \rightarrow 2NaOH(aq) +$
$\qquad H_2(g)$

9. (a) $Na_2CrO_4(aq) + PbCl_2(aq) \rightarrow$
      $2NaCl(aq) + PbCrO_4(s)$
   (b) $Cl_2(g) + 2NaBr(aq) \rightarrow 2NaCl(aq)$
      $+ Br_2(g)$
   (c) $Mg(ClO_3)_2(s) \xrightarrow{\Delta} MgCl_2(s) + 3O_2(g)$
   (d) $2H_2(g) + O_2(g) \rightarrow 2H_2O(1)$
   (e) $3Ca(OH)_2(aq) + 2FeCl_3(aq) \rightarrow$
      $2Fe(OH)_3(s) + 3CaCl_2$

10. 8.(a) double replacement
    (b) synthesis
    (c) decomposition
    (d) single replacement
    (e) single replacement
   9.(a) double replacement
    (b) single replacement
    (c) decomposition
    (d) synthesis
    (e) double replacement

Page 196. INVESTIGATIONS

1. (a) Bubbles of gas are given off
   (b) sodium hydrogen carbonate in water solution plus heat yields carbon dioxide
   (c) $2NaHCO_3(aq) \rightarrow Na_2CO_3 + CO_2$
      $+ H_2O$
   (d) Reaction occurs, heat is given off, a gas escapes.
   (e) Reaction occurs, heat is given off, a gas escapes. Cream of tartar tastes sour.
   (f) Baking powder fizzes in water (gas is given off). Baking powder contains sodium bicarbonate and cream of tartar.
   (g) Biscuits, cakes, some types of breads need baking powder to make them rise.

2. In water, a salt releases ions which become surrounded by water molecules. A central ion surrounded by water molecules makes up a complex ion or a coordination compound. The number of molecules which are attached to the central ion is the coordination number.

Chapter 10 Acids, Bases, and Salts

Equipment and Reagents for Experiments

Equipment

balance
beaker
Bunsen burner
buret
buret holder
drinking straw
evaporating dish
graduated cylinder
labels
litmus, red and blue
ring stand
safety glasses
safety apron
6 test tubes
test tube rack
universal indicator paper
wire gauze

Reagents

calcium oxide
fruit juice
hydrochloric acid, dilute
lemon juice
liquid soap
milk (fresh, sour)
phenolphthalein
soda pop
soda water
sodium bicarbonate, dilute
sodium hydroxide, $0.1M$
sulfuric acid, dilute, concentrated
table sugar
vinegar
zinc (mossy)

Page 203. PROBLEM

(a) $Pb(s) + H_2SO_4(aq) \rightarrow PbSO_4(s) +$
   $H_2(g)$
(b) $2Al(s) + 6HCl(aq) \rightarrow 2AlCl_3(aq)$
   $+ 3H_2(g)$
(c) $2Al(s) + 3H_2SO_4(aq) \rightarrow Al_2(SO_4)_3$
   $(s) + 3H_2(g)$

39

Page 204. PROBLEM

2. HBr, HI, HF

Page 205. PROBLEM

3. (a) one (b) two (c) one (d) three (e) two

Page 206. PROBLEM

4. (a) one (b) two (c) one (b) two

Page 209. PROBLEMS

5. (a) $2 KOH(aq) + H_2SO_4(aq) \rightarrow K_2SO_4(aq) + 2H_2O$
   (b) $HBr(aq) + NaOH(aq) \rightarrow NaBr(aq) + H_2O$
   (c) $Ca(OH)_2(s) + 2HNO_3(aq) \rightarrow Ca(NO_3)_2(aq) + 2H_2O$
   (d) $Mg(OH)_2(s) + 2HCl(aq) \rightarrow MgCl_2(aq) + 2H_2O$
   (e) $Zn(s) + 2HBr(aq) \rightarrow ZnBr_2(aq) + H_2(g)$

6. (a) potassium sulfate
   (b) sodium bromide
   (c) calcium nitrate
   (d) magnesium chloride
   (e) zinc bromide

Page 210. PROBLEM

7. (a) basic
   (b) acid
   (c) acid
   (d) basic

Page 213. EXPERIMENT

Acid-base titration is a very important procedure for the student to learn to use. In many reactions in which no precipitate is formed it is very difficult to separate and weigh the products of the reaction while they are still in solution. But it is possible to measure the amounts of products by titration if the product is an acid or a base.

Make sure that the buret is clean before you begin the titration. Rinse it with distilled water and then rinse with some of the solution to be used in the buret.

A base of known concentration ($0.1M$ NaOH) is carefully measured out into an acid of unknown concentration (CH_3COOH) in which some acid-base indicator is present. When the end point of the reaction (neutralization) occurs, the indicator changes color. Make sure that the students read the buret carefully before the titration and at the end point. The difference in these readings is the volume (in liters) of the known base used to neutralize the acid.

Calculate the molarity of acid:
volume NaOH × molarity NaOH = volume CH_3COOH × molarity CH_3COOH

Sample calculation:
0.02 l NaOH × $0.1M$ NaOH = 0.06 l CH_3COOH × x

$$x = \frac{0.02 \text{ NaOH} \times 0.1\,M}{0.06 \text{ CH}_3\text{COOH}}$$

$$= 0.0033M \text{ CH}_3\text{COOH}$$

Since the vinegar was diluted first, the molarity of the undiluted vinegar will be six times as great.

The equation for the neutralization reaction:

$$NaOH + CH_3COOH \rightarrow CH_3COONa + H_2O$$

Page 213. PROBLEM

8. (a) $.015\,l \times \dfrac{0.3 \text{ moles NaOH}}{1 \text{ liter}} =$
   .0045 moles NaOH

   (b) 1 mole NaOH neutralizes 1 mole HNO_3 so .0045 moles NaOH = .0045 moles HNO_3

   (c) $.045\,l \times M \text{ HNO}_3 = .0045$ moles

   $$M = \frac{.0045 \text{ moles}}{.045\,l}$$

   $$M = 0.1 \text{ HNO}_3$$

Pages 214-216. STUDY QUESTIONS

D. *How and Why*

1. Examples of reactions that could be used:

40

(a) $Zn(s) + 2\,HCl \rightarrow Zn\,Cl_2 + H_2\ (g)$
(b) $HCl + NaOH \rightarrow NaCl + H_2O$
(c) $SO_2\ (g) + H_2O \rightarrow H_2SO_3$
(d) $HCl + AgNO_3 \rightarrow AgCl\ (s) + HNO_3$

2. Cl^- and Na^+

3. (a) H_2SO_4 acid   NaOH base
   (b) HCl acid   NaOH base
   (c) HNO_3 acid   NaOH base

4. pH is a measure of the hydrogen ion concentration of a solution (negative log of $[H_3O^+]$). If a solution has a pH $<$ 7 the solution is acid; if the pH = 7, the solution is neutral; if the pH $>$ 7, the solution is basic. The addition of a base increases the pH.

5. 50 ml KOH

$$\frac{2\ \text{moles}}{1\ \text{liter}} \left|\ \frac{.05\ \text{liter}}{} \right. = 0.1\ \text{mole HCl}$$

$$\frac{.1\ \text{mole}}{.05\ \text{liter}} = \frac{.1\ \text{mole KOH}}{x\ \text{liter KOH}}$$

$$x = .05\ \text{liter KOH (50 ml)}$$

6. sulfuric acid—fertilizers, dyes, petroleum refining, explosives, electroplating, dehydrating agent
hydrochloric acid—dyes, metal plating, digestive juice, producing other chemicals
nitric acid—fertilizers, explosives, manufacturing plastics

7. An acid is a substance which, when placed in water, increases the hydronium ion concentration. A base is a substance that increases the hydroxide ion concentration of a solution. A salt is a substance which is formed in a neutralization reaction.

8. (a) hydroiodic acid   (c) formic acid
   (b) nitrous acid   (d) chloric acid

Page 216. INVESTIGATIONS

1. Examples are:

Acids

Aspirin
Buttermilk
Cream of Tartar
Vinegar
Copper cleaner

Bases

Window cleaner
Washing soda
Milk of Magnesia
Baking soda

2. Results will vary depending on type of detergent.

3. Synthetic fibers hold up in acid since they are "hardened" in acid bath; natural fibers break down. Synthetic fibers react in basic solution.

4. Carbon dioxide in water produces carbonic acid. Oxides of sulfur produce sulfuric acid and other sulfur acids. Oxides of nitrogen form nitric acid and other nitrogen acids. Various chlorine compounds form hydrochloric acid and other chlorine acids.

Chapter 11 Force and Work

Equipment and Reagents for Experiments

bathroom scale
board
brick
cardboard
clamp
marble
masking tape
metal washers
meter stick
paper clip
paper cup
pencil
pulley, 1 movable
        1 fixed
        2 fixed in tandem
ring stand
ruler
scissors
spring
2 spring balances
string
thimble

weights, 2 equal
      2 unequal
      0.5 lb
watch

Page 221. PROBLEMS

1. A student's arms could lift or push it if the desk is not bolted down. If the desk is bolted down it would require a jack to lift it or a very large push or pull by many students.

2. The forces of muscles pulling on the bones inside body limbs move your body parts.

3. Sit on a chair, place hands on the chair, and push down.

Page 223. PROBLEMS

4. $W = FD$
   $W = 15\ \text{lb} \times 2\ \text{ft}$
   $W = 30\ \text{ft-lb}$

5. $W = FD$
   $W = 3\ \text{lb} \times 2\ \text{ft}$
   $W = 6\ \text{ft-lb}$

6. Lifting the suitcase might take more work. The distance component in each case is the same but the force needed to overcome gravity is probably more than the force needed to overcome inertia.

7. $W = FD$
   $W = 40\ \text{nt} \times 4\text{m}$
   $W = 160\ \text{nt-m}$

8. $F = \dfrac{W}{D}$

   $F = \dfrac{500\ \text{ft-lb}}{100\ \text{ft}}$

   $F = 5\ \text{lb}$

Page 224. PROBLEM

9. (a) force used to move pedals converted into larger force of the wheel pushing on the road
   (b) oar acts as a lever to push boat
   (c) the needle acts as a wedge, great gain in speed

(d) elevator uses pulleys to reduce force needed to lift objects
(e) block and tackle sets several pulleys in tandem to distribute force
(f) crowbar acts as a lever

Page 225. ACTIVITY

Use this activity to illustrate the types of levers and the properties of each type. Refer to Figure 11-11 for the types of levers. In Part 1 the second class lever is considered. The fulcrm is under the book at the point that the ruler touches the table. In Part 2, the pivot point is at the edge of the table. Since the fulcrum is between the effort arm and the resistance arm, this is a first class lever like a crowbar. In Part 3, the third class lever is presented. The effort force lies between the resistance and the fulcrum.

The second class lever has the highest M.A. and makes the task the easiest. The third class has the lowest M.A.

Page 226. PROBLEM

10. First Class Lever
    effort/fulcrum/resistance
    Second Class Lever
    effort/resistance/fulcrum
    Third Class Lever
    resistance/effort/fulcrum

Page 228. PROBLEMS

11. $F_e \times D_r = F_e \times D_e$
    $100\ \text{lb} \times 4\ \text{ft} = F_e \times 5\ \text{ft}$

    $F_e = \dfrac{400\ \text{ft-lb}}{5\ \text{ft}} = 80\ \text{lb}$

12. $F_r \times D_r = F_e \times D_e$
    $100\ \text{lb} \times 3\ \text{ft} = 75\ \text{lb} \times D_e$
    $300\ \text{ft-lb} = 75\ \text{lb} \times D_e$
    $D_e = 4\ \text{ft}$

13. $50\ \text{nt} \times 1\ \text{m} = F_e \times 2\text{m}$
    $50\ \text{nt-m} = F_e \times 2\text{m}$
    $F_e = 25\ \text{nt}$

14. $(5\ \text{nt} + 3\ \text{nt})1\ \text{m} = F_e \times 1.5\ \text{m}$
    $8\ \text{nt-m} = F_e \times 1.5\ \text{m}$
    $F_e = 5.3\ \text{nt}$

42

15. $I.M.A. = \dfrac{\text{Effort Arm}}{\text{Resistance Arm}}$

    $I.M.A. = \dfrac{10 \text{ ft}}{5 \text{ ft}}$

    $I.M.A. = 5$

16. $I.M.A. = \dfrac{\text{Effort Arm}}{\text{Resistance Arm}}$

    $I.M.A. = \dfrac{1.0 \text{ m}}{0.2 \text{ m}}$

    $I.M.A. = 5$

Page 230. PROBLEM

17.

Pulleys	Effort Force	Distance	Resistance Force
Set A	10 lb	2 ft	20 lb
Set B	10 lb	3 ft	50 lb
Set C	5 lb	20 ft	20 lb

Resistance Distance	Support Ropes	I.M.A.
1 ft	2	2
0.6 ft	5	5
5 ft	4	4

Page 230. EXPERIMENT

In Part 1 each spring balance should register ¼ lb. In Part 2 when the single movable pulley is used the force on the spring balance should still be ¼ lb. The movable pulley has a mechanical advantage of 2. When the fixed pulley and movable pulley are used as in Figure 11-15c the mechanical advantage is increased to 3. In Figure 11-15d the force needed to lift the weight will be 1/6 lb (M.A. = 3) since only three support ropes involve the movable pulley. The addition of the third pulley allows for a change in the direction of the force. The addition of support ropes increases the mechanical advantage. Try to keep the length of the string as equal as possible for all setups for the sake of experimental control. The students might want to measure the distance the effort and resistance forces move to reinforce the idea of mechanical advantage.

Page 231. PROBLEM

18. automobile, lawnmower, bicycle, wagon, egg beater
Answers given by students.

Page 232. PROBLEMS

19. roads to higher elevations, stairs from one floor of house to another, loading ramps, ramps over curbs, boards to load trucks, trailer hitches for transporting cars

20. Rather than lifting an object straight up, the force needed to overcome gravity changes direction and is spread over a distance. The overall force required is greater but the average force/unit time is less.

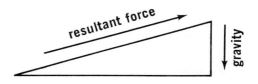

Page 234. PROBLEMS

21. knife, razor blade, hatchet, ice pick, wood planer, chisel

22. $I.M.A. = \dfrac{\text{circumference}}{\text{pitch}}$

    $I.M.A. = \dfrac{2(3.14)\,(42 \text{ in.})}{0.25 \text{ in.}}$

    $I.M.A. = \dfrac{263.76 \text{ in.}}{0.25 \text{ in.}}$

    $I.M.A. = 1055$

23. decreases to 353.6

Page 236. PROBLEM

24. $W_i = F_e \times D_e$
    $W_i = 100 \text{ nt} \times 6 \text{ m}$
    $W_i = 600 \text{ nt-m}$

    $W_o = F_r \times D_r$
    $W_o = 200 \text{ nt} \times 2 \text{ m}$
    $W_o = 400 \text{ nt-m}$

Page 237. PROBLEM

25. % Efficiency = $\dfrac{\text{Work output}}{\text{Work input}} \times 100\%$

$\% E = \dfrac{W_o}{W_i} \times 100$

$\% E = \dfrac{400 \text{ nt-m}}{600 \text{ nt-m}}$

$\% E = 66.7\%$

26. $\% E = \dfrac{W_o}{W_i} \times 100$

$\% E = \dfrac{400 \text{ nt-m}}{600 \text{ nt-m}} \times 100$

$\% E = 66.7\%$

Page 238. PROBLEMS

27. $P = \dfrac{W}{t}$

$P = \dfrac{2000 \text{ ft-lb}}{4 \text{ sec}}$

$P = 500 \text{ ft-lb/sec}$

$P(\text{hp}) = \dfrac{500 \text{ ft-lb/sec}}{550 \text{ ft-lb/sec}}$

$P = 0.91 \text{ hp}$

28. $P = \dfrac{W}{t}$

$P = \dfrac{3000 \text{ ft-lb}}{60 \text{ sec}} \times \dfrac{1 \text{ hp}}{550 \text{ ft-lb/sec}}$

$P = 50 \text{ ft-lb/sec} \times \dfrac{1 \text{ hp}}{550 \text{ ft-lb/sec}}$

$P = 0.09 \text{ hp}$

29. $W = FD$

$W = 40,000 \text{ lb} \times 100 \text{ ft}$

$W = 4,000,000 \text{ ft-lb}$

$P = \dfrac{4,000,000 \text{ ft-lb}}{120 \text{ sec}} \times \dfrac{1 \text{ hp}}{550 \text{ ft-lb/sec}}$

$P = 60.7 \text{ hp}$

Page 239. PROBLEM

30. lowest (a), (b), (d), (c), (f), (e), highest

Page 240-242. STUDY QUESTIONS

D. *How and Why*

1. $W = F \times D$
   $W = 25 \text{ nt} \times 10 \text{ m}$
   $W = 250 \text{ nt-m}$

2. (a) oar—oarlock, blade, handle
   (b) pliers—bolt, jaws, handles
   (c) wheelbarrow—axle, box, handles

3. Effort force will move 5 in.

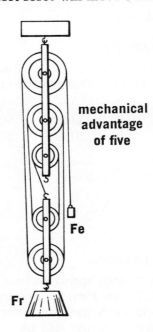

mechanical advantage of five

4. They all make work easier by changing the direction, size, or distance through which a force moves.

5. typewriter—lever
   car—wheel and axle, lever, screw
   record player—wheel and axle
   can opener—wedge
   lawn mower—wheel and axle
   tape dispenser—wheel and axle

6. $\% E = \dfrac{W_o}{W_i} \times 100$

$\% E = \dfrac{200 \text{ nt-m}}{250 \text{ nt-m}} \times 100$

$\% E = 80\%$

7. $F_e \times D_e = F_r \times D_r$

$F_e \times 1 \text{ ft} = 50 \text{ lb} \times 10 \text{ ft}$

$F_e = \dfrac{500 \text{ ft-lb}}{1 \text{ ft}}$

$F_e = 500 \text{ lb}$

8. $W = Pt$

$W = \frac{1}{4} \text{ hp} \times 180 \text{ sec}$

$W = \frac{1}{4}\text{hp} \left(\dfrac{550 \text{ ft lb/sec}}{1 \text{ hp}} \right) \times 180 \text{ sec}$

$W = (137.5 \text{ ft-lb/sec}) \times 180 \text{ sec}$

$W = 24{,}750 \text{ ft-lb}$

9. Since power is work per unit time, the more powerful engine (1 hp) will be able to do the work twice as fast.

10. $W = F \times D$

$W = 175 \text{ lb} \times 16 \text{ ft}$

$W = 2{,}800 \text{ ft-lb}$

Pages 242-243. INVESTIGATIONS

1. Tuning the engine means making sure the engine's ignition system fires the spark plugs at the correct time. Contact points, distributor, rotor, and spark plugs are checked.

2. Sample set up:

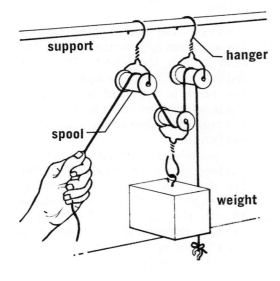

3. Find out about the r.p.m. "power bands" of different motorcycles.

4. Try to build a model of an early "perpetual motion" machine.

Chapter 12 Moving Bodies

Equipment and Reagents for Experiments

beaker, 400 ml
board, 2 m × 15 cm
  plywood, 60 cm^2
lead sinker
marble
meter stick
pan balance
rubber band
ruler
2 screw eyes
2 spring scales
stopwatch
string
3 weights (metric masses), 100 g, 250 g, 500 g

Page 245. PROBLEM

1. As submarine submerges it takes on water to reduce its boyuancy. To surface it forces water out of the ballast tank with compressed air. It decreases in weight and floats to the surface.

Page 247. PROBLEM

2. (a) decrease weight to one fourth

(b) $\dfrac{1}{9}$ of surface weight

Page 249. PROBLEMS

3. $v = \dfrac{d}{t}$

$v = \dfrac{100 \text{ m}}{50 \text{ sec}}$

$v = 2 \text{ m/sec}$

4. $v = \dfrac{d}{t}$

$$\dfrac{50 \text{ m}}{\text{sec}} = \dfrac{d}{600 \text{ sec}}$$

$$d = \dfrac{50 \text{ m}}{\text{sec}} \times 600 = 30,000 \text{ m}$$

5. train

6. The speed of car in Figure 12-11 is constant but the speed of the car in Figure 12-12 changes. Since each speed shown is maintained for the same time, average speed may be computed by finding the arithmetic average of the speeds shown in the graph.

average speed =
$$\dfrac{(30 + 20 + 40 + 10 + 20) \text{ mi}}{5 \text{ hr}} =$$

$$\dfrac{120 \text{ mi}}{5 \text{ hr}} = 24 \text{ mi/hr}$$

Page 250. PROBLEMS

7. $v = \dfrac{d}{t}$

$$v = \dfrac{2560 \text{ mi}}{5 \text{ hr}}$$

$$v = 512 \text{ mi/hr}$$

8. $v = \dfrac{d}{t}$

$$v = \dfrac{2000 \text{ m}}{4 \text{ sec}}$$

$$v = 500 \text{ m/sec}$$

Page 250. EXPERIMENT

The marble does not have a constant speed. It is accelerating due to the force of gravity. Therefore the results will be average speed over the entire run not the actual speed of any moment.

Page 252. PROBLEM

9. $a = \dfrac{v_2 - v_1}{t}$

$$a = \dfrac{585 - 450 \text{ km/hr}}{15 \text{ sec}}$$

$$a = \dfrac{135 \text{ km/hr}}{15 \text{ sec}}$$

$$a = 9 \text{ km/hr/sec}$$

Page 254. PROBLEMS

10. $a = \dfrac{v_2 - v_1}{t}$

$$a = \dfrac{400 \text{ mi/hr} - 500 \text{ mi/hr}}{20 \text{ sec}}$$

$$a = \dfrac{-100 \text{ mi/hr}}{20 \text{ sec}}$$

$$a = -5 \text{ mi/hr/sec}$$

11. $a = \dfrac{v_2 - v_1}{t}$

$$a = \dfrac{80 - 160 \text{ mi/hr}}{8 \text{ sec}}$$

$$a = \dfrac{-80 \text{ mi/hr}}{8 \text{ sec}}$$

$$a = -10 \text{ mi/hr/sec}$$

12. Passenger car and drag race car— forces produced by the engine and the tires against the road.
Jet plane—reaction forces produced by jet engines, force of gravity if the plane falls a short distance in a low pressure pocket.

13. Passenger car—forces produced by brake drums against the wheels and road against the wheels. Drag race car—same as for passenger car or, if the racer is equipped with a drag chute which is released at the end of the run, the force of air against the drag chute.
Jet plane—force of air against the airplane, force produced by reversing the engines just after landing. The engines produce a force opposite to the direction the plane is moving. Brakes and the ground produce forces against the wheels which stop the plane after landing.

Page 256. PROBLEMS

14. 50 lb + 100 lb = 150 lb

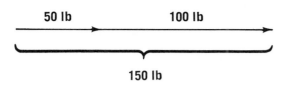

15.

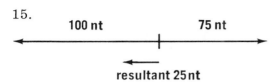

16. Answers will vary depending on accuracy of drawing. The students
may be interested to note that the
larger the scale of the parallelogram
the greater the accuracy of the calculation when the same method and
tools are used. Pythagorean Theorem
can be used: $c^2 = a^2 + b^2$

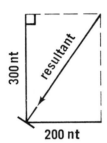

Resultant = 360 nt

17. Subtract the N from the S force and
then subtract the E from the W
force. Use these two resultants in a
diagram to find the resultant force
on the ball.
7 lb S — 4 lb N = 3 lb S
5 lb W — 2 lb E = 3 lb W

Resultant = 4.2 lb SW

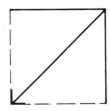

Page 258. PROBLEM

18. Scale ½ in. or 1 cm = 5 km
Resultant = 21 km
Answers will vary according to
accuracy.
Using Pythagorean Theorem
$c^2 = a^2 + b^2$
$c^2 = (20)^2 + 5^2$
$c^2 = 425$ km^2
c = 20.6 km

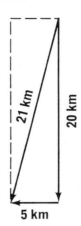

5 km

Pages 260-262. STUDY QUESTIONS

D. *How and Why*

1. $\bar{v} = \dfrac{d}{t} = \dfrac{80 \text{ mi}}{2 \text{ hr}} \left| \dfrac{1 \text{ hr}}{60 \text{ min}} \right. = 0.67$ mi/min

2. $\bar{a} = \dfrac{v_2 - v_1}{t} = \dfrac{50 \text{ mi/hr} - 10 \text{ mi/hr}}{6 \text{ sec}} =$
   6.7 mi/hr/sec

3. $\bar{v} = at = \dfrac{1 \text{ m}}{\text{sec/sec}} \left| 6 \text{ sec} \right. = 6$ m/sec

4. $\bar{v} = \dfrac{v_1 + v_2}{2} = \dfrac{0 \text{ m/sec} + 6 \text{ m/sec}}{2} =$
   $\qquad\qquad\qquad\qquad$ 3 m/sec

5. $d = \bar{v}t = \dfrac{3 \text{ m}}{\text{sec}} \left| 6 \text{ sec} \right. = 18$ m

6. a. 23 mi/hr b. 2 mi/hr c. 2 min to
   2.7 min d. 0.5 min to 2 min, 2.7
   min to 4.2 min and 4.8 min to 5
   min

7. $t = \dfrac{v}{a} = \dfrac{80 \text{ ft/sec}}{20 \text{ ft/sec/sec}} = 4 \text{ sec}$

$\bar{v} = \dfrac{v_1 + v_2}{2} = \dfrac{80 \text{ ft/sec} + 0 \text{ ft/sec}}{2} =$

40 ft/sec

$d = \bar{v}t = \dfrac{40 \text{ ft}}{\text{sec}} \left| \dfrac{4 \text{ sec}}{} \right. = 160 \text{ ft}$

8. Winds affect the velocity and direction of the airplane's flight. Head-winds decrease velocity with respect to the ground and tailwinds increase the velocity. Crosswinds may force an airplane off a direct course and must be compensated for in air navigation.

9. No. The forward push of air by the fan (action force) is equal to the opposing reaction force of the air against the fan. The blast of air pushes forward against the sail and the fan pushes backwards against the boat. Since action and reaction forces are equal and opposite, the boat does not move.

10. A hammer's weight is the force of gravity acting on the hammer. For example, a 0.5 lb hammer exerts 0.5 lb of force when lying at rest. When a hammer is swung to strike a nail, it is accelerated; both the force of gravity and the force of the arm accelerate it. This force, which is larger than the hammer's weight, is exerted against the nail.

Page 262. INVESTIGATIONS

1. A flight instructor at a local airport will probably have information and might be willing to talk to the class.

2. A sailboat can sail against the wind if there is a resultant force vector opposite the wind direction.

Equipment and Reagents for Experiments

aluminum foil
ball, rubber
    Ping-Pong
    metal
balloon
2 boards, 15 cm × 4 m
clock (to dismantle)
2 coins
dry cell, 6 v
electric bell
glass, 8 oz tumbler
hammer
metronome
nails
paper, 8 × 15 cm card
        graph
protractor
rulers
solder, liquid
3 spring scales
stick (60-cm)
stopper, rubber
string
tube, plastic 2 cm × 15 cm
9 washers
wire hanger
wire, bell

Page 266. PROBLEMS

1. c a r—tires against road; bullet—explosion of gunpowder; arrow—snap of the bow after it is stretched and released; jet airplane—hot gases escaping from engine; roller skates—push of skate against the sidewalk or floor.

2. rocket—atmosphere when a rocket enters the earth's atmosphere, gravity and earth when a rocket falls back to the ground; submarine—water against the hull, rudder pushing against water when course is changed, gravity when submarine submerges buoyant force of the

water; surfboard—wave against board, beach against board at end of ride, gravity in a wipe out; car—road against tires; bowling ball—force of floor on a spinning ball will cause it to curve, backstop stops ball at end of alley.

3. Gravity is involved when a rocket falls back to earth, a submarine submerges, a surfboard wipes out; by shifting his weight a rider controls surfboard. In each case gravity forces the body toward the earth.

4. Seat belts hold the passenger in his seat if the car stops suddenly and prevents him from being thrown forward and possibly injured. Also, the seat belt may prevent injury by holding a passenger in his seat during an accident.

Page 268. PROBLEMS

5. A fly. A fly has less mass; therefore less inertia. Its wings can create more force per unit of body mass.

6. The moving van needs more force to stop than a sports car at the same speed. The moving van has more mass; therefore, for the same deceleration, it will need more force.

7. Pedaling a bicycle hard to make it go faster. Jumping up out of a chair. Throwing a ball. Other examples given by students.

8. In each case a force causes a body to accelerate.

9. $a = F/m$
$a = 10$ nt/20 kg
$a = .5$ m/sec^2
Remember: $F = ma$, nt = $\dfrac{\text{kg}}{}\bigg|\dfrac{\text{m}}{\text{sec}^2}$

Page 270. PROBLEMS

10. Your weight, a force, down on the earth.

11. Upward force of the floor on your feet.

12. Recoil, the sharp backward movement of the gun, is the reaction force that fires the bullet out of the gun barrel.

13. Action force of pencil against paper is opposed by the reaction force of paper against pencil.

14. The Hero's engine would have the same motion. The balloon and rocket would continue in a path out to space. The motions would be faster since there would be no opposing friction force due to air resistance.

15. (a) Newton's third law—action and reaction forces

(b) Newton's first law—inertia

(c) Newton's third law—action and reaction forces

(d) Newton's first law—inertia

(e) Newton's third law—action and reaction forces

Page 273. PROBLEMS

16. $v = gt = \dfrac{9.8\text{m}}{\text{sec}^2}\bigg|\dfrac{2\text{ sec}}{} = 19.6$ m/sec

17. $d = \frac{1}{2}gt^2 \qquad d = \dfrac{1}{2}\bigg|\dfrac{32\text{ ft}}{\text{sec}^2}\bigg|\dfrac{9\text{ sec}^2}{}$

$d = 144$ ft

18. $d = \frac{1}{2}gt^2$

$d = \dfrac{1}{2}\bigg|\dfrac{9.8\text{ m}}{\text{sec}^2}\bigg|\dfrac{1\text{ sec}^2}{}$

$d = 4.9$ m

Page 275. PROBLEMS

19. $v = -gt$

$v = \dfrac{-9.8\text{ m}}{\text{sec}^2}\bigg|\dfrac{2\text{ sec}}{} = -19.6$ m/sec

$v = (30.0$ m/sec$) + (-19.6$ m/sec$) =$

10.4 m/sec

20. $t = \dfrac{v}{-g}$

$= \dfrac{30\text{m}}{\text{sec}}\bigg|\dfrac{\text{sec}^2}{9.8\text{m}} = 3.06$ sec

21. Due to inertia the car tends to keep moving in a straight line rather than rounding the curve. Ice decreases the friction between the tires and the road (centripetal force).

22. Inertia tends to cause it to go off in a straight line instead of curving in a circle; your hand must keep pulling inward.

23. More of the car's weight is centered over the wheels. This increases the centripetal force and makes it less likely for the car to slide off the road.

24. (a) automobile

    (b) electric vacuum cleaner

    (c) wristwatch

    (d) piano

    (e) satellite

25. tennis ball has more momentum because it has more mass

26. The momentum of the tennis ball is equal to the momentum of the golf ball because both have the same mass and velocity.

D. *How and Why*

1. Pendulum swinging back and forth. Coasting automobile. Trying to move a heavy boulder. Other examples given by students. Passenger in an automobile thrown forward when car stops suddenly and passenger hits dashboard. Other examples given by students.

2. a. 1st—inertia

   b. 3rd—action and reaction forces

   c. 2nd—deceleration

   d. 3rd—action and reaction

3. $v = gt = 32 \text{ ft/sec}^2 \times 3 \text{ sec} = 96 \text{ ft/sec}$

4. Drop the stone off the bridge and time the seconds it falls. Use the formula $d = \frac{1}{2} g t^2$

5. $t = v/\text{-}g = \dfrac{32 \text{ ft/sec}}{32 \text{ ft/sec}^2} = 1 \text{ sec}$

6. The resultant of the horizontal and vertical motion is a parabola.

7. The force of gravity pulls the arrow toward the ground while it is moving forward. An arrow aimed above the mark would land on target.

1. Pollution is caused by many sources giving out various quantities of wastes. A systems approach would try to determine the most feasible and economical method of dealing with each kind to reduce the cumulative effect.

Chapter 14 Heat Energy

Equipment and Reagents for Experiments

aluminum foil
balance
ball, iron with ring
2 beakers (1 large, 1 small)
bottles, glass pint
Bunsen burner
calorimeter (or materials to make calorimeter—cans, #2½ and #1; electric drill; glass wool; wood to cover large can)
candle
clamp, flask
cork
dowel, ¼ in.
dye
glass rod
glass tubing
glass wool
graduated cylinder (250-ml)
graph paper
hammer
ice

knitting needle, metal
masking tape
nail
2 paper cups
paraffin
refrigerator
ring
ring stand and ring
rubber bands
rubber stoppers
ruler
sand
steam boiler
test tube (large Pyrex)
test tube clamp
4 thermometers, Celsius
vacuum bottle, pint
watch (with second hand)
wood block

Page 293. PROBLEM

1. (a) falling rock (b) sled going downhill (c) swinging baseball bat (d) car in motion (e) quarterback Many examples from students.

Page 293. ACTIVITY

Book loses potential energy because it is converted into kinetic energy as the book falls.

Page 294. PROBLEM

2. (a) mainspring unwinds

   (b) rubber band contracts when released

   (c) opens when released

   (d) moves when air rushes out

   (e) diver jumps off board

   (f) changed to chemical energy when struck

Page 296. PROBLEMS

3. sun, lamp, warm food

4. clouds cut out some radiant heat from sun, turn off lamp or insulate it, cover food or keep in reflective container

Page 297. PROBLEMS

5. metal knitting needle—conductor glass rod insulator

6. conductors—metal in pans, water in bath, air in furnace insulators—air in glass wool, wood, brick

7. reflects incoming heat. See Experiment on p. 296.

Page 298. PROBLEMS

8. In steam radiator, heat is given off as steam condenses. Heat rises from hot radiator setting up convection currents.

9. Air space surrounded by insulating materials.

10. Hot water will rise in middle of beaker and cold water will sink along sides. Hot air will rise along outside wall. Colder air will sink and travel along floor.

Page 300. PROBLEM

11. Heat lost to surroundings cannot be calculated so only a well insulated calorimeter would give an accurate measurement.

Page 301. PROBLEMS

12. 5,000 calories heat gained by the water equals heat lost by the metal, excluding heat left in inner chamber.

13. $H = (t_2 - t_1)\, m$
    $= (100°C - 25°C)\,(500\ g)$
    $= (75°C)\,(500\ g)$
    $= 37,500\ cal$

14. $H = (t_2 - t_1)\, m$
    $= (60°C - 40°C)\,(20\ g)$
    $= (20°C)\,(20\ g)$
    $= 400\ cal$

Page 302. PROBLEMS

15. Answers will vary.

16. 1 cal = 4.4×10^{-3} B.T.U.
    1 B.T.U. = 252 cal

17. Each gram of ice absorbs 80 calories as it forms.

18. Water as it evaporates from the skin absorbs 540 cal/g.

19. Since steam releases 540 cal/g as it condenses, it would take 54 g of water changing $10°C$ to produce as much heat.

Pages 308-309. STUDY QUESTIONS

D. How and Why

1. Heat is the total kinetic energy in the molecules of a substance. Temperature is the average kinetic energy, a relative measure of its hotness or coldness

2. kinetic energy—a person walking, an airplane flying, snow falling, a football pass, the wind blowing
potential energy—water behind a dam, snow on the side of a mountain, a hung-up coat, a person sitting on a chair, an unburnt piece of paper

3. If you measure the mass of the water in a calorimeter and the change in temperature that occurs, you can calculate the amount of heat in the substance burned.

4. The heat might cause the parts to expand. They then might "freeze" together.

5. The ether absorbs heat as it evaporates. If it drew enough heat from the water, the water would freeze.

6. $H = (t_2 - t_1) m$
$= (1.5°C) 1000 g$
$= 1500 cal$

7. Gain in kinetic energy causes molecules to move apart and the parts to expand.

8.

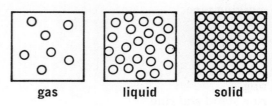

gas   liquid   solid

9. When liquid freon, under pressure, evaporates to a gas, the molecules gain molecular potential energy (heat of fusion), taking on heat from the inside of the refrigerator.

Page 310. INVESTIGATIONS

1. Thermal pollution results when some part of the natural surroundings are abnormally heated. For example, a power plant discharges hot water into a river and the temperature of the river rises. Cooling towers are a partial solution to the problem.

2.

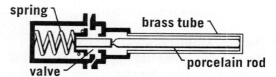

Brass Tube Type Thermostat

3. Building supply stores or hardware stores would have this type of material.

Chapter 15 Heat and Its Uses

Equipment and Reagents for Experiments

balloon
2 beakers
bimetallic strip
broom straw
Bunsen burner
dish (for mercury)
dye, dark-colored
ether

flask (500-ml)

glass tubing, 10 cm of 1 mm bore
    80 cm

graph paper

hot plate

ice

mercury

2 metal cans

3 metal pieces (Al, Fe, Cu—all same
    mass)

paraffin

refrigerator

ring stand and ring

rubbing alcohol

rubber band

ruler

sand

tape measure

2 test tube clamps

2 thermometers

tongs

vacuum bottle

Page 313. PROBLEMS

1. The specific heat of water is higher than sand, glass, and air.

2. Because it has a high specific heat, it absorbs a relatively large amount of heat per gram.

3. Nearby bodies of water make climate warmer in winter and cooler in summer. The water is warmer than the land in winter and cooler in summer.

Page 316. PROBLEM

4. Air pressure is greater at sea level and greater under the water's surface. Air pressure is caused by the weight of the atmosphere's mass. The earth at sea level has more atmosphere above it, thus greater force pushing down (weight) than at the top of the mountain. The weight of water above a submerged body makes the force on the body greater than force at the water's surface.

Pages 328-330. STUDY QUESTIONS

D. How and Why

1. The partial vacuum between the two glass walls and the metallic coating reduces heat loss or gain by radiation, conduction, and convection.

2. Changes in density cause liquids to rise or sink, thereby producing movements called convection currents.

3. Heat in the large bodies of water may prevent late spring frosts that would damage fruit blossoms.

4. A hot water heating system transfers heat by moving hot water from a boiler to radiators inside rooms.

5. Heating and cooling causes the bimetallic strip in the thermostat to bend back and forth. When the temperature becomes too low the strip bends to touch an electrical contact that turns on the heating unit. When the right temperature is reached the bimetallic strip bends away from the contact and the heater shuts off.

6. Burning of the gasoline inside the engine's cylinders produces heat which causes gases in the cylinders to expand and exert a force on the pistons. Force makes the pistons move up and down and thereby turn a crankshaft to which they are attached. Motion of the pistons and crankshaft produces power, work (f × d) per unit time.

7. The Wankel, or rotary engine, has a rotor that rotates inside a chamber. A mixture of gasoline and air is sent into the chamber where it is compressed and then ignited by a spark plug. This causes the release of hot gases which exert a force on the rotor, making it rotate in a clockwise direction. The rotor is attached to a crankshaft that turns the wheels of a car.

8. Thermal pollution can warm the temperature of water in rivers and lakes several degrees. This aids the growth of some plants causing them to overpopulate the water. Animals often die because the water can no longer provide enough oxygen or because the water is clogged with algae and bacteria.

9. Their molecules decrease vibration and take on more orderly arrangements. The resistance to flow of electrical current in metals approaches zero.

Page 330. INVESTIGATIONS

1. Models are available at hobby shops or department stores.

2. A good geology book would be a reliable source.

3. Some students might be interested in reporting on air conditioning units.

4. A good source would be recent yearbooks for encyclopedias.

5. In certain places, geothermal power has been used for many years.

6. Have rotating blades, stationary blades, direction of hot gas labeled.

Chapter 16 Waves

Equipment and Reagents for Experiments

bottle
dowel
dry cell
electric bell
glass plate (to fit in ripple tank)
glass tube, 2.5 × 45 cm
hacksaw blade
medicine dropper
metal washers
overhead projector
pan, flat glass
protractor
rope
rubber bands
ruler
"Slinky" coil spring
6 test tubes
test tube rack
tubing, glass
        rubber (heavy wall)
3 tuning forks, various frequencies
    attached to resonator boxes
vacuum pump
2 whistles
wooden block

Page 334. PROBLEMS

1. $\dfrac{10 \text{ vib}}{30 \text{ sec}} = 0.3$ vib/sec

2. 256 vib/sec

Page 335. ACTIVITY

The loudness decreases since there is less matter (air) inside the jar to transmit the sound waves.

Page 337. PROBLEMS

3. $\lambda = \dfrac{v}{f}$

$= \dfrac{1130 \text{ ft}}{\text{sec}} \left| \dfrac{\text{sec}}{256 \text{ vib}} \right.$

$= 4.4$ ft or 1.32 m

4. $f = \dfrac{v}{\lambda}$

$f = \dfrac{335 \text{ m}}{\text{sec}} \left| \dfrac{}{1 \text{ m}} \right.$

$f = 335$ vib/sec

Page 338. PROBLEMS

5. $f = \dfrac{v}{\lambda}$

$f = \dfrac{34{,}400 \text{ cm/sec}}{6 \text{ cm}}$

$f = 5{,}733$ vib/sec

6. $f = \dfrac{v}{\lambda}$

$f = \dfrac{344 \text{ m/sec}}{12 \text{ m}}$

$f = 28.7$ vib/sec

7.
$$f = \frac{v}{\lambda}$$

$$f = \frac{347 \text{ m/sec}}{12 \text{ m}}$$

$$f = 28.9 \text{ vib/sec}$$

8. $v = 1,130$ ft/sec (at $20°$ C)

$$\frac{5,280 \text{ ft}}{1,130 \text{ ft/sec}} = 4.7 \text{ sec}$$

$$\frac{4.7 \text{ sec}}{1 \text{ mile}} = \frac{10 \text{ sec}}{x}$$

$$4.7 \text{ x} = 10 \text{ miles}$$

$$x = 2.1 \text{ miles}$$

Page 340. PROBLEMS

9. Dogs can hear sound frequencies beyond the range of human hearing. The frequency of the whistle exceeds the range of human hearing.

10. The bat emits sounds of very high frequency as it flies. The echoes reflected back to the bat are used to locate surrounding objects and their distances.

11. Sonar sound waves are sent out through the bottom of the ship. By timing the return of the echo, the depth and the location of submerged objects may be determined.

Page 348. PROBLEM

12. violet light 4×10^{-5} cm
red light 7×10^{-5} cm
cosmic rays $-\lambda = 1 \times 10^{-11}$ cm to 1×10^{-15} cm

Cosmic rays have the highest frequency; red light has the lowest frequency in the visible spectrum.

Pages 349-351. STUDY QUESTIONS

D. *How and Why*

1.

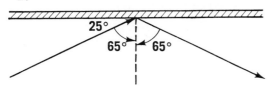

2. $\frac{15 \text{ waves}}{3 \text{ sec}} = 5$ waves/sec

3. Their speed changes and they are refracted.

4. Transverse wave vibrations are at right angles to the direction the wave is moving. In a compressional wave the vibrations are in the same direction the wave is moving. Transverse wave: light, X rays; compressional wave: sound, wave in a metal spring.

5. It cannot be done. All forms of communication from one point to another require energy waves.

6.

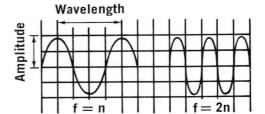

7. The electromagnetic spectrum is a set of invisible, transverse energy waves, ranging from very low frequency to very high frequency. All travel at the speed of light.

8. Infrared waves have a longer wavelength. Ultraviolet waves have a shorter wavelength. They are all forms of radiant energy.

9. Place a vibrator or rippler in the water and slowly move it in the direction of the waves. Then move the rippler away from the waves.

10.
$$\lambda = \frac{v}{f}$$

$$= \frac{3 \times 10^8 \text{ m}}{\text{sec}} \left| \frac{\text{sec}}{540 \times 10^3 \text{ vib}} \right| =$$

555 m, round off to 600

Page 351. INVESTIGATIONS

1. Relate this to other examples of the Doppler effect. In this case it applies

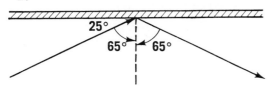

55

to light waves. This is also another example of spectroscopic observation—similar to but much more refined than flame tests for cation analysis.

2. How does radar relate to echolocation in bats and certain fish?

3. Large lakes often have regular oscillations. Is the motion of waves in them similar to ocean waves?

4. Find out how dimensions and the arrangement of a building are important to its acoustic qualities. Can the actual building materials affect its quality?

5. What factors affect the accuracy of these results? How does averaging the results of several trials improve accuracy?

Chapter 17 Optics

Equipment and Reagents for Experiments

aluminum foil
2 candles
cardboard, piece
  shoe box
coin
convex lens
cup
diffraction grating, 3 cm^2
glass, clear block
  8 oz tumbler
index card, white
knife
lamp (flashlight)
light meter (or camera with coupled light
  meter)
meter stick
mirror, plane
  shaving (magnifying)
paper, white
pencil
2 polarizing filters
prism

protractor
ruler
straight pins

Page 353. PROBLEM

1. pond, window, car fender, refrigerator, eyeglasses

Page 356. PROBLEMS

2. $S_i = \dfrac{f^2}{S_o}$

$S_i = \dfrac{(2 \text{ cm})^2}{10 \text{ cm}} = \dfrac{4 \text{ cm}^2}{10 \text{ cm}} = 0.4 \text{ cm}$

3. $S_i = \dfrac{f^2}{S_o}$

$24 \text{ cm} = \dfrac{f^2}{6 \text{ cm}}$

$f^2 = 144 \text{ cm}^2$

$f = 12 \text{ cm}$

Page 359. PROBLEMS

4.

5. index of refraction =

$\dfrac{\text{speed of light in vacuum}}{\text{speed of light in glass}}$

$1.75 = \dfrac{3 \times 10^8 \text{ m/sec}}{\text{speed of light in glass}}$

speed of light $= \dfrac{3 \times 10^8 \text{ m/sec}}{1.75}$

speed of light (glass) =
$1.71 \times 10^8 \text{ m/sec}$

6. index of refraction (quartz) =

$\dfrac{3 \times 10^8 \text{ m/sec}}{\text{speed of light in quartz}}$

index $= \dfrac{3 \times 10^8 \text{ m/sec}}{1.94 \times 10^8 \text{ m/sec}}$

index of refraction (quartz) = 1.60

7. $1.46 = \dfrac{3 \times 10^8 \text{ m/sec}}{\text{speed of light (oleic acid)}}$

speed of light (oleic acid) =

$$\dfrac{3 \times 10^8 \text{ m/sec}}{1.46}$$

speed of light = 2.05×10^8 m/sec

Page 362. PROBLEMS

8. $\dfrac{H_i}{H_o} = \dfrac{D_i}{D_o}$

$\dfrac{10 \text{ cm}}{2 \text{ cm}} = \dfrac{24 \text{ cm}}{D_o}$

$D_o = 48$ cm

9. $\dfrac{H_i}{H_o} = \dfrac{D_i}{D_o}$

$\dfrac{2.5 \text{ cm}}{H_o} = \dfrac{100 \text{ cm}}{10 \text{ cm}}$

$H_o = .25$ cm

10. increases

Page 363. PROBLEM

11. real images, otherwise they could not be used to photograph stars

Page 365. PROBLEMS

12. violet

13. red

14. violet

15. red

Page 367. PROBLEM

16. violet — highest frequency
    red — lowest frequency

Pages 371-373. STUDY QUESTIONS

D. *How and Why*

1. Particle theory states that light is a stream of particles and wave theory states that light is composed of waves. Particle theory: photoelectric effect; wave theory: refraction, polarization, interference.

2. Interference causes reinforcement and cancellation of different wavelengths. At points where a certain wavelength is reinforced a color appears and wavelengths for all other colors are canceled.

3. Light consists of tiny "bundles" of energy. The energy of a photon varies directly with the wave frequency of light. This means the higher the wave frequency the greater the energy in a photon of the light.

4. An electron microscope is a microscope which can magnify objects more than 100,000X using electron beams and magnets.

5. Two sides of the tank and the vertical edge between the sides are a prism which can disperse light.

6. Light ray bends toward the normal, indicating that it is entering a medium with greater index of refraction. Substance (b) is the glass.

7. Sunlight is refracted as it passes from space into the atmosphere. Therefore, the light from the sun which enters our eyes has been bent from a straight path and the sun appears at a point higher than it really is.

Chapter 18 Electricity

Equipment and Reagents for Experiments

ammeter
2 bar magnets
2 beakers
bottle, glass
comb
copper, strip
  wire
cork
curtain rod (with ball end)
dry cell, 6 volt
  several used
galvanometer
glass rod

graphite
hacksaw
iron filings
metal, foil
  rod
  wire
nail, large
paper, thin
plastic rod
silk, cloth
  thread
sulfuric acid, dilute
variable resistor
wire
wool cloth
zinc strip

Page 376. PROBLEMS

1. rubbed amber, combing clean hair, electrostatic generator, Leyden jar

2. from the hair

Page 378. PROBLEMS

3. rubber, ceramics, glass

4. to ground the truck

5. Conduction involves direct contact and produces the same charge as the original charged object. Induction does not involve contact and produces a charge opposite to the charge on the original object.

6. With a rubber stopper (or other suitable nonconducting material). Leaves are often enclosed in glass container to prevent discharge to air.

Page 381. PROBLEM

7. Substances cannot ionize unless in solution and will not effectively carry current.

Page 386. PROBLEM

8. Magnetic field induces current in the wire coil.

Page 388. PROBLEM

9. house current

Page 390. PROBLEMS

10. $I = \dfrac{V}{R}$

   $I = \dfrac{12 \text{ volt}}{3 \text{ ohms}}$

   $I = 4 \text{ amp}$

11. $R = \dfrac{V}{I}$

   $R = \dfrac{120 \text{ volt}}{5 \text{ amp}}$

   $R = 24 \text{ ohms}$

12. one millivolt = one thousandth of a volt

13. $R = \dfrac{V}{I}$

   $R = \dfrac{6 \text{ volt}}{30 \text{ amp}}$

   $R = 0.2 \text{ ohm}$

14. $500 \text{ w} \times 10 \text{ hr} = 5000 \text{ w-hr} = 5 \text{ kw-hr}$

Pages 391-393. STUDY QUESTIONS

D. *How and Why*

1. friction between two bodies

2. kinetic energy

3. A chemical reaction between the chemical solution and metals immersed in the solution releases electrons which form an electric current through an outside circuit.

4. Both are vacuum tubes and both contain a cathode and anode. The heated cathode in the diode releases electrons and these electrons travel to the anode, forming an electric current. The cathode in a photoelectric cell releases electrons when light strikes it and these electrons travel to the anode, forming an electric current.

5. Both the generator and galvanometer contain a wire coil and magnets. The coil of the generator produces an electric current when turned. The coil in a galvanometer rotates when an electric current flows through it.

6. $I = \dfrac{V}{R} = \dfrac{12 \text{ v}}{2 \text{ ohms}} = 6 \text{ amp}$

7. The Canadian nickel contains nickel metal which is ferromagnetic and attracted to magnets. An American nickel does not contain nickel or any other ferromagnetic metal.

Page 393. INVESTIGATIONS

1. Study the various kinds of electricity generation plants and the environmental effects of each kind.

2. Some students might be interested in finding out about different kinds of motors for various purposes.

3. When working with magnets always be sure to remove your watch. Magnetic fields often affect watch movements.

Chapter 19 Electronics

Equipment and Reagents for Experiments

aluminum foil
ammeter
bar magnets, varying strength
battery, 6 v
bell
bell wire
copper wire
Crookes tube (cathode ray tube or television set)
diodes, used
dry cell
electroscope
electrostatic generator
glass plate
jar, glass
magnesium wire

match
3 micro lamps
plastic rod
rubber band
sandpaper
switch
tongs
triode, used
wire loop (connected to nonconducting handle)
wool cloth
zinc strip

Page 395. PROBLEM

1. battery, coil, switch

Page 396. PROBLEM

2.

Page 401. PROBLEM

3. Alternating current would not completely reverse the chemical reaction that produced electrons in the first place.

Page 402. PROBLEM

4. The electrons rather than returning to original positions are constantly attracted to the positively charged grid thus forcing them to move in one direction in the circuit.

Page 410. PROBLEM

5. (a) hourglass
   (d) slide rule
   (a) clock
   (d) Geiger counter
   (d) abacus
   (d) fingers

(d) telephone dial

(a) hygrometer

(a) ammeter

(a) voltmeter

(a) odometer

(a) spring balance

D. *How and Why*

1. The triode contains a grid which regulates the flow of electrons from filament to plate.

2. One set of plates is positively charged and the other set is negatively charged. The insulator between the plates prevents the electrons from traveling from the negative plate to the positive plate so the electrons are "stored."

3. In both cases the electric current is a flow of ions from cathode to anode.

4. In a triode an alternating current heats the filament; electrons leave the filament and travel to the plate. When the germanium transistor is connected to A.C. current, electrons move through the transistor in one direction only, producing D.C. current.

5. D.C. current is produced by the battery through a chemical change between lead oxide plates and sulfuric acid solution. The battery is charged by reversing the chemical reaction. This is done by passing D.C. current through the battery in the direction opposite to the D.C. current generated by the battery.

6. Bring a magnet near an operating Crookes tube, or cathode ray tube (*e.g.*, T.V. tube) and the path of the beam will be deflected. In a T.V. the picture on the screen will be distorted.

7. Transistors are smaller, cheaper, use less voltage, and do not produce much heat when operating.

8. An analog is something which is similar to something else. The movement of mercury in a thermometer varies directly with changes in temperature. The movement of the needle on a speedometer varies directly with changes in speed (distance/time). Annual rings in a tree trunk equal years of time through which the tree has grown. Thickness of the annual rings represents the amount of rainfall during the tree's growth.

1. Learn what some of the various kinds of vacuum tubes do in an electronic circuit.

2. Find out what kinds of tests can be performed on a cathode ray oscilloscope.

3. Find out how to test a color television set for proper color function.

4. Find out the differences between a radio transmitter and receiver; what laws govern radio transmitters.

Chapter 20 Radiation

Equipment and Reagents for Experiments

aluminum sheet, 2 mm thick
box, square or rectangular
cathode ray tube
100 corn kernels
electroscope
Geiger counter
meter stick
radiation source
watch

1. X rays—wavelength 1×10^{-9} to 5×10^{-6} cm. The longest X rays have a

wavelength one tenth as long as the wavelength of blue light. Radio waves are 10^6 to 10^{15} times longer than X rays.

Page 419. PROBLEMS

2. $f = \dfrac{c}{\lambda}$

$f = \dfrac{3 \times 10^8 \text{ m/sec}}{1 \times 10^{-3} \text{ m}}$

$f = 3 \times 10^{11}$ vib/sec

3. $\lambda = \dfrac{c}{f}$

$= \dfrac{3 \times 10^8 \text{ m/sec}}{5 \times 10^{15} \text{ vib/sec}}$

$\lambda = 6 \times 10^{-8}$ m

Page 421. PROBLEM

4. 0.5 roentgen/month $\times \dfrac{12 \text{ mo}}{\text{year}} =$

6 roentgen/year

0.3 roentgen/week $\times \dfrac{52 \text{ weeks}}{\text{year}} =$

15.6 roentgen/year

One X ray per month would fall well below the maximum safe dosage for a year.

Page 423. PROBLEMS

5. Radioactive isotopes are produced artificially by bombarding an element with high speed neutrons or charged particles.

6. Elements whose atoms have a high binding energy per particle or that contain equal numbers of protons and neutrons or that have an even number of both protons and neutrons tend to be stable. Most heavy elements contain more neutrons than protons and have very low binding energies per particle so they tend to decay.

Page 425. PROBLEMS

7. Gamma rays have higher frequencies and shorter wavelengths than X rays. Both travel at the speed of light and penetrate solid substances to some degree. Neither are charged. Both can be diffracted by a crystal.

8. Cosmic rays have shorter wavelengths.

Page 426. PROBLEMS

9. 86 min = 5 grams
2 hr 52 min = 2.5 grams
4 hr 18 min = 1.25 grams

10. Technically forever because a very small fraction would always be left. 99.9% would have decayed after 104 hours.

11. Radon 222—3.82 days
Polonium 214—0.0001 seconds
Uranium 238—4.5 billion years
Uranium 238 is much less radioactive than radon 222. Both are less radioactive than polonium 214.

Page 428. PROBLEM

12. A charged electroscope loses its charge faster when ionizing radiation is present. The ions formed in the air are attracted to the knob of the electroscope causing the leaves to drop.

Page 429. PROBLEM

13. They are bent in opposite directions because they have opposite charges.

Page 430. PROBLEM

14. The charged particles "expose" grains of silver bromide in the emulsion. In chemical developer, the exposed grains are reduced to silver which appears black. The path of the particles shows up as very short black lines.

D. How and Why

1. Inside a vacuum tube a stream of electrons from a cathode are accelerated toward a tungsten anode. When the electrons strike the anode X rays are emitted.

2. The target is heated and would soon melt if it were not cooled. Heat is produced by the impact of the electrons. Energy lost by the electrons is changed to X rays and heat.

3. X rays and radioactivity ionize the air. Ions (charged particles) are attracted to the electroscope and neutralize the charge on it.

4. Alpha and beta rays are deflected in opposite directions by a magnetic field because they have opposite charges. The magnetic forces set up by the particles as they move have opposite polarity.

5. A cloud chamber contains a supersaturated vapor in which visible cloud tracks are produced by radioactive particles. A bubble chamber contains a superheated liquid in which a trail of bubbles is produced by radioactive particles passing through it. A nuclear emulsion is a thick layer of gelatin containing silver bromide. It is similar to photographic emulsion. When developed after exposure to radioactivity, a black streak produced in the nuclear emulsion indicates the path of a radioactive particle.

6. The Geiger tube has two electrical connections which are separated from each other by a gas. Radioactivity ionizes particles in the gas, causing a brief current to be carried between the two electrical connections. The current is amplified and detected by a click or a light.

7. Alpha particles are positively charged particles each consisting of a helium nucleus. Speed is between 10,000 and 20,000 mi/sec; they are stopped by a thin piece of paper and are deflected by a magnetic field. Beta particles are electrons (negative charge) which originate from the nucleus. They travel at speeds 100 times that of alpha particles; they are deflected by a magnetic field. Gamma rays are waves of radiant energy having wavelength of about 10^{-10} cm. They travel at the speed of light, are not deflected by a magnetic field, and are stopped by several feet of concrete or by several inches of lead.

8. X rays have the longest wavelength of the three; cosmic rays have the shortest wavelength.

9. Of the three, cosmic rays have the most energy per photon; X rays have the least energy per photon.

Page 435. INVESTIGATIONS

1. Find out how radiation is used to diagnose diseases. What kinds of radiation-detection devices are used?

2. Obtain X-ray photographs from a dentist. Find out how to identify signs of disease from the photographs.

Chapter 21 Nuclear Reactions

Equipment and Reagents for Experiments

None

Page 439. PROBLEM

1. Attractive forces between nuclear particles that exist over very short distances.

Page 440. PROBLEM

2. $^4_2 He$ The helium nucleus contains two protons and two neutrons for an atomic mass of four a.m.u.'s.

3. uranium 238, uranium 234, thorium 230, radium 226, radon 222, polonium 218, polonium 214, polonium 210

4. thorium 234, protactinium 234, lead 214, bismuth 214, lead 210, bismuth 210

5. helium, oxygen, calcium, tin, lead

6. Stable elements are more common because unstable nuclei naturally decay into more stable nuclei.

D. *How and Why*

1. Energy is needed to overcome the nuclear forces which hold the neutrons and protons together.

2. The universe is held together by gravitational, nuclear, electrostatic, and magnetic forces.

3. transmutation $^{226}_{88}Ra \rightarrow ^{222}_{86}Rn + ^{4}_{2}He$

fission $^{235}_{92}U + ^{1}_{0}n \rightarrow ^{144}_{56}Ba + ^{90}_{36}Kr + 2^{1}_{0}n$

fusion $^{2}_{1}D + ^{2}_{1}D \rightarrow ^{3}_{2}He + ^{1}_{0}n$

In transmutation a particle is ejected from the nucleus and in fission a nucleus splits into nearly equal parts. Fusion results when two light particles join to form a heavier particle.

4. Carbon 14 with a half-life of 5,600 years decays to form carbon 12. The amount of undecayed carbon 14 in a fossil indicates its age.

5. Elements with high average binding energy are manganese, iron, and chromium. Their stability is higher than carbon 12 and uranium 235.

1. Report on chemical chain reactions and physical chain reactions and how they differ from nuclear chain reactions.

2. Find out about "heavy water" and what it is used for.

3. Find out how research in plasma state of matter is related to sustained nuclear fusion reactions.

Chapter 22 Nuclear Technology

Equipment and Reagents for Experiments

None

D. *How and Why*

1. A cyclotron is used to accelerate atomic particles to high speeds in magnetic fields. The magnetic field is produced inside the dees of the cyclotron by a large electromagnet. High voltage alternating current produces an electric field along the slit separating the dees. The electric field is constantly reversing from negative to positive many times per second. Protons injected into the center of the dees are forced by the magnetic and electric fields into a circular path, and are accelerated to very high speeds. The particles travel in an ever widening circle, constantly accelerating, until they exit through a window at the edge of the dees.

2. If air or any other material were present the atomic particles would strike the molecules and be stopped before they accelerated to high speeds.

3. Uranium 235 is a fissionable material and undergoes a chain reaction, emitting heat energy and radiation.

4. If the fuel cans absorbed neutrons there would not be sufficient neutrons to maintain the chain reaction.

5. Large amounts of heat are produced in the chain reaction inside a nuclear

reactor. If a nuclear fuel had a low melting point, it would melt and the reaction could become uncontrolled.

6. This is a safety device used to stop the reaction in an emergency. The control rods absorb the neutrons and completely stop the chain reaction.

7. Both iron ore and uranium ore are oxides mixed with mineral impurities. Iron ore is mixed with carbon and limestone and heated to high temperatures. Carbon reduces the iron oxide by removing the oxygen and forming carbon dioxide. The limestone removes sand and other minerals, forming slag. Uranium oxide is removed from mineral impurities by dissolving it in nitric acid and tributyl phosphate and kerosene and filtering off the impurities. Next the uranium oxide is changed to uranium fluoride which is reduced to uranium metal by heating it with calcium or magnesium.

8. One experiment for producing a controlled thermonuclear reaction is the heating of hydrogen gas inside a magnetic "bottle." Heavy hydrogen gas is enclosed in a circular aluminum tube and high voltage alternating current is used to heat the gas to a few million degrees for less than a second. Magnetic fields produced by an electromagnet "pinch" the gas and keep it away from the walls of the tube. If a temperature of 100 million degrees can be reached, a thermonuclear reaction will occur inside the tube.

Page 462. INVESTIGATIONS

1. Reports will vary. An example is: Electronics technician—requires two to three years beyond high school for certification.

2. For information look in an encyclopedia or a college physics text.

3. Some students might be interested in reporting on fast-breeder reactors.

Films and Filmstrips

Catalogs listing films and filmstrips for purchase or rental may be obtained from the following distributors. (Most filmstrips are not distributed on a rental basis.)

Some of the larger companies maintain branch offices in various regions of the country. In requisitioning films, it is desirable to locate a branch office or nearby film library when one is available. Films must be ordered months in advance, with alternate choice of dates for their use. Therefore, it is advisable to order films for specific units of study at least three months in advance of the time you wish to use them.

You should preview films and filmstrips before they are shown to the class. Often a class will benefit most if a film is viewed twice—the first time to overview the material and the second time to identify specific principles and concepts. Also, the teaching value of a film may be increased if students are given a list of five to ten questions covering the main ideas in the film. Students should be directed to answer the questions on the basis of what they have learned from the film. This technique increases student attention and retention.

DISTRIBUTORS

United States

Almanac Films, Inc., 915 Broadway, New York, New York 10010

Alturas Films, P.O. Box 940, Stanford, California 94305

American Film Registry, 24 East 8th Street, Chicago, Illinois 60415

Arco Film Productions, 580 Fifth Avenue, New York, New York 10032

Associated Films, Inc., 79 East Adams Street, Chicago, Illinois 60003

Association Films, Inc., 866 Third Avenue, New York, New York 10022

Athena Films, Inc., 165 West 45th Street, New York, Yew York 10019

Audio Film Center, 34 MacQuesten Parkway South, Mt. Vernon, New York 10550

Audio Productions, Inc., 630 Ninth Avenue, New York, New York 10036

Bailey Films, Inc., 6509 De Longpre Avenue, Hollywood, California 90028

Stanley Bowmar Co., 4 Broadway, Valhalla, New York 10595

Brandon Films, Inc., 34 MacQuesten Parkway South, Mt. Vernon, New York 10550

Bray Studios, Inc., 630 Ninth Avenue, New York, New York 10036

Colonial Films, 752 Spring Street N.W., Atlanta, Georgia 30308

Contemporary Films, Inc., 330 West 42nd Street, New York, New York 10036

Coronet Films, 65 East South Water Street, Chicago, Illinois 60601

William Cox Enterprises, 2900 South Sawtelle Boulevard, Los Angeles, California 90024

Walt Disney Productions, 800 Sonora Avenue, Glendale, California 91201

Eastman Kodak Co., Audio-Visual Service, 343 State Street, Rochester, New York 14604

Educational Film Library Association, Inc., 19 West 60th Street, New York, New York 10023

Encyclopaedia Britannica Films, Inc., 425 North Michigan Avenue, Chicago, Illinois 60611

Farm Film Foundation, 1425 H Street N.W., Washington, D.C. 20005

Films of the Nation Distributors, Inc., 5113 16th Avenue, Brooklyn, New York 11204

Filmstrip House, 432 Park Avenue S, New York, New York 10016

Film Strip of the Month Club, Inc., 353 4th Avenue, New York, New York 10010

Gateway Productions, Inc., Bureau of Audio-Visual Services, Univ. of Arizona, Tucson, Arizona 85721

Golden Key Productions, Inc., Film Distributors, 1921 Hillhurst Avenue, Hollywood, California 90027

Handel Film Corporation, 8730 Sunset Boulevard, Los Angeles, California 90069

Harcourt, Brace, Jovanovich, Inc., 750 Third Avenue, New York, New York 10017

Heidenkamp Nature Pictures, 538 Glen Arden Drive, Pittsburgh, Pennsylvania 15208

Huyck Corp., 200 East 42nd Street, New York, New York 10017

Ideal Pictures Corp., 3910 Harlem Road, Buffalo, New York 14226

Indiana University Films, Audio-Visual Center, Bloomington, Indiana 47401

Institutional Cinema Service, Inc., 915 Broadway, New York, New York 10010

Instructional Films, Inc., 1150 Wilmette Avenue, Wilmette, Illinois 60091

International Film Bureau, Inc., 332 South Michigan Avenue, Chicago, Illinois 60604

International Film Foundation, Inc., Suite 916, 475 Fifth Avenue, New York, New York 10017

Jam Handy Organization, 2821 East Grand Boulebard, Detroit, Michigan 48211

Library Films, Inc., 25 West 45th Street, New York, New York 10019

Life Filmstrips, P.O. Box 834, Radio City P.O., New York, New York 10019

McGraw-Hill Publishing Co., 330 West 42nd Street, New York, New York 10036

Modern Talking Picture Service, Inc., 1145 North McCadden Pl., Los Angeles, California 90038

National Audubon Society, Photo and Film Department, 1130 Fifth Avenue, New York, New York 10028

National Film Board of Canada, Suite 819, 680 Fifth Avenue, New York, New York 10019

Samuel Orleans and Associates, Inc., 211 West Cumberland Avenue, Knoxville, Tennessee 37915

Photolab, Inc,., 3825 Georgia Avenue N, Washington, D.C. 20011

Society for Visual Education, Inc., 1345 Diversey Parkway, Chicago, Illinois 60614

Sterling-Movies, U.S.A., Inc., 241 East 34th Street, New York, New York 10016

Teaching Films Custodians, Inc., 25 West 43rd Street, New York, New York 10036

United World Films, Inc., 1445 Park Avenue, New York, New York 10029

Venard Organization, P.O. Box 1332, Peoria, Illinois 61601

Visual Education Consultants, P.O. Box 52, Madison, Wisconsin 53701

Visual Sciences, P.O. Box 599RB, Suffern, New York 10901

Ward's Natural Science Establishment, P.O. Box 1712, Rochester, New York 14603

Wilner Films and Slides, P.O. Box 231, Cathedral Station, New York, New York 10025

Young America Films, Inc., 18 East 41st Street, New York, New York 10017

U.S. Government Agencies

Fish and Wildlife Service, 6010 Executive Boulevard, Rockville, Md. 20852

National Aeronautics and Space Administration, Washington, D.C. 20546

Soil Conservation Service, Washington, D.C. 20250

U.S. Atomic Energy Commission, Washington, D.C. 20545

U.S. Department of Agriculture, Washington, D.C. 20250

U.S. Forest Service, Washington, D.C. 20250

U.S. Public Health Service, Communicable Disease Center, Atlanta, Georgia 30303

Canada

Audio-Visual Supply Co., Toronto General Trusts Building, Winnipeg, Manitoba

Canadian Film Institute, 142 Sparks Street, Ottawa, Ontario

General Films Limited, 1534 13th Avenue, Regina, Saskatchewan

Radio-Cinema, 5011 Verdun Avenue, Montreal, Quebec

BEHAVIORAL OBJECTIVES

INTRODUCTION

An unlimited number of behaviors could be cited which indicate a student has learned something. Basically, **a behavioral objective is a description of the behavior you might observe in a student if he is achieving an educational goal.**

What Is a Good Behavioral Objective?

Statements of behavioral objectives can usually be divided into three distinct parts. First is a **description of the conditions under which the desired behavior will be observed.** Here are some examples which describe the condition:

"When presented with samples of metals and nonmetals . . ."

"When asked to list the three basic particles which make up an atom . . ."

"When presented with the materials suggested on page . . ."

"After having read and discussed . . ."

"In groups of five students, given beam balances and five objects per group . . ."

A good behavioral objective includes a condition which tells what causes, stimulates or motivates the student to perform the behaviors or under what circumstances those behaviors will be performed.

The second part of a well-stated behavioral objective is a **clear description of exactly what behavior you're looking for.** A good behavioral objective would avoid using such terms as "know about," "appreciate," or "sense the relationship between." Rather, a good behavioral objective will include terms which describe what you could observe students doing if they do "know about" or "appreciate." It's almost impossible to observe a student "appreciating," but you can gather some evidence that he is appreciating science if he is:

voluntarily reading science books instead of comic books.

coming to class early to manipulate science materials.

requesting that a science demonstration be repeated or expressing a desire to perform it himself.

expressing to you a liking for science.

In other words, **a good behavioral objective uses verbs which express some type of observable action.** Here are some examples of action verbs which describe observable behaviors:

states orally	manipulates
matches	measures
distinguishes between	expresses
constructs	watches
identifies	states hypotheses
lists	recalls

The third part of a well-stated behavioral objective is a **description of some level of performance or criteria which may help you to know if the student or class has performed to the degree which you hoped for.**

For example, if you were teaching students to use a ruler, would you want all of your class to be able to accurately measure the perimeter of a desk or table? Would you feel satisfied if 90% of your class could perform this skill? 80%? 50%? Would you be happy if just one student did it? Obviously, this level of performance would vary for each class, each student, each teacher, and each task. In some classrooms a teacher might think that all students should be able to measure accurately. In other classrooms, a teacher would be elated if even a few students could measure accurately.

What do we mean by accurately? Would you be satisfied if students could measure the perimeter of a tabletop to the nearest foot? Inch? Half-inch? Quarter inch? More accurately than that? Just how accurately would be acceptable to you? Here, then, is another aspect of a level of performance: A well-stated behavioral objective might also include some description of **how precise, how accurate, how well** the behavior should be performed in order for you to know that the student has really achieved the objective.

Another kind of criterion measure or performance level which might be included in a behavioral objective is a statement of **how often or how many times** a student must perform the behavior in order to demonstrate that he has learned something. For example, if he measured the perimeter of the table-top with a ruler accurately just one time, would you conclude that he has learned how to measure? What if you asked him to measure the length of five objects with a ruler, and you were looking for his ability to measure correctly to the nearest half-inch? Would you be satisfied if he measured the length of four of them correctly? The length of three out of the five? Or would you only be satisfied if he measured the length of all five of them correctly?

Again, this decision will have to be made on the basis of what you know about the student's ability, and the task at hand. For some students, you'd be happy if they could do it just once; for other students, you might expect perfection four out of five trials.

Now let's put all these parts together and see what a well-stated behavioral objective looks like:

Conditions
(tell you how to plan and organize your class and what materials you'll need)

Working in groups of five students, when presented with a beam balance and five objects, and without the aid of labeled diagrams or charts,

Performance
(tells you what behaviors of students to look for)

students will recall the names of the parts of a beam balance and label each on a blank diagram. Students will place an object on the pan of the balance and accurately measure the mass of the object to the nearest 0.1 gram. Students will evaluate the performance of each of the other members of the group as he measures the mass of an object to the nearest 0.1 gram with the beam balance.

Criterion Measure
(tells you how many of the students or to what degree the objective should be achieved)

Of all the students, 85% will achieve 100% of the above objectives.

Why Should You Use Behavioral Objectives?

A behavioral objective cannot and should not tell you how to teach. Your teaching strategy is a product of your own creativity as a professional teacher, your knowledge of science and teaching methodology, suggestions from teacher's guides and textbooks, and immediate clues from your students. A behavioral objective is only a suggested outcome of what students will be able to do after or during your teaching.

Planning instruction is one use of a behavioral objective. It can help you decide what materials, classroom conditions, grouping and teaching strategies you must acquire or develop prior to meeting with your students. This description of conditions is part of the well-stated objective. It helps you think through what you, the teacher, must do to cause the desired behavior to happen.

Another use of a behavioral objective is to help you **gather and provide evidence** that students in your class are learning. It allows you to become **accountable for time and energy** you spend teaching science. It means, however, that you have to evaluate and keep records of student progress. Some suggestions for record keeping are in the EVALUATION section of this guide. If you do keep such records, then, you or anyone else—parent, teacher, administrator or supervisor—could observe and evaluate your teaching of science. If anyone were to ask you how you know your students are learning something, you could provide them with some behavioral evidence that the goals of your science program were being achieved. Of course, students may not exhibit the desired behaviors. If they don't, you have a basis for examining your own teaching, the instructional materials, the classroom and the school environment and changing them to make them more conducive to learning. But you wouldn't know what changes to make unless you knew what behavioral outcomes you desired. Part of the well-stated behavioral objective describes the performance. A precise description tells you what behaviors you should be able to observe if students are achieving the goals of science.

Diagnosing a student's abilities is another use of behavioral objectives. When you can observe and evaluate certain behaviors, it is easier to determine what a student is capable of doing, or what he has accomplished in the past, and what he has yet to master. It more clearly defines the boundaries between what he knows and what he doesn't know. With this information, you can provide a better individualized learning situation for each student. If the students already have demonstrated to you that, for example, they can distinguish between physical and chemical changes around them, why dwell on that? Go on to another objective. Or, perhaps some of your students can do this while others cannot. If it is an important goal, then you'll need to provide some individual or small group activities for some of your students while others might be pursuing other goals. An effective teacher will provide for these individual differences. It is the criterion measure part of the well-stated behavioral objective that allows you to diagnose which students have accomplished the objective and to what degree they have achieved it.

In addition, behavioral objectives are helpful because they **tune students in** to what it is you're trying to achieve. When it is apparent to students what it is you and they are trying to accomplish, when it is clear to all what is meant by successful completion, then students may use their energies to achieve the objective rather than try to "psych-out" what the teacher wants them to do. Many teachers have found that when they share with students what objectives are sought (if they are reasonable), much of the teaching job is accomplished. Most students will accept the challenge rather than try to "play games" with the teacher.

Where Do Behavioral Objectives Come From?

Statements of behavioral objectives come in many forms, and no given number of them constitute a science curriculum. You could never say that students, having achieved the objectives contained in this booklet, will then "know" science. The behavioral objectives for each school, class, group of students, or individual student will vary according to the students, the teacher, the resources available in the learning environment, and the task at hand.

Books are available which contain behavioral objectives for science. Several are listed in the BIBLIOGRAPHY section of this guide. There is even an Instructional Objectives Exchange to which you can subscribe.* It is difficult for teachers in New York or Washington or Los Angeles to write adequate behavioral objectives for teachers to use with their students in Centerville, Garden City, or Westberg. Even school districts which employ science curriculum specialists cannot decide what objectives are appropriate for you and your students in your situation with the materials and resources you have available.

Ultimately, the task of selecting, composing and evaluating behavioral objectives is up to you. You should draw upon the behavioral objectives in this guide and upon other sources or other people who could help you. Students are good, if not the best, sources of behavioral objectives. When they can express to you their questions, their interests, and their goals, then you can cooperatively decide what objectives shall be reached. The next section of this guide and any other list of behavioral objectives provides a basis for selecting what is appropriate for your students. Select from these lists, seek objectives from other teachers and consultants, and create some of your own. **The ultimate**

*Information and a catalog of objective collections can be obtained from: Instructional Objectives Exchange, Center for the Study of Evaluation, Graduate School of Education, University of California, Los Angeles, California 90024.

decision of what to teach is yours; the decision of what to learn is the student's.

Any behavioral objective for teaching science should be based upon one or more of the goals of science education. You should be able to say that the reason you're working to accomplish this particular objective is because it's one step or one part of a long range goal of science education. For example, if one of the goals of science education is to develop the student's ability to utilize some of the methods and processes by which problems are solved scientifically, then one of the purposes of a lesson might be to develop an understanding of what an experiment is. If a student does understand what an experiment is:

When asked to define an experiment, he will state that it is a test or a way of proving some theory or principle.

When asked what he would do to find out if food coloring diffuses faster in warm water than in cold water, he will describe what he would do and uses the term "experiment" in his description.

When asked for examples of experiments which have been conducted so far this semester, he will cite at least three.

Specific behavioral objectives such as the above are only examples of one small part of that larger, broader goal for science education. However, each behavioral objective should be consistent with one or more of those goals so that you can justify what you are teaching, and so that you can see students progress toward that goal.

How to Use the Behavioral Objectives for *Focus on Physical Science*

In the next section of this guide, behavioral objectives for *Focus on Physical Science* are related to four broad goals of science education.

A 1. **Attitudes:** To develop students' attitudes of curiosity, of wonderment about and involvement with phenomena in their natural environment; to develop an appreciation for the contributions of science to daily living; and to develop the value and inclinations toward solving problems in a scientific manner.

P 2. **Processes:** To develop those intellectual processes of inquiry by which scientific problems and phenomena are explained, predicted and/or controlled.

K 3. **Knowledge:** To develop knowledge of facts, terminology, concepts, generalizations, and principles which help the students confront and interpret their environment.

S 4. **Skills:** To develop the student's ability to handle, construct, and manipulate materials and equipment in a productive and safe manner, and to develop his ability to measure, organize, and communicate scientific information.

In the margin next to each behavioral objective you will find one or more of the following capital letters: **A, P, K, S.** They indicate the goal on which the behavioral objective is based— Attitudes, Processes, Knowledge, Skills. Designed to help you see a consistency between the specific objectives and the goals of science education, it may serve to help you keep in mind a balance between each of these four goals since they are all of equal priority.

1. The statements of behavioral objectives which are identified as "A" — developing Attitude goals — are behaviors which you might observe as students increase their enjoyment of science activities, and as they demonstrate an interest in the scientific objects and events in their environment. You will find such statements as:

Students will request that the demonstration be repeated.
Students will volunteer to conduct an experiment outside the classroom or laboratory.
Students will request the use of science equipment during free periods.
Students will volunteer to do research and report their findings in class.

As you can see, few of these behaviors are prompted by the teacher. They are voluntary behaviors which indicate an affinity for, an inclination toward, and a preference for science. You will find suggested attitudinal behaviors throughout the list and particularly at the end of each chapter when students may have an opportunity to go beyond the information presented in the text.

2. The statements of behavioral objectives which are identified as "P" — developing Process goals — are behaviors which you might observe as students use the thinking processes of analyzing, experimenting, applying, hypothesizing, theorizing, comparing and contrasting, classifying, observing, etc. You will find such statements as:

When presented with various objects, students will compare and contrast their similarities and differences and place them in groups of metallic and nonmetallic.

Given data about weather fronts, temperature and barometric readings, students will predict the weather conditions in their area.

Given pictures of various land forms, students will apply their information of wind and water erosion and glaciation to describe how the land was shaped.

When asked to suggest ways of testing the hypothesis that electromagnets are stronger than bar magnets, students will devise experiments to find out.

3. The statements of behavioral objectives which are identified as "K" — developing Knowledge goals — are behaviors which you might observe as students demonstrate they have gained an understanding and use of certain terms, concepts, and generalizations of science.

You will find such statements as:

When asked, students will define the term "electrolysis" correctly.

Students will explain the reason why objects fall toward the earth by using the term gravity, gravitational pull or force of gravity.

Students will correctly identify the elements represented by symbols in the chemical formula for a compound.

Students will describe the effects of very low temperatures on the electrical conductivity of many metals.

Generally, a knowledge objective is one which calls upon the student to recall or explain information, concepts, or principles which he has learned in the past or which have been presented in the text and other materials.

4. The statements of behavioral objectives which are identified as "S" — developing Skills goals — are behaviors which you might observe as students gain skill in using scientific equipment correctly, and organizing, recording or reporting information accurately. Some examples of such statements are:

Students will strip the insulation from the wires and correctly connect the wires to each pole of the dry cell.

Using a stopwatch, students will count the number of swings a pendulum makes in one minute.

While observing the demonstration, students will record their observations in their notebooks.

Using a yardstick or tape measure and chalk, students will construct a model of the solar system on the playground, using the ratio: 1 foot equals 10,000,000 miles.

In this guide, each chapter begins with a goal statement. The goal statement is also found at the beginning of each chapter in the student's text.

Following the goal statement, the specific objectives for each section of that chapter are stated. There may be several objectives in each section. Each objective is numbered to correspond to that section of the chapter. For example, 22:5 identifies an objective for Chapter 22, section 5. From this you should be able to determine and plan for the achievement of the objectives for each small section of a chapter.

Remember, **the behavioral objectives in this guide are not meant to be all inclusive.** You should supplement them with behavioral objectives from other sources and with those you create yourself.

As you examine these objectives, you will find many of them include a description of the conditions. Feel free to alter these conditions according to your own classroom situation. For example, the objectives may state a condition: "When presented with three types of magnets: bar, horseshoe and cylindrical . . ." You may not have these types of magnets in your classroom. Change the statement of conditions to reflect those particular materials you have available. Another example: "When asked to state . . ." Maybe you'd prefer your students to write or to demonstrate a certain response. Make adjustments as required.

You will also find that the criterion or level of performance for each objective is not included. The intent was to create guidelines and not to state levels of expectancies for you. Only you can decide if 100% or only 50% of your students should be able to accomplish each task. You will need to develop and insert these criterion levels for your own students based upon your knowledge of their abilities, the available materials, and your own situation.

1 Introduction to Physical Science

Goal:

Students will gain knowledge and understanding of the nature of science and methods of science.

Objectives:

Upon completion of the reading and activities and when asked to diagram, demonstrate, or respond either orally or on a written test, students will:

**Section
Number**

1:1-2   K   differentiate between science and technology.

1:3   K   list the methods used by scientists in developing and testing scientific knowledge.

1:3   S/P   conduct an experiment to demonstrate some methods of science.

1:4   K   define the role of a control in experimentation.

1:5   K   differentiate between theory and law.

1:6   K   define physical science.

1:7   P   explain the importance of measurements in science.

1:7-10   K   compare units of measure in the metric system and English system.

1:8-10   S   measure specified bodies with recommended measuring instruments.

1:11   P   compare and contrast the Celsius and Fahrenheit temperature scales.

1:12   S/K   conduct an experiment to demonstrate a method of indirect measurement.

1:12   K   distinguish among mass, weight, and density.

1:13   S   conduct an experiment to determine the density of a substance.

       S/A   When conducting activities and experiments, students will use laboratory materials and equipment in the prescribed manner.

            Upon completion of the reading and activities, students will exhibit an interest in science by:

       A   reading unassigned literature related to ideas presented in the chapter.

       A/S   voluntarily measuring a number of objects with different measuring instruments.

       A/S   volunteering to design and conduct a demonstration for the class.

       A/S   volunteering to help maintain and care for laboratory equipment.

2 Classification of Matter

Goal:

Students will gain an understanding of the ways in which matter is classified and the differences between physical changes and chemical changes.

Objectives:

Upon completion of the reading and activities and when asked to diagram, demonstrate, or respond either orally or on a written test, students will:

2:1   K define matter and inertia.

2:1   S conduct an experiment to demonstrate that no two pieces of matter can occupy the same place at the same time.

2:2-4 P distinguish between elements, compounds, and mixtures.

2:4   S/P conduct an experiment to separate a mixture of salt and sand.

2:5   S/P conduct an experiment to demonstrate how iodine can be separated from a mixture by sublimation.

2:5   S/P conduct an experiment to demonstrate how water can be purified by evaporation and condensation.

2:5-6 P contrast the physical properties of objects with the chemical properties of objects.

2:7-8 P contrast physical changes with chemical changes.

2:8   S/P conduct an experiment to demonstrate the difference between a mixture of iron and sulfur and a compound of iron and sulfur (iron sulfide).

2:8   S/P conduct an experiment to demonstrate a way of producing hydrogen and to determine if hydrogen has been produced.

2:8   S/P conduct an experiment to demonstrate methods of making physical separations.

2:8   S/P conduct an experiment to demonstrate distillation.

2:8   S/P experiment to demonstrate some characteristics of a chemical change.

       S/A   When conducting activities and experiments, students will use laboratory materials and equipment in the prescribed manner.
              Upon completion of the reading and activities, students will exhibit an interest in science by:

       A reading unassigned literature related to ideas presented in the chapter.

       A/S voluntarily helping to maintain and care for laboratory materials and equipment.

3 Atoms and Compounds

Goal:
   Students will gain an understanding of the atomic theory of matter and the importance of the electron in both ionic and covalent chemical bonds.

Objectives:
   Upon completion of the reading and activities and when asked to diagram, demonstrate, or respond either orally or on a written test, students will:

Section
Number

3:1   K state the atomic theory and define atom.

3:2   K define and list the characteristics of electrons, protons, and neutrons.

3:3   P discuss the value of models in explaining scientific ideas.

3:3   P compare and contrast the Bohr model of the atom with the electron cloud model of the atom.

3:3   K define isotope.

3:4   K explain electron energy levels or shells.

3:5   P compare the properties of an element with the properties of a compound.

3:6   P differentiate between ionic and covalent bonding.

3:6   S/K diagram and explain the covalent bond between chlorine and hydrogen.

3:6   S/K diagram and explain the ionic bond between sodium and chlorine.

3:7   K define valence and list the valences of some common elements.

3:7   K write the chemical formulas for a given list of combinations of elements.

3:8-9 P compare and contrast binary compounds with compounds containing polyatomic ions.

3:9   S/P conduct an experiment to determine the percent of oxygen in potassium chlorate.

    S/A   When conducting activities and experiments, students will use laboratory materials and equipment in the prescribed manner.

        Upon completion of the reading and activities, students will exhibit an interest in science by:

    A reading unassigned literature related to the ideas presented in the chapter.

    A/S volunteering to construct models of atoms and molecules.

4 The Periodic Table

Goal:

Students will gain an understanding of the periodic table of the elements and will learn how to predict the relative activity of elements by applying the periodic law.

Objectives:

Upon completion of the reading and activities and when asked to diagram, demonstrate, or respond either orally or on a written test, students will:

Section
Number

4:1   K define atomic mass.

4:1   S/P conduct an experiment with marbles and steel balls to demonstrate the value of using relative mass rather than actual mass when determining mass ratios.

4:2   S/P conduct an experiment to demonstrate how sodium, potassium, calcium, and magnesium might be grouped into two chemical families based upon their observed properties.

4:2-3 P compare and contrast the periodic table developed by Mendeleev with the periodic table developed by Moseley.

4:3   K list the meanings of the symbols and numbers contained in a square of the periodic table of the elements.

4:4   K define isotopes.

4:4   K list and explain the two methods used to distinguish between isotopes of an element.

4:5   P explain why the average atomic mass is used when referring to the atomic weight of an element.

4:5-6 K differentiate between the atomic mass number of an element and its average atomic mass.

4:7-8 P compare and contrast the patterns in the periodic table of the elements when reading from left to right in a row and when reading from top to bottom in a column.

4:9   P predict the chemical activity and probable bond types of some elements based on the position of each in the periodic table.

4:9   S/P conduct an experiment to demonstrate the relative chemical activity of the halogens.

       S/A   When conducting activities and experiments, students will use laboratory materials and equipment in the prescribed manner.

             Upon completion of the reading and activities, students will exhibit an interest in science by:

       A reading unassigned literature related to ideas presented in the chapter.

       A voluntarily visiting a chemical laboratory and reporting to the class.

5 Families of Elements

Goal:

Students will gain an understanding of the properties of chemical families, diatomic gases, allotropy, photoconductivity, multiple proportions, and spectrum analysis.

Objectives:

Upon completion of the reading and activities and when asked to diagram, demonstrate, or respond either orally or on a written test, students will:

Section
Number

5:1   K list the elements in the halogen family and indicate the characteristics of each.

5:1   K define electrolysis.

5:1   S/P conduct an experiment to devise a test for starch.

5:1   S/P conduct an activity to test various foods for starch.

5:2   K list the elements in the oxygen family and indicate the characteristics of each element.

5:2   K define allotropes and list examples.

5:2   S/P conduct an experiment to demonstrate that there is free oxygen in the atmosphere and that approximately 20% of air by volume is free oxygen.

5:2   S/P conduct an experiment to demonstrate how oxygen can be produced in the laboratory and to test some of the chemical properties of oxygen.

5:2 S/P conduct an experiment to demonstrate a method of determining the identity of sulfides of some metals.

5:2 K define photoconductivity and indicate two elements which are good photoconductors.

5:3 K list the elements in the nitrogen family and indicate the characteristics of each element.

5:3 S/P conduct an experiment to demonstrate a test for the nitrate ion.

5:3 K state the law of multiple proportions and list examples of this law.

5:4 K list the alkali metals and indicate the characteristics of each alkali metal.

5:4 K/A explain the importance of knowing the spectrum of an element.

5:4 S/P conduct an experiment to demonstrate the identification of some elements on the basis of their characteristic flame tests.

5:5 K list the alkaline earth metals and describe the characteristics of each alkaline earth element.

5:6 K list the elements in the noble gas family and describe the characteristics of these elements.

S/A When conducting activities and experiments, students will use laboratory materials and equipment in the prescribed manner.

Upon completion of the reading and activities, students will exhibit an interest in science by:

A reading unassigned literature related to ideas presented in the chapter.

A voluntarily visiting a plant which produces chemicals commercially and reporting to the class.

6 Carbon and Its Compounds

Goal:
Students will gain an understanding of the reasons for the large number of carbon compounds, catenation, multiple bonding, and substitution.

Objectives:
Upon completion of the reading and activities and when asked to diagram, demonstrate, or respond either orally or on a written test, students will:

Section
Number

6:1 K explain the different ways carbon atoms can bond with each other.

6:2 P/A explain why the structural formulas of carbon compounds are important.

6:3 K explain what isomers are and diagram examples.

6:4-6 P compare and contrast saturated hydrocarbons and unsaturated hydrocarbons.

6:4 S/P conduct an experiment to demonstrate a method of producing methane gas and testing its properties.

6:5   S/P conduct an experiment to demonstrate the paper chromatography method of separating chemical compounds.

6:6   P explain how fractionation is used to produce different petroleum products.

6:6   K define octane rating for gasoline and indicate how the octane rating can be changed.

6:7   S/P conduct an experiment to demonstrate a method of producing acetylene gas and testing its properties.

6:8   S/P conduct an experiment to demonstrate polymerization in the manufacture of the plastic Bakelite.

6:8   S/P conduct an activity to test the properties of both natural and synthetic fibers.

6:9   K list some ring compounds of carbon, some substituted hydrocarbons, and some common alcohols and their uses.

      S/A When conducting activities and experiments, students will use laboratory materials and equipment in the prescribed manner.

Upon completion of the reading and activities, students will exhibit an interest in science by:

      A reading unassigned literature related to ideas presented in the chapter.

      A voluntarily tracing the history of the discovery of an organic compound and its uses and report findings to the class.

7 Solids and Fluids

Goal:

Students will gain an understanding of solids and fluids, the arrangements and bonding of particles within solids and fluids, and factors which cause changes in state of solids and fluids.

Objectives:

Upon completion of the reading and activities and when asked to diagram, demonstrate, or respond either orally or on a written test, students will:

**Section
Number**

7:1   K define solid and list examples of solids.

7:2   K define crystal and list examples of crystalline substances.

7:2   S/P conduct an activity to compare crystals of different substances and list similarities and differences for these crystals.

7:2   S/P examine a mica crystal under the microscope, diagram the crystal's shape, and explain the cleavage pattern.

7:3-6 P compare types of bonding in crystals including ionic bonding, bonding resulting from Van der Waals forces and from dipole-dipole attraction, covalent bonding, and metallic bonding.

7:3   S demonstrate the growth of macromolecular crystals from a solution of sodium hydroxide, sodium dichromate dihydrate, lithium carbonate, and water.

7:6 S/P conduct an experiment to demonstrate the crystallization of mercury-sodium alloy.

7:6 P explain why metals are good conductors of electricity and how this property is related to crystal structure.

7:7 P compare the formation of crystals from a melt with the formation of crystals from a solution.

7:8 K define amorphous solid and list examples of amorphous solids.

7:9 K define fluids and list examples of fluids.

7:10 K define liquids and list examples of liquids.

7:10 S/P conduct an experiment to demonstrate that alcohol molecules move into space between water molecules.

7:11 P compare physical characteristics of gases with physical characteristics of liquids.

7:12 K state and explain Pascal's Law.

7:12 S/P conduct an experiment to demonstrate Pascal's Law.

7:12-16 K explain what happens when matter changes phase.

7:13 S/P conduct an experiment to demonstrate that the temperature of water does not change as it boils.

7:16 P explain how the type of bonding in a crystal affects the melting point of the crystal.

7:16 P explain how the type of bonding in a liquid affects the boiling point of the liquid.

S/A When conducting activities and experiments, students will use laboratory materials and equipment in the prescribed manner.

Upon completion of the reading and activities, students will exhibit an interest in science by:

A reading unassigned literature related to ideas presented in the chapter.

A/S voluntarily building and demonstrating a crystal model.

A/S voluntarily growing a large alum crystal and bringing it to class.

A voluntarily visiting a local garage, examining the hydraulic lift, and calculating the force exerted on the small piston when it lifts a 3000-pound automobile.

8 Solutions

Goal:

Students will gain an understanding of solutes, solvents, concentration, and saturation.

Objectives:

Upon completion of the reading and activities and when asked to diagram, demonstrate, or respond either orally or on a written test, students will:

**Section
Number**

8:1 P compare and contrast liquid, gaseous, and solid solutions.

8:1 K differentiate between miscible and immiscible.

8:2	S/P	conduct an experiment to demonstrate the energy change which occurs as a solid dissolves in a liquid.
8:3	S/P	conduct an experiment to demonstrate the difference in the rate a large crystal and the rate the same quantity of small crystals will dissolve in a solvent.
8:3	K	list the three factors which affect the solution rate of a solid in a liquid.
8:3	K	list the factors which affect the solution rate of gases in a liquid.
8:4	K	state the general rule concerning organic solvents and inorganic solvents and the materials they dissolve.
8:4	S/P	conduct an experiment to demonstrate the solubility of oil in an organic solvent and in an inorganic solvent.
8:5	P	compare and contrast the solutions made from polar compounds and nonpolar compounds and explain the reasons for the electrical conductivity of these solutions.
8:6	S/P	experiment to determine the solubility of salt in water.
8:7	S/P	conduct an experiment to determine the concentration of a solute in a solvent.
8:8	P	compare and contrast a mixture and a solution.
8:8	S/P	experiment to demonstrate that crystallization occurs in a supersaturated solution as it cools.
8:9	S/P	conduct an experiment to devise a test for water of hydration in crystals.
8:10	K	describe the effect of a solute on a solvent's boiling point and on a solvent's freezing point.
	S/A	When conducting activities and experiments, students will use laboratory materials and equipment in the prescribed manner.
		Upon completion of the reading and activities, students will exhibit an interest in science by:
	A	reading unassigned literature related to ideas presented in the chapter.
	A/S	voluntarily conducting experiments at home to determine the boiling points and freezing points of various solutions.

9 Conservation of Mass

Goal:

Students will gain an understanding of the principle of conservation of matter and energy and the manner in which energy changes accompany chemical reactions.

Objectives:

Upon completion of the reading and activities and when asked to diagram, demonstrate, or respond either orally or on a written test, students will:

**Section
Number**

| 9:1 | S/P | conduct an experiment to demonstrate that there is no change in mass as a result of a chemical change. |

9:1	P	compare and contrast precipitates, reactants, and products.
9:2	K	define and give an example of double replacement reactions, single replacement reactions, decomposition reactions, and synthesis reactions.
9:2	S	write the equations for a given set of reactions.
9:2	S/P	conduct an experiment to demonstrate a double replacement reaction.
9:2	S/P	conduct an experiment to demonstrate a single replacement reaction.
9:2	S/P	conduct an experiment to illustrate a decomposition reaction.
9:2	S/P	conduct an experiment to illustrate a synthesis reaction.
9:3	P	compare and contrast exothermic reactions and endothermic reactions and indicate an example of each.
9:4	K	differentiate between molecular mass and formula mass.
9:5	K	define the mole and list examples of this unit.
9:6	S/P	conduct an experiment to demonstrate the use of an indicator to determine when neutralization occurs between an acid and a base.
9:6	K	explain a one-molar solution.
	S/A	When conducting activities and experiments, students will use laboratory materials and equipment in the prescribed manner.
		Upon completion of the reading and activities, students will exhibit an interest in science by:
	A	reading unassigned literature related to ideas presented in the chapter.
	A/S	volunteering to help care for and maintain laboratory materials and equipment.

10 Acids, Bases, and Salts

Goal:

Students will gain an understanding of the properties of acids, bases, and salts and various means of measuring the relative strengths of these materials.

Objectives:

Upon completion of the reading and activities and when asked to diagram, demonstrate, or respond either orally or on a written test, students will:

**Section
Number**

10:1	P	compare the properties of acids with the properties of bases and indicate examples of acids and bases.
10:2	K	describe the purpose of indicators and list examples of indicators used.
10:2	S/P	conduct an experiment to demonstrate the use of an indicator in determining which solutions are acids and which solutions are bases.
10:3	S/P	conduct an experiment to demonstrate the dehydrating power of concentrated sulfuric acid.

10:3   S/P conduct an experiment to demonstrate the different activity rates of three different acids when these acids are in contact with mossy zinc.

10:4-5 K describe the relationship between electrical conductivity and the strength of acids and bases.

10:6   S/P conduct an experiment to produce a salt as a result of mixing an acid and a base.

10:7   K define anhydride and list examples of anhydrides.

10:8   S use Universal Indicator Paper to test the pH of liquids.

10:8   P compare the pH values of some common acids and bases.

10:9   S/P conduct an experiment to demonstrate the titration method of determining the concentration of acids or bases.

10:9   S/P conduct an experiment to determine the molarity of a solution.

S/A   When conducting activities and experiments, students will use laboratory materials and equipment in the prescribed manner.

Upon completion of the reading and activities, students will exhibit an interest in science by:

A reading unassigned literature related to ideas presented in the chapter.

A/S volunteering to help prepare materials for use in experiments.

A/S volunteering to help care for and maintain laboratory materials and equipment.

11 Force and Work

Goal:

Students will gain knowledge and understanding of forces, work, simple machines, mechanical advantage, and power.

Objectives:

Upon completion of the reading and activities and when asked to diagram, demonstrate, or respond either orally or on a written test, students will:

**Section
Number**

11:1   P compare and contrast force and resistance.

11:1   S/P conduct an experiment to demonstrate how the force of gravity can be measured with a spring.

11:2   P explain how work is related to force and distance.

11:2   P compare and contrast the unit of force in the English system and the unit of force in the metric system.

11:3-11 K list the six simple machines and indicate examples of each.

11:4   P compare and contrast ideal mechanical advantage and actual mechanical advantage.

11:5-11 S/P conduct experiments to demonstrate how machines make work easier.

11:6-11   P explain how the ideal mechanical advantage of the six simple machines can be calculated.

11:12   P relate the efficiency of a machine to work input and work output.

11:13   P explain the relationships of power, work, horsepower, and watt.

S/A   When conducting activities and experiments, students will use laboratory materials and equipment in the prescribed manner.

Upon completion of the reading and activities, students will exhibit an interest in science by:

A reading unassigned literature related to ideas presented in the chapter.

A/S volunteering to develop and conduct a demonstration for the class.

A relating ideas presented in this chapter to things which happen in everyday life.

12 Moving Bodies

Goal:

Students will gain an understanding of the difference between weight and mass, the difference between speed and velocity, and the relationship between forces and motion.

Objectives:

Upon completion of the reading and activities and when asked to diagram, demonstrate, or respond either orally or on a written test, students will:

**Section
Number**

12:1   P/K compare and contrast the meanings of weight and mass.

12:1   S/P conduct an experiment to demonstrate the difference between mass and weight.

12:2   P state Newton's law of gravitation and explain how it can be used to predict what an object will weigh at a particular altitude.

12:3   P compare and contrast the meanings of constant speed and average speed.

12:4-5   P compare and contrast the meanings of acceleration and deceleration.

12:6   K define vector.

12:6   S/P conduct an activity to illustrate the parallelogram method for determining a resultant force.

12:7   P compare and contrast the meanings of velocity and speed.

12:7   P/S solve assigned problems which require the use of vectors to determine the velocity of a body.

S/A   When conducting activities and experiments, students will use laboratory materials and equipment in the prescribed manner.

Upon completion of the reading and activities, students will exhibit an interest in science by:

A reading unassigned literature related to ideas presented in the chapter.

A/S volunteering to develop and conduct a demonstration for the class.

A relating ideas presented in this chapter to things which happen in everyday life.

13 Laws of Motion

Goal:

Students will gain an understanding of Newton's laws, effects of gravity on motion, projectile motion, motion in curves, systems, and momentum.

Objectives:

Upon completion of the reading and activities and when asked to diagram, demonstrate, or respond either orally or on a written test, students will:

**Section
Number**

13:1-3   K   state Newton's three laws of motion and give examples of each.

13:1-3   S/P   conduct experiments to demonstrate Newton's three laws of motion.

13:4   S/P   conduct an experiment to demonstrate the effects of gravity on falling bodies.

13:4-5   P   compare and contrast the effects of gravity on falling bodies and bodies thrown vertically upward.

13:6   S/P   conduct an experiment to illustrate how the velocity of a projectile changes during its flight.

13:7   P/K   compare and contrast centrifugal force and centripetal force.

13:8   K   compare and contrast simple systems and complex systems.

13:8   S/K   dismantle and assemble a machine and explain how the component parts act together to form a system.

13:9   K   indicate the relationships among mass, velocity, and momentum.

13:10   K   indicate the relationship between impulse and momentum.

13:11   K   state and explain the mathematical equations for conservation of momentum.

S/A   When conducting activities and experiments, students will use laboratory materials and equipment in the prescribed manner.

Upon completion of the reading and activities, students will exhibit an interest in science by:

A   reading unassigned literature related to ideas presented in the chapter.

A   relating ideas presented in the chapter to things which happen in everyday life.

A/S   calculating the momentum of various moving bodies and explaining the results to the class.

A   requesting permission to perform demonstrations to the class.

14 Heat Energy

Goal:

To gain an understanding of kinetic energy and the relationship between heat and kinetic energy.

Objectives:

Upon completion of the reading and activities and when asked to diagram, demonstrate, or respond either orally or on a written test, students will:

**Section
Number**

14:1   P   explain the relationship between kinetic energy and potential energy.

14:1   S/P   experiment to demonstrate how heat is produced from kinetic energy in particles of matter.

14:2   S/P   experiment to demonstrate the transfer of heat from a hot body to a cooler body.

14:2   P   compare and contrast conduction, convection, and radiation as methods of heat transfer.

14:2   S/P   experiment to demonstrate the transfer of heat by conduction, convection, and radiation.

14:3   S/P   experiment to determine how much heat is produced by a Bunsen burner in one minute.

14:3   S/P   experiment to demonstrate how a calorimeter is used to measure heat energy.

14:4   K   define British thermal unit and describe Joule's experiment in which he determined the mechanical equivalent of heat.

14:5   K   define temperature in terms of molecular kinetic energy.

14:6   P   relate the change in state in a quantity of matter to the amount of heat possessed by that quantity of matter before and after the change of state.

14:6   S/P   experiment to demonstrate that steam loses heat when it condenses to water.

14:6   P   compare and contrast heat of fusion and heat of vaporization.

      S/A   When conducting activities and experiments, students will use laboratory materials and equipment in the prescribed manner.

Upon completion of the reading and activities, students will exhibit an interest in science by:

      A   reading unassigned literature related to ideas presented in the chapter.

      A/S   volunteering to design and conduct a demonstration for the class.

      A   voluntarily relating ideas presented in the chapter to everyday occurrences and informing class members.

15 Heat and Its Uses

Goal:

Students will gain an understanding of heat energy and its practical applications.

Objectives:

Upon completion of the reading and activities and when asked to diagram, demonstrate, or respond either orally or on a written test, students will:

16 Waves

Goal:

Students will gain an understanding of the properties of waves and the electromagnetic spectrum.

Objectives:

Upon completion of the reading and activities and when asked to diagram, demonstrate, or respond either orally or on a written test, students will:

16:1   K   define wavelength, frequency, and amplitude and indicate their relationships.

16:2   S/P   conduct an experiment to determine wave frequency.

16:3   S/P   conduct an experiment to determine the length of a sound wave.

16:3   S/P   conduct an experiment to demonstrate how beats may be produced by two sounds.

16:4   K   explain the use of a ripple tank in wave studies.

16:5   S/P   conduct an experiment to demonstrate that waves can be reflected.

16:6   S/P   experiment to demonstrate that waves can be refracted.

16:7   S/P   conduct an experiment to demonstrate the Doppler effect and explain what happens.

16:8   K   define and describe the electromagnetic spectrum.

      S/A   When conducting activities and experiments, students will use laboratory materials and equipment in the prescribed manner.

           Upon completion of the reading and activities, students will exhibit an interest in science by:

      A   reading unassigned literature related to ideas presented in the chapter.

      A/S   volunteering to help maintain and care for laboratory equipment.

      A/S   volunteering to design and conduct a demonstration for the class.

17 Optics

Goal:

Students will gain an understanding of the properties of light and how to use mirrors and lenses to produce images through reflection and refraction.

Objectives:

Upon completion of the reading and activities and when asked to diagram, demonstrate, or respond either orally or on a written test, students will:

**Section
Number**

17:1   S/P   conduct an experiment to demonstrate the characteristics of an image formed by a plane mirror.

17:1   K   list the physical properties of light which cause a mirror to produce an image.

17:1-2   P   compare and contrast real images and virtual images and the ways they can be produced.

17:2   S   demonstrate the production of a real image and a virtual image with a concave parabolic mirror.

17:3   S/P   conduct an experiment to demonstrate and determine the index of refraction of glass.

17:3   S/P   experiment to demonstrate and determine the index of refraction of a clear liquid.

17:4	P	compare convex lenses with concave lenses.
17:4	S	use a convex lens to produce a real image and diagram the paths of the light rays producing the image.
17:5	P	compare and contrast refracting telescopes and reflecting telescopes.
17:6	S	use a prism to separate white light into its component colors.
17:6	K	explain how ROY G. BIV is related to the visible light spectrum.
17:6-7	P	explain how wavelength and frequency are related to color.
17:8	P	compare and contrast the wave theory of light and the particle theory of light.
17:8	S	use polaroid filters to demonstrate the polarization property of light.
17:8	S	use a diffraction grating to demonstrate interference of light waves.
17:8	K	describe the photoelectric effect and indicate a device which works on this principle.
S/A		When conducting activities and experiments, students will use laboratory materials and equipment in the prescribed manner.

Upon completion of the reading and activities, students will exhibit an interest in science by:

| A | reading unassigned literature related to ideas presented in the chapter. |
| A/S | requesting permission to conduct further experiments related to ideas presented in the chapter. |

18 Electricity

Goal:

Students will gain an understanding of the different kinds of electricity and the relationship between electricity and magnetism.

Objectives:

Upon completion of the reading and activities and when asked to diagram, demonstrate, or respond either orally or on a written test, students will:

**Section
Number**

18:1	S	conduct an experiment to demonstrate how electrons can be added to or removed from a substance by rubbing two substances together.
18:1	P	compare and contrast positive static electric charges and negative static electric charges.
18:1	P	compare electrons with protons.
18:2	P	contrast electrical conductors and insulators.
18:2	S	use an electroscope to determine when an object is charged positively, negatively, or is neutral.
18:2	S	conduct an experiment to demonstrate the charging of a metal rod by induction.

18:2-3   P   compare and contrast the charging of an electroscope by induction and by conduction.

18:4   P   compare and contrast wet cells and dry cells and explain how they can make up a battery.

18:5   K   describe two ways in which electric current can be produced by heat energy.

18:6   S   construct an electromagnet and demonstrate its use.

18:6   K   list the properties of a magnet.

18.6   S   conduct an experiment to demonstrate the presence of a magnetic field around a magnet.

18:7   S/P   conduct an experiment to produce an electric current through the use of a magnet and a coil of wire.

18:7   P   compare direct current with alternating current.

18:8   K   define ampere, coulomb, volt, ohm, and watt.

18:8   S/P   conduct an experiment to demonstrate the relationship among volts, amperes, and ohms in a circuit.

S/A   When conducting activities and experiments, students will use laboratory materials and equipment in the prescribed manner.

Upon completion of the reading and activities, students will exhibit an interest in science by:

A   reading unassigned literature related to ideas presented in the chapter.

A/S   voluntarily constructing a direct current motor and demonstrating its use to the class.

A/S   voluntarily converting the kilowatt hours listed on a monthly electric bill to British thermal units.

19 Electronics

Goal:

Students will gain an understanding of principles involved in electronic devices such as diodes, triodes, rectifiers, transistors, and cathode ray tubes.

Objectives:

Upon completion of the reading and activities and when asked to diagram, demonstrate, or respond either orally or on a written test, students will:

Section
Number

19:1   S/P   conduct an experiment to demonstrate a simple series circuit and a simple parallel circuit.

19:2   P   compare the cathode with the anode found in vacuum tubes.

19:2   S/P   conduct an experiment to demonstrate that zinc loses electrons when exposed to ultraviolet light.

19:2   P   compare a diode vacuum tube with a triode vacuum tube.

19:3   S/P   conduct an experiment to demonstrate one way of storing an electric charge.

19:3   P   describe the principle of a capacitor and explain how it is used in a radio circuit.

19:4   K   explain what a rectifier is and what it is used for.

19:5   P   compare *n-type* transistors with *p-type* transistors.

19:6   S/P   experiment with a cathode tube and a magnet to demonstrate the effect of a magnet on a stream of electrons.

19:7-8   P   compare and contrast a digital computer and an analog computer.

       S/A   When conducting activities and experiments, students will use laboratory materials and equipment in the prescribed manner.

          Upon completion of the reading and activities, students will exhibit an interest in science by:

       A   reading unassigned literature related to ideas presented in the chapter.

       A   voluntarily visiting a computer center and reporting to the class.

       A   voluntarily visiting an electric power plant and reporting to the class.

20 Radiation

Goal:

Students will gain an understanding of radiation and the detection and measurement of radiation.

Objectives:

Upon completion of the reading and activities and when asked to diagram, demonstrate, or respond either orally or on a written test, students will:

Section Number

20:1   K   describe the characteristics of X rays.

20:1   S/P   conduct an experiment to demonstrate the effect of lead shielding on X rays produced by a Crookes tube.

20:1   K   indicate the relationships among frequency, wavelength, and velocity.

20:2   K   define roentgen.

20:3   P   contrast stable nuclei with unstable nuclei.

20:3   K   describe transmutation.

20:4   P   contrast the differences among alpha, beta, and gamma radiation.

20:5   K   explain the half-life concept as it applies to a radioactive material.

20:6   K   explain the detection of radiation with an electroscope.

20:7   P   compare and describe uses of a cloud chamber and a bubble chamber.

20:8-9   P   compare nuclear emulsions, Geiger counters, and scintillation counters and describe the uses of each.

20:9   S/P   conduct an experiment to detect radioactivity with a Geiger counter.

20:9   S/P   conduct an experiment to illustrate the relationship between the level of radiation and distance from the radioactive source.

  S/A   When conducting activities and experiments, students will use laboratory materials and equipment in the prescribed manner.

  Upon completion of the reading and activities, students will exhibit an interest in science by:

  A   reading unassigned literature related to ideas presented in the chapter.

  A/S   voluntarily constructing and using a cloud chamber to detect background radiation.

  A/S   voluntarily constructing and using an electroscope to determine relative radiation levels in the home.

21 Nuclear Reactions

Goal:
   Students will gain an understanding of the structure of the atomic nucleus, transmutation, fission, and fusion.

Objectives:
   Upon completion of the reading and activities and when asked to diagram, demonstrate, or respond either orally or on a written test, students will:

**Section
Number**

21:1   P   explain the relationship between mass defect and binding energy.

21:1   P   compare and contrast nuclear forces, electrostatic forces, and gravitational forces.

21:2   P   explain nuclear transmutation.

21:3   K   list and explain three uses of radioactive isotopes.

21:3   P   compare a positron with an electron.

21:3   K   explain the relationship between average binding energy and the stability of a nucleus.

21:3   K   explain the relationship between the magic number sequence and the shell theory.

21:3   K   explain how carbon 14 can be used to determine the age of an object.

21:4   K   explain the relationship between a nuclear chain reaction and critical mass.

21:4   K   indicate what the symbols represent in $E=mc^2$.

21:4-5   P   compare nuclear fission with nuclear fusion.

  S/A   When conducting activities or experiments, students will use laboratory materials and equipment in the prescribed manner.

Upon completion of the reading and activities, students will exhibit an interest in science by:

A   reading unassigned literature related to ideas presented in the chapter.

A/S   volunteering to collect materials and help set up a demonstration of the rates at which different plants absorb radioactive isotopes.

A/S   volunteering to help care for and maintain laboratory materials and equipment.

A/S   volunteering to help inventory laboratory materials and equipment.

22 Nuclear Technology

Goal:

Students will gain an understanding of the relationship between nuclear science and technology.

Objectives:

Upon completion of the reading and activities and when asked to diagram, demonstrate, or respond either orally or on a written test, students will:

**Section
Number**

22:1   K   describe the operation of a cyclotron.

22:1   P   explain why all of the particles used as "bullets" in nuclear accelerators possess an electrical charge.

22:1   P   compare the process of accelerating nuclear particles with the principles which cause the armature in an electric motor to turn.

22:2   K   list the six main parts of a nuclear reactor and describe the major functions of each part.

22:2   K   explain why nuclear reactors are not considered efficient energy sources for airplanes and rocket ships.

22:2   P   explain how energy from nuclear reactor fuel is converted to electrical energy.

22:3   K   describe the process of extracting uranium from its ore.

22:4   P   explain why scientists are not able to produce a controlled thermonuclear fusion reaction.

     S/A   When conducting activities or experiments, students will use laboratory materials and equipment in the prescribed manner.

Upon completion of the reading and activities, students will exhibit an interest in science by:

A   reading unassigned literature related to ideas presented in the chapter.

A   voluntarily contacting the Atomic Energy Commission to determine the location of the closest nuclear reactor or particle accelerator, visiting the installation, and reporting observations to the class.

A/S   voluntarily constructing a model of a nuclear reactor or particle accelerator.

EVALUATION

How Do You Know You've Achieved Your Objectives?

When you try to find out if students have learned anything, you probably give some form of written test — true-false, completion, matching or essay type of examination. All of these forms of evaluation are important in determining whether or not students have achieved their objectives.

Some of the behavioral objectives in this guide do not lend themselves to a written evaluation. It is very difficult to assess through written tests the degree to which students are developing attitudes toward science. Therefore, some other ways of evaluating the achievement of your objectives may be necessary.

Personal observation is probably the best way to evaluate student growth toward the goals of science education. But if you have a large class or are in a departmentalized system, personal observation becomes an overwhelming task. If there were a quick way of recording your observations of student behavior to indicate the achievement of an objective, the task might be easier.

Behavioral checklists molded to your needs can be used to collect evidence of the achievement of your objectives. **Caution:** Don't try to observe all students performing all the behaviors at once. Select several students to observe at one time; the next day, observe several more. Record your observations soon after or during the lesson.

In the simple behavioral checklist given below, enter the behavioral objectives by number or by statement for each section. Then, as you observe your students, mark the square which corresponds to the student and the objective he performs.

Date _January 9_   Topic _Controlling Sound Waves_

Page _40-45_

OBJECTIVE	Bates, W.	Bush, S.	Corson, C.	Dawes, D.	Elkins, H.	
1. Uses term "reflected" correctly	✓	✓				
2. Compares materials which absorb/ reflect sound		✓		✓		
3. Describes function of megaphone			✓			
4. Suggests ways to soundproof building					✓	
5.						

Another type of checklist may help you to record attitudinal objectives. You might keep one of these for each student, and record his growth as he demonstrates some of the behaviors which indicate to you he is developing a positive attitude toward science. It would be impossible to keep a daily record; however, you could complete it five or six times a year. Just before sending out progress reports is a good time.

STUDENT _Maria Robinson_

Date _January 9_   Observation period _2nd 6 weeks_

BEHAVIOR	Never	Sometimes	Always
1. Expresses a liking for science		✓	
2. Requests to use science materials		✓	
3. Reads science books		✓	
4. Does activities and experiments at home			
5. Volunteers to bring in equipment			✓
6. Asks questions beyond the text material			✓
7. Volunteers to do research	✓		

Another way of eliciting students' attitudes is through opinion surveys. These are helpful in determining how a student feels about himself, the subject, your teaching strategies, his own learning style and the other students in class, and the materials of instruction. Following is only a sample of the type of questions which you might use to construct an opinion survey:

OPINION SURVEY   Name _____

Section _____   Date _____

1. While studying this chapter, I found it most difficult to:
   (Check the three answers which best describe your feelings)

   _____   understand the diagrams

   _____   work in the laboratory

   _____   do the experiments suggested

   _____   understand the new vocabulary

   _____   express my opinion

   _____   understand the written assignments

   _____   discuss my misunderstandings with the teacher

2. Which do you enjoy doing most? (Check three answers)

_____ performing experiments in the laboratory

_____ reading the textbook

_____ answering the questions at the end of the unit

_____ asking questions of the teacher

_____ listening to the teacher

_____ listening to the opinions of other students

_____ doing research on my own in the library

_____ watching films

_____ experimenting on my own

_____ other (describe)

3. I have learned the most about the unit from:

_____ watching films

_____ doing my own experiments

_____ listening to the discussion

_____ asking questions about something that interests me

_____ listening to the teacher explain

_____ reading the text

_____ reading other supplementary materials

_____ participating in class discussions

_____ participating in small group discussions

Recording group behavior allows you to estimate the number of students who have completed each activity, and the time you've spent on each. This information might indicate whether you should spend more time with the whole class or with individual students.

Chapter_____

Topic _____   No. of students in class_____

Page(s)	Date(s)	Activity	Number of students completing	Total time spent
335-340	1/22-2/2	Experiments with sound waves.	21	2 hours, 32 minutes
340-342	2/5-2/8	Observing reflection of waves in a ripple tank.	25	1 hour, 20 minutes

These forms of evaluation are merely suggestions intended to supplement the many other forms of evaluation with which you may be familiar. All are intended to help you answer the question: "How do you know you're achieving the goals of science education?"

BIBLIOGRAPHY

Bloom, Benjamin, Hastings, J. Thomas, and Madaus, George, *Handbook on Formative and Summative Evaluation of Student Learning.* McGraw-Hill Book Co., New York, 1971.

Bloom, Benjamin and others, *Taxonomy of Educational Objectives, Handbook I: Cognitive Domain.* David McKay, New York, 1956.

California State Department of Education, *Science Framework for California Public Schools.* Sacramento, Calif., 1970.

Costa, Arthur, Lowery, Lawrence, and Strasser, Ben, *Strategies for Science Instruction: A Personal Workshop.* Hayward, Calif., Rapid Printers, Inc., 1972.

Eiss, Albert F., and Harbeck, Mary B., *Behavioral Objectives in the Affective Domain.* National Science Teachers Association, National Education Association, Washington, D.C., 1969.

Krathwohl, D. R., Bloom, Benjamin, and Masia, Bertram R., *Taxonomy of Educational Objectives, Handbook II: Affective Domain.* David McKay, New York, 1956.

Lindvall, C. M., ed., *Defining Educational Objectives.* University of Pittsburgh Press, Pittsburgh, 1964.

Mager, Robert, *Preparing Instructional Objectives.* Fearon Publishers, Inc., Palo Alto, Calif., 1962.

Picard, Anthony and Sund, Robert, *Behavioral Objectives and Evaluational Measures for Science and Mathematics.* Charles E. Merrill Publishing Co., Columbus, Ohio, 1971.

Plowman, Paul, *Behavioral Objectives in Science.* Science Research Associates, Chicago, 1969.

Popham, W. James, *The Teacher-Empiricist.* Aegeus Publishing Co., Los Angeles, 1965.

Popham, W. James, and Baker, Eva L., *Establishing Instructional Goals.* Prentice-Hall, Inc., Englewood Cliffs, N.J., 1970.

Walbesser, Henry H., *Constructing Behavioral Objectives.* Bureau of Educational Research and Field Services, University of Maryland, College Park, Md., 1970.

4 5 6 7 8 9 10 11 12 13 14 15-80 79 78 77 76

FOCUS ON
PHYSICAL
SCIENCE

Charles H. Heimler

California State University, Northridge
Northridge, California

Jack Price

San Diego City Schools
San Diego, California

CHARLES E. MERRILL PUBLISHING CO.
A Bell & Howell Company
Columbus, Ohio

FOCUS ON
PHYSICAL
SCIENCE
SECOND EDITION

A Merrill Science Text

Focus on Physical Science
Focus on Physical Science, Teacher's Annotated
Edition and Solutions Manual
Evaluation Program for Focus on Physical Science
(Spirit Duplicating Masters)
Physical Science: Activity-Centered Program Teacher's Guide
Physical Science: A Learning Strategy
for the Laboratory
Physical Science Skillcards

Focus on Life Science Program
Focus on Earth Science Program

COVER PHOTO: A map of the sun taken by the Orbiting Solar Observatory-7 is presented here as a computerized color display. The display shows temperature differences as color differences. Colors range from black, blues, and greens, for cool areas to reds and yellows for warm regions. The coldest areas on the sun (about one million degrees Kelvin) are black in this display. The hottest places (about forty million degrees Kelvin) are white.

ISBN 0-675-07510-6

Published by
CHARLES E. MERRILL PUBLISHING CO.
A Bell & Howell Company
Columbus, Ohio 43216

Focus on Physical Science provides a practical experience in science. Through a carefully-planned learning sequence, students employ observation and experimentation to develop and test their own hypotheses. Memorization is minimized. Rather, necessary principles of physics and chemistry are introduced through student involvement in the process of science.

While student experimentation is emphasized, expensive or complicated equipment is avoided. This program is especially useful in classrooms lacking extensive laboratory facilities. Most materials used are readily available around the home or at school. Apparatus is easily assembled and experimental procedures are kept simple so that manipulations do not obscure the basic concepts being explored.

Each of the twenty-two chapters in *Focus on Physical Science* is divided into sections of related material. These sections form logical teaching blocks and convenient units for student assignments. Chapters may be studied in a variety of sequences and can be easily organized into either semester or quarter programs.

Throughout the text, reading level has been carefully controlled without diluting the content presentation. Photographs, illustrations, charts, graphs, and tables allow the student to visualize ideas presented in the text and therefore to read with greater understanding. New science words are defined, spelled phonetically, and printed in italic or boldface type when introduced.

Focus on Physical Science: Careers, People, Frontiers—newspaperlike pages with photographs and articles on current topics—bring an additional contemporary emphasis to *Focus on Physical Science.* Some selections illustrate the relevance of physical science to everyday life. Others describe technical developments based on the concepts being studied. Still others point to career opportunities in physical science and related fields through job descriptions or brief biographical sketches.

Questions in the Margin help the student identify important concepts as he reads. Margin questions may also be used to introduce new topics in class discussions and, after a topic has been covered, for review.

Problems interspersed throughout each chapter enable the student to immediately apply newly-learned concepts. Problems are also useful for identifying and correcting individual difficulties and for ensuring that basic concepts are mastered before complicated topics are introduced. Mathematics required to do problems is integrated within the text. Thus, the student learns mathematical skills as he needs them to employ physical science concepts. Metric units are emphasized throughout.

Chapter-end features of *Focus on Physical Science* encourage student involvement and increase the flexibility of the program. These features are

- *Main Ideas*—list of important concepts
- *Vocabulary*—list of important science words
- *Study Questions*—questions and additional problem-solving applications of scientific knowledge
- *Investigations*—selected thought-provoking problems and projects
- *Suggested Readings*—literature references to topics discussed

CONTENTS

Unit Three discusses differences and similarities of various elements and shows how elements are organized into the Periodic Table.

UNIT Three   Structure of Matter

Chapter 4   Periodic Table
Chapter 4 includes the history and detailed description of the Periodic Table and its applications.

Chapter 5   Families of Elements
Chapter 5 describes the major families of elements.

Chapter 6   Carbon and Its Compounds
Chapter 6 explains basic carbon bonding and describes different types of carbon compounds.

Unit Four   treats changes in matter. Including phase changes, solutions, reactions, and acid or base behavior.

UNIT Four   Changes in Matter

Chapter 7   Solids and Fluids

Chapter 7 includes the basic characteristics of solids, liquids, and gases.

Chapter 8   Solutions

Chapter 8 explains how solutions form and the properties of dissolved substances.

Chapter 9 Conservation of Mass

Chapter 9 introduces basic chemical reactions and describes how to balance chemical equations.

Chapter 10 Acids, Bases, and Salts

Chapter 10 describes basic acid and base properties and titration.

Unit Five includes the properties of motion, force, and work.

UNIT Five   Motion

Chapter 11 introduces force, work, simple machines, mechanical advantage and power.

Chapter 11 Force and Work

Chapter 12   Moving Bodies

Chapter 12 expands the weight and mass discussion of Chapter 1, defines speed and velocity, and illustrates relationships between force and motion.

Chapter 13   Laws of Motion

Chapter 13 covers Newton's laws and special types of motion.

Chapter 18 Electricity

Chapter 18 introduces static and current electricity, describes conductors, and relates electricity to magnetism.

Chapter 19 Electronics

Chapter 19 covers many of the applications of electricity.

Unit Seven includes the science and technology of nuclear energy.

UNIT Seven Nuclear Energy

Chapter 20 Radiation

Chapter 20 includes a basic discussion of radiation.

Chapter 21   Nuclear Reactions

Chapter 21 describes nuclear reactions within the atom.

Chapter 22   Nuclear Technology

Chapter 22 introduces practical applications of nuclear energy.

Physical Science

"The more we know; the more we feel our ignorance; the more we feel how much remains unknown—

Sir Humphry Davy (1778-1829)

Through the study of physical science, students will develop an understanding of natural laws. They will observe natural phenomena and collect information by performing simple experiments. They will learn to search for regular patterns in experimental results by asking the questions How and Why. The study of physical science demands that the student learn to make accurate observations, use problem-solving techniques, and to reason to a logical conclusion.

Science is man-made. It applies human curiosity, reasoning, and creativity to the solution of problems. Physical science is the study of matter and energy. Man is able to transform matter and control energy. Through application of basic discoveries in physical science, man has developed space rockets, plastics, computers, television, and many other inventions. Yet many problems, such as pollution and energy shortages, remain to be solved.

Science is as old as ancient Greece and as new as today. Discoveries by future scientists, you and your classmates, will bring changes to your world. Perhaps you yourself will develop methods to recycle wastes, prevent diseases, reduce pollution, and . . . it's your world . . . your future.

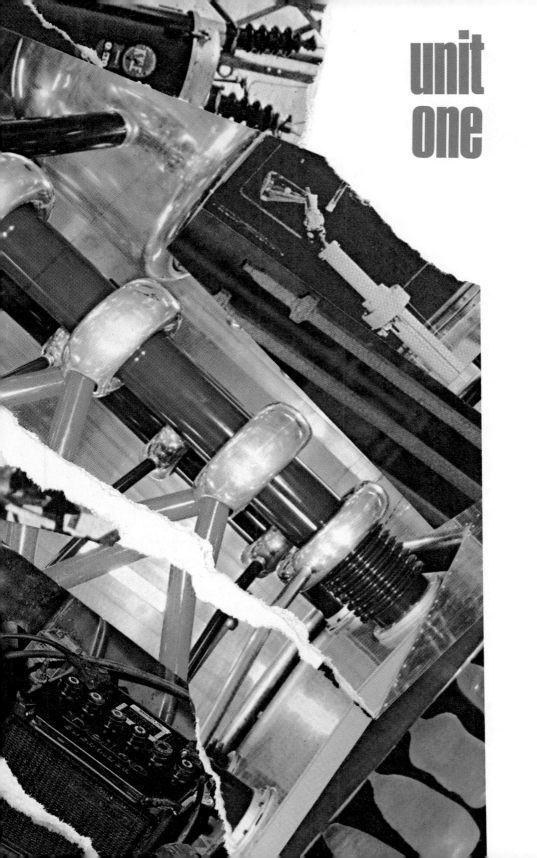

unit
one

The nature of physical science is discussed in this chapter. A distinction is made between science and technology. Students will be made aware of the importance of measurements in science and will be given opportunities to become familiar with the methods of science as well as metric, English, and other systems of measurement as they perform a wide variety of experiments.

Introduction to Physical Science

For Behavioral Objectives for each section, see the Teacher's Guide at the front of this book.

GOAL: You will gain an understanding of the nature of science and methods of science.

Review briefly the major concepts in MAIN IDEAS at the end of each chapter prior to intensive study of each chapter. Stress the use of the study-guide questions printed in the margin to guide student's reading and learning. See introduction to Teacher's Guide at the front of this book.

With today's emphasis on the environment, many people are becoming more interested in natural processes and the laws that govern them. Is modern civilization too dependent on instruments? What happens when instruments fail? Guide discussion to help students understand that even today observations of nature are important and that instruments help in observing and measuring changes that take place.

Man has always been curious. He has always tried to learn more about his environment. Ancient peoples observed the seasons and day to day changes in the weather. They felt earthquakes and tried to understand and control what caused them. Early men explained their world as best they could. Much of their world, however, remained a mystery to them.

Today we know much more about our world than did ancient peoples. Yet we still seek to understand our environment more fully. Science is one of the methods that we use. Through science, we have discovered many things about our environment. We have learned to understand and control our surroundings. Yet, there are still many unsolved problems and unanswered questions. Perhaps what you learn in physical science will help you find answers to some of these questions.

By studying physical science, you will learn new and interesting facts. You will also learn how to use these facts to help you understand your environment. The more facts you know, the more questions about your environment you can answer. You can ask questions and find answers most effectively if you ask the questions and search for the answers in an organized way. This is the purpose of physical science.

Figure 1-1. Stonehenge, a group of huge, rough-cut stones in Wiltshire, England, is estimated to be over 3,500 years old. Scientists believe the monument may have served as an ancient calendar.

Aerofilms and Aero Pictorial Limited

Figure 1-2. Alchemists tried to transform lead and other metals into silver and gold. Their work eventually lead to the branch of physical science called chemistry.

Margin questions are a reading aid as well as study guide. Students might use margin questions as a basis for self evaluation of learned concepts.

1:1 Product of Science

Emphasized words and phrases appear in bold type. Suggest to the students that they pay particular attention to these terms. Guide students to the pronunciations and definitions which are also included in the Glossary (pp. 473-498).

Science has two parts—*process* and *product*. The **process of science** is the use of scientific methods. It is a special way of exploring our world. The **product of science** is information—the facts discovered and ideas developed by people using the process of science.

What is the difference between product and process of science?

The product of science exists in science books, journals, tapes, films, and other records. Information in the science books in your library is part of the product of science.

Figure 1-3. The camera has wide impact in all areas of life, from sports to education to space technology.

1:2 Technology

The product of science often leads to new inventions. Antismog devices, photography, and plastics are applications of science. The application of science for practical benefits is called **technology.**

Photography is one example of technology. The design of a camera begins with knowledge of light and materials. Before a photographic film is designed, the way certain chemicals change when exposed to light must be known.

Science and technology are interrelated. Scientific knowledge is used to develop new inventions such as the electron microscope or space rockets. In turn, such inventions further scientific discovery. For example, many facts about living cells have been discovered through use of electron microscopes. Rockets make it possible to send scientific instruments into space.

Richard M. Fetters

5

Vincent McGuire

How does technology relate to science?

Technology is based on scientific knowledge.

Problems are placed within the chapter to stimulate student involvement with concepts.

PROBLEM

1. Here are some problems of modern technology. Name some of the products of science which could help to solve these problems.   *Answers will vary. Examples are:*
   (a) Heating and cooking with heat from the sun.   *solar cells*
   (b) Recycling of wastes.   *chemical precipitation*
   (c) Producing fresh water from seawater.   *nuclear reactor*
   (d) Finding replacements for fossil fuels.   *seismograph*

1:3   Process of Science

Scientists use special methods to develop and test scientific knowledge. These methods include making observations, proposing and testing hypotheses, and stating theories.

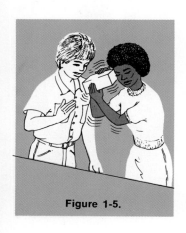

Figure 1-5.

ACTIVITY. Your teacher has placed an object in a box and sealed it. Without opening the box, try to find out what is inside. Use your powers of observation. Write down what you know is true about the object in the box. For example, could the object be larger than the box? Is there only one object in the box? From what you know, make a "best guess" about what the object is. This is your hypothesis. Test your hypothesis. Does your "guess" fit all the facts you know about the object? The interaction of the object and box gives clues. If the object were taped inside the box, it would be a difficult problem indeed.

The above activity is sometimes called a "black box" experiment. This is because the box contains an unknown object which you cannot observe directly.

6

American Society of Agricultural Engineers

Figure 1-6. Scientific investigations can yield many practical benefits, in this case better apples.

Observation is basic to the process of science. For example, you look at the thermometer. It reads 75°F. This is an observation. Scientists often use tools to make their observations. Some tools like the metric ruler, mercury thermometer, and graduated cylinder are simple. Other tools are complex. The microscope, sextant, and telescope are examples of complex tools.

Scientific observations are usually made under carefully controlled conditions. When several scientists make the same observation time and time again, the observation is considered to be a **fact**. For example, air is about 21% oxygen. This is a fact because it fits all known observations of air. Water contains hydrogen and oxygen. This is also a fact. No one has discovered any water that does not contain these two elements.

A **hypothesis** is a scientific "guess." It is a proposed answer to a question or solution to a problem. Based on observations and facts, a scientist can propose a hypothesis. Then he must test his hypothesis. In the "black box" activity, you could have tested your hypothesis by opening the box and finding out what really was inside. It is not so simple in most scientific investigations. For example, a scientist makes this hypothesis: A homing pigeon uses its ears to find its way to its home loft. Now he must test his hypothesis. He takes 25 pigeons and masks their ears. Then he releases them at various points far away from their loft. He then waits to see how many pigeons return to the loft.

Scientists form *conclusions* based on observations. A **conclusion** is a judgment or decision based on observation. For

Figure 1-7. To test his hypothesis, a scientist releases pigeons with masked ears from various points away from the loft.

General Electric Research and Development Center

example, you read a room thermometer. The temperature reads 90°F. You may conclude that the room is too warm. You see the sun shining when you wake up in the morning. You might conclude that it is going to be a nice day. In either case, you might be right or wrong. You have made a judgment based on what you observed. In the pigeon experiment, none of the 25 pigeons with masked ears returned to their loft. The scientist concluded that pigeons use their ears in finding their way home. However, his conclusion need not be correct. Perhaps a storm prevented the flock from returning. Can you think of other possibilities? *Answers will vary.*

How does a conclusion relate to a hypothesis?

Conclusion should support or deny hypothesis.

1:4 *Experiments*

In your study of science you will conduct experiments and other activities. **Experiments** are designed to yield observations under carefully controlled conditions. Keep a record of your work in a notebook. Organize your experimental work as follows:

In what steps are experiments organized?

(1) Problem or purpose. Why is this experiment done? What question do you hope to answer?

(2) Procedure. List the steps in the experiment or activity. What things are you doing?

(3) Observations. What happens? What do you see, hear, or smell? What changes have occurred? How do you know?

(4) Conclusion. Based on your observations, what is your explanation or answer to the question?

PROBLEMS

2. What is the problem, procedure, observations, and conclusion for the pigeon experiment?

3. Write down the problem, procedure, observations, and conclusion for the following experiment.

Problem: Does a pigeon use its ears to find its way home?
Procedure: Take pigeons from home, mask ears, let them go.
Observation: No pigeons returned.
Conclusion: Pigeons use ears.

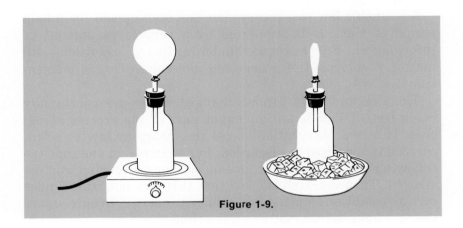

Figure 1-9.

EXPERIMENT.   Does air expand when it is heated? A balloon is attached to a glass tube. The tube and balloon are attached to a flask with a rubber stopper. The flask is heated on a hot plate. The balloon expands. The flask is set on a pan of ice. The balloon contracts.   Conclusions will vary. Discuss all possibilities.

Problem: Does air expand when heated?
Observations: Balloon expands when flask heated; contracts when flask cooled.
Conclusion: Air in balloon expands when flask heated.

In the above experiment could you be sure that only heat is affecting the balloon? Perhaps, any balloon in a flask will expand. One way to be sure is to use a *control*. A **control** is a standard for comparison. It is an important feature of many experiments. The control can be part of the procedure. In the heated air experiment, you could assemble two balloons and flasks. You could then treat both exactly the same except that one you would heat and one you would not. The heated balloon would be your control.

PROBLEMS

4. A medical scientist tests a new drug. Two groups of people who have the disease the drug is intended to cure are selected. One group is given the drug. The other is not. What is the control?   group not given drug

5. How would a control improve the pigeon experiment? Describe such a control.   Answers will vary. Example: have half of birds with ear masks, half without, test several times from different directions.

1:5   *Theories and Laws*

A scientific **theory** is an explanation based on current facts. For example, there are several theories to explain how birds navigate when they migrate. One theory is that they use the earth's magnetic field. Another is that they are guided by the sun. Both theories fit current facts.

How does a scientific law differ from a theory?

Law has stood the test of time.

A scientific **law** is a theory that has been upheld for a long period of time. It is supported by a very large amount of information. For example, under ordinary conditions, all matter is composed of atoms and molecules. This is a scientific law.

Laws of nature merely summarize the effects of certain conditions. Laws do not change; our understanding of them does. Experiments are investigations of the various conditions that produce given results.

Theories and laws can be changed. They are continually being tested. This is an important part of the process of science. If a new observation shows the theory or law to be incorrect, it is revised or discarded. For example, at one time the following was a law: Matter can neither be created nor destroyed. Then research showed that this was not true. Under certain conditions matter does change to energy. In outer space energy changes into matter all the time.

In actual practice the methods of science are not cut and dried. The work of successful scientists shows that problem solving is not always a step-by-step process. Skill, luck, trial and error, and intelligent guessing all play their part.

1:6   *Physical Science*

Physical science is a branch of science. Physical science has two main categories—*chemistry* and *physics*. **Chemistry** is mainly concerned with what matter is made of and changes in matter. It includes such topics as solutions, acids, and bases. **Physics** is mainly concerned with how matter and energy are related. It includes such topics as motion, electricity, magnetism, gravity, sound, heat, and light. Simply stated, it includes the study of matter and energy.

Figure 1-10. To build a birdhouse, you must measure and cut each part carefully.

1:7   *Measurements*

How much material do you need to make a shirt? How much flour, milk, and eggs do you need to make a cake? Without numbers and units you could not answer these questions. Numbers and units are used to express measurements. Measurements are necessary for keeping records, solving problems, and doing jobs.

Suppose you wanted to build a birdhouse. First you need a plan. You need materials: wood and nails. You also need tools: hammer, saw, and ruler. You begin by measuring and cutting the birdhouse parts. Then you nail the parts together. If you do not measure correctly, your birdhouse will not be tight and trim. It may not even fit together.

The following scientific questions can only be answered with numbers and units.

(1) How far is the sun?

(2) How long would it take to go to Jupiter?

(3) How far can you see?

(4) How large is the earth?

You are already familiar with English units of measure. For example, the wheelbase of a car is measured in inches. Cloth is measured in yards. Baking powder can be weighed in ounces or measured in teaspoons. Milk is measured in quarts and gallons. Appendix A lists English units for length, weight, and volume.

Figure 1-11.

ACTIVITY. Obtain a meter stick and yardstick or a metric ruler and English ruler. Compare their lengths and the units into which they are divided. How are they different? How are units on the meter stick similar to units in United States money?   *divided into tenths*

How is the metric system like the U. S. money system?

both are decimal systems
Figure 1-12. Some new road signs give distances in both miles and kilometers.

Ohio Dept. of Transportation, Div. of Highways

Most people in the world do not use English units to express measurements. They use another system of units called the **metric system.** Scientists in all countries know and use metric units in their work. This makes it easier for scientists to understand each other's measurements. There is another advantage to the metric system. It is a decimal system just like the United States money system. Metric units are based on 10 and multiples of 10. This makes changing from one unit to another very easy.

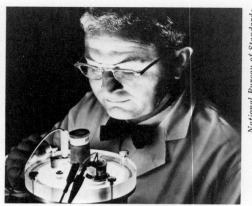

Figure 1-13. In 1960, the wavelength of the orange-red light emitted by a krypton-86 lamp was adopted as the international standard of length. Here a scientist adjusts such a lamp to make sure it remains accurate.

National Bureau of Standards

1:8 Measuring Length

The **meter (m)** is the unit of length in the metric system. One meter is the same length as 39.37 inches (1 m = 39.37 in.). A meter stick is a little more than 3 inches longer than a yardstick.

The meter is divided into 100 units called centimeters (cm). Note the prefix *centi-* is similar to cent in the United States coin. There are 100 cents in a dollar. There are 100 centimeters in a meter (100 cm = 1 m). One centimeter (1 cm) is 1/100 of a meter.

One millimeter (1 mm) is 1/1000 of a meter. The prefix *milli-* means 1/1000. There are 10 millimeters in a centimeter (10 mm = 1 cm) and 1000 millimeters in a meter (1000 mm = 1 m). Thus, 945 mm equals 94.5 cm or 0.945 m.

ACTIVITY. Use a meter stick and a metric ruler to measure the following: (a) length and width of this book in centimeters; (b) length and width of a room in meters, (c) your height in metric units. Results will vary.

Figure   1-14.

You usually think of distance in miles. For example, it is about 3000 miles from the east coast to the west coast of the United States. In most other countries, however, distance is measured in a metric unit called the kilometer (km). The prefix *kilo-* means 1000. So a kilometer is 1000 meters (1 km = 1000 m). One mile is the same distance as 1.61 kilometers (1 mile = 1.61 km).

PROBLEM   For complete numerical solution, see Teacher's Guide at the front of this book.

6. The speed limit on some highways is 65 mi/hr. Is a driver speeding if he goes 65 km/hr? Explain. *No. 65 km/hr ≈ 40 mi/hr*

12

National Bureau of Standards

Figure 1-15. The covered containers in the upper part of this photograph are used as standards for measuring volume. Standards of mass are shown in the lower part of the photograph.

1:9   *Measuring Volume*

The **liter (1)** is the unit of volume in the metric system. One liter is equal to about 1 quart. One liter contains 1000 milliliters (ml). One milliliter is 1/1000 of a liter.

Graduated cylinders are used for measuring volumes of liquid. They are made in many sizes (Figure 1-16). The level of a liquid in a graduated cylinder shows the volume of the liquid.

A milliliter is about the same volume as 1 cubic centimeter. One milliliter of water has a mass of about 1 gram. Therefore, a liter of water is 1000 grams.

> *EXPERIMENT.   Obtain three test tubes of different size. Fill the smallest test tube with water. Pour the water into an empty graduated cylinder. How much water does the test tube hold? Repeat with the other two test tubes.*
> *Results will vary.*

PROBLEM

7. How much water will fill a dish 10 cm × 10 cm × 5 cm? How many grams of water will fill this dish?
   Volume = 500 cm³ mass = 500 g

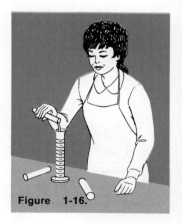

Figure   1-16.

1:10   *Measuring Mass and Weight*

Pounds and ounces are English units used to measure weight. Weight is a measure of the force or pull of gravity on a body. Your own weight is the *force* of gravity that pulls you down to earth. Weight may be measured with a spring balance The unit of force in the metric system is the **newton (nt)** (Section 11:1).

Mass is the amount of material in a body. Mass does not depend on gravity. The more you weigh, however, the more

How are weight and force related?

Weight is force due to gravity.

Figure 1-17. The international standard of mass is a platinum-iridium cylinder. The cylinder is assigned a mass of exactly 1 kilogram.

mass you have. Mass may be measured with a pan balance (Figure 1-18). A body of unknown mass is placed on the left pan of the balance. Metal pieces of known mass are placed on the right pan. When the unknown and known bodies balance, they both have the same mass. The total mass of the pieces on the right pan is the mass of the object on the left pan.

The **gram (g)** is the unit of mass in the metric system. One kilogram is equal to 1000 grams (g). Remember, the prefix *kilo-* means 1000 ×. A mass of one kilogram weighs about 2.2 pounds.

One page of this book has a mass about 3.25 g. A cubic centimeter of water has a mass of 1 g.

Figure 1-18.

EXPERIMENT. Obtain a beam balance and measure the mass of 5 bodies such as a paper clip, pen, notebook, ring, and block of wood. Record your results. How is a beam balance different from a spring balance? When would you use each one?

PROBLEMS   *Answers will vary.*

8. What is the total mass in grams for the three objects in the experiment above? Change this figure into kilograms.
9. What is your weight in pounds? What is your mass in kilograms?

1:11 *Measuring Temperature*

Temperature is a measure of the "hotness" or "coldness" of an object. Temperature does not tell us matter is hot or cold. It merely helps us compare heat energy of one object with heat energy of another object. Temperature indicates the direction in which heat will travel. Heat goes from matter of high temperature to matter of low temperature. Temperature scales

What determines the direction heat moves?

are based on a standard unit called a *degree* (°). The freezing point of pure water is 32° on the *Fahrenheit* (far' en hiet) *scale*. The boiling point of water is 212°. There are 180° (212° − 32°) between the freezing and boiling points of pure water on the Fahrenheit scale. One Fahrenheit degree (1F°) is 1/180 of the difference between the freezing point and boiling point of water.

The *Celsius temperature scale* was devised by Anders Celsius (1701-1744), a Swedish astronomer. It is also known as the *Centigrade* (sent' i graed) *temperature scale*. Celsius temperature has international use in science and everyday use in many countries. The freezing point of pure water is 0° on the Celsius scale. The boiling point is 100°C. There are 100° (100° − 0°) between the freezing and boiling points on the Celsius scale. One Celsius degree is 1/100 of the difference between the freezing and boiling points of water.

Compare the Fahrenheit scale with the Celsius scale (Figure 1-19). The amount of heat needed on each scale to make pure water boil or freeze is the same. Therefore, 180 Fahrenheit degrees are equivalent to 100 Celsius degrees.

The difference between Fahrenheit and Celsius degrees can be shown as follows:

$$\frac{\text{Fahrenheit (freezing to boiling)}}{\text{Celsius (freezing to boiling)}} = \frac{180°}{100°} = \frac{9}{5}$$

One Celsius degree is 9/5 of one Fahrenheit degree.

$$\frac{\text{Celsius (freezing to boiling)}}{\text{Fahrenheit (freezing to boiling)}} = \frac{100°}{180°} = \frac{5}{9}$$

One Fahrenheit degree is 5/9 of one Celsius degree.

To convert one temperature scale to another, you use either 9/5 or 5/9. The 32° difference in freezing points between the two scales is used also.

To change a Fahrenheit read-temperature to Celsius, subtract 32 F° and multiply by 5/9:

$$\frac{(°F - 32°)}{} \bigg| \frac{5}{9} = °C$$

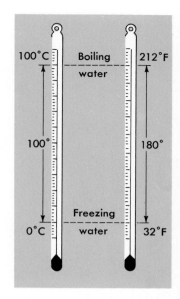

Figure 1-19. Heat added to a thermometer causes the mercury column to expand in length.

Which is larger, a Fahrenheit degree or a Celsius degree?

Celsius degree

EXAMPLE

Change 77°F to °C.

Solution: (a) Write the equation: $\dfrac{(°F - 32°)}{} \bigg| \dfrac{5}{9} = °C$

(b) Substitute 77° for °F: $\dfrac{(77° - 32°)}{} \bigg| \dfrac{5}{9} = °C$

(c) Subtract and then multiply to find the answer:
$$\frac{45° \quad | \quad 5}{\quad | \quad 9} = °C$$

(d) Answer: $77°F = 25°C$

To change a Celsius temperature to Fahrenheit, multiply the Celsius temperature by 9/5. Then add 32°:

$$\left(\frac{9 \quad | \quad °C}{5 \quad |}\right) + 32° = °F$$

EXAMPLE

Change 90°C to °F.

Solution: (a) Write the equation:
$$\left(\frac{9 \quad | \quad °C}{5 \quad |}\right) + 32° = °F$$

(b) Substitute 90° for °C
$$\left(\frac{9 \quad | \quad 90°}{5 \quad |}\right) + 32° = °F$$

(c) Multiply and then add to find the answer:
$$162° + 32° = °F$$

(d) Answer: $90°C = 194°F$

PROBLEMS

10. Change the following temperatures to °C: 32°F, 100°F, 40°F, 10°F, 25°F. *0°C, 37.8°C, 4.4°C, -12.2°C, -3.9°C*

11. Change the following temperatures to °F: 0°C, 100°C, 25°C, 50°C, 37°C. *32°F, 212°F, 77°F, 122°F, 98.6°F*

1:12 *Indirect Measurement*

When you measure your height, you are making a direct measurement. You can mark your height on a wall and measure the distance to the floor with a meter stick. Finding your weight is another example of a direct measurement. You step on a scale and read your weight in pounds. Many measurements, however, are made by indirect methods.

Indirect measurement is a way of measuring something you cannot measure directly. For example, how high is the flagpole at your school? You could directly measure the flagpole with a tape measure. You would need a very long tape measure. How would you get the tape measure to the top of the pole?

You can indirectly measure the height of your school's flagpole by triangulation. In this method you measure the distance

Figure 1-20. Why is measuring this flagpole called indirect measurement?

from the base of the flagpole to a certain point on the ground. Then measure the angle from this point to the top of the flagpole with a sextant. A sextant is an instrument used to measure angles (Figure 1-21).

The angle and distance of the flagpole are used to draw a triangle. The flagpole is one of the three sides of the triangle. The diagram is drawn to scale. For example, 1 centimeter in the diagram might equal 1 meter on the flagpole. By measuring the length of the flagpole in centimeters on the diagram, you can find the actual height of the flagpole in meters.

See Teacher's Guide at the front of this book for suggestions.

ACTIVITY. Make a simple sextant with a soda straw, protractor, masking tape, string, and metal washer. Tie one end of a 10-cm string to the center of the protractor's straight edge. Tie the other end to the metal washer. Tape the straw lengthwise to the straight edge of the protractor. Objects are sighted by looking through the straw with one eye closed. The string on the curved scale indicates the angle of the object. Students will need help reading the angle.

Measure the distance from a point on the ground to the base of a flagpole. Then use the sextant to sight the angle of the top of the flagpole from this point. Using a scale of 1 cm = 1 m, draw a triangle. First draw a horizontal line to scale, representing the ground. Draw a perpendicular line (90°) to represent the flagpole. Draw a third line at the angle you measured to complete the three sides of the triangle. Measure the perpendicular line to find the flagpole's height. Each centimeter of line equals 1 meter of pole. Students will need help making the diagrams.

When is indirect measurement used?

When measurement to be taken is outside range of common measuring device.

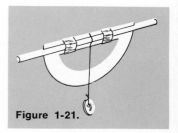
Figure 1-21.

1:13   *Density*

Density is the mass of a substance per unit volume. Density can be expressed in both English and metric units. For example, the density of lead is 11 g/cm³. The density of mercury is 13.5 g/cm³, and the density of liquid oxygen is 1.14 g/cm³.

You have probably heard the old riddle: Which weighs more, a pound of lead or a pound of feathers? Both have the same weight, one pound. However, lead has a greater density. Density is a basic property of a substance. Often a substance can be identified by its density. Steel and polished aluminum may look alike but they have different densities. You would easily know the difference between a sack of lead and a sack of feathers because of their difference in density. Minerals also have characteristic densities and are often identified by this trait.

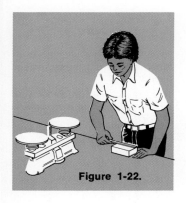

Figure 1-22.

ACTIVITY. Find the density of a rectangular wooden block. Measure the length, width, and height of the block in centimeters. Calculate the volume of the block by the formula: volume = length × width × height (v = lwh). Use a balance to find the mass of the block in grams. Calculate the density of the block by the method given below. Results will vary.

To calculate the density of a substance, you must know its mass and volume. For example, a block with a volume of 5 cm³ has a mass of 4 grams. Its density is:

$$\text{Density} = \frac{\text{mass}}{\text{volume}}$$

$$\text{Density} = \frac{4 \text{ g}}{5 \text{ cm}^3} = 0.8 \text{ g/cm}^3$$

How can you find the density of a stone? It has uneven surfaces so you cannot find its volume by measuring with a ruler. You can find the volume of the stone through an indirect measurement. Tie a string around the stone and lower it into a graduated cylinder containing water (Figure 1–23). Water rises in the graduate as it is displaced by the stone. The amount the water rises is the volume of the stone.

Figure 1-23.

EXPERIMENT.   Find the density of a small stone. First use a balance to find the mass of the stone. Then fill a 25-ml graduate to the 15-ml mark. Tie a string around the stone and lower it into the water until it is completely submerged. Record the increase in water level. This is the volume of the stone. Use the formula to find the density of the stone.

PROBLEMS   *See Teacher's Guide at the front of this book.*

12. Density determines the use of many materials. Explain how the density of each substance listed affects its uses: aluminum, balsam wood, lead, cast iron, styrofoam.

13. What is the density of water?   *1 g/cm³*

MAIN IDEAS

p. 5   1. Science may be thought of as having two parts—product and process.

pp. 5,6   2. Scientific knowledge is the product of science.

pp. 5,6   3. The process of science includes methods used to solve scientific problems.

p. 9   4. A control is an important part of most experiments.

p. 8 **5.** An experiment may be recorded in four parts: problem or purpose, procedure, observations, and conclusion.

p. 10 **6.** Hypotheses, theories, and scientific laws are tested by experiments and observations.

p. 5 **7.** Technology is the practical use of scientific knowledge.

p. 12 **8.** The meter (m), centimeter (cm), and millimeter (mm) are metric units of length.

p. 14 **9.** The kilogram (kg) and gram (g) are metric units of mass.

p. 13 **10.** The liter (l) and milliliter (ml) are metric units of volume.

p. 17 **11.** Density is mass per unit volume.

For a discussion of the suggested methods of using the materials at the end of the chapter, see the introduction to Teacher's Guide at the front of this book.

VOCABULARY

Write a sentence in which you correctly use each of the following words or terms.

chemistry	gram	observation
conclusion	hypothesis	physics
control	law	scientist
density	liter	technology
experiment	mass	temperature
force	meter	theory

STUDY QUESTIONS

A. True or False   *Have students rewrite false statements to make the statements correct.*

Determine whether each of the following sentences is true or false. (Do not write in this book.)

T **1.** A metric ruler, graduated cylinder, and microscope are tools used in science.

F **2.** Product and process of science are ~~both~~ the same.   *not*

F **3.** A hypothesis ~~is always~~ true.   *may be*

T **4.** Every experiment has a procedure.

F **5.** The control in an experiment is the same as a conclusion.   *not*

F **6.** A scientific law can ~~never~~ be disproved.

T **7.** Metric units have international use in science.

F **8.** The English system of measurement is a decimal system.   *metric*

F **9.** A meter stick and a yardstick ~~both~~ have the same length.   *do not*

T **10.** A Celsius degree is smaller than a Fahrenheit degree.

Some questions in Part B may have more than one correct answer. Only one answer is required.

B. Multiple Choice

Choose one word or phrase that correctly completes each of the following sentences. (Do not write in this book.)

1. A meter equals (10, 100, 1000, 10,000) centimeters.
2. The prefix centi- means (10, 100, 1/100, 1/1000).
3. There are (1, 10, 100, 1000) millimeters in a centimeter.
4. The prefix milli- means (10, 100, 1000, 1/1000).
5. The prefix kilo- means (10, 100, 1000, 1/1000).
6. There are (10, 100, 1000, 10,000) grams in a kilogram.
7. A kilogram is the mass of about (1.5, 2, 2.2, 10) pounds.
8. A milliliter of water has a mass of about (0.1, 1, 10, 100) grams.
9. 1 cm³ equals (1 ml, 1 l, 1 kg, 1 km).
10. 25°C equals (102°F, 77°F, 45°F).

C. Completion

Complete each of the following sentences with a word or phrase that will make the sentence correct. (Do not write in this book.)

1. length
2. 10
3. Density
4. cm³
5. 0.5 g/cm³
6. 15
7. 4
8. 2.5 g/cm³
9. volume
10. Lead

1. A meter stick is used to measure __?__.
2. On a scale of 1 mm = 1 m, a centimeter equals __?__ meters.
3. __?__ is an example of indirect measurement.
4. Density is expressed as grams per __?__.
5. A block has a volume of 1 liter and a mass of 500 grams. Its density is __?__.
6. A graduated cylinder contains 15 ml of water. The mass of this water is __?__ g.
7. A stone is dropped into a graduated cylinder. The volume of water rises from 18 ml to 22 ml. The volume of the stone is __?__ ml.
8. A stone has a mass of 10 g and a volume of 4 ml. Its density is __?__.
9. The volume of a pound of feathers is greater than the __?__ of a pound of lead.
10. __?__ is the mineral with a density of 11 g/cm³.

D. How and Why

Answers to this section are given in the Teacher's Guide at the front of this book.

1. Name five instruments used to make measurements. What units are used with each instrument?

2. Name five branches of science. Define each.

3. Describe three methods used by scientists.

4. How is science different from technology?

5. What are the advantages of the use of metric units?

6. You are riding in an American-made car in a foreign country. A sign you pass shows a maximum speed of 50 km/hr. What reading on the car's speedometer is equal to the posted speed limit?

7. Change the following to liters: 250 ml, 1000 ml, 5000 ml.

8. How do you measure mass and volume in a laboratory?

9. How is triangulation used to find height?

10. Design an experiment to determine the density of vegetable oil.

Answers to this section are given in the Teacher's Guide at the front of this book.

INVESTIGATIONS

1. Obtain a few mineral samples and measure their densities. Use the densities to identify the samples from tables in a rocks and minerals handbook.

2. Use a 10-ml graduate to measure the volume of a thimble, water glass, teacup, medicine dropper, and soda straw.

3. Use a sextant and triangulation to measure some tall buildings, towers, or other tall structures. Report your results to your class.

INTERESTING READING

Bendick, Jeanne, *How Much and How Many: The Story of Weights and Measures.* New York, McGraw-Hill Book Co., 1961.

Bendick, Jeanne, *Measuring.* New York, Franklin Watts, 1971.

Breeden, Richard, *Those Inventive Americans.* Washington, D.C., National Geographic Society, 1971.

Chandler, M. H., *Science and the World Around Us.* Chicago, Rand McNally, 1968.

Hayden, Robert C., *Seven Black American Scientists.* Reading, Mass., Addison-Wesley, 1970.

Siedel, Frank, and James Siedel, *Pioneers in Science.* Boston, Houghton Mifflin Company, 1968.

Matter

Albert Einstein was a great American physicist and Nobel prize winner whose creative work led to the special and general theories of relativity and the photon theory of light.

The most incomprehensible thing about the world is that it is comprehensible.

Albert Einstein (1879-1955)

Robert Boyle in the seventeenth century revived the atomic theory of Democritus and formulated the first working definition of an element. His experiments on the compressibility of gases (the gas law expressing the relationship between pressure and volume later bore his name) provided proof for the discontinuous nature of matter.

Jacques Charles, a French mathematician and physicist, was the first to use hydrogen gas to inflate balloons. The gas law stating the relationship between volume and temperature carries his name.

All properties of matter are believed to depend upon the kinds of atoms it contains. The order and arrangement of these atoms in elements and compounds also determines how they react. The ancient Greeks developed the idea of a basic element from which all other substances could be produced. Long years of research since have shown that there are not one, two, or three basic elements but at least 104. Each element has its own particular physical and chemical properties. Robert Boyle and Jacques Charles experimented with the properties of gases. Other scientists like Thomas Edison and Albert Einstein investigated the physical properties of elements.

Physical and chemical properties determine the way matter may be used. Dry ice is used as a refrigerant because it is a solid at low temperatures and changes to a gas when its temperature is raised. Transistors were made possible by defects in the structure of crystals. The bonding of atoms in metals provides free electrons for conducting electricity. In engineering and technology, the practical use of materials rests on a scientific understanding of their composition and structure. Many future uses of matter are limited only by the imagination and skill of scientists, engineers, and technicians . . . perhaps expanded by you and your classmates in your own careers.

unit
two

GOAL: You will gain an understanding of the ways in which matter is classified and the differences between physical and chemical changes.

Metal and wood have great strength compared to air, water, and paper.

Because of this strength, metal and wood can be used for structures, equipment, or any other man-made items meant to last indefinitely.

The objectives of this chapter are: to learn some ways in which matter is classified, to study some differences between chemical and physical changes, and to perform some activities to observe chemical and physical changes in matter.

Classification of Matter

One reason a scientist studies the world around him is to learn how materials are alike and different. By applying this knowledge, man improves the products he uses. For example, aluminum is lighter than steel, so it is used in making airplanes and boats. Metal filing cabinets are often used in place of wooden filing cabinets. Metal is more fire resistant than wood. Each material has at least one property that makes it different from any other material. How are water, air, and paper different from metal and wood? How are these differences related to the uses of these materials?

2:1 Matter

Matter is anything that has mass and takes up space. Can you think of anything that is not matter? Are thoughts and ideas matter? Is heat matter? Is air matter?

No   *No*   *Yes*

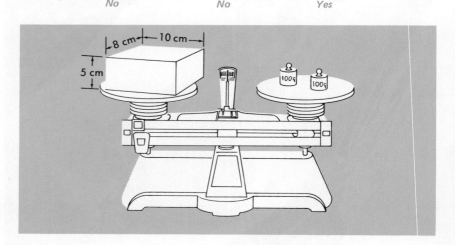

Figure 2-1. A pan balance is used to measure the mass of matter.

EXPERIMENT. Obtain a glass milk bottle and a two-hole rubber stopper to fit the neck of the bottle. Insert a funnel into one hole of the stopper. CAUTION: Moisten the stem of the funnel tube with water or mineral oil. Hold it with a rag or towel as you slide it into the stopper. In the same way, insert a 10-cm piece of glass tubing into the other stopper hole. Now fit a 15-cm piece of rubber tubing over the top end of the glass tube. Insert the stopper firmly in the bottle neck. Clamp the rubber tube so no air can escape through it. Pour 10 ml of water into the funnel. What do you observe? Next, unclamp the rubber tube. What happens to the water? Explain what you observe.   Some water will run into the bottle as the air compresses. As the tube is unclamped, the water will displace air in the bottle. Since air occupies space, it is matter.

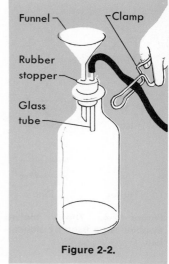

Figure 2-2.

The experiment above illustrates that no two pieces of matter can occupy the same place at the same time. This is one property of matter. When a ship sinks, it displaces enough water to make room for the ship. When a nail is pounded into a board, the nail displaces some of the wood.

Inertia (in er′ shuh) is a second general property of all matter. Because of inertia, a body at rest tends to remain at rest, and a body in motion tends to remain in motion. Inertia is used to explain why a shovelful of dirt continues moving in the air after the shovel is stopped. Inertia causes passengers in a bus to sway forward when the bus makes a quick stop.

Would melting ice in an iced drink make it overflow?

Melting ice in a glassful of liquid does not cause an overflow. Ice displaces the same volume of water that it will create when melted.

How can a magician pull a tablecloth from under dishes?

The inertia of the dishes causes them to stay if the cloth is jerked quickly.

2:2   Elements

Matter is made up of certain basic substances called *elements*. An **element** cannot be broken down into simpler sub-

Carl England

Figure 2-3. What makes the shovelful of dirt continue to move after the shovel stops?

inertia

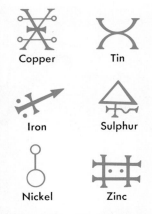

Copper | Tin

Iron | Sulphur

Nickel | Zinc

Figure 2-4. These ancient symbols were used by alchemists.

Element 104 has been produced but has not yet been officially accepted by IUPAC.

What other elements can you name?

Many elements could be named; steel is not an element, nor is brass or bronze.

stances by ordinary means. At present, 88 elements have been found naturally on the earth. Fifteen have been produced in the laboratory. Two elements found in air are oxygen and nitrogen. Carbon, iron, and aluminum are other common elements.

There is a shorthand way to write the names of elements. Circles, dots, and lines were once used as symbols for elements. Today scientists use letters of the alphabet. Table 2–1 gives the names of some of the common elements and the symbols used to represent them.

Table 2–1. Some Common Elements

Element	Symbol
Aluminum	Al
Carbon	C
Chlorine	Cl
Copper	Cu
Hydrogen	H
Iron	Fe
Magnesium	Mg
Mercury	Hg
Nitrogen	N
Oxygen	O
Silver	Ag
Sodium	Na
Sulfur	S

PROBLEMS

1. Use Table 2–1 to find the name of each of the following elements: O, C, Mg, Hg, Ag, Na, Cl, Fe.
2. Name the element in Table 2–1 that:
    (a) rusts   *iron*
    (b) is black   *carbon*
    (c) is used in thermometers   *mercury*
    (d) you need to breathe   *oxygen*
    (e) is added to water in swimming pools   *chlorine*

2:3 Compounds

Two or more elements can be combined chemically to make a **compound.** "Combined chemically" means the elements are joined together in a way that makes them very difficult to separate. All samples of a given compound are made of the same elements. For example, sodium chloride (table salt) is a compound. It is always composed of sodium and chlorine. No other elements are included. Carbon dioxide is also a compound. It is always composed of carbon and oxygen.

Elements in a given compound are always combined in the same ratio. The ratio between sodium and chlorine in sodium chloride is always one part sodium to one part chlorine (1:1). The ratio between carbon and oxygen in carbon dioxide is always one part carbon to two parts oxygen (1:2). Water is another example of a compound. Every sample of water contains two parts hydrogen to one part oxygen (2:1).

Formulas are often used to represent compounds. In chemical formulas, symbols show which elements are present. The formula for sodium chloride is NaCl. The formula for carbon dioxide is CO_2. A small number to the right and slightly lower than the symbol is called a *subscript*. **Subscripts** give the ratio in which the elements are combined in the compound. The subscript 2 in CO_2 means two parts oxygen to one part carbon. Absence of a subscript next to C means one part carbon. A subscript 1 is never used in a chemical formula. The symbol for the element stands for one part. For example, NaCl means a ratio of one part sodium to one part chlorine.

Water has the formula H_2O. The subscript 2 means two parts hydrogen. What does the symbol O show? *one part oxygen*

Figure 2-5. A chemical formula indicates the kind of atoms in a compound. Name the elements in each of these compounds.

HCl (hydrochloric acid) - hydrogen, chlorine; H_2SO_4 (sulfuric acid) - hydrogen, sulfur, oxygen; HNO_3 (nitric acid) - hydrogen, oxygen, nitrogen.

What are the subscripts in H_2CO_3?

2H, 1C, 3O

PROBLEMS

nitrogen, hydrogen

3. NH_3 is the formula for ammonia. What elements does it contain? What is the ratio between these elements? *1:3*

4. Laughing gas is a compound containing a ratio of two parts nitrogen to one part oxygen. What is its formula? *N_2O*

5. Name the elements in each of the compounds in Table 2–2.

Table 2–2. Some Common Compounds and Their Formulas

Compound	Formula	
Ammonia	NH_3	*nitrogen, hydrogen*
Cane sugar	$C_{12}H_{22}O_{11}$	*carbon, hydrogen, oxygen*
Rust	Fe_2O_3	*iron, oxygen*
Table salt	NaCl	*sodium, chlorine*
Water	H_2O	*hydrogen, oxygen*

What are some other compounds?

Other compounds include sand (SiO_2), grain alcohol (ethyl) C_2H_5OH; rubbing alcohol (isopropyl) C_3H_7OH, and chalk ($CaCO_3$).

Richard M. Fetters

Figure 2-6. Is ice cream a mixture or a compound?

Other mixtures: ice cream, pond water, chocolate nut fudge.

2:4 Mixtures

Two or more elements or compounds can be mixed together yet not combined chemically. This is called a **mixture.** Each element or compound in a mixture keeps its identity. Mixtures can be separated by physical or mechanical means. Sifting or pouring are examples. A mixture may or may not have the same composition throughout. Air is a mixture. Air contains nitrogen, oxygen, and several other gases. However, the composition of air varies from place to place. Air in a large industrial city may contain smoke and dust particles that would not be found in the air over a mountain lake. Other examples of mixtures are a cement sidewalk, a glass of iced tea, and a handful of soil. Can you name the parts which make up these mixtures? What other mixtures can you name?

PROBLEM   *Cement sidewalk: Calcium sulfate ($CaSO_4$), sand (SiO_2), water*   *(H_2O); iced tea: tea, water, ice; soil: sand, clay, rocks, etc.*

6. How could you separate a mixture of iron filings and salt?   *iron filings attracted by magnet*

Sand-salt mixture

250 ml of water

EXPERIMENT. CAUTION: All experiments using chemicals should be performed only under the direct supervision of a teacher. Mix 25 g of sand and 25 g of table salt together on a piece of paper. Examine the mixture. How can you separate the two substances? First, add the mixture to 250 ml of hot water. Stir. Pour off the water into a glass funnel fitted with a paper filter. Catch the filtrate in a clean 400-ml beaker. Allow the filtrate to evaporate over a warm hot plate.

Sulfur is insoluble in water. How would you separate a mixture of sulfur and sand?   *Sulfur and sand can be separated by the use of carbon disulfide*

How does a scientist determine which substances make up air or soil? Each of these decisions is made on the basis of certain characteristics, or properties, of matter. There are two types of properties: physical properties and chemical properties.   *(CS_2) or carbon tetrachloride (CCl_4) which dissolve sulfur. Neither experiment should be carried out by the students.*

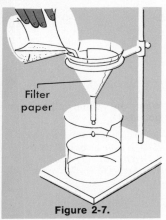

Filter paper

Figure 2-7.

2:5 Physical Properties

Suppose you have four test tubes in a rack. Each test tube is filled with a liquid. Here is the problem. How can you determine if any of the liquids is water? What properties of water do you know already?

The liquid in the first test tube is blue. In the second test tube, the liquid has a bad odor. A small steel ball floats on the

Observe caution! Make a filter to fit the funnel by folding the filter paper in half and then in quarters. Pull one side out to make the cone. Two substances in   *a mixture can be separated physically if a solvent for only one can be found. If the substance can then be separated from the solvent by evaporation or some*   *similar means, the substances are separated. In this case salt dissolves in water and passes through the filter. If the filtrate is allowed to evaporate, salt crystals appear.*

First has color, second has odor, third is dense, fourth has low boiling point.

liquid in the third test tube. When you hold the fourth test tube in your hands, the liquid evaporates rapidly.

Do you think any of the liquids in the test tubes is water? *no* What properties not typical of water does each liquid have? The properties we have just mentioned are called *physical properties*. A **physical property** depends only upon the substance itself. It may be observed without changing the chemical composition of the substance.

> EXPERIMENT. Mix 5 g of iodine crystals with 5 g of iron filings in a clean, dry 400-ml beaker. Cover with a large watch glass. Place an ice cube in the watch glass. Heat the beaker with a low flame for a few minutes. What do you observe? Describe another way to separate iodine and iron.

Color, odor, density, and boiling point are physical properties. You can observe these from the test tubes. Other physical properties are taste*, freezing point, shape, and hardness. Sometimes odor and taste are also considered to be chemical properties.

> EXPERIMENT. Place 250 ml of a mixture of salt and water in a 400-ml flask. Bend a piece of glass tubing so that one part is 10 cm long and the other part is 30-35 cm long. Moisten the tube with water or mineral oil. Hold it with a rag or towel. Then slide it through the hole in the stopper. Set the stopper tightly in the neck of the flask. Cover the opposite end of the glass tube with a test tube. Heat the mixture with a Bunsen burner flame and allow it to boil gently for 10 min. How is the water in the test tube different from the water in the flask?

The water in the flask is salty; in the test tube, pure.

* Do not test the property of taste in the laboratory.

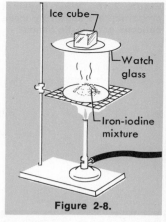

Figure 2-8.

Do not allow I_2 vapor to escape into the room. This may be a class demonstration. Purple fumes (I_2 vapor) rise from the mixture and condense in steel gray crystals on the watch glass. I_2-Fe mixture could also be separated by a magnet or by dissolving iodine in alcohol or carbon tetrachloride.

Some chemists classify odor and taste as chemical properties because it is felt chemical reactions are necessary for taste and odor identification.

Use care in inserting tubing. Glass tubing can be bent using a wing tip covered flame, heating thoroughly, and bending quickly against gravity. This is a simple distilling apparatus.

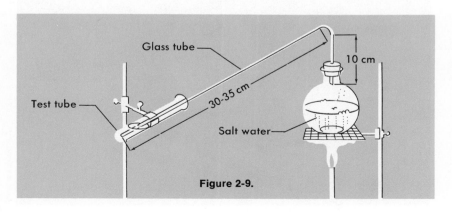

Figure 2-9.

Figure 2-10. What physical properties are shown by these balloons and elastic bands?

Answers will vary. color, elasticity, shape, etc.

Figure 2-11. A football and a baseball have different physical properties.

PROBLEM

7. What physical properties could you use to distinguish between the following pairs of materials?
   (a) Coal and snow *color, melting point, density*
   (b) Strawberry ice cream and vanilla ice cream *color, taste*
   (c) Soda pop and water *density*
   (d) Lead and aluminum *density*
   (e) Salt and sugar *taste*
   (f) A baseball and a football *shape*

2:6 Chemical Properties

Suppose you have four test tubes containing liquids. Some iron filings are sprinkled into the first test tube. The liquid

Figure 2-12. Chemical properties depend upon a substance's reactions with other substances.

bubbles and a gas escapes. The gas burns with a blue flame. Iron filings are sprinkled into the second test tube. Again, a gas is given off. But this time it has an unpleasant odor. Does either of these two test tubes contain only pure water? What does water do when iron filings are added to it? Try it. Observe any change that takes place.

In the meantime, the liquid in the third test tube has turned black. In the fourth test tube, a small metal nail has taken on a coating of some other metal. Is either of these two liquids pure water?   *Neither is water.*

The properties that we have described in these liquids are *chemical properties*. **Chemical properties** are those that depend upon the material's reaction with other materials. For example, some materials combine with oxygen and burn. Some materials react with other materials to produce gases or metals.

Name a chemical property of iron.

It rusts (combines with oxygen).

You might want to carry out this experiment. In the first test tube use dilute HCl; in the second, concentrated H_2SO_4; $AgNO_3$ solution in the third; $CuSO_4$ in the fourth. The first gas is H_2 and the second is H_2S. Neither test tube contains water. Water does not react with iron filings when they are sprinkled into it. Try it as a control to the first two test tubes. When silver nitrate is exposed to light it turns black (silver is formed). The coating on the nail in the fourth test tube is copper.

2:7 Physical Change

A pane of glass breaks. Breaking is a physical change. The size of the glass changes. The pieces, however, still contain the same substances in the same ratios as the original pane of glass. When a piece of wood is shaped into a shelf or a chair, a physical change takes place. When an object changes in size, shape, or form, it undergoes a *physical change*.

In a **physical change,** only physical properties are altered. One of the most common physical changes is a change of state. Matter may be divided into three states or phases: solid, liquid,

What are the three physical forms of water?

ice, liquid water, water vapor

Carl England

Figure 2-13. Physical changes involve changes in size, shape, or form.

and gas. All substances have their own special physical state at room temperature and normal atmospheric conditions. For example, at room temperature and normal pressure, oxygen is a gas. Marble is a solid and mercury is a liquid under the same conditions.

Temperature and pressure can affect the state of a substance. A substance may change its state if the temperature or pressure is changed. Water can be changed to ice by lowering the temperature. Water can be changed to steam by raising the temperature. Have you ever packed a snowball? The pressure of your hands causes the snow to melt. The water then refreezes to ice when you release the pressure. Because the snow changes in form, it has undergone a physical change. Water and ice have the same composition. Ice melting is a physical change because only a physical property has changed.

The pressure of the skates on the ice produces friction. The heat generated by the friction melts the ice. Thus the skater moves along on a film of water.

2:8   Chemical Change

Substances remaining after a chemical change are different from the original substances.

A piece of wood is burned. What happens? Heat, light, and smoke are given off. A small pile of ashes is left. Has the substance been changed? More has occurred than just a change in appearance. The composition of the materials has changed. In *chemical change*, substances disappear. New substances with different properties appear. **Chemical changes** usually involve the release of heat, light, or electricity.

What energy is released in a battery?

electrical energy

Compounds can be broken down, or decomposed, by chemical change. For example, electric current can be passed through water. The water will then decompose into hydrogen and oxygen. The properties of hydrogen and oxygen are different from the properties of water. Pour a few drops of vinegar on some baking soda. Is this a physical change or a chemical change? Why? *If vinegar (acetic acid, CH_3COOH) is poured on baking soda ($NaHCO_3$) a chemical change takes place. CO_2 is released along with heat.*

EXPERIMENT. *Mix equal parts of powdered sulfur and iron filings on a piece of paper. Wrap a magnet in a plastic bag. Pass it through the mixture several times. What do you observe? How can you separate the two elements without a magnet?* *Iron filings attracted by magnet. Dissolve sulfur.*

Mix the sulfur and iron filings again. Fill a Pyrex test tube one-third full of the mixture. Heat with a Bunsen burner until the mixture becomes red hot. Allow the test tube to cool. Wrap it in a towel and break the glass with a hammer. Pass a magnet over the material left in the test tube. Now can you separate the iron from the sulfur? What change took place?

No, a chemical change has taken place. Iron and sulfur have formed a compound (iron sulfide, FeS).

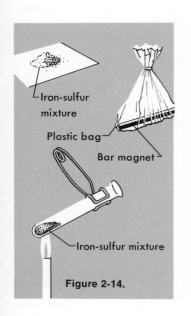

Iron-sulfur mixture

Plastic bag

Bar magnet

Iron-sulfur mixture

Figure 2-14.

EXPERIMENT. CAUTION: Do this experiment under teacher supervision. Wear protective glasses. Place 3 ml of dilute hydrochloric acid in a test tube. Add a tiny piece of mossy zinc to the acid. Loosely cover the end of the test tube for a few seconds. Then cautiously point the test tube toward a Bunsen burner flame. Did a chemical change take place? How do you know? *Bubbles of gas, test tube warms. Hydrogen gas evolves which burns with a "bark."*

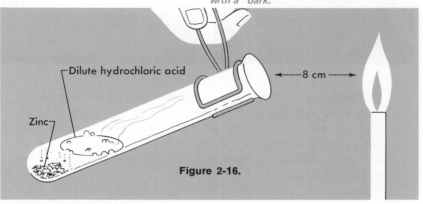

Dilute hydrochloric acid

Zinc

←— 8 cm —→

Figure 2-16.

Use care! Wear safety glasses!

Figure 2-15. Acid should always be handled with care. Remove the stopper with your second and third fingers, palm up. Hold the stopper there while pouring. Then replace the stopper in the bottle.

Table 2–3 compares physical and chemical changes.

Table 2–3. *Physical and Chemical Changes*	
Physical Change	*Chemical Change*
Little or no energy lost or gained	Heat, light, or some other form of energy lost or gained
Original substances remain; however, size or form may change	Original substances are changed to other substances
Can be used to separate mixtures	Can be used to decompose or form compounds

PROBLEMS

8. Which of the following is a chemical change?
   (a) Piling rocks on top of each other
   (b) Burning sulfur
   (c) Breaking a window
   (d) Baking a cake
9. Which of the following is a physical change?
   (a) Opening an envelope
   (b) Burning paper
   (c) Paneling a room

Figure 2-17. Chemical changes involve changes in composition.

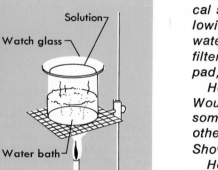

Figure 2-18.

It might not be necessary to do this experiment if previous ones have been done successfully.

EXPERIMENT. What are some methods of making physical separations? For this experiment, you will need the following materials: mixtures of water and sand, sugar and water, salt and sand, salt and iron; test tubes, beakers, funnel, filter paper, Bunsen burner, ring stand and ring, asbestos pad, watch glass. *By physical means.*

How can you separate a mixture of sand and table salt? Would it be possible to pick out all the crystals of salt? Is there *no* some liquid that will dissolve one substance and not the other? Devise a method to separate the salt and sand mixture. *water* Show your instructor the two separated substances.

How can you separate a mixture of salt and iron filings? Is there something that will dissolve one and not the other? *water* Is there something else that will affect one but not the other? *magnet* Devise a method to separate the mixture of salt and iron filings. Show your instructor the two separated substances.

A sugar solution is a mixture of sugar and water. How can you recover the sugar? How can you separate the mixture of sand and water? *Evaporate the water.*

Evaporate the water or pour it off through a filter.

Figure 2-19. What properties of aluminum make it a suitable material for canoes?

PROBLEMS

10. How could you separate the following mixtures?
   (a) sulfur-sand   (c) salt-iodine
   (b) iodine-iron filings   (d) copper-nickel

10. (a) carbon disulfide
(b) heat or magnet
(c) heat or alcohol
(d) magnet

11. How could you separate water into hydrogen and oxygen? What kind of change is this?   *electrolysis, chemical change*

    EXPERIMENT. How can liquids be separated? For this experiment, you will need the following materials: 5% alcohol-water mixture, distilling flask, condenser, rubber tubing, stopper and thermometer, ring stand and ring, asbestos pad, Bunsen burner, watch glass. CAUTION: Alcohol burns easily. Handle it with care.

The first drops should fall in the beaker about 75-80°C.

    Into the distilling flask, pour the alcohol-water mixture. Place the stopper with the thermometer into the neck of the flask and begin heating the flask gently. Record the temperature at which the first drops fall into the beaker. Continue recording the temperature at one-minute intervals. How will you be able to tell when all the alcohol is gone? Have you separated the two liquids? Where is the water?   *Yes. In the flask.*

The temperature will rise quickly to 100°C.

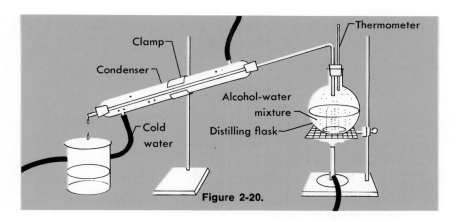

Figure 2-20.

PROBLEMS

12. What kind of separation is in this experiment?   *12. physical*

13. What is the purpose of the water in the condenser?   *13. Cold water cools the gas to condense it.*

14. How could you separate a mixture of carbon tetrachloride and water? Would you use the method used in the experiment? Why?   *14. CCl₄ has boiling point of 76.8°C, far enough below H₂O to make the distillation possible. No. Dangerous unless in hood.*

15. Could you separate sulfur and iron in the same way you would separate the iodine-iron mixture?   *15. no*

16. How could you separate sulfur and iron?   *16. magnet, CS₂, CCl₄*

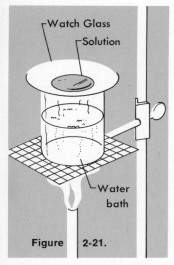

Watch Glass

Solution

Water bath

Figure   2-21.

Aluminum dissolves, bubbles of gas formed, test tube becomes warm.

EXPERIMENT.   How can you identify a chemical change? For this experiment, you will need dilute hydrochloric acid, aluminum squares, beakers, watch glasses, ring stand and ring, asbestos pad, and Bunsen burner.

Pour a little of the dilute hydrochloric acid in a watch glass. Evaporate the acid to dryness over a water bath. Describe the result. Nothing left in the watch glass.

Observe and record the physical properties of the small square of aluminum. bright, shiny, metallic, thin sheet

Place the square of aluminum in a test tube. Add hydrochloric acid slowly. Continue to add acid very slowly until the aluminum has disappeared. Record what you observe. Feel the test tube bottom.

Pour a little of the liquid from the test tube into a watch glass. Evaporate it to dryness over a water bath. Describe what you observe. White crystals ($AlCl_3$) left on watch glass.

PROBLEMS

Aluminum dissolves in HCl, new compound formed (white crystals), H_2 gas formed, test tube became warm.

17. Why do you evaporate the hydrochloric acid in this experiment? To show that HCl did not leave the crystals.

18. What chemical changes did you observe in this experiment?

19. What substance is left after you evaporate the test tube solution? Aluminum chloride ($AlCl_3$).

MAIN IDEAS

p. 24   1. Matter is anything that has mass and takes up space.

p. 25   2. Elements are basic substances. They cannot be broken down by ordinary means.

p. 26   3. Two or more elements can combine to form a compound.

p. 28   4. Mixtures are made of elements or compounds which are not chemically united.

p. 29   5. The physical properties of a substance depend only on the substance. Some physical properties are color, melting point, and density.

p. 31   6. The chemical properties of a substance depend upon its reaction with other substances.

p. 31   7. A physical change does not change the composition of a substance. Only its size, shape, or form changes.

p. 32   8. In a chemical change, some substances disappear. Others with different properties appear.

VOCABULARY

Write a sentence in which you correctly use each of the following words or terms.

chemical change	gas	mixture
chemical formula	inertia	physical change
compound	liquid	solid
element	matter	subscript

STUDY QUESTIONS

A. True or False

Determine whether each of the following sentences is true or false. (Do not write in this book.)

T 1. Water is matter because it has mass and takes up space.

F 2. Ideas are *not* matter because they have *no* mass.

F 3. Making ice cubes is a ~~chemical~~ change. *physical*

T 4. Boiling point and density are physical properties of matter.

F 5. Sodium chloride is ~~an element.~~ *a compound*

T 6. Air is a mixture.

F 7. Elements in compounds can be separated by ~~physical~~ means. *chemical*

T 8. All objects have inertia.

T 9. Chemical changes produce new substances with new chemical properties.

T 10. A substance in the solid phase can be changed to the liquid phase.

B. Multiple Choice

Some questions in part B may have more than one correct answer. Only one answer is required.

Choose one word or phrase that correctly completes each of the following sentences. (Do not write in this book.)

1. Air is a(n) (element, <u>mixture</u>, solid).

2. Compounds are (mixtures, <u>substances</u>, elements).

3. (Breaking, Melting, Grinding, <u>Burning</u>) is an example of a chemical change.

4. Mixtures can be separated by (<u>physical</u>, chemical) means.

5. (Taste, <u>Odor</u>, Color) is not a physical property.

6. Iron usually exists as a (<u>solid</u>, liquid, gas).

7. The composition of air (<u>varies</u>, remains the same).

8. Carbon is an example of a(n) (compound, <u>element</u>, mixture, liquid).

C. Completion

Complete each of the following sentences with a word or phrase that will make the sentence correct. (Do not write in this book.)

mixture **1.** Matter which has varying composition is called a(n) __?__.

physical **2.** Heating a frying pan is an example of a(n) __?__ change.

temperature, pressure **3.** Substances can be forced to change their states through changes in __?__ and __?__.

inertia, mass **4.** Two properties of all matter are __?__ and __?__.

chemical **5.** Compounds are decomposed by __?__ changes.

low **6.** Something which evaporates easily usually has a(n) __?__ boiling point.

physical **7.** Shape is a(n) __?__ property.

1. chemical - unites with some elements, does not support combustion
physical - colorless, odorless, tasteless, etc.

D. How and Why

1. What are some chemical and physical properties of water?

2. Not necessarily. Someone may have put a dye in it.

2. If a liquid turns blue while you are not in the room, has a chemical change taken place? Explain your answer.

3. Shape, size, color, taste, etc.

3. What properties would help you to describe an apple?

4. What kinds of properties are listed in your answer to Question 3? *physical*

5. See Experiment on page 25.

5. How could you prove that helium has mass?

6. What are the basic differences between mixtures and compounds?

7. mixtures - lemonade, concrete, soil, air, etc.
compounds - water, sugar, ammonia, salt

7. Name three common mixtures. Name three common compounds.

8. strength, resilience, color, wearability

8. What properties would a manufacturer look for in a material suitable for auto seat covers?

9. Evaporate a small amount to determine whether there is a crystalline residue.

9. How could you find out if a liquid is pure water or salt water without tasting it?

10. How could distillation be used to separate two liquids?
See Experiment on page 35.

INVESTIGATIONS

See Teacher's material at front of book for suggestions.

1. Obtain various samples of wood and/or metal. Devise tests to compare the physical properties of the samples.

6. mixture	*substance*
not the same throughout	*same composition throughout*
can be separated by physical means	*decomposed by chemical means*
no definite proportions	*definite proportion by weight*

2. Determine the boiling points of vegetable oil, salt water, and ethylene glycol (antifreeze) mixed with water.

3. Visit a materials testing laboratory. Learn what a Brinell test is. Find out how it is used in the laboratory.

INTERESTING READING

"Fingerprinting Marble." *Science Digest*, LXXII (December, 1972), pp. 30–31.

Jaffe, Bernard, *Chemistry Creates a New World*. New York, Thomas Y. Crowell Company, 1957.

Kelman, Peter and Stone, A. Harris, *Mendeleyev: Prophet of Chemical Order*. New York, Prentice-Hall, 1969.

Kendall, James, *Great Discoveries by Young Chemists*. New York, Thomas Y. Crowell Company, 1954.

Lapp, Ralph E., *Matter*. Time-Life Books, New York, Time Inc., 1969.

Vaczek, Louis, *The Enjoyment of Chemistry*. New York, Viking Press, Inc., 1965.

Nonmetals

III A	IV A	V A	VI
5 B 10.81	6 C 12.011	7 N 14.007	8 O 15.99
13 Al 26.98	14 Si 28.09	15 P 30.9	16 S 2.0
31 Ga 69.72	32 Ge 72.59	33 A 74.	34 Se 8.9
49	50	51	52

3

GOAL: You will gain an understanding of the atomic theory of matter and the importance of the electron in both ionic and covalent chemical bonds.

Chapter 3 introduces the atomic theory of matter and discusses the concept of a model to represent an atom which cannot be observed directly. The importance of the electron in chemical bonds, both ionic and covalent, is stressed.

Atoms and Compounds

A scientist can often predict what will happen when substances come in contact with other substances. As a result, man can make new products with completely different properties from the original materials. For example, sodium is a soft light metal which burns easily. Chlorine is a yellowish-green gas which is extremely poisonous. These two elements, sodium and chlorine, can combine. The compound they form is sodium chloride. Sodium chloride is a white crystalline substance that is called table salt.

How are compounds formed? Why are compounds different from the original substances? By studying atoms, combinations of atoms, and even parts of atoms, you may find answers to these questions.

3:1 *Atomic Theory*

Suppose you could divide an element into two pieces. Then you continued to divide each piece into smaller and smaller pieces. Finally, you would not be able to divide a piece and still have pieces of the same element. The smallest piece of an element which still has the properties of that element is called an **atom.** All elements are composed of atoms.

At one time, scientists believed that all matter was continuous. *Continuous* means not made of particles. Then, based on experiments, the English chemist John Dalton (1766-1844) proposed his atomic theory. Dalton's atomic theory states that all matter is made of small particles called atoms. Dalton also believed that all atoms of the same element were exactly the same. Later experiments have supported some of Dalton's ideas. Some of his views, however, have been proven incorrect.

What is Dalton's atomic theory?

Dalton believed that all matter is composed of small particles called atoms, that these particles cannot be divided, and that all atoms of the same element are exactly the same.

40

3:2 Subatomic Particles

Dalton correctly believed that all matter is made of atoms. He wrongly assumed that atoms cannot be divided. Scientists have found more than one hundred smaller (subatomic) particles. Some of these form part of the atom. Chemists are usually concerned with only three of these subatomic particles: *electron*, *proton*, and *neutron*.

An **electron** has a negative charge. Its mass is very small. 1×10^{29} electrons (1 followed by 29 zeros) have a total mass of only about one gram. It has a radius so small that 25×10^{11} (25 followed by 11 zeros) electrons could fit on an one-centimeter line. There is some disagreement about whether the electron is a wave, a particle, or both. For our purposes, it will be considered a particle.

A **proton** has a mass more than 1800 times larger than an electron. Yet the proton is still very small. More than 6×10^{23} protons (6 followed by 23 zeros) have a mass of only about one gram. The positive charge on a proton is the same size as the negative charge on an electron. A proton has a slightly smaller radius than the electron.

A **neutron** has a slightly larger mass than a proton. As its name suggests, the neutron is neutral. It carries no charge.

3:3 Atomic Structure

Scientists often use models to help explain a scientific idea. A *model* is simply a way of looking at an idea in order to make it more understandable. Many people make model airplanes or ships. Often social studies classes will make

What are the three subatomic particles of interest to chemists?

proton, neutron, electron

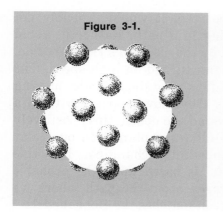

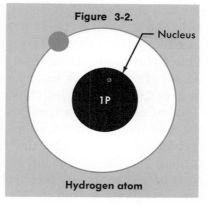

Figure 3-1. An early concept of the atom showed the electrons imbedded in the nucleus.

Figure 3-2. A later concept, the Bohr model, was patterned after the solar system.

Figure 3-3. A model shows certain properties of the original. What properties of the original do these models show?

models of frontier villages or old castles. Architects and engineers make models of homes or bridges they plan to build. In each case new ideas may cause the model to be changed. The model is never exactly the same as what it represents. It may be smaller or larger. Often it is made from different materials. A model shows certain properties of the original as accurately as possible based on known facts and ideas.

One early model of the atom showed electrons lying in a ball of positively-charged material. This model is similar to a snowball with pebbles in it. Later experiments led to the *Bohr model*, named after the Danish scientist Niels Bohr (1885-1962). In this model, the atom is similar to our solar system. The protons and neutrons form a central core or nucleus. The electrons revolve around this nucleus in certain paths called orbits.

Again, more experiments with better equipment have led to a new atomic model, the *electron cloud model*. In this model the nucleus also contains protons and neutrons. The electron moves very fast. If it could be seen, it would probably not look like a small particle moving in a path. Rather it would look like a cloud that is formed by the electron's rapid motion. This cloud is something like a fan turned on high speed. The blades of the fan look like a cloud, not like single blades moving in a certain path. Electrons as they move appear to form a cloud of negative electricity around the dense, tiny, positively charged nucleus of an atom. Unlike the planets in our solar system, electron paths are constantly changing. For this reason, the electron cloud model is based upon the probable path of electrons. In the hydrogen atom the path where we are most likely to find the electron matches the Bohr model.

How does the electron cloud model differ from the Bohr model?

In the Bohr model, the electrons follow definite paths around the nucleus. In the electron cloud model, the electron is moving so rapidly that it seems to enclose the entire nucleus in a cloud of negative electricity.

42

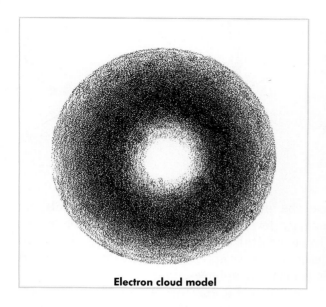

Electron cloud model

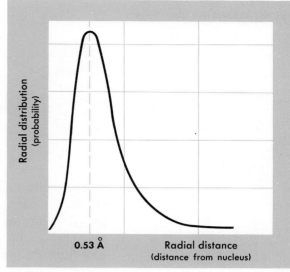

Figure 3-4. The current model of the atom is the electron cloud model. The density of negative charge in an electron cloud is greatest where the number of electrons traveling around the nucleus are most concentrated.

Most of the mass of the atom is found in the nucleus. The protons and neutrons are in the nucleus. All atoms of the same element have the same number of protons. For example, any hydrogen atom has one proton in its nucleus. Any carbon atom has six protons in its nucleus. However, some atoms of an element may have more neutrons than other atoms of the same element. Atoms of the same element with different numbers of neutrons are called **isotopes**. For example, hydrogen has three isotopes. A hydrogen atom may contain no neutrons. Another hydrogen atom may contain one neutron. Still another may contain two neutrons. The number of protons in the nucleus of an atom determines the element. The number of neutrons determines the isotope of the element. Every element has at least two isotopes.

What are isotopes?
Isotopes are atoms of the same element with different numbers of neutrons.

PROBLEM

1. How does the number of neutrons in an atom affect the mass of an element?

Deuterium

Figure 3-5. Deuterium is an isotope of hydrogen which has one neutron and one proton.

3:4 *Electron Location*

An atom is electrically neutral. The number of electrons and protons in an atom is equal. The positive charge of the protons balances the negative charge of the electrons. Thus, for each proton in the nucleus, one electron is in orbit around the nucleus.

Why are atoms neutral?
The positive charges of the protons balance the negative charges of the electrons.

Figure 3-6. Some atomic orbitals are shaped like dumbbells.

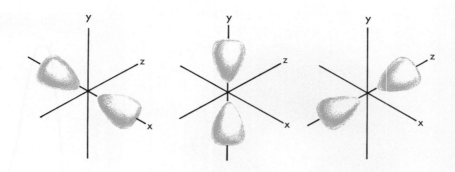

Electrons circle the nucleus in certain **energy levels,** or **shells.** In each energy level are one or more electron paths called *orbitals*. Each orbital can contain no more than two electrons (one pair of electrons). The orbitals are shaped like dumbbells or concentric spheres.

Only two electrons can orbit the nucleus in the first shell. The first shell is the energy level closest to the nucleus. Thus, the first energy level can contain one orbital of two electrons. The second shell of an atom can hold up to eight electrons arranged in four orbitals. The third shell can hold up to 18 electrons. Higher shells sometimes hold as many as 32 electrons.

Electrons in energy levels are normally as close as possible to the nucleus. A magnesium (Mg) atom contains 12 protons, 12 electrons, and 12 neutrons. In the nucleus of the atom are 24 particles—12 protons and 12 neutrons. The 12 electrons are arranged in pairs within the shells. The first shell has one pair of electrons. The second shell has four pairs of electrons. However, one pair is slightly closer to the nucleus than the other three pairs. Thus, within a shell there can be *subshells*. The two remaining electrons of the magnesium atom are in a third shell.

Some atoms have more than three occupied energy levels and further divisions of electrons into subshells. Lawrencium (Lw), an element with 103 electrons, has seven shells containing electrons. Other elements may have electrons in fewer than three shells. Each hydrogen (H) atom contains only one electron. How many occupied shells does hydrogen have?

Electrons in the outer energy level have the most effect on an element's chemical properties. These electrons are most commonly involved in chemical change. They also determine some physical properties. For these reasons, the number of electrons in the outermost shell of an atom is extremely important.

Figure 3-7. Electrons are found in specific energy levels. Each energy level can contain one or more orbitals. Each orbital can contain one or two electrons.

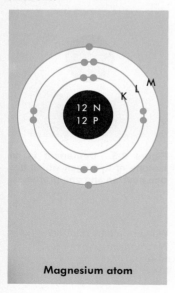

Magnesium atom

Table 3–1. Electrons in Energy Levels

Energy Level	Total Electrons Possible in Each Shell	Electrons Possible in Subshells	Cumulative Number of Electrons
1	2	2	2
2	8	2, 6	10
3	18	2, 6, 10	28
4	32	2, 6, 10, 14	60
5	32	2, 6, 10, 14	92
6	10	2, 6, 2	102
7	2	2	104

3:5 Molecules

An atom is the smallest particle of an element. It is the smallest part of an element that can take part in a chemical change.

When atoms combine chemically, they form molecules. A **molecule** (mahl′ i kewl) is the smallest part of a substance (either element or compound) as it normally exists. A molecule of a *compound* always contains two or more atoms of different elements. A molecule of an element always contains two or more atoms of the same kind. Thus, it is impossible to speak of an "atom of a compound," since a molecule is the smallest portion of a compound that can exist. If a molecule is subdivided, it is decomposed into the atoms which make it up. Figure 3–8 shows how atoms may combine to form molecules.

What is the difference between an atom and a molecule?

The atom is the smallest particle that can exist as an element; a molecule is a group of two or more atoms.

carbon, oxygen

O = C = O

CO₂

oxygen

O = O

O₂

O = C O — Na
       O — H

NaHCO₃

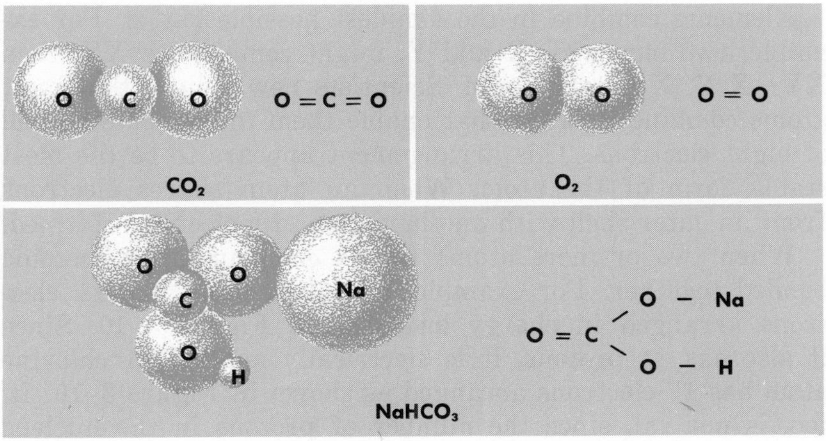

sodium, hydrogen, carbon, oxygen

Figure 3-8. If each of the molecules illustrated were decomposed, atoms of what elements would result?

Figure 3-9. Sodium bicarbonate is commonly known as baking soda.

What does S_8 represent?

S_8 means a molecule of sulfur composed of eight sulfur atoms.

1 hydrogen, 1 chlorine
2 sodium, 1 oxygen
1 potassium, 1 oxygen
1 hydrogen
2 hydrogen, 1 sulfur
4 oxygen

Carbon dioxide has the chemical formula CO_2. The subscript 2 means that two atoms of oxygen are combined with one atom of carbon. If only one atom of oxygen combines with one atom of carbon, a different compound, carbon monoxide (CO), is formed. A chemical formula may also be used to represent two or more atoms of the same element combined chemically. For example, oxygen atoms in air are usually combined in pairs. Thus, the formula for free oxygen is O_2. This represents one molecule of oxygen.

Sodium bicarbonate, a household chemical, has the formula $NaHCO_3$. This formula shows that each molecule of sodium bicarbonate contains one sodium atom (Na), one hydrogen atom (H), one carbon atom (C), and three oxygen atoms (O_3). Aluminum sulfide has the formula Al_2S_3. Each molecule of aluminum sulfide contains two aluminum atoms (Al_2) and three sulfur atoms (S_3).

PROBLEMS

2. Assume that each of the following formulas represents one molecule of a substance. What kinds of atoms and how many of each are represented?
   (a) HCl
   (b) Na_2O
   (c) KOH
   (d) H_2SO_4
   (e) F_2
   (f) Fe_2S_3
   (g) Br_2
   (h) NH_3

   2 fluorine
   2 iron, 3 sulfur
   2 bromine
   1 nitrogen, 3 hydrogen

3. Which of the formulas in Problem 2 represent compounds? What do the other formulas represent?

   compounds - a, b, c, d, f, h
   elements - e, g

3:6 Bonding

Elements combine in the simplest possible ratios. For example, two elements, X and Y, might combine as XY, then XY_2, X_2Y, XY_3, and so on. Scientists now believe that most atoms combine in ways that enable them to complete a shell of eight electrons. This arrangement appears to be the most stable form of the atom. When an atom shares electrons from its outer shell with another atom, a molecule is formed.

When two or more atoms form a compound, they become bonded together. For example, a sodium atom has 11 electrons arranged in energy levels as in Figure 3–10. Since it also has 11 protons, it is electrically neutral. A chlorine atom has 17 electrons arranged as shown in Figure 3–10. It, too, is neutral, since the number of protons in the nucleus

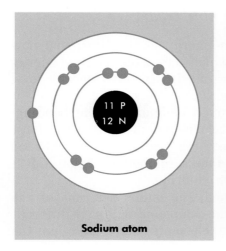

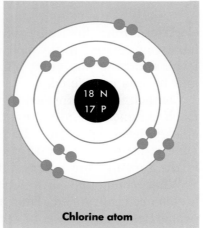

Sodium atom   Chlorine atom

is 17. Suppose a sodium atom and a chlorine atom come close together. The electron in the outer shell of the sodium atom may transfer to the outer shell of the chlorine atom. The sodium atom loses an electron and becomes positively charged. The chlorine atom gains an electron and becomes negatively charged. The two atoms now have opposite charges. They are attracted to each other and bond together to form a compound. In the new compound, the number of electrons and protons is equal. Thus, the compound is neutral.

When an atom loses or gains an electron, the atom becomes a charged particle called an **ion.** Therefore, the type of bonding in which electrons are transferred is called *ionic* (ie awn' ik). The positive sodium ion is shown as Na$^+$. The negative chloride ion is shown as Cl$^-$.

Another type of bonding is called covalent bonding. In *covalent* (koh vae' lent) *bonding*, electrons are shared by atoms in the molecule. Hydrogen has one electron and one proton. Figure 3–11 shows how chlorine and hydrogen share

How would lithium and fluorine combine?

The electron in the outer shell of lithium would transfer to the vacancy in the outer shell of the fluorine atom.

Why is a compound neutral?

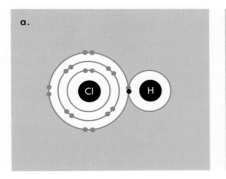

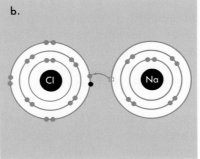

Figure 3-11. Both hydrogen and chlorine contribute one electron to a covalent bond. They share the two electrons to complete their energy levels. In effect, chlorine has eight electrons, hydrogen has two. What kind of bonding occurs in sodium chloride?

ionic

electrons. Both fill their outer energy levels. Hydrogen now has two electrons in its shell which completes the first energy level. Chlorine has eight electrons in its third energy level and is thus completed.

Compounds are formed through ionic or covalent bonding. Each magnesium atom has two electrons in its outermost energy level (pg. 44). It requires two atoms of chlorine (one electron to each) to produce a compound. Thus, $MgCl_2$ is the formula for magnesium chloride.

When compounds are formed, the outer electrons of the atoms are rearranged. Thus, the compound will have different properties than those of the elements that make up the compound.

PROBLEMS

4. Draw a diagram of a molecule of chlorine gas (Cl_2).
5. Draw a diagram of $MgCl_2$. *See Teacher's Guide at the front of this book.*

See Teacher's Guide at the front of this book.

3:7 Valence

The combining capacity of an atom or group of atoms determines how compounds are formed. This combining ability is called *valence* (vae' lens). Sodium loses one electron as it forms a compound. Therefore, its valence is +1. Chlorine gains one electron as it forms a compound. The valence of chlorine is —1. The valence of a compound is zero. Therefore, one atom of sodium combines with one atom of chlorine. The formula for the compound is NaCl.

Hydrogen has a valence of +1. When hydrogen (+1) and chlorine (—1) combine, the formula for the compound is HCl. Magnesium gives one electron to each of two chlorine atoms. Magnesium has a valence of +2. The formula for this compound is $MgCl_2$.

Table 3–2 lists some elements with two valences. Unusual placement of electrons in the shells of some atoms give them more than one valence. Such an element may combine with one element differently from the way it combines with another element. It may even combine in two or more different ways with the same element. For example, carbon has valences of +2 and +4. Thus carbon forms two compounds with oxygen, CO and CO_2. The valence of oxygen is —2. Iron can have +2 or +3 valences. If more than one valence is possible, the valence intended is written in parentheses after the element's name. For example, iron (II) always has the valence +2; iron (III) always has the valence +3.

Valences of come common elements are listed in Table 3–2. A more complete list of valences is in Appendix E.

Table 3–2. *Valences of Some Common Elements*				
+1	*+2*	*+3*	*−1*	*−2*
silver, Ag^+	iron (II), Fe^{+2}	iron (III),	chlorine, Cl^-	sulfur,
sodium, Na^+	calcium, Ca^{+2}	Fe^{+3}	iodine, I^-	S^{-2}
potassium, K^+	barium, Ba^{+2}	aluminum,	bromine, Br^-	oxygen,
hydrogen, H^+	copper (II),	Al^{+3}	fluorine, F^-	O^{-2}
lithium, Li^+	Cu^{+2}			
copper (I),	magnesium,			
Cu^+	Mg^{+2}			

What elements in the list have two valences?

EXAMPLE

Find the formula for a compound of silver and sulfur.

Solution: Silver has a valence of +1, and sulfur, in this case, has a valence of −2. Thus, two atoms of silver are needed to combine with one atom of sulfur. The formula for this compound is written Ag_2S. (Note: The symbol of the element with the metallic or positive valence is always written first.)

PROBLEM

6. Write formulas for the following combinations of elements:
   (a) sodium and bromine   *NaBr*
   (b) potassium and iodine   *KI*
   (c) hydrogen and bromine   *HBr*
   (d) hydrogen and sulfur   *H_2S*
   (e) magnesium and fluorine   *MgF_2*
   (f) calcium and chlorine   *$CaCl_2$*
   (g) lithium and sulfur   *Li_2S*
   (h) aluminum and chlorine   *$AlCl_3$*
   (i) copper (II) and sulfur   *CuS*

3:8   Binary Compounds

All of the compounds in the preceding problem are binary compounds. *Binary* (bie′ na ree) means composed of only two

What are binary compounds?

Compounds composed of only two elements.

elements. To name binary compounds, the element with the positive valence is mentioned first. Then the element with the negative valence is named, using the ending -ide. Thus, $MgCl_2$ is magnesium chloride. HCl is hydrogen chloride. $FeCl_2$ is iron (II) chloride, read as "iron two chloride." BaS is barium sulfide. $CaBr_2$ is calcium bromide. CuF is copper (I) fluoride, read as "copper one fluoride."

EXAMPLE

What is the name of FeS?

Solution: Iron can have a valence of either $+2$ or $+3$. In most binary compounds, sulfur has a valence of -2. Only one atom of iron and one atom of sulfur are indicated in this molecular formula. Thus the valences must be equal and opposite. The formula means iron (II). The name is iron (II) sulfide.

PROBLEMS

7. Name each of the following compounds:
    (a) NaCl   sodium chloride
    (b) CuBr   copper (I) bromide
    (c) BaS   barium sulfide
    (d) MgO   magnesium oxide
    (e) KI   potassium iodide
    (f) $MgBr_2$ magnesium bromide
    (g) CaS   calcium sulfide
    (h) CuO   copper (II) oxide
    (i) $FeCl_3$ iron (III) chloride
    (j) FeO   iron (II) oxide

8. Write formulas for each of the following compounds:
    (a) calcium bromide $CaBr_2$
    (b) potassium oxide K_2O
    (c) aluminum chloride $AlCl_3$
    (d) iron (III) iodide FeI_3
    (e) copper (I) sulfide Cu_2S
    (f) lithium fluoride LiF
    (g) sodium bromide $NaBr$
    (h) copper (II) chloride $CuCl_2$

Figure 3-12. This mass spectrograph can detect the one different atom among a billon or more identical atoms.

Radio Corporation of America

People in Physical Science

Some of the people who work in physical science are scientists, but many are not. There are teachers, plant operators, technical artists and many other specialists.

American Society of Agricultural Engineers

Dr. Chokyun Rha is an agricultural engineer. She studies the texture and chemical properties of food. Such research may lead to synthetic foods which taste and look like their natural counterparts.

RCA Corp.

Ann Nieroda might be called a "space age seamstress." She designs and sews special mylar blankets for space equipment. Mylar is a material which is resistant to the intense heat and cold of space.

Associated Photographers, Inc.

Many people who work in physical science are directly concerned with the quality of our environment. Here a water treatment specialist examines the water supply used by a manufacturing plant.

Scientific glassblowing combines artistry and craftsmanship with a knowledge of the physics and chemistry of glass.

General Motors Corporation

Shirley Carrie Williams

Shirley Carrie Williams is a technical writer. Her knowledge of science and her writing skills help to ensure that scientists all over the world learn about new discoveries.

3:9 *Polyatomic Ions*

Not all compounds are binary compounds. Often, compounds contain more than two elements. Two or more elements may sometimes be found in a polyatomic ion. A *polyatomic* (pawl' ee ah taw' mik) *ion* is a group of atoms which act together as one ion or charged atom. Table 3–3 lists some common polyatomic ions and their valences.

Table 3–3. Some Common Polyatomic Ions and Their Valences

Name	Valence	Representation
ammonium	+1	$NH_4{}^+$
chlorate	−1	$ClO_3{}^-$
nitrate	−1	$NO_3{}^-$
carbonate	−2	$CO_3{}^{-2}$
sulfate	−2	$SO_4{}^{-2}$
phosphate	−3	$PO_4{}^{-3}$

How many oxygen atoms in a sulfate ion?

Four oxygen atoms in a sulfate ion.

Compounds which contain polyatomic ions are named in much the same way as binary compounds. The positive part of the compound is named first, followed by the name of the negative polyatomic ion. For example, the compound formed by sodium and the sulfate ion has the formula Na_2SO_4. It is called sodium sulfate. The compound formed by the ammonium ion and sulfur is treated just as a binary compound. Its formula is $(NH_4)_2S$. Its name is ammonium sulfide because the polyatomic ion is the positive ion. Parentheses and the subscript 2 indicate that two ammonium ions balance the valence of sulfur.

EXAMPLE

What kinds of atoms and how many of each are in one molecule of barium nitrate?

Figure 3-13. The compound $(NH_4)_2S$ has a complex bonding structure. The double dots around N represent an electron pair (covalent bond) while the + and = represent ionic bonding between ammonium ion and the sulfide ion.

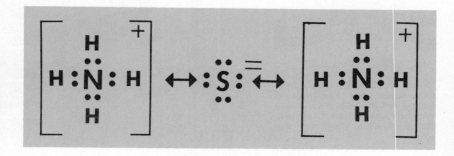

Solution: First, a formula for barium (Ba^{+2}) nitrate (NO_3^-) must be found. Based on valences, this formula could be $Ba(NO_3)_2$. One barium atom is in a molecule of this compound. Each nitrate ion has one nitrogen atom and three oxygen atoms. The subscript applies to the whole nitrate ion. Two nitrogen atoms and six oxygen atoms must be in one molecule of barium nitrate.

See Teacher's Guide at the front of the book for answers and suggestions.

PROBLEMS

9. Write a formula for each of the following compounds:
   (a) sodium nitrate $NaNO_3$ (d) potassium phosphate K_3PO_4
   (b) silver sulfate Ag_2SO_4 (e) copper (II) iodide CuI_2
   (c) iron (II) chloride $FeCl_2$

10. Name the following compounds:
   (a) Na_2SO_4 (c) FeO (e) KBr
   (b) $(NH_4)_3PO_4$ (d) $AgNO_3$

10. a. sodium sulfate
    b. ammonium phosphate
    c. iron (II) oxide
    d. silver nitrate
    e. potassium bromide

11. What kinds of atoms and how many of each are present in the compounds listed in Problems 9 and 10?

See Teacher's Guide at the front of this book.

EXPERIMENT. CAUTION: *This experiment is to be done only under direct supervision of the teacher. Wear eye protection. Find the percent of oxygen in potassium chlorate. Find the mass of a clean, dry test tube and add about 3 g of powdered potassium chlorate to the tube. Hold the tube with a test tube clamp. Heat the lower end of the test tube with a low Bunsen burner flame for 5 min. Gradually make the flame stronger, until it reaches its hottest point. Heat for 10 min. Allow the test tube to cool. Find its mass again. To find the percent of oxygen compute the mass of oxygen lost. Divide by the original mass of the potassium chlorate. Multiply by 100.*

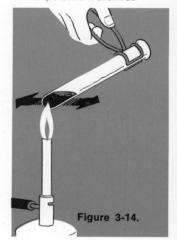

Figure 3-14.

Use extreme care in performing this experiment. Use U.S.P. $KClO_3$. The test tube may be clamped to a ring stand for the ten minute heating. Help the students devise a chart for data. A possible chart is given in the Teacher's Guide at the front of this book. Be sure to demonstrate to the students the calculation of finding the percentage of composition. Students will be confused if they do not understand this thoroughly.

MAIN IDEAS

p. 40   **1.** All elements are made of atoms.

p. 41   **2.** Three major subatomic particles are the proton, neutron, and electron.

p. 42   **3.** The present "model" of the atom is a nucleus containing the protons and neutrons. An "electron cloud" surrounds the nucleus.

p. 43   **4.** Isotopes are atoms with the same number of protons but different numbers of neutrons.

p. 44   **5.** Electrons are arranged in shells surrounding the nucleus.

p. 45   **6.** Atoms combine chemically to form molecules.

p. 47   **7.** In ionic bonding, electrons are gained or lost. In covalent bonding, electrons are shared.

p. 48   **8.** The combining capacity of an atom or group of atoms is called "valence."

p. 49   **9.** Binary compounds are composed of two elements.

p. 52   **10.** Some compounds contain polyatomic ions. A polyatomic ion is a group of atoms which act together as one ion.

VOCABULARY

Write a sentence in which you correctly use each of the following words or terms.

atom	ion	neutron
atomic shell	ionic bond	orbital
covalent bond	isotope	proton
electron	model	valence
electron cloud	molecule	

STUDY QUESTIONS

A. True or False

Have students rewrite false statements to make the statements correct.

Determine whether each of the following sentences is true or false. (Do not write in this book.)

T   **1.** Models are used to explain theories.

T   **2.** Dalton stated that matter was composed of small indivisible particles called atoms.

T   **3.** Electrons have a negative electric charge.

many times smaller   *F*   **4.** The mass of an electron is greater than the mass of a proton.

T   **5.** All atoms of the same element contain the same number of protons.

T   **6.** Atoms of the same element may contain different numbers of neutrons.

different masses   *F*   **7.** All atoms of the same element have the same mass.

T   **8.** The positive charge of the protons in an atom is equal to the negative charge of the electrons.

F **9.** Electrons in the outer shell of an atom have ~~little~~ effect upon its chemical properties. *great*

T **10.** The valence of an element tells the number of electrons which may be lost, gained, or shared by atoms of that element in chemical reactions.

B. Multiple Choice

Some questions in part B may have more than one correct answer. Only one answer is required.

Choose one word or phrase that correctly completes each of the following sentences. (Do not write in this book.)

1. Modern atomic theory is based on the work of (Kepler, Aristotle, <u>Dalton</u>).

2. A compound is (<u>matter</u>, an element, a liquid).

3. The compound $Mg(NO_3)_2$ contains some (mercury, neon, <u>oxygen</u>).

4. Sodium chloride is formed by (<u>ionic</u>, covalent) bonding.

5. The compound iron (II) sulfide has the formula (<u>FeS</u>, Fe_2S, FeS_2).

6. A polyatomic ion is a group of atoms which act together as (<u>one ion</u>, two ions, three ions).

7. A magnesium atom can form a compound by giving up (one, <u>two</u>, three) electrons.

8. A(n) (neutron, <u>proton</u>, electron) has a positive charge.

9. The first energy level can contain at most (<u>2</u>, 6, 8) electrons.

10. The greatest number of electrons in an energy level is (10, 18, <u>32</u>, 64, 104).

C. Completion

Complete each of the following sentences with a word or phrase that will make the sentence correct. (Do not write in this book.)

1. Potassium has a valence of __?__ .   *+1*

2. In forming compounds, potassium __?__ electrons.   *loses*

3. The formula X_3Y shows that for every one atom of Y, there are __?__ atoms of X.   *three*

4. A molecule of $Al_2(SO_4)_3$ contains __?__ atoms of oxygen.   *twelve*

5. Ions are __?__ atoms or groups of atoms.   *charged*

6. Elements which have the same number of protons but different numbers of neutrons are called __?__ .   *isotopes*

two

7. A binary compound contains atoms of __?__ elements.

covalent

8. The chlorine molecule (Cl_2) is formed by __?__ bonding.

electron cloud

9. The model of the atom which is in use today is called the __?__ model.

nucleus

10. Neutrons and protons are found in the __?__ of the atom.

D. How and Why

See Teacher's Guide at the front of this book.

1. How does covalent bonding differ from ionic bonding?

2. Name the compounds represented by the following formulas: (a) NaCl, (b) NH_4NO_3, (c) $Ca_3(PO_4)_2$.

3. Write the formulas for the following compounds: (a) potassium sulfate, (b) sulfur dioxide, (c) mercury (I) sulfide.

4. Draw a diagram to show how magnesium bromide might be formed.

5. What are the differences between a proton, electron, and neutron?

6. What is the location of electrons in energy levels in an oxygen atom?

7. What are the main ideas in Dalton's theory? How have these ideas been modified by later experimentation?

8. An atom of an element has electrons distributed in energy levels in this manner: 2, 8, 2. What would you expect its valence to be? Why? What kind of bonding might it have?

9. What kind of atoms and how many of each are represented by the formula $Mg(NO_2)_2$?

INVESTIGATIONS

See Teacher's material at front of book for suggestions.

1. Find the chemical formulas for a number of common household compounds.

2. Report on the life of Niels Bohr.

3. Using the Bohr model, draw the electron structure of an atom with nine electrons.

4. Construct Bohr models of atoms. Use clay or styrofoam spheres to represent electrons, protons, and neutrons. Thin copper wire will hold the spheres in place.

5. Construct some molecular models. Use styrofoam spheres, or gumdrops, and toothpicks.

INTERESTING READING

Adler, Irving, *The Elementary Mathematics of the Atom.* New York, John Day Company, 1965.

Freeman, Ira M., and Patton, A. Rae, *The Science of Chemistry.* New York, Random House, Inc., 1969.

Grunwald, Ernest, and Johnsen, Russell H., *Atoms, Molecules and Chemical Change.* New York, Prentice-Hall, Inc., 1965.

Jensen, W. B., "Chemist's Annotated Mother Goose of Modern Bonding Theory." *Chemistry*, XLV (June, 1972), pp. 13-15.

Silverstein, Alvin and Silverstein, Virginia, *Frederick Sanger: The Man Who Mapped Out a Chemical of Life.* New York, John Day Publishing Co., 1969.

Structure of Matter

No law of nature, however general, has been established all at once; its recognition has always been preceded by many presentments.

Dmitri Mendeleev (1834-1907)

Scientists search for meanings and patterns in nature. They look for ways in which substances are alike and different. Through research, scientists develop new knowledge of matter. Then this scientific knowledge is woven together and organized by classification. Matter can be classified in many ways. One system divides matter into three groups: element, compound, and mixture. Another system divides all matter into living and nonliving. Matter can also be classified by its three physical states: solid, liquid, and gas. A fourth state of matter, plasma, is currently being studied. As new knowledge is gained, new ways of classifying matter are developed.

Scientists learn from the ideas and experiments of others. Each builds on the genius of those who came before. Often, a new discovery results after long periods of time. Efforts of groups of scientists in different countries, often looking at a problem in different ways, are behind many discoveries. The ways of discovery are open to you . . . now in the classroom, later in the laboratory.

unit
three

GOAL: You will gain an understanding of the periodic table of the elements and will learn how to predict the relative activity of elements by applying the periodic law.

The concept of classification by similar characteristics is an important one in all branches of science. Emphasize this.

Why is relative atomic mass rather than actual atomic mass used?

Actual atomic mass is too small to be measured accurately in ordinary laboratory conditions.

The concept of the combining capacity of elements is studied in greater depth as the student learns about the Periodic Table of elements. Quantitative aspects are emphasized with the study of atomic mass and atomic number. Students will learn to predict the relative activity of elements by applying the periodic law.

Periodic Table

Perhaps you or one of your friends collect stamps. When you collect many different stamps, you can identify them by size, color, shape, value, or country of issue.

Suppose a line of students is waiting in the school cafeteria. You do not know the students' names. But, you notice that some have the same features. For example, they have blue eyes, brown hair, and the same shape nose. You conclude that these students could be members of the same family.

In much the same way, elements are grouped into families. Elements are classified by the similarities and differences in their physical and chemical properties.

4:1 *Atomic Mass*

Early classifications of elements were based on atomic mass. Atomic mass is not the actual mass of an atom. It is a mass which is relative to a set standard. For example, Tom has a mass of 75 kilograms. Jim has a mass of 25 kilograms. Tom, then, has a mass of three "Jims." Tom's mass is given in relation to Jim's mass. In this case, Jim's mass is the standard. A

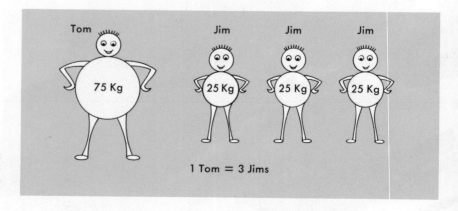

1 Tom = 3 Jims

Figure 4-1. Tom's mass is 75 kilograms. Jim's mass is 25 kilograms. If Tom's mass is the standard, what is Jim's mass?

Jim has a mass of 1/3 "Tom".

relative scale for the masses of atoms is needed because actual masses are very small. For example, the mass of a hydrogen atom is 1.66×10^{-24} grams (a decimal point followed by 23 zeros before the 166). It has a relative mass of 1.0080. Which of these numbers would you find easier to use?

The purpose of this experiment is to give insight into determination of relative mass. See Teacher's

EXPERIMENT. Find the mass of an empty beaker. Place an equal number of steel ball bearings and glass marbles into the beaker. Find the mass again. Subtract the mass of the empty beaker from the mass of the full beaker. What is the mass of the contents? Take the marbles out of the beaker and find the mass of the beaker and ball bearings. Subtract this mass from the mass of the total contents. What is the mass of the marbles? Subtract the mass of the empty beaker from the mass of the beaker and ball bearings. What is the mass of the ball bearings? Find the simplest ratio of the mass of the marbles to the mass of the ball bearings. Assign the lightest object a mass of 1. By applying the ratio, find the mass of the second object on the same scale. Why is the lightest object instead of the heaviest object given a mass of 1?

If you used twice as many marbles as ball bearings, how would the problem be changed? Why is it necessary to know the ratio of numbers of objects?

Figure 4-2.

Guide at the front of this book for a sample data table and answers to questions.

You could find the relative mass of other spherical objects. Then you might assign a mass of 10 to the base marble. Why?

See Teacher's Guide.

Compare the beaker, marbles, and ball bearings to a compound whose molecules are composed of two elements. Name one way a scientist might figure the atomic masses of the elements. Why must he know the ratio of numbers of atoms of each element in a compound? *See Teacher's Guide.*

The *carbon 12 isotope* now is the standard for atomic mass. The carbon 12 isotope may be subdivided into smaller units. These are called *atomic mass units* (a.m.u.). An **atomic mass unit** is $\frac{1}{12}$ the mass of the carbon 12 isotope. The masses of all other elements are related to this standard.

An atom of carbon 12 isotope has six protons, six neutrons, and six electrons. The electrons contribute almost no mass. The neutrons and protons have nearly the same mass. Each has a relative mass of one. If you know the number of protons and neutrons in an atom, you can find its relative mass. For example, a certain atom has 4 protons and 5 neutrons. Its atomic mass, relative to carbon 12, is 9; $4 + 5 = 9$. What is the

What is the standard for relative atomic mass?

Figure 4-3. The carbon-12 isotope is the standard for atomic mass.

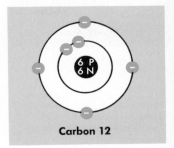

Carbon 12

atomic mass of an atom with 24 protons and 28 neutrons? How many electrons would this element have?

4:2 Mendeleev's Table

Early in the 1800's, the elements were grouped according to similar properties and atomic masses. Elements were arranged in groups of three and seven. Even spiral arrangements were tried. None of these methods proved effective. This was because the atomic masses of many elements were not known exactly. Also, many elements had not been discovered.

What did Mendeleev use to build his table?

Mendeleev built his table on the basis of atomic mass.

Finally, an acceptable arrangement was worked out by Mendeleev (1834-1907), a Russian scientist. Mendeleev arranged the known elements according to their atomic masses. He learned that, with this method, some physical properties and some chemical properties periodically were repeated. He called this repetition of properties the **periodic** (peer i aw' dik) **law.** The chart he drew up became known as the **periodic table.**

Use caution with this experiment.

EXPERIMENT. CAUTION: This experiment should be done only under direct teacher supervision. Wear eye and clothing protection. Obtain sodium, potassium, calcium, and magnesium metal. Fill a large beaker or jar three-fourths full of water. Remove the sodium metal from its container with a forceps and cut off a piece smaller than a pea. Replace the sodium in its container. Drop the pea-size piece of sodium into the water. Repeat the steps separately with potassium, calcium, and magnesium. Why are sodium and potassium kept under kerosene? Based on your observations, group these four metals into two families. List the observed properties of each family. *See Teacher's Guide at the front of this book.*

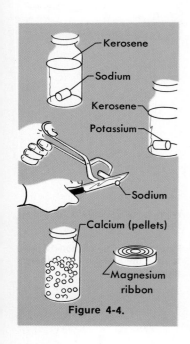

Figure 4-4.

Kerosene
Sodium
Kerosene
Potassium
Sodium
Calcium (pellets)
Magnesium ribbon

Elements not yet known could be predicted from Mendeleev's periodic table. There were places in the table where properties seemed to skip an element. These suggested to Mendeleev that some other element might belong there. Three elements which Mendeleev suggested—gallium (Ga), scandium (Sc), and germanium (Ge)—were later discovered. All have properties similar to those he predicted.

4:3 Moseley's Table

Chemists who used Mendeleev's table found errors. Mendeleev arranged elements in order of increasing atomic mass.

Try this before the students do to decide whether you want them to attempt it. Sodium and potassium react violently with water. Lithium could also be used here. Magnesium and calcium will not react with cold water.

At least three pairs of elements, however, seemed out of order. Mendeleev's table had pairs of elements with properties different from other elements in the same period. These errors were believed to be caused by inaccurate measurement of the masses.

Henry Moseley (1877-1915), a young English scientist, solved the problems in Mendeleev's table. Moseley thought that the periodic repetition of properties was due to the number of protons in an atom. He believed that the atomic number rather than the atomic mass was the key factor. And this was found to be true!

Atomic number is the number of protons in the nucleus. Z is the symbol for atomic number. For example: H, $Z = 1$; N, $Z = 7$; O, $Z = 8$. The number of protons equals the number of electrons in an atom. Therefore, the atomic number is also the number of electrons in an atom. No two elements have the same atomic number. Why?

The periodic table used by chemists today is not the same as Mendeleev's. In the modern periodic table (Table 4–1), elements are arranged by atomic number and *not* atomic mass. Find three pairs of elements in the modern periodic table that do not fit Mendeleev's table.

If elements are arranged in order of increasing atomic number, there is a periodic repetition of properties. This is now called the **periodic law.**

The periodic table (pages 64–65) shows how elements are classified today. Each box represents one element. The symbol for the element is in the center of the box. The number at the top is the atomic number of the element. This is the number of protons in the nucleus. The number at the bottom is the average atomic mass of the element relative to carbon 12. For example, find zinc (Zn). Its atomic number is 30, and its average atomic mass is 65.37. The number at the side of each box shows how electrons are distributed into shells.

Figure 4-5. How could you classify these stamps?

What is the modern table based on?

atomic number (number of protons)

Argon-potassium, tellurium-iodine, cobalt-nickel are three pairs that could be reversed in Mendeleev's table.

All elements have different numbers of protons. Atoms of the same element have the same number of protons. If two elements had the same number of protons, they would be the same element.

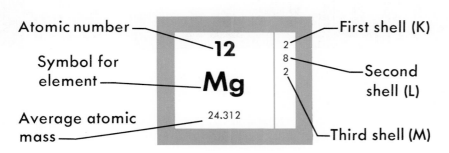

Atomic number

12

Symbol for element

Mg

Average atomic mass

24.312

First shell (K)

2

8

2

Second shell (L)

Third shell (M)

Figure 4-6. Each box in the periodic table gives the symbol for the element, its atomic number, its average atomic mass, and the number of electrons in each shell.

Table 4–1.

Periodic table of the elements
(Based on Carbon 12 = 12.0000)

Metals

Transition elements

Rare earth elements

	IA	IIA	IIIB	IVB	VB	VIB	VIIB	VIIIB		
1	1 **H** 1.00797 (1)									
2	3 **Li** 6.939 (2/1)	4 **Be** 9.0122 (2/2)								
3	11 **Na** 22.9898 (2/8/1)	12 **Mg** 24.312 (2/8/2)								
4	19 **K** 39.102 (2/8/8/1)	20 **Ca** 40.08 (2/8/8/2)	21 **Sc** 44.956 (2/8/9/2)	22 **Ti** 47.90 (2/8/10/2)	23 **V** 50.942 (2/8/11/2)	24 **Cr** 51.996 (2/8/13/1)	25 **Mn** 54.9380 (2/8/13/2)	26 **Fe** 55.847 (2/8/14/2)	27 **Co** 58.9332 (2/8/15/2)	
5	37 **Rb** 85.47 (2/8/18/8/1)	38 **Sr** 87.62 (2/8/18/8/2)	39 **Y** 88.905 (2/8/18/9/2)	40 **Zr** 91.22 (2/8/18/10/2)	41 **Nb** 92.906 (2/8/18/12/1)	42 **Mo** 95.94 (2/8/18/13/1)	43 **Tc** [99*] (2/8/18/13/2)	44 **Ru** 101.07 (2/8/18/15/1)	45 **Rh** 102.905 (2/8/18/16/1)	
6	55 **Cs** 132.905 (2/8/18/18/8/1)	56 **Ba** 137.34 (2/8/18/18/8/2)	Lanthanide Series / 71 **Lu** 174.97 (2/8/18/32/9/2)	72 **Hf** 178.49 (2/8/18/32/10/2)	73 **Ta** 180.948 (2/8/18/32/11/2)	74 **W** 183.85 (2/8/18/32/12/2)	75 **Re** 186.2 (2/8/18/32/13/2)	76 **Os** 190.2 (2/8/18/32/14/2)	77 **Ir** 192.2 (2/8/18/32/15/2)	
7	87 **Fr** [223] (2/8/18/32/18/8/1)	88 **Ra** [226] (2/8/18/32/18/8/2)	Actinide Series / 103 **Lw** [257] (2/8/18/32/32/9/2)							

Lanthanide Series

57 **La** 138.91 (2/8/18/18/9/2)	58 **Ce** 140.12 (2/8/18/20/8/2)	59 **Pr** 140.907 (2/8/18/21/8/2)	60 **Nd** 144.24 (2/8/18/22/8/2)	61 **Pm** [147*] (2/8/18/23/8/2)	62 **Sm** 150.35 (2/8/18/24/8/2)	63 **Eu** 151.96 (2/8/18/25/8/2)

Actinide Series

89 **Ac** [227] (2/8/18/32/18/9/2)	90 **Th** 232.038 (2/8/18/32/18/10/2)	91 **Pa** [231] (2/8/18/32/20/9/2)	92 **U** 238.03 (2/8/18/32/21/9/2)	93 **Np** [237] (2/8/18/32/23/8/2)	94 **Pu** [242] (2/8/18/32/24/8/2)	95 **Am** [243] (2/8/18/32/25/9/2)

NOBLE GASES

		IIIA	IVA	VA	VIA	VIIA	VIIIA
							2 **He** 4.0026 (2)
		5 **B** 10.811 (2,3)	6 **C** 12.01115 (2,4)	7 **N** 14.0067 (2,5)	8 **O** 15.9994 (2,6)	9 **F** 18.9984 (2,7)	10 **Ne** 20.183 (2,8)
		13 **Al** 26.9815 (2,8,3)	14 **Si** 28.086 (2,8,4)	15 **P** 30.9738 (2,8,5)	16 **S** 32.064 (2,8,6)	17 **Cl** 35.453 (2,8,7)	18 **Ar** 39.948 (2,8,8)

Nonmetals

1B	2B	IIIA	IVA	VA	VIA	VIIA	VIIIA
28 **Ni** 58.71 (2,8,16,2)	29 **Cu** 63.54 (2,8,18,1)	30 **Zn** 65.37 (2,8,18,2)	31 **Ga** 69.72 (2,8,18,3)	32 **Ge** 72.59 (2,8,18,4)	33 **As** 74.9216 (2,8,18,5)	34 **Se** 78.96 (2,8,18,6)	35 **Br** 79.909 (2,8,18,7) — 36 **Kr** 83.80 (2,8,18,8)
46 **Pd** 106.4 (2,8,18,18,0)	47 **Ag** 107.870 (2,8,18,18,1)	48 **Cd** 112.40 (2,8,18,18,2)	49 **In** 114.82 (2,8,18,18,3)	50 **Sn** 118.69 (2,8,18,18,4)	51 **Sb** 121.75 (2,8,18,18,5)	52 **Te** 127.60 (2,8,18,18,6)	53 **I** 126.9044 (2,8,18,18,7) — 54 **Xe** 131.30 (2,8,18,18,8)
78 **Pt** 195.09 (2,8,18,32,16,2)	79 **Au** 196.967 (2,8,18,32,18,1)	80 **Hg** 200.59 (2,8,18,32,18,2)	81 **Tl** 204.37 (2,8,18,32,18,3)	82 **Pb** 207.19 (2,8,18,32,18,4)	83 **Bi** 208.980 (2,8,18,32,18,5)	84 **Po** [210*] (2,8,18,32,18,6)	85 **At** [210] (2,8,18,32,18,7) — 86 **Rn** [222] (2,8,18,32,18,8)

64 **Gd** 157.25 (2,8,18,25,9,2)	65 **Tb** 158.924 (2,8,18,27,8,2)	66 **Dy** 162.50 (2,8,18,28,8,2)	67 **Ho** 164.930 (2,8,18,29,8,2)	68 **Er** 167.26 (2,8,18,30,8,2)	69 **Tm** 168.934 (2,8,18,31,8,2)	70 **Yb** 173.04 (2,8,18,32,8,2)
96 **Cm** [247] (2,8,18,32,25,9,2)	97 **Bk** [249*] (2,8,18,32,27,8,2)	98 **Cf** [251*] (2,8,18,32,28,8,2)	99 **Es** [254] (2,8,18,32,29,8,2)	100 **Fm** [253] (2,8,18,32,30,8,2)	101 **Md** [256] (2,8,18,32,31,8,2)	102 **No** [253] (2,8,18,32,32,8,2)

Brackets indicate that the mass number for the isotope of longest known half-life is given. An asterisk indicates that the mass number for the best known isotope is given.

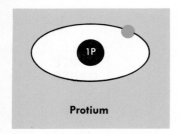

Figure 4-7. Protium is the isotope that is normally thought of as hydrogen: one proton, no neutrons.

In fact, no elements in the table have relative masses which are exactly whole numbers.

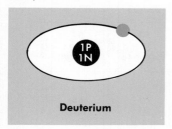

Figure 4-8. Deuterium, an isotope of hydrogen, has one proton and one neutron.

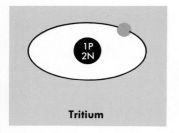

Figure 4-9. Tritium, a third isotope of hydrogen, has one proton and two neutrons.

How many protons are there in $^{25}_{12}$ Mg?

12 protons

PROBLEMS

1. What is the atomic number (Z)? *number of protons*
2. What is the atomic number of tungsten (W)? *74*

4:4 *Isotopes*

Study the periodic table. Count the number of elements whose masses are given in whole numbers. The number of these elements is smaller than you might think. Scientists consider the relative mass of both the proton and the neutron to be 1. The relative mass of the electron is zero (Section 3:2). These three particles are ordinarily indivisible. Then atomic masses should be whole numbers. They would be if Dalton had been correct in saying that all atoms of the same element are exactly the same.

However, some atoms of an element may have more neutrons than other atoms of the same element. Atoms of the same element with different numbers of neutrons are called **isotopes** (ie′ soh tohpz) (Section 3:3). Every element has at least two isotopes.

Protium is the most common isotope of hydrogen. It has an atomic mass of one. It contains one proton in its nucleus (Figure 4-7). A second isotope of hydrogen is called deuterium or heavy hydrogen. It has an atomic mass of two. Tritium is the third isotope of hydrogen. It has an atomic mass of three. This is because it contains two neutrons and one proton in its nucleus (Figure 4-9). How do you think these isotopes were named?

There are two methods to show the difference between isotopes of an element. One method uses the name of the element followed by the atomic mass. For example, oxygen 16 means the isotope of oxygen which has an atomic mass of 16. Carbon 12 is the isotope of carbon which has an atomic mass of 12. The numeral indicates which isotope is being discussed. Thus, an isotope of hydrogen might be called hydrogen 2, instead of deuterium. What is another name for tritium? *hydrogen 3*

The second method to show the difference between isotopes uses the isotope's symbol, atomic number, and atomic mass. For example, $^{12}_{\ 6}C$ is the carbon 12 isotope. The 12 is the atomic mass of this isotope. The 6 is the atomic number of the element. $^{23}_{11}Na$ tells the mass (23) and the atomic number (11) of an isotope of sodium. How many protons does this sodium isotope contain? How many protons and neutrons are in the nucleus? How many electrons are in an atom of this isotope?

$^{23}_{11}$ Na contains 11 protons and 12 neutrons in the nucleus and 11 electrons arranged 2 in the first energy level, 8 in the second, and 1 in the third.

6	2 4	19	2 8 8 1	9	2 7
C		**K**		**F**	
12.01115		39.102		18.9984	

Figure 4-10. What is the atomic number of each of these atoms?

Carbon - 6, Potassium - 19, Fluorine - 9

4:5 *Average Atomic Mass*

Every element with natural isotopes usually is found in nature as a mixture of these isotopes. For example, a sample of chlorine gas is likely to be a mixture of two isotopes. These are chlorine 35 and chlorine 37. The average mass of the atoms in this sample would be greater than 35 but less than 37. Thus, the atomic masses given for elements in the periodic table are **average atomic masses.** They are based upon the atomic masses of the naturally occurring isotopes. This average mass of an element is sometimes called the *atomic weight.*

Scientists can separate the isotopes of elements. They can determine how much of each is in the mixture of isotopes. From this, the average atomic mass is found.

Why is an average atomic mass needed?

Average atomic mass is needed because a mixture of isotopes occurs naturally.

EXAMPLE

Suppose scientists find an element which they call gymnasium. They determine that it has two isotopes: gymnasium 25, which makes up 40% of the sample; and gymnasium 30, which makes up 60% of the sample. What average atomic mass should they assign to gymnasium?

Solution 1: Since gymnasium 25 contributes 40% of the sample, it must contribute 40% of its mass to an average atomic mass. In the same manner, gymnasium 30 must contribute 60% of its mass to an average atomic mass.

Average atomic mass $= 0.40(25) + 0.60(30)$
$= 10 + 18 = 28$ a.m.u.

Solution 2: Consider 100 of the atoms. Since 40 of the atoms of gymnasium have mass 25 and 60 atoms have mass 30, the solution can be found simply by averaging.

Average atomic mass $= \dfrac{40(25) + 60(30)}{100} =$

$\dfrac{1000 + 1800}{100} = \dfrac{2800}{100} = 28$ a.m.u.

PROBLEMS

20.2 a.m.u.

3. Neon exists as two isotopes: 90% is neon 20 and 10% is neon 22. What is the average atomic mass of neon?

32.5 a.m.u.

4. The fictitious element, cranium, exists as 20% cranium 30, 50% cranium 32, and 30% cranium 35. What is the average atomic mass of cranium?

The element has isotopes.

5. The atomic mass of chlorine on the periodic table is not a whole number. What does this show?

4:6 Atomic Mass Number

Figure 4-11. Members of the halogen family are active non-metals. In density, color, and chemical activity are caused by differences in atomic structure.

Chemists often use the atomic mass number rather than the average atomic mass. The **atomic mass number** (A) of an element is its average atomic mass rounded to the nearest whole number. (Atomic mass number is sometimes called mass number.) For example, the average atomic mass of cobalt (Co) is 58.93. Its mass number is 59 (or A = 59). Barium (Ba) has an average atomic mass of 137.34. Its mass number is 137.

9 F 18.9984	2 7
17 Cl 35.453	2 8 7
35 Br 79.904	2 8 18 7
53 I 126.9044	2 8 18 18 7
85 At 210	2 8 18 32 18 7

PROBLEMS

6. An element has 30% isotope with atomic mass 27 and 70% isotope with atomic mass 30. What is its average atomic mass? *29.1 a.m.u.*

7. An element has 20% isotope 15 and 35% isotope 16. What remains is isotope 18. What is the element's average atomic mass and mass number? *16.7 a.m.u.*

8. Find Z and A for iron, radon, ytterbium, vanadium, and copper. *Fe, 26, 56; Rn, 86, 222; Yb, 70, 173; V, 23, 51; Cu, 29, 64. See Appendix C, page 464.*

4:7 Reading the Periodic Table—Columns

You can learn much about elements by understanding the periodic table. Each small block within the table contains the symbol, atomic number (Z), and average atomic mass of an element. The symbol represents the name of the element. What can you learn about an element from its atomic number?

Now study the periodic table. What happens to the atomic masses and atomic numbers as you read from left to right? What happens to them as you read down? Imagine you are given a periodic table without any numbers. How could you determine if one element had more protons than another?

Number of protons in the nucleus; number of electrons.

Z and A increase.

An element has more protons than any element above it or to the left of it.

Z and A increase.

In the periodic table, elements are arranged in *vertical columns*. Each column lists elements with similar properties. For example, fluorine, chlorine, bromine, iodine, and astatine are all in column VIIA. They are called the *halogen* family. These elements have similar properties.

In column VIIA, the elements have electrons in different shells. However, each element in this column has seven electrons in its outer shell. Therefore, these elements often react in the same way.

All but one of the elements in column VIIIA have eight electrons in their outer shells. Helium has two electrons in its outer shell. Why does helium not have eight electrons in its outer shell? How many electrons do you think an element in column IA has in its outer shell? The Roman numerals of the A columns show the number of electrons in the outer shell of each element. Nearly all elements in the B columns have two electrons in their outer shells.

Elements may be classified as *metals* or *nonmetals*. Look at the elements in column VIIIB and column IB. These elements are metals. They have many properties which are alike. Elements in column IA and column IIA are also classified as metals. In general, **metals** have one, two, or three electrons in their outer shells. Elements with more than four electrons in the outer shell are **nonmetals**.

How many electrons are in the outer shell in column VIA members?

Six electrons.

One electron is in the outer level.

Is sodium a metal?

Sodium is a metal; it has one electron in the outer shell and has other physical and chemical properties generally associated with metals such as luster, hardness, etc.

4:8   *Reading the Periodic Table—Rows*

The periodic table is also arranged in horizontal rows. Look at row two. This row lists lithium through neon (atomic numbers

Figure 4-12. Position of an element in the periodic table indicates its properties. The elements become less metallic from left to right across the periodic table.

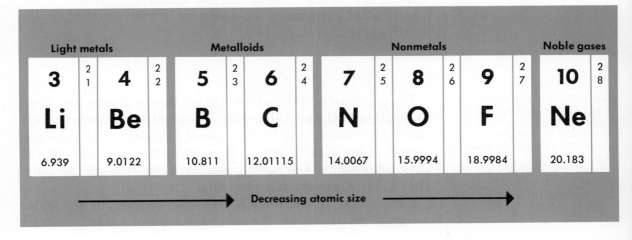

Light metals		Metalloids		Nonmetals			Noble gases
3 (2, 1) Li 6.939	4 (2, 2) Be 9.0122	5 (2, 3) B 10.811	6 (2, 4) C 12.01115	7 (2, 5) N 14.0067	8 (2, 6) O 15.9994	9 (2, 7) F 18.9984	10 (2, 8) Ne 20.183

Decreasing atomic size

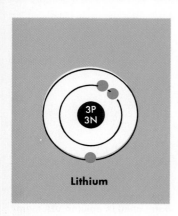

Figure 4-13. Lithium has three electrons. How many electrons does cesium have?

3 through 10). Lithium has one electron in its outer shell. Thus, it is a metal. Lithium forms compounds by giving up an electron. Beryllium (Z = 4, column IIA) has two electrons in the outer energy level. It is a metal. Beryllium forms compounds by giving up its two outer electrons. Boron (Z = 5) is listed as a *metalloid* (met''l oid). A metalloid is neither a metal nor a nonmetal. A **metalloid** has properties of both. Boron usually shares its three outer electrons. Boron combines covalently with other elements and forms compounds.

Carbon (Z = 6) is the first nonmetal in the second row. Carbon has four electrons in the outer shell. It forms compounds covalently. Carbon is also the last element in this row which occurs naturally as a solid. Nitrogen (Z = 7) occurs as a gas. Its five valence electrons are shared as it forms compounds covalently. The next element in the row is oxygen (Z = 8). Oxygen is a gas. It contains six electrons in the outer shell. Oxygen usually forms compounds covalently. In some cases, however, oxygen accepts electrons. Then it forms compounds through ionic bonding. Fluorine (Z = 9) is a gas. It has seven electrons in the outer shell. Fluorine forms compounds by gaining an electron.

Each row ends with a gas that contains eight electrons in the outer shell. These gases are very stable. They are called the *noble gases*. Until 1962, it was believed that noble gases did not form compounds. However, covalent compounds of these elements have now been formed. Neon (Z = 10) is the last member of the second row. It is the gas in neon signs.

Row four elements occur in columns which have not appeared in rows one, two, and three. These are the B columns. The metals in the B columns are called transition metals. Nearly all of them have two electrons in their outer shell, the fourth energy level.

Name another noble gas.
Helium, xenon, argon, radon are other noble gases.

4:9 *Chemical Activity*

The *chemical activity* of an element can be determined from its position in the periodic table. **Chemical activity** means how easily an element reacts with other elements. For example, oxygen is chemically active. It reacts with most elements to form compounds. The noble gases have low chemical activity. They react with very few elements.

Each metal in column IA has one electron in the outer energy level. However, the outer electron of cesium is much

The column IA metals (alkali metals) easily lose the single outer electron and form extremely stable inert gas configuration. Column IB metals (coinage metals) are noncorrosive and relatively unreactive because loss of the single outer shell electron does not result in the formation of an appreciably more stable ion.

farther from its nucleus than the outer electron of lithium. Cesium has a larger nuclear charge than lithium (more protons in the nucleus). It also has more electrons than lithium. In cesium, the electrons between the nucleus and the electron in the outer energy level tend to screen the attractive force of the nucleus. Thus, the outer electron is held more loosely in the cesium atom than in the lithium atom. Cesium can lose its electron more easily than lithium can lose its electron. Therefore, cesium is more chemically active than lithium. The same idea holds true for the other metals. The most chemically active metals are on the bottom left portion of the chart.

Can you tell the chemical activity of nonmetals by reading the periodic table? Fluorine and iodine combine with other elements. They attract an electron from another atom. The electrons of the fluorine atom are relatively close to the nucleus. This means the nuclear charge is effective in attracting other electrons. However, the outer energy level of iodine is far away from the nucleus. Its nuclear charge is screened by the electrons. Fluorine has greater attraction for other electrons. It is more active than iodine. The most active nonmetals are at the top right of the periodic table.

Which is more active, magnesium or barium?

Barium is more active than magnesium. On the periodic table barium is found on the lower left below magnesium.

Name another active nonmetal.

oxygen, sulfur, nitrogen

Note: Active metals are in the lower left; active nonmetals are in the upper right of the periodic table.

> EXPERIMENT. CAUTION: This experiment should be done only under the direct supervision of the teacher. When two or more substances are mixed, a color change may indicate a chemical change. Compare the chemical activity of the halogens. Obtain a test tube rack and five test tubes. To each test tube, add the materials indicated: (1) Add 5 ml of carbon tetrachloride to 10 ml of potassium iodide solution and shake. Add 5 ml of chlorine water and shake again. (2) Repeat, using bromine water instead of chlorine. (3) Repeat, using potassium bromide solution and chlorine water. (4) Repeat, using potassium bromide solution, iodine solution, and carbon tetrachloride. (5) Repeat, using sodium chloride solution, iodine solution, and carbon tetrachloride. Based on your observations, list chlorine, bromine, and iodine in order of decreasing chemical activity. How are your results related to the position of these elements in the periodic table? Why is fluorine not used in this experiment? *Too reactive.*

See Teacher's Guide at the front of this book.

Activity series: chlorine, bromine, iodine

Same as the order in the periodic table.

Figure 4-14.

The patterns that have been seen so far are repeated in each row of the periodic table. Move across the table from left to right. The elements change from metals to nonmetals. Bonding changes from ionic to covalent to ionic. In the columns, the most active metals are at the bottom left. The most active non-metals are at the upper right. Elements in the same column have different sizes and different chemical activities. Yet they exhibit similar properties.

MAIN IDEAS

p. 61   **1.** The atomic mass of an element is a relative value with respect to a standard mass.

p. 61   **2.** The carbon 12 isotope is the standard for atomic mass. One atomic mass unit (1 a.m.u.) $= \frac{1}{12}$ the mass of the carbon 12 atom.

p. 62   **3.** Mendeleev organized the elements according to their atomic masses.

p. 63   **4.** Moseley rearranged the periodic table according to atomic number.

p. 63   **5.** When elements are arranged in order of increasing atomic number, there is a periodic repetition of properties.

p. 63   **6.** The atomic number (Z) of an element is the number of protons in the nucleus.

p. 67   **7.** Average atomic mass of an element is the average mass of the element's isotopes.

p. 68   **8.** The mass number (A) of an element is its average atomic mass rounded to the nearest whole number.

p. 69   **9.** In the periodic table, families of elements occur in columns.

pp. 70-71   **10.** The most active metals are at the lower left of the periodic table. The most active nonmetals are at the upper right.

VOCABULARY

Write a sentence in which you correctly use each of the following words or terms.

atomic mass unit	metal
atomic number	metalloid
chemical activity	noble gas
halogen	nonmetal
isotope	periodic table
mass number	

STUDY QUESTIONS

Have students rewrite false statements to make the statements correct.

A. True or False

Determine whether each of the following sentences is true or false. (Do not write in this book.)

T **1.** Carbon 12 isotope has a mass of 12 atomic mass units.

T **2.** An atomic mass unit (a.m.u.) is equal to $\frac{1}{12}$ the mass of a carbon 12 atom.

T **3.** An atom with 6 protons, 6 neutrons, and 6 electrons has a mass of 12 a.m.u.

F **4.** Mendeleev's periodic table was arranged according to increasing atomic ~~number~~. *mass*

F **5.** Atomic number of an element equals the total number of protons, ~~neutrons, and~~ electrons in an element's atom. *or* *A*

F **6.** The letter ~~(Z)~~ is used as a symbol for atomic mass. *an electron*

F **7.** The mass of ~~a proton~~ is so small that it is considered zero. *an electron*

F **8.** Noble gases are chemically ~~active~~. *inactive*

T **9.** The most chemically active nonmetals are at the top right of the periodic table.

T **10.** The most chemically active metals are at the bottom left of the periodic table.

Some questions in part B may have more than one correct answer. Only one answer is required.

B. Multiple Choice

Choose one word or phrase that correctly completes each of the following sentences. (Do not write in this book.)

1. The first member of group VIIIA is (neon, <u>helium</u>, argon).

2. (<u>Moseley</u>, Mendeleev, Berzelius) discovered that periodic repetition of properties depends on the number of protons in an atom.

3. (Helium, Carbon, Sulfur) was not known to Mendeleev.

4. Hydrogen has (0, 1, 2, <u>3</u>, 4, 5) natural isotopes.

5. Isotopes differ in the number of (protons, electrons, <u>neutrons</u>).

6. The most active metals are found at the (upper left, <u>lower left</u>, lower right, upper right) of the periodic table.

7. Nonmetals are found on the (left, <u>right</u>, <u>top</u>, bottom) of the periodic table.

8. According to the periodic table, calcium should be more active than (<u>magnesium</u>, barium, <u>iron</u>, potassium).

9. According to the periodic table, sulfur should be less active than (<u>oxygen</u>, <u>chlorine</u>, selenium, phosphorus).

10. Boron has (0, 1, 2, <u>3</u>, 4, 5, 6, 7, 8) electrons in the outer energy level.

C.   Completion

Complete each of the following sentences with a word or phrase that will make the sentence correct. (Do not write in this book.)

ionic

1. Sodium will form compounds through __?__ bonding.

Na₂O, H₂S, etc.

2. An example of a compound formed between elements of group IA and group VIA is __?__.

Mendeleev

3. The "father" of the periodic table is __?__.

Francium

4. __?__ is the most active member of group IA.

three

5. Group IIIA elements have __?__ electrons in the outer shell.

cobalt, nickel

6. Two members of the transition elements are __?__ and __?__.

26, 30

7. Iron 56 has 26 protons, __?__ electrons, and __?__ neutrons.

protons, electron

8. Z = 9 tells us that an element has nine __?__.

transition

9. Metals in the B columns of the periodic table are called __?__ elements.

fluorine

10. The most chemically active halogen is __?__.

D.   How and Why

Iodine's outer electrons are farther from nucleus.

1. Why is iodine less chemically active than fluorine or chlorine?

Active nonmetals in the upper right corner; active metals in the lower left corner.

2. List some general rules for using the periodic table to discuss the activities of metals and nonmetals.

Metals - 1 to 3 e⁻ in outer shell, luster, malleable, conductor. Nonmetals - 4 to 8 e⁻ in outer shell, no luster, brittle, nonconductor.

3. An element is found 60% as isotope 30 and 40% as isotope 32. What is its mass number? *30.8 a.m.u.*

4. What are some differences between metals and nonmetals?

5. How do the transition metals differ from the other elements along a row? *Add e⁻ to inner shells, 2 e⁻ in outer shell.*

15 p, 15 e⁻, isotopes, A = 33, electron structure 2, 8, 5 probably a nonmetal

6. An element has Z = 15 and an atomic mass of 32.7. What can you tell about the element?

Mg has +2 valence
Cl has −1 valence
See Problem 4 for differences between metals and nonmetals.

7. Using only the periodic table, tell how magnesium differs from chlorine.

8. How could you remember the valences of the A groups on the periodic table? *The same as the Roman numeral.*

INVESTIGATIONS

1. The search for helium is an interesting story. Find out how helium got its name. Why was its discovery so unusual?

2. How did the rare earths get their name? Study one of these elements. Determine why they are "rare."

3. John Newlands and Johann Dobereiner made early attempts at classifying the elements. Find out about their work.

See Teacher's material at front of book for suggestions.

INTERESTING READING

Asimov, Isaac, *The Search for the Elements*. New York, Fawcett World Library, 1971.

"Evidence for Element 112." *Science News*, XCIX (February 20, 1971), pp. 127-128.

Sanderson, R. T., "How Should Periodic Groups Be Numbered?" *Chemistry*, XLIV (November, 1971), pp. 17-18.

Seaborg, Glenn T., and Valens, Evans G., *Elements of the Universe*. New York, E. P. Dutton & Company, 1958.

Wiegand, C. E., "Exotic Atoms." *Scientific American*, CCXXVII (November, 1972), pp. 102-108.

Wohlrabe, Raymond A., *Metals*. Philadelphia, J. B. Lippincott Company, 1965.

Included in the Teacher's Section is a review of the periodic table. The students are asked to fill out, from the information known, a blank periodic table of the thirty known elements found on Mars. The exercise could be used as an open book test to determine how well the students understand the chapter.

Columns of the periodic table are called families. Elements in families exhibit similar properties. The study of families leads to generalizations about chemical properties. Among these are diatomic gases, allotropy, photoconductivity, multiple proportions, and spectrum analysis.

Families of Elements

GOAL: You will gain an understanding of the properties of chemical families, diatomic gases, allotropy, photoconductivity, multiple proportions, and spectrum analysis.

Every known element is unique—it has its own individual properties. However, scientists classify elements into families because some elements have similar properties. Each vertical column on the periodic table represents a **family**, a group of elements with a few similar properties. *Alkali metals, alkaline earth metals, halogens,* and *noble gases* are examples of families of elements.

5:1 Halogen Family

The family is usually given a name. The members of a family have a similar arrangement of valence electrons, and they tend to react similarly.

Table 5–1. The Halogen Family

Element	Z	A	M.P.(°C)	B.P.(°C)	Description
Fluorine (F)	9	19	−223	−187	pale yellow gas
Chlorine (Cl)	17	35	−102	−34.6	greenish-yellow gas
Bromine (Br)	35	80	−7.3	58.8	reddish-brown liquid
Iodine (I)	53	127	114	183	steel-gray crystals
Astatine (At)	85	(210)	—	—	radioactive solid

Students could be assigned elements for reports.

Chlorine (kloh′ reen) is added to swimming pool water to kill germs and to laundry water to bleach clothes. In its element form, chlorine is a yellowish-green gas with a sharp odor. Chlorine is a member of the **halogen family**, Column VIIA of the periodic table. In addition to chlorine, the halogen family includes **fluorine** (floo′ ren), **bromine** (broh′ meen), **iodine** (ie′ oh dien), and **astatine** (ahs′ tah teen). In their uncombined (element) form all the halogens are poisonous and burn the skin.

Halogen means "salt-producer." Halogen elements combine with metals to form compounds called *salts*. Table salt (sodium chloride, NaCl) is the salt with which you are most familiar.

Sodium

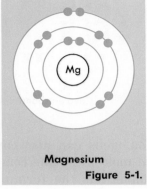

Magnesium

Figure 5-1.

Chlorine

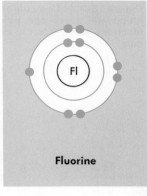

Fluorine

Each halogen has seven electrons in its outer shell. One more electron is needed to complete the outer shell. When a halogen atom combines with a metal, the halogen atom gains that one electron. For example, potassium combines with chlorine to form the salt called potassium chloride (KCl). An ionic bond is formed. The chlorine atom gains one electron. The potassium atom loses one electron. As a result, a negatively charged chloride ion is formed. Also, a positively charged potassium ion is formed. *Potassium has one more proton than electron and chlorine has one more electron than proton.*

How many electrons "complete" an outer shell?

An atom with eight electrons in its outer level represents a very stable electron configuration. (Helium with two electrons is also stable.) In bonding, atoms gain or lose or share enough electrons to complete the octet configuration.

PROBLEMS

1. Draw a diagram of a chlorine atom and potassium atom. Begin by finding their atomic numbers in the periodic table. Show how these atoms become ions and form a compound.

See Teacher's material for this chapter.

2. Draw a diagram of a sodium atom and bromine atom. Show how these atoms combine to form the salt called sodium bromide (NaBr).

See Teacher's material for this chapter.

Halogens can also form covalent bonds (Section 3:6). Two like halogen atoms can share one pair of electrons between them and form a halogen molecule (Figure 5–3). In the gaseous phase, the halogens exist as *diatomic* molecules. **Diatomic** means that each molecule is composed of two atoms.

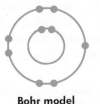

Bohr model

Electron dot model

Figure 5-2. Fluorine may be represented by several different models.

Cl_2
Covalent-bond

BrCl
Covalent-bond

Figure 5-4. Bromine and chlorine each contribute an electron to form a BrCl molecule.

Mention the value of fluorine compounds (in small amounts) in toothpaste and water to prevent tooth decay. Perhaps a student would like to report on this to the class.

What kind of bond would hydrogen and fluorine form?

covalent bond

Where is the most plentiful source of brine?

seawater

Figure 5-5. Teflon® is a compound of fluorine and carbon.

Two different halogens can also combine covalently with each other to form molecules. One compound of bromine and chlorine, for example, has the formula BrCl. Its electronic structure is shown in Figure 5–4. Many other halogen molecules of this type can form.

In addition to the properties common to this family, each halogen has special properties of its own.

Fluorine. Fluorine is the most reactive nonmetallic element. It is an extremely corrosive, pale yellow gas. It is never found free in nature. Compounds containing fluorine are called *fluorides*. Free fluorine is obtained by passing an electric current through molten fluorides. The decomposition of a compound into simpler substances by passing an electric current through the compound is called **electrolysis** (ee lek trawl′ i sis).

Fluorine reacts explosively with hydrogen to form hydrogen fluoride (HF). In water solution, hydrogen fluoride can be used to etch glass. Fluorine also combines with oxygen to form many different compounds. Among these are OF_2 and O_2F_2. The "non-stick" material on cooking utensils is a compound made from fluorine and carbon.

Chlorine. Chlorine is the most abundant halogen. It is twice as plentiful in nature as fluorine and one hundred times more abundant than bromine. Chlorine does not occur free in nature. It is usually found chemically combined with sodium, potassium, magnesium, or calcium. It is usually obtained by the electrolysis of molten sodium chloride or saltwater brine.* It is only slightly less active than fluorine. Unlike fluorine, chlorine can be liquefied easily under pressure.

Chlorine forms compounds with hydrogen and oxygen. The gas, hydrogen chloride, is a compound of hydrogen and chlorine. It becomes hydrochloric acid (HCl) in water solution. Hypochlorous acid (HClO) is a bleach commonly used in laundries. Chlorine dioxide (ClO_2) is the best known of the oxygen-chlorine compounds. It has wide use in bleaching flour

_____
* Brine is a very concentrated saltwater or ocean water solution. Chlorides and other compounds such as bromides are also present in a brine.

Bruce Charlton

Figure 5-6. Chlorine compounds have many everyday uses. One of the most common is disinfectant for swimming pools.

and paper. It is also used in preparing other chlorine compounds. Chlorine compounds are also used to disinfect drinking water.

Bromine. In nature, bromine is never found as an element. It is always combined as a bromide. Bromides are generally found in seawater and brine wells. Bromine is prepared commercially by treating seawater or brine with chlorine. Chlorine is more reactive than bromine. Thus, chlorine replaces bromine in compounds and free bromine is released. At room temperature, bromine is a dark red liquid with a reddish-brown cloud above it.

Bromine in the form of silver bromide (AgBr) is used to make photographic film. Bromine compounds are added to gasoline to prevent the poor combustion that causes "knock" in car engines.

Iodine. Iodine, like the other halogens, is found only in the combined state in nature. Like bromine, iodine can be obtained from seawater. Free iodine also results from the burning of

What kind of bond would ClO_2 have?

covalent

Carl England

Figure 5-7. Iodine crystals.

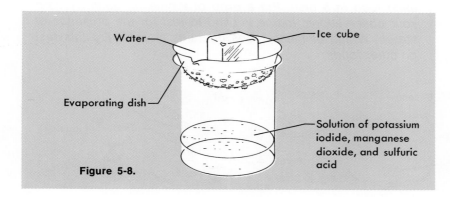

Water

Ice cube

Evaporating dish

Solution of potassium iodide, manganese dioxide, and sulfuric acid

Figure 5-8.

certain kinds of seaweed. Iodine has a property called *sublimation*. **Sublimation** (sub' li mae' shun) is the change of a solid directly to a vapor without passing through a liquid phase. Iodine is purified by first making the impure iodine sublime. Then its vapor is crystallized on another surface (Figure 5–8).

At room temperature, iodine is a gray, lustrous solid. It has many of the physical properties of a metal. Iodine compounds are essential to the human diet. They are also used in medicine.

This conforms to the general rule that elements on the right of the periodic table become more metallic near the bottom.

CAUTION: Use a well-ventilated room for this experiment. Do not expose students to direct skin contact or allow them to breathe the vapors of iodine or CCl₄.

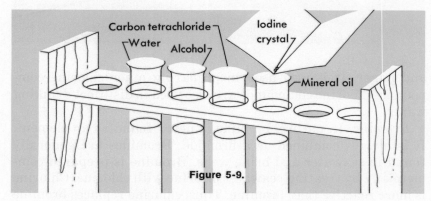

Figure 5-9.

This experiment should be performed only as a teacher demonstration.

You may wish to try other solvents also.

EXPERIMENT. Set up a series of labeled test tubes. Each should contain a single liquid: water, alcohol, carbon tetrachloride, mineral oil. Add a crystal of iodine to each liquid. Mix. In which of the four liquids does iodine dissolve? Add a drop of liquid starch solution to each and observe any change. Devise an experiment to determine whether it is the iodine or the liquid which reacts with starch.

You might like to use a control such as distilled water. Add a drop of liquid starch to each test tube.

ACTIVITY. Obtain a potato, a piece of bread, a banana, a carrot, and some tincture of iodine. Place a small piece of each food in a dish. Put a drop of iodine on each. Record your observations. Iodine is used to test for the presence of starch. Which of these foods contains starch? Try this test on other foods.

What is a test for starch?

iodine forms a blue complex with starch

Figure 5-10.

Astatine. The last member of the halogen family is a man-made element, astatine. It has properties similar to iodine but is a radioactive element. Most of its isotopes have short half-lives. This means the nuclei of these atoms break up rapidly to form other elements. Astatine can form compounds with other halogens.

PROBLEMS

3. Write the chemical formula for a molecule of fluorine, of chlorine, of bromine, and of iodine. F_2, Cl_2, Br_2, I_2

4. Draw a diagram of an atom of fluorine and an atom of bromine. How are they alike?

See Teacher's Material for diagram. Each has seven electrons in its outer shell.

5. The formula for calcium fluoride is CaF_2. Draw a diagram of these atoms and show how they combine to form a compound.

See Teacher's Material.

5:2　Oxygen Family

Element	Z	A	M.P.(°C)	B.P.(°C)	Description
Oxygen (O)	8	16	−219	−183	colorless gas
Sulfur (S)	16	32	119	445	yellow solid
Selenium (Se)	34	79	220	685	reddish solid
Tellurium (Te)	52	128	450	1390	gray solid
Polonium (Po)	84	(210)	—	—	radioactive solid

Table 5–2. The Oxygen Family

What members of the oxygen family are gases at room temperature?

The name oxygen is derived from the Greek words oxys (sharp) and genes (to form). Lavoisier believed that oxygen was an essential part of every acid. Oxygen is the most abundant element on our earth and is necessary for the continuous existence of most living things. Twenty-one percent of the atmosphere is oxygen. It accounts for 50% of the weight of rocks and eight-ninths of the weight of water.

Column VIA in the periodic table is called the **oxygen** (ahk′ si jen) **family.** Unlike the halogens, the oxygen family members are all found in nature both in the free state and chemically combined. Most members form covalent bonds. Each atom has six electrons in its outer shell. Each has two electrons to share with atoms of other elements to form compounds. Sulfur in hydrogen sulfide (H_2S) is an example of an element sharing electrons (Figure 5–11).

The elements of the oxygen family form *allotropes* (al′ oh trohps). **Allotropes** are different molecular forms of the same element. They result from the formation of molecules with different numbers of the same atoms. Oxygen, for example, exists free as the diatomic molecule, O_2. However, under certain conditions, some molecules of O_2 can be changed into ozone, O_3. During thunderstorms, for example, some oxygen in the air is changed to ozone. Both diatomic oxygen molecules

Figure 5-11. In H_2S, sulfur forms a covalent bond with each hydrogen atom.

Electronic structure of H_2S

Paul Nesbit

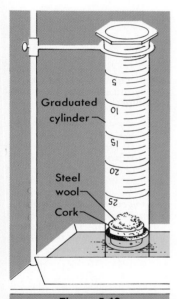

Graduated cylinder

Steel wool

Cork

Figure 5-13.

The water has risen in the cylinder to replace the oxygen which united with the steel wool.

Why is the oxygen molecule paramagnetic?

The unpaired electron in each atom can be affected by a magnetic field.

and *triatomic* ozone molecules (composed of three atoms of oxygen) are allotropes of oxygen. Oxygen is the only member of the oxygen family which exists as a diatomic gas at room temperature. All other members are solids. Their properties become more metallic as the atomic masses increase.

Oxygen. Oxygen is one of the most reactive nonmetallic elements. (Fluorine is the most reactive nonmetallic element.) Oxygen can be found in chemical combination with nearly every other element. Combined oxygen makes up nearly 50 percent by weight of the earth's crust. Approximately 20 percent of the total volume of air is free oxygen.

ACTIVITY. Place a piece of steel wool on a cork floating in a pan of water. Cover with an inverted 25-ml graduated cylinder. Allow to stand for one week. Observe the water level and the appearance of the steel wool during this time. Explain your observations.

Diatomic oxygen (O_2) does not appear to follow the *rule of eight*. This rule states that a molecule is formed if the combining atoms have a shared total of eight electrons in the outer shell. The oxygen molecule appears to share only one pair of electrons. Each atom has an unpaired electron. This causes the molecule to be *paramagnetic* (par' ah mag net' ik). **Paramagnetic** means attracted or repelled by a magnetic field. One possible structure for the oxygen molecule is given in Figure 5–15a. Molecules of ozone (O_3) are not affected by a magnetic field. Thus, we assume that all the electrons are paired. One possible structure for ozone is shown in Figure 5–15b.

Figure 5-14. The sand on this beach is an oxygen compound called silicon dioxide, or silica. What other oxygen-containing materials are shown?

air, water, many organic materials

Without free oxygen, most life on earth could not exist. Compounds of oxygen are also extremely important to man. Water (H_2O) is perhaps the most important oxide. Another compound of hydrogen and oxygen is hydrogen peroxide (H_2O_2). It is used as a disinfectant and as a bleach. Common sand is an oxygen compound called silicon dioxide, or silica (SiO_2). Rust is iron oxide (Fe_2O_3).

In the laboratory, oxygen is usually prepared by heating potassium chlorate ($KClO_3$) and manganese dioxide (MnO_2). Manganese dioxide is a *catalyst* (kat′ ah lizt) here. A **catalyst** is a substance which increases or decreases the speed of a chemical reaction but is not itself changed in the reaction. In this experiment, the MnO_2 is used to speed up the reaction.

Figure 5-15. Unpaired electrons in the oxygen molecule (a) cause it to be paramagnetic. Ozone (b) is not paramagnetic. All its electrons are paired.

EXPERIMENT. Gently mix 5 g of potassium chlorate with 2.5 g of manganese dioxide. DO NOT GRIND THE MIXTURE. Place the mixture in a Pyrex test tube. Arrange the apparatus as shown in Figure 5–16. Heat the test tube. Collect one bottle of oxygen gas by water displacement. Discard the contents of the first bottle since it contains mostly air from the test tube and delivery tube. Collect three more bottles of oxygen. Cover each with a glass plate and stand them upright. Remove the delivery tube from the water as soon as you stop the heating. Light a wooden splint and blow it out so it glows red. Thrust the glowing splint into the first bottle of oxygen. What do you observe? Hold a piece of fine steel wool with tongs and heat it until it glows red. Lower it into the second bottle. What do you observe? In a deflagrating spoon, heat a small piece of sulfur until it glows red. Lower it into the third bottle. What do you observe? Name the three oxygen compounds you think are produced.

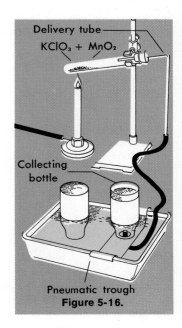

Delivery tube
$KClO_3 + MnO_2$
Collecting bottle
Pneumatic trough
Figure 5-16.

Splint bursts into flame (O_2 supports combustion). The steel wool glows brightly (rapid oxidation). Sulfur burns with a blue flame. Carbon dioxide, iron (III) oxide, sulfur dioxide are formed.

B.F. Goodrich Co.

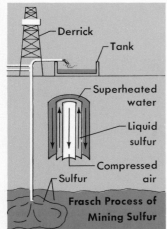

Frasch Process of Mining Sulfur

Figure 5-18. In mining sulfur, superheated water and compressed air are forced down the outer and inner of three concentric pipes. The molten sulfur and water foam are forced up the middle pipe. The sulfur mixture is sprayed into molds where the water evaporates and the sulfur remains.

The atoms within the molecules are held together by covalent bonds. The molecules are attached to other molecules by weak van der Waals forces.

Figure 5-19. The formula for a rhombic sulfur molecule is S_8.

Sulfuric acid is the most widely used of all industrial chemicals. There are not many industries that do not use sulfuric acid in some manner.

Oxygen is most often prepared commercially by the *distillation* (dis' tah lae shun) of liquid air. In **distillation,** a gas mixture is liquefied and cooled to a low temperature. The liquefied gases with lower boiling points are then allowed to boil off first. When air is distilled, liquid oxygen begins to boil at −183°C. It is drawn off into another container. Repeated liquefaction and distillation produces an almost pure oxygen sample. Large amounts of oxygen can be produced by electrolysis of water. However, this method is expensive on a commercial scale.

Sulfur. Sulfur (sul' fer), like oxygen, is found both free and combined in nature. Sulfur is generally found chemically combined with metals in the form of mineral ores. Most commercial sulfur is obtained from deposits in the southern and southwestern United States. Sulfur is "mined" by the Frasch process (Figure 5–18). This process produces sulfur which is more than 90 percent pure. Like iodine (p. 80), sulfur can be further purified through sublimation.

Sulfur also exists in several allotropic forms. The most common form is *rhombic* (rahm' bik) sulfur. In this form, eight sulfur atoms are joined in a ring (Figure 5–19). Many other allotropes of sulfur exist. Most of these are long chains of sulfur atoms.

Sulfur unites with some metals to form compounds called sulfides. An example is sodium sulfide (Na_2S). Sulfur unites directly with oxygen to form sulfur dioxide (SO_2) or, in some cases, sulfur trioxide (SO_3). Sulfur compounds in the air, such as hydrogen sulfide (H_2S), are responsible for the tarnish on silver (Ag_2S). Certain compounds which contain sulfur, oxygen, and a third element have commercial value. These compounds may be sulfates, such as sodium sulfate (Na_2SO_4), or sulfites, such as sodium sulfite (Na_2SO_3). Sulfuric acid (H_2SO_4) is one of the most important compounds containing sulfur and oxygen. Commercial products which contain sulfur include insecticides, fertilizers, drugs, and rubber.

EXPERIMENT. Place 5 ml of cadmium nitrate, zinc sulfate, antimony chloride, and copper sulfate solutions separately in four test tubes. Label each tube. Cover the label with a blank piece of paper. Have a classmate arrange the test tubes in a rack so you do not know the contents of each. Add a few drops of hydrogen sulfide solution to each. From the color of the solid formed, try to identify the metal. Then check your results against the labels. Table 5–3 lists the colors of various metal sulfides.

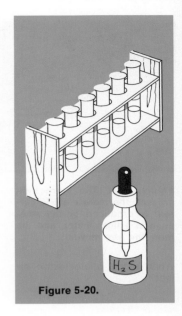

Figure 5-20.

This is a method of determining the identity of compounds.

Table 5–3. *Sulfides*	
Sulfide Compound	*Color*
Antimony (Sb_2S_3)	orange
Arsenic (As_2S_3)	yellow
Bismuth (Bi_2S_3)	brown
Cadmium (CdS)	yellow
Copper (CuS)	black
Lead (PbS)	black
Silver (Ag_2S)	black
Zinc (ZnS)	white

Selenium. Selenium (see le′ nee um) can be found in deposits of free sulfur. It is also an impurity in sulfides and in copper. Most selenium is obtained as a by-product in the electrolysis of copper ore to produce copper.

Selenium is a poison. Plants can absorb selenium from soil. They then pass the poison along to animals that eat the plant. Insects which feed on plants are often killed in this way. Often small amounts of selenium are put in the soil or sprayed on the leaves. Selenium then passes through the entire plant without hurting it. Eating the plant poisons the insect.

Selenium has metallic properties. It can conduct an electric current (Section 18:2). An electric current is a flow of electrons. Metals tend to give up electrons readily (Section 4:7). This property makes metals good conductors because the electrons can move through the metal. Nonmetals tend to hold electrons tightly. Therefore, nonmetals are poor conductors. In the dark, selenium is a poor conductor. However, when exposed to light, it becomes a good conductor. Selenium gives up electrons when exposed to light. For this reason, selenium

Kenn Knowlton

Figure 5-21. The more light present, the more electric current is produced by the selenium in a light meter, and the more the arm moves.

Figure 5-21. The more light present, the more electric current is produced by the selenium in a light meter, and the more the arm moves.

What is the photoelectric effect?

Light shining on some metals releases electrons.

Richard M. Fetters

Figure 5-22. The red color of the glass used in traffic lights is produced by adding large amounts of selenium to the glass.

Polonium was first discovered by the Curie's during the same experiments in which they discovered radium. Formerly it was extracted from pitchblende but now it is synthesized in nuclear reactors. Polonium has a half-life of 138 days which makes it extremely radioactive. After about 138 days a sample of polonium emits only half as

is called a *photoconductor*. This means that its ability to pass along electrons is controlled by light.

Photoconductors find good use in photographic light meters. One kind of light meter uses a selenium *photocell*. This **photocell** is made with a small plate of copper, a selenium layer, and a gold film that transmits light. Electric wires go to both the copper film and the gold film. Electricity does not flow through the wires until light hits the meter. Then the electrons in the selenium move. An electric current is produced. This causes an arm to move on a dial which indicates the light intensity. As the light intensity increases, the current increases, and the arm moves a greater distance. Selenium photocells are also used in counting people as they enter buildings and for setting off burglar alarms.

Small amounts of selenium are added during the manufacture of glass. Selenium counteracts the green color due to iron impurities in glass. If a great deal of selenium is used, the glass becomes red. This red glass is used in traffic lights.

Tellurium. Tellurium (te leu' ree um), like selenium, is found in many minerals. It is prepared as a by-product in the refining of ores. Its photoconductivity is small, but tellurium has some use in the electronics industry. Tellurium is poisonous. It produces a garlic odor on the breath and in the perspiration of people working with it.

Polonium. Polonium (poh loh' nee um) is an extremely radioactive metal (Section 20:3). It occurs naturally in pitchblende ore. Madame Curie, a French chemist (1867-1934), discovered this element in 1898.

PROBLEMS   See Teacher's material for
diagram.   six

6. Draw a diagram of an atom of oxygen and an atom of sulfur. How many electrons are in the outer shell of each?

7. How many electrons are in the outermost shell of each element of the oxygen family? *six*

many particles per minute as at the start. After 138 more days its activity is again halved and so on.

8. How can you account for the similarity in the chemical properties of the elements of the oxygen family?

They have similar electron configurations. Each have six electrons in the outer shell.

5:3 Nitrogen Family

Table 5–4. *The Nitrogen Family*

Element	*Z*	*A*	*M.P.(°C)*	*B.P.(°C)*	*Description*
Nitrogen (N)	7	14	−210	−196	colorless gas
Phosphorus (P)	15	31	44.1	280	white or red solid
Arsenic (As)	33	75	—	—*	gray or yellow solid
Antimony (Sb)	51	122	631	1380	gray solid
Bismuth (Bi)	83	209	271	1500	gray metal

*Gray arsenic sublimes at 450°C.

Column VA in the periodic table is called the **nitrogen** (nie′ troh jen) **family.** Each member of the nitrogen family has five electrons in its outer shell. Thus, these elements usually form covalent compounds. The family contains a wide range of physical properties. For example, nitrogen is a gas. Both nitrogen and phosphorus are nonmetals. Bismuth is a metal. Arsenic and antimony have some properties of both metals and nonmetals. For this reason these two elements are called *metalloids* (met′ l oids).

What are covalent compounds?

Covalent compounds are formed when atoms share electrons.

Elements in the nitrogen family are generally less reactive than elements in the halogen and oxygen families. The five electrons in the outer shell are responsible for this property. It is unlikely that these elements will gain three electrons or lose five electrons. However, they do share electrons with atoms of other elements. In some instances, they share three or even all five electrons.

Figure 5-23. The outer energy level of each member of the nitrogen family contains five electrons.

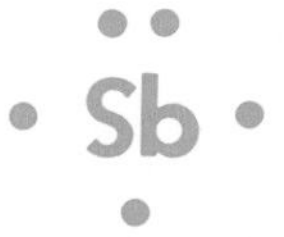

Nitrogen. Nitrogen is required by every living thing. Air is approximately 79 percent free nitrogen. However, most living things can not get nitrogen directly from the air. Nitrogen for life comes from compounds found as minerals in the ground, formed during electrical storms, or produced by bacteria.

Like oxygen, nitrogen is usually prepared by the distillation of liquid air. Liquid nitrogen boils at —196°C. Very pure nitrogen can be formed by heating some nitrogen compounds. For example, ammonium nitrite (NH_4NO_2) can be carefully heated to produce nitrogen (N_2) and water (H_2O).

Figure 5-24. The triple bond (three pairs of electrons) of the N_2 molecule makes it extremely stable.

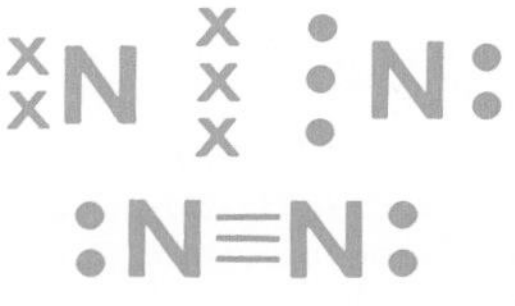

Free nitrogen is found as a diatomic molecule. The two nitrogen atoms are held together with a triple covalent bond

Be sure that the students understand the idea of double and triple covalent bonds before proceeding further.

Sulfuric acid

Mixture of nitrate and iron sulfate solutions

Figure 5-25.

What is the test for the nitrate ion?

State the law of multiple proportions.

The chemical name is generally preferred, but there are many compounds that have long been named by their common names. These more common names are usually retained. Examples are nitrous oxide, nitric oxide.

(Figure 5–25). Two nitrogen atoms each share three electrons. Thus, the nitrogen molecule has little chemical activity. However, the molecule does form many compounds which are important to man. One of these compounds is ammonia (NH_3). Others are Chile saltpeter, a common name for sodium nitrate ($NaNO_3$); saltpeter, a common name for potassium nitrate (KNO_3); and nitric acid (HNO_3).

EXPERIMENT. This is a test for the nitrate ion (NO_3^-). CAUTION: This activity should be done only under the supervision of your teacher. (1) Add 5 ml of a solution of sodium or potassium nitrate to a large Pyrex test tube. Add 5 ml of a freshly prepared saturated iron sulfate ($FeSO_4$) solution. Mix. Then slant the tube. Carefully add 1 to 2 ml of concentrated sulfuric acid by allowing it to run down the inside of the test tube. Look for a "brown ring" at the line between the acid and mixed solutions.

Repeat Part 1 using 5 ml of distilled water in place of nitrate solution. Does a brown ring form? Why?

Many different nitrogen-oxygen compounds exist. These compounds are excellent for illustrating the *law of multiple proportions*. The **law of multiple proportions** states that the same two or more elements may unite to form different compounds. If the mass of one element is held constant, the ratio of the combining masses of the other elements will be in whole numbers. Various nitrogen oxides are shown in Table 5–5. What is the ratio of the masses in each compound?

Table 5–5.	Nitrogen Oxides		
Formula		Chemical Name	Common Name
N_2O	7:4	nitrogen (I) oxide	nitrous oxide
NO	7:8	nitrogen (II) oxide	nitric oxide
N_2O_3	7:12	nitrogen (III) oxide	dinitrogen trioxide
NO_2	7:16	nitrogen (IV) oxide	nitrogen dioxide
N_2O_5	7:20	nitrogen (V) oxide	dinitrogen pentoxide

Phosphorus. Like oxygen and sulfur, phosphorus (faws' foh rus) has allotropes. The two most common are white phosphorus and red phosphorus. White phosphorus is produced from calcium phosphate ($Ca_3(PO_4)_2$). It is first formed as a gas. Then the gas is condensed under water in the form of P_4 molecules. The water also prevents the phosphorus from reacting immediately with the oxygen in air.

Oxides of phosphorus are phosphorus (III) oxide, P_2O_3; phosphorus (IV) oxide, P_2O_4; and phosphorus (V) oxide, P_2O_5.

Chemists

If you were a chemist, what would you do? There are thousands of possibilities. You might work in a small college or in the research laboratories of a large industry. Perhaps you would study the impurities in polluted water or help develop a better method for sewage treatment. Right now there are chemists doing these things.

Chemists are seeking new detergents and safer insecticides. As a chemist you might develop a new textile or improve gasolines for car engines. By using your skills to examine clues, you might even help to solve crimes.

Chemistry is the largest area of employment in physical science. According to the 1970 census, the United States had almost 137,000 chemists. About three-fourths of all chemists work for private in-

dustry. Nearly half of these work for companies which manufacture chemicals. The rest are employed by firms which make textiles, foods, paper, paints, and hundreds of other products.

Chemists study matter. They seek to learn all they can about the properties of matter. Much of a chemist's work is research. Man-made textiles for clothing, hundreds of kinds of plastics, and synthetic rubber are some of the applications of chemical research.

Chemistry is a vast field. No chemist can hope to know everything about it. Most chemists specialize. Organic chemists, for example, study only carbon and compounds containing carbon. Analytical chemists try to identify and measure components in mixtures and compounds.

Associated Photographers, Inc.

Instruments such as this infrared spectrophotometer help chemists identify the different materials in waste water.

solve manufacturers' production problems. These problems could include what to do with chemical wastes or how to get the most product from a given amount of raw material.

Like chemists, chemical engineers usually specialize in a particular production problem or type of chemical product.

Focus on Physical Science Chemical Engineer

Chemical engineers find ways to apply the laboratory discoveries of chemists. Using the principles of both chemistry and engineering, they develop equipment in which chemical or physical changes take place. The machines they build are designed to do the best job at the lowest cost. Chemical engineers also help

General Motors Corp.

Chemistry sometimes requires careful work with complicated and fragile equipment.

E. I. duPont de Nemours & Co.

This organic chemist is preparing a compound which may eventually become a new polymer.

Figure 5-26. Phosphorus is necessary to both plant and animal life.

Red phosphorus is formed slowly from chains of white phosphorus molecules. Red phosphorus is more stable than white phosphorus. At room temperature, red phosphorus normally has little chemical activity. However, at higher temperatures it forms many compounds. Phosphine (PH_3), with a structure like ammonia (NH_3), is one such compound.

Like nitrogen, phosphorus forms a number of oxides. Phosphates are an important class of phosphorus compounds. Phosphates are compounds of metals with phosphorus and oxygen. For example, calcium phosphate ($Ca_3(PO_4)_2$) is present in bones. Some phosphates serve as water softeners. Some are used as fertilizers. Ammonium phosphate ($(NH_4)_3PO_4$) is used as a fertilizer because of its nitrogen and phosphorus content. Both nitrogen and phosphorus are essential to plant growth.

Phosphorus is essential for life. In small amounts, phosphorus provides a means for storing energy in the body. It is a constituent of DNA, a compound found in genes. The ease with

Name a phosphate found in fertilizer.

ammonium phosphate, $(NH_4)_3PO_4$

DNA is short for deoxyribonucleic acid. Molecules of DNA are long chains interlocked to form a double helix. The molecules are formed by the repetition of a small number of different and comparatively simple chemical compounds.

Figure 5-27. Excess phosphorus in water may cause plant life to multiply until it uses up all the oxygen dissolved in the water.

which phosphorus burns makes it useful in matches. In large amounts it harms the human nervous system. Excessive use of phosphates in detergents may contribute to water pollution. Waste water from the laundry is joined by the runoff from fields fertilized with phosphates and nitrates. These wastes often end up in lakes and rivers. As a result, water plants and lower life forms are fed a diet rich in nutrients. They increase rapidly and use up the supply of oxygen dissolved in the water. Thus, they deprive fish and other aquatic life of oxygen.

Arsenic. Arsenic (ahr sen' ik) compounds are widespread in nature. The most common consist of arsenic and sulfur. Two allotropic forms of arsenic can be prepared from these compounds. Yellow arsenic exists as As_4 molecules. It is a nonmetal. Yellow arsenic will slowly change to gray arsenic. Gray arsenic is a metal. Perhaps you know that arsenic is a poison. However, it also has uses in medicine. Salvarsan, an arsenic compound, was the forerunner of many of the modern "miracle" drugs.

Antimony and Bismuth. Both antimony (an' ti mohn ee) and bismuth (biz' muth) have metallic properties. Bismuth is a true metal. These two elements have many properties in common with phosphorus and arsenic. They form similar compounds. Both antimony and bismuth can be used in *alloys* with other metals. Bismuth is often included in alloys because it has a low melting point. It is used in automatic sprinkler systems. Heat from a fire melts the bismuth alloy plugs in water pipes. The sprinklers then turn on.

Both antimony and bismuth are used in plates of storage batteries. Antimony and bismuth also have the unusual property of expanding when they are cooled. Thus, when these metals are cooled, they expand to fill molds. Most metals would contract away from the walls of the molds. This makes antimony and bismuth useful in casting type metal for sharp printing.

Figure 5-28. Because it ignites easily, phosphorus is used in match heads.

Carl England

Figure 5-29. Fire damage to many buildings has been prevented by automatic sprinklers. Bismuth alloys are used in a plug which melts when heated. Water then sprays out.

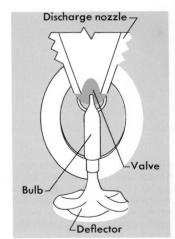

PROBLEMS   *See Teacher's material for diagram.*

9. Draw a diagram of a nitrogen atom and a phosphorus atom. How many electrons are in the outer atomic shell of each? *five*

10. How many electrons are in the outer shell of each member of the nitrogen family? *five*

11. What types of bonds are most often formed by members of the nitrogen family? *covalent*

5:4 Alkali Metals

Table 5–6. The Alkali Metals					
Element	Z	A	M.P.(°C)	B.P.(°C)	Description
Lithium (Li)	3	7	186	1336	
Sodium (Na)	11	23	97.5	880	All are silver-
Potassium (K)	19	39	62.3	760	gray metals
Rubidium (Rb)	37	85	38.5	700	
Cesium (Cs)	55	133	28.5	670	
Francium (Fr)	87	(223)	—	—	radioactive solid

How would sodium and fluorine combine?

ionically

The properties of metals are determined by the number of valence electrons available. Column IA metals have only one valence electron per atom and are soft. Column IIA metals have two valence electrons and are harder than Column IA metals. As metallic valence increases, the metals become harder and stronger. Metallic valence refers to the number of free electrons available for metallic bonding.

Metals can be defined as those elements which give up their outer shell electrons easily. Metals usually are shiny and reflect light. Metals can be pounded into sheets and pulled into wires. They are good conductors of electricity and heat. These properties describe the **alkali** (al' kah lie) **metals** very well. The alkali metals are in column IA of the periodic table. Lithium (lith' ee um), sodium (soh' dee um), potassium (poh tas' ee um), rubidium (roo bid' ee um), cesium (see' zee um), and francium (fran' see um) are the most reactive of all the metals. They are never found in the free state in nature. In their element form, the alkali metals are kept under kerosene so they will not react directly with oxygen or water vapor in the air.

All the alkali metals form compounds by ionic bonding. They readily give up their one outer electron to form ions. Cesium, in fact, gives up its electron when hit with a beam of light. This photoelectric effect is used in a photocell to convert light energy into electrical energy (Section 5:2).

Figure 5-30. Many metals have properties which make them useful in manufacturing. These newly-formed metal pellets, for example, may be easily packaged, moved, then eventually remelted.

Dravo Corp.

The alkali metals can be identified by *flame tests*. When these elements are heated in a flame some of their electrons take on energy. As the atoms cool the electrons lose this energy in the form of light. In the case of potassium, violet light is emitted. Sodium gives a yellow flame.

The names for rubidium and cesium were derived from Latin words describing the color they give off in a flame test. Rubidium gives a red flame. Cesium gives a blue flame. Lithium produces a red flame. These flame colors are one way to identify the elements in a compound.

EXPERIMENT. Place 5 ml each of solutions of chlorides of lithium, potassium, sodium, barium, calcium, strontium, and copper into seven test tubes. Label each test tube. Clean a platinum or nichrome wire by dipping it in hydrochloric acid and distilled water in two separate test tubes. Dip the clean wire into one of the sample test tubes. Then hold the wire at the tip of the inner cone of a Bunsen burner flame. Record the color of the flame test for each solution. Clean the wire after each test. When you have become familiar with the colors of flames for each of the samples, ask your instructor for an unknown sample. Identify the metal in the unknown.

Compare with photos on page 94.

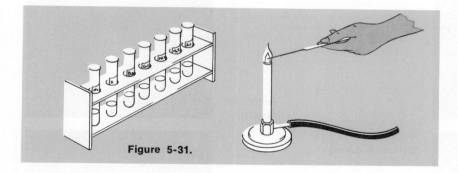

Figure 5-31.

PROBLEMS

12. Draw diagrams of an atom of lithium and an atom of sodium. How many electrons are in the outer shell of each of these atoms? *one*

See Teacher's material for diagrams.

13. How many electrons are in the outer shell of an atom of each of the alkali metals? *one*

14. Why are these elements in the free state stored under kerosene? *They combine explosively with oxygen or water vapor in the air.*

**Copper
(emerald green)**

Qualitative analysis is the determination of the elements that are contained in a sample of a substance. The students have already been exposed to one method — the formation of identifiable precipitates. Other methods that they will become acquainted with are electrolysis, titration, flame test, and paper chromatography.

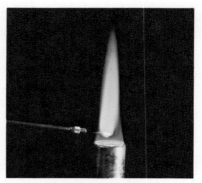

**Sodium
(yellow)**

**Calcium
(yellowish red)**

The flame test is an older technique than the other methods and is still extremely important. The flame test method led to the development of the very refined spectrographic techniques that are used in almost every laboratory today. Originally, spectroscopy meant viewing the spectrum produced by a substance, such as that produced

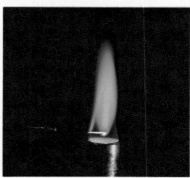

**Potassium
(violet)**

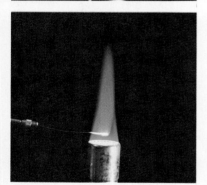

**Strontium
(scarlet red)**

when light passes through a prism. It has now come to have a much broader meaning. Spectroscopy now might be interpreted as the broad set of reactions of a substance when it is submitted to a continuous exciting force (heat, in the case of the flame test).

If solutions are relatively pure, some cations can be identified by

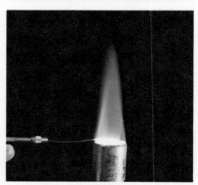

**Rubidium
(violet)**

**Barium
(yellowish green)**

characteristic flame tests. Use a length of platinum (or nichrome) wire, clean it and insert it into a solution of the unknown solution. Place the wire in the oxidizing flame of a Bunsen burner. Note the color of the flame. You must be careful that none of the solution falls into the burner, otherwise the succeeding flame tests will be inconclusive.

**Cesium
(violet)**

Lester V. Bergman & Associates, Inc.

Figure 5-32.   Flame tests

5:5   *Alkaline Earth Metals*

Table 5–7. *The Alkaline Earth Metals*

Element	Z	A	M.P.(°C)	B.P.(°C)	Description
Beryllium (Be)	4	9	1280±5	2970	very hard silvery metal
Magnesium (Mg)	12	24	651	1107	hard silvery metal
Calcium (Ca)	20	40	842–8	1487	hard silvery metal
Strontium (Sr)	38	88	769	1384	soft silvery metal
Barium (Ba)	56	137	725	1638	soft silvery-white metal
Radium (Ra)	88	(226)	700	1737	radioactive silvery metal

The elements in column IIA of the periodic table are called the **alkaline** (al′ kah lin) **earth metals.** They are also known as the calcium (kal′ see um) family. This family includes beryllium (be ril′ lee um), magnesium (mag nee′ zhee um), calcium, strontium (strawn′ tee um), barium (bar′ ee um), and radium (raed′ ee um).

The alkaline earth metals are very reactive. They are not found in the free state in nature. These elements readily give up their two outer electrons and form ions. For this reason, they tend to form compounds by ionic bonding. All of these metals react with water.

Beryllium. Beryllium is found chemically combined in nature in the form of a green mineral. The element itself is usually obtained by the electrolysis of its molten chlorides. Beryllium forms compounds with all of the halogens.

Magnesium. In nature, magnesium is found chemically combined in mineral deposits and in compounds dissolved in seawater. Free magnesium burns with a very bright flame. For this reason it has been used in photographic flashbulbs.

Magnesium is one of the elements found in the green plant pigment, chlorophyll. Some compounds of magnesium are used as medicine. An example is magnesium sulfate. It is marketed as Epsom salt.

Calcium. Calcium is one of the most abundant elements in the crust of the earth. About 3 percent of the weight of the earth's crust is calcium compounds. Calcium is never found in the free state in nature. It is usually prepared by the electrolysis of molten calcium chloride.

Calcium compounds are important commercially. Calcium oxide is commonly known as lime. Lime mixed with sand,

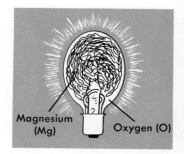

Figure 5-33. The flash you see when a flashbulb goes off is magnesium burning in oxygen.

Figure 5-34. Calcium mining.

Caterpillar Tractor Co.

water, and other additives is used in making mortars and plaster. Lime is also used in making glass, dehairing hides, and softening hard water. Calcium sulfate is used in making paints and plasterboard. Calcium compounds are also used in treating soils that are too acid.

Calcium is an essential component of bones and teeth. It is also found in the shells of many aquatic animals. Calcium is essential to humans and other animals. Milk and other dairy products are excellent sources of calcium.

Strontium. Because strontium is a very reactive metal, it is not found free in nature. It is usually prepared by the electrolysis of molten strontium chloride. Strontium reacts readily with air and water. Therefore, it must be stored under a special liquid in a tightly stoppered bottle. The chemical properties of strontium are very similar to those of calcium.

When vaporized in a flame, strontium compounds cause the flame to appear a beautiful shade of red. For this reason, strontium compounds are often used in the manufacture of fireworks.

Barium. Like the other alkaline earth metals, barium is always found in the combined state in nature. Chemically, barium is very similar to calcium and strontium. However, it tends to react more rapidly than calcium and strontium. Barium reacts readily with water, halogens, and oxygen. When vaporized in a flame, barium compounds cause the flame to appear green.

Barium sulfate is important in medicine. It is used to study the digestive tract. Patients swallow a liquid mixture containing barium sulfate. Because barium sulfate absorbs X rays, the physician can study the digestive tract as the barium sulfate moves through it.

Figure 5-35. Barium sulfate X rays are used to detect disorders in the digestive tract.

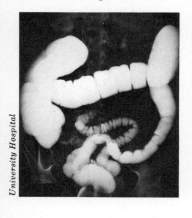

University Hospital

Radium. Radium is even more chemically reactive than barium. It is also radioactive. In nature, it is found in uranium ores such as pitchblende. Usually, it is obtained in the free state by electrolysis of fused radium salts. The metal is silvery white but turns black rapidly on exposure to air.

Radium is used in medicine to treat malignant growths. At one time, it was used to make luminous watch dials. *Luminous* means to glow in the dark.

Figure 5-36. Radium glows in the dark.

See Teacher's material for diagrams.

PROBLEMS

15. Draw a diagram of an atom of beryllium and an atom of magnesium. How many electrons are in the outer shell of each of these atoms? *two*
16. How many electrons are in the outer shell of each of the alkaline earth metals? *two*
17. Chlorine combines with all of the alkaline earth metals. Write a chemical formula for the chloride of each of the alkaline earth metals. *$BeCl_2$, $MgCl_2$, $CaCl_2$, $SrCl_2$, $BaCl_2$, $RaCl_2$*

5:6　Noble Gases

Table 5–8.	The Noble Gases				
Element	Z	A	M.P.(°C)	B.P.(°C)	Description
Helium (He)	2	4	−272	−269	
Neon (Ne)	10	20	−249	−246	All are
Argon (Ar)	18	40	−189	−186	colorless gases
Krypton (Kr)	36	84	−157	−153	
Xenon (Xe)	54	131	−112	−107	
Radon (Rn)	86	(222)	−71	−61.8	

What is a use for neon?

display lighting (neon signs)

Figure 5-37. A helium-filled balloon is lighter than the volume of air it replaces.

Column VIIIA of the periodic table includes helium (hee′ lee um), neon (nee′ ahn), argon (ar′ gahn), krypton (krip′ tahn), xenon (zee′ nahn), and radon (rae′ dahn). These elements are known as the **noble gases.** Until 1962 it was believed that the noble gases would not combine with other elements. However, experiments now show that xenon, for example, can form compounds with fluorine, oxygen, and platinum. Compounds of the noble gases are formed covalently since in each case the outer shell of the noble gas is already complete.

Most of the members of this family were found by chance. Helium, for example, was found in a study of light from the sun before it was discovered on earth. Argon was found when

Some of the compounds of noble gases are: xenon hexafluoroplatinate, $XePtF_6$; xenon difluoride, XeF_2; and xenon trioxide, XeO_3. Some of these compounds are being used experimentally as industrial fluorinating agents.

Ria C. Parody

Figure 5-38. When electricity is applied to the neon gas in the tube, the gas glows.

See Teacher's material for diagrams.

not all of the sample of a distillation of liquid air could be accounted for. Xenon, neon, and krypton were found by using the techniques that led to the discovery of argon. The last member of the family, radon, is the heaviest gas known. It is the product of the radioactive decay of radium and is itself radioactive (Section 20:3).

PROBLEMS

18. Draw diagrams of an atom of helium, an atom of neon, and an atom of argon. How many electrons are in the outer shell of each of these atoms? *two, eight, eight*

19. How many electrons are in the outermost shell of an atom of each of the noble gases? *eight for all but helium*

20. Why does helium not follow the rule of a stable outer shell of an octet of electrons? *Its outer shell is completely filled by 2 electrons*

MAIN IDEAS

p. 76   **1.** Chemical elements can be grouped in families. Elements in a family all have similar chemical properties.

pp. 78-79   **2.** Halogens are the most reactive nonmetals.

p. 92   **3.** Alkali metals are the most reactive metals.

p. 81   **4.** Allotropes are different molecular forms of the same element.

p. 86   **5.** A photoconductor is a substance whose ability to conduct electrons is controlled by light.

p. 88   **6.** Two or more of the same elements may combine in different ways to form different compounds.

p. 84, p. 87, p. 98   **7.** Nitrogen, oxygen, and the noble gases can be produced from the distillation of liquid air.

p. 93, p. 94   **8.** Some metals can be identified by flame tests.

p. 97   **9.** Noble elements are chemically the least active elements.

VOCABULARY

Write a sentence in which you correctly use each of the following words or terms.

allotropes	electrolysis	paramagnetic
catalyst	law of multiple	photoconductor
diatomic	proportions	sublimation
distillation	metals	triatomic

STUDY QUESTIONS

A. True or False   *Have students rewrite false statements to make the statements correct.*

Determine whether each of the following sentences is true or false. (Do not write in this book.)

T 1. The elements in the halogen family are all poisonous or harmful in the uncombined state.

F 2. Under normal room temperature and pressure, all of the halogen elements exist as ~~monatomic~~ particles.   *diatomic*

F 3. Uncombined fluorine is found in the atmosphere.   *not*

T 4. At room temperature and pressure bromine is a red liquid.

F 5. At room temperature and pressure iodine is a ~~red liquid~~.   *gray crystalline solid*

T 6. All elements in the oxygen family have two electrons to share in chemical bonds.

T 7. Although arsenic is a poison, it is used in some medicines.

T 8. Selenium is a good electrical conductor when exposed to light.

T 9. Heavy growth of algae in lakes and streams may result from excess phosphate in the water.

F 10. The ~~high~~ melting point of bismuth makes it suitable for use in automatic sprinkler systems used for fire prevention.   *low*

B. Multiple Choice   *Some questions in part B may have more than one correct answer. Only one answer is required.*

Choose one word or phrase that correctly completes each of the following sentences. (Do not write in this book.)

1. (Helium, Nitrogen, <u>Sodium</u>, Oxygen) is a solid at room temperature.

2. Selenium exhibits (<u>photoconductivity</u>, photosynthesis, heliotrope).

3. All members of the halogens have (0, 1, 2, 3, 4, 5, 6, <u>7</u>, 8) electrons in their outer shells.

4. Halogen atoms form compounds with other elements by (covalent, ionic, <u>covalent and ionic</u>) bonding.

5. Phosphorus is not used in the manufacture of (matches, fertilizers, poison gas, <u>ice cream</u>).

6. Ammonia contains (oxygen, <u>nitrogen</u>, helium).

7. (<u>Bismuth</u>, Sulfur, Nitrogen, Antimony) is a true metal.

8. Sulfur has many (<u>allotropes</u>, ions, crystals).

9. (<u>Phosphorus</u>, Arsenic, Selenium) is essential for life.

10. (Nitrogen, Carbon, <u>Helium</u>) is a noble gas.

C. Completion

Complete each of the following sentences with a word or phrase that will make the sentence correct. (Do not write in this book.)

diatomic

multiple proportions

light

oxygen

distillation of air

distillation of air

flame

bismuth

selenium

1. Nitrogen is found free as __?__ molecules.

2. The compounds of nitrogen and oxygen illustrate the law of __?__.

3. The ability of cesium and selenium to conduct electrons is affected by __?__.

4. Twenty percent of air is __?__.

5. Pure nitrogen is produced by __?__.

6. Argon is a by-product of __?__.

7. Each alkali metal has a characteristic __?__ test.

8. The most metallic member of the nitrogen family is __?__.

9. __?__ is the element most like sulfur in physical and chemical properties.

D. How and Why

1. elements in same column of periodic table - all under oxygen

2. NH_3, ammonia; N_2H_4CO, urea: HNO_3, nitric acid

3. nitrogen - covalent alkali metals and halogens - ionic

4. Differences in properties - those with higher atomic numbers are more metallic

5. atomic structure, physical state, color, allotropic forms, m.p. and b.p.

6. See Teacher's material

7. allotropes - different molecular forms of an element; isotopes - different number of neutrons in atoms of same element

8. None combine easily with other elements. After the first one was found it was easier because properties were then known.

9. molecular form has two atoms- Cl_2, chlorine; O_2, oxygen; N_2, nitrogen

10. See Teacher's material.

1. What is a family of elements? Give an example.

2. What are the names and formulas of three nitrogen compounds?

3. What kind of bonding is present in binary compounds containing nitrogen? How does this compare with binary compounds between alkali metal and halogen families?

4. How can you distinguish between metallic and nonmetallic members of a family of elements?

5. In what specific ways is sulfur different from oxygen?

6. State the law of multiple proportions. How does it differ from the law of definite proportions?

7. How do allotropes differ from isotopes?

8. Hypothesize: Why were the noble gases difficult to discover?

9. What is a diatomic gas? Name three and give their formulas.

10. (a) Name a binary compound that could be formed from each of the following pairs of elements: (1) boron-nitrogen, (2) iron-oxygen, (3) magnesium-chlorine, (4) sulfur-carbon, (5) hydrogen-lithium.

    (b) What kind of bonding do you think each compound would have? Why?

INVESTIGATIONS

1. Visit a nursery or garden shop. (1) From the labels on the pesticides, determine which elements are most used. (2) From the labels on the fertilizers, determine which elements are most often used.

2. Conduct a survey in your local grocery store to determine which detergents have phosphates in them.

3. Obtain a photographic light meter. Use it to determine the relative amounts of light given off by various size light bulbs.

4. Visit your local municipal water supply headquarters. Find out how drinking water is purified. List any chemicals added to drinking water in your area.

See Teacher's material for suggestions.

INTERESTING READING

Asimov, Isaac, *The World of Nitrogen.* New York, Abeland-Schuman, Ltd., 1958.

Flaschen, Steward, *Search and Research: The Story of the Chemical Elements.* Boston, Allyn and Bacon, Inc., 1965.

Freeman, Ira M., and Patton, A. Ral, *The Science of Chemistry.* New York, Random House, 1968.

Froman, Robert, *The Science of Salt.* New York, David McKay Company, Inc., 1967.

"Making Hydrogen a Metal." *Science News*, XCIX (April 3, 1971), p. 231.

Pratt, C. J., "Sulfur." *Scientific American*, CCXXII (May, 1970), pp. 63–72.

Sootin, Harry, *Experiments with Water.* New York, W. W. Norton & Co., 1971.

GOAL: You will gain an understanding of the reasons for the large number of carbon compounds, chain formation, multiple bonding, and substitution.

What is organic chemistry?

Organic chemistry is the study of carbon compounds.

How does a carbon atom form compounds?

Carbon forms covalent bonds. Atoms join in chains or rings. Many elements bond to carbon and its chains or rings.

Figure 6-1. Balls of various sizes are often used to make models of carbon molecules. On the left is a tetrahedron; on the right a double tetrahedron.

Ward's Natural Science Establishment

Carbon forms an exceedingly large number of compounds. A very large percentage of the chemical research in the last few years has involved organic chemistry. In this chapter the students will learn some of the reasons for the large number of carbon compounds— catenation, multiple bonding, and substitution. Saturated and unsaturated hydrocarbons and homologous series are discussed.

Carbon and Its Compounds

What do a diamond and a pencil lead have in common? For one thing, both are carbon (kahr′ buhn). A great many things have carbon in them. Most foods, medicines, cloth materials, plastics, and detergents contain carbon. Name some other carbon-containing materials.

6:1 *Organic Chemistry*

The term "organic" means living. At one time, **organic** (or gan′ ik) **chemistry** was the study of materials found in living things, plants and animals. All of these materials contain *carbon*. Later, chemists were able to make some of these carbon materials without using any animal- or plant-made substances. Thus, organic chemistry came to include all carbon compounds.

Carbon is one of the least reactive elements. It combines easily with only a few of the other elements. Yet, roughly ninety percent of all known compounds contain carbon. More than one million different carbon compounds have been found.

One reason for so many carbon compounds is the way carbon atoms bond. Atoms of carbon can join together in long chains or in rings. Other elements may also bond with carbon atoms or with carbon chains or rings. In this way, a great variety of compounds is possible.

In the periodic table, carbon is a member of family IVA. This family also includes silicon (sil′ i kahn) (Si), germanium (jur mae′ nee um) (Ge), tin (Sn), and lead (Pb). Each element in the carbon family has four electrons in its outer shell. Thus, carbon atoms can share electrons with as many as four other atoms.

When a carbon atom shares electrons with four other atoms, the molecule formed has a shape called a *tetrahedron* (tet′ rah

Carl England

Figure 6-2. All of the items shown here contain carbon.

The geometry of carbon compounds is very important.

The structure of 1 carbon atom bonded to 4 hydrogen atoms:

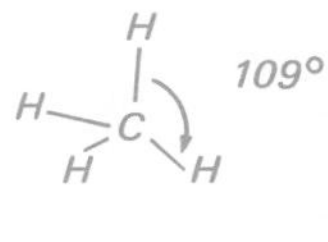

$$H-\underset{\underset{H}{|}}{\overset{\overset{H}{|}}{C}}\diagdown\!\!\!_H \quad 109°$$

The angle between a double bond and the other single bonds is about 120°.

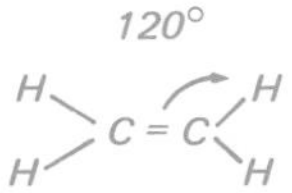

$$120°$$
$$\underset{H}{\overset{H}{\diagdown}}C = C\underset{\diagdown H}{\overset{\diagup H}{}}$$

A triple bond forms a linear molecule. $H-C \equiv C-H$

hee′ drun). The angle between each pair of bonds is about 109°. This shape permits each shared pair of electrons to be as far as possible from the other three shared pairs.

A carbon atom can bond with another atom in several different ways by sharing electrons. A single covalent bond is made when one electron pair is shared between atoms. A double covalent bond is formed when two electron pairs are shared. A triple covalent bond is formed when three electron pairs are shared between two atoms.

When double or triple bonds are formed, the tetrahedral shape is lost. For this reason, carbon compounds with double or triple bonds are sometimes unstable. They may react to form compounds with only single bonds. Thus, the more stable tetrahedron shape is regained.

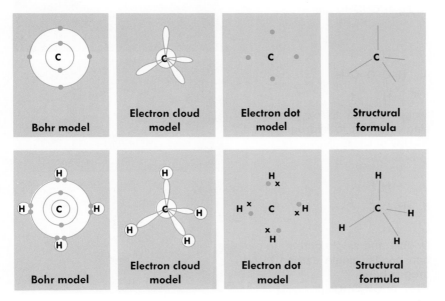

| Bohr model | Electron cloud model | Electron dot model | Structural formula |

Figure 6-3. Models of the carbon atom.

Figure 6-4. Models of the methane (CH_4) molecule.

Double bond

Triple bond

Figure 6-5. Carbon atoms can form double covalent bonds and triple covalent bonds.

Have the students construct the models of molecules illustrated on pages 104 and 105. Styrofoam balls and florists chenille or pipe cleaners are all the materials that you require. Flattening the sides of the styrofoam balls where they are to be joined makes the models more compact. Toothpicks may be used in place of the pipe cleaners if the models are to be glued. Each carbon atom has 4 bonds. Each hydrogen atom has 1 bond. Single, double, and triple bonds are indicated by varying degrees of flatness of the joint between two atoms.

6:2   *Structural Formulas*

A *structural formula* is a simple way to show the bonding between atoms. One straight line between symbols represents one covalent bond. Two lines means a double bond. Three lines means a triple bond.

Figure 6–6 shows some structural formulas and picture models for carbon compounds containing hydrogen.

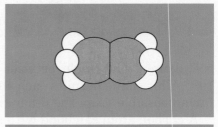

1.

Single carbon to carbon bond; single carbon to hydrogen bond.
(C_2H_6 or CH_3CH_3)   *ethane*

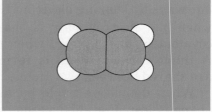

2.

Double carbon to carbon bond; single carbon to hydrogen bond.
(C_2H_4 or CH_2CH_2)
ethene or ethylene

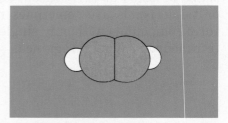

3.   H–C≡C–H

Triple carbon to carbon bond; single carbon to hydrogen bond.
(C_2H_2 or $CHCH$)   *ethyne*

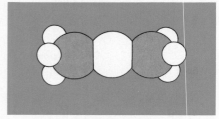

4.

Single carbon to oxygen bond; single carbon to hydrogen bond.
(C_2H_6O or CH_3OCH_3)

dimethyl ether

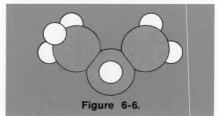

5.

Double and single carbon to carbon bonds; single carbon to hydrogen bond.
(C_3H_6 or CH_3CHCH_2)   *propene*

Figure 6-6.

6. H–C–C
   (H H above/below left C, H O above right C)

Double carbon to oxygen bond;
single carbon to carbon bond;
single carbon to hydrogen bond.
(C_2H_4O or CH_3CHO)

ethanal or ethyl adehyde

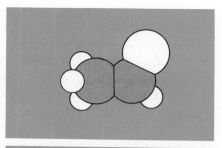

7. H–C–C–N
   (H H H above, H H H below)

Single carbon to carbon bond;
single carbon to nitrogen bond;
single carbon to hydrogen bond;
single nitrogen to hydrogen bond.
(C_2H_7N or $CH_3CH_2NH_2$)

ethyl amine

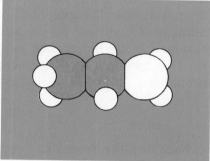

8. H–C–C–C–H
   (H H Cl above, H H H below)

Single carbon to chlorine bond;
single carbon to carbon bond;
single carbon to hydrogen bond.
(C_3H_7Cl or $CH_3CH_2CH_2Cl$)

1-chloropropane

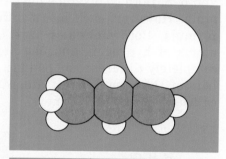

9. H–C–C–C–H
   (H Cl H above, H H H below)

Single carbon to chlorine bond;
single carbon to carbon bond;
single carbon to hydrogen bond.
(C_3H_7Cl or $CH_3CHClCH_3$)

2-chloropropane

10. H–C–C–C–H
    (H O H above, H H below)

Single carbon to carbon bond;
single carbon to hydrogen bond;
double carbon to oxygen bond.
(C_3H_6O or CH_3COCH_3)

*dimethyl ketone or methyl
methanone*

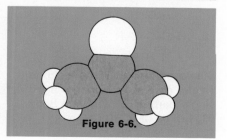

Figure 6-6.

Figure 6–6 also shows two other formulas for each compound. One formula, the *simple molecular formula*, tells the number of atoms of each element in a molecule of the compound. The second formula is the *graphic formula*. It shows number and kinds of atoms and the structure of the molecule. For example, the simple molecular formula, C_3H_8, shows that one molecule contains three carbon atoms and eight hydrogen atoms. The graphic formula, $CH_3CH_2CH_3$, shows the number of hydrogen atoms attached to each carbon atom. Location of atoms in a carbon compound is important. A different location means a different compound with different chemical properties.

6:3   Isomers

Examine the formulas for the compounds in Figures 6–7 and 6–8. Both compounds have the same simple molecular formula. However, each has a different graphic and structural formula. Both molecules have three atoms of carbon, seven atoms of hydrogen, and one atom of chlorine. Yet they are completely different compounds. Compounds with equal numbers of the same kind of atoms, but different structures, are called **isomers** (ie′ soh mers).

What are isomers?

Isomers are compounds which have the same simple molecular formulas but different structural formulas. They might be compared to allotropes.

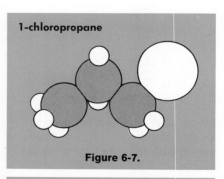

1.
```
    H  H  Cl
    |  |  |
 H–C–C–C–H
    |  |  |
    H  H  H
```

Single carbon to chlorine bond; single carbon to carbon bond; single carbon to hydrogen bond. (C_3H_7Cl or $CH_3CH_2CH_2Cl$)

1-chloropropane

Figure 6-7.

2.
```
    H  Cl H
    |  |  |
 H–C–C–C–H
    |  |  |
    H  H  H
```

Single carbon to chlorine bond; single carbon to carbon bond; single carbon to hydrogen bond. (C_3H_7Cl or $CH_3CHClCH_3$)

2-chloro-propane

Figure 6-8.

Often, more than two compounds will have the same simple formula. For example, there are three compounds with the formula C_5H_{12}:

H H H H H
H–C–C–C–C–C–H,   *normal pentane*
H H H H H

isopentane or 2-methylbutane

H
H   H H–C–H H
H——C——C——C——C——H,   and
H   H   H   H

H
H H–C–H H
H——C——C——C——H.   *neopentane or*
H H–C–H H   *2,2-dimethylpropane*
H

ACTIVITY. *Seven isomers have been found for $C_5H_{11}Cl$. Draw structural formulas for each isomer. Write the graphic formula for each isomer. Obtain styrofoam balls and pipe cleaners. Make a model of at least two of the isomers.*

See Teacher's Guide at the front of book.

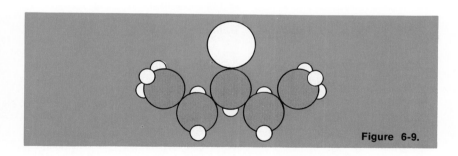

Figure 6-9.

As the number of carbon atoms in a molecule increases, the number of possible isomers also increases. All these isomers may not exist. But the structure of each is possible. Isomers are another reason why there are so many carbon compounds.

What are two reasons for the large number of carbon compounds?

Carbon-to-carbon bonding (catenation); isomeric forms; single, double, and triple bonds

PROBLEMS

1. Draw the structural formulas for three isomers of C_4H_9Cl. (Note: All carbon atoms in these isomers are bonded to each other by single covalent bonds.)

H H Cl H
H–C–C–C–C–H .
H H H H

H H H H
H–C–C–C–C–Cl
H H H H

H
H–C–H
H H
H–C–C–C–H
H Cl H

H H H
H–C–C–C–H
H   H
H–C–H
Cl

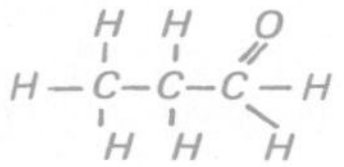

2. Draw a structural formula for CH_3CH_2CHO.
3. What is the simple molecular formula for the compound in Problem 2? C_3H_6O

6:4 Saturated Hydrocarbons

Can you find a general formula for the relationship between the hydrogen and carbon atoms in the alkane series?

There should be two hydrogen atoms for each carbon atom plus one hydrogen at each end. If the number of carbons is n, then there should be 2n + 2 hydrogens or in general,

$$C_nH_{2n+2}$$

Many of the compounds discussed in the preceding sections contain only carbon and hydrogen. These compounds are called **hydrocarbons** (hie′ droh kahr′ buhns). Hydrocarbons can be classified into two groups. Those in which all carbon atoms are joined by single bonds are *saturated* (sach′ u raet ed) *hydrocarbons*. If, however, two or more carbon atoms are joined by double or triple bonds, the hydrocarbon is *unsaturated*.

Hydrocarbons are classified into series of compounds with similar structure. One group of saturated hydrocarbons is called the *alkanes* (al′ kaenz). Since the first member of the alkane series is methane (CH_4), the series is sometimes also called the *methane* (meth′ aen) series. Ethane (C_2H_6), propane (C_3H_8), and butane (C_4H_{10}) are the next three members of the series. Methane is found in natural gas. Propane and butane are used as "bottled" gas. Each successive alkane has one more CH_2 group than the alkane before it. How many hydrogen atoms would one molecule of the alkane containing twenty carbon atoms have? *42 — two for each carbon atom and two on each end.*

Table 6–1. Methane Series			
Name	Simple Molecular Formula	Graphic Formula	Normal State
Methane	CH_4	CH_4	Gas
Ethane	C_2H_6	CH_3CH_3	Gas
Propane	C_3H_8	$CH_3CH_2CH_3$	Gas
Butane	C_4H_{10}	$CH_3CH_2CH_2CH_3$	Gas
Pentane	C_5H_{12}	$CH_3CH_2CH_2CH_2CH_3$	Liquid
Octane	C_8H_{18}	$CH_3CH_2CH_2CH_2CH_2CH_2CH_2CH_3$	Liquid

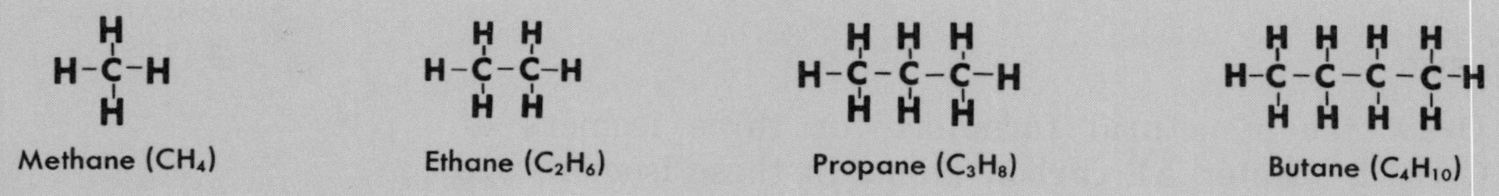

Figure 6-10. Saturated hydrocarbons are single-bonded compounds of hydrogen and carbon.

Methane (CH_4)   Ethane (C_2H_6)   Propane (C_3H_8)   Butane (C_4H_{10})

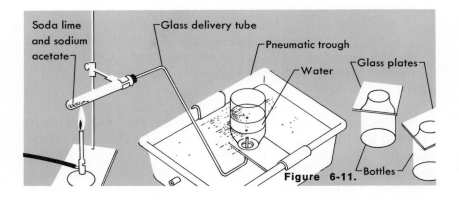

Safety precautions: 1. Keep the gas collection bottles away from open flames.
2. Maintain proper ventilation or use the fume hood.
3. Have students wear goggles when they perform this experiment.

Have students note the physical properties of the gas.

Figure 6-11.

Methane burns with a blue flame.

EXPERIMENT. Crush together 15 g of sodium acetate with 5 g of dry soda lime in a mortar. Fill a test tube one-third full of the mixture. Arrange the apparatus as shown in the diagram. Heat the test tube. Collect the methane in bottles by water displacement. CAUTION: Keep the bottles of gas away from the open flame of the gas burner. Discard the contents of the first bottle of gas. Then collect four bottles. Place the bottles upside-down on the glass slide when they are filled. Insert a burning splint into one bottle. Add 5 ml of limewater and shake. To the second bottle, add 2 ml of bromine water. To the third bottle, add 2 ml of potassium permanganate solution. Shake each bottle. Note any changes in the three bottles. Record your results. How can you prove that methane in the fourth bottle has a smaller mass than an equal amount of air?

Hold the bottle upside down — the gas remains in the bottle.

Limewater turns milky indicating that CO_2 was a product.

Bromine water remains red in color.

Methane does not change $KMnO_4$ solution.

Structural formulas of some members of the methane series are given in Figure 6–10. The chains are written as straight lines to make them less confusing. Actually, the carbon chains are not straight. Remember, the angle between each pair of bonds is 109°, not 90°. As a chain grows longer, it is more likely to bend back and forth.

Demonstrate the correct bond angles with ball and stick or styrofoam models.

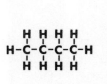

Structural formula

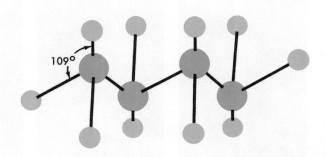

Structural model

Figure 6-12. Hydrocarbon chains are usually represented as straight chains. However, carbon covalent bonds are actually 109°.

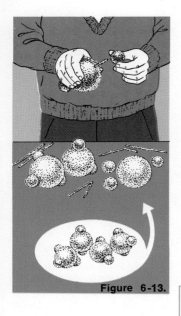

ACTIVITY. Using styrofoam balls and toothpicks, construct a model of the butane molecule, CH₃CH₂CH₂CH₃. Remember that angles between pairs of bonds should be about 109°.

As the number of carbon atoms in the methane series increases, the physical state of the compounds that are formed changes. The first four members of the methane series are gases at room temperature. Starting with five carbon atoms (pentane, C_5H_{12}), a shift from the gas to the liquid form occurs. Saturated hydrocarbons with more than eighteen carbon atoms ($C_{18}H_{38}$) are waxy solids.

Hydrocarbons with 40 carbon atoms in a chain are known to exist naturally. How many hydrogen atoms would a 40-carbon chain require? Can you imagine the possible number of isomers of that compound? To give you an idea of the number, more than 350,000 isomers which have the formula $C_{20}H_{42}$ are possible.

Figure 6-13.

82

PROBLEM

4. Identify each of these alkanes as either a solid, liquid, or gas.
   (a) C_2H_6 *gas*
   (b) $C_{30}H_{62}$ *solid*
   (c) C_8H_{18} *liquid*
   (d) CH_4 *gas*
   (e) $C_{16}H_{34}$ *liquid*

6:5 Separating Organic Mixtures

Organic compounds are usually found in mixtures. Separating these mixtures into their parts is often difficult. Chemists have developed many methods for separating materials.

Figure 6-14. Column chromatography is another way of separating organic mixtures. Different substances move at different rates through the column.

Bell & Howell

EXPERIMENT. Prepare a mixture of four or five vegetable dyes. Cut a piece of filter paper as shown in the diagram. Place a drop of the dye mixture on the cut strip of filter paper. Fill a small beaker one-half full of water and add 2 drops of white vinegar. Cover the beaker with the paper, and allow the tip of the cut strip to stand in the water for a few hours. What happens? This method of separating chemical compounds is known as paper chromatography *(kroh'ma tahg'ra fee).*

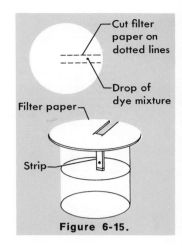

Figure 6-15.

Paper chromatography is a useful way of separating chemical compounds for qualitative analysis.

Boiling points cover quite a range.

6:6 Fractionation

Petroleum is one of the most important sources of saturated hydrocarbons. Most of our petroleum comes from deep underground deposits. Wells are drilled to reach the petroleum. Depending on the location of the well, 60 to 90 percent of the petroleum is composed of mixtures of saturated hydrocarbons. The various kinds of alkanes are separated by a process called **fractionation** (frak' shun ae' shun), a type of distillation. *Distillation* is a physical separation which depends upon boiling point differences.

How is fractionation like distillation?

Fractionation is carried out in large towers. Each fraction, or compound, is piped off at a different level. The level depends on the boiling point of the fraction.

Fractionation separates mixtures of hydrocarbons by piping off compounds as they boil.

For example, natural gas is distilled from 0° to 30°C. Gasoline is distilled from 30° to 200°C. Kerosene and fuel oil are

The Standard Oil Co.

Figure 6-16. A fractionating tower separates the various compounds in petroleum.

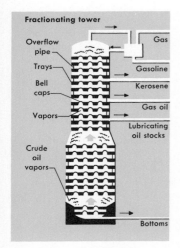

Figure 6-17. Fractional distillation is used to refine crude petroleum.

A gasoline rated at 90 octane has the same performance as a mixture which contains what percent isooctane?

ninety percent

distilled from 200° to 325°C. Lubricating oil is distilled at 325°C and higher. The remaining material, or residue, is used for asphalt or similar products. Each fraction is distilled over a wide range of temperatures and may still contain a large number of different alkanes. Using a smaller temperature spread, further fractionation can be carried out to separate some of these alkanes.

Each petroleum fraction has its own specific purpose. However, gasoline is the fraction of most commercial importance. Direct from fractionation, gasoline is not a good fuel. Additional processing must be done to convert it for use in high compression engines.

Engine gasoline is rated on the basis of *octane* (ahk′ taen) numbers. Octane numbers indicate the smoothness or uniformity of burning inside a combustion engine. Zero octane is the performance rating given to normal (straight-chain) heptane (C_7H_{16}). The rating 100 octane is given to isooctane (C_8H_{18}), a highly branched hydrocarbon. Performances of gasoline mixtures are compared to the octane values of *n*-heptane (normal heptane) and isooctane. If a gasoline gives the same performance as a mixture of 80 percent isooctane and 20 percent *n*-heptane, it has a rating of 80 octane. This is so even if the gasoline contains no octane. The higher the octane rating, the better is the performance of the engine. Octane rating is a performance rating, not a power rating. In other

Figure 6-18. This machine determines octane ratings in gasoline.

Exxon Co.

words, gas with high octane does not give more power when burned than gas with a low octane rating. More of the fuel is completely burned so less can escape in exhaust fumes to pollute the air.

There is a direct relationship between the shape of gasoline molecules and the performance of the gasoline. Straight-chain molecules tend to give poorer performance (more "knock") than branched-chain or ring-shaped molecules. Look at the structural formulas of the standards:

n-heptane,

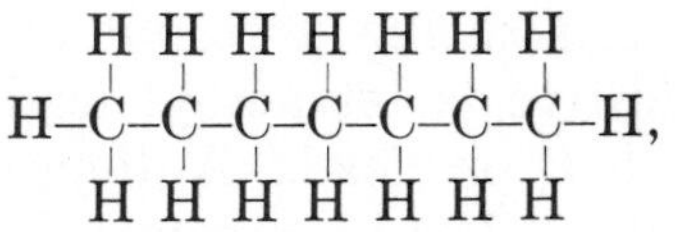

$$H-\overset{\displaystyle H}{\underset{\displaystyle H}{C}}-\overset{\displaystyle H}{\underset{\displaystyle H}{C}}-\overset{\displaystyle H}{\underset{\displaystyle H}{C}}-\overset{\displaystyle H}{\underset{\displaystyle H}{C}}-\overset{\displaystyle H}{\underset{\displaystyle H}{C}}-\overset{\displaystyle H}{\underset{\displaystyle H}{C}}-\overset{\displaystyle H}{\underset{\displaystyle H}{C}}-H,$$ is a straight chain, and

isooctane,

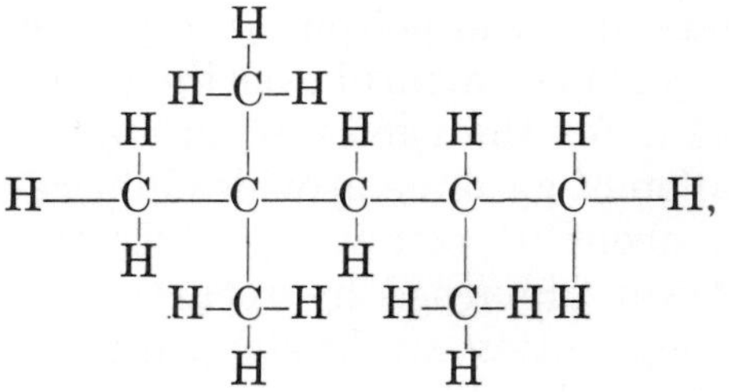

is a branched chain.

n-heptane is 0 octane
isooctane is 100 octane

Branched means that some carbon atoms are connected to three other carbon atoms. Are their performance ratings high or low?

The octane rating of a fuel can be increased in two ways. One way is to make straight-chain hydrocarbons form branched chains through chemical reactions. If the fraction containing larger carbon molecules is "cracked," a greater yield of gasoline can be obtained. The term cracked means chemically broken down into molecules which contain no more than seven or eight carbon atoms. These molecules are then processed chemically to form branched chain hydrocarbons.

How can octane rating be increased?

Increase the amount of branched carbon atoms and put in additives.

Figure 6-19. Normal butane, a straight-chain hydrocarbon, can be broken down chemically to produce isobutane, a branched-chain hydrocarbon.

Normal butane

Isobutane

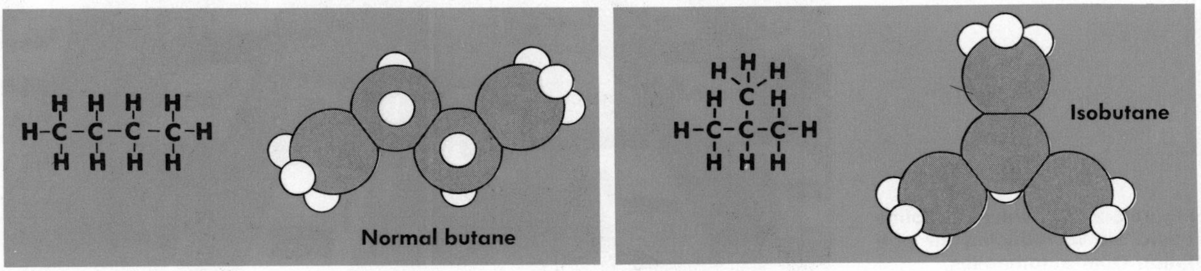

Figure 6-20. Gasoline and other petroleum products are stored in tanks until needed.

The second way to improve the octane rating is to put an "additive" into the gasoline. One additive is tetraethyl lead $(Pb(C_2H_5)_4)$, commonly known as "ethyl" or "lead." Automobile exhaust adds lead to air as a pollutant. Lead is a very poisonous substance. To date, no direct connection has been made between lead in the atmosphere and lead poisoning in people. Yet lead in the air we breathe could be harmful over the years.

Lead is a necessary lubricant for the valves of an engine. About ½ gram of lead per gallon of gasoline provides lubrication. A "low lead" gasoline, about 91 octane, provides this amount. It will also cause fewer unburned hydrocarbons to enter and pollute the air. Some pollution can be stopped if the gasoline used in the auto has just a high enough octane rating to produce good engine performance.

6:7 Unsaturated Hydrocarbons

Among the major by-products of "cracking" are unsaturated hydrocarbons. Unsaturated hydrocarbons have double or triple carbon bonds. The term unsaturated is sometimes used to describe cooking oils and vegetable shortenings. Why?

Figure 6-21. Low-lead gasoline could aid in reducing air pollution from automobiles.

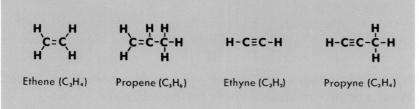

Ethene (C_2H_4)   Propene (C_3H_6)   Ethyne (C_2H_2)   Propyne (C_3H_4)

Unsaturated hydrocarbons with one double bond are called **alkenes** (al′ keenz). Ethylene (eth′ i leen), or ethene (CH_2= CH_2), is the smallest possible chain. It is also the most common alkene produced by cracking. Other members of the alkene series include propene,

1 - butene

H–C=C–C–H, and the two isomers of butene, H–C=C–C–C–H

Richard M. Fetters

Have the students develop a general formula for the alkenes.

2 - butene

and H–C–C=C–C–H. Each isomer simply has the double bond

A new way to form isomers is to change the location of the double bond.

in a different location.

Figure 6-23. Acetylene burns with a high temperature. It is used in welding and soldering.

Another group of unsaturated hydrocarbons is the alkyne series. *Alkynes* (al′ kinz) have one triple bond. The most common triple-bond compound is acetylene (ah set′ i leen), or ethyne (H–C≡C–H). It is the simplest member of the alkyne series. Among others, the alkyne series includes propyne and the two isomers of butyne.

Develop a general formula for the alkynes (C_nH_{2n-2}).

PROBLEM

See Teacher's material

5. Write structural formulas for the two butyne isomers.

Observe the same safety precautions as in the experiment on page 109.

EXPERIMENT. CAUTION: Do not perform this experiment near an open flame. Wear eye protection. Place 2 g of calcium carbide in a flask. Obtain a two-hole rubber stopper to fit the flask. Insert a medicine dropper into one hole of the stopper. Insert a glass delivery tube into the other hole. Fill the medicine dropper with water. Fit the stopper into the flask. Squeeze a few drops of water onto the calcium carbide. Collect three bottles of acetylene gas by water displacement. Discard the first bottle of gas. To the second bottle, add 2 ml of bromine water. To the third bottle, add 2 ml of potassium permanganate solution. Compare your results with the experiment on methane.

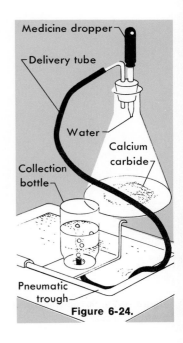

Medicine dropper

Delivery tube

Water

Calcium carbide

Collection bottle

Pneumatic trough

Figure 6-24.

Be extremely careful. Acetylene is very flammable. Bromine water bleaches to   *colorless. $KMnO_4$ solution is bleached from purple to colorless.*

115

1, 2-butadiene

$$H\text{-}C=C=C\text{-}\underset{\underset{H}{|}}{\overset{\overset{H}{|}}{C}}\text{-}H \quad \overset{H}{|}\; \overset{H}{|}$$

1, 3-butadiene

$$H\text{-}\underset{\underset{H}{|}}{\overset{\overset{H}{|}}{C}}=C\text{-}C=\underset{\underset{H}{|}}{\overset{\overset{H}{|}}{C}}\text{-}H$$

Other unsaturated hydrocarbons include the *alkadienes* (al′ ka die′ eens) or *dienes*. These compounds have two double bonds. Propadiene, $H\text{-}\overset{\overset{H}{|}}{C}=C=\overset{\overset{H}{|}}{C}\text{-}H$, is a member of this series. What are two possible isomers for butadiene?

As with the alkanes, the alkenes and alkynes with short carbon chains are gases at room temperature. Pentene is a liquid. So is one of the butynes. The larger carbon chains are waxy solids.

6:8   Polymers

The molecules of many compounds can join together to form a very large molecule called a *polymer* (pahl′ i mer). This process is called *polymerization*. The dienes discussed in Section 6:7 form polymers.

Pentadiene, $H\text{-}\overset{\overset{H}{|}}{C}=\overset{\overset{H}{|}}{C}\text{-}\underset{\underset{H}{|}}{\overset{\overset{H}{|}}{C}}\text{-}\overset{\overset{H}{|}}{C}=\overset{\overset{H}{|}}{C}\text{-}H$, has an isomer called iso-

prene, $H\text{-}\overset{\overset{H}{|}}{C}=\overset{}{C}\text{-}\overset{\overset{H}{|}}{C}=\overset{\overset{H}{|}}{C}\text{-}H$, which in nature polymerizes to form

$$\underset{\underset{H}{|}}{\overset{\overset{H\text{-}\overset{\overset{}{|}}{C}\text{-}H}{|}}{}}$$

rubber. Synthetic rubber has been made from isoprene, from butadiene, and from isomers of hexadiene. Neoprene rubber, one of the most successful, is made using acetylene. Part of the chain of this rubber has the following structural formula:

$$\cdots\text{-}\overset{\overset{H}{|}}{C}=\overset{\overset{H}{|}}{C}\text{-}\overset{\overset{H}{|}}{C}=\overset{\overset{H}{|}}{C}\text{-}\cdots$$

Figure 6-25. A polymer is a giant molecule.

Fossil Fuels — How Long Will They Last?

We may be running out of fuel. Today, most energy comes from fossil fuels, such as coal, gas, and oil. These fuels are carbon compounds. They were formed from the remains of ancient plants which died, decayed, and were buried millions of years ago. Fossil fuels store chemical energy which can be released as heat energy during burning. A large portion of the fossil fuels used is burned to heat water to make steam. The steam is used to drive a turbine generator which produces electric energy.

The supply of these common fossil fuels is limited. According to the U.S. Geological Survey, the United States has enough oil for 10 more years and enough gas for 11 more years. About ¼ of our oil is already shipped in from other parts of the world. U.S. coal reserves could last 500 years at present rates of use. However, much of this coal is rich in sulfur. When burned, this high-sulfur coal releases large amounts of sulfur into the air. Since about 50% of our electricity comes from the burning of coal, electric generating plants can be major sources of pollution. As yet there is no completely adequate method for removing sulfur from smokestack gases.

Not all coal is high-sulfur. Low-sulfur coal is abundant in some parts of the U.S. A large portion of both high- and low-sulfur coal is, however, strip mined. This creates additional environmental problems.

Fremont Davis, Science Service

Even a pile of garbage is a potential source of fuel.

Many possible new sources for gas and oil are now under study. One plan is to "gasify" coal; that is, to manufacture methane (CH_4) gas from coal. Another possible source is oil shale, a type of rock in which tiny bits of oil hold the rock particles together. About 40 gallons of oil could be extracted from a ton of this rock. Even garbage can be converted into oil. One ton of waste yields about one barrel (55 gallons) of a low-sulfur fuel oil.

Another possible energy source is hydrogen. It can be produced by electrolysis of water. As a gas, hydrogen could replace natural gas (methane). When liquefied, hydrogen might be burned in automobile or airplane engines. At present hydrogen, like many of the possible new fuels, is too expensive to produce to make its use practical. By the year 2000, 75% of our energy will still be produced from ordinary fossil fuels—oil, gas, and coal.

Exxon Co.

Many scientists are seeking new ways to remove sulfur from petroleum.

As yet there is no adequate method for removing sulfur from smokestack gases.

This experiment can be done as a demonstration to illustrate the manufacture of a plastic.

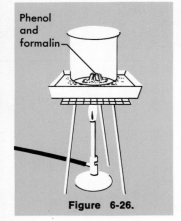

Phenol and formalin

Figure 6-26.

The formation of Bakelite results from the polymerization of phenol by formaldehyde in the presence of the basic catalyst NaOH.

EXPERIMENT. CAUTION: The chemicals used in this experiment are very corrosive to the skin. Use eye and clothing protection. Mix 50 g of phenol and 80 g of formalin in a beaker. Heat the beaker in a pan of water until the crystals melt. Add ½ g of solid sodium hydroxide and heat gently. If needed, add a small amount of solid sodium hydroxide to thicken the mixture. What kind of organic compound have you prepared? a plastic (Bakelite)

Alkenes also form polymers. Plastic bags, refrigerator storage containers, toys, utensil handles, and many other everyday items are made of polyethylene. Polyethylene, as its name implies, is a polymer of ethylene. It is more rigid than the synthetic rubbers. Other compounds based on ethylene are vinyl products. These polymers may include elements other than hydrogen and carbon. Polyvinyl chloride, for example, includes chlorine. Its large molecules may be composed of from 100 to 500 smaller units. Polyvinyl compounds are used in phonograph records, garden hoses, floor tiles, sprinkler tubing, and many other items.

Some polymers do not include hydrogen. Tetrafluoroethylene,

$$\begin{array}{c} F \quad F \\ | \quad | \\ C = C \\ | \quad | \\ F \quad F \end{array}$$

, polymerizes and forms the compound used in "non-stick" utensils. Because its fluorine-carbon bond is so strong, tetrafluoroethylene resists heat and chemicals. It is so tightly bonded that it will not allow anything to "stick" to it. Thus, it can be used as the lining for many kitchen pots and pans. It is also of great use in industry and in the chemistry laboratory for the same reasons.

What are some man-made fibers?

acrilan, polyester fiber, dacron, kodel, rayon, etc.

General Motors Corp.

Figure 6-27. Many everyday items are made from polymers.

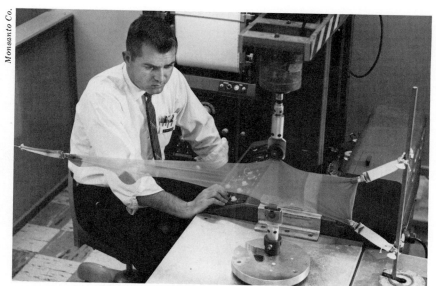

Figure 6-28. Nylon stockings, a product of polymerization, are fragile in appearance but relatively strong and durable.

Figure 6-29. Polyesters are not used only to make textiles. These bowling balls are polyester.

Many man-made fibers, such as nylon and orlon, are produced by polymerization. Some are tougher, stronger, and more elastic than many natural fibers. The popular knit clothes are "polyester," polymers of organic compounds called esters. They have properties similar to nylon and orlon.

ACTIVITY. Collect small samples of textile materials from home. Wool, cotton, nylon, rayon, orlon, dacron, silk, and linen are good choices. Your instructor may supply some of these. Hold one sample of each over a flame with forceps. Which samples burn? Put a second sample of each in a test tube containing 5 ml of dilute hydrochloric acid. Which samples are affected? Put a third sample of each in a test tube containing 5 ml of sodium hydroxide solution. Which are affected? What does this tell you about the relative properties of the materials? Make a chart to explain your results.

Figure 6-30.

6:9   *Other Organic Compounds*

Not all hydrocarbons are found as chain molecules. Many form *ring compounds*. Both saturated and unsaturated hydrocarbons may form rings. Two compounds which have six carbon atoms in each molecule are cyclohexane (C_6H_{12}) and benzene (C_6H_6). Are these compounds isomers? The structural formulas for the two compounds are

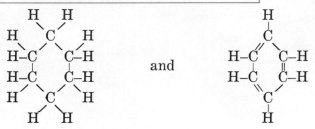

and

Cyclohexane has all single bonds. Benzene has alternating double bonds. To save time and space, cyclohexane is often

written as ⬡. Benzene is ⬡. A carbon atom bonded

to hydrogen atoms is at each vertex. A vertex is a point where two lines intersect at an angle.

PROBLEMS

6. Draw a structural formula for cyclopentane. Its simple molecular formula is C_5H_{10}.

7. Draw a structural formula for $C_6H_4Cl_2$ (dichlorobenzene). How many structural formulas for $C_6H_4Cl_2$ can you draw? *Three, with chlorine ortho-, meta-, para-*

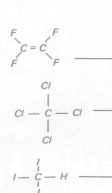

Among the reasons for the great number of carbon compounds is the existence of substituted hydrocarbons. *Substitution* means that atoms of some other element replace one or more hydrogen atoms in a certain compound. Tetrafluoroethylene is a substituted hydrocarbon. Each hydrogen atom in the ethylene molecule is replaced by a fluorine atom.

Carbon tetrachloride (tetrachloromethane) is another substituted hydrocarbon. In this case, each hydrogen atom is replaced by an atom of chlorine. Similar products, such as iodoform (CHI_3) and chloroform ($CHCl_3$), are formed with members of the halogen family.

If a hydrogen atom in a hydrocarbon is replaced by an –OH group, an alcohol is formed. You may be familiar with two common alcohols: methyl alcohol (methanol, CH_3OH) and ethyl alcohol (ethanol, CH_3CH_2OH). Table 6–2 lists some of the alcohols with their structural formulas and their uses. Notice that some of the alcohols have more than one –OH substitution.

What is a common use for isopropyl alcohol ($CH_3CHOHCH_3$)?

rubbing alcohol

Table 6–2. *Some Common Alcohols*

Name	Structural Formula	Uses
Methanol	H—C—OH (with H top and bottom)	fuel for high-performance engines, solvent, preparation of other compounds
Ethanol	H—C—C—OH	solvent, preparation of other compounds, germicide, grain spirits, fuel
Propanol-2 (isopropyl alcohol)	H—C—C—C—H (OH on middle carbon)	common rubbing alcohol, preparation of other organic compounds
Phenol	(benzene ring)—OH	preparation of plastics, disinfectant, preparation of other compounds
Ethylene glycol	H—C—C—H (OH OH on top)	solvent, coolant, antifreeze
Glycerol	H—C—C—C—H (OH OH OH on top)	moistening agent, lubricant, preparation of explosives (nitroglycerin)

Have some of the students prepare reports on organic compounds such as amino acids, fats, proteins, and nucleic acids that are important in biology. For example, have them find out how the structural formula for hemoglobin compares with the structural formula of chlorophyll.

See Teacher's material for additional experiment with esters.

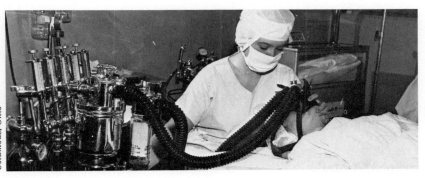

Courtesy of University Hospital, Columbus, Ohio

Figure 6-31. An anesthetist administers an anesthetic to a patient. Most anesthetics are carbon compounds, the most common being diethyl ether ($C_2H_5OC_2H_5$).

MAIN IDEAS

p. 102 **1.** Organic chemistry is the study of carbon compounds.

p. 102, p. 103 **2.** A carbon atom can form four covalent bonds. Carbon combines with other atoms in single, double, or triple covalent bonds.

p. 102 **3.** There are a great number of carbon compounds because:
   a. carbon atoms can unite with other carbon atoms to form long chains or rings;
   b. carbon atoms can combine with single, double, or triple bonds;
   c. carbon compounds may have many isomers;
   d. carbon compounds can be formed by substituting an atom of one element for another in a compound that already exists.

p. 106 **4.** Isomers have the same molecular formulas, but different structural formulas.

p. 108 **5.** Hydrocarbons contain carbon and hydrogen.

p. 108 **6.** In saturated hydrocarbons all carbon atoms are bonded with single covalent bonds.

p. 108 **7.** Hydrocarbons with double or triple carbon to carbon bonds are called unsaturated.

p. 108 **8.** Alkanes are a group of saturated hydrocarbons.

p. 115, p. 116 **9.** Alkenes, alkynes, and alkadienes are unsaturated.

p. 111 **10.** Crude oil is refined by fractionation.

p. 112 **11.** Gasoline is rated on the basis of octane number.

p. 116 **12.** Polymers are large molecules formed through the bonding together of smaller molecules.

p. 120 **13.** Ring compounds may be saturated or unsaturated.

VOCABULARY

Write a sentence in which you correctly use each of the following words or terms.

alkane	hydrocarbon	polymer
alkadiene	isomer	saturated
alkene	molecular formula	substitution
alkyne	octane rating	tetrahedron
fraction	organic	unsaturated
graphic formula		

STUDY QUESTIONS

A. True or False *Have students rewrite false statements to make the statements correct.*

Determine whether each of the following sentences is true or false. (Do not write in this book.)

F **1.** Carbon is in the ~~VA~~ column of the periodic table. *IVA*

F **2.** A carbon atom has ~~6~~ electrons in its outer shell. *4*

T **3.** Carbon atoms can form double and triple covalent bonds.

T **4.** H–C–C–H is the structural formula for ethane.

T **5.** CH_3CH_3 is a graphic formula for ethane.

T **6.** Isomers are compounds which have the same simple formula but different structural formulas.

F **7.** Propane, H–C–C–C–H, is a member of the ~~alkene~~ series. *alkane*

T **8.** Petroleum may be separated into gasoline, kerosene, and other fuels and oils.

T **9.** Automobile exhaust contains unburned hydrocarbons.

F **10.** A substituted hydrocarbon contains atoms of hydrogen and carbon ~~only~~. *and other elements*

B. Multiple Choice *Some questions in part B may have more than one correct answer. Only one answer is required.*

Choose one word or phrase that correctly completes each of the following sentences. (Do not write in this book.)

1. All hydrocarbons contain (<u>carbon</u>, chlorine, oxygen).

2. The carbon atom has (0, 1, 2, 3, <u>4</u>, 5, 6, 7) electrons in its outer shell.

3. Carbon chains are limited to (5, 18, 25, <u>no known limit of</u>) carbon atoms.

4. All alcohols have at least one (NO_3, <u>OH</u>, SO_4) group.

5. Neoprene rubber is a(n) (<u>polymer</u>, isomer, isotope, allotrope).

6. Gasoline may contain (<u>octane</u>, ethylene, potassium chloride).

7. Ethene is a(n) (saturated, <u>unsaturated</u>) hydrocarbon.

8. Acetylene is an (alkane, alkene, <u>alkyne</u>).

9. C_2F_4 is a(n) (isomer, <u>polymer</u>, allotrope).

C. Completion

Complete each of the following sentences with a word or phrase which will make the sentence correct. (Do not write in this book.)

structural

1. $H-\underset{\underset{H}{|}}{\overset{\overset{H}{|}}{C}}-\underset{\underset{H}{|}}{\overset{\overset{H}{|}}{C}}-H$ is a(n) __?__ formula.

Covalent

2. Carbon compounds are formed by __?__ bonding.

isomers

3. $CH_2ClCH_2CH_3$ and $CH_3CHClCH_3$ are __?__.

cracking

4. Long chains of carbon atoms can be broken down by the process called __?__.

fractionation

5. Gasoline is produced from crude oil by __?__.

polymers

6. Vinyl compounds are examples of __?__.

CCl_4

7. The formula for tetrachloromethane is __?__.

$\underset{\underset{F}{|}}{\overset{\overset{F}{|}}{C}}=\underset{\underset{F}{|}}{\overset{\overset{F}{|}}{C}}$ _____

8. Tetrafluoroethylene has the structural formula __?__.

methane

9. The first member of the alkane family is __?__.

D. How and Why

1. $H:\overset{\cdot\cdot}{\underset{\cdot\cdot}{C}}:H$
    $\quad\;\;H$

1. Draw a diagram of methane (CH_4). Show the electrons.

2. Isomers are compounds with the same formula but different structure; isotopes are elements with the same number of protons but different number of neutrons.

2. How do isomers differ from isotopes?

3. See p.122.

3. What facts account for so many carbon compounds?

4. See p.120.

4. Benzene and cyclohexane have similarities and differences. What are some of each?

5. See Teacher's Guide at the front of this book.

5. Draw structural formulas for the organic compounds that are isomers of C_4H_9Br.

6. (a) C_2H_6 (b) $Hg\,I$ (c) $NaBr$ (d) $(NH_4)_3PO_4$

6. Write formulas for each of the following: (a) ethane, (b) mercury (I) iodide, (c) sodium bromide, (d) ammonium phosphate.

7. See Teacher's material.

7. Draw a structural formula for each of the following compounds. C_2H_5OH, C_2H_3OH, and C_5H_{10}.

8. Fractionation is a form of distillation.

8. How is distillation related to fractionation?

9. See Teacher's Guide at the front of this book.

9. Give a structural formula for a representative from each of these families: alkane, alkene, alkyne, diene. How can you tell which compound is in which family?

10. C-C bonds are 109°.

10. Why are "straight" carbon chains crooked?

INVESTIGATIONS

See Teacher's material at front of book for suggestions.

1. Chlorophyll is necessary for plant life. Hemoglobin is basic to life in human beings and warm-blooded animals. Find

the chemical composition and structure of these two compounds. Compare them. How are they alike? How are they different?

2. Visit a service station and determine what different petroleum products are used or sold to the public. Explain the characteristics which make each product useful.

3. Prepare a report on natural gas. Include the history of its use, sources of the gas, uses of the gas, and any current information about shortages of natural gas.

4. Organic compounds are used for textile dyes. Prepare a report on the history and uses of dyes.

INTERESTING READING

Asimov, Isaac, "Is Silicon-Life Possible?" *Science Digest*, LXXII (July, 1972), pp. 56–57.

Asimov, Isaac, *The World of Carbon*. New York, Abelard-Schuman, Ltd., 1962.

Chase, Sara H., *First Book of Diamonds*. New York, Franklin Watts, Inc., 1971.

Kaufman, Morris, *Giant Molecules: The Technology of Plastics, Fibers, and Rubber*. Garden City, New York, Doubleday & Company, Inc., 1968.

Klein, S. A., "Methane Gas: An Overlooked Energy Source." *Organic Gardening and Farming*, XIX (June, 1972), pp. 98–101.

Lambert, Joseph B., "The Shapes of Organic Molecules." *Scientific American*, CCXXII (January, 1970), pp. 58–70.

Squires, Arthur M., "Clean Power from Dirty Fuels." *Scientific American*, CCXXVII (October, 1972), pp. 26–35.

Wohlrabe, Raymond A., *Exploring Giant Molecules*. New York, World Publishing Co., 1969.

Changes in Matter

Alfred Werner was a French-Swiss chemist whose work on molecular structure led to the electronic theory of valency.

Chemistry must become the astronomy of the world of molecules.

Alfred Werner (1866-1919)

Some of the first matter-energy relationships to be observed by early scientists were those involving chemical changes. It has taken many years of labor to gain insight into the matter-energy changes on the molecular and atomic levels. Manipulation and control of chemical changes have given the foundation for many facets of technology.

Astronomers explore heavenly bodies in the universe; chemists probe the structure of molecules in matter. Knowledge of new stars and comets is added to the science of astronomy. In the same way, new knowledge is added to the science of chemistry. Theories about the structure of matter make it possible for man to begin to understand the principles that explain physical and chemical changes. Evaporation, freezing, and boiling are examples of physical changes which can be explained by atomic theory. Chemical changes, such as burning and rusting, are related to the bonds which hold atoms together.

Chemists have special ways to communicate with each other. Chemical equations are a shorthand for showing changes in a chemical reaction. Letters are used as abbreviations for elements and compounds. Chemists have developed systems for naming and classifying elements and compounds. Numbers are included in equations to show the amounts of substances in a reaction. In the eighteenth century, chemists recognized the importance of accurate measurements in their experiments. They came to agree on special ways to measure the reactants and products involved in chemical changes.

New theories give unity and simplicity to the chemical knowledge of today. Much more is still to be done . . . perhaps by you.

unit
four

Bruce Charlton

Solid substances with a regular geometric form are called crystals. Particles in crystals are held together through ionic bonding, covalent bonding, metallic bonding, van der Waals attraction, or dipole-dipole attraction. Solids which have no crystalline shape are said to be amorphous. Fluids are substances which flow. By altering conditions, changes of state can take place for most substances.

Solids and Fluids

GOAL: You will gain an understanding of solids and fluids, arrangement and bonding of particles in solids and fluids, and factors which cause changes of state.

Have you ever watched a candle burn? Is wax a solid or liquid? Matter exists in three common phases (states): *solid*, *liquid*, and *gas*. Sometimes, however, it is difficult to decide which phase a material is in.

Each phase of matter has different properties. Changing the phase of a material means changing some of the material's properties.

7:1 Solid Phase

Ice is a solid. What other solids can you think of? **Solids** have a definite shape and a constant volume. The particles in solids are held together by strong attractive forces. Solids can be classified as either crystalline or amorphous.

7:2 Crystals

Crystals are regular, solid, geometric forms. Every crystalline element or compound has a characteristic geometric form. The crystal form of a compound may aid in its identification.

Figure 7-1. When a candle burns, wax changes from solid into liquid and then back to solid again.

Do all crystals have the same shape?

Crystals of the same substance have the same shape. However, crystals of each substance have characteristic shape.

Figure 7-2. Snowflakes are crystals. They are always six-sided but no two are exactly alike.

Charles and Nancy Knight, National Center for Atmospheric Research

ACTIVITY. *One common crystalline solid is table salt (NaCl). Pour a few crystals of table salt onto a piece of colored paper. Examine the salt with a magnifying glass. Compare the shape of the crystals. Compare the size of the crystals. Draw the shape of a salt crystal. Is each side the same or are some sides different from others?*

Sides are squares or rectangles.

Figure 7-3.

ACTIVITY. *Obtain some different kinds of crystals from home or the school home economics department. Sugar and Epsom salts are examples. Observe each type of crystal under a magnifying glass. Try to pulverize (crush) several crystals of each type. Prepare a chart showing relative size, shape, strength (pulverizing) of each type. Include other properties you observe.*

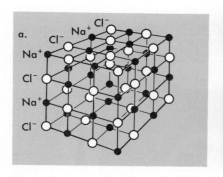

Pacific Gas & Electric Co.

Regularly patterned wallpaper is an example of a two-dimensional pattern. Each unit of the pattern is repeated either vertically, horizontally, or in both directions.

Figure 7-4. (a) Two kinds of ions make up the sodium chloride crystal. (b) A crystal of sodium chloride looks like a cube.

In crystals, atoms or ions are held together in organized patterns. The pattern of atoms or ions in a crystal extends in three dimensions. Thus, a three-dimensional structure forms.

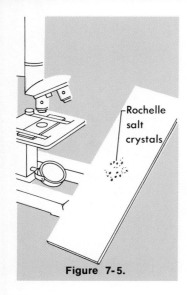

Figure 7-5.

The crystal may be thought of as identical blocks arranged in straight lines in three dimensions (Figure 7–4).

Surfaces of crystals are called **faces.** The faces form definite angles with each other. For example, the faces of a salt crystal are at 90-degree angles to each other. How many faces does a salt crystal have? A crystal may be *cleaved* (split). Still each piece will have the same number of faces and the same angles. The same basic structure is repeated throughout each piece. In other words, a large crystal of a substance will have the same shape as a small crystal of the same substance.

EXPERIMENT. Place several Rochelle salt crystals on a glass slide. Observe under a microscope. Make a sketch of their shape. Repeat with alum, nickel sulfate, and sodium nitrate crystals. Compare the crystal shapes. See Teacher's Guide at the front of this book.

What things in nature might exhibit symmetry?

butterflies, leaves, seeds, plants, etc.

If you examine a crystal, you see that some of the faces look alike. A cube like the salt crystal, for example, looks the same if you turn it 90 degrees left or right or up or down. This property is called *symmetry.* Symmetric objects can be divided by a plane, line, or point, so that each half is equal in size, shape, and function (Figure 7–6). Thus, some crystals are symmetric with respect to a plane and some with respect to a point. Some are symmetric with respect to an *axis.* This axis is called an *axis of symmetry.* Figure 7–6 shows some examples of symmetry.

Demonstrate the building of a two-dimensional pattern from a unit cell such as a square. Repeat the square in both the horizontal and the vertical directions. Have the students visualize the repetition of the square in the third dimension. The three-dimensional pattern will be cubic.

Axes of symmetry are important when considering cleavage of a crystal. **Cleavage** is the tendency of a crystal to come

Figure 7-6. A person and a butterfly are symmetric with respect to a plane. A wheel is symmetric with respect to a point.

apart between planes of atoms or ions when hit by a sharp blow. A cubic crystal can be split along any direction perpendicular to an edge of the cube. Thus it has three axes of symmetry. Along each axis it can be broken apart along definite smooth planes. Not all crystals have this property to the same degree. Some crystals simply crumble when hit. Others, such as mica, can be pulled apart by hand along the cleavage planes (Figure 7–8). The shape and cleavage of a crystal depends upon the kinds of particles in the crystal and the bonds which hold the particles together. The types of particles and bonds also determine many of the crystal's properties. When *melting* for instance, a crystal goes from the solid to the liquid phase. The stronger the bonds between particles in the crystal, the higher the **melting point.** (The melting point is the temperature at which a material goes from the solid to the liquid phase.) Also, strongly bonded crystals can not usually conduct an electric current (Section 18:2). Their **melts** (liquid formed by melting the crystal), however, often can conduct a current.

Figure 7-7. These two large tourmaline crystals are two inches in diameter and four inches long. They rest in a 6-inch quartz crystal. Because of their beauty, both quartz and tourmaline are often used in jewelry.

Van Pelt, courtesy of Pala Properties

EXPERIMENT.　*Obtain a piece of mica. Stick a pin into the edge of the crystal. Work the pin back and forth to cleave off a small piece. Observe the mica crystal under a microscope. Draw a diagram of its shape.*

7:3　Ionic Bonding in Crystals

Particles in crystals may be held together by *ionic bonding*. In **ionic bonding,** attraction between oppositely charged ions holds the crystal together. Sodium chloride crystals, for example, are made of sodium ions and chloride ions. Each sodium ion is surrounded by six chloride ions. Each chloride ion is surrounded by six sodium ions.

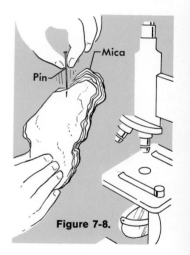

Figure 7-8.

ACTIVITY.　*Obtain six small styrofoam balls, one large styrofoam ball, and some toothpicks. Arrange all seven balls to form the most compact structure possible. Use toothpicks to hold the balls together. Does your model look like Figure 7–9? The small balls represent sodium ions. The large ball represents a chloride ion. Combine your model with those of several of your classmates. Each sodium should be separated by only one chloride. Compare your model to Figure 7–4. What does this larger model represent?*

Figure 7-9.

Emphasize that there is no such thing as a sodium chloride molecule.

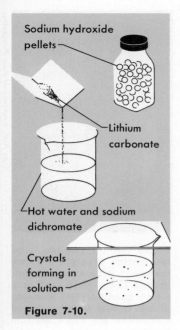

Sodium hydroxide pellets

Lithium carbonate

Hot water and sodium dichromate

Crystals forming in solution

Figure 7-10.

What is the relationship between melting point of a crystal and the bonding in the crystal?

the ratio of ions in compound

The van der Waals radius is the minimum distance that can exist between nonbonded atoms.

EXPERIMENT.   CAUTION: Do not touch either sodium dichromate or sodium hydroxide. Wear eye and clothing protection. Mix 60 g of sodium dichromate dihydrate in 130 ml of hot water in a beaker. Slowly add 7.5 g of lithium carbonate. When the bubbling of carbon dioxide stops, add 8 g of solid sodium hydroxide. Cover and allow to stand. Observe any crystals which form. If crystals do not form in a day, add a few tiny sodium dichromate crystals. The crystals are yellow and hexagonal.

A crystal built up by ionic bonding is called an ionic crystal. Ionic bonding produces crystals which are hard and brittle. These crystals have high melting points. They do not conduct electricity. This is because the outer electrons in each ion in the crystal are held tightly. However, a *melt* can conduct a current. When an ionic crystal melts, its ions are no longer held together. The ions are free to move in a melt.

Sodium chloride and other crystalline ionic compounds do not have a molecular arrangement. The formula NaCl gives only the ratio of sodium ions to chloride ions in a crystal. It is not a formula for a molecule. What are some other common examples of ionic crystals? Look at the periodic table in Chapter 4. Where are the elements most likely to form ionic crystals located in the table? *KCL, NaI, CaBr$_2$*

In general, metals at the far left of the table combine with nonmetals of Groups VI and VII to form ionic crystals.

7:4 *Other Attractive Forces in Crystals*

Some crystals are held together by *van der Waals forces*. **Van der Waals forces** are the attraction of the positively charged nucleus of one atom for the electrons of another atom. Van der Waals forces are very weak compared to ionic bonds.

Another force is the *dipole-dipole attraction*. When two atoms form a covalent bond, the shared electrons are not always shared equally. For example, two hydrogen atoms and one oxygen atom form one molecule of water through covalent bonding. Oxygen has eight protons in its nucleus. Hydrogen has one proton. Therefore, oxygen has a greater positive nuclear charge (Section 3:2) than hydrogen. For this reason, electrons in the water molecule spend more time near the oxygen nucleus than the hydrogen nucleus. Thus, the oxygen end of the molecule has a negative charge. The hydrogen end of the molecule is positively charged; it has an absence of elec-

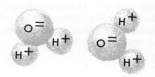

trons (Figure 7–11). Since the water molecule has a positive end and a negative end, it is called a **dipole** (two poles).

In effect, a dipole molecule acts like a magnet. It has positive and negative ends like a magnet's north and south poles. In **dipole-dipole attraction,** the positive end of one molecule attracts the negative end of other molecules. The positive end of the others will attract the negative end of still other molecules, and so on. This produces a crystal that is held together by weak attractive forces. These forces are far weaker than the ionic attraction in a crystal such as sodium chloride.

Crystals formed by van der Waals and dipole forces have some similar properties. They are soft and have low melting points. They do not conduct electricity. Iodine crystals are a good example of crystals formed by van der Waals bonding.

Figure 7-11. The water molecule is a dipole.

Would HCl be a polar molecule?

HCl is polar because chlorine controls the shared electrons more than the hydrogen. Chlorine has a greater nuclear charge.

7:5   Covalent Bonding in Crystals

Some crystals are formed by only covalent bonding. In **covalent bonding,** attraction between atoms holds the crystal together. The entire crystal becomes one huge molecule called a macromolecule. Diamonds are formed by this type of bonding. Each carbon atom in a diamond crystal is bonded covalently to four other carbon atoms. Such a crystal is said to have a *three-dimensional strong bond.* The properties of diamonds are typical of crystals which are covalently bonded throughout. They are extremely hard and have high melting points. They do not conduct electricity. Some compounds also crystallize covalently in a three-dimensional

The carbon atoms in the "giant molecule" of diamond are bound together by strong covalent bonds. The molecules of molecular compounds are held to each other by much weaker van der Waals forces. To melt diamond or other compounds having a covalent lattice crystalline structure, the individual covalent bonds must be broken. This requires energy and such compounds melt at high temperatures.

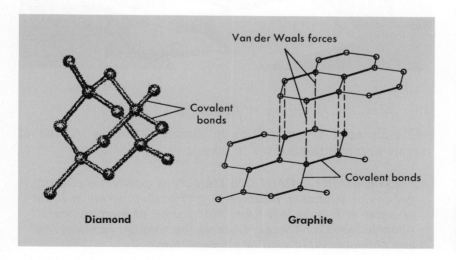

Van der Waals forces

Covalent bonds

Covalent bonds

Diamond

Graphite

Figure 7-12. The differences in the properties of diamond and graphite are the result of different crystal structures.

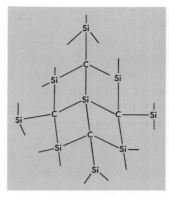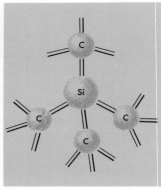

Diamonds and graphite are allotropes because they are different molecular (crystalline) forms of the same element, carbon.

strong bond. In these cases the attraction is between molecules. Silicon carbide (SiC) is an example (Figure 7–13).

Some molecules with covalent bonding do not form crystals held together entirely by covalent bonds. Graphite in your pencil is one example. In graphite, each carbon atom is covalently bonded to three others in the same plane. These are *two-dimensional strong bonds*. However, the bonding between the planes is probably weak van der Waals bonding. The distances between the atoms in the plane are much smaller than the distances between the planes (Figure 7–12). This partly accounts for the fact that graphite is not as hard as diamond. The planes in graphite easily slide over each other. This property makes graphite a very good lubricant and a useful writing material. As it moves across the paper, your pencil lays down a thin but continuous layer of graphite (Figure 7–14).

What kind of bonding does graphite have?

*Two-dimensional.
Recall experiment with mica.*

Figure 7-14. The "lead" in pencils is really graphite. Because it is soft, graphite glides easily over paper and is a good writing material.

Carl England

7:6 Metallic Bonding in Crystals

Metals tend to crystallize in simple patterns. Atoms of metals arrange themselves in layers.

EXPERIMENT. CAUTION: *Mercury is poisonous. Do not get any on your skin. Dissolve ¼ g of sodium nitrate in 10 ml of water in a large test tube. Add 1 drop of mercury metal. Allow to stand for 1 week. Observe the solution and describe any changes. What kind of crystals form?*

Needle-shaped crystals of metal grow.

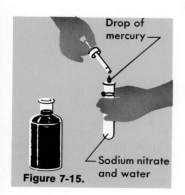

Drop of mercury

Sodium nitrate and water

Figure 7-15.

Mfg. Jewelers & Silversmiths

The Reveker Hill Co

In metallic bonding, the outer electrons of the atoms move throughout the crystal and are shared equally by all the ions.

The free electrons in a metal help explain some of the properties of metals (Section 5:4). Because electrons are free to move throughout the structure, metals conduct electricity. Metals are not brittle because metallic ions in layers can slide over each other and may be shifted without shattering the crystal. This allows the metals to be pulled out into wire or hammered into thin sheets without breaking.

Figure 7-16. Metals are ductile (able to be pulled out into wires). Metals are malleable (able to be hammered into thin sheets).

7:7   Crystallization

Solid crystals of a substance form under varying conditions. Crystals are formed from solutions, hot melts, or vapor. In a solution, particles of solid substance are mixed throughout another substance, usually a liquid. An example of this is a solution of salt in water. Particles of solid salt mix into the water as the salt dissolves. Under certain conditions, the salt will come out of solution and form crystals of salt again.

From what three sources do crystals form?

Nonmetallic elements which have relatively low melting points (sulfur and iodine) form crystals in which the positions in the crystal pattern are occupied by molecules. The atoms within the molecules are held together by covalent bonds. The molecules are attached to other molecules by weak van der Waals forces.

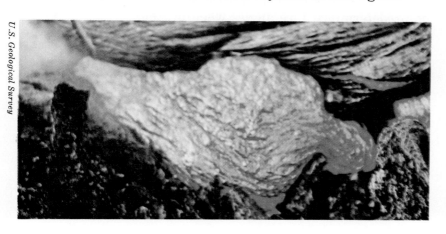

U.S. Geological Survey

Figure 7-17. Lava is liquid rock.

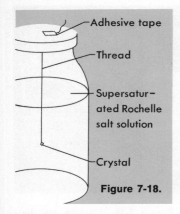

Adhesive tape

Thread

Supersatur-
ated Rochelle
salt solution

Crystal

Figure 7-18.

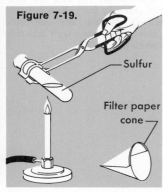

Figure 7-19.

Sulfur

Filter paper
cone

EXPERIMENT. Add 130 g of Rochelle salt to 100 ml of water in a beaker. Heat the mixture and stir until all the salt is dissolved. Allow the solution to cool. Add 9 g of Rochelle salt to the mixture. Pour the solution into a small cap-covered jar. Attach a large Rochelle crystal to a thread, suspend it in the solution, and allow the crystal to stand undisturbed for a week. Does the size of the crystal <u>increase</u>, decrease, or remain the same? Does the shape of the crystal change? How?

EXPERIMENT. Slowly melt some sulfur in a test tube over a Bunsen flame. Describe your observations. Pour the liquid into a paper cone of filter paper. How is this process different from dissolving sugar in water? When a crust forms on the melted sulfur, break it open. Do you observe any crystals?

PROBLEMS

1. How is melting of a substance different from dissolving?

2. How does the formation of crystals from a melt differ from formation of crystals from a solution?

See Teacher's Guide at the front of the book.

How do glasses differ from crystals?

Glasses have no regular pattern, no cleavage axes, no specific face angles, no specific structure.

7:8 *Amorphous Solids*

Many solids have no regular crystalline shapes. These are amorphous solids. Glass is the most common amorphous solid. It has two properties of a solid—definite shape and constant volume. Glass, however, has no regular crystalline structure. Plastics, such as lucite and celluloid, are also amorphous solids.

What happens when glass breaks? Amorphous solids do not have cleavage axes. They chip or leave depressions when broken. They are brittle and break easily. However, they have no predetermined face angles when broken.

Figure 7-20. Glass has no crystal structure. It does not form specific shapes or angles when broken.

Figure 7-21. Glass can be molded into a variety of shapes.

Edward Sonner

RCA Corp.

At one time, some allotropic forms of carbon and sulfur were believed to be amorphous. However, further study, using X-ray diffraction (Section 20:1), showed that soot (amorphous carbon) and amorphous sulfur have crystal structures. Name some amorphous solids.   *Answers will vary. Examples are wax, fat, and plastics.*

7:9 *Fluids*

The term **fluid** is applied to both liquids and gases because both substances flow. A garden hose with holes punched in it can be used as a water sprinkler. When the water is turned on, it sprays out all along the hose at the same height. The principle that explains how all the jets of water rise to the same height also explains how a service station hoist can lift an automobile. Water and all other fluids can exert or transfer forces which move things.

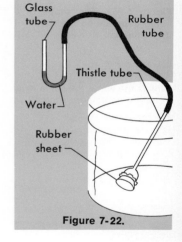

Figure 7-22.

> *EXPERIMENT. Stretch a piece of rubber tubing over the mouth of a thistle tube. Attach with a rubber band. Insert the end of the thistle tube into one end of a rubber tube. Connect the other end of the rubber tube to a U-shaped glass tube which is one-third full of water. Hold the thistle tube at various depths in a large, deep container of water. Point the mouth of the thistle tube up, down, and sideways and observe the movement of water in the U-tube. How is pressure in a liquid affected by depth and direction?*

The pressure is affected only by depth.

7:10 *Liquids*

Liquids have no definite shape. They take the shape of their container. The volume of a liquid, however, remains constant except when the temperature is changed. Molecules of liquid

Figure 7-23. When two containers are connected, the water levels become equal.

Figure 7-24. Particles are constantly in motion. The movement of suspended particles is called Brownian motion.

The random motion of particles in a suspension is caused by the unbalanced force of many molecules bombarding the particle. Although the molecules move extremely fast (100 mi/hr) they go only a short distance before bumping into another molecule or some other particle.

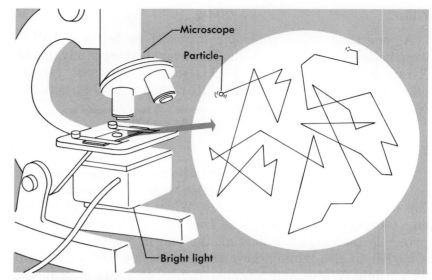

Microscope

Particle

Bright light

Figure 7-25. The shape of a liquid depends on the shape of its container.

Why is the water the same level in all the containers shown?

The molecules at the top are all at the same potential energy level. The level of the water is the lowest potential energy level of the system.

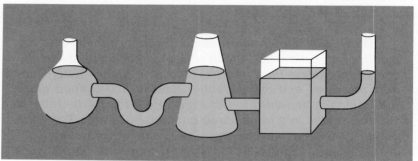

are not tightly bonded. They are free to move and slide freely over each other. Because liquids have no rigid form, the molecules tend to move toward the area closest to the ground. Thus, in a series of interconnected containers, the liquid will be at the same level across all the containers (Figure 7–25). Particles of a solid vibrate about a fixed point. Liquid particles move more or less independently throughout the liquid.

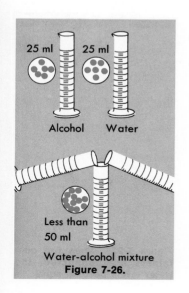

25 ml   25 ml

Alcohol   Water

Less than 50 ml

Water-alcohol mixture
Figure 7-26.

EXPERIMENT. Obtain a 25-ml and a 50-ml graduate. Measure exactly 25 ml of water with the small graduate and then pour this water into the 50-ml graduate. Measure 25 ml more of water with the small graduate and pour it into the 50-ml graduate. Repeat the procedure using alcohol instead of water. How much is 25 ml plus 25 ml? Using the small graduate, measure and add exactly 25 ml of water and 25 ml of alcohol to the 50-ml graduate. Why is the combined volume of the alcohol and water less than 50 ml? Explain what you observe.

50 ml

The alcohol molecules move into spaces between the water molecules. The mixture of alcohol and water is a liquid-liquid solution since the mixture is uniform throughout.

In most cases, the particles in a liquid are farther apart than the particles in a crystal of the same substance. There is more empty space between liquid particles. Other particles can move into these spaces. This can also occur in solids, although not to the same extent.

ACTIVITY. Fill a 250-ml beaker with marbles to the 100-ml mark. Fill another 250-ml beaker with BB pellets to the 100-ml mark. What is the total volume of both? Add the BB's to the marble. What is the new total volume? Explain the change. BB's fit between marbles.

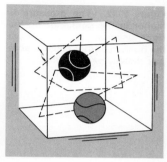

Figure 7-27. Balls in a vibrating box collide with the walls and with each other.

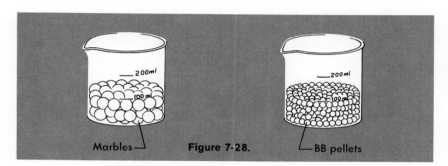

Marbles   **Figure 7-28.**   BB pellets

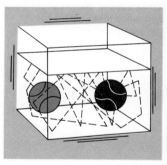

Figure 7-29. If the volume is decreased, the pressure increases.

7:11 Gases

Gases have no definite shape and no constant volume. The atoms or molecules in gases are separated by large distances. Because gases are mostly empty space, the gas molecules can be forced closer together. Also, since gas molecules are very weakly attracted to one another, they can move further apart. This ability allows gases to completely fill containers of various volumes and shapes. Gas molecules are constantly in rapid random straight line motion. The average gas particle travels at about 400 meters per second at standard conditions. However, particles collide with (bump into) each other and with the sides of their container. The average distance traveled without collision is 0.000001 centimeter. Collisions of gas molecules with the walls of the container create pressure in the container. If the collisions are increased, the pressure is increased.

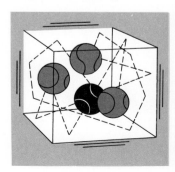

Figure 7-30. Increasing the number of balls, increases the number of collisions.

PROBLEMS   *Gas molecules collide with sides of balloon.*

3. How do gases cause balloons to inflate?
4. What happens to an auto tire as air is released?

Air molecules rush out, tire deflates.

Figure 7-31. The pressure is higher in the container on the left, because none of the gas is being released and more of the gas molecules are colliding.

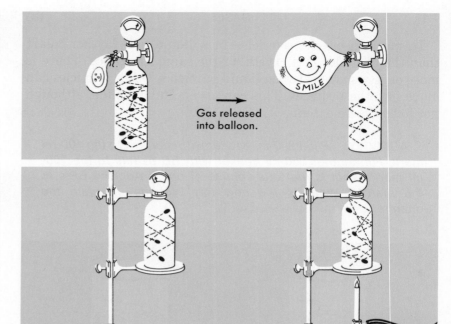

Gas released into balloon.

Figure 7-32. The pressure is higher in the container on the right because the heat from the Bunsen burner causes more gas molecules to collide.

What causes the pressure on a container filled with a gas?
collision of molecules

If the volume of a gas is reduced without any change of temperature, the pressure increases.

As the number of gas molecules in a container increases, the pressure increases (Figure 7–30). This is due to an increased number of collisions with the container wall. Does the pressure in a car tire <u>increase</u> or decrease as it rolls over hot pavement at high speeds? Why?

Heat causes molecules to move more rapidly. When gas molecules are heated, they move faster and hit the walls of the container more often. This causes a flexible container such as a balloon to expand. Closed rigid containers, such as the one in Figure 7–32, register a pressure increase.

Like liquids, the volume of a mixture of gases is not equal to the sum of the volumes of the individual gases. Suppose one liter of oxygen at a given temperature and pressure were added to a container holding one liter of hydrogen at the same conditions. Only one liter of the oxygen-hydrogen mixture of gases would result. However, the pressure of the mixture would be equal to the sum of the individual gas pressures. The pressure would be twice the original pressure because twice as many molecules occupy the same volume.

PROBLEM

5. When you blow up a balloon, how does your breath cause the balloon to expand? *Addition of more and more molecules causes more collisions.*

7:12 Pascal's Law

If the external pressure on a gas in a closed container is increased, the volume of the gas decreases. The particles move closer together. If the pressure on a crystal is increased, the crystal may crumble or shatter. The crystal will not noticeably decrease in size.

When pressure is applied to a liquid, however, changes do occur. For example, suppose that you had a jug of water that was completely full. Then you put a cork in the mouth of the jug and hit the cork with a hammer. If you hit it hard enough, the bottom of the jug might fall out. A balloon filled with water reacts differently when dropped than a balloon filled with air. The air-filled balloon will absorb the pressure of hitting the ground by compressing the air in the balloon. The water-filled balloon, however, will transmit the pressure to all surfaces of the balloon. If there is a weakness, the balloon will break.

Blaise Pascal (1623–1662), a French scientist, proposed what is now called *Pascal's law:* If pressure is applied to a liquid in a closed container, the pressure is transmitted unchanged to all surfaces of the container. Thus, the pressure put on the cork in the jug (Figure 7–33) is transmitted unchanged to the bottom of the jug. Because it works on a much greater area, the force is much greater and the bottom is forced out.

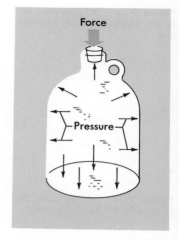

Figure 7-33. Pressure applied to a liquid in a container is transmitted to all surfaces.

Why may an empty bottle bounce and a full one break?

The liquid inside does not compress and transmits the force of the fall to all the surfaces.

EXPERIMENT.   *Obtain a hollow rubber ball. Bore ten small holes evenly spaced over the ball. Insert a glass tube into the ball and connect the tube to a piece of rubber tubing. Connect the rubber tube to a water faucet and place the ball in a sink. Make sure all connections are tight and then turn on the water. How does this experiment illustrate Pascal's law? How does a sprinkler hose illustrate it?*

Pressure is equal in all directions.

Be careful when performing this experiment because the water sprays in all directions. It would be a good idea to do it in the yard with a hose if possible. The pressure exerted by the water is transmitted equally to all surfaces. Water flows from each hole at the same speed.

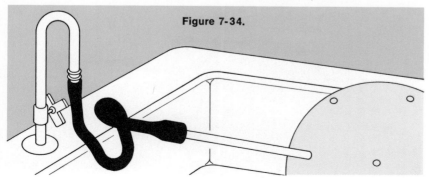

Figure 7-34.

Abraxas Studio, Columbus, Ohio

Figure 7-35. The hydraulic lift is an application of Pascal's law.

$$P = \frac{f}{a} \qquad P = \frac{F}{A}$$

$$\frac{f}{a} = \frac{F}{A}$$

$$\frac{1 \, nt}{1 \, cm^2} = \frac{F}{100 \, cm^2}$$

$$F = \frac{100 \, cm^2}{1 \, cm^2} \cdot \frac{1 \, nt}{}$$

$$F = 100 \, nt$$

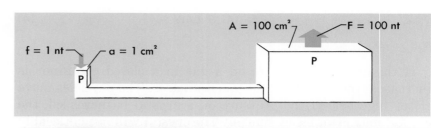

Figure 7-36. A hydraulic lift is used to lift heavy objects.

Carl England

Figure 7-37. The balloons filled with air bounce. The balloons filled with water break. Why?

A similar principle is at work on a hydraulic lift. The diagram in Figure 7–35 shows Pascal's law in use.

A force exerted on a small area causes a pressure in the liquid. This pressure is transmitted equally throughout the liquid. Since the pressure is the same throughout the system, a small force on the small piston produces a large force on the large piston. A force of 1 newton exerted on 1 cm² (small piston) will transfer 100 newtons of force to the piston with an area of 100 cm². In service stations, compressed air is used to apply a force to a small piston. This raises an auto on a hydraulic hoist.

Paul Nesbit

Figure 7-38. Ice melting into water is one kind of change of phase.

7:13   *Change of Phase*

Most substances can be changed from solid to liquid to gas and also from gas to liquid to solid (Section 2:7.) Change of state can readily be explained by the kinetic theory and the structure of substances. The **kinetic theory** states that particles of matter are constantly in motion. As heat is added to a substance, its particles move faster. If the substance is cooled, its particles slow down. Change in speed of particles means change in temperature. Thus, heat plays an important part in change of temperature and change of phase.

Have the students record the temperature and the time as they observe the mixture.

EXPERIMENT.   Place a few ice cubes in a glass of water. Place a thermometer in the mixture. Check the temperature every few minutes until the ice cubes are entirely melted. Where did the heat come from that melted the ice? melted ice *Was there a change in temperature of the solution while the ice was melting? What happened to the heat?*
No.

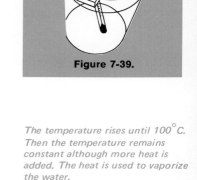

Figure 7-39.

EXPERIMENT.   Suspend a thermometer in a beaker of boiling water. Record the temperature every few minutes as you gradually increase the heat under the beaker. Continue until the water is nearly gone. Was there a change in temperature? What happened to the heat? vaporized water
No.

The temperature rises until $100^{\circ}C$. Then the temperature remains constant although more heat is added. The heat is used to vaporize the water.

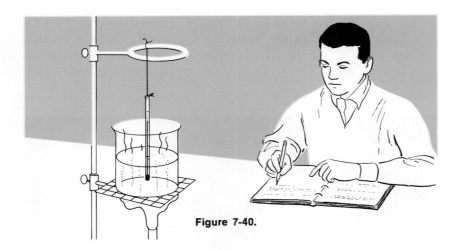

Figure 7-40.

During phase change, particles may separate or move closer together. They may become more or less attracted to each other. Their speed, however, does not change. Therefore, there is no change in temperature.

7:14 Solid-Gas Change

Particles in solids vibrate about fixed points. If heat is added to the solid, the rate of the vibrations increases. The particles in the crystal move back and forth and collide with each other with a greater force. Because the particles are forced farther apart, most solids expand when they are heated. As more heat is added, some of the particles may acquire enough energy to break the bonds that hold them to other particles. In that case, they escape into the air and form a vapor or gas.

Iodine is a solid which changes directly from the solid phase to the gaseous phase. Iodine crystals are formed from diatomic molecules of iodine (I_2). The atoms of iodine in the molecules are much closer together than the molecules in the crystal. The crystal is held together by van der Waals forces. The molecules are held together by covalent bonding. Thus, the particles that eventually escape from the crystal are I_2 molecules. If iodine crystals are in a closed container, purple iodine vapor can be seen over the crystals. Substances which change directly to the gas phase from the solid phase are said to *sublime* (Section 5:1).

To crystallize a substance from the gas form, two processes may be used. The gas may be cooled, or it may be subjected to pressure, or both. In some cases, the gas may become a liquid as an intermediate step before it becomes a solid. However, it is possible for the solid to be formed immediately. The CO_2 (carbon dioxide) fire extinguisher is a good example. In this extinguisher, CO_2 gas is kept under pressure. As the pressure is released, some of the high energy molecules escape. This

What does it mean if a solid sublimes?

changes directly from a solid to a gas

Phosphorus is condensed from a gas to a solid under water.

Figure 7-41. Gaseous carbon dioxide is changed to solid dry ice at low temperatures and a pressure of more than 5.6 atmospheres. At room temperature, dry ice sublimes.

Liquid Carbonic Corp.

lowers the average kinetic energy of the remaining molecules. Their temperature drops to a point below the freezing temperature of carbon dioxide. These molecules form a solid and fall as "snow" to smother the fire.

7:15 *Liquid-Solid Change*

The most common way to cause a liquid to crystallize is to cool the liquid. The liquid particles begin to slow down and move closer together. In their movements, they may try to crystallize in many different forms. However, the liquid will not crystallize until its normal structure is reached. This can happen by seeding or by chance. An impurity in the substance may provide the needed pattern. The particles then begin to crystallize around the impurity. The substance then remains at the freezing temperature until the entire substance is crystallized.

When a liquid fails to crystallize at its freezing point, it is *supercooled*. Normally, water freezes at 0°C. Under some conditions, however, water may exist as a liquid at temperatures below 0°C.

7:16 *Liquid-Gas Change*

Suppose a solid is changed to a liquid by adding heat. If the addition of heat is continued, the particles continue to gain kinetic energy. By successive collisions, they may acquire enough energy to escape the liquid and become part of a vapor. The temperature at which bubbles of a gas or vapor form

The solid carbon dioxide has several advantages over water: it does not conduct electricity; it is much colder than water, thus lowering the kindling temperature; it replaces oxygen essential for combustion to continue; it sublimes making cleaning no problem.

Crystals form around impurities in the substance or around irregularities in the container. Once a small crystal is started, the rest of the substance crystallizes on this base.

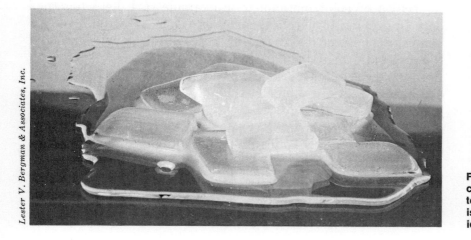

Lester V. Bergman & Associates, Inc.

Figure 7-42. Water and ice can exist at 0°C. Heat is added to change ice to water. Heat is removed to change water to ice.

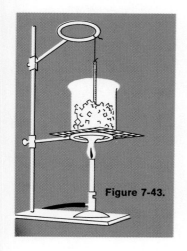

Figure 7-43.

Would krypton or hydrogen be more easily liquefied?

Krypton would be more easily liquefied.

Figure 7-44. Chlorine can be liquefied in the laboratory.

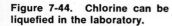

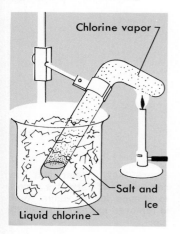

within the liquid is called the vaporization, or boiling, point. For water, this point is 100°C at standard pressure. Whether this can occur depends upon the nature of the substance and the bonds holding the particles together in the liquid.

Generally, in a liquid there are two bond forces acting: dipole-dipole and van der Waals.

> *EXPERIMENT. Fill a beaker two-thirds full of ice. Clamp a thermometer midway into the ice and let it stand until the temperature no longer decreases. Heat gently with a Bunsen burner flame. Does the temperature decrease as the ice melts?* The temperature remains constant as the ice melts.

The van der Waals forces appear to get larger as more electrons and protons are involved in the substance. This would be expected, since van der Waals attraction occurs between the electrons of one particle and the protons of another. Radon gas is composed of atoms with 86 protons and 86 electrons. Thus, it would more likely be found as a liquid than would helium. Helium has atoms with only two electrons and two protons. In liquids, the molecules with the greater number of electrons should attract each other more strongly and be less likely to change to a gas.

Since dipoles attract each other, liquids whose molecules are dipoles tend to be less likely to form a gas than do similar compounds whose molecules are not dipoles. Dipoles have greater attraction to each other, and additional heat is needed to break these bonds.

Bonding type also has some effect on the melting points of substances which occur as solids at normal temperatures. Molecules of solid methane, for example, are held together only by weak van der Waals forces. Thus, methane crystals have a much lower melting point than sodium chloride crystals (ionic bonds) or diamond (covalent bonds).

In the same manner, elements or compounds which normally are gases are more difficult to liquefy the fewer the number of electrons and protons.

For example, chlorine gas is easy to liquefy. Figure 7-44 shows one laboratory method for liquefying chlorine. Pressure forces the gas molecules closer together. Reduced temperature causes them to slow down. The van der Waals forces then take over and cause the gas molecules to come together in a liquid form. Helium and hydrogen are extremely difficult to liquefy.

What to do With Trash

Much valuable material goes into the trash pile. Think of all the paper, steel and aluminum cans, and metal foil you yourself throw away. Most of this ends up in dumps, landfills, or incinerators. Usually little if anything is recycled. This is no longer the case in a few places. For example, the small city of Franklin, Ohio, has one of the most advanced waste treatment plants in the world. This plant removes paper and metal from the city's garbage and trash. The city is able to sell the paper and metal that its recycling plant recovers. This money helps to pay for operating the plant. Here's how it works. A conveyor belt dumps the refuse into a big tub of water. The tub has rotating blades which move the trash around to start separation. Big and heavy pieces sink to the bottom of the tub and are removed. A magnet then passes over the big pieces and picks out the iron mate-

rials. The tub water and those pieces that didn't sink pass through a series of screens and centrifuges. Here paper fibers are recovered. Eventually the plant will also be able to recover glass and aluminum.

Iron is one of the few materials now recycled in large amounts.

Inland Steel Co.

Recycling one ton of paper saves seventeen trees from being cut down to make paper pulp.

The Mead Corp.

Each of us uses about 70 gallons of water every day for drinking, bathing, and waste disposal. Millions of gallons more are used every year by industry and agriculture. Mr. Shiro G. Kimura, a chemical engineer, is one of the people exploring ways to quickly transform this used water into pure drinking water. Here he is inspecting a transparent membrane which allows water to pass through but blocks bacteria, viruses, and particles like clay. Such membranes may someday be used in home water-purification units.

General Electric Research and Development Center

MAIN IDEAS

p. 128
1. Crystals are solid elements or compounds having characteristic geometric form.

pp. 131-135
2. Particles in crystals may be bonded together through:
    a. ionic bonds
    b. covalent bonds
    c. van der Waals forces
    d. dipole-dipole attraction
    e. metallic bonding

pp.131-135
3. The type of bonding in a crystal determines many properties of the crystal.

pp.134-135
4. In metals, free electrons conduct electricity.

p.136
5. Amorphous solids have no regular crystalline shape.

p. 137
6. Fluids—gases and liquids—have no fixed shape. Fluids take the shape of their containers.

p.137
7. Particles of fluids move almost independently of each other.

p. 141
8. Pascal's law states that pressure applied to a liquid in a closed container is transmitted unchanged to all sides or surfaces of the container.

p p.139-140
9. The volume of a gas equals the volume of the container.

p. 143
10. Changes of phase are caused by a change of energy.

VOCABULARY

Write a sentence in which you correctly use each of the following words or terms.

amorphous	dipole	macromolecule
cleavage	fluids	pressure
covalent	gas	solid
crystal	ionic	symmetry
crystal face	liquid	

STUDY QUESTIONS

A. True or False

Have students rewrite false statements to make the statements correct.

Determine whether each of the following sentences is true or false. (Do not write in this book.)

strong ionic, covalent, dipole-dipole, or metallic bonds

F **1.** The molecules of a solid are held together by ~~weak attractive forces~~.

T 2. The surfaces of crystals are called faces.

F 3. Ionically bonded crystals are usually ~~soft~~.   *hard*

T 4. Ionic crystals have high melting points.

T 5. Van der Waals forces are weak bonding forces in some crystals.

T 6. Metals are good conductors of electricity because they contain free electrons.

T 7. Glass is a solid that has no definite crystal structure.

F 8. The volume of a ~~liquid~~ can be decreased by increasing the pressure on the ~~liquid~~ in a closed container.   *gas*   *gas*

F 9. If 10 ml of water is mixed with 10 ml of alcohol the total volume of the mixture will be ~~more~~ than 20 ml.   *less*

T 10. Gas pressure in balloons results from the collision of gas molecules with the inside surface of the balloon.

B. Multiple Choice *Some questions in part B may have more than one correct*   *answer. Only one answer is required.*

Choose one word or phrase that correctly completes each of the following sentences. (Do not write in this book.)

1. Ionic bonding produces crystals which are (soft, <u>brittle</u>, malleable).

2. Metals conduct electricity through their (central ions, <u>electrons</u>, atoms).

3. (<u>Metals</u>, Nonmetals, Metalloids) normally conduct electricity.

4. Particles in solids (always, <u>sometimes</u>, never) move.

5. In an iodine crystal, the distance between iodine atoms in a molecule is (greater than, <u>less than</u>, the same as) the distance between iodine (I_2) molecules.

6. As the temperature increases, the motion of particles in a liquid (<u>increases</u>, decreases, remains the same).

7. Covalent bonding in a crystal is (<u>stronger than</u>, weaker than, the same as) van der Waals bonding.

C. Completion

Complete each of the following sentences with a word or phrase that will make the sentence correct. (Do not write in this book.)

1. Covalent crystals have __?__ melting points.   *low*

2. Van der Waals forces are caused by __?__.   *attraction of nucleus for other electrons*

3. Two crystalline forms of sulfur are ____ and __?__.   *crystalline, amorphous*

glass, wax

4. One example of an amorphous solid is __?__ .

freezing

5. The melting point of a solid is the same as the __?__ point of its liquid state.

temperature, pressure

6. A substance can be liquefied from a gas by __?__ and __?__ .

dipole

7. The water molecule is an example of a(n) __?__ .

increases

8. As the temperature of a gas increases, the particle motion __?__ .

See Teacher's Guide at the front of this book.

D. How and Why

1. What causes dipole molecules?

2. Make a chart showing the properties of different types of crystal bonding.

3. How does a melt of an ionic solid conduct electricity?

4. Two liters of gas A at a pressure of 3 atmospheres are added to one liter of gas B which has a pressure of 2 atmospheres. The combined volume of the two gases is one liter and the temperature remains unchanged. What is the pressure due to both gases?

5. What is a macromolecule?

6. Why should van der Waals forces generally be larger for the heavier elements than for the lighter elements?

7. How does Pascal's law explain the hydraulic lift?

8. Why do you think carbon compounds would not necessarily be found as polar molecules?

9. What type of bonding would you expect crystals of each of the following to have: (a) KBr, (b) diamond, (c) graphite, (d) ethane, (e) hydrogen chloride? Why?

See Teacher's Guide at the front of this book.

INVESTIGATIONS

1. Find out how synthetic diamonds are made. Prepare a report for the class.

2. Obtain samples of various kinds of minerals and chemical compounds. Try to separate them into different kinds of crystal formations. Observe them closely under a magnifying glass or binocular microscope.

3. Obtain a book on refrigeration. Learn how evaporation and condensation are employed in mechanical refrigeration. Make a model or diagram to show the major parts of some refrigeration unit.

4. Visit a service station. Under the supervision of the station attendant, find out how the hydraulic lift works.

INTERESTING READING

Apfel, R. E., "Tensile Strength of Liquids." *Scientific American*, CCXXVII (December, 1972), pp. 58–62.

Boys, Charles V., *Soap Bubbles.* New York, Thomas Y. Crowell Company, 1962.

Burke, John G., *Origins of the Science of Crystals.* Berkeley, University of California Press, 1966.

Griesbach, R. J., "Growing Metallic Crystals." *Chemistry*, XLV (December, 1972), pp. 25–26.

Holden, Alan, and Singer, Phyllis, *Crystals and Crystal Growing.* New York, Doubleday & Company, Inc., 1960.

Hyde, Margaret, *Molecules Today and Tomorrow.* New York, McGraw-Hill Book Company, 1966.

Wohlrabe, Raymond A., *Crystals.* Philadelphia, J. B. Lippincott Company, 1962.

Solutions

GOAL: You will gain an understanding of solutes, solvents, concentration, and saturation.

Magnesium is a shiny metal. Oxygen is a colorless and odorless gas. When magnesium burns, it combines with oxygen. A very large amount of heat and light is produced during this reaction. The product formed is magnesium oxide, a white, powdery compound. It is completely different from the two separate elements, magnesium and oxygen. This reaction is striking evidence of a chemical change.

A chemical change involves the formation of a new substance and an energy change. For example, when magnesium burns chemical energy changes into heat or light. Is the formation of a solution a chemical change? Some evidence suggests that it is a chemical change. Some evidence suggests that it is not. As you read and discuss this chapter, you can come to your own conclusions.

8:1 *Solutions*

ACTIVITY. (1) To four 15-ml test tubes add 5 ml of water. In the first test tube place a small amount of table salt. To the second add 4 drops of mineral oil. To the third add 4 drops of ethyl alcohol. To the fourth add a small amount of sugar. Place stoppers in each test tube and shake. Record what you observe. Empty and rinse your test tubes with distilled water. (2) Repeat Part 1 using 5 ml of alcohol in each test tube. Add water to the third test tube instead of alcohol. Compare the results of Parts 1 and 2. See Teacher's Guide at the front of this book.

What is a solution?* A solution is formed when a substance, called the **solute** (sohl' eut), is dissolved in another substance,

5 ml of water **Figure 8-1.**

---

* The term "solution" is also used to describe the process of dissolving or going into solution.

called the **solvent** (sahl' vent). In a solution, separate substances are completely mixed. The new material formed is exactly the same throughout. When sugar is dissolved in water, sugar is the solute and water is the solvent. Molecules of sugar are distributed uniformly throughout the molecules of water.

In the most common solutions, solids, liquids, or gases are dissolved in liquids. These solutions are called **liquid solutions.** Liquids which dissolve each other are said to be *miscible* (mis' ah bl). Liquids which do not dissolve each other are said to be *immiscible.* Water is probably the most common solvent. Unless some other solvent is specified, we assume the solvent is water. For example, a sugar solution is a solution of sugar and water.

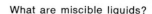

What are miscible liquids?

Liquids are miscible if they dissolve each other.

Figure 8-2.

EXPERIMENT. Half fill a small beaker with cold soda water (carbonated water). (1) Stir the liquid. Explain what you observe. (2) Test the liquid with litmus paper. Explain what you observe. (3) Heat the liquid until boiling. Allow it to cool and test again with litmus paper. Explain. What is the solute in this solution? What is the solvent?

Before boiling - acid.
After boiling - neutral.
CO_2 more soluble in cold liquid.

Solution takes place as the solvent molecules separate.

Solutions can also be formed by dissolving solids, liquids, or gases in gases. In this case, a **gaseous solution** is formed. Air is a gaseous solution.

A third type of solution is the **solid solution.** Solid solutions are formed by dissolving solids, liquids, or gases in solids. Carbon

Figure 8-3. Alloys, such as bronze or carbon steel, are made by dissolving solids in other solids.

What is an alloy?

Solid solution of two or more metals.

steel is a solid solution of carbon in iron. Bronze is a solution of copper and zinc. Such solid solutions of metals are called **alloys** (al' oiz).

By mixing certain metals together in the right proportions, an alloy with properties to suit a special purpose can be made. For example, chromium can be alloyed with steel. The chromium-iron-manganese alloy is called stainless steel. It does not rust as does pure steel. Brass is an alloy of copper and zinc. It is stronger and more resistant to corrosion than either copper or zinc alone. Table 8–1 shows common alloys and their uses.

Table 8–1. Some Alloys and Their Uses		
Alloy	Metals	Typical Uses
Wood's metal	Bi, Pb, Sn, Cd	automatic sprinklers
Commercial bronze	Cu, Zn	jewelry, screens, nuts, and bolts
German silver	Cu, Zn, Ni	silver platings, jewelry
Gold, 14 carat	Au, Cu, Ag	jewelry
Solder	Sn, Pb	electrical wire soldering
Dentist's amalgam	Hg, Ag	tooth fillings
Nichrome	Ni, Cr	electrical heating elements
Monel metal	Ni, Cu, Fe	household appliances
Dow metal	Mg, Al, Mn	aircraft parts

Alloying metals produces changes in density. Alloying may also produce changes in electrical conductivity, strength, hardness, heat conductivity, and melting point.

Figure 8-4. The formula for copper sulfate is $CuSO_4$. The actual formula for copper sulfate crystals is $CuSO_4 \cdot 5H_2O$ (Section 8:9).

8:2 Formation of Solutions

The atoms or molecules of all elements and compounds attract each other (Section 7:4). A solvent often reduces the attractive force between the molecules of the solute. Sugar crystals, for example, are formed because the sugar molecules attract each other. If these crystals are placed in water, the attraction between sugar molecules and water molecules is greater than the attraction between sugar molecules. The water molecules then surround each sugar molecule. Motion

of both water and sugar molecules causes the sugar molecules to spread out evenly in the solution. Figure 8–16 shows the change in salt crystals when they are placed in water.

A solid solute goes into solution along its surface. Surface molecules of solute first come into contact with the solvent. For example, sugar crystals placed in water dissolve along the surface of the crystal. As layers of molecules dissolve along the outer surface more surface is exposed. The dissolving continues through new layers of molecules.

How do crystals dissolve?

Molecules or ions of crystal disperse into solvent.

PROBLEM

1. You are given two 1-gram samples of copper (II) sulfate crystals. One sample contains very small crystals. The other contains large crystals. Which crystals will dissolve faster? Explain. *Small crystals have larger total surface area.*

EXPERIMENT. CAUTION: This experiment should be done only under the direct supervision of the teacher. (1) Place a thermometer in a 250-ml beaker one-half full of water at room temperature. Record the temperature. Add 25 g of ammonium chloride (NH₄Cl) and stir to dissolve the solid. Does the temperature increase, decrease, or remain the same? (2) Repeat Part 1 with 10 g of solid sodium hydroxide (NaOH). Compare the results from Parts 1 and 2. *The temperature increases greatly in Part 2; decreases in Part 1.*

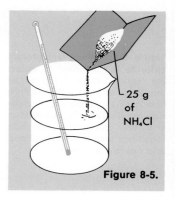

Figure 8-5.

Energy changes occur when a solution is formed. Energy is needed to break the chemical bonds that hold the solvent particles together (solvent-solvent bond). Energy is needed to break the chemical bonds that hold the particles of solute together (solute-solute bond). Energy is released when the solvent and solute particles unite (solute-solvent bond).

PROBLEM

2. How is the formation of a solution similar to a chemical change? *Energy change occurs.*

When ammonium chloride dissolves in water, heat energy first breaks the solute-solute bonds between the ammonium and chloride ions. Then new solute-solvent bonds form and energy is released. The overall effect of dissolving NH₄Cl in water is a decrease in the temperature of the solution. This means that the amount of heat absorbed to break the bonds in the NH₄Cl crystal is greater than the heat released in the formation of the new solute-solvent bonds.

How is heat used in the solution process?

Energy breaks bonds of the reactants and an energy interchange forms new bonds.

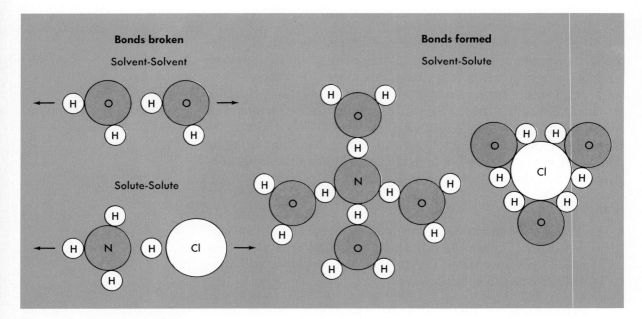

Bonds broken

Solvent-Solvent

Solute-Solute

Bonds formed

Solvent-Solute

Figure 8-6. When ammonium chloride is dissolved in water, the solvent-solvent bonds of the water and the solute-solute bonds of the ammonium chloride are broken. The water ions and the ammonium chloride ions form a solvent-solute bond and energy is released.

Make sure the students understand that the sugar has not changed to a liquid (melted). The sugar is still in its solid state but the molecules are evenly distributed throughout the solvent. The melting of sugar is a completely different process.

Figure 8-7. Stirring helps a solute dissolve faster because it exposes molecules more quickly to the solvent.

PROBLEM

3. As sodium hydroxide is dissolved in water, the temperature of the solution rises. The water becomes hot. Heat is absorbed in breaking the solute-solute bonds. Heat is released in the formation of solute-solvent bonds. Which is the larger: heat absorbed or heat released?

8:3 Rate of Solution

Suppose you stir some coffee or tea after adding sugar to it. Does the stirring help the sugar dissolve? Will sugar dissolve faster in iced tea or in hot tea? Will powdered granulated sugar dissolve faster than cubes of granulated sugar? The answers to these questions are based upon factors that affect the rate at which a solute dissolves.

When a solution is stirred, surface molecules of the solute are pulled away faster. Other surface molecules are exposed more quickly to the action of the solvent. Does stirring cause a solution to form faster?

Energy is needed to break the solute-solute bonds and the solvent-solvent bonds. The addition of energy in the form of heat should cause the bonds to break and speed the dissolving process. Heat causes molecules to move faster. Dissolving solute particles then move away from the surface faster. Other particles at the surface are exposed.

The small crystals, though they have the same mass, have more surface area and will dissolve faster. Periodic checks should be made throughout the week.

8:3   RATE OF SOLUTION   157

EXPERIMENT. Find the mass of a large crystal of copper (II) sulfate on a balance. Measure an equal mass of the small copper (II) sulfate crystals. Put the large crystal in a 250-ml flask full of water. Seal with a stopper. Put the small crystals in a second 250-ml flask full of water. Seal this flask with a stopper. Allow the flasks to stand for one week. Check the flasks several times during the week. Compare the results.

A crushed crystal has more surface area than the original crystal. Consider a cube 20 centimeters on a side. The area of each face of the cube is 400 square centimeters (20 cm $\times$ 20 cm = 400 cm²). Since a cube has six faces, the total area of the cube is 2,400 square centimeters (400 cm² $\times$ 6 = 2,400 cm²). If the cube is cut so that it forms eight equal cubes, each 10 centimeters on a side, the total area will be 4,800 square centimeters. Suppose the original cube is cut so that it forms 8,000 cubes, each one centimeter on a side. Then the total area will be 48,000 square centimeters (Figure 8–9). As the cubes are made smaller, more and more area is exposed. If a cube of granulated sugar is crushed (powdered) and put into water, the area exposed to the solvent is tremendous. More particles will be dissolved in a shorter period of time than with a large size cube. *For calculations, see the Teacher's Guide at the front of this book.*

To summarize, three ways to hasten the solution (dissolving) of a crystalline substance in a liquid are: (1) heat the solution, (2) stir or shake the solution, and (3) crush the solute.

How does heat affect the solution of a gas in a liquid? Heat increases the amount of solid that can dissolve in a liquid. Just the opposite holds true for gases. Gas molecules are normally farther apart than molecules in a solid. Cooling a gas causes its volume to contract. The molecules slow down and pull closer together. More molecules are packed into a given

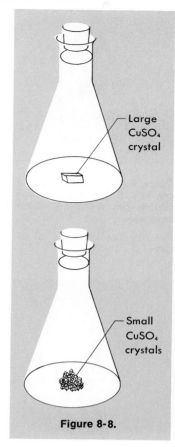

Large CuSO₄ crystal

Small CuSO₄ crystals

Figure 8-8.

What are three ways to speed solution of a solid?

If a glass of cold water stands at room temperature air which was in solution forms bubbles as it comes out of solution.

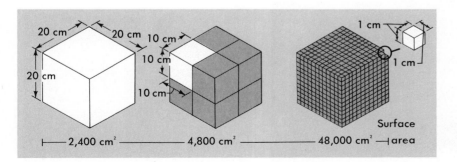

20 cm 20 cm 20 cm

10 cm 10 cm 10 cm

1 cm 1 cm

2,400 cm²   4,800 cm²   48,000 cm² Surface area

Figure 8-9. As a cube is divided into smaller pieces, its total surface area increases.

Carl England

Figure 8-10. The bubbles we see in soft drinks are carbon dioxide gas dissolved in the beverage.

no

How can gases be made to dissolve?

Cool them under pressure.

Carl England

Figure 8-11. Water and oil are immiscible.

Point out this rule.

Remember organic compounds contain carbon.

Figure 8-12. Dry cleaning fluid removes most soil on clothing because both the fluid and the soil are organic.

space. This greater number of gas molecules can form more bonds with a liquid solvent. Therefore, cooling a liquid allows more gas to dissolve in the liquid.

Do you think that stirring would speed or slow solution of a gas in a liquid? Carbon dioxide gas (CO_2) is dissolved in many kinds of beverages. Have you ever stirred a glass of ginger ale or some other carbonated drink? Does the gas stay in solution? Before the bottle of soda pop is opened, the gas is under pressure. What happens when the cap is removed from a warm bottle of soda pop which has been shaken? Gas rushes out of the bottle and takes some of the liquid along with it. Gases dissolve better in liquids if the solution is cooled and if pressure is increased. *Demonstrate this with a cold bottle of carbonated beverage.*

8:4   Solvents

Early chemists searched to find a "universal solvent." But no known solvent will dissolve everything. Water is probably the most nearly universal solvent. It can dissolve many gases, liquids, and solids. However, water will not readily dissolve a number of substances. Grease and carbon tetrachloride are two materials that do not dissolve in water.

Generally, solvents will dissolve solutes which are chemically like them. Usually, organic solvents will dissolve organic solutes. Inorganic solvents will dissolve inorganic solutes. Remember, organic compounds contain carbon. Both grease and carbon tetrachloride are organic substances. Carbon tetrachloride, a liquid organic solvent, readily dissolves grease. Benzene, another liquid organic solvent, dissolves grease and carbon tetrachloride. Water, however, is inorganic. Water and

American Institute of Drycleaning

Figure 8-13. Because water and oil are immiscible, the oil in this river lies on the surface of the water.

Vincent McGuire

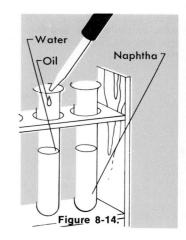

Figure 8-14.

carbon tetrachloride will not mix. Water dissolves many inorganic substances, such as table salt.

General rules for solution are not always followed. For example, ethyl alcohol is an organic compound. However, water and alcohol are miscible. Water also dissolves some organic substances, such as sugar.

> EXPERIMENT.   Place 10 ml of water in one test tube, and 10 ml of naphtha (lighter fluid) in another test tube. Add 5 drops of vegetable oil to each and shake. Add ½ ml of liquid soap to the water and shake again. Note the solubility of oil in water, naphtha, and soapy water.

Oil will not dissolve in water but will dissolve in naphtha. When liquid soap is added, vegetable oil forms a suspension in water.

Organic solvents are usually used as "dry cleaning" agents because most soil on clothing is organic soil. Before you try to remove some foreign matter from your clothing with a solvent, consider what it is that you are trying to remove. A solvent that will remove chewing gum may also dissolve nylon. Care should be exercised in using any solvent.

What kind of solutes do organic solvents usually dissolve?

organic

8:5   Polarity

Most chemical reactions in the laboratory and in nature occur in water. A review of the structure of water molecules and other types of molecules might help you understand why. Water molecules are composed of one oxygen atom and two hydrogen atoms. The oxygen atom shares electrons with the two hydrogen atoms forming two covalent bonds. The shared electrons spend most of their time around the oxygen atom. Therefore, the oxygen end of the water molecule has a slight negative electrical charge. The hydrogen end of the molecule has a slight positive charge. But the molecule as a whole is still neutral. Why? This bonding structure with an unsymmetrical charge distribution causes the molecules to be **polar.** A polar molecule is sometimes called a *dipole* because of the two oppositely charged ends.

The polarity of the water molecule helps it dissolve inorganic substances. Most inorganic substances are composed of polar molecules or charged particles. Sodium chloride, for example, is an ionic compound. It is formed through ionic bonding of sodium ions (Na^+) and chloride ions (Cl^-) (Section 7:3). When sodium chloride is placed in water, the attractive force between the ions in the crystals is lessened. Water molecules surround the ions (Figure 8–16), and the ions are distributed

What is a polar molecule?

Molecule with unsymmetric charge distribution.

Figure 8-15. Water is a polar molecule. The hydrogen end is positive and the oxygen end is negative.

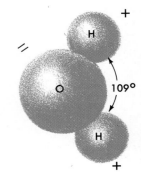

Figure 8-16. Salt crystals dissolve as the sodium and chloride ions are hydrated and carried apart.

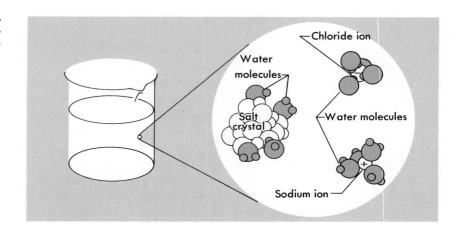

rapidly throughout the solution. When an ionic compound dissolves in water and forms ions, the process is called **dissociation** (di soh' see ae shun).

Hydrogen chloride (HCl) is a molecular compound. It is formed through covalent bonding between hydrogen and chlorine. This molecule is bonded by the sharing of an electron pair. The charge of chlorine is large compared to that of hydrogen. Therefore, chlorine controls the electrons most of the time. Thus, the electrons are more likely to be at the chlorine end of the molecule, causing that end to be a negative end. The hydrogen end is positive. Hydrogen chloride, then, is a polar molecule (Figure 8–17).

When hydrogen chloride is placed in water, it forms ions. Both the chloride ion (Cl^-) and the hydrogen ion (H^+) form in the water solution. The hydrogen ion (H^+) combines with a molecule of water (H_2O) to produce an ion called the *hydronium* (hie drohn' ee um) *ion* (H_3O^+) ($H^+ + H_2O \rightarrow H_3O^+$). When a molecular compound dissolves in water to form ions, the process is called **ionization** (ie an i zae'shun).

It is now assumed that H^+ ions (free protons) are nearly impossible to find in any solution. Free protons would combine instantaneously with a water molecule.

Figure 8-17. The hydrogen choride molecule is polar.

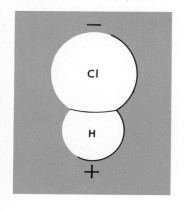

PROBLEM

4. What is the difference between ionization and dissociation? Give an example of each. *See Teacher's Guide at the front of this book.*

Some compounds do not ionize or dissociate when placed in water. For example, sugar is such a compound. The atoms in its molecules are held together by covalent bonds. Sugar is nonpolar. That is, its electric charges are shared equally throughout the molecule. Neither end is charged. In water, it dissolves but remains a molecule. It does not break up into ions.

Electric current in a wire is a flow of electrons (Section 18:2). In a solution, an electric current is a flow of ions. Both electrons and ions are charged particles. For an electric current to pass through a solution, ions must be present in the solution.

The apparatus in Figure 8–18 is used to determine if a substance produces ions when it dissolves in water. Can an electric current move through pure water? A current can move through water solutions which contain ions. Such solutions are said to conduct an electric current. They are called *conductors* (Section 19 : 2). Solutions which contain only molecules cannot conduct a current. In general, inorganic compounds which dissolve in water will produce ions. Organic compounds, with a few exceptions, will not produce ions and will not conduct electricity.

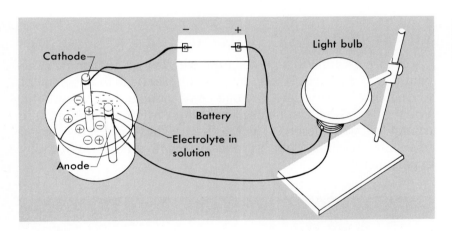

Figure 8-18. Positively charged ions move to the cathode (−) and negatively charged ions move to the anode (+).

Potassium bromide (KBr) is an ionic compound. It dissociates in water. The ions present (K^+ and Br^-) make the solution a conductor. Substances such as potassium bromide are called *electrolytes* (ee lek′ troh lietz). In water solution, **electrolytes** can conduct electric currents. Such solutions are called electrolytic solutions.

Sugar in solution does not ionize. A sugar solution contains nonpolar sugar molecules. Because the solution cannot conduct electric currents, it is called a *nonelectrolyte*. A **nonelectrolyte** is a substance which does not conduct an electric current when dissolved in water. An alcohol-water solution cannot conduct a current because alcohol is an organic compound that does not ionize. Alcohol is a nonelectrolyte.

Name a nonelectrolyte.

alcohol

Figure 8-19.

EXPERIMENT.   Prepare a test device for electrolytes similar to that in Figure 8–19. Connect two dry cells to an electric socket containing a 3-v flashlight bulb. Cut one wire in the circuit and bare the wires for about an inch. Obtain five small beakers (125 ml) and pour 50 ml of distilled water in each. Put the two bare wires into the water in one beaker. Be sure that the wires do not touch each other. What change occurs? Sprinkle a few grams of sodium chloride into the water. What happens? Is sodium chloride an electrolyte?

Clean the wires by rinsing in distilled water. Then place them in the second beaker. What is your observation? Pour 5 ml of alcohol in the water. Is alcohol an electrolyte?

Clean the wires and repeat with hydrochloric acid, sugar, and potassium sulfate in the other three beakers. Which are electrolytes? What "carries" the current through the solution? How could you make the bulb burn brighter? Devise an experiment to test your hypothesis. See Teacher's Guide at the front of this book.

8:6   Solubility

Often it is difficult to determine whether an inorganic compound will dissolve. It also may be impractical to experiment to find out. Fortunately, chemists have determined a few solubility rules which can be used to predict whether an inorganic compound will dissolve (Table 8–2). These rules are based upon observations that have been made during laboratory experiments.

Figure 8-20. Over hundreds of years, a solution of calcite (CaCO$_3$) drips from the ceiling of a cave. Calcite is practically insoluble in water and precipitates out as the water flows away. Eventually, enough calcite accumulates to form stalactites (top) and stalagmites (bottom) such as these.

Point out the usefulness of this table.

Table 8–2.   *Solubility of Common Compounds in Water*

1. Common compounds which contain the following ions are *soluble:*
   a. sodium (Na^+), potassium (K^+), ammonium (NH_4^+).
   b. nitrates (NO_3^-).
   c. acetates ($C_2H_3O_2^-$), except silver acetate, which is only moderately soluble.
   d. chlorides (Cl^-), except silver, mercury (I), and lead chlorides. $PbCl_2$ is soluble in hot water.
   e. sulfates (SO_4^{-2}), except barium and lead sulfates. Calcium, mercury (I), and silver sulfates are slightly soluble.

2. Common compounds which contain the following ions are *insoluble:*
   a. silver (Ag^+), except silver nitrate and silver perchlorate.
   b. sulfides (S^{-2}), except those of sodium, potassium, ammonium, magnesium, barium, and calcium.
   c. carbonates (CO_3^{-2}), except those of sodium, potassium, and ammonium.
   d. phosphates (PO_4^{-3}), except those of sodium, potassium, and ammonium.
   e. hydroxides (OH^-), except those of sodium, potassium, ammonium, and barium.

Figure 8-21.

EXAMPLE

Will mercury (II) sulfide dissolve in water?

Solution: Check Table 8–2. All sulfides are insoluble, except those listed. Mercury (II) sulfide is not listed. It will not dissolve in water.

Any salt such as NaCl, NaNO₃, or KNO₃ will work.

EXPERIMENT. *Find the solubility of a salt in water. Place 20 ml of water in a beaker. Slowly dissolve the salt, with constant stirring, until a small amount of salt lies on the bottom of the beaker and does not dissolve. Filter the solution through a piece of filter paper in a funnel. Find the mass of an evaporating dish. Place the filtrate in an evaporating dish and find the mass of the dish and contents. Heat with a Bunsen burner flame until all the liquid is evaporated. Allow to cool and find the mass of the dish again. From your measurements, compute the mass of salt dissolved in 20 ml of solution.* *See Teacher's Guide at the front of this book for sample data.*

PROBLEMS

5. Which of the following compounds is (are) soluble in water?
   (a) sodium nitrate *yes*   (d) ammonium chloride *yes*
   (b) silver phosphate *no*   (e) aluminum hydroxide *no*
   (c) barium chloride *yes*   (f) magnesium carbonate *no*
6. If any of the compounds in Problem 5 is (are) soluble in water, what ions, if any, will be found in solution?

   (a) Na^+, NO_3^- (c) Ba^{++}, Cl^- (d) NH_4^+, Cl^-

8:7 Concentration

A dilute solution has less solute per given volume than a concentrated solution. They are relative terms.

To some people, a glass of lemonade may be too sour. To others, the same lemonade may not be sour enough. To describe a solution such as lemonade, people often use the terms "dilute" or "concentrated." These terms are sometimes misleading. It is often difficult to determine what is concentrated and what is dilute, except in extreme cases. A solution is generally described as containing a ratio of so many grams of solute in each liter of solution $\left(\dfrac{\text{grams of solute}}{\text{one liter of solution}} \text{ or g/l} \right)$. Other units of measure are also used, but this one is the most common in science.

Suppose a solution contains 50 grams of sugar per liter of water solution. The sugar is distributed uniformly throughout the solution. There are 25 grams of sugar in 500 milliliters and five grams in 100 milliliters. Suppose you needed five grams of sugar. You simply pour out 100 milliliters, ¹⁄₁₀ of a liter, and evaporate the water.

EXPERIMENT. (1) Place 35 ml of water in a beaker. Slowly add table salt with constant stirring until no more will dissolve. A small amount of salt will remain on the bottom of the beaker undissolved. Pour the solution into a 25-ml graduated cylinder or large test tube. Take a specific gravity reading with a straw hydrometer (Figure 8–22). (2) Repeat Part 1 with four other salts. Make a table to compare the specific gravities of the solutions. How might a difference in temperature affect your results? *Temperature determines amount of solute to go into solution.*

8:8 Saturation

Not all compounds dissolve at the same rate. For example, at 60°C approximately 110 grams of potassium nitrate (KNO_3) dissolve in 100 milliliters of water. Less than 40 grams of

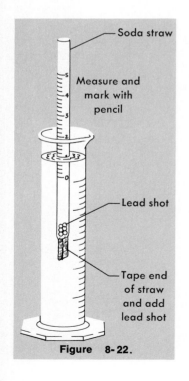

Soda straw

Measure and mark with pencil

Lead shot

Tape end of straw and add lead shot

Figure   8- 22.

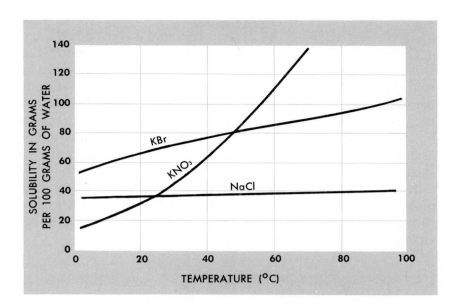

Figure 8-23. Solubility of KNO_3, KBr, and NaCl at various temperatures.

sodium chloride dissolve in the same amount of water at the same temperature.

At room temperature, 20°C, 100 milliliters of water will hold about 40 grams of potassium nitrate (KNO_3). If any more KNO_3 is added to the solution, it appears to fall to the bottom undissolved. A solution is said to be **saturated** (sach' u raet ed) when it will hold no more solute. If the solution is heated to 60°C, however, the same amount of water can hold nearly three times as much KNO_3. At 60°C, then, the solution is **unsaturated**. It does not hold all of the solute that it can hold at that temperature. *No more will dissolve.*

Now suppose that the KNO_3 and H_2O solution is cooled to 10°C slowly, so that no crystals form. At 10°C, 100 milliliters of H_2O are expected to contain only 25 grams of KNO_3. This solution, however, contains 40 grams of KNO_3. The solution is called *supersaturated*. It contains more solute than is expected at that temperature. Thus, the same solution could be saturated, unsaturated, or supersaturated.

Care must be taken not to agitate the flask.

EXPERIMENT. Dissolve 100 g of "hypo" (sodium thiosulfate) in 100 ml of water in a 250-ml flask. Heat until all the solid dissolves. Remove the flask from the flame, stopper the flask with a wad of cotton. Allow it to cool. Then remove the cotton and drop a crystal of "hypo" into the liquid. Crystallization should occur. Design an experiment to prove that crystallization would not occur if a crystal of sodium chloride were added to a supersaturated sodium thiosulfate solution.

Crystallization should occur as soon as the crystal is dropped in.

The same experiment could be repeated and a crystal of sodium chloride added to the hypo solution. Because sodium chloride is not the

How can you determine whether a solution is saturated or not?

Figure 8-24.

right shape, crystallization would not take place. Sodium chloride is the wrong model for hypo crystallization.

Figure 8-25. Orange juice is more concentrated than orange drink.

This is an example of dynamic equilibrium.

A solution is a mixture rather than a compound. It does not have a definite composition by weight. The solute can be recovered by physical means. The process of solution may be chemical but the material formed is a mixture.

One way to determine whether or not a solution is saturated is to put more solute into the solution. A saturated solution contains all of the solute it is expected to contain at that temperature. Additional solute put into a saturated solution will not dissolve. At least, it appears not to dissolve. What actually happens is that some of it does dissolve. And some solute crystallizes out at the same time. The amount of solute in the saturated solution remains the same.

If the solution is unsaturated, the additional solute will dissolve. If the solution is supersaturated, however, the excess solute in solution will crystallize immediately. Why is a solution a mixture and not a compound?

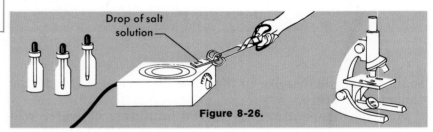

Drop of salt solution

Figure 8-26.

Use the solutions prepared for the experiment on p. 163.

EXPERIMENT. Prepare saturated solutions of various salts in small dropper bottles. Use the solutions prepared for the experiment on page 164. Place one drop of a salt solution on a slide and gently heat over a burner or on the edge of a hot plate. Place the slide under the low power lens of the microscope and watch for crystals to form as the liquid cools. If no crystallization occurs, reheat and observe again. If crystallization is too rapid, add water with the end of a toothpick and repeat.

8:9 Hydrated Crystals

Many substances which ionize or dissociate in water solution produce ions that are strongly attached to water molecules. Therefore, when they crystallize from solution, water molecules form a part of their crystalline structure. For example, when copper (II) sulfate ($CuSO_4$) crystallizes out of solution, four water molecules are attached to each Cu^{+2} ion and one water molecule is attached to each SO_4^{-2} ion. Thus the ions are said to be **hydrated**. The crystal formed is called a *hydrate*. Many ionic substances form hydrated crystals. The water they contain is called **water of hydration**.

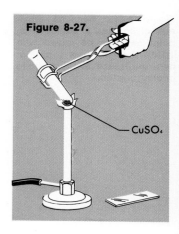

Figure 8-27.

—CuSO₄

EXPERIMENT. Place a few crystals of CuSO₄ in the bottom of a Pyrex test tube. Hold the test tube at a 45-degree angle and heat the bottom strongly. What happens to the crystals? What happens at the mouth of the test tube? What do you suppose causes the color of the CuSO₄ crystals? Place some of the powder remaining in the test tube on a slide. Put a few drops of water on the powder. What happens? Warm the slide gently over the burner. Does a crystal form? What is it? Devise an experiment which uses copper sulfate to test for water. See Teacher's Guide at the front of this book.

Some substances give up their waters of hydration much easier than others. In fact, some release them quickly into the air. These compounds are said to be *efflorescent* (ef loh res′ ent).

On the other hand, some crystals hold their water of hydration so strongly that water from the air is attracted to the crystal. These substances may even gather enough water to form a solution. Compounds which do this are said to be *deliquescent* (del′ i kwes′ ent).

Name a deliquescent compound.

Calcium chloride

EXPERIMENT. Weigh four small beakers, watch glasses, or petri dishes. Place approximately 10 grams of sodium sulfate crystals (Na₂SO₄ · 10 H₂O) in the first dish. In the second dish place 10 g of CaCl₂; in the third, 10 g of CuSO₄ · 5 H₂O; and in the fourth, 10 g of Na₂CO₃ · 10 H₂O. Record the mass of each dish every fifteen minutes for an hour or wait until the following day. Has anything appeared to happen? What change occurs in the mass of each container and its contents? Which crystals, if any, are deliquescent? Which, if any, are efflorescent? Which show no signs of change?

CaCl₂

CuSO₄ · 5 H₂O

Na₂ CO₃ · 10 H₂O

Na₂ SO₄ · 10 H₂O

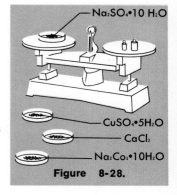

—Na₂SO₄•10 H₂O

—CuSO₄•5H₂O
—CaCl₂
—Na₂Co₃•10H₂O

Figure 8-28.

Dow Chemical Co.

Figure 8-29. Deliquescent materials attract and hold water. They are used where a dry environment is desired.

Marathon Oil Co.

8:10 Properties of Solutions

Why do some motorists put ethylene glycol (antifreeze) in the radiator of their cars? How does this substance prevent the water in the cooling system from freezing? You may know someone who adds salt to water "to make it hotter" when heated to boiling. Does the addition of salt make water boil at a higher temperature? *The addition of salt raises the B.P. of water.*

Cold weather may cause the radiator to freeze and crack.

How does a dissolved substance affect the boiling point of a liquid?

EXPERIMENT. *Place 100 ml of tap water in a flask. Insert a thermometer and a glass tube into a two-hole rubber stopper. Place the stopper assembly into the flask. The thermometer bulb should be submerged. Attach one end of a heavy walled rubber hose to the glass tube. Attach the other end to an aspirator (Figure 8–31). Record the temperature of the water. Turn on the tap and observe any changes. Record the temperature of the water as changes occur. Explain what you observe. Repeat the experiment using hot water.*

Temperature remains same but water boils when pressure decreases.

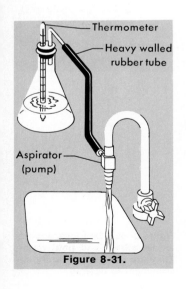

Figure 8-31.

The particles of a liquid are held together by attractive forces. The temperature of the liquid is a measure of the average kinetic energy of the particles (Section 14:1). However, not all the particles have the same velocity. Some have above-average velocity; others have below-average velocity. As the particles collide, one particle may take on some of the energy

168

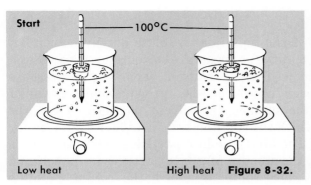

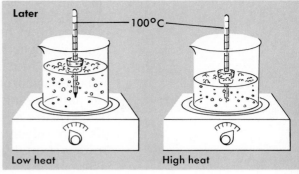

Start — 100°C — Low heat / High heat **Figure 8-32.** **Later** — 100°C — Low heat / High heat

of another particle. Through successive collisions, a particle can attain a great velocity. If one such particle is near the surface of the liquid, it may escape from the attractive force of the other particles. This process is called **evaporation** (e vap' ah rae' shun). Thus, for a particle to escape from a liquid by evaporation, it must have sufficient movement (kinetic energy) to overcome the attractive force of the other particles. Also, it must be near the surface.

The particles which leave the surface of a liquid form a vapor above it. When the pressure of this vapor equals the existing atmospheric pressure, the boiling point of the liquid is reached. At this point, vapor can form within the liquid as bubbles. This increases the liquid/vapor surface and gives more particles of liquid an opportunity to escape. Thus, any heat that is added to a boiling liquid tends to make it evaporate faster but does not raise the temperature of the liquid. This occurs because the particles with higher kinetic energy leave the liquid. The average kinetic energy of the remaining particles is lowered. The liquid remains at the boiling temperature until it is evaporated completely.

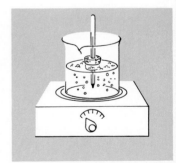

PROBLEM

7. In climbing a mountain, the atmospheric pressure decreases as the altitude increases. At an altitude of 10,000 ft above sea level would you expect water to boil at a higher or lower temperature than at sea level?

EXPERIMENT. Bring water in a beaker to a boil. Record the temperature. Stop heating the beaker. Allow the water to cool slightly. Add 10 grams of salt (NaCl) to the water and stir. Heat the water until it boils. Record the temperature again. Was there any change in boiling temperatures? What caused the change? Adding salt raised boiling point.

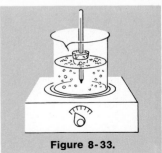

Figure 8-33.

169

What happens if the liquid has a solute dissolved in it? A smaller proportion of the particles are solvent particles. Therefore, more heat is needed to produce a vapor with a pressure equal to atmospheric pressure. Also, proportionally fewer of the particles at the surface are solvent particles. Thus, the temperature at which the solution boils is higher than it is for the pure solvent. The kind of solute particles in the solution is unimportant, but the amount of solute particles in the solution is important. As more solute is added, the boiling point is increased. A smaller proportion of the particles in the solution is solvent particles. More of the solution consists of solute particles.

PROBLEM

8. Would salt water from the ocean have the same boiling point as fresh water from the Great Lakes?

Salt water has higher boiling point.

The addition of a solute to a liquid lowers the freezing point in much the same way that it raises the boiling point. When a substance freezes, it changes from liquid to solid state. The substance forms characteristic crystal patterns. When a substance is dissolved in the liquid, the particles of this solute interfere with formation of the regular crystalline shape of the solvent. More heat must be removed for the crystals to form. Thus, the temperature at which the solution freezes is lower than the temperature of the pure solvent. The freezing point decreases as more solute is dissolved in the solvent.

In general, the addition of a solute to a pure liquid causes an increase in the boiling point of the liquid. Addition of a solute causes a decrease in the freezing point.

PROBLEM

9. Why is salt spread on ice-covered sidewalks?

The solution has lower freezing point, ice melts.

ACTIVITY. *Partially fill a glass with ice and add a small amount of water. Place a thermometer in the glass, stir, and record the temperature. Add a large amount of salt to the ice and water and record the temperature. What changes do you observe?* *Ice melts, temperature lowers.*

Figure 8-34.

MAIN IDEAS

pp. 153-154

1. Solutions are mixtures of matter which are the same throughout.

pp. 152-153
2. A solute dissolves in a solvent to form a solution.

p. 157 3. Solution of a solid in a liquid may be aided by heating the solution, pulverizing the solute, or stirring.

p. 158 4. Solution of a gas in a liquid may be aided by cooling the solution or by increasing the pressure.

p. 158 5. Organic solvents usually will dissolve organic solutes. Inorganic solvents usually will dissolve inorganic solutes.

p. 160 6. When an ionic compound dissolves in water, it dissociates to form ions.

p. 159 7. When a polar molecular compound dissolves in water, it releases polar molecules into solution.

p. 160 8. Substances that form ions in solution and conduct electric current are called electrolytes.

p. 164 9. The concentration of a solution may be described as the number of grams of solute per liter of solution.

p. 165 10. Solutions may be saturated, unsaturated, or supersaturated.

p. 168 11. The boiling point of a solution is generally higher than that of the pure solvent.

p. 170 12. The freezing point of a solution is lower than that of the pure solvent.

VOCABULARY

Write a sentence in which you correctly use each of the following words or terms.

alloy	immiscible	solute
deliquescent	ionization	solution
density	miscible	solvent
dissociation	nonelectrolyte	supersaturated
efflorescent	polar	unsaturated
electrolyte	saturated	water of hydration
evaporation		

STUDY QUESTIONS

A. True or False *Have students rewrite false statements to make the statements correct.*

Determine whether each of the following sentences is true or false. (Do not write in this book.)

F 1. To form a solution a ~~solvent~~ must be dissolved by a ~~solute~~. *solute, solvent*

T **2.** Oil is immiscible in water.

gaseous *F* **3.** A ~~solid~~ solution can be formed by dissolving a gas in another gas.

most inorganic compounds *F* **4.** Water is a solvent that will dissolve ^ ~~everything~~.

T **5.** Ethyl alcohol and water can form a mixture.

F **6.** Organic solvents usually dissolve ~~inorganic~~ solutes.

T **7.** Stirring increases the rate of solution.

T **8.** Ions conduct electricity in a liquid.

efflorescent *F* **9.** Crystals which lose their waters of hydration easily are ~~deliquescent~~.

T **10.** The addition of solute usually raises the boiling point of a pure liquid.

Some questions in part B may have more than one correct answer. Only one answer is required.

B. Multiple Choice

Choose one word or phrase that correctly completes each of the following sentences. (Do not write in this book.)

1. Water will not dissolve (salt, copper sulfate, <u>naphtha</u>, alcohol).

2. (Nitrate, <u>Silver</u>, Phosphate, Sulfate) compounds are all insoluble in water.

3. Adding solute to a solution causes its boiling point to (<u>rise</u>, go down, remain the same).

4. A solution conducts electricity through its (electrons, <u>ions</u>, polar molecules, atoms).

5. If you could dissolve 10 lb of salt in a quart of water, the solution would probably be (saturated, unsaturated, <u>supersaturated</u>).

6. (Ag_2S, Sugar, <u>$NaNO_3$</u>) would produce the most ions when added to water.

7. Adding solute to a solution causes (increase, <u>decrease</u>, no change) in the freezing point.

8. Organic solids will generally dissolve in (water, ammonia, <u>naphtha</u>).

9. Concentration of solution is usually expressed as (<u>g/l</u>, g/ft^3, lb/ft^3, lb/l, oz/ml).

10. One gram of salt in 10 l of water would make a (<u>dilute</u>, concentrated, saturated, unsaturated, supersaturated) solution.

C. Completion

Complete each of the following sentences with a word or phrase that will make the sentence correct. (Do not write in this book.)

1. __?__ is the most common solvent.

2. When ionic compounds dissolve in water, they __?__.

3. __?__ does not ionize when it dissolves.

4. Water is a good solvent for inorganic compounds because it has __?__ molecules.

5. __?__ is the process in which molecular compounds form ions in solution.

6. Organic solvents generally dissolve __?__ solutes.

7. __?__ is a good solvent for grease.

8. The water molecule has a bond angle of approximately __?__ degrees.

water

dissociate

sugar

polar

ionization

organic

naphtha

109°

D. How and Why   *See Teacher's Guide at the front of this book.*

1. If a solution of NaCl contains 50 g in 1 l, how much salt would 50 ml contain?

2. List three factors that contribute to rapid solution of a solid solute.

3. From the graph on page 165, estimate how many grams of KNO_3 will dissolve in 100 ml of water at 20°C. How does this compare with the amount that will dissolve at 40°C?

4. List the following in order of solubility in water, using Table 8–2 on page 163: (a) lead chloride, (b) ammonium nitrate, (c) silver chloride, (d) calcium sulfate.

5. One hundred milliliters of a solution contain 50 g of solute. How could you make 100 ml of solution of the same material which contained only 30 g of the solute?

6. A solution conducts electricity. What do you know about the solution?

7. A solution contains 50 g of solute in 300 ml of solution. What is the concentration in grams per liter?

8. What are some household substances that will dissolve in water? In alcohol?

2.5 g

agitation, pulverization, heat

35-40 g at 20° C
60-65 g at 40° C
about half

b   a   d   c

100 ml contains 50 g,
60 ml contains 30 g,
Add 40 ml water to 60 ml solution

It contains ions, probably inorganic

167 g

salt, sugar

INVESTIGATIONS   *See Teacher's Guide at the front of this book.*

1. Find out how to make a "silica garden."

2. Prepare a report on purification of chemicals by crystallization.

3. Visit a service station to determine how the device for testing antifreeze works. You may find it very close to something you may have already made.

4. Using table salt (NaCl), 100 ml of water, and a thermometer determine the solubility of NaCl in water at various temperatures. NOTE: Form a saturated solution at room temperature first. Record the mass of salt used—or the volume of the salt if a balance is not available. Make a graph of your results.

5. Grow a large crystal of copper (II) sulfate or alum from a saturated solution.

INTERESTING READING

Asimov, Isaac, "Are Oceans Getting Too Salty?" *Science Digest*, LXXII (April, 1972), pp. 73–74.

Coulson, E. H., Trinder, A. E. J., and Kleith, Aaron E., *Test Tubes and Beakers: Chemistry for Young Experimenters.* Garden City, Doubleday & Company, Inc., 1971.

Holden, Alan, and Singer, Phyllis, *Crystals and Crystal Growing.* Garden City, Doubleday & Company, Inc., 1960.

Technical Careers in Science

If you enjoy science and like laboratory work, you may wish to consider a career as a technician.

Technicians are found in all aspects of science and engineering. Usually they work directly with scientists and engineers performing jobs that range from writing to building production equipment.

The term "technician" is used to describe many different types of workers with many different types of skills. A person doing a somewhat routine experiment in a research laboratory is usually called a technician. Someone who writes technical reports or someone who builds scale models of new equipment might also be known as a technician.

This chemical technician works in a research laboratory. His experiments are designed to develop materials which will improve the quality of paper products.

Some technicians schedule construction work on buildings. Some act as salesmen. Others advise companies on how to install complex machines. These are only a few of hundreds of different technicians.

Physical science technician Barbara Rasnick prepares radioactive tracer materials. These materials are used to follow water as it moves through plants.

Whatever his specific job, a technician's work must in some way *assist* the scientists or engineers he works with. He may take over work that a scientist or engineer would otherwise need to do. He may possess abilities—carpentry, writing, drawing, special laboratory skills—that the scientist and engineer do not have. Whatever his type of employment, the technician is a valued and important member of the scientific team.

Technicians work both in research and in production.

In research, technicians conduct experiments, set up and operate equipment, and analyze the results of experiments. They may design new instruments or procedures for new experiments or tests.

In production work, technicians often follow a set plan for assembling or testing a complex product. Some help to design the manufacturing steps and pick out the materials that will be used in the new product.

Here a technician tests paint. He pours a sample into a machine that grinds up the tiny particles of color pigment. The result is a paint which is very smooth and uniform in texture.

Darla Higgs, a technician, is part of a research group studying the element nickel. Here she extracts nickel from the liver of a chick. These experiments help to determine how much nickel humans need for good health.

GOAL: You will gain an understanding of the principle of conservation of matter and energy and how energy changes accompany chemical reactions.

One of the most basic concepts of all science is the principle of conservation of matter and energy. Chemical equations are used by the chemist to describe chemical change and to demonstrate the law of conservation of mass. Common types of reactions are synthesis, decomposition, single replacement, and double replacement. One of the important ideas in this chapter is that energy changes accompany chemical reaction. Energy is released in an exothermic reaction and absorbed in an endothermic reaction. The concept of the mole is introduced.

Conservation of Mass

Some silver nitrate solution is placed in a small flask. Some sodium chloride solution is poured into a small test tube. The test tube is placed inside the flask (Figure 9–1). The flask is closed with a rubber stopper. The mass of the complete system is then found on a balance. The flask is then gently inverted. Solution in the test tube flows into the solution in the flask. When the solutions come in contact with each other, a thick, cloudy substance forms. A small amount of heat is generated.

chemical change — What kind of change occurs in the experiment? The mass of the system is found after the experiment. The mass is the same as before the solutions were mixed. Did the chemical reaction change the mass of the system?

A chemical change does not change the mass that is present.

9:1 *Chemical Equations*

What is the law of conservation of mass? — In ordinary chemical changes, no matter is lost. The mass of all the substances before a reaction equals the mass of all the substances after the reaction. This statement is called the **law of conservation of mass.** It is a basic principle in the study of chemical reactions.

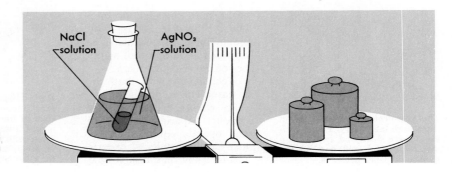

Figure 9-1. Does a chemical change cause a change in mass? *no*

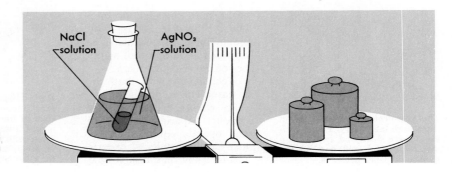

Labels in figure: NaCl solution, AgNO₃ solution

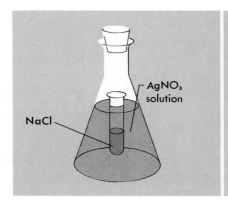
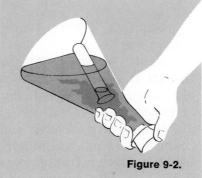

AgNO₃ solution

NaCl

Figure 9-2.

EXPERIMENT. CAUTION: This experiment should be done only under the direct supervision of the teacher. Dissolve 5 g of silver nitrate in 150 ml of water in a 250-ml flask. Add 5 ml of sodium chloride solution to a small test tube. Place the test tube inside the flask. Seal with a stopper. Find the mass of the flask and its contents. Tip the flask over so the contents of the test tube mix with the liquid in the flask. Determine the total mass of the flask, test tube, and contents. Does the mass increase, decrease, or remain the same? Explain your experimental results.

The mass remains the same. No weight is gained or lost in a chemical change.

A chemical change does not change the total mass.

How does one chemist tell another chemist about a chemical change he has observed? To describe chemical reactions, scientists have developed chemical equations. **Chemical equations** are a shorthand made up of symbols and formulas. For example, the chemical equation for the oxidation of carbon is: $C + O_2 \rightarrow CO_2$.

What does a chemical equation represent?

How do you describe the reaction between solutions of silver nitrate ($AgNO_3$) and sodium chloride ($NaCl$)? Chemical reactions can be described by using two types of chemical equations: the *word equation* and the *formula equation*. Using a **word equation** you can say that silver nitrate reacts with sodium chloride to produce silver chloride and sodium nitrate: silver nitrate + sodium chloride → silver chloride + sodium nitrate. A simpler way to explain the reaction is to write a **formula equation:** *Point out the symbol (s).*

Figure 9-3. Silver nitrate and sodium chloride solutions react to produce a precipitate of silver chloride.

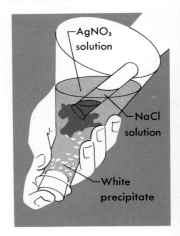

AgNO₃ solution

NaCl solution

White precipitate

$$AgNO_3(aq) + NaCl(aq) \rightarrow AgCl(s) + NaNO_3(aq)$$

Symbols in a formula equation describe how atoms are rearranged in a chemical reaction. The letter (s) means "solid." It shows that a *precipitate* (pre sip′ i taet) forms. A **precipitate** is a substance which is separated from a solution by a chemical or physical change. A precipitate is usually a solid which does not dissolve in the solvent. Silver chloride is

Monsanto Co.

Figure 9-4. Industrial precipitators remove waste gas pollutants from the atmosphere.

What do you suppose (g) in an equation would mean?

A gas is formed.

Figure 9-5. Double replacement reactions result in the formation of a precipitate, a gas, or water.

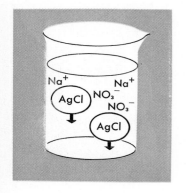

a precipitate. The (aq) means the compound is dissolved in water; (aq) stands for *aqueous*. The arrow which points to the right (→) means "yields" or "produces." Substances to the left of → are called the **reactants**. Substances to the right of → are called the **products**.

Some reactants will not take part in a chemical reaction unless they are in water solution. In these cases, chemical change takes place through the action of ions. The reaction between silver nitrate and sodium chloride is such a reaction. Both silver nitrate and sodium chloride are ionic compounds. Their ions are held tightly to each other in their crystalline forms. In order for the compounds to react, these ionic bonds must be broken. One way to break these bonds is to dissolve the compound in water.

When silver nitrate and sodium chloride are dissolved in water, the water molecules separate the ions. The ions are distributed throughout the solution. Silver, sodium, chloride, and nitrate ions are in the solution. When silver ions and chloride ions collide, they bond to form silver chloride. The water molecules are not able to break this bond to any extent. Thus silver chloride, because it is not soluble in water, settles out of solution (precipitates). Free sodium ions and free nitrate ions remain in solution. The precipitate AgCl may be filtered out. Then, when the water is evaporated, sodium nitrate will remain. Since the water molecules no longer hold the ions apart, the compound $NaNO_3$ forms.

Sometimes a gas is formed in solution as a result of a chemical reaction. In this case, the gas bubbles out of solution, leaving the other ions behind. For example, if zinc is added to a water solution of hydrogen chloride, hydrogen gas is formed. Zinc ions and chloride ions are left in solution.

Balanced chemical equations indicate the kind and quantity of the reactants and products in reactions. Our example equation shows that one unit of silver nitrate reacts with one unit of sodium chloride. The reaction produces one unit of silver chloride and one unit of sodium nitrate.

9:2 *Common Chemical Reactions*

There are many different types of chemical reactions. Four main kinds are *double replacement, single replacement, decomposition*, and *synthesis*.

Double Replacement Reaction. The reaction between silver nitrate and sodium chloride is called a *double replacement reaction.* In this type of reaction, the reactants switch ions. A precipitate, a gas, or water is also formed.

A general form of the double replacement reaction is shown below. Letters are used to represent the compounds.

General equation for a double replacement reaction

Word equation:

AB plus CD yields AD and CB

Formula equation:

AB + CD → AD + CB

Actual double replacement reaction

Word equation:

| barium chloride (solution) | plus | sodium sulfate (solution) |

| yields | barium sulfate (solid) | plus | sodium chloride (solution) |

Formula equation:

$$BaCl_2 (aq) + Na_2SO_4 (aq) \rightarrow BaSO_4 (s) + NaCl (aq)$$

In the above reaction, the barium ion (Ba^{+2}) combines with the sulfate ion (SO_4^{-2}) replacing the sodium. The sodium ion (Na^+) combines with the chloride ion (Cl^-), replacing the barium. The newly formed barium sulfate $(BaSO_4)$ is an insoluble precipitate. The sodium chloride $(NaCl)$ is soluble. The sodium (Na^+) and the chloride (Cl^-) ions remain dissolved.

NaCl is in solution as Na^+ and Cl^- ions.

Count the number of sodium atoms on the left and right sides of the equation. Does the number of sodium atoms on the left side equal the number of sodium atoms on the right side? Now count the chlorine atoms. Is the number the same on both sides? According to the law of conservation of mass, the number of atoms of an element should be the same on both sides of an equation. By writing the numeral 2 in front of NaCl, the equation can be *balanced.* An equation is **balanced** when the number and kind of atoms to the left of → equal the number and kind of atoms to the right of →. The equation is now balanced:

no

no

How do you know when an equation in balanced?

$$BaCl_2 (aq) + Na_2SO_4 (aq) \rightarrow BaSO_4 (s) + 2 NaCl (aq)$$

NaCl is in solution as Na^+ and Cl^- ions.

Numerals used to balance a chemical equation are called **coefficients** (coh ih fish′ nts). Subscript numbers in a formula should not be added or changed to balance an equation. Changing a subscript changes the formula into a formula for a different compound.

Equations represent chemical changes or reactions. To write a correct equation, first write a word equation for the reaction, then write proper formulas for all reactants and products. See if the equation is balanced. Place coefficients in front of the formulas if needed to balance the equation. *Do not change formulas to balance equations.*

EXAMPLE

Make sure that the students understand the example before you proceed.

Sodium hydroxide ($NaOH$) and iron(III) chloride ($FeCl_3$) react to form sodium chloride ($NaCl$) and iron (III) hydroxide ($Fe(OH)_3$). $NaOH$, $FeCl_3$, and $NaCl$ are in solution. $Fe(OH)_3$ is a precipitate. You can write an equation for this reaction. This is a double replacement reaction. Iron (III) means that each iron atom has lost three electrons to chloride ions.

Solution: When the iron ions (Fe^{+3}) unite with the hydroxide ions (OH^-), a precipitate forms.

(a) Write the formulas: $NaOH(aq) + FeCl_3(aq) \rightarrow NaCl(aq) + Fe(OH)_3(s)$

(b) Check the balance: hydroxide ions and chloride ions do not balance.

(c) Balance: Three chlorine atoms are on the left. To have three chlorine atoms on the right, place the numeral 3 in front of $NaCl$:

$$NaOH(aq) + FeCl_3(aq) \rightarrow$$
$$3\,NaCl(aq) + Fe(OH)_3(s)$$

Now three sodium atoms are on the right. To have three sodium atoms on the left, place the numeral 3 in front of $NaOH$:

$$3\,NaOH(aq) + FeCl_3(aq) \rightarrow$$
$$3\,NaCl(aq) + Fe(OH)_3(s)$$

Three hydroxide ions are needed on the right. The formula already has three. The iron atoms are equal. The equation is balanced.

PROBLEM

1. Complete and balance the following equations:

(a) $NaBr(aq) + AgNO_3(aq) \rightarrow$ __?Ag__ $Br(s) +$ __?Na__ $NO_3(aq)$

(b) $Ca(NO_3)_2(aq) + K_2SO_4(aq) \rightarrow Ca$ __?SO4__ $(s) +$ $2K$ __?NO3__ (aq)

(c) $2KCl(aq) + Pb(NO_3)_2(aq) \rightarrow 2K$__NO?__ $(aq) +$ Pb __?Cl2__ (s)

(d) $AlCl_3$ (aq) $+\overset{3\,LiCl}{3}LiOH$ (aq) $\rightarrow$ __?__ (aq) $+$ __?__ (s)

(e) $3\,Ca(OH)_2$ (aq) $+2\,Fe(NO_3)_3$ (aq) $\rightarrow 2\,Fe\,(OH)_3$ (s) $+$
$3\,Ca(NO_3)_2$ (aq)

(f) $3\,MgSO_4$ (aq) $+2\,Na_3PO_4$ (aq) $\rightarrow \overset{Mg_3(PO_4)_2}{\_\_?\_\_}$ (s) $+ \overset{3Na_2SO_4}{\_\_?\_\_}$ (aq)

(g) Hydrogen sulfide plus mercury (II) chloride in water yields __?__ $+$ __?__.   *2 hydrogen chloride plus mercury (II) sulfide*

Sodium hydroxide solution

Copper sulfate solution   **Figure 9-6.**

EXPERIMENT. Place 5 ml of copper (II) sulfate solution in a test tube and add three drops of sodium hydroxide solution. What do you observe? What compound is formed? What color is characteristic of most copper compounds? What other substance must have been formed? Write an equation for the reaction that you think took place.

Filter the solution. Can you tell if all of the copper (II) sulfate in the solution has reacted? How? Add an additional drop of sodium hydroxide solution. What change occurs? What does this prove about the first addition of sodium hydroxide?   *If more precipitate forms, all copper sulfate did not react initially.*

Blue precipitate forms. Copper compounds are generally blue.
$$CuSO_4 + 2NaOH \longrightarrow Cu(OH)_2 + Na_2SO_4$$

All reactions in which a gas, a precipitate, or water is formed are said to "go to completion." What could you use to test the completeness of any reaction which involves precipitation?

What is an "end" reaction?

Reaction that goes to completion

Single Replacement Reaction. In the *single replacement reaction,* a free element replaces an element which is combined in a compound. The element being replaced must be similar to the element replacing it. Metals replace metals. Nonmetals replace nonmetals. Many metals will also replace hydrogen.

EXPERIMENT. Dissolve 2 grams of silver nitrate ($AgNO_3$) in 100 ml of distilled water. Place this solution in an 150-ml beaker. Wind a clean bare copper wire around a pencil to form a coil. Remove the pencil. Leave enough wire to form a handle so that the wire can be hung on the lip of the beaker. Place the coil in the beaker. Explain what you observe. Allow the reaction to continue overnight. What happens to the copper wire? What is the gray material that forms? Why does the liquid turn blue?   *Silver crystals grow on copper wire. Copper ions in solution give blue color.*

General equation for single replacement reactions

Word equation:

   A plus BC yields AC plus B

Formula equation:

   $A + BC \rightarrow AC + B$

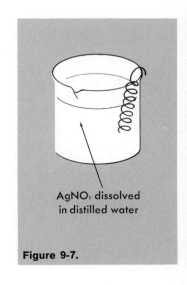

$AgNO_3$ dissolved in distilled water

Figure 9-7.

Figure 9-8. A series of chemical reactions take place when metal is refined.

Actual single replacement reaction

Word equation:

| copper (solid) | plus | silver nitrate (solution) | yields | copper (II) nitrate (solution) | plus | silver (solid) |

Formula equation:

$$Cu(s) + 2AgNO_3(aq) \rightarrow Cu(NO_3)_2(aq) + 2Ag(s)$$

In the experiment, a deposit of silver forms on the coil. The solution turns blue. This indicates that a copper (II) nitrate solution has formed. Notice that the equation is balanced in the same manner as the equation for a double replacement reaction. Remember, (s) represents "solid."

Can zinc replace copper? *yes*

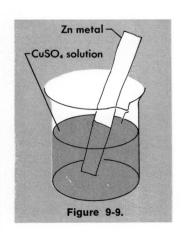

Zn metal

CuSO₄ solution

Figure 9-9.

copper metal

EXPERIMENT. Dissolve 10 g of powdered copper (II) sulfate in 100 ml of water. Place a strip of zinc (Zn) metal in the water. What substance forms on the zinc? Write an equation for the reaction. Repeat the procedure using silver nitrate and a strip of lead. $CuSO_4 + Zn(s) \longrightarrow ZnSO_4 + Cu(s)$

Silver is deposited $2AgNO_3 + Pb(s) \longrightarrow Pb(NO_3)_2 + 2Ag(s)$

Sometimes it is difficult to determine whether one substance can replace another. An element can usually replace any element of the same kind below it or to the right of it in the periodic table (Section 4:7). For example, iron will replace copper, and chlorine will replace bromine. This rule, however, does not always hold true. Lead, for example, will replace silver. Fortunately, an experiment can show which substances

Engelhard Industries

Figure 9-10. Silver plate is made by coating base metals with silver through electrolysis.

will replace each other. If you do not know whether a reaction will occur, set up an experiment to find out.

Decomposition Reaction. Sometimes a compound breaks down, or decomposes, into other compounds and/or elements. This is called a *decomposition* (dee' kom poh zish' un) *reaction.*

General equation for decomposition reaction

Word equation:
   AB yields A plus B
Formula equation:
   $AB \rightarrow A + B$

Actual decomposition reaction

Word equation:

potassium chlorate (solid)	yields	potassium chloride (solid)	plus	oxygen (gas)

The Continental Baking Co.

Figure 9-11. Bubbles of CO_2 in a decomposition reaction cause bread to "rise."

Formula equation:

$$2 \, KClO_3 \, (s) \rightarrow 2 \, KCl \, (s) + 3 \, O_2 \, (g)$$

In the above reaction, potassium chlorate is heated. The heat energy causes the potassium chlorate molecules to break apart (decompose) into oxygen gas and solid potassium chloride. When oxygen is free, it exists as a diatomic molecule (Section 5:1). The symbol (g) indicates that a gas is formed. Bubbles that cause cakes and bread to "rise" are caused by carbon dioxide (CO_2) gas produced by decomposition reactions.

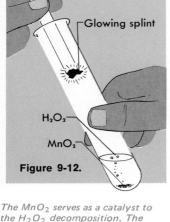

Figure 9-12.

The MnO_2 serves as a catalyst to the H_2O_2 decomposition. The wooden splint bursts into flame, signifying the presence of oxygen gas.

EXPERIMENT. Place 5 ml of hydrogen peroxide H_2O_2 in a test tube. Drop a pinch of manganese dioxide (MnO_2) into the liquid. Insert a glowing wooden splint into the mouth of the test tube. What gas is released by the decomposition of the hydrogen peroxide? Write an equation for the reaction. NOTE: The MnO_2 only serves to start the reaction. It is not chemically changed so it should not be considered part of the reaction.   oxygen $2H_2O_2 \longrightarrow 2H_2O + O_2 \, (g)$

Some compounds decompose when they are exposed to a form of energy, generally heat, light, or electrical energy. Usually, the form of energy is indicated above the arrow in the equation as $\overset{\Delta}{\rightarrow}$ (heat), $\overset{lt}{\rightarrow}$ (light), or $\overset{elec}{\rightarrow}$ (electrical). When a compound is decomposed by electrical energy, the reaction is called **electrolysis.**

Synthesis reaction. A synthesis is a process by which something is put together. A *synthesis reaction* occurs when two or more elements or compounds unite to form one compound.

Figure 9-13.   By the single re-placement reaction that com-bines fuel and oxygen to form carbon dioxide and water, this jet engine produces heat.

General Electric Research & Development Center

General equation for synthesis reaction

Word equation:

A plus B yields AB

Formula equation:

$A + B \rightarrow AB$

Actual synthesis reaction

Word equation:

sodium (solid) plus chlorine (gas) yields sodium chloride (solid)

Formula equation:

$$2\,Na\,(s) + Cl_2\,(g) \rightarrow 2\,NaCl\,(s)$$

In the above reaction, sodium and chlorine combine directly to form sodium chloride. Notice the symbols (s) and (g) indicate the state of the substances.

Iron rusting is a synthesis reaction. Iron (Fe) combines with oxygen (O_2) in the air and produces iron (III) oxide (Fe_2O_3):

$$4\,Fe\,(s) + 3\,O_2\,(g) \rightarrow 2\,Fe_2O_3\,(s)$$

Addition of elements or compounds to unsaturated hydrocarbons (Section 6:9) is also a synthesis reaction. Bromine (Br_2) can be added to ethene (C_2H_4) to form ethylene dibromide ($C_2H_4Br_2$):

What could bromine replace? *iodine*

$$C_2H_4\,(g) + Br_2\,(l) \rightarrow C_2H_4Br_2\,(l)$$

The symbol (l) indicates liquid state.

Thus, a variety of reactions can be thought of as belonging to four different types. In using equations to describe each type of reaction, the same general rules apply. To help determine what products will be formed, try to recognize the kind of reaction taking place. After identification, write correct formulas for the reactants and the products. Then, if necessary, balance the equation by placing coefficients in front of the formulas.

PROBLEMS

2. Complete and balance each of the following equations. In Parts (e) and (f), what type of reaction is taking place?

    (a) Single replacement: $Fe\,(s) + Cu\,(NO_3)_2\,(aq) \rightarrow$ *Cu*? (s) + *Fe*? $(NO_3)_2\,(aq)$

    (b) Synthesis: $Mg\,(s) + O_2\,(g) \rightarrow MgO\,(s)$ *2Mg (s) + O₂(g) ⟶ 2MgO(s)*

    (c) Decomposition: $2Hg_2O\,(s) \xrightarrow{\Delta}$ *? 4Hg*(s) + $O_2\,(g)$

    (d) Double replacement: $AgNO_3\,(aq) + KI\,(aq) \rightarrow$ *? Ag*$I\,(s) +$ *? K*$NO_3\,(aq)$

(e) $CaI_2(aq) + Cl_2(g) \rightarrow$ __?__ $\overset{CaCl_2}{}$ $(aq) + I_2(g)$

(f) $2\,H_2O(l) \rightarrow$ __2H₂__ $(g) + O_2(g)$

3. When sulfur is burned, a very disagreeable substance is produced:

$$S(s) + O_2(g) \rightarrow SO_2(g)$$

   (a) Is this equation balanced?
   (b) Is this an end reaction?
   (c) What does (s) after the symbol for sulfur mean?
   (d) What does the → mean?
   (e) What kind of chemical reaction does this represent?
   (f) What is the name of the gas, $SO_2(g)$?

9:3 Energy Relationships in Chemical Change

Energy is either gained or lost during chemical change. In some reactions, energy is given up as the reactants regroup themselves into new compounds. In other reactions, energy must be continually added to the reactants for a chemical change to occur. If energy is given up, the reaction is called **exothermic** (eks' oh thur' mik). This means that heat is given off during the reaction. If heat or some other form of energy is taken on during the reaction, the reaction is **endothermic** (en' doh thur' mik). $2H_2O(l) \overset{elec}{\longrightarrow} 2H_2(g) + O_2(g)$

EXPERIMENT. Add 150 ml of water containing 5 ml of concentrated H_2SO_4 to a Hoffman electrolysis apparatus (Figure 9–16). CAUTION: When mixing water and acid, always add the acid to the water. Wear eye and clothing protection. Connect the terminals to four dry cells connected in series (Section 19:1), or to a lead storage battery, or to a 6-v D.C. power supply. Collect the gases produced. Test each gas by holding a glowing splint above the stopcock and opening the stopcock. What reaction has occurred? Is the reaction exothermic or _endothermic_? Write an equation to show the reaction. *Alternating current would change the polarity of the electrodes 60 times a second. The ions would not collect at either electrode.*

The burning of magnesium is an exothermic reaction. Little heat is needed to start the reaction. After the reaction starts, the tremendous amount of heat given off by the union of magnesium atoms and oxygen atoms is more than enough to keep the reaction going.

Electrolysis of water is an endothermic reaction. Because water is a stable compound, it does not decompose readily.

Ria C. Parody

Figure 9-14. When iron rusts, what type of reaction is taking place? *synthesis*

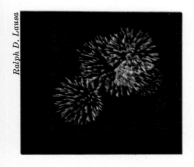

Ralph D. Lawsa

Figure 9-15. Does a fireworks display require _exothermic_ or endothermic reactions?
There will be twice as much H_2 as O_2 produced. H_2 will burn with a blue flame. O_2 will cause a glowing splint to burst into flame.

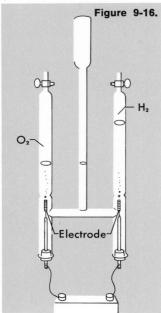

Figure 9-16.

O_2
H_2
Electrode

Figure 9-17. During a volcanic eruption much heat is given off. Rock is melted. Water is changed into steam (Section 7:13).

However, by passing an electric current through water, it can be forced to decompose into hydrogen gas and oxygen gas. The reaction stops as soon as the electric current is stopped. Atoms of hydrogen and oxygen are produced. These give up little energy as they combine to form H_2 and O_2, the normal diatomic forms of the gases. A great deal of energy is added to keep the reaction going. Little energy is given up as the products form. Thus, this reaction is endothermic.

What kind of a reaction is the burning of magnesium?

exothermic

Flask: $CaCO_3 (s) + 2 HCl \rightarrow CaCl_2 (aq) + CO_2 (g)$

EXPERIMENT. *Place 25 g of limestone and 50 ml of water in a flask. Insert a thistle tube and a glass delivery tube into a two-hole rubber stopper. Seal the flask with the stopper. Place the tip of the glass delivery tube in a solution of limewater (calcium hydroxide). Add 25 ml of dilute hydrochloric acid through the thistle tube. Be certain the bottom of the thistle tube is submerged underneath the surface of the liquid. Note the change in the flask and the limewater. Does an* <u>exothermic</u> *or an endothermic reaction occur in the flask? How do you know?* *Beaker:* $CO_2 (g) + Ca(OH)_2 (aq) \rightarrow CaCO_3 (s) + H_2O$

Use care in putting the thistle tube into the stopper. Lubricate with water or glycerin. Hold both parts in several layers of cloth to avoid getting glass into hands if breakage should occur.

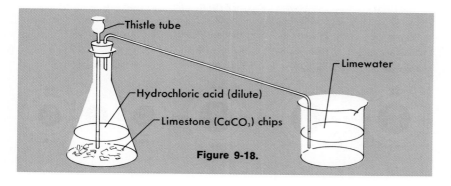

Thistle tube

Limewater

Hydrochloric acid (dilute)

Limestone (CaCO₃) chips

Figure 9-18.

In the flask, chips begin to disappear as they react. Heat is produced (exothermic reaction). Bubbles of CO_2 gas move through the delivery tube to the limewater. $CaCO_3$ disappears in the flask forming CO_2 which reacts with $Ca(OH)_2$ in the beaker to form $CaCO_3$ again. Ask students to give equations for reactions taking place. All three types of end reactions (gas, precipitate, water) are present here.

9:4 *Molecular Mass and Formula Mass*

In a chemical reaction, the sum of the masses of the reactants is equal to the sum of the masses of the products. This is the law of conservation of mass. Conservation of mass does not tell the number of grams of materials that are needed to react. Nor does it indicate the number of grams of products that are formed. How can you predict the quantities?

You can answer the preceding question by using mass numbers (Section 4:6). From the masses of atoms, it is possible to find the molecular mass of a compound. The *molecular mass* of a compound is the sum of the mass numbers of the atoms in a molecule of the compound. (The symbol for mass number is A.) For example, in one molecule of carbon dioxide (CO_2) there is one atom of carbon ($A = 12$) and two atoms of oxygen ($A = 16$). The molecular mass of CO_2 is 44, the sum of the mass numbers. For your work in this course, you can simply use the atomic mass number rather than the atomic mass, which is carried out to four or five significant digits. Hydrogen has an atomic mass number of 1, and chlorine has an atomic mass number of 35. Add these together and you get 36 ($1 + 35 = 36$). Thus, the molecular mass of hydrogen chloride (HCl) is 36.

Ionic compounds do not exist as molecules. The mass of the smallest possible unit of an ionic compound is called the *formula mass*. The **formula mass** is the sum of the mass numbers of the atoms present in a formula of an ionic compound. Molecular mass and formula mass can be calculated in the same way. Sodium chloride, an ionic compound, does not exist as a molecule. It is possible, however, to find the formula mass of NaCl. According to the periodic table, sodium has a mass of

What is the molecular mass of oxygen?   *32*

What is formula mass?

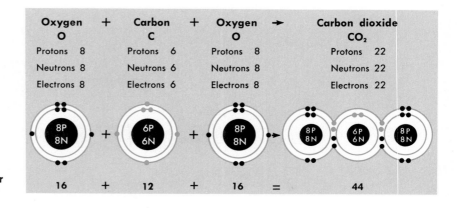

Figure 9-19. The molecular mass of CO_2 is 44.

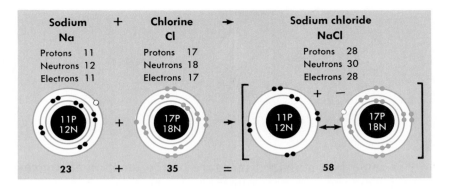

Sodium +	Chlorine →	Sodium chloride
Na	Cl	NaCl
Protons 11	Protons 17	Protons 28
Neutrons 12	Neutrons 18	Neutrons 30
Electrons 11	Electrons 17	Electrons 28

23 + 35 = 58

Figure 9-20. The formula mass of NaCl is 58.

Some mass numbers you will find useful:

Al	27	Pb	207
Ba	137	Hg	201
B	11	N	14
Br	80	O	16
Ca	40	P	31
C	12	K	39
Cl	35	Si	28
Cu	64	Ag	108
F	19	Na	23
H	1	S	32
I	127	Sn	119
Fe	56	Zn	65

What is the formula mass of KBr? *119*

23 and chlorine has a mass of 35. Therefore, NaCl has a formula mass of 58, $(23 + 35 = 58)$.

Molecular mass should be used only for molecular compounds. Formula mass may be used for all compounds. Formula mass is a more general term than molecular mass.

EXAMPLE

Find the formula mass of calcium phosphate.

Solution: (a) Write the correct formula: $Ca_3(PO_4)_2$

(b) Analyze the compound:

Number of Atoms	Mass Number	Formula Mass
3 calcium	40	$3 \times 40 = 120$
2 phosphorus	31	$2 \times 31 = 62$
8 oxygen	16	$8 \times 16 = 128$
		310

(c) Answer: Formula mass = 310

PROBLEM

4. Find the formula mass for each of the following compounds: *Appendix D*

(a) Na_2SO_4 *142*   (d) copper (II) sulfate *160*
(b) $CaCO_3$ *100*   (e) silver bromide *188*
(c) NH_4NO_3 *80*   (f) potassium phosphate *212*

El Paso Natural Gas Company

Figure 9-21. This pipe is being cleaned and coated with tar. The tar prevents the iron in the pipe from coming into contact with air and rusting.

Figure 9-22. Mass is conserved in a chemical reaction.

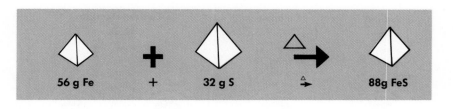

56 g Fe   +   32 g S   →   88g FeS

Suggestion:"Since the mole concept is central to much of chemistry, do not proceed quickly to the next section. Instead, give extra time to this section. Emphasize its importance, and give the students a chance to become familiar with it.*

9:5   The Mole

Define mole.

What is a mole of a substance?

The **mole** is a standard measure of the amount of a compound. One mole of any substance is the formula mass expressed in grams. Since the formula mass of sodium chloride is 58, one mole of NaCl is 58 grams. Since the formula mass of calcium phosphate is 310, one mole of $Ca_3(PO_4)_2$ is 310 grams.

Read the equation for the reaction between silver nitrate and sodium chloride:

$$AgNO_3(aq) + NaCl(aq) \rightarrow AgCl(s) + NaNO_3(aq)$$

This equation could be read as: one unit (formula unit) of $AgNO_3$ reacts with one unit (formula unit) of NaCl to produce one unit (formula unit) of $NaNO_3$ and one unit (formula unit) of AgCl. The equation can also be read as: 170 grams of $AgNO_3$ unite with 58 grams of NaCl to produce 143 grams of AgCl and 85 grams of $NaNO_3$. The total mass of the reactants equals the total mass of the products. The totals are both equal to 228 grams. How does this illustrate the law of conservation of mass? Table 9–1 shows the relationships of formula units, moles, and grams.

Find the total mass of the reactants and compare it to the total mass of the products. They should be equal.

Table 9–1. *A Chemical Reaction*			
$AgNO_3$ (aq)	+ NaCl (aq)	→ AgCl(s)	+ $NaNO_3$ (aq)
1 formula unit	+ 1 formula unit	= 1 formula unit	+ 1 formula unit
1 mole	+ 1 mole	= 1 mole	+ 1 mole
170 g	+ 58 g	= 143 g	+ 85 g
	228 g	= 228 g	

Important.

Nitrogen (N_2) and hydrogen (H_2) can combine to form ammonia (NH_3):

$$N_2(g) + 3 H_2(g) \rightarrow 2 NH_3(g)$$

This equation can be read three different ways:
(1) One formula unit of nitrogen combines with three formula units of hydrogen to produce two formula units of ammonia
(2) One mole of nitrogen combines with three moles of hydrogen to produce two moles of ammonia

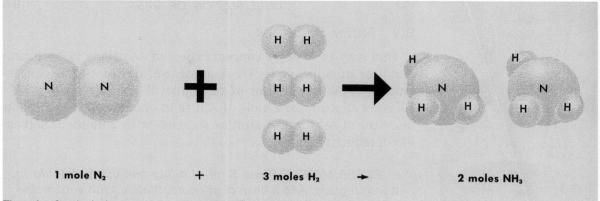

1 mole N₂   **+**   **3 moles H₂**   →   **2 moles NH₃**

The ratio of moles is the same as
the ratio of atoms for a given
formula unit because there are
exactly N (6.02×10^{23}) atoms in

one mole of an element. N is called
Avogadro's number.

**Figure 9-23. Four molecules
combine to form two molecules
through rearrangement of
atoms. In the same manner,
four moles can yield two moles.**

(3) 28 grams of nitrogen combine with 6 grams of hydrogen
to produce 34 grams of ammonia

PROBLEM

How is a chemical equation
used to determine the amount
of products in a chemical reaction?

*A chemical equation is used to
determine the ratio of moles of
product to the moles of reactant.*

5. Fill in the blanks:

(a) $C_2H_4(g) + Br_2(l) \rightarrow C_2H_4Br_2(l)$

$C_2H_4(g)$ $+$ $Br_2(l)$ $\rightarrow$

_1?_ formula unit(s) $+$ _1?_ formula unit(s) $\rightarrow$

_1?_ mole(s) $+$ _1?_ mole(s) $\rightarrow$

_28?_ g $+$ _160?_ g $\rightarrow$

$C_2H_4Br_2(l)$

_1?_ formula unit(s)

_1?_ mole(s)

_188?_ g

(b) $3\,NaOH(aq) + FeCl_3(aq) \rightarrow$

$3\,NaCl(aq) + Fe(OH)_3(s)$

$3\,NaOH(aq) + FeCl_3(aq)$ $\rightarrow$

_3?_ mole(s) $+$ _1?_ mole(s) $\rightarrow$

_120?_ g $+$_161?_ g $\rightarrow$

$3\,NaCl(aq)$ $+$ $Fe(OH)_3(s)$

_3?_ mole(s) $+$ _1?_ mole(s)   _3_

_174?_ g $+$_107?_ g

(c) _2?_ $Na_3PO_4(aq) +$ _3?_ $MgSO_4(aq) \rightarrow$

_2?_ mole(s) $+$ _3?_ mole(s) $\rightarrow$

_328?_ g $+$ _360?_ g $\rightarrow$

3Na₂SO₄

$Mg_3(PO_4)_2$_?_ (aq) $+$ _?_ (s)

_1?_ mole(s) $+$ _3?_ mole(s)

_?_ g $+$ _?_ g

262   426

191

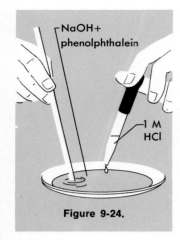

NaOH+
phenolphthalein

1 M
HCl

Figure 9-24.

9:6   *Molar Solutions*

One way to express concentration of solutions is by grams per liter of solution (g/l). A more useful measure of concentration is moles per liter of solution (M). A *one-molar* (1M) *solution* contains one mole of solute in enough solvent to make one liter of solution. A similar solution with 2 moles of solvent has a molarity of 2. See Teacher's Guide at the front of this book.

EXPERIMENT.   Place 5 ml of dilute sodium hydroxide in a watch glass. Add a drop of phenolphthalein. With a medicine dropper, add 1M hydrochloric acid. Add one drop at a time and stir gently until a color change occurs. Twenty drops equal about 1 ml. In this particular example, the molarity of the sodium hydroxide can be calculated with this formula:

(acid)   (base)
Volume × Molarity = Volume × Molarity
Why is phenolphthalein used in this experiment?

Suppose you have a 1M solution of sodium sulfide (Na_2S). You want this solution to react with a 1M solution of lead nitrate ($Pb(NO_3)_2$). The equation for the reaction is: $Na_2S(aq) + Pb(NO_3)_2(aq) \rightarrow 2\,NaNO_3(aq) + PbS(s)$. One mole of Na_2S reacts with one mole of $Pb(NO_3)_2$. You have 1M solutions of both reactants. Thus, in this example, if you mix equal volumes of each, you will have a complete reaction.

Suppose you want to know the number of grams of a substance in a given volume. How many grams of silver nitrate are in 500 milliliters of a 0.1M solution? One liter of a 1M solution contains 170 grams of $AgNO_3$. One-half liter, or 500 milliliters, contains 85 grams. Since this solution is a 0.1M solution, it must contain 0.1 of 85 grams, or 8.5 grams of

One liter of 0.25M NaCl contains how many grams of NaCl?

14.5 g

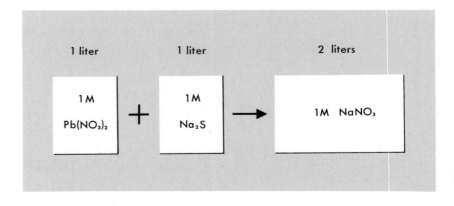

1 liter	1 liter	2 liters
1 M $Pb(NO_3)_2$	1 M Na_2S	1M $NaNO_3$

Figure 9-25. Even though two moles of NaNO$_3$ would be formed, two liters of solution would reduce the molarity to 1M.

AgNO₃. Another way to approach this problem is to use this formula:

grams of   = volume of solution ×   molarity   × formula mass
solute   (in liters)   (in moles per liter)   (grams)

> What is a 2M solution?
>
> *Contains 2 moles solute in one liter solution*

(a)   volume: 500 ml = 0.5 liter
(b)   molarity: 0.1M = 0.1 mole/liter
(c)   formula   Ag   = 108 g
      mass of   N   = 14 g
      AgNO₃: O₃   = 3 × 16 g
                       ‾‾‾‾‾‾‾‾
                        170 g

$$\text{grams of solute (AgNO}_3) = \frac{0.5 \text{ liter}}{} \left| \frac{0.1 \text{ mole}}{1 \text{ liter}} \right| \frac{170 \text{ grams}}{1 \text{ mole}}$$

$$\text{grams of AgNO}_3 = \frac{0.5 \times 0.1 \times 170}{1} \text{ grams} = 8.5 \text{ grams}$$

EXAMPLE

How many grams of potassium chloride are needed to make 200 ml of a 0.2M solution?

Solution: (a)   Write the correct formula: KCl
          (b)   Find the correct formula mass: 39 + 35 = 74
              One mole of KCl weighs 74 g
          (c)   Change volume to liters: 200 ml = 0.2 l
          (d)   Use formula:
              grams = volume × molarity × formula mass

$$\text{grams} = \frac{0.2 \text{ l}}{} \left| \frac{0.2 \text{ mole}}{1 \text{ l}} \right| \frac{74 \text{ g}}{1 \text{ mole}}$$

          (e)   grams of KCl = 2.96 g

PROBLEMS

6. How many grams of barium chloride are needed for 1 l of a 0.5M solution?   *104 g*

7. How many grams of sodium sulfate are needed for 400 ml of a 0.3M solution?   *17 g*

8. How many milliliters of a 2M solution of AgNO₃ are needed to react with 10 ml of a 2M solution of NaCl? How many milliliters of 1M, 0.5M, and 0.2M solutions of AgNO₃ are needed?   *10 ml, 20 ml, 40 ml, 100 ml*

MAIN IDEAS

p. 176. **1.** The law of conservation of mass states that in an ordinary chemical reaction, no matter is lost.

p. 177   **2.** Chemists use chemical equations to describe chemical changes.

p. 178   **3.** Reactions that can be represented by chemical equations include:
- (a) double replacement reactions
- (b) single replacement reactions
- (c) decomposition reactions
- (d) synthesis reactions

p. 181   **4.** If a water, a gas, or a precipitate is formed in a chemical reaction, the reaction is said to go to completion and is called an end reaction.

p. 188   **5.** Each formula in an equation may represent a formula unit, or it may represent a mole of a compound or element.

p. 190   **6.** A mole is a formula mass or a molecular mass expressed in grams.

p. 192   **7.** A one-molar ($1M$) solution contains one mole of solute per liter of solution.

p. 190   **8.** Balanced equations aid in determining the amounts of reactants used and products formed.

VOCABULARY

Write a sentence in which you correctly use each of the following words or terms.

aqueous	endothermic	molecular mass
coefficients	equation	precipitate
conservation of mass	exothermic	product
decomposition	formula mass	reactant
electrolysis	molar solution	subscript
end reaction	mole	synthesis

STUDY QUESTIONS

A. True or False   *Have students rewrite false statements to make the statements correct.*

Determine whether each of the following sentences is true or false. (Do not write in this book.)

is a liquid   F   **1.** The (1) after H_2O_2 in the equation means that the substance ~~decomposes when exposed to light~~.
$$H_2O_2(l) \rightarrow H_2(g) + O_2(g)$$

T   **2.** In ordinary chemical reactions no mass is lost.

T **3.** When a gas is formed, the reaction is known as an end reaction.

T **4.** A precipitate is a relatively insoluble solid that forms during a chemical reaction.

T **5.** Electrolysis is decomposition of a compound by electricity.

F **6.** An equation may be balanced by changing ~~subscripts~~.   *coefficients*

F **7.** A molar solution contains one ~~gram~~ of solute per liter.   *gram formula weight*

T **8.** A mole of oxygen (O_2) has a molecular mass of 32 grams.

T **9.** The symbol (aq) after a chemical formula means "dissolved in water."

T **10.** The formula mass of potassium bromide (KBr) is 119.

B.   Multiple Choice   *Some questions in part B may have more than one correct answer. Only one answer is required.*

Choose one word or phrase that correctly completes each of the following sentences. (Do not write in this book.)

1. A reaction that gives off heat is (exothermic, endothermic, stable).

2. Bromine can replace (fluorine, iodine, iron) in a chemical reaction.

3. When hydrogen chloride dissolves in water, (ions, molecules, atoms) are formed.

4. In a reaction, 10 g of X produces 5 g of Y. Fifty grams of X would produce (1, 25, 10, 250) g of Y.

5. The formula mass for $NaNO_3$ is (85, 85 g, 170, 170 g).

6. Fifty grams of calcium carbonate in 1 l of solution is (1M, 0.5M, 2M).

7. To balance equations, (coefficients, subscripts, formulas) should be changed.

8. A 0.30M solution of NaBr would require (31, 310, 3.1, 103) g of NaBr in 1 l of solution.

9. Fifty ml of a 0.1M Na_2S solution contain (3.9, 39, 0.39, 78, 7.8, 0.78) g of Na_2S.

C.   Completion

Complete each of the following sentences with a word or phrase that will make the sentence correct. (Do not write in this book.)

1. $C(s) + O_2(g) \rightarrow CO_2(g)$ is an equation which represents a(n) __?__ reaction.   *synthesis*

mass

decomposition

136

silver chloride

K^+, NO_3^-

ionization

100

2. A chemical change involves no change in __?__.

3. Electrolysis of water is an example of a(n) __?__ reaction.

4. One mole of calcium sulfate has a mass of __?__.

5. If silver nitrate solution reacts with potassium chloride solution, __?__ is the precipitate that forms.

6. In the reaction in Question 5, __?__ and __?__ are the ions left in solution.

7. When molecular compounds dissolve to form ions, the process is called __?__.

8. Ten ml of $2M$ sodium chloride solution should react exactly with __?__ ml of $0.2M$ silver nitrate solution.

D. How and Why

1. In the reaction represented by $Fe(s) + S(s) \rightarrow FeS(s)$, how many grams of iron (II) sulfide will be produced from 28 g of iron?   *44 g*

water, a gas, a precipitate

2. An end reaction occurs when certain types of products are formed. What are the three types of products?

3. Three hundred ml of $0.2M$ KCl solution requires how many grams of solid KCl?   *4.4 g*

4. A reaction yields 20.2 g of potassium nitrate. How many moles is this?   *0.2 mole*

5. Endothermic reactions absorb heat as they proceed; exothermic reactions give off heat as they proceed.

5. How do endothermic reactions differ from exothermic reactions?

6. Which contains more carbon: 88 g of CO_2, or 76 g of CS_2?

7. How many moles are in 640 g of bromine gas (Br_2)?   *4 moles*

double replacement

synthesis

decomposition

single replacement

single replacement

8. Balance the following equations:
   (a) $Na_2S(aq) + 2AgNO_3(aq) \rightarrow NaNO_3(aq) + Ag_2S(s)$
   (b) $3H_2(g) + N_2(g) \rightarrow 2NH_3(g)$
   (c) $2KClO_3(s) \rightarrow 2KCl(s) + 3O_2(g)$
   (d) $3CuSO_4(aq) + 2Al(s) \rightarrow Al_2(SO_4)_3(aq) + 3Cu(s)$
   (e) $2Na(s) + 2H_2O(l) \rightarrow 2NaOH(aq) + H_2(g)$

double replacement

single replacement

decomposition

synthesis

double replacement

9. Complete and balance the following equations:
   (a) $Na_2CrO_4(aq) + PbCl_2(aq) \rightarrow$ *2NaCl(aq) + PbCrO$_4$(s)*
   (b) $Cl_2(g) + NaBr(aq) \rightarrow$ *2NaCl(aq) + Br$_2$(l)*
   (c) $Mg(ClO_3)_2(s) \rightarrow$ *MgCl$_2$(s) + 3O$_2$(g)*
   (d) $2H_2(g) + O_2(g) \rightarrow$ *2H$_2$O(l)*
   (e) $3Ca(OH)_2(aq) + 2FeCl_3(aq) \rightarrow$ *2Fe(OH)$_3$(s) + 3CaCl$_2$(aq)*

10. What type of reaction is represented by each equation in Questions 8 and 9?

INVESTIGATIONS

See Teacher's Guide at the front of this book.

1. Sodium hydrogen carbonate is the chemical name for baking soda. In baking, carbon dioxide gas is produced as baking soda is heated. (Baking soda is also called bicarbonate of soda.)

   (a) Place a teaspoon of baking soda in a beaker. Add water. Heat your mixture. What happens?

   (b) Write a word equation for the decomposition of $NaHCO_3$ to carbon dioxide (CO_2) when it is heated.

   (c) Write a chemical equation for the decomposition.

   (d) Place a teaspoon of baking soda in water. Add a drop of vinegar. What happens?

   (e) Place a teaspoon of baking soda in water. Add cream of tartar. What happens? Taste cream of tartar. How is it like vinegar?

   (f) Place a teaspoon of baking powder in water. How does it react? How does baking powder differ from baking soda? Read the ingredients on the label of the baking powder can.

   (g) What types of baked goods require baking soda or baking powder?

2. Do a library research project about coordination compounds. Find out how they relate to solubility and solutions.

INTERESTING READING

Haensel, V. and Burwell, R. L., Jr., "Catalysis." *Scientific American*, CCXXV (December, 1971), pp. 46-58.

Kuslan, Louis, and Stone, A. Harris, *Liebig, The Master Chemist*. New York, Prentice-Hall, 1969.

Marcus, Rebecca B., *Antoine Lavoisier and the Revolution in Chemistry*. New York, Franklin Watts, Inc., 1965.

10

Some of the most important compounds in chemistry are the acids, bases, and salts. This chapter will introduce the student to some properties of these substances. The students will become acquainted with various means of measuring relative strengths of acids, bases, and salts.

Acids, Bases, and Salts

GOAL: You will gain an understanding of the properties of acids, bases, and salts and the various means for measuring the relative strengths of these materials.

Vinegar is acid. Sodium bicarbonate in water is a base. Sodium chloride is common table salt. Man needs *acids*, *bases*, and *salts*. However, acids, bases, and salts can be harmful. Some are poisons.

Acids, bases, and salts provide much of the flavor in foods. The sour flavor in lemons is caused by an acid. Just as acids often taste sour, bases often taste bitter. Never taste unknown chemicals. It can be dangerous. In the laboratory, acids, bases, and salts can be detected in many other safe ways.

10:1 *Ionization of Water*

A solution must contain ions to conduct electricity. Sensitive instruments reveal that pure water conducts electricity to a very small degree. Where do ions come from in pure water?

ionization of water

Water molecules are always in motion. Some of them have greater velocity than others. If two molecules collide, they may form a *hydronium* (hie drohn' ee um) *ion* (H_3O^+) and a *hydroxide* (hi drok' sid) *ion* (OH^-):

$$H_2O(l) + H_2O(l) \rightleftharpoons H_3O^+(aq) + OH^-(aq)$$

Hydronium ion (H_3O+) is formed instead of H+ ion (free proton) because the free proton is so strongly attracted to the electrons of the polar water molecule that it would be virtually impossible for them to exist in solution.

Water molecules ionize only slightly. Only one in every 500 million molecules of water ionizes.

Many acids contain hydrogen ions. Hydrogen ions become hydronium ions in water. **Acids** placed in water increase the hydronium ion (H_3O^+) concentration. **Bases** add hydroxide ions (OH^-) to a solution. Bases when placed in water increase the hydroxide ion (OH^-) concentration. For example, place hydrogen chloride (HCl) in water. It ionizes and produces hydronium ions:

$$HCl(g) + H_2O(l) \rightarrow H_3O^+(aq) + Cl^-(aq)$$

198

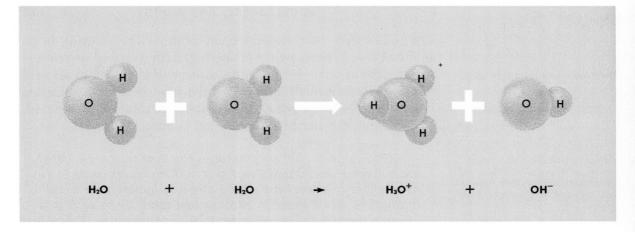

$$H_2O \quad + \quad H_2O \quad \rightarrow \quad H_3O^+ \quad + \quad OH^-$$

Figure 10-1. On the average, there is one H^+ ion and one OH^- ion for every 500 million H_2O molecules.

Organic acids such as acetic acid (CH_3COOH) ionize in a similar way.

$$CH_3COOH\,(l) + H_2O\,(l) \rightarrow H_3O^+\,(aq) + CH_3COO^-\,(aq)$$

Bases produce hydroxide ions. The base sodium hydroxide ($NaOH$), for example, dissociates in water as follows:

$$NaOH\,(s) + H_2O\,(l) \rightarrow Na^+\,(aq) + OH^-\,(aq) + H_2O\,(l)$$

10:2 *Indicators*

Taste is a dangerous way to determine that acids are sour and bases are bitter. Chemicals can harm the tongue, as well as other parts of your body. The use of an **indicator** is a more exact test for an acid or base. Indicators turn different colors.

Carl England

Figure 10-2. Litmus papers dipped in ammonia and vinegar indicate whether the solutions are acidic or basic.

Ohio Environmental Protection Agency

Figure 10-3. Sulfur dioxide in smog can combine with water to form sulfuric acid.

The colors they turn depend upon whether the solution is an acid or base. *Litmus paper* is one indicator you can use to test for an acid or base. Blue litmus paper will turn red in an acid solution. Red litmus paper will turn blue in a base solution. If neither color of paper changes color, the solution is *neutral.* This means it is neither an acid nor a base.

These indicators are organic dyes.

EXPERIMENT. Set six test tubes in a test tube rack. Label each appropriately. Dissolve 1 g of sodium bicarbonate in 10 ml of water in a test tube. Use a straw to bubble your breath through 10 ml of water in another test tube. Dissolve 5 g of calcium oxide in 10 ml of water in a third test tube. Place 5 ml each of milk, soda pop, and vinegar in separate test tubes. Add a piece of red and blue litmus to each of the six test tubes. Determine which are acids and which are bases.

sodium bicarbonate, base; breath + water, acid; calcium oxide, base; milk (fresh), neutral; milk (sour), acid; soda pop, acid; vinegar, acid

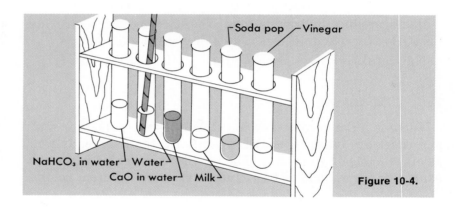

Figure 10-4.

Indicators are only approximate for judging acidity and basicity because of the limitations of the human eye to perceive color change.

Other common indicators may be used. Some are methyl orange, methyl red, bromthymol blue, and *phenolphthalein* (fee' nohl thal' een). Each has a characteristic color change for acids and bases. Phenolphthalein indicator is colorless in an acid solution and pink in a basic solution. For most laboratory tests, only litmus and phenolphthalein are needed.

10:3   *Acids*

Common acids play an important part in daily life. The label on a bottle of vinegar lists one of its components as acetic acid. Automobile batteries contain a sulfuric acid solution. Some household bleaches are weak solutions of hypochlorous acid. We eat citric acid in lemons and oranges. Hydrochloric acid in the stomach aids digestion. There are three important

Name some common acids.

Some common acids: sulfuric acid, acetic acid, citric acid, hydrochloric acid, tannic acid, boric acid, acetylsalicylic acid (aspirin).

commercial acids. They are sulfuric acid, nitric acid, and hydrochloric acid.

Sulfuric (sul feu' rik) *acid* (H_2SO_4) is an oily, thick liquid. It is used to prepare other acids and to act as a dehydrating agent. (Dehydrate means to take water away.) A wooden stick placed in sulfuric acid becomes charred as the acid removes water from it. Because it is a dehydrating agent, sulfuric acid can burn skin and seriously damage fibers. Always handle it with care.

Sulfuric acid is used as an oxidizing agent and as a dehydrating agent.

Sulfuric acid can be produced in the laboratory. Sulfur dioxide is dissolved in water and the solution is treated with hydrogen peroxide (H_2O_2). Sulfur dioxide can be produced by burning sulfur and collecting the gas. The following equations show the steps used in this method:

$$S(s) + O_2(g) \rightarrow SO_2(g)$$
$$SO_2(g) + H_2O(l) \rightarrow H_2SO_3(aq)$$
$$H_2SO_3(aq) + H_2O_2(aq) \rightarrow H_2SO_4(aq) + H_2O(l)$$

Dilute sulfuric acid will react with zinc or iron to produce hydrogen:

$$Zn(s) + H_2SO_4(aq) \rightarrow ZnSO_4(aq) + H_2(g)$$
$$Fe(s) + H_2SO_4(aq) \rightarrow FeSO_4(aq) + H_2(g)$$

H_2S is very poisonous.

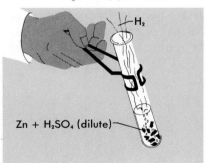

$Zn(s) + H_2SO_4(dil.) \longrightarrow ZnSO_4(s) + H_2(g)$

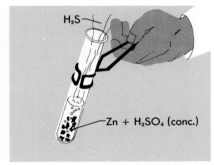

$4(Zn)(s) + H_2SO_4(con.) \longrightarrow 4ZnO(s) + H_2S(g)$

Figure 10-5. Concentrated and dilute H_2SO_4 react differently.

Reaction depends on the number of electrons transferred as sulfur changes oxidation states.

However, concentrated sulfuric acid may produce sulfur dioxide (SO_2) and hydrogen sulfide (H_2S) rather than hydrogen when reacting with zinc or iron. Various other sulfides are also formed in the reaction.

EXPERIMENT. CAUTION: Conduct this experiment only under the direct supervision of your teacher. Wear eye and clothing protection. (1) Place 25 g of table sugar in a beaker. Add 10 ml of concentrated sulfuric acid. (2) Repeat Part 1 with dilute sulfuric acid. Compare your results.

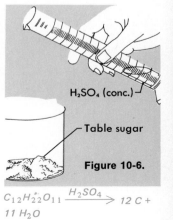

Figure 10-6.

$$C_{12}H_{22}O_{11} \xrightarrow{H_2SO_4} 12\,C + 11\,H_2O$$

This experiment demonstrates the dehydrating power of concentrated H_2SO_4. The concentrated acid removes hydrogen and oxygen from the sugar. The dilute acid does not remove water from sugar since the acid is already in water solution.

Figure 10-7. Each of these materials is acidic or becomes acidic when mixed with water.

Nitric (nie′ trik) *acid* (HNO₃) is oily but not as thick as sulfuric acid. Nitric acid should be handled with care. If it touches skin, it combines chemically with the protein. A yellow stain results which only gradually will wear away.

Nitric acid can be produced in the laboratory. This is done by heating sodium nitrate with concentrated sulfuric acid:

$$NaNO_3(s) + H_2SO_4(aq) \rightarrow NaHSO_4(aq) + HNO_3(g)$$

Nitric acid does not normally produce hydrogen when it reacts with metals. This is the difference between it and most dilute acids. Some products of nitric acid-metal reactions are nitrogen oxides and various nitrates. Nitrates are important commercially. They are used in making fertilizers and explosives.

Figure 10-8. Nitrates are an important component of fertilizer.

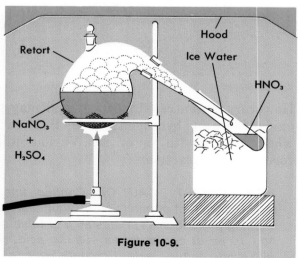

Figure 10-9.

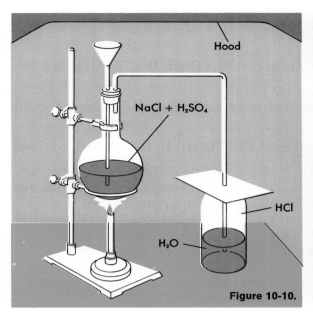

Figure 10-10.

Engelhard Industries

Engelhard Industries

Figure 10-11. Hydrochloric acid is used to clean metals before they are plated.

Hydrochloric (hie′ droh kloh′ rik) *acid* (HCl) is produced by dissolving hydrogen chloride gas in water. The hydrogen chloride gas can be produced by heating sodium chloride with concentrated sulfuric acid:

$$NaCl(s) + H_2SO_4(aq) \rightarrow NaHSO_4(aq) + HCl(g)$$

The resulting gas is collected in distilled water and forms hydrochloric acid.

Hydrochloric acid will produce hydrogen when reacted with metals such as zinc and iron. This acid is not as destructive as sulfuric acid or nitric acid. However, care should be taken when using HCl. HCl fumes can harm the lungs and will react on skin. However, hydrochloric acid has many uses. One of these is to clean metals. Also, when present in the human stomach in a dilute form, it helps in digestion.

Figure 10-12. Hydrochloric acid is sometimes sold under the name "muriatic acid." Muriatic acid is used to remove some types of stains from brick and cement surfaces.

PROBLEM   *(a) Pb (s) + H_2SO_4 (aq) $\longrightarrow$ $PbSO_4$ (s) + H_2(g)*

1. Write balanced equations for the following reactions:
   (a) sulfuric acid (dilute) with lead
   (b) hydrochloric acid with zinc   *(b) Zn(s) + 2HCl(aq)$\rightarrow$ $ZnCl_2$(aq) + H_2(g)*
   (c) sulfuric acid (dilute) with aluminum
   (c) 2Al(s) + 3 H_2SO_4 (aq) $\longrightarrow$ $Al_2(SO_4)_3$ (aq) + 3H_2(g)

Many other acids are also important. Organic acids contain hydrogen, carbon, and oxygen. Formic acid (HCOOH,

$$\overset{\text{O}}{\underset{}{\text{H–C–OH}}}$$ *methanoic acid*

) was first found in ant bites and was isolated by

203

distilling ants. Acetic acid (CH_3COOH, ethanic acid — H–C–C–OH, with $\overset{H}{\underset{H}{|}}$C and $\overset{O}{||}$C) is a fermentation product and a part of vinegar. A third organic acid, propanoic acid (CH_3CH_2COOH, H–C–C–C–OH, with H, H, and O groups), is used to retard spoilage in such foods as bread. Citric, salicylic, and oleic acids are among other common organic acids.

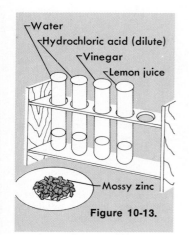

Water
Hydrochloric acid (dilute)
Vinegar
Lemon juice

Mossy zinc

Figure 10-13.

> EXPERIMENT. Add 5 ml of each of the following liquids to separate test tubes: water, dilute hydrochloric acid, vinegar, and lemon juice. Add a small piece of mossy zinc to each liquid. Compare and explain the activity of the acids. What control is used in this experiment?

PROBLEM

2. In addition to hydrochloric acid (HCl), other acids are formed from the other halogens. What would you expect the formulas to be for: hydrobromic acid, hydriodic acid, and hydrofluoric acid? *HBr, HI, HF*

Some inorganic acids contain both oxygen and hydrogen (oxyacids). Among these are phosphoric acid (H_3PO_4), chloric acid ($HClO_3$), and carbonic acid (H_2CO_3). See Table 10–1 for some acids and their formulas. Each acid has the property of increasing the hydronium ion concentration in a water solution.

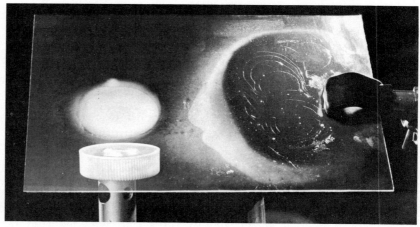

Figure 10-14. Glass can be etched by hydrofluoric acid. In what kind of a container could HF be stored? *wax containers*

	Table 10–1. *Acids*		
Acetic	CH_3COOH	Hydrobromic	HBr
Carbonic	H_2CO_3	Hydrochloric	HCl
Nitric	HNO_3	Hydrosulfuric	H_2S
Phosphoric	H_3PO_4	Sulfurous	H_2SO_3
Hydrofluoric	HF	Sulfuric	H_2SO_4

PROBLEM

3. The following acids ionize in water to produce hydronium ions. How many hydronium ions could be produced
   by one molecule of each of the following acids?
   (a) HCl *one*   (d) phosphoric *three*
   (b) H_2SO_4 *two*   (e) carbonic *two*
   (c) HBr *one*

10:4 *Bases*

Bases generally taste bitter and feel slippery. However,
taste and touch are not safe and accurate methods to identify
a base. Use the indicator phenolphthalein to test for a base.
Phenolphthalein is colorless in an acid solution and pink in a
basic solution.

Name some common bases.

*ammonia, lye, baking soda, washing
soda, milk of magnesia*

The most common base is *sodium hydroxide* (NaOH). It is
a part of lye and is used in making soap. Sodium hydroxide
can be produced in the laboratory. To do this, place a piece
of sodium in a beaker of water. CAUTION: The reaction is
violent. Hydrogen gas is released in the reaction. Sodium
hydroxide forms in the water.

$$2\,Na(s) + 2\,H_2O(l) \rightarrow 2\,NaOH(aq) + H_2(g)$$

Sodium hydroxide is commercially prepared by the electrolysis
of brine.

$$2\,NaCl(aq) + 2\,H_2O(l) \rightarrow$$
$$2\,NaOH(aq) + H_2(g) + Cl_2(g)$$

*Suggestion: The experiment on
page 62 illustrates the production of
various metallic hydroxides. Ask
students to write equations to
represent the reactions on page 62:*
$2K(s) + 2H_2O\ (l) \longrightarrow 2KOH(aq)$
$+ H_2(g)$
$Ca(s) + 2H_2O\ (l) \longrightarrow Ca\ (OH)_2(aq)$
$+ H_2(g)$
*Magnesium has no reaction at room
temperature.*

Not all compounds which contain an OH group are bases.
Some organic compounds known as alcohols contain an OH
group. However, they do not ionize in water to form hydroxide
ions (OH^-). Therefore, they are not classified as bases. Although most hydroxides of metals are bases, a few can act as
acids or bases. Zinc hydroxide and aluminum hydroxide can
act as acids or bases. Reaction conditions determine how each
of these compounds will act.

Figure 10-15. Each of these materials is basic or becomes basic when mixed with water.

Carl England

Table 10–2. *Bases*	
Ammonium hydroxide	NH_4OH
Calcium hydroxide	$Ca(OH)_2$
Potassium hydroxide	KOH
Aluminum hydroxide	$Al(OH)_3$
Sodium hydroxide	$NaOH$
Iron (III) hydroxide	$Fe(OH)_3$

PROBLEM

4. The following bases provide hydroxide ions (OH^-) in water solution. How many hydroxide ions are represented by each of the following formulas?
   (a) $NaOH$ *one*
   (b) $Ca(OH)_2$ *two*
   (c) NH_4OH *one*
   (d) $Mg(OH)_2$ *two*

10:5   *Strength of Acids and Bases*

Acids and bases are classified as strong or weak. The dividing line between strong and weak is not distinct. In general, strong acids and bases ionize readily to form a large number of ions. Weak acids and bases do not ionize readily. Nitric acid, sulfuric acid, and hydrochloric acid are strong acids. Most organic acids are considered weak acids. These include acetic acid and citric acid. Bases formed by metals of columns I and II in the periodic table are strong bases (example: sodium, potassium, and calcium). Bases formed by the heavier metals, such as iron and lead, are weak bases. Ammonium hydroxide (NH_4OH) is a weak base. Ammonium hydroxide is formed when ammonia gas is dissolved in water ($NH_3 + H_2O \rightarrow NH_4OH$). The common household ammonia used in cleaning is ammonium hydroxide.

Figure 10-16. The strength of acids and bases can be determined by their electrical conductivity. This apparatus is a simple means for determining electrical conductivity. The greater the strength of the acid or base, assuming that they have the same degree of dilution, the brighter the light.

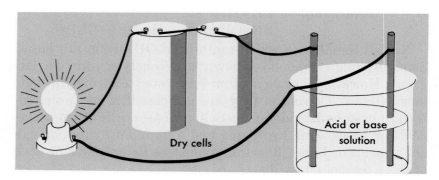

Dry cells

Acid or base solution

Relative strength for acids and bases can be determined by electrical conductivity (Section 18:2). Strong acids and bases produce more ions in water solution than do weak acids or bases. Thus, solutions of strong acids and bases conduct more electric current. If solutions with equal concentrations of acids and bases are tested for conductivity, the stronger acids and bases will conduct more current. Why is it important that the concentrations be equal? Table 10-3 lists some strong and weak acids and bases.

The strength, number of ions, might result from the increased concentration rather than the type of acid or base.

Table 10-3. **Strength of Acids and Bases**		
	Strong	*Weak*
ACIDS	nitric acid	oxalic acid
	hydrochloric acid	citric acid
	sulfuric acid	acetic acid
	hydrobromic acid	carbonic acid
BASES	sodium hydroxide	ammonium hydroxide
	calcium hydroxide	iron (III) hydroxide
	potassium hydroxide	aluminum hydroxide

10:6 Salts

Acids and bases react with each other in a chemical reaction called neutralization. In **neutralization** (neu' tral i za' shun), hydronium ions (H_3O^+) of the acid unite with the hydroxide ions (OH^-) of the base to form water (H_2O). The positive ion from the base and the negative ion from the acid remain as ions in solution. If the water is evaporated after a neutralization reaction, a solid substance remains. This substance is called a **salt.**

What is a salt?

An example of a neutralization reaction is:

$$HCl(aq) + NaOH(aq) \rightarrow NaCl(aq) + H_2O(l)$$

Since this reaction occurs in water solution, the equation may be written:

$$(H_3O^+ + Cl^-) + (Na^+ + OH^-) \rightarrow$$
$$(Na^+ + Cl^-) + 2\,HOH$$

Water may be written as HOH. This helps in determining the products of a reaction and in writing the correct equation. Note that the sodium ion and the chloride ion remain in solution after the reaction has taken place. Ions which do not take part in a reaction are called *spectator ions*. In this reaction, the sodium ion and the chloride ion are spectator ions.

The only ions that change are the hydronium ion and the hydroxide ion. That reaction can be written in the ionic form as:

$$H_3O^+ + OH^- \rightarrow 2HOH$$

This equation is called a *skeleton equation*. It represents only the "bones" of the reaction, only those ions which actually change. Spectator ions are not included in the ionic equation. In this neutralization reaction, the salt sodium chloride forms.

> EXPERIMENT. Place 10 ml of dilute sodium hydroxide in an evaporating dish. Add 2 drops of phenolphthalein as an indicator. What do you observe? Stir this solution carefully while slowly adding dilute HCl. Add HCl until the solution just becomes colorless. Evaporate slowly over a low Bunsen burner flame. Name the residue which remains.

If the acid and base are chemically equivalent (both about 0.1M) only NaCl should remain. Do not taste, however, since some NaOH may still be present. Litmus and/or phenolphthalein could be used to determine neutrality before evaporation.

$HCl + NaOH \longrightarrow NaCl + H_2O$ (l)
$H_3O^+ + OH^- \longrightarrow H_2O + H_2O$

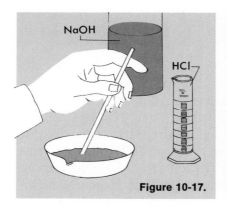
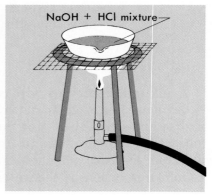

Figure 10-17.

When sulfuric acid reacts with sodium hydroxide, the salt sodium sulfate is formed:

$$H_2SO_4\,(aq) + 2\,NaOH\,(aq) \rightarrow Na_2SO_4\,(aq) + 2\,HOH\,(l)$$

Write this equation as an ionic equation. Which ions in this reaction are spectator ions? Write the skeleton equation for this reaction.

$(2H_3O^+ + SO_4^=) + 2(Na^+ + OH^-) \longrightarrow Na^+ + SO_4^= + 4HOH$

Salts also are formed when an active metal reacts with an acid. A single replacement reaction produces the salt (Section 9:2). For example, iron filings in hydrochloric acid will produce hydrogen gas. Iron (II) chloride crystals remain upon evaporation of the water:

$$Fe\,(s) + 2\,HCl\,(aq) \rightarrow FeCl_2\,(aq) + H_2\,(g)$$

PROBLEMS

See Teacher's Guide at the front of this book.

5. Write balanced equations for each of the following reactions:
   (a) potassium hydroxide + sulfuric acid
   (b) hydrobromic acid + sodium hydroxide
   (c) calcium hydroxide + nitric acid
   (d) magnesium hydroxide + hydrochloric acid
   (e) zinc + hydrobromic acid
6. Name the salt produced in each of the preceding reactions.

10:7 *Anhydrides*

When magnesium is burned, magnesium oxide (MgO) is formed. Magnesium oxide is slightly soluble in water. An aqueous solution of MgO is colorless. When a drop of colorless phenolphthalein is added to a MgO solution, the solution turns pink. This color change indicates a base. When sulfur is burned, sulfur dioxide (SO_2) is formed (Figure 10–18). Sulfur dioxide is a gas which is very soluble in water. An aqueous solution of sulfur dioxide is colorless. When a piece of blue litmus paper is added to an aqueous solution of sulfur dioxide, the paper turns red. What does this color change indicate?   *acid present in solution*

Similar reactions occur if calcium oxide and carbon dioxide are dissolved in water and tested with indicators. The results show that the calcium oxide solution is a base and the carbon dioxide solution is an acid.

These oxides are called anhydrides. *Anhydride* (an hie′ dried) means "without water." Most metallic oxides are bases "without water," or basic anhydrides. Most nonmetallic oxides are acids "without water," or acid anhydrides.

When water is added to magnesium oxide, the following changes occur:

$$MgO(s) + H_2O(l) \rightarrow Mg(OH)_2(aq)$$
$$Mg(OH)_2(aq) \rightarrow Mg^{+2}(aq) + 2OH^-(aq)$$

Since the hydroxide ion concentration of the solution is increased, MgO is a basic anhydride.

When carbon dioxide is dissolved in water, the following reactions occur:

$$CO_2(g) + H_2O(l) \rightarrow H_2CO_3(aq)$$
$$H_2CO_3(aq) + 2H_2O(l) \rightarrow 2H_3O^+(aq) + CO_3^{-2}(aq)$$

What is an anhydride?

$$S(s) + O_2(g) \longrightarrow SO_2(g)$$
$$H_2O(l) + SO_2(g) \longrightarrow$$
$$H_2SO_3(aq)$$

Ask students why this occurs. Sulfur burned in oxygen produces SO_2. When dissolved in water, it produces sulfurous acid, H_2SO_3. This gives the acid reaction to litmus.

Figure 10-18. When sulfur is burned in oxygen and the gas formed is dissolved in water, blue litmus placed in the solution will turn red.

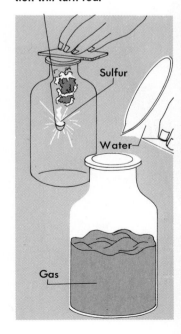

Since the hydronium ion concentration is increased, CO_2 is an acid anhydride.

Like acids, acid anhydrides will react with bases to form salts. Like bases, basic anhydrides will react with acids to produce salts. The following reactions illustrate neutralization of anhydrides:

$$CaO(s) + H_2SO_4(aq) \rightarrow CaSO_4(s) + H_2O(l)$$
$$CO_2(g) + Ba(OH)_2(aq) \rightarrow BaCO_3(s) + H_2O(l)$$

Many bases and acids form anhydrides when heated. This occurs when water is driven off:

$$Ba(OH)_2(s) \rightarrow BaO(s) + H_2O(g)$$
$$H_2CO_3(aq) \rightarrow CO_2(g) + H_2O(g)$$

PROBLEM

7. Label the following oxides as basic or acidic anhydrides.
   (a) MgO __?__ *basic*   (c) CO_2 __?__ *acidic*
   (b) SO_2 __?__ *acidic*   (d) CaO __?__ *basic*

10:8   *pH of a Solution*

The acidity of a solution is expressed in terms of its hydronium ion concentration. The symbol for hydronium ion concentration is **pH**. Water ·ionizes to the extent that the hydronium ion concentration is 10^{-7} mole/liter (0.0000001 mole/liter) (Appendix C). The hydroxide concentration of pure water must also be 10^{-7} mole/liter. This is because for each hydronium ion there is one hydroxide ion. Scientists have agreed on pH as a measure of acidity of a solution. The pH of pure water is given the value 7 (Table 10–5). Acid solutions have pH between 0 and 7. Bases have pH between 7 and 14. Strong acids may have a pH range of 1 to 2. Weaker acids may have a pH range of 3 to 5. Strong bases may have a pH of 13. Weaker bases may have a pH of 11. pH usually ranges from 0 to 14.

What is the pH of pure water?

pH=7 (neutral)

> EXPERIMENT. *Test a variety of liquids with Universal Indicator Paper. They may be any number of common household liquids. Make a chart indicating the pH of each liquid.*

Any number of liquids could be used. Try any of those on p. 211.

Suppose that the hydronium ion concentration of a solution is increased. This increases the possibility that some of the hydronium ions will unite with hydroxide ions in solution to form water. As the hydronium ion concentration increases,

Figure 10-19.

the hydroxide ion concentration decreases. Suppose that the hydroxide concentration of a solution is increased. This increases the possibility that some of the hydroxide ions will unite with some of the hydronium ions in solution to form water. Thus, as the hydroxide ion concentration increases, the hydronium ion concentration decreases.

Suppose that enough hydronium ions were added to a solution to make the concentration of the hydronium ion 10^{-3} mole/liter. The pH of the solution would be 3. A solution with a hydronium ion concentration of 10^{-6} mole/liter has a pH of 6. What is the pH of a solution with a hydronium ion concentration of 10^{-8} mole/liter? Is this solution acidic or basic? Is this acid or base strong or weak?   *weak base*

Table 10–4 lists some common acids and bases and the pH of their solutions of equal concentrations. Table 10–5 lists some common substances and their pH values.

Corning Glass Works

Figure 10-20. A pH meter can be used to determine the acidity of a solution.

pH can be described as log $\frac{1}{[H^+]}$ where

$[H^+]$ is the molar concentration of hydrogen. However, students do not need this concept for the material in the book and probably do not have a working knowledge of logarithms.

Figure 10-21. Which substance has the highest pH? Which has the lowest pH?

highest — shrimp; lowest - apples

Table 10–4. *pH Values of Solutions of Some Common Acids and Bases*

Hydrochloric acid	1.1	Ammonium hydroxide	11.1
Sulfuric acid	1.2	Sodium hydroxide	13.0
Citric acid	2.2	Potassium hydroxide	14.0
Acetic acid	2.9		

Table 10–5. *Approximate pH Values of Some Common Substances*

Stomach contents	1.6	Milk	6.5
Apples	3.0	Shrimp	7.0
Carrots	5.0	Blood	7.35
Urine	6.0	Milk of magnesia	10.5

Carl England

10:9   *Titration*

Neutralization reactions can be used to determine the concentration of acids or bases. One laboratory procedure for this determination is called *titration* (tie trae′ shun). In the titration process, a sample of the solution whose concentration is unknown is measured out. Several drops of an appropriate indicator are added to the solution. A standard solution is then used in the determination of the concentration sample solution. A *standard solution* is one whose concentration is known exactly. The standard solution is added carefully to the solution of unknown concentration until a color change indicates that the sample has been neutralized. The amount of

Figure 10-22. An indicator shows when the titration is complete.

Carl England

Editorial Photocolor Archives, Inc.

Figure 10-23. Titrations have many uses in industrial chemistry. The pH of the solution is determined by measuring the voltage developed across the electrode-pair assembly immersed in the solution.

What is a titration?

Titration is a process used to determine concentration of acids or bases.

standard solution used in this titration is carefully noted. From this information, it is possible to determine the unknown concentration of the solution.

EXAMPLE

Suppose that 20 ml of a standard solution of potassium hydroxide is required to neutralize 40 ml of hydrochloric acid solution of unknown concentration. The concentration of the standard potassium hydroxide solution is 0.1 M. (a) How many moles of potassium hydroxide are required? (b) How many moles of hydrochloric acid are present in the 40 ml of solution? (c) What is the molarity of the hydrochloric acid solution?

Solution: (a) The number of moles of potassium hydroxide can be found by multiplying the molarity of the potassium hydroxide solution by the volume (expressed in liters) of the potassium hydroxide solution used in the titration .

$$0.02 \text{ liters} \times \frac{0.1 \text{ mole KOH}}{1 \text{ liter}} = 0.002 \text{ mole of KOH}$$

(b) The balanced equation for this reaction is:
$$KOH(aq) + HCl(aq) \rightarrow KCl(aq) + HOH(l)$$

From this equation, you can see that one mole of potassium hydroxide is required to neutralize one mole of hydrochloric acid. Thus, 0.002 mole of potassium hydroxide will neutralize 0.002 mole of hydrochloric acid.

(c) Since 40 ml of the unknown solution contains 0.002 mole of hydrochloric acid, a liter of hydrochloric acid of the same concentration would contain

$$\frac{0.002 \text{ mole}}{0.04 \text{ liter}} = \frac{X}{1 \text{ liter}}$$

$$X = 0.05 \text{ mole}$$

Thus, the molarity of the hydrochloric acid solution is 0.05 molar.

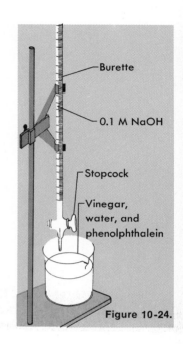

Figure 10-24.

When solution turns pink, neutralization has been reached.

EXPERIMENT. *Place 50 ml of water in a beaker. Add 10 ml of vinegar. Add a few drops of phenolphthalein. Fill a burette with 0.1M sodium hydroxide. Release the base from the burette into the acid, drop by drop, with constant stirring. Be certain that you record the starting point and ending point. Stop as soon as a faint pink color is detected. Why? Compute the number of moles of acetic acid in the vinegar. Bring some other acids from home for similar study. Examples are fruit juices and soda water.* *After molarity of acetic acid solution is found, the molarity of acetic acid in vinegar should be six times as great since it has been diluted five to one.*

PROBLEM

8. Fifteen milliliters of a standard 0.3M solution of sodium hydroxide are required to neutralize 45 ml of a nitric acid solution of unknown concentration. (a) How many moles of sodium hydroxide are required? (b) How many moles of nitric acid are present in the 45 ml of solution? (c) What is the molarity of the nitric acid solution?

(a) 0.0045 moles
(b) 0.0045 moles
(c) 0.1M HNO₃

MAIN IDEAS

p. 198 **1.** Water ionizes slightly to form hydronium ions (H_3O^+) and hydroxide ions (OH^-).

p. 198 **2.** Acids increase hydronium ion concentration of a solution; bases increase hydroxide ion concentration of a solution.

p. 199 **3.** Indicators turn different colors in solutions, depending upon the acidity of the solution.

p. 206 **4.** Strong acids and bases provide large numbers of ions in solution.

p. 207   **5.** A salt is a product of a neutralization reaction.

p. 209   **6.** An anhydride is a substance "without water."

p. 209   **7.** Oxides of most metals are basic anhydrides.

p. 209   **8.** Oxides of most nonmetals are acid anhydrides.

p. 210   **9.** The pH values of acid solutions range from 0 to 7.

p. 210   **10.** The pH values of basic solutions range from 7 to 14.

VOCABULARY

Write a sentence in which you correctly use each of the following words or terms.

acid	hydroxide ion	pH
anhydride	indicator	phenolphthalein
base	litmus paper	salt
hydronium ion	neutralization	standard solution
		titration

STUDY QUESTIONS

Have students rewrite false statements to make the statements correct.

A. True or False

Determine whether each of the following sentences is true or false. (Do not write in this book.)

F   **1.** The formula for nitric acid is ~~NH₃~~.   *HNO₃*

F   **2.** Vinegar contains a ~~base~~.   *acid*

T   **3.** The strength of an acid can be determined by electrical conductivity.

T   **4.** The concentration of an acid or base can be found by titration.

F   **5.** In a water solution, ~~citric~~ acid is more highly ionized than ~~hydrochloric~~ acid.   *Hydrochloric, citric*

T   **6.** A neutralization reaction is a reaction between an acid and a base.

T   **7.** OH^- is the formula for an hydroxide ion.

T   **8.** An indicator may be used to determine the acidity or basicity of a solution.

F   **9.** A base which has a pH of 8 is a ~~stronger~~ base than a base with a pH of 10.   *weaker*

T **10.** An acid anhydride will react with a base in the same way that an acid will.

B. Multiple Choice

Choose one word or phrase that correctly completes each of the following sentences. (Do not write in this book.)

Some questions in part B may have more than one correct answer. Only one answer is required.

1. Acids taste (sour, sweet, bitter, salty).
2. A strong acid will usually have a pH of (2, 5, 7, 8, 11).
3. (Phenolphthalein, Methyl orange, Benzene, Litmus) are indicators.
4. An oxide of a metal usually is a(n) (acid anhydride, basic anhydride, mole).
5. A 1M sodium hydroxide solution has (a higher, a lower, the same) pH as a 1M HCl solution.
6. Examples of a basic anhydride are (magnesium oxide, carbon dioxide, sulfur dioxide, calcium oxide).
7. Which of the following is an acid (H_2O, MgO, HCl)?
8. Neutralization reactions produce a salt and (a gas, light, water).
9. Equal volumes of solutions of the same molarity have the same (reactants, concentrations, molecular mass, pH, color).
10. The strongest bases are formed by (light metals, heavy metals, light nonmetals, heavy nonmetals).

C. Completion

Complete each of the following sentences with a word or phrase that will make the sentence correct. (Do not write in this book.)

1. Hydrogen ions consist of free __?__.
2. A hydrogen ion combines with a water molecule to form __?__.
3. Common bases taste __?__.
4. CO_2 is an example of a(n) __?__ anhydride.
5. When an active metal reacts with dilute H_2SO_4, __?__ gas is formed.
6. When an extremely active metal reacts with water, __?__ gas is formed.
7. As the acidity of a solution rises, its pH value __?__.
8. Water will not conduct electricity unless __?__ are present.
9. Two liters of 0.5M KOH will neutralize __?__ liters of 1M HCl.

1. protons
2. hydronium ion
3. bitter
4. acid
5. hydrogen
6. hydrogen
7. decreases
8. ions
9. one

D. How and Why

1. Write an equation which could represent involvement of acids or bases in each of the following: (a) single replacement reaction, (b) neutralization, (c) formation of acid from acid anhydride, (d) double replacement reaction.

2. Which ions in the following reaction are spectator ions? $HCl(aq) + NaOH(aq) \rightarrow NaCl(aq) + H_2O(l)$ *Cl⁻ and Na⁺*

3. What are the parent acids and bases for these salts: (a) Na_2SO_4, (b) NaCl, (c) $NaNO_3$?

4. What is pH?

5. How many milliliters of *2M* KOH are required to neutralize 50 ml of *2M* HCl? *50 ml*

6. List three important industrial acids. What are the primary uses of each?

7. Give definitions for acid, base, and salt.

8. On the basis of information contained in Table 10–1, what name would you give to each of the following acids: (a) HI, (b) HNO_2, (c) HCOOH, (d) $HClO_3$?

(a) hydroiodic acid   (c) formic acid
(b) nitrous acid   (d) chloric acid

INVESTIGATIONS

1. Check the labels on many household products such as patent medicines, kitchen aids, and foods. See how many involve acids or bases.

2. Prepare solutions from liquid synthetic detergents of different brands. Use the same number of drops of each detergent in the same volumes of water. Use a universal indicator to determine the pH of each.

3. Boil some natural and man-made fibers for about 5 minutes in a weak solution of sodium hydroxide. Test the same type of fibers in dilute sulfuric acid. What do you conclude?

4. Certain gases in the air form acids when dissolved in water. What gases are they? Where do they come from? How do the acids they form affect the environment?

5. Using information from garden books, farm publications, your local garden store, or florist make a list of plants that require acid soil and those that require basic soil. If available, give pH requirements. Find out what methods can be used to make soil basic or acidic.

INTERESTING READING

Beeler, Nelson F., *Experiments in Chemistry*. New York, Thomas Y. Crowell Company, 1952.

Cooper, Elizabeth K., *Discovering Chemistry*. New York, Harcourt Brace Jovanovich, Inc., 1959.

Motion

But nearly all the grandest discoveries of science have been but the reward of accurate measurement and patient, long-continued labor in the minute sifting of numerical details.

William Kelvin (1824-1907)

From prehistoric times, man has been interested in how objects move. Early man ascribed the movement of wind and tides and the sun and stars to gods actually causing matter to move. They used some simple machines such as the lever and inclined plane. Yet they probably did not understand why such devices did change the direction or amount of force needed to perform some work. The Greeks at the height of their civilization could develop logical theories to explain movement, but they rarely put their theories to experimental test.

Not until 1543 when Copernicus' book *On the Revolution of the Celestial Spheres* came out, did motion really come under scrutiny again. This book introduced (actually reintroduced) the idea that the sun was the center of the solar system. The earth, therefore, revolved around the sun.

Since the seventeenth century, the widespread use of machines has been increasing. Use of the machine, coupled with man's increasing control of energy, changed the world. Automobiles and airplanes greatly improved transportation. Practical application of the action-reaction idea, developed thousands of years before, has enabled man to send rockets to explore the moon and to find out more about the solar system and universe. What will you uncover in your lifetime?

unit
five

Introduce Chapter 11 by having students read the introductory paragraph. Have them make a list of objects in motion and at rest. Examples of objects in motion: earth, second hand in a watch, beating heart, digestive tract, blood in arteries, moon. Let students speculate on answers to the last question which is answered in detail in the sections that follow. Concepts of work and power are also developed in this chapter. The six simple machines are discussed in detail.

Force and Work

GOAL: You will gain an understanding of forces, work, simple machines, mechanical advantage, and power.

Is the second hand of a clock at rest or in motion? Look at this page. Is it at rest or in motion? On a separate sheet of paper, list five objects which are in motion. Then list five objects which are at rest. Why are some objects in motion and other objects at rest?

11:1 Force

What is force?

All sports involve forces and motion. Relate these principles to baseball, basketball, football, hockey, and other sports. Have students name the forces they experience in their home or school.

It takes *force* to put an object at rest into motion. How can you set an object in motion? Kick a can. Throw a stone. Pound a nail into a board. In each case an object is moved. It took a force to do it.

A **force** is a push or a pull. For example, a boy can pull a wagon or he can push it. In either case, he exerts a force to move the wagon. When the wagon moves, it is in motion.

Many forces are at work. A force pushes against a passenger in an automobile when the auto changes speed. Another

Figure 11-1. When we pull or push an object, we are exerting a force on that object.

force, gravity, holds the automobile on the road. The force produced in the engine makes the car move by transferring this force to the drive wheels.

If you kick a football, the force exerted by your foot sets the ball in motion. If you kick a large boulder, you might hurt yourself. Why? Does a force always produce motion? Push down on your desk top as hard as you can or push against the wall in your room. A force does not always produce motion. Only an unbalanced force produces motion. This means that the force you or something exerts must be greater than the opposing force (*resistance*). When this happens, motion occurs.

Resistance is the force which slows down or prevents motion. *Friction* and *weight* are examples of resistance. **Weight** is a measure of the force of gravity on an object.

Figure 11-2.   A force only produces motion when it is greater than the opposing force.

PROBLEMS   *If not fixed in place, a student's arms.*

1. What could exert a force great enough to move your desk top?
2. What force moves your body parts?   *The forces of muscles on bones.*
3. How could you exert a force to lift yourself?
    Sit on chair, place hands on chair, and push down.

EXPERIMENT. You can measure the force of gravity with a spring. (1) Cut off the bottom half of a paper cup. With a small piece of string, attach the cup bottom to a spring. Tie the opposite end of the spring to a clamp supported by a ring stand. Bend a paper clip to form a pointer and attach it to the bottom end of the spring. Attach a piece of cardboard in back of the spring with masking tape. Mark a zero on the cardboard opposite the pointer. Now place a metal washer in the paper cup. Mark the new position of the pointer. Add a second washer and mark the new position of the pointer. Repeat this procedure until you have a total of ten washers in the cup. Mark the scale each time. DO NOT OVERLOAD THE SPRING. Why? Remove the washers from the cup. (2) Now weigh separately a marble, thimble, pencil, and pen. Read and record the weight of each in terms of your washer weight scale. Which weighed the most? Why aren't washers used as standard units of force?   *Washers are not uniform in weight.*

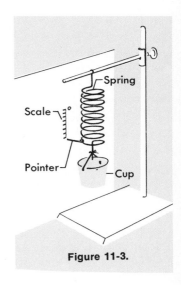

Figure 11-3.

11:2   *Work*

A force is needed to do *work*. Mowing a lawn is work. Washing a car and lifting barbells are other examples of work.

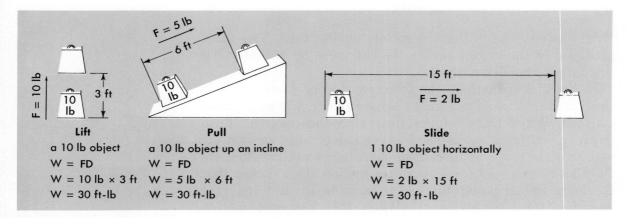

Figure 11-4. Work is done only when a body is moved a distance. The amount of work done is not affected by the speed with which the body is moved.

Lift
a 10 lb object
W = FD
W = 10 lb × 3 ft
W = 30 ft-lb

Pull
a 10 lb object up an incline
W = FD
W = 5 lb × 6 ft
W = 30 ft-lb

Slide
1 10 lb object horizontally
W = FD
W = 2 lb × 15 ft
W = 30 ft-lb

What equation is used to calculate work?

W = F × D

A force does not always result in work. Work is done only when the force moves through a distance. If a person holds a 10 lb sack of potatoes he does not do work even though he exerts a force.

Work can make a person tired. *Trying* to lift a house can also make you tired. However, this kind of activity is not called work by a scientist.

In science, work has a precise definition. **Work** is the product of the force applied to an object and the distance the object moves. The object must move, otherwise, no work is done.

To calculate work done, use the equation $W = F \times D$.

$$W = \text{Work}$$
$$F = \text{Force}$$
$$D = \text{Distance}$$

In the English system, the unit of force is the pound (lb). Distance is usually measured in feet (ft). Thus, in the English system, work is expressed in *foot-pounds* (ft-lb). In the metric system, the unit of force is the newton (nt) and distance is measured in meters (m). Thus, in the metric system, work can be expressed in *newton-meters* (nt-m) (Appendix C, page 468).

EXAMPLE

Weight of the object can be ignored.

How much work is done when a force of 100 pounds is used to slide a 600-pound piano 5 feet across a floor?

Solution: (a) Write the equation: $W = F \times D$
(b) Substitute 100 pounds for F, and 5 feet for D
$W = 100 \text{ lb} \times 5 \text{ ft}$
(c) Multiply to find the answer: $W = 500$ ft-lb
(d) Answer: Work = 500 ft-lb

EXAMPLE

How much work is done when a force of 98 newtons is applied in lifting a concrete block 1.5 meters?

Solution:　(a)　Write the equation: $W = F \times D$
　　　　　　(b)　Substitute 98 newtons for F, and 1.5 meters
　　　　　　　　　for D
　　　　　　　　　$W = 98 \text{ nt} \times 1.5 \text{ m}$
　　　　　　(c)　Multiply to find the answer: $W = 147$ nt-m
　　　　　　(d)　Answer: Work $= 147$ nt-m

PROBLEMS

4. A 15-lb suitcase is lifted 2 ft. How much work is done?　　　*30 ft-lb*

5. How much work is done when a force of 3 lb is used to　　　*6 ft-lb*
   move the suitcase in Problem 4 a distance of 2 ft across
   the floor?

6. Which takes more work, lifting a suitcase 2 ft or sliding　　　*See Teacher's Guide.*
   it a distance of 2 ft across a smooth floor? Why?

7. Calculate the amount of work done when a force of 40 nt　　　*160 nt-m*
   is used to push a desk 4 meters across a room.

8. Jim figured that he did 500 ft-lb of work in pushing a　　　*5 lb*
   wagon 100 ft. What average force did he exert?

11:3　*Machines*

Suppose you want to dig a hole to plant a tree. Can you do it
using just your fingers? A shovel would make it much easier.
A shovel is one kind of *simple machine*. A **machine** makes

What is a machine?

A machine changes the direction, size, or distance through which a force moves.

Figure 11-5.　Many of the simple tools we use daily are machines.

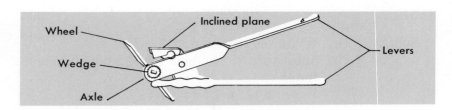

Figure 11-6. One type of can opener is a combination of several machines: wheel and axle, inclined plane, wedge, and lever.

Labels: Wheel, Inclined plane, Wedge, Axle, Levers

work easier by changing the direction, size, or distance through which a force moves.

Name some simple machines.

There are six simple machines. They are the *lever*, *pulley*, *inclined plane*, *wedge*, *screw*, and *wheel and axle*. Notice that some of these machines are variations of another.

Define compound machine.

two or more simple machines working together

A *compound machine* is two or more simple machines working together. A sewing machine, gasoline engine, and a washing machine are examples of compound machines. Some can openers, for example, contain inclined planes, a lever, and a wheel and axle. This makes the can opener a compound machine.

PROBLEM

See Teacher's Guide at the front of the book.

9. How does each machine make work easier?
   (a) bicycle   (d) elevator
   (b) oar   (e) block and tackle
   (c) sewing machine (f) crowbar

Figure 11-7. Without a lever, a paint can would be very difficult to open.

11:4 *Mechanical Advantage*

Have you ever opened a can of paint using a screwdriver to pry off the lid? It was easy. But how hard would it have been if you had only your fingers? You used the screwdriver as a lever and gained a large force to open the can. This gain in force is called the machine's *mechanical advantage*.

All machines have a mechanical advantage. This tells us how the machine changes the force it uses. The amount by which the applied force is multiplied by a machine is called the **mechanical advantage** (M.A.). This value is not always greater than one. Sometimes a gain in force is sacrificed for a gain in speed or a change in direction.

We can talk about the *ideal mechanical advantage* (I.M.A.) of a machine or about the *actual mechanical advantage* (A.M.A.) of a machine. The **ideal mechanical advantage** tells us how the machine can ideally change the force. Ideal means neglecting friction. The **actual mechanical advantage** tells us how a machine actually changes a force. It includes the effects of friction. In your measurements of mechanical advantage, you will be working with objects in contact with one another. Is it possible to completely eliminate friction in a machine? Thus, in your experiments with machines involving moving parts, will you be measuring ideal mechanical advantage (I.M.A.) or actual mechanical advantage (A.M.A.)? Explain.

Why is I.M.A. different from A.M.A.?

A.M.A. takes into account friction which will decrease any advantage.

11:5   *Levers*

A *lever* is a simple machine. Crowbar, seesaw, shovel, oar, scissors, and bottle opener are examples of levers. They can make work easier. A **lever** is a bar that is free to rotate around

Name four examples of levers.

broom, wheelbarrow, crowbar, tweezers

Figure 11-8. A seesaw is a lever. The point where it is attached is the fulcrum.

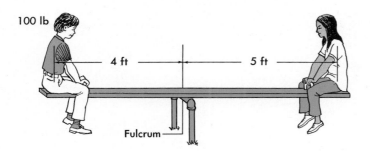
100 lb   4 ft   5 ft   Fulcrum

Vickiann Bennett

a point. The point where it rotates is called the *fulcrum* (ful′ cruhm) (Figure 11–9). When an effort force is applied to a lever, a resistance can be overcome.

ACTIVITY. (1) Place a book or some heavy object on the edge of a table or desk. Place a ruler under the book with most of the ruler extending beyond the table. Pull up on the end which is not under the book. Notice how easy it is to raise the book. What type of lever have you used? Where is the fulcrum? (2) Now push down on the end of the ruler extending beyond the table. Where is the fulcrum this time? (3) Place the book in the center of the table. Again put the end of the ruler under the edge of the book. Place one hand on the other end of the ruler. With your other hand, lift up on the center of the ruler. Which type of lever does this represent? Where is the fulcrum? Notice the different forces you had to exert to lift the book. Which type of lever made the task easiest? Hardest? Which had the highest M.A.? The lowest?

Every lever has two arms. These are called the *effort arm* and the *resistance arm*. The **effort arm** is the distance from the fulcrum to the effort force. The **resistance arm** is the distance from the fulcrum to the resistance force.

Figure 11-9. The fulcrum of this lever is where the bottle cap and the opener touch.

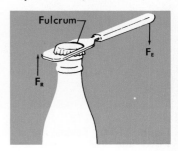
Fulcrum F_E F_R

Figure 11-10.

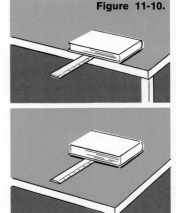

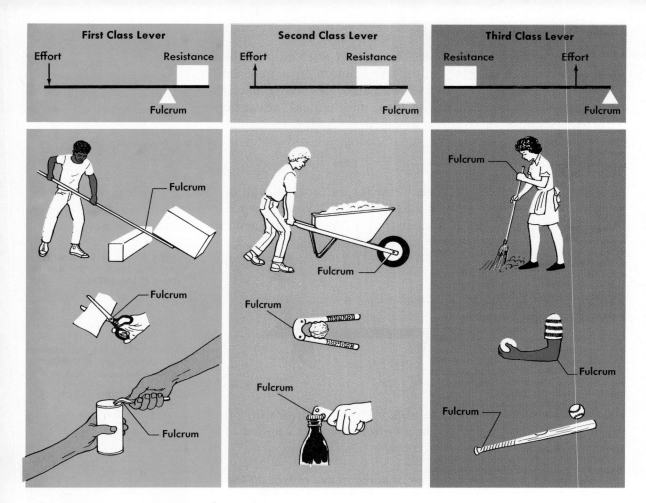

Figure 11-11. Levers are divided into first, second, and third class levers based on the position of the fulcrum, resistance, and effort.

How is M.A. for a lever calculated?

See Teacher's Guide.

PROBLEM

10. Three classes of levers are shown in Figure 11–11. How do they differ? Notice the position of the fulcrum for each class of lever. *See Teacher's Guide.*

Every lever also has two **moments**, effort moment and resistance moment. To calculate the *moment*, multiply the force by the length of the lever arm. In the English system, force is measured in pounds and distance in feet. Thus, the English unit for a moment is *pound-foot* (lb-ft). In the metric system, force is measured in newtons and the distance in meters. The metric unit for a moment is *meter-newton* (m-nt). The equation below can be used to calculate the moments of a lever.

$$M = F \times D$$

M = Moment
F = Force
D = Lever arm length

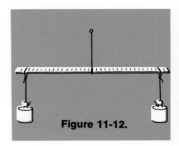

Figure 11-12.

ACTIVITY. (1) Obtain a yardstick, two equal weights, string, and scissors. Tie a piece of string around the exact center of the yardstick. Then hang the yardstick from a hook or nail on a wall. Or, hang it from an iron stand on a table. Tie string to both weights and hang them on opposite ends of the yardstick. Move the string in the center back and forth until the yardstick is balanced. When the yardstick is balanced, find the distance from the fulcrum to each weight. Record your data in a chart. Was the yardstick with the two equal weights balanced when the string was tied at the center of the stick? If not, explain. (2) Repeat the procedure with two unequal weights. Again, record your results.

The two moments of a balanced lever are equal. *Balanced* means the lever is not turning. Note that the units for moment (lb-ft and m-nt) are the reverse of those for work. When a lever is balanced, you can use the following equation to find the unknown force on a lever or the length of a lever arm.

$$F_R \times D_R = F_E \times D_E$$

F_R = resistance force
D_R = resistance arm length
F_E = effort force
D_E = effort arm length

EXAMPLE

Using a lever, how much force must be applied on a bar to move a rock? Necessary facts are given below.

Given:

Resistance Force = 150 lb

Resistance Arm = 1 ft

Effort Arm = 5 ft

Solution:

$F_R \times D_R = F_E \times D_E$

150 lb $\times$ 1 ft = $F_E \times$ 5 ft

150 lb-ft = $F_E \times$ 5 ft

F_E = 30 lb

EXAMPLE

A pipe 5 meters long is supported at the center. A bag of nails is hung 1 meter from the center of the pipe. The bag exerts a force of 100 newtons on the pipe. In order to balance this sack, how far from the center on the opposite side of the fulcrum must a 40-newton sack be hung?

Given:

Resistance Force = 100 nt

Resistance Arm = 1 m

Effort Force = 40 nt

Solution:

$F_R \times D_R = F_E \times D_E$

100 nt $\times$ 1 m = 40 nt $\times D_E$

100 m-nt = 40 nt $\times D_E$

D_E = 2.5 m

PROBLEMS

80 lb

four feet from fulcrum on opposite end

25 nt

5.3 nt

11. In Figure 11–8, how much does the girl weigh?
12. A 100-lb boy sits on a seesaw 3 ft from the fulcrum. Where must a 75-lb boy sit to balance the seesaw?
13. A board 4 m long is supported at the middle. A force of 50 nt is exerted 1 m from the center of the board. What force must be applied at the opposite end of the board to balance the 50-nt force?
14. A board 3 m long is supported at the middle. A crate weighing 5 nt is placed 1 m from the center of the board. On top of this crate is placed another crate weighing 3 nt. What force must be applied at the opposite end of the board to balance the two crates?

11:6 *Mechanical Advantage for a Lever*

A lever has a mechanical advantage. To find the I.M.A., measure the length of the effort arm and the length of the resistance arm. Divide the effort arm length by the resistance arm length.

$$\text{I.M.A.} = \frac{\text{Effort Arm}}{\text{Resistance Arm}}$$

EXAMPLE

Find the I.M.A. for a lever with a resistance arm 5 ft long. The effort arm is 15 ft.

Given:
Effort Arm = 15 ft
Resistance Arm = 5 ft

Solution:
$$\text{I.M.A.} = \frac{\text{Effort Arm}}{\text{Resistance Arm}}$$
$$\text{I.M.A.} = \frac{15 \text{ ft}}{5 \text{ ft}}$$
$$\text{I.M.A.} = 3$$

Remember, I.M.A. is the ratio of the effort arm length to the resistance arm length. In this case, an effort force applied to the lever is multiplied by 3. The A.M.A. for a lever is less than the I.M.A. Explain.

PROBLEMS

two

five

15. What is the I.M.A. for a lever with an effort arm of 10 ft and a resistance arm 5 ft long?
16. What is the I.M.A. for a 1-m crowbar when the fulcrum is 0.2 m from the resistance end?

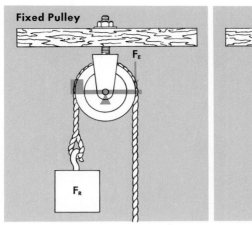

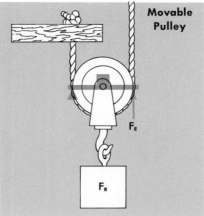

Figure 11-13. A pulley may be either fixed or movable.

11:7 *Pulleys*

A *pulley* is a simple machine. Study Figure 11–13 and you will see that a **pulley** is really a form of a lever. It is used to move bodies and do work. It can be fixed in one spot or movable.

You can use a pulley to make work easier by changing the direction of a force. For example, you can use a rope around a single fixed pulley to raise some object. You can pull the object up when you are standing on the ground. With a single, fixed pulley the effort force is applied in one direction. The resistance moves in the opposite direction.

Two or more pulleys used together can decrease the force needed to move a body. The I.M.A. of a pulley system equals the number of *supporting strands* (Figure 11–14).

How does a pulley make work easier?

By changing the direction or magnitude of the force required to do some work.

Figure 11-14. The number of supporting strands a movable pulley has determines its ideal mechanical advantage.

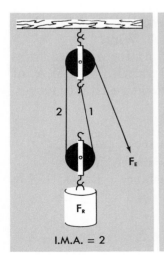

I.M.A. = 2

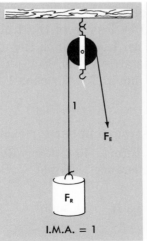

I.M.A. = 1

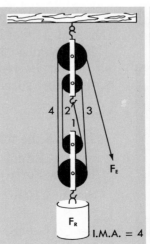

I.M.A. = 4

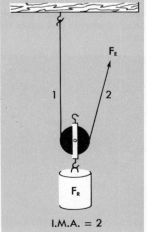

I.M.A. = 2

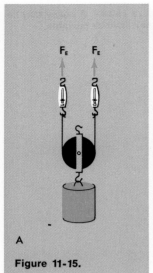
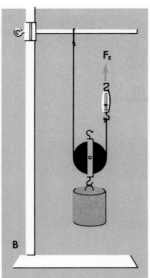
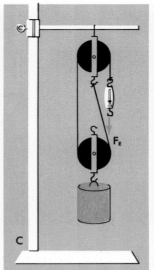
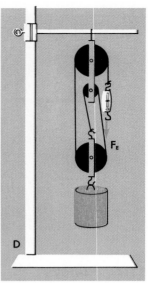

Figure 11-15.

EXPERIMENT. A pulley may be used to lift objects. (1) Lift a ½-lb weight with a spring balance and observe the reading of the balance. Next, run a piece of string 2 ft long through a single movable pulley. Attach each end of the string to a different spring balance as shown in Figure 11–15a. Attach a weight to the pulley. Lift the weight by lifting the spring balances and record the reading on each balance. (2) Arrange pulleys as shown in Figures 11–15b and c. Find the force needed to lift the weight. The force is the reading on the spring balance. How does the number of supporting strings affect the force needed to lift a weight? Predict the force needed to lift the weight in Figure 11–15d.

Figure 11-16. The wheel is a special kind of lever. Combinations of wheels can make work easier.

Richard M. Fetters

In calculating the I.M.A. of pulleys, friction and the weight of the movable pulley are not considered. In actual practice, the A.M.A. would be less than the I.M.A. Why?

Note that with an I.M.A. of 2, the effort force moves twice as far as the resistance force. For pulleys with an I.M.A. of 3, the effort force moves 3 ft for each 1 ft the resistance moves.

PROBLEM

17. Give the missing number for each set of pulleys.

Pulleys	Effort Force	Effort Distance	Resistance Force	Resistance Distance	Support Ropes	I.M.A.
Set A	10 lb	?	?	1 ft	2	2
Set B	?	3 ft	50 lb	?	5	?
Set C	5 lb	?	?	5 ft	?	4

See Teacher's Guide.

11:8   *Wheel and Axle*

Bicycles, trains, cars, motorcycles, printing presses, and pulleys run on *wheels*. Most compound machines have at least one wheel. Often the wheel has teeth cut into it and is called a gear.

Observe the wheel and axle in Figure 11–18. **A wheel and axle** can be considered a variation of a lever. Note that the wheel turns through a larger diameter than the axle. This difference gives a wheel and axle its mechanical advantage.

How can you find the I.M.A. of a wheel and axle? Divide the diameter of the wheel by the diameter of the axle. What is the I.M.A. for a 15.0-cm wheel with a 2.5-cm axle?

$$\text{I.M.A.} = \frac{\text{wheel diameter}}{\text{axle diameter}}$$

$$\text{I.M.A.} = \frac{15.0 \text{ cm}}{2.5 \text{ cm}}$$

$$\text{I.M.A.} = 6$$

Figure 11-17. The I.M.A. of a wheel and axle is determined by dividing the diameter of the wheel by the diameter of the axle.

How is M.A. for a wheel and axle calculated?

PROBLEM

18. Make a list of machines containing a wheel and axle which you use in everyday life. Which part of the machine is the wheel? Which part is the axle?

See Teacher's Guide .

11:9   *Inclined Plane*

Examine a ramp or stairs. These are examples of inclined planes. An inclined plane is a slanted surface used to raise

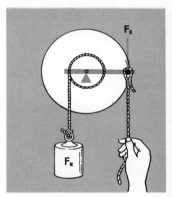

Figure 11-18. `The wheel turns through a larger diameter than the axle.

Figure 11-19. An inclined plane, such as a stairway, makes work easier by changing the angle of the moving force.

objects to higher elevations. A mountain road is an inclined plane. Cars increase their elevations as they go up the road.

Less force is needed to lift a body when it is on an inclined plane. Why? There are two reasons for this. The angle of the moving force now has changed. Also, the body is moved through a longer distance than if the body were moved straight up.

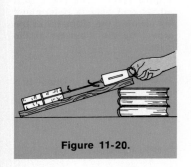

Figure 11-20.

> EXPERIMENT. Tie a string to a brick or wooden block. Weigh it with a spring scale. The reading on the spring scale is also the force needed to lift the brick. Set a smooth board against a pile of books to make an inclined plane. Drag the brick up the inclined plane by holding the spring scale attached to the string. Drag the brick at constant speed. Don't jerk it. Read the scale while the brick is moving. The reading on the spring scale gives the force used to pull the brick. Compare the forces needed to lift and pull the brick. What is the A.M.A. of the inclined plane?

The I.M.A. of an inclined plane is its length divided by its height. The longer the inclined plane, the smaller the force needed to move a body on it.

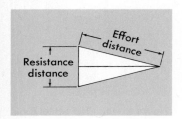

Figure 11-21. A wedge is two inclined planes.

PROBLEMS   *See Teacher's Guide.*

19. What are some practical uses of the inclined plane?
20. With a diagram, explain how the inclined plane is used.

11:10 *Wedge*

Put two inclined planes together and you have a **wedge.** A knife, an axe blade, and a can opener blade are wedges. The wedge is a variation of the inclined plane. This simple machine is used for work such as splitting logs. The thin edge of the wedge is placed in a crack in a log and driven deeper with blows from a sledgehammer or mallet. This forces the sides of the log further apart and it finally splits. The I.M.A. of a wedge is equal to the I.M.A. of one of the inclined planes making up the wedge multiplied by 2.

EXAMPLE

$$\text{I.M.A.} = \frac{20 \text{ cm}}{5 \text{ cm}} = 4$$

$$\text{Total I.M.A.} = 4 \times 2 = 8$$

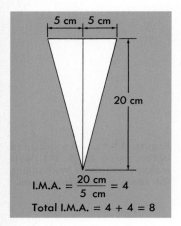

Figure 11-22. Find the I.M.A. of a wedge by multiplying the I.M.A. of one of its inclined planes by 2.

$$\text{I.M.A.} = \frac{20 \text{ cm}}{5 \text{ cm}} = 4$$
$$\text{Total I.M.A.} = 4 + 4 = 8$$

All kinds of engineers

Designers of washing machines and designers of spacecraft have something in common. They are engineers. Next to teaching, engineering is the largest professional occupation. According to the 1970 census, the U. S. has more than one million engineers.

What do all these men and women do? Some are designing better bicycles. Others are developing machines that will safely harvest delicate crops. Even our food and clothing are engineered.

Engineering is so vast and varied that an engineer is usually identified by his specialty: chemical engineer, electrical engineer, civil engineer, mining engineer. There are 25 officially recognized engineering categories. Each speciality is often subdivided. Highway engineering, for example, is a subdivision of civil engineering (construction engineering).

All members of this diverse profession, however, have a few things in common. All engineers use scientific principles to solve design and production problems. Their work emphasizes *applying* existing scientific information rather than *discovering* new information. The engineer's concerns range from raw materials and ideas through design and manufacturing. His interests may even go beyond the finished product to packaging, distribution, and sales.

The engineer must answer some very practical questions about his product. Will it cost too much or take too long to produce? Will an average person be able to use the product he has engineered?

Copley News Service

Yvonne Brill is a propulsion engineer. She has played a major role in the design of many weather and communication satellites.

General Electric Research and Development Center

This experimental laser was designed and built by engineers. Myung K. Chun, also an engineer, is using it to study new ways lasers could aid manufacturing.

U. S. Department of Agriculture

Agricultural engineers have designed machines which sort and grade vegetables.

Associated Photographers, Inc.

An environmental engineer takes a sample of the waste water from an industrial plant. Later he will analyze this sample and recommend steps to improve water quality.

Vickiann Bennett

Figure 11-23. An axe is a wedge used to split wood.

Why is a screw an inclined plane?

Figure 11-24. You can make a screw by wrapping an inclined plane around a pencil.

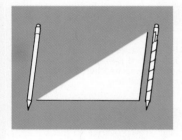

Figure 11-25. The distance between the threads of a screw is called the pitch.

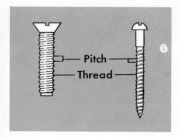

A common example of a wedge is a knife. When you sharpen a knife, you make the wedge longer and thinner and thereby increase the mechanical advantage. This makes it easier to do work (cut things) with the knife.

PROBLEM

21. List some everyday uses of the wedge.

knife, razor blade, hatchet, ice pick, wood planer, chisel

11:11   *Screw*

A *screw* is an inclined plane wound around a center to form a cylinder. By twisting a screw into wood or metal, a small effort force is used through a longer distance. In contrast, when hammering a nail you use a large force. The large force drives the nail a short distance.

A common use for this type of machine is the jackscrew. The jackscrew is used in raising cars, houses, or other heavy objects. The distance between threads of a screw is called the *pitch*. A screw has a large mechanical advantage. A very large resistance can be overcome with a comparatively small force. Let's take an example.

Suppose a jackscrew has a pitch of ¼ inch and a 3-foot handle to turn the jack. For one revolution of this handle, the jack will go up a vertical distance of ¼ inch. Remember, the I.M.A. for a simple machine is found by dividing the distance the resistance moves into the distance the effort moves. Suppose it takes an input force of 40 pounds to turn the jack handle. The handle moves in a circle. The radius of this circular path is 36 inches. Using the formula $C = 2\pi r$, the circumference of this circular path can be calculated. The circumference is equal to 2 (3.14) (36 in.) or 226.1 in. At the same time the jack moves up 0.25 in. Therefore the I.M.A. is $\dfrac{226.1 \text{ in.}}{0.25 \text{ in.}} = 904.4$.

This means an input force of 40 lb can move a resistance force of 40 lb × 904.4, or 36,176 lb. No wonder it is so easy to jack up an automobile! This same principle is used in the nut and bolt and such things as a vise.

PROBLEMS

22. A jackscrew has a pitch of ¼ inch and a handle 42 inches long. What is its I.M.A.?   *I.M.A. = 1055*

23. If the length of the handle in Problem 22 is changed to 30 inches, does the I.M.A. increase or decrease?

decreases to 753.6

Richard M. Fetters

Figure 11-26. All car "jacks" do not have jackscrews. This one is hydraulic. It uses levers and the pressure of a fluid to lift the car (Section 7:12).

11:12 *Efficiency*

Most people think machines do work. A machine does not do work. A machine only helps you do work.

Work must be put into the machine before it can do any work for you. A machine merely converts the *work input* into more useful *work output*. It does this by changing force, distance, or direction. The useful work obtained by a machine is always less than the work put into it. Why? Some of the input work is used to overcome friction. The ratio of work output to work input is called the **efficiency** of a machine. A scissors, knife, and can opener do work when someone uses them. In each case, an effort force must be applied to overcome a resistance. Electric motors and engines are used to operate many machines.

Every machine has a work input and work output. **Work input** is the effort force multiplied by the effort distance. **Work output** is the resistance force multiplied by the resistance distance.

What is the efficiency of a machine?

ratio of work output to work input

Work Input = Effort Force × Effort Distance
$$W_i = F_e \times D_e$$

Work Output = Resistance Force × Resistance Distance
$$W_o = F_r \times D_r$$

EXAMPLE

A crate is dragged up a ramp 20 m long. One end of the ramp is on the ground. The raised end is 5 m above the ground. The crate has a force of 300 nt. The effort force is 100 nt. Find the work input and work output.

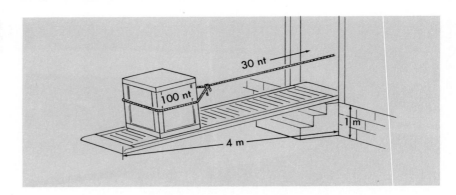

Given:

Effort force = 100 nt

Effort distance = 20 m

Resistance force = 300 nt

Resistance distance = 5 m

Solution:

$W_i = F_e \times D_e$

$W_i = 100 \text{ nt} \times 20 \text{ m}$

$W_i = 2000 \text{ nt-m}$

$W_o = F_r \times D_r$

$W_o = 300 \text{ nt} \times 5 \text{ m}$

$W_o = 1500 \text{ nt-m}$

Why is work output always less than work input?

Some work must be done to overcome friction.

In the example above, work output is less than work input. For an ideal machine they would be the same. But for real machines, work output always is less than work input. You get less work out of a machine than you put into it.

Efficiency of a machine may be calculated as a percent. Divide the work output by the work input. Then multiply by 100.

$$\% \text{ Efficiency} = \frac{\text{work output}}{\text{work input}} \times 100$$

The following shows how efficiency is calculated for the inclined plane described above.

EXAMPLE

Given:

Work input = 2000 nt-m

Work output = 1500 nt-m

Solution:

$\% E = \dfrac{W_o}{W_i} \times 100$

$\% E = \dfrac{1500 \text{ nt-m}}{2000 \text{ nt-m}} \times 100$

$= 75\%$

PROBLEMS

24. A loading area is 2 meters above the ground. A ramp 6 meters long extends from the ground to the edge of the loading area. A box of books with a force of 200 nt is

dragged up the ramp. The force necessary to drag this box is 100 nt. Calculate the work input and the work output. $W_i = 600$ nt-m $W_o = 400$ nt-m

25. Calculate the efficiency of the inclined plane described in Problem 24. $E = 66.7\%$

26. Calculate the efficiency of a set of pulleys. Work output is 400 ft-lb and work input is 600 ft-lb. $E = 66.7\%$

How can you increase the efficiency of a machine? One way is to reduce friction. For example, sanding the surface of a ramp or waxing the hull of a boat. Sanding or waxing smooths a surface and reduces friction. Oil and grease are used in many machines to decrease friction. Ball bearings in bicycle wheels and other machines decrease friction. Thus, efficiency is increased.

How do lubricants and bearings increase efficiency?

decrease friction

Increasing the efficiency of machines is an important step in conserving natural resources. Many machines are run by electricity or fuels such as gasoline. When efficiency is increased, less fuel or electricity is needed to do a given amount of work. Thus, resources are conserved. Also, reducing friction cuts down on wear and makes a machine last longer. The gasoline engine in cars is not very efficient. Someday some gasoline engines may be replaced by the more efficient turbine engine.

11:13   *Power*

Power has a precise meaning in science. **Power** is the amount of work done per unit time. The more rapidly work is done, the greater is the power. For example, a large engine is more powerful than a small engine. The large engine can do more work in less time. The less time it takes to do work, the more power is used. To find the power for a machine, divide the work done by the time. Use this equation:

What equation is used to calculate power?

$P = \frac{W}{t}$

$$P = \frac{W}{t}$$

In the equation, P represents power, W represents work, and t represents time.

EXAMPLE

A man uses a set of pulleys to lift a 200-pound boat 5 feet in 50 seconds. What is the power?

Figure 11-28. This train engine is powered by steam. The steam is produced in a boiler heated by burning coal.

Solution: (a) Write the equation: $P = \dfrac{W}{t}$

(b) Calculate the work done: $W = F \times D = 200$ lb $\times 5$ ft $= 1{,}000$ ft-lb

(c) Substitute 1,000 ft-lb for W and 50 sec for t:

$$P = \frac{1{,}000 \text{ ft-lb}}{50 \text{ sec}}$$

(d) Divide to find the answer: $P = 20$ ft-lb/sec

(e) Answer: Power $= 20$ ft-lb/sec

Horsepower is an English system unit of power. This term was first defined by James Watt, the inventor of the steam engine. Watt determined how much work the average horse could do and compared this with the work done by his steam engine. One **horsepower** (hp) is now defined as exactly 550 ft-lb of work per second. Gasoline engines and other engines are also rated in horsepower.

To calculate horsepower, find the ft-lb of work done per second. Then divide by 550 ft-lb/sec, the work equal to one horsepower (1 hp).

EXAMPLE

A 150-pound boy walks up a flight of stairs 30 feet high in 10 seconds. What horsepower does he use?

Solution: (a) Calculate the work done: $W = F \times D$
150 lb $\times$ 30 ft $= 4{,}500$ ft-lb

(b) To find power, divide work by the time:

$$P = \frac{W}{t} = \frac{4{,}500 \text{ ft-lb}}{10 \text{ sec}} = 450 \text{ ft-lb/sec}$$

(c) To find horsepower, divide power by 550 ft-lb/sec

$$\frac{450 \text{ ft-lb/sec}}{550 \text{ ft-lb/sec}} = 0.82 \text{ hp}$$

(d) Answer: 0.82 hp

PROBLEMS

27. What is the horsepower of an engine which does 2,000 ft-lb of work in 4 sec? *0.91 hp*

28. A sewing machine operated at full speed does 3,000 ft-lb of work in 1 min. What is the horsepower of the sewing machine motor? *0.09 hp*

29. A bulldozer pushes 20 tons of soil 100 ft in 2 minutes. What is the horsepower of the bulldozer? *60.7 hp*

EXPERIMENT. How many horsepower do you use when you go up a flight of stairs? Measure the height of a flight of stairs. Do this by measuring the height of a single step and then multiplying by the total number of steps. Have a classmate clock the time it takes for you to walk and trot up the stairs. Measure and record your weight on a bathroom scale. Power is the rate at which work is done. One horsepower is 550 ft-lb of work per second or 33,000 ft-lb of work per minute (550 ft-lb × 60 sec = 33,000 ft-lb/min). Calculate the horsepower used when you walk and trot up the stairs.

(a) Calculate work: W (ft-lb) = F × D

(b) Calculate power: $P = \dfrac{W}{t}$

(c) Calculate horsepower: $hp = \dfrac{P}{\dfrac{550 \; ft\text{-}lb}{sec}}$

Figure 11-29.

Electric motors and many power tools are rated in horsepower. For example, electric hand drills use a ¼- or ½-hp electric motor. An electric household mixer uses a ¼-hp motor. Name two home appliances powered by an electric motor.

The *watt* (*w*) is the basic unit of power in the metric system. One **watt** is one newton-meter per second $\left(\dfrac{nt\text{-}m}{sec}\right)$. This unit was named in honor of James Watt, the inventor of the steam engine. One horsepower is equal to 746 watts.

PROBLEM

30. Use your own experience. You have probably seen each of these machines around your home or school. Rank each machine from the lowest to highest horsepower.

(a) egg beater   (d) minibike
(b) washing machine   (e) jet transport plane
(c) compact car   (f) subway train

lowest (a), (b), (d), (c), (f),(e) highest

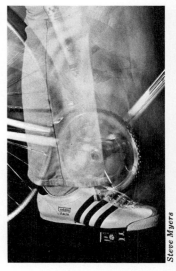

Figure 11-30. The horsepower of a bicycle depends on the rider. The harder he pedals, the faster he moves.

MAIN IDEAS

p. 221 **1.** Unbalanced forces can produce motion.

p. 222 **2.** Work is done when a force is exerted through a distance.

p. 224 **3.** Machines help us do work.

p. 224 **4.** Machines can change the speed or direction of a force.

p. 224   **5.** Machines can decrease the amount of force needed to do work.

p. 224   **6.** Most machines may be classified as compound machines. Compound machines are two or more simple machines working together.

p. 224   **7.** The mechanical advantage of a machine is the ratio of the resistance force to the effort force M.A. $= F_R/F_E$

p. 225   **8.** In figuring I.M.A. friction, weight, and bending are not considered.

p. 235   **9.** Work output is always less than work input.

p. 235   **10.** Efficiency is work output divided by work input.

p. 237   **11.** Power is the rate at which work is done.

p. 238   **12.** Power in the English system is measured in horsepower.
1 hp = 550 ft-lb/sec

p. 239   **13.** Power in the metric system is measured in watts.
1 w = 1 nt-m/sec
1 hp = 746 watts

VOCABULARY

Write a sentence in which you use correctly each of the following words or terms.

actual mechanical	fulcrum	moment
advantage	gravity	power
compound machine	horsepower	resistance
efficiency	ideal mechanical	simple machine
force	advantage	watt
friction	mechanical advantage	weight

STUDY QUESTIONS

A. True or False   *Have students rewrite false statements to make the statements correct.*

Determine whether each of the following sentences is true or false. (Do not write in this book.)

T   **1.** A compound machine is more complex than a simple machine.

simple   *F*   **2.** A pulley is an example of a ~~compound~~ machine.

not   *F*   **3.** The M.A. of a machine is always greater than one.

T **4.** A force is a push or pull.

F **5.** An egg beater is an example of a ~~simple~~ machine.   *compound*

F **6.** ~~Pound~~ is the metric unit of force.   *Newton*

F **7.** The efficiency of a machine is calculated by dividing work ~~input~~ by work ~~output.~~   *output, input*

T **8.** There are six simple machines.

F **9.** One horsepower is 550 ft-lb of work per ~~minute.~~   *second*

T **10.** To do work an object must be moved.

B. Multiple Choice *Some questions in part B may have more than one correct answer. Only one answer is required.*

Choose one word or phrase that correctly completes each of the following sentences. (Do not write in this book.)

1. Work is done when a body is moved through a distance by a (force, moment, M.A., fulcrum).

2. Work is equal to $\left(F \times D, \dfrac{F_R}{F_E}, \dfrac{D_R}{D_E} \right)$.

3. A (sewing machine, gasoline engine, washing machine, lever) is a simple machine.

4. A compound machine has (one, two, two or more) simple machines.

5. A single fixed pulley has an I.M.A. of (1, 2, 3, 4).

6. I.M.A. is (less than, greater than, the same as) the A.M.A. for a given machine.

7. (Moment, Resistance, Effort, Fulcrum) is the point around which a lever rotates.

8. Every lever has (4, 3, 2, 1) moments.

9. The moments of a balanced lever are (equal, unequal, less than the M.A.).

10. You can measure force with a(n) (ruler, pulley, inclined plane, spring scale).

C. Completion

Complete each of the following sentences with a word or phrase that will make the sentence correct. (Do not write in this book).

1. The pivot point of a lever is called the __?__ .   *fulcrum*

2. The arms of a lever are 8 ft and 2 ft long. Its I.M.A. is __?__ .   *four*

3. A block and tackle has four support ropes. The I.M.A is __?__ .   *four* *moments*

4. The __?__ of a balanced lever are equal.

output, input

5. The work __?__ of a machine is always less than the work __?__.

lubricants

6. __?__ are used to decrease friction.

time

7. Power is the amount of work done per unit of __?__.

550

8. One horsepower is __?__ ft-lb of work/sec.

power

9. A ½-hp motor has more __?__ than a ¼-hp motor.

less than

10. The efficiency of a machine is always __?__ 100%.

D. How and Why

1. How much work is done when a force of 25 nt is used to slide a 150-nt sofa 10 m across a floor? *250 nt-m*

See Teacher's Guide.

2. Where is the fulcrum, resistance force, and effort force in (a) the oar of a rowboat, (b) a pair of pliers, (c) a wheelbarrow?

See Teacher's Guide.

3. Draw a set of pulleys with an I.M.A. of 5. How far will the effort force move if the resistance force moves 1 in.? *5 in.*

Simple machines; make work easier; change direction, magnitude or distance of force

4. In what three ways are a lever, wheel and axle, and pulley alike?

5. List six compound machines. Name one simple machine in each. *See Teacher's Guide.*

6. Work input for a block and tackle is 250 nt-m. Work output is 200 nt-m. Find the percent efficiency. *E = 80%*

7. Given: effort arm = 1 ft, resistance arm = 10 ft, resistance force = 50 lb. Find the effort force. *F_e = 500 lb*

8. An electric mixer has a ¼-hp motor. It beats cake batter for 3 minutes. How much work did the motor do? *24,750 ft-lb*

9. A 1-hp gasoline engine and a ½-hp motor both do 100 ft-lb work. Which machine can do the work faster? Explain your answer. *1 hp*

10. A pole vaulter weighing 175 lb leaped 16 ft over a bar. How much work did he do in lifting himself? *W = 2,800 ft-lb*

INVESTIGATIONS

See Teacher's Guide at the front of the book for answers and suggestions.

1. Automobile engines must be "tuned" every so often to maintain their performance. Obtain a book on automobile mechanics and visit a service station to learn how an engine is "tuned."

2. Pulleys may be made from empty thread spools and wire clothes hangers. Cut off the wire of a hanger eight inches

on each side of the hook. Bend the ends and slip them through a spool. Make three spool pulleys in this manner. Using some string, hook two pulleys together to indicate an I.M.A. of 2. Then hook three pulleys together to indicate an I.M.A. of 3. Use a spring scale to measure the effort force needed to lift various objects with the pulleys. Record your observations.

3. Obtain advertising material for different kinds of motorcycles, dirt bikes, and minibikes. Make a chart comparing horsepower, gear ratios, and torque.

4. Look up "perpetual motion" in the library and give a report on the perpetual motion machine.

INTERESTING READING

Bulman, A.D., *Models for Experiments in Physics*. New York, Thomas Y. Crowell Co., 1968.

Burlingame, Roger, *Machines That Built America*. New York, New American Library, Inc., 1955.

Gamow, George, *Gravity*. Garden City, New York, Doubleday & Company, Inc., 1962.

12

The objectives of this chapter are to discuss the difference between mass and weight and to further develop the concepts of motion including speed, acceleration, and velocity. Vectors are introduced and used in problem solving.

Moving Bodies

GOAL: You will gain an understanding of weight and mass, speed and velocity, and relationships between forces and motion.

You walk on the earth with no fear of falling into space. A ball that you hold in your hand will not fall into space. To get the ball or any other body into the air, you apply a force. Your muscles provide the force needed to throw a ball. What force brings the ball down to the ground? What force prevents all bodies from falling off the earth?

Man has learned how to exert a force great enough to send a satellite into orbit. He now launches spacecrafts beyond the earth to the moon, sun, and planets. Man has learned how to overcome the earth's force on bodies.

12:1 *Weight and Mass*

All things are attracted to the earth. A skydiver leaping from an airplane falls swiftly toward the ground. Jump up in the air and you come down again. If you accidentally let go of a ball during a game, it falls to the ground. Bodies fall because the earth exerts a force on them. This force is **gravity.** Gravity acts upon all bodies on or near the earth's surface. The newton is a unit of force in the metric system. Ounce and pound are units of force in the English system. **Weight** is a measurement of the force of gravity. You can measure weight with a spring scale.

Mass is different from weight (Section 1:10). Mass is the quantity or amount of matter in an object. Examine a book, a pencil, or any solid body near you. Notice that it has a definite mass and occupies space. Gases and liquids also have definite mass and occupy space. Anything that occupies space and has mass is called matter. Unlike weight, the mass of a given body remains constant.

Figure 12-1. The stretch of the spring inside the scale is proportional to the force which stretches it.

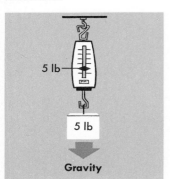

5 lb

5 lb

Gravity

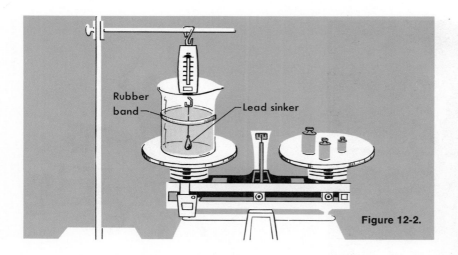

Rubber band

Lead sinker

Figure 12-2.

EXPERIMENT. Does a body lose mass or weight when submerged in water? (1) Fill a 400-ml beaker half full of water. Place a rubber band around the beaker at the level of the water. Set the beaker on the pan of a balance and balance it. Record the mass. (2) Attach a spring scale to a body (lead sinker) with a string and record the weight. Lower the body into the water until it is submerged. Record the decrease in weight observed on the spring balance. Now move the rubber band to the new level of the water. Remove the body from the water. (3) Add water to raise the water level in the beaker to the rubber band. Record the new reading on the balance (beaker and water). (4) Find the mass of the water added by subtracting the original mass of the beaker plus water from the new mass of the beaker plus water.

Does the beaker gain mass or weight, or both, when water is added? Why does the body lose weight and not mass when submerged? Compare the change in mass of the beaker plus water with the weight loss of the submerged body. Explain your answer.

The beaker gains both mass and weight.

Buoyancy, a force exerted by the water, decreases weight.

The weight loss of the submerged object is equal to the weight of the water added to the beaker. Explanation above.

PROBLEM

1. How does a submarine change its weight when it dives and surfaces?

To submerge it takes on water to reduce buoyancy. To surface, it forces water out to reduce weight.

The mass of a body is constant and unchanged, regardless of its location. However, the weight of a body can change. Differences in the force of gravity cause differences in weight. For example, on the moon you would weigh ⅙ of your weight on earth. Why the difference? Gravity on the moon is only ⅙ as great as gravity on the earth. Yet your mass would be the

How is weight different from mass?

Weight is the amount of force of gravity acting on a body and mass is the quantity of matter or "stuff" in the body.

Figures 12-3 and 12-4. A person can jump higher and much more easily on the moon than on earth because of the difference in gravity.

same on the moon as it is on the earth. Two masses that exactly balance each other on the moon would also balance on earth.

Weight of a body varies slightly from place to place on earth. A man who weighs 200 lb at the equator would weigh 201 lb at the North Pole. Weight decreases by about 0.5% when a body is moved from the North Pole to the equator. The earth is not a perfect sphere. If the earth were a perfect sphere, your weight would be the same anywhere on its surface. The earth is slightly flattened at the poles and thicker at the equator. From the North Pole to the equator, the distance from the center of the earth increases by about 12½ miles. As a body moves away from the center of the earth, gravity decreases. Gravity is less at the equator; weight is less, too. Your weight would be about ½ pound less at the equator than at the North Pole. Suppose the earth were a perfect sphere. Then your weight would be the same at both places.

Figure 12-5. A man who weighs 160 lb at the surface of the earth would weigh 40 lb at 8000 mi from the center of the earth and 18 lb at 12,000 mi from the center.

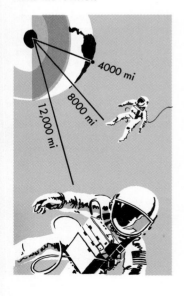

4000 mi

8000 mi

12,000 mi

12:2 *Gravity*

Most things fall down and not up if you drop them. Gravity pulls bodies to the earth. However, gravity is a property not only of the earth but of all matter. Every body in the universe pulls on every other body. Every body has its own force on other objects. The pull between most objects is too small to be measured except with precise scientific instruments. For example, a five-ton lead ball attracts a baseball at its surface with a force less than the weight of one mosquito!

Sir Isaac Newton (1642-1727) formulated the law of gravitation during the seventeenth century. A scientific law is an accepted statement based upon a large amount of scientific evidence. Any scientific law, however, may be disproved by new evidence. A scientific law is, therefore, subject to change.

Newton's law of gravitation states: the gravitational attraction between two bodies is proportional to the product of the mass of the bodies divided by the square of the distance between them.

Equation: Newton's Law of Gravitation

$$F \propto \frac{Mm}{d^2}$$

F = force of gravity
$\propto$ = is proportional to
M = mass of one body
m = mass of a second
d^2 = distance between two bodies squared

Bodies with a large mass exert a greater gravitational force than bodies with a small mass. For example, the earth exerts a greater force on bodies near its surface than does the moon. This is so because the earth has a greater mass. As the distance between two bodies increases, the attraction between them decreases. For example, as the distance between a rocket and the earth increases, the attraction between them decreases. Double the distance between two bodies and their attraction decreases to ¼ (or $[½]^2$).

PROBLEM

2. Suppose you were 4,000 miles above the surface of the earth. You would be twice as far from the center of the earth as you are now. The force of gravity on your body would decrease to ¼ (or $[½]^2$). How would this affect your weight? What would you weigh if you were 8,000 miles above the earth's surface? *1/9 surface weight*

1/4 surface weight

Figure 12-6. As a rocket travels farther away from the earth, the gravitational attraction between rocket and earth decreases proportionately.

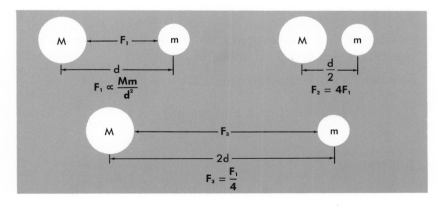

Figure 12-7. How does distance affect gravitational attraction between two objects?

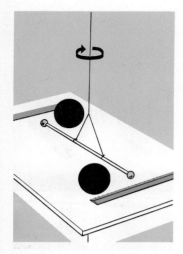

Figure 12-8. Cavendish used his calculations of gravitational force to find the earth's mass, 6.6 sextillion (6.6 $\times$ 10²¹) tons.

Henry Cavendish (1731-1810), an English scientist, accurately measured the gravitational attraction between two bodies. He mounted two small balls on opposite ends of a horizontal rod 2 meters long. Then he hung the rod horizontally from a wire (Figure 12–8). Cavendish set rulers at each end of the rod to measure its position. He placed two large masses near the balls at the ends of the rods. The balls were attracted to the large masses. As the small balls moved toward the large masses, the wire twisted. Cavendish measured the change in position of the balls. He used this measurement to calculate the gravitational force between the balls and the large masses.

12:3   *Speed*

A force can set a body in motion. Every body in motion moves a distance in a certain unit of time: second, minute, hour. **Speed** is defined as the distance a body travels per unit of time. Speed = distance/time.

What equation is used to calculate speed?

Have students consult Appendix A, pages 460-461. Explain the tables listed and how they may be used as an aid in solving problems.

Figure 12-9.   A car could travel at a speed of 45 miles per hour on this highway.

An automobile speedometer usually indicates speed in miles per hour (mi/hr). Automobiles on a highway may move for a time at a constant speed. Constant speed means that the speed does not vary. For example, a car travels at a constant speed of 30 mi/hr. The car travels 30 miles in the first hour and 30 miles in the second hour. Thus, it travels a total of 60 miles in two hours. It goes 30 miles every hour it maintains this constant speed.

You can calculate speed, distance, or period of time in motion for a moving body. Use the equation below:

$$v = \frac{d}{t} \qquad \begin{aligned} v &= \text{speed} \\ d &= \text{distance} \\ t &= \text{time} \end{aligned}$$

EXAMPLE 1

What distance is covered by a police car that travels at a constant speed of 1.5 mi/min for 5 min?

Solution: (a) Write the equation: $v = \frac{d}{t}$; $d = vt$

(b) Substitute and simplify $d = \frac{1.5 \text{ mi}}{\text{min}} \times 5 \text{ min}$

$d = 7.5$ mi

EXAMPLE 2

What is the speed of a truck which travels 5 kilometers in 10 minutes at constant speed?

Solution: (a) Write the equation: $v = \dfrac{d}{t}$

(b) Substitute 5 km for d and 10 min for t:

$$v = \frac{5 \text{ kilometers}}{10 \text{ min}}$$

(c) Divide to find the answer: $v = 0.5$ kilometers/min

Review the factor-label method of solving problems. The units for each numerical value are listed in setting up the problem. By canceling units, the correct units for the answer may be obtained. Explain how the factor-label method applies to Examples 1 and 2. Explain and work out the examples on a chalkboard. Problems may be done in class or for homework. If given as a homework assignment it is helpful to do at least one problem in class so students understand the methods involved.

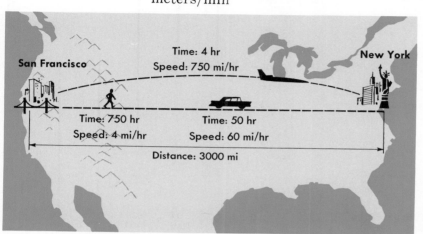

Figure 12-10. To find the average speed between San Francisco and New York, divide the distance (3000 mi) by total hours of time.

PROBLEMS

3. What is the speed of a bicycle that travels 100 meters in 50 sec at constant speed?   *2 m/sec*

4. What distance would be covered in 10 min by a train that travels at a constant speed of 500 meters in 10 sec?   *30,000 m*

5. Which has the greatest constant speed, the bicycle in Problem 3 or the train in Problem 4?   *train*

Cars, trucks, trains, and bicycles seldom travel at a constant speed for very long. The speed of a moving body usually increases or decreases as it moves. For this reason, the speed of a body usually means its average speed. To find average speed, use this equation:

$$v \text{ (average)} = \frac{d \text{ (total)}}{t \text{ (total)}}$$

Divide the total distance by the total time it takes to travel this distance.

How is average speed different from constant speed?

Average speed is total distance traveled divided by the time required to travel the total distance. Constant speed means that a body moves the same distance in each unit of time.

PROBLEMS

6. Compare the motion of the car in Figure 12–11 with that of the car in Figure 12–12. How do they differ? What is the average speed of the car in Figure 12–11?

car in Figure 12-11 has constant speed
car in Figure 12-12 has average speed of 24 mi/hr

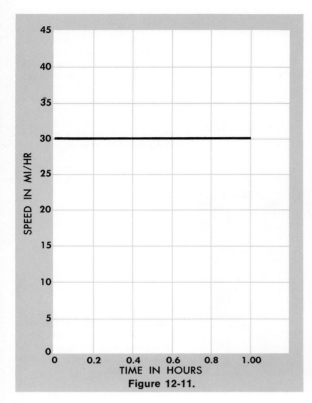

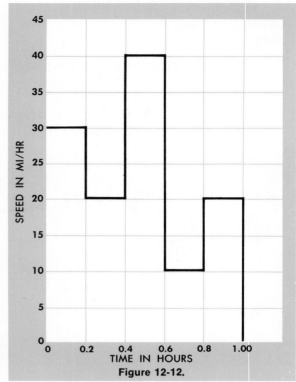

Figure 12-11.

Figure 12-12.

Figures 12-11 and 12-12 distinguish between constant speed and motion in which speed changes (accelerated motion).

7. What is the average speed of a jet plane which travels from New York City to Los Angeles (2,560 mi) in 5 hr?

8. What is the average speed of a bullet which travels 2,000 meters in 4 sec? *500 m/sec*   *512 mi/hr*

Figure 12-13.

EXPERIMENT. Obtain a board at least 2 m long and 15 cm wide. Place it on a table with one end on a pile of books about 40 cm high. Place a ball or large marble at the high end of the board and gently release it (do not push it). Time its trip down the board with a stopwatch. Mark off and measure in centimeters the distance the marble travels. Find the speed of the ball in cm/sec. Repeat three times and average your answers. Does the marble have constant speed? Is your answer the speed or average speed of the marble? Explain. See Teacher's Guide.

12:4 Acceleration   *Acceleration is produced by a force.*

From the starting line, a drag racer accelerates his car to a speed of 100 mi/hr. The driver increases his speed from 0 mi/hr to 100 mi/hr in 10 seconds. What is the acceleration? **Acceleration** is the rate at which speed is changing. Accelera-

Ronald Appelbe, Texaco Inc.

Figure 12-14. A race car has a high rate of acceleration.

tion is caused by a force. The force of a drag racing car's wheels on the road makes the car accelerate. In a rocket, the engine produces the force that accelerates the rocket up and away from the launching pad. To find acceleration, divide the change in speed by the time taken to change speed. Use the equation:

$$a = \frac{v_2 - v_1}{t}$$

a = acceleration
v_1 = original speed
v_2 = final speed
t = time

What equation is used to calculate acceleration?

$$a = \frac{v_2 - v_1}{t}$$

Acceleration of the drag race car is:

$$a = \frac{v_2 - v_1}{t} = \frac{100 \text{ mi/hr} - 0 \text{ mi/hr}}{10 \text{ sec}} = 10 \text{ mi/hr/sec}$$

The acceleration is read as 10 miles per hour per second. In each second the drag racer increases his speed 10 miles per hour.

Dragsters accelerate rapidly because the engines have a high horsepower and the rear wheels rotate rapidly.

EXAMPLE

A car starts from a standstill and accelerates to a speed of 50 km/hr in 10 sec. What is its acceleration?

Solution: (a) Write the equation: $a = \dfrac{v_2 - v_1}{t}$

(b) Substitute 50 km/hr for v_2, 0 km/hr for v_1, and 10 sec for t:

$$a = \frac{50 \text{ km/hr} - 0 \text{ km/hr}}{10 \text{ sec}}$$

(c) Subtract and divide to find the answer:
$a = 5$ km/hr/sec

PROBLEM

9. The speed of a jet plane increases from 450 km/hr to 585 km/hr in 15 sec. Find the acceleration.   *9 km/hr/sec*

How is average acceleration different from acceleration?

Average acceleration is total gain in speed divided by total time in which speed increases. Acceleration is the rate of increase in the speed at a given time.

The acceleration of a vehicle is not always constant. The rate of change in speed may increase or decrease while accelerating. Thus, acceleration often means the average acceleration during a period of time. To find average acceleration, use the equation:

$$a \text{ (average acceleration)} = \frac{v_2 - v_1}{t} \frac{\text{(change in speed)}}{\text{(total time)}}$$

Most amusement rides provide thrills by rapid accelerations and decelerations which produce forces on the riders.

Divide the overall change in speed by the total time. As with speed, it is common to use acceleration when referring to both acceleration and average acceleration. This practice is followed throughout this book.

Figure 12-15.   Forces and speed provide fun and excitement for amusement park riders. Is the roller coaster accelerating or decelerating?

Courtesy of Cedar Point, Sandusky, Ohio

12:5   *Deceleration*

How does a pilot stop a jet airliner after it lands? Reversing the engines of a jet airplane causes it to slow down. The driver of a car applies the brakes to slow it down. Both the airplane and car are stopped by forces. Decreasing speed is the opposite of increasing speed. The rate at which the speed of an object decreases is called deceleration. The greater the force applied, the greater the deceleration. *Deceleration* means negative acceleration. To find deceleration, use the acceleration equation:

How is deceleration different from acceleration?

Decreasing speed is the opposite of increasing speed (acceleration).

$$a = \frac{v_2 - v_1}{t}$$

Application of forces required to decelerate a body results in the generation of heat. A heat shield on a space capsule returning to earth   glows red as it decelerates while falling through the atmosphere. Air exerts the force which decelerates the space capsule.

EXAMPLE

A car traveling at 30 km/hr is stopped in 3 sec. Find the deceleration.

Solution: (a) Write the equation: $a = \dfrac{v_2 - v_1}{t}$

(b) Substitute 0 km/hr for v_2, 30 km/hr for v_1, and 3 sec for t: $a = \dfrac{0\ \text{mi/hr} - 30\ \text{mi/hr}}{3\ \text{sec}}$

(c) Subtract and divide to find the answer: Note: Subtracting 30 from 0 gives —30, a negative number.

$$a = \frac{-30\ \text{km/hr}}{3\ \text{sec}} = -10\ \text{km/hr/sec}$$

Figure 12-17. A jet airplane decelerates when its engines are reversed, its flaps lowered to increase air friction, and its wheel brakes applied.

Deceleration has a negative value. Deceleration is the opposite of acceleration and is in the opposite direction. Acceleration problems have (+) answers. Deceleration problems have negative (—) answers. It is standard practice not to write a + sign before a positive number. However a — sign is always written before a negative number.

PROBLEMS

−5 mi/hr/sec

10. The speed of a jet plane is decreased from 500 mi/hr to 400 mi/hr in 20 sec. What is the deceleration?

−10 mi/hr/sec

11. When a parachute on a drag race car opens, it slows the speed of the car from 160 mi/hr to 80 mi/hr in 8 sec. What is the deceleration?

How is a moving body accelerated and decelerated?

application of a force

Acceleration and deceleration are opposites. Yet both are produced by forces. Any change in the speed of an object requires the application of a force.

PROBLEMS   *See Teacher's Guide.*

12. What forces accelerate a passenger car, a drag race car, and a jet plane?
13. What forces decelerate a passenger car, a drag race car, and a jet plane?

12:6 *Vectors*

What information is needed to draw a vector?

magnitude and direction of force

Figure 12-18. The resultant or sum of the force vectors for a body at rest is zero.

A **vector** is used to represent the quantity of a force and its direction of action. The direction the vector points shows the direction in which the force is applied. The length of the vector shows the amount of force applied. Figure 12–18 shows vectors for several different forces. When indicating vector

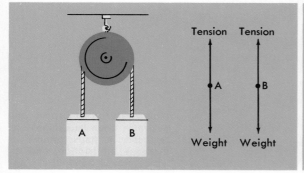
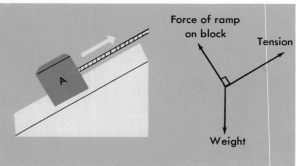

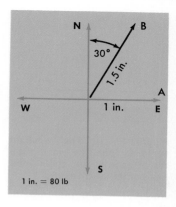

direction on paper, north is toward the top of the paper. East is toward the right.

To express a quantity of force as a vector, you must choose a scale to represent the quantity. For example, use ⅛ inch to represent one pound of force. Convert the size of the force into equivalent units of length. Using this scale, a line 1¼ inches long would represent a force of ten pounds.

Three boys push a car and each exerts 70 pounds of force in the same direction. These three forces act as a single force of 210 pounds. The single force which arises from the effects of two or more forces is called the *resultant force.* The **resultant** is the net effect of several forces. In this case, it is equal to the sum of the individual forces. The resultant is also in the same direction as the three forces acting on the car. In effect, the car is pushed by a force of 210 pounds. Remember each vector has both magnitude and direction.

In a football game, a player may be tackled by several opposing players. The force from each player acts at an angle to the other forces. You can find the resultant force by drawing a force diagram. Each force vector is represented by an arrow. This arrow has a definite length and direction. It is wise to use

Figure 12-19. A vector shows the direction and quantity of a force. Describe vector B.

Force B = 1.5 in. = 120 lb, 30°E

What method is used to find the resultant of forces acting in the same direction?

If forces are in the same direction, simply add them together.

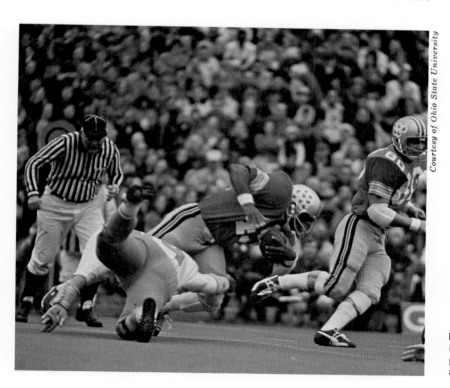

Courtesy of Ohio State University

Figure 12-20. A football player is often tackled by several players coming from different angles.

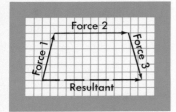

Figure 12-21. The resultant vector is found by placing the tail of each vector against the head of the next vector.

150 lb in direction all cars were moving.

a ruler and protractor when making vector diagrams. To add force vectors (arrows), place the tail of the second arrow on the head of the first arrow. Then place the tail of the third arrow on the head of the second arrow, etc. Vectors may be added in any sequence. To find the resultant of these vectors, draw a final arrow from the tail of the first vector to the head of the last vector. This is the resultant vector and has both direction and magnitude.

PROBLEM

14. Three cars collide at the same time. The second car hits the rear of the first car with a force of 100 lb. The third car hits the rear of the second car with a force of 50 lb. Find the resultant force on the first car.

In Figure 12–22, two forces oppose each other. To find the resultant of two opposite forces, find the difference between them. What is the resultant of the forces represented in Figure 12–22? In a basketball game, two players may collide. Here two forces may act at an angle to each other. You can find the resultant force in a problem of this kind by drawing a parallelogram. A parallelogram is a four-sided figure with opposite sides parallel.

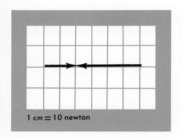

Figure 12-22. Opposing forces are shown by these vectors.

What method is used to find the resultant of several forces acting at angles to each other?

Draw a parallelogram using the vector forces as sides. The diagonal is the resultant force.

First, represent each force with a force vector. Draw the vectors from the same point to form two sides of a parallelogram. The point represents the place where the two forces act on a body. Then complete the parallelogram. Draw two sides parallel to the vectors that you have drawn to represent the forces. Draw a diagonal through the point where the forces act. The diagonal is a vector for the resultant force. Measure the diagonal. Use your scale to convert the measured length to an amount of force.

PROBLEMS

25 nt in the direction of the first team.

15. Two teams play tug-of-war. One team pulls with a force of 100 newtons. The other pulls with a force of 75 newtons. Using vectors, find the resultant force.

360 nt

16. At an intersection, two cars strike a third car at right angles to each other. One car exerts a force of 300 newtons. The other car exerts a force of 200 newtons. Find the resultant force by the parallelogram method.

4.2 lb sw

17. Four different feet kick a soccer ball at the same time. The forces are: 4 lb north, 2 lb east, 7 lb south, and 5 lb

west. Using a protractor, ruler, and paper make a scale drawing. Find the resultant force on the soccer ball and the direction it will go.

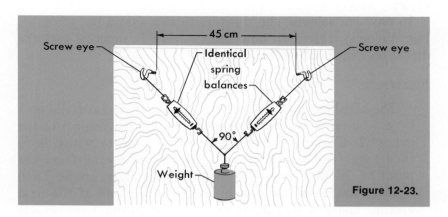

The angle between the two strings may be measured with a protractor or drawn on the student's paper by placing the paper behind the strings.

Figure 12-23.

If angle is <120°, each force is <W. If angle = 120°, each force = W. If angle is >120°, each force is >W.

EXPERIMENT.   How can spring balances be used to find the components of a force? (1) Fasten two screw eyes about 45 cm apart near one edge of a 60-cm² piece of plywood. Support the board in a vertical position. Hang two identical spring balances, one from each eye. Connect the hooks of the spring balance with a string. (2) Attach a weight, equal to one-half of the maximum load of a spring balance, to the center of the string. The two components of the force exerted by the weight are the two readings on balances. The resultant force is vertical to the weight. (3) Move the weight to different points on the string so that the force components form different angles. Each time record the reading of each balance. (4) Using a ruler and pencil, draw a vector diagram to show the components and resultant for three different angles between the two force components. How is the size of the angle related to the size of the forces?

Square and add the value of the force components when the components are at a right angle. How does this figure compare with the force of the weight? Use different weights and repeat the calculations for each weight. What is your conclusion?

12:7 *Velocity*

The speed and direction of an airplane traveling north at 300 knots (kn)* may be shown by a vector. To draw this

Why is velocity a vector quantity?

_____

* Knots represents nautical miles per hour. One nautical mile is approximately 6,076 feet.

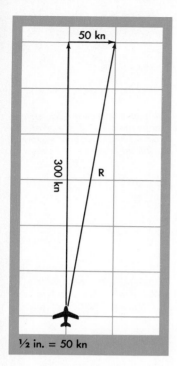

Figure 12-24. Velocity of airplanes is often expressed in knots. Plotting a course must include an allowance for wind speed and direction.

Scale: 1/2 in. or 1 cm = 5 km

vector, use a scale of 50 knots = ½ in. Draw a line 6 inches long pointing to the top of your paper (north). The vector you have drawn shows both speed and direction. It is called a velocity vector.

In physical science, speed refers to how fast a body is moving. **Velocity** refers to how fast a body is moving and the direction in which it is moving.

EXAMPLE

The airplane in Figure 12–24 is blown toward the east by a 50-knot wind. What is its velocity with respect to the ground? To solve this problem, draw a vector which is ½ inch long (equal to 50 knots). Draw the vector from the point of the first vector to the east at a right angle. Then connect the tip of this vector with the far end of the first vector. The line you draw to close the triangle represents the true velocity of the airplane. It shows the speed and direction relative to the ground over which the airplane flies. In what approximate direction does the airplane travel? What is the speed of the airplane? *310 km*
NNE

PROBLEM

18. A motorboat moves south across a river at 20 kn. The river current moves at 5 kn. Use vectors to find the velocity of the motorboat.

MAIN IDEAS

p. 244   **1.** Weight and mass are different. Weight is the amount of force earth exerts on a body due to gravity. Mass is the amount of matter in a body.

p. 248, p. 254 p. 256,   **2.** Motion starts and stops through the action of forces.

p. 248, p. 258   **3.** Speed is the distance covered per unit time. Velocity is speed in a given direction.

p. 254   **4.** A force must be applied to vary speed or velocity.

p. 254   **5.** Acceleration and deceleration result from the action of forces.

p. 244   **6.** The amount of force may be measured in pounds.

p. 254   **7.** A vector represents both magnitude and direction.

p. 255   **8.** Force vectors are used to find the resultant of two or more forces acting together.

Physicists

A safer family car, atomic power plants, tiny radios, and televisions . . . all these are based on the research of physicists.

Physicists study energy and the relationships between matter and energy. Such studies

Dr. George R. Carruthers is a research physicist. He was the first person to detect hydrogen molecules in newly-forming stars. To do this, he first designed the instrument shown here. It is a special type of electronic image-intensifier. When flowing in a rocket, Dr. Carruthers' intensifier recorded the light coming from stars. Dr. Carruthers analyzed data collected by the intensifier and found that part of the light from a new star called Xi Persei came from hydrogen.

have changed the way we live, especially in the last few decades. For example, research by physicists has led to the development of the transistor.

In turn, transistors make possible hundreds of products—from hand-size radios to guidance systems for spaceships.

There are about 48,000 physicists in the United States today. Most of these work in basic or applied research. Physicists in basic research are sometimes divided into two main groups—experimental and theoretical. Experimental physicists design and conduct experiments to study matter and energy. Theoretical physicists seek to describe the basic concepts of matter and energy in mathematical terms. Many researchers combine theoretical and experimental physics. They both conduct experiments and

Instruments such as this help physicists measure light intensity.

seek basic mathematical formulas to fit the data they gather.

Physicists in applied research use the principles of physics to solve practical problems. They often work

closely with engineers to apply the results of basic research and to develop new products.

The work of an experimental physicist may include building his own equipment.

Physics is such a diverse profession that most physicists specialize. Mechanics (forces and machines), optics (light), and acoustics (sound) are among the main divisions. Each main division has several subdivisions. For instance, one division is called solid-state physics (behavior of materials in the solid state). Within this division are such subdivisions as ceramics (clay and glass) and crystallography (crystal structure). Of course, as in all areas of science, a particular physicist's work may overlap several different subdivisions.

p. 258
9. Velocity vectors are used to find the resultant or true velocity of a body in motion.

VOCABULARY

Write a sentence in which you correctly use each of the following words or terms.

acceleration	mass	speed
deceleration	resultant	vector
force	scale	velocity
gravity	scientific law	weight

STUDY QUESTIONS

A. True or False   *Have students rewrite false statements to make the statements correct.*

Determine whether each of the following sentences is true or false. (Do not write in this book.)

T 1. It takes a force to produce motion.

T 2. A body would have the same mass on the moon as it has on earth.

T 3. It takes a force to change the velocity of a body.

T 4. Force may be measured in newtons.

F 5. Gravity is ~~not~~ a force.

T 6. Weight is measured in newtons.

lower than *F* 7. Gravity is ~~the same~~ on the moon as it is on earth.

T 8. A vector may be used to indicate speed.

T 9. The resultant is the sum of two or more vectors.

T 10. The mass of a body may be measured in kilograms.

not a vector quantity *F* 11. Speed is ~~the same as velocity~~.

only *F* 12. Speed has ~~both~~ magnitude and direction.

varies from place to place *F* 13. The force of gravity ~~is the same everywhere~~ on earth.

miles/hour *F* 14. ~~The mile~~ is a unit of speed.

B. Multiple Choice   *Some questions in part B may have more than one correct answer. Only one answer is required.*

Choose one word or phrase that correctly completes each of the following sentences. (Do not write in this book.)

1. The (newton, centimeter, pound) is a unit of force.

2. A car traveling 60 km in 2 hr has an average speed of (30 km/2 hr, 30 km/hr, 30 km/min, 30 km/sec).

3. The formula for speed is $(v = \dfrac{d}{t}, \; v = \dfrac{t}{d}, \; v = \dfrac{s}{d}, \; s = \dfrac{t}{d})$.

4. When an automobile driver steps on the brake pedal, the automobile (accelerates, loses velocity, changes direction).

5. An example of acceleration is (15 km/hr, 15/min, 15 km/min/sec, —15 km/min/sec).

6. Velocity may be shown by a (force, line, vector, unit).

7. To find the resultant of two forces acting in the same direction, (add, subtract, multiply, draw a parallelogram).

8. To find the resultant of two forces acting at right angles, (add, subtract, multiply, draw a parallelogram).

9. Mass is measured in (feet, kilograms, ounces).

C. Completion

Complete each of the following sentences with a word or phrase that will make the sentence correct. (Do not write in this book.)

1. __?__ is a vector quantity.   *velocity*

2. Velocity has both speed and __?__.   *direction*

3. The resultant of three forces (30 lb, 50 lb, 100 lb) all acting in the same direction is __?__ lb.   *180 lb*

4. To find the resultant for two forces acting at a right angle to each other, draw a __?__.   *parallelogram*

5. A vector shows both the amount and __?__ of a force.   *direction*

6. When a drag racer leaves the starting line and increases his speed, he must __?__ his car.   *accelerate*

7. One __?__ is the force required to accelerate 1 kg of mass 1 m/sec/sec.   *newton*

8. Acceleration is produced by a __?__.   *force*

9. The brakes of a bicycle cause it to stop by supplying the necessary __?__.   *deceleration*

D. How and Why

1. A car travels 80 mi in 2 hr. What is its average speed in mi/min?   *0.67 mi/min*

2. A car going 10 mi/hr accelerates to 50 mi/hr in 6 sec. Find the average acceleration.   *6.7 mi/hr/sec*

3. A bobsled has an average acceleration of 1 m/sec/sec, starting from rest. How fast is it going after 6 sec?   *6 m/sec*

4. What is the average speed of the bobsled in Question 3?   *3 m/sec*

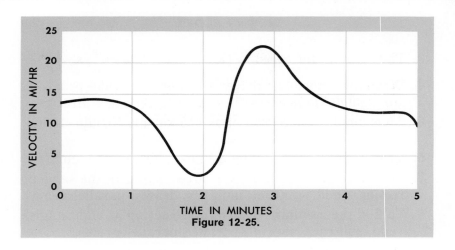

TIME IN MINUTES
Figure 12-25.

5. How much distance is covered in 6 sec by the bobsled in Question 3? *18 m*

6. A boy rides a bicycle as fast as he can from his home to a store 1 mi away. On the way he goes over a hill. Look at Figure 12-25 and find:
   (a) the rider's greatest velocity
   (b) the rider's least velocity
   (c) the time at which the rider is accelerating
   (d) the time at which the rider is decelerating

7. A car traveling at a speed of 80 ft/sec is stopped with a deceleration of 20 ft/sec/sec. How far does the car go before stopping? How long does it take to stop the car?

8. Why must a pilot include headwinds, tailwinds, and cross-winds when making a flight plan?

9. A sailor attaches a large fan to the stern of his sailboat. The fan is powered with a gasoline engine so that it will blast air against the sail. Will the fan move the boat? Explain your answer.

10. Why can a hammer exert a force many times its own weight?

INVESTIGATIONS

1. Find out how forces can make an airplane accelerate, decelerate, and change direction in flight. Learn the use of ailerons, flaps, and elevators. Using a model airplane, report your findings to the class.

2. Obtain a book on sailboats and learn how wind and water forces can make a sailboat sail against the wind.

INTERESTING READING

Burlingame, Roger, *Machines That Built America.* New York, New American Library, Inc., 1955.

Gamow, George, *Gravity.* Garden City, New York, Doubleday & Company, Inc., 1962.

13

Laws of Motion

The objectives of this chapter are: To discuss Newton's laws, projectile motion, and motion in curves; to discuss the effects of gravity on motion; and to develop an understanding of momentum, impulse, and systems.

GOAL: You will gain an understanding of Newton's laws, effects of gravity on motion, projectile motion, motion in curves, systems, and momentum.

Men dreamed about space travel for thousands of years before astronauts went to the moon. To enter space a spaceship must overcome the earth's gravitational attraction. To do this the spaceship must travel at a velocity of about 7 mi/sec. This velocity is called escape velocity. Both movements of spacecraft and movements of bodies here on earth are explained by the laws of motion.

13:1 First Law of Motion

You are riding in an automobile. The driver suddenly applies the brakes. You tend to keep moving. The tendency of a body to keep its present state of motion is called **inertia** (in er' shuh). Inertia keeps you moving in a straight line, even though the car has stopped. The pull of a seat belt brings you to a halt. If you do not wear a seat belt, you may get hurt. You may continue to move forward and hit the windshield.

What is inertia?

Inertia is the reluctance of a mass to change its state of rest or motion.

Figure 13-1. When a moving automobile crashes into an object, inertia throws its passengers forward.

Ford Motor Co.

ACTIVITY. Set a glass tumbler on a desk or table. Lay a card flat on top of the tumbler. Place a coin on the center of the card. Flick the card with your finger so it moves out from under the coin. If you do this fast enough, the coin will fall into the glass when the card flies away.

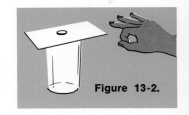

Figure 13-2.

ACTIVITY. Tie a light string to a heavy hammer or flat-iron. Pull the object slowly up from the floor. Then pull hard on the string while the object is on the floor. Record and explain your observations.

Sir Isaac Newton (1642-1727) formed three scientific laws which explain the movement of bodies. **Newton's first law of motion** states:

A body continues in a state of rest unless a force causes it to move. A body continues in motion at constant speed along a straight line unless a force causes a change in the speed of the body or the direction in which the body is moving.

Newton's first law means that it takes a force to start and stop motion. It takes a force to change the speed or direction of a body in motion. In other words, bodies have inertia. Bodies at rest tend to remain at rest. Bodies in motion tend to keep moving. It takes a force to overcome the effects of inertia. A force is required to accelerate a body. A force is required to decelerate it. Here are three examples of the first law of motion:

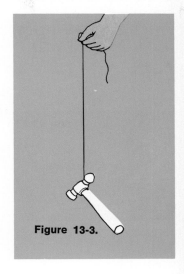

Figure 13-3.

A well known example of inertia is the magician's trick of pulling a tablecloth out from underneath a table set with dishes.

EXAMPLES

1. The electric motor in a slot car makes the wheels turn. The force of the wheels against the track makes the car move forward. As the car rounds a curve, the force of the track against the car makes it change direction. When the power is shut off, friction force gives the car a negative acceleration and makes it stop.

2. A sailboat floats on a lake with no wind. The sailors have two choices: (1) start to paddle, (2) wait for the wind. A breeze comes up and exerts a force on the sails. The boat moves. To change direction, the skipper moves the rudder right or left. The force of water on the rudder makes the boat turn.

3. A young girl is standing on a bus. The bus suddenly moves forward and the girl falls backward. Her body tends

Figure 13-4. The force of wind moves a sailboat through the water. The force of water on the rudder makes the boat turn.

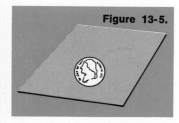

Figure 13-5.

to remain at rest (motionless) while the bus moves. The same thing happens when the bus stops suddenly. The girl tends to fall forward because of inertia.

ACTIVITY. Stand a nickel or quarter on edge on a 3 x 5-inch paper. Try to jerk the paper from under the coin without upsetting the coin. What does this illustrate?

PROBLEMS *Problems 1-9 should be discussed in class. Ask students to name* *additional examples which illustrate the principles involved.*

1. What forces put the following objects in motion: car, bullet, arrow, jet airplane, roller skates? *See Teacher's Guide.*
2. What forces stop or change the motion of the following objects: rocket, submarine, surfboard, car, bowling ball?
3. In which of the cases in Problem 2 is gravity involved? Explain your answer. *See Teacher's Guide.*
4. Why are seat belts important in an automobile?
   See Teacher's Guide.

Figure 13-6. The acceleration of gravity (32 ft/sec²) on the 2M body is the same as on the M body. Double the accelerating force on a body and the rate of acceleration doubles.

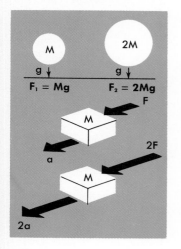

13:2 *Second Law of Motion*

See Teacher's Guide.

Hit a ball with a bat and the ball flies away. The ball is accelerated by the bat at the moment the bat strikes the ball. Acceleration of the ball depends on mass and force. The harder you hit the ball, the faster it moves. Hit with the same force, a ball with small mass travels faster than a ball with large mass. How far can you hit a baseball? A man can drive a golf ball 250 yards if he hits it hard enough.

Hitting a ball illustrates **Newton's second law of motion:**

The acceleration of a body varies directly with the size of the force producing the acceleration. Acceleration varies inversely with the mass of the body.

266

Figure 13-7. The greater the force with which the bat strikes the ball, the greater the acceleration of the ball as it moves away from the bat.

$$a = F/m \text{ or } F = ma$$

a = acceleration
F = force
m = mass

The second law of motion means that the harder you hit a ball, the faster it goes and the farther it travels. It also means that a ball with twice the mass will go one-half as far.

A ball has a mass of 0.5 kg. It is hit with a force of 50 nt and travels 100 m. If the mass of the ball had been 1 kg, it would have gone half as far or 50 m. If the force had been 100 nt, the ball would have traveled twice as far or 200 m. The larger the force the greater the acceleration, if the mass remains constant. The larger the mass the smaller the acceleration, if the force remains constant.

Here are four examples of the second law of motion:

EXAMPLES

1. The explosion of gunpowder accelerates a bullet out of a gun barrel. The large force on a small mass makes the bullet move swiftly. Its speed on impact may be 2000 ft/sec or more.

2. A driver controls the acceleration of his car with the gas pedal, called the accelerator. By feeding more gas into the engine, more force is created. The car speeds up.

Iroquois Publishing Co.

Figure 13-8. A bee has a very small mass and relatively powerful wings. It accelerates quickly.

3. Heavy (more massive) football players often are used as linemen. They can exert a large force to stop players on the other team. Players with less mass than linemen often are used as backfield players. They carry the ball and catch passes. Backfield players must be able to accelerate quickly. Less mass makes for faster acceleration since there is less mass to put in motion. Backfield players crouch in a way that allows them to spring forward when the ball is snapped from center.

4. The fastest drag racers have a small car with a large horsepower engine for rapid acceleration.

PROBLEMS

5. Is it easier for a fly or a bee to accelerate when taking off? Explain. *The fly. It has less mass.*

The van. It needs more force since it has more mass for the same amount of deceleration.

6. When a sports car and a loaded moving van both are traveling at a speed of 50 mi/hr, which vehicle requires more force to stop? Explain.

7. List three examples of the second law of motion from your everyday life. *Student answer.*

8. Explain how each example above illustrates the second law of motion. *Student answer.*

9. A force of 10 nt is applied to a 20-kg mass. What is the acceleration of the mass? *0.5 m/sec²*

13:3 Third Law of Motion

Motion is produced by an unbalanced force. Two teams have a tug-of-war. The winning team exerts more force than the

268

Carl England

Figure 13-9. In a tug-of-war, the team that exerts greater force is able to do work by moving the other team.

losing team and pulls them across the line. This is an example of an unbalanced force.

Push down on your desk top as hard as you can. The desk does not collapse. It exerts an upward force on your hand. The forces are equal and in opposite directions The net force is zero. How does the force of water in a rotary sprinkler make it spin? Water is forced out of the sprinkler by pressure. The water exerts a back force that makes the sprinkler arm turn. This is an example of unbalanced forces.

When a force (the *action force*) is exerted on an object, the object exerts an equal force (*reaction force*) in the opposite direction. How, then, do objects move? Movement requires an unbalanced force. Once inertia is overcome, forces are unbalanced.

O.M. Scott and Sons

Figure 13-10. When the water is turned on, its force turns the sprinkler arm.

EXPERIMENT. *Attach a spring balance to the leg of a desk or table. Connect the balance hook to the hook of a second spring balance. Exert a force on the balance. Keep the force constant and read both balances. Repeat with different amounts of force. What do you observe?*
The force readings on the two balances are always equal.

Forces described above are examples of **Newton's third law of motion:**

For every force, there is an equal and opposite force.

The two forces that always act together are called action force and reaction force. Exert an action force on an object and the object exerts a reaction force. The reaction force is equal in amount to the action force and acts in the opposite direction.

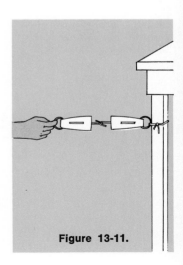

Figure 13-11.

PROBLEMS

10. The earth exerts a force on you. What is the reaction force? *Your weight, a force, down on the earth.*

11. As you stand, you exert a force on the floor. What is the reaction force? *Upward force of the floor on your feet.*

12. How does the recoil of a gun illustrate Newton's third law? How does it illustrate Newton's second law?
See Teacher's Guide.

ACTIVITY. Obtain a toy balloon and blow it up. Hold the open end of the inflated balloon closed, then release it. Explain why the balloon moves. What causes the action force and the reaction force? *Air pushes against inside of balloon as it escapes. The balloon at the same time pushes against air.*

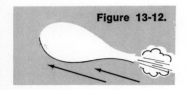

Figure 13-12.

ACTIVITY. Take two spring scales. Fasten them together. One person holds one scale while another person pulls on the other scale. Look at the reading on the scales and see who is pulling the hardest. This shows Newton's third law. Fasten three scales together in a line. Again one person holds the scale on one end while another person pulls on the scale on the other end. What is the reading on all three scales? *All three scales have the same reading.*

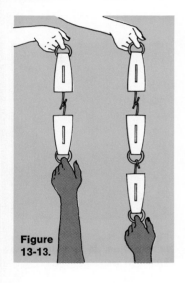

Figure 13-13.

PROBLEMS

Pencil pushes on paper; paper pushes against pencil.

13. How are action and reaction forces produced as you press a pencil against a paper while writing?

14. How would the motions of a toy balloon and rocket engine be different if there were no gravity? How would these motions be different if there were no air resistance? *See Teacher's Guide.*

15. Which law of motion is illustrated by each of the following examples?

(a) A boy jumps to a dock from a boat. The boat moves away from the dock. *Newton's third law.*

(b) A galloping horse comes to a sudden stop. Its rider is thrown over the head of the horse and lands on the ground. *Newton's first law.*

(c) A cannon moves backward as a shell is fired from it. *Newton's third law.*

(d) A playing card is set on top of a drinking glass. A coin is set in the center of the card. The card is swiftly moved away, and the coin drops into the glass. *Newton's first law.*

(e) A rotary water sprinkler rotates when the water is turned on. *Newton's third law.*

action — bullet flies out of barrel reaction — recoil force against arm or hand holding gun

13:4 *Falling Bodies*

From a tenth-story window, a bowling ball and a golf ball are dropped. Which ball strikes the ground first?

Aristotle (384-322 B.C.), a Greek philosopher, stated that when two different bodies are dropped from the same height at the same time, the heavy body will strike the ground first. Aristotle's theory claimed that a heavy body (large mass) falls faster than a lighter body (small mass). A theory is an explanation based on available information. We do not know if Aristotle ever performed an experiment to test his theory.

Neglecting air resistance, the bowling ball and golf ball will strike the ground at the same time.

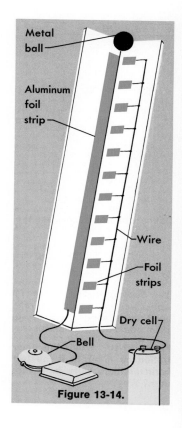

Figure 13-14.

EXPERIMENT. How does the speed of a body change as it falls? (1) Motion along an inclined plane is a special case of free fall. Nail two 15-cm wide 4-m long boards together to form a trough. Paste a 5-cm strip of aluminum foil alongside of the trough. Paste 1-cm square pieces of foil along the opposite side as shown in the diagram. The aluminum squares must be 2.5 cm apart. Connect each foil piece to a long wire connected to a dry cell. Connect the dry cell to a bell and then connect the bell to the aluminum strip. "Liquid" or "cold" solder can be used to attach the wire to the foil. (2) Set the trough at an angle of 10° to the horizontal. Run a metal ball down the trough. If a metronome is available, set it for 4 beats/sec and use it to time the speed of the ball. Why does the bell ring more often as the ball goes down the ramp? At what point is the ball's speed greatest?

The bell rings often farther down the ramp because it accelerates (its velocity increases) as it goes down the ramp. Velocity is greatest at the end of the ramp.

Aristotle's theory was accepted until the time of Galileo (1564-1642), an Italian scientist. Galileo believed that all bodies, regardless of mass, fall at the same rate. Galileo performed an experiment to test his hypothesis. A *hypothesis* (hie pahth' e sis) is a proposed solution or explanation for a problem. Galileo timed the motion of a ball rolling down a smooth groove on an inclined board. The movement of a ball down an inclined board is caused by gravity. Speed of the ball can be measured in the same way as a freely falling body. At equal intervals of time, Galileo marked the distance the ball had traveled.

Galileo's hypothesis was that the distance a ball travels increases with each unit of time. What did he discover in his experiment? Galileo found that this distance traveled was always proportional to the square of the time elapsed. The ball moved four times as far the second time interval as it did the

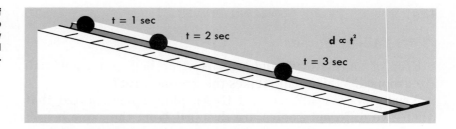

t	t^2	d spaces	Final v spaces/sec
1	1	1	2
2	4	4	4
3	9	9	6
4	16	16	8

first time interval and nine times as far the third time interval. The distance traveled was always proportional to the square of the time elapsed (Figure 13–15). The relationship that Galileo discovered is expressed as:

$$d \propto t^2$$

$d =$ distance object travels
$\propto =$ varies directly
$t =$ time

Suppose you repeated the above experiment with a bowling ball and a golf ball. Would the time intervals differ? No. The distance traveled per second is the same for the bowling ball and the golf ball. Acceleration for both balls is the same.

Near the surface of the earth, falling bodies of high density accelerate at a rate of about 9.8 meters/second/second (32/ft/sec²). This means the speed of a falling body increases 9.8 m/sec for each second it falls. At the end of one second, it is traveling at 9.8 m/sec. At the end of the next second, its speed is 19.6 m/sec. How fast will it be falling after 3 seconds? 29.4 m/se Eventually the object will reach a point where it will stop accelerating. This is known as the *terminal velocity* and is reached when the upward force caused by air resistance is equal to the downward force of gravity. The net force is then zero. The body will keep falling at a constant speed, no acceleration.

The value 9.8 m/sec² is usually labeled as g. g is the acceleration caused by gravity. In English units g is 32 feet/sec/sec (32 ft/sec²).

Low density bodies, such as feathers, Ping-Pong balls, and open handkerchiefs, fall more slowly. They encounter more air resistance when they fall. If you measured the fall of feathers, Ping-Pong balls, and handkerchiefs in a vacuum, you would find that they also accelerate at a rate of 9.8 m/sec².

To find the velocity of a falling object, use this equation:

$$v = gt$$

$v =$ velocity
$g =$ gravitational acceleration (9.8 m/sec² or 32 ft/sec²)
$t =$ time

Define uniform acceleration.

Yes. Released at the same time both would accelerate at the same rate and have the same velocity because there would be no air resistance.

Figure 13-16. Would this illustration be different if the two handkerchiefs were in a vacuum? Why?

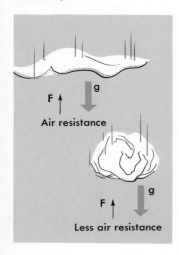

F ↑
g
Air resistance

F ↑
g
Less air resistance

Due to air resistance, a parachutist in a free fall may reach a terminal or maximum velocity of about 120 mi/hr before opening his chute. When the chute is open velocity may be reduced to about 14 mi/hr.

EXAMPLE

A billiard ball is dropped from the roof of a building. It takes 3 sec to strike the ground. What is the velocity of the billiard ball at the instant it strikes the ground?

How can you calculate the velocity of a falling body?

Solution: (a) Write the equation: $v = gt$

(b) Substitute 9.8 m/sec² for g and 3 sec for t:

$$v = \frac{9.8 \text{ m}}{\text{sec}^2} \left| \frac{3 \text{ sec}}{} \right.$$

(c) Multiply 9.8 m by 3 sec to find v

(d) Answer: $v = 29.4$ m/sec

According to legend Galileo (1564-1642) dropped two cannon balls, one ten times heavier than the other, from the leaning tower of Pisa. Both cannon balls were seen to strike the ground simultaneously.

PROBLEM

16. A rock falls from a cliff and takes 2 sec to reach the ground below. What is the velocity (m/sec) of the rock as it strikes the ground? *19.6 m/sec*

To calculate the distance that a body travels when it falls from rest, use the equation:

$$d = \tfrac{1}{2}\, gt^2$$

$d =$ distance
$g =$ gravitational acceleration
$t =$ time

EXAMPLE

A stone falls from the edge of a roof to the ground. If it takes 2 sec for the stone to fall, how high is the building in meters?

How can you find the distance a body falls during a given time?

Solution: (a) Write the equation: $d = \tfrac{1}{2}\, gt^2$

(b) Substitute 9.8 m/sec² for g and 2 sec for t:

$$d = \frac{1}{2} \left| \frac{9.8 \text{ m}}{\text{sec}^2} \right| \frac{(2 \text{ sec})^2}{}$$

(c) Square the 2 sec, multiply by 9.8 m and 1/2, and divide by sec²

(d) Answer: $d = 19.6$ m

PROBLEMS

17. A boy drops a rock from the center of a bridge. He sees the rock splash in the water 3 sec later. How high is the bridge in feet? Use 32 ft/sec² for g to solve this problem.   *144 ft*

18. A ball is thrown straight up into the air. The ball takes 1 sec to fall to the ground from its highest point. How high does the ball go?   *16 ft or 4.9 m*

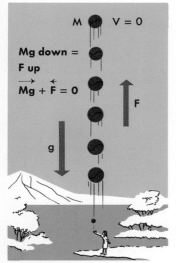

Figure 13-17. The ball's velocity is greatest the instant it leaves the thrower's hand. On the way up, velocity decreases; on the way down, velocity increases.

No. It would continue to fall back and forth through the tube. When falling towards the center of the earth it would accelerate. After passing the center of the earth

Figure 13-18. If a ball was dropped into a tube extending through the center of the earth, would the ball come to rest? Why?

it would decelerate until it reached zero velocity at the end of the tube (earth's surface) and then start falling again back down through the tube.

Figure 13-19. The drag force of a parachute prevents acceleration. This causes a body to fall at a constant velocity.

13:5   *Deceleration by Gravity*

When you throw a ball up into the air, it decelerates. The ball's velocity decreases as it goes up. The deceleration (negative acceleration) is caused by gravity. Rate of deceleration is the same as the rate of acceleration caused by gravity acting on a falling body (9.8 m/sec² or 32 ft/sec²). To find the deceleration, use the equation:

$$v = -gt$$

v = decrease in velocity
$-g$ = 9.8 m/sec², 32 ft/sec²
t = time

Note: In the equation g is the same as for acceleration, except for the negative sign. The negative sign shows deceleration.

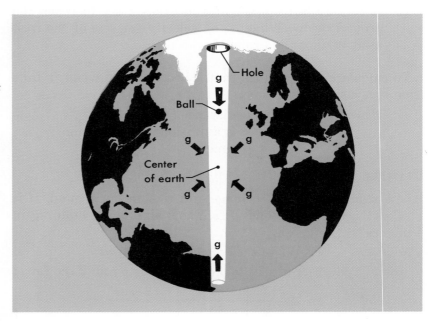

EXAMPLE

A boy throws a ball straight up into the air. It starts upward with a velocity of 12 m/sec. The ball begins to decelerate the instant it leaves the boy's hand. How fast will the ball be going after 1 sec?

Solution: (a) Use the equation: $v = -gt$

(b) Substitute 9.8 m/sec² for g and 1 sec for t:

$$v = \frac{-9.8 \text{ m}}{\text{sec}^2} \left| \frac{1 \text{ sec}}{} \right.$$

(c) Multiply —9.8 m by 1 sec and divide by sec²
to find v

(d) $v = $ —9.8 m/sec

(e) Subtract the loss of velocity, 9.8 m/sec,
from the initial velocity:

$$\begin{array}{r} 12.0 \text{ m/sec} \\ -9.8 \text{ m/sec} \\ \hline 2.2 \text{ m/sec} \end{array}$$

(f) Answer: 2.2 m/sec

Deceleration causes a decrease in the velocity of a moving body.

PROBLEMS

19. An archer shoots an arrow straight up into the air. The upward velocity of the arrow as it leaves the bow is 30 m/sec. What is the velocity of the arrow after 2 sec? *10.4 m/sec*

20. How long does it take for the arrow in Problem 19 to reach zero velocity at the top of its rise? *3.06 sec*

13:6 *Relative Motion*

Suppose you are standing in a moving jet airplane. You jump up two feet off the floor. Will you land in the same spot on the floor when you come down from your jump? Remember, you are moving forward all the time you go up and come down. On a separate sheet of paper, draw a figure of the approximate path of your jump. What is this curved path called?

A large stone is dropped from the top of the mast of a moving ship. Does the stone fall to the deck directly below the point from which it was dropped? Or does the stone land in front of or behind the mast? Assume that the mast is perpendicular to the water's surface. Also, remember the ship is moving forward as the stone falls.

The falling stone lands on the deck directly below the point from which it was dropped. Before it was released, the stone was moving forward at the same velocity as the moving ship. The stone maintained its forward velocity during its fall. While falling, the stone had two velocities: forward and downward. The forward motion caused it to continue in the same path as the boat during its fall. The stone did not land behind the mast. It fell to a point on the deck directly below the place from which it was dropped. The path followed by the stone is a curved path, a parabola (puh rab' ah luh).

Frame of reference applies here. An observer inside the plane sees the girl go straight up and down. The path shown in the drawing is the path as it would appear if it could be observed from outside the plane.

Figure 13-20. **Because the girl and the jet have the same forward velocity, she lands in the same spot from which she jumped. The path of the girl is parabola.**

which satisfies the general equation for a parabola, $y = kx^2$. The parabola is the curve formed by the intersection of a cone with a plane parallel to the side of the cone.

You will land in the same spot. You are traveling forward at the same speed as the airplane and you keep moving forward with the airplane while jumping. The graph of the motion, on x and y

coordinates satisfies two equations at the same time:
$x = vt$ and $y = 1/2 \, gt^2$. Substituting for t in the second equation, the result is the equation $y = gx^2/2v^2$

The path of the ball has two components. To the left of the ruler the components are up and to the right of the ruler the components are down and to the right. Gravity decelerates the ball as it goes up and accelerates it as it comes down. Velocity is greatest at the beginning of the motion. Change in velocity (deceleration) is greatest in the path to the left of the ruler. Two forces acting on ball: gravity and the throwing force which propelled it forward.

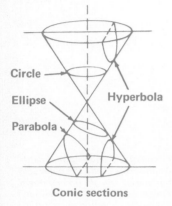

Circle

Ellipse

Parabola

Hyperbola

Conic sections

What is a parabola?

EXPERIMENT. How does the velocity of a projectile change during its flight? (1) Figure 13–21 shows a projectile in motion. The ball was thrown into the air at a trajectory of 27°. The time interval between each position of the ball is 1/30 sec. Place a piece of thin centimeter graph paper on top of the drawing. Mark each position of the ball with a dot. (2) Remove the graph paper. Draw straight lines connecting every third position of the ball. The time between three positions of the ball is 0.1 sec, because 3 × 1/30 sec = 1/10 = 0.1 sec.

Each straight line (covering three positions of the ball) represents the average velocity during each 0.1 sec of flight. At what point is the velocity greatest? At what point in its flight is the change in velocity greatest? What two forces are acting on the ball?

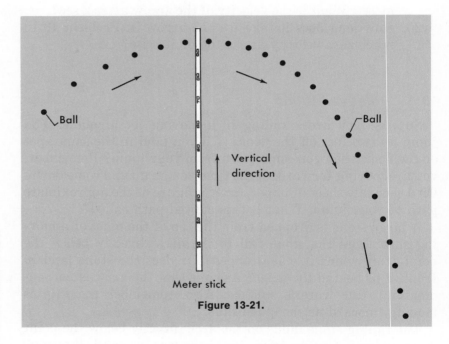

Ball

Vertical direction

Ball

Meter stick

Figure 13-21.

A gun fires a bullet horizontal to the ground. How long does it take for the bullet to strike the ground? The time depends only on the bullet's downward acceleration caused by gravity. The forward velocity has no effect on the time it takes to fall. Experiments prove this fact. The time it takes for a bullet to strike the ground when it is fired from a gun is clocked. Then the time is clocked for a bullet to strike the ground when it is dropped from the gun's muzzle. The forward velocity has no

The sights on a gun are adjusted so that a person aiming at a target actually shoots above the target to compensate for the fall of the bullet.

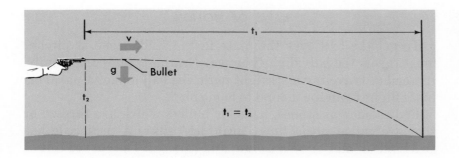

Figure 13-22. Both the fired bullet and a bullet dropped from the same height as the muzzle hit the ground at the same time.

effect on the downward velocity. The force on the bullet from the gun is horizontal and the force of gravity on the bullet is downward.

ACTIVITY. Nail the center of a 60-cm stick to the corner of an old wooden table. Be certain you have permission to put a nail in the table. The stick should be free to rotate around the nail. Set it so half the stick is over the table and half is over the floor. Place a coin on the end of the stick over the table. Place another coin on the end of the stick over the floor. With a ruler, strike sharply the end of the stick on the table. Do both coins hit the floor at the same time? How is this activity related to the path of a bullet (Figure 13–22)?

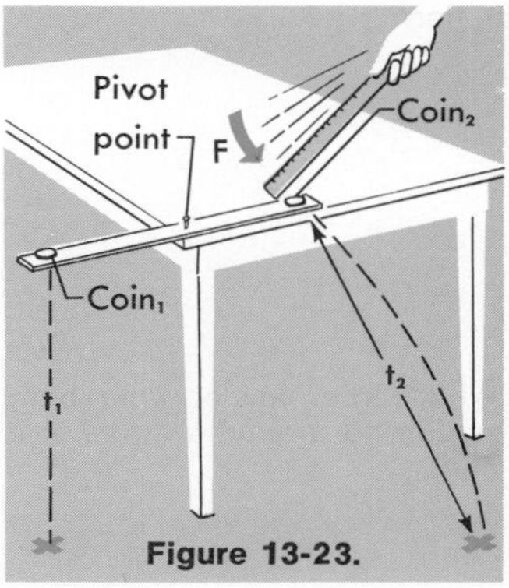

Does a pitcher throw a baseball in a straight line or in a parabola? Suppose the pitcher throws a ball horizontally 3 ft above the ground. The ball's velocity is 120 ft/sec. It takes 1/2 second for the ball to travel 60 ft from the pitcher's mound to home plate ($d = vt = 120$ ft/sec $\times$ 1/2 sec = 60 ft). During this time (1/2 sec), the ball falls 3 ft to the ground. It strikes the plate rather than passing over it. Why? Recall that you can find the distance that an object falls with the formula $d = 1/2\ gt^2$. By substituting 32 ft/sec^2 for g and 1/2 sec for t, you will find that d is equal to 4 ft.

Figure 13-23.

The inertia of the coin on the left causes it to fall off the stick when it is struck out from underneath the coin.

Can a pitcher throw a strike in a straight line?

No. The path of a pitched ball is always a parabola because the ball begins falling as soon as it leaves the pitcher's hand. Velocity of a fast ball in the major leagues averages about 100 mi/hr.

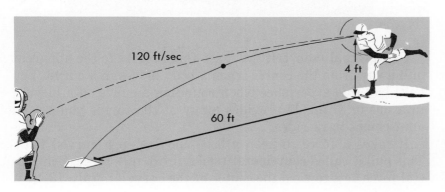

120 ft/sec

4 ft

60 ft

Figure 13-24. If a pitcher throws a ball with a velocity of 120 ft/sec, the ball is traveling 82 mi/hr!

To get the ball over the plate in the strike zone, a pitcher must throw the ball slightly upward rather than horizontally. Instead of traveling a straight path, the ball makes a parabola in its flight from the mound to home plate.

What is a projectile?

Bodies such as stones, balls, or bullets which are thrown or shot are called *projectiles* (prah jek′ tils). A projectile has two kinds of motion: *horizontal* and *vertical*. The curved line of a parabola shows the result or combination of these two motions. To hit a target you cannot throw or shoot straight at it. You must allow for the object's downward velocity caused by gravity. The paths of baseballs, footballs, bullets, arrows, and all other projectiles are explained by the laws of motion.

What are the horizontal and vertical parts of a projectile's motion?

13:7 *Motion in Curves*

What forces act on your body as you go around a curve in a car?

What kind of push or pull do you feel in a car when it rounds a sharp curve? Your body may slide toward the door. You feel as though you are being pushed outward.

Inertia forces the rider outward and centripetal force pulls the rider inward.

Figure 13-25. Inertia causes the passenger to travel in a straight line as the car curves to the left. Centripetal force of the car door is equal and opposite to the outward force of the girl.

Centrifugal force is a fictitious or imaginary force used to explain motion along a curve. Centripetal force is a real force which causes bodies to travel in a curved path.

Gravity of the sun is the centripetal force which causes planets to travel in orbits around the sun.

The earth's gravity is the centripetal force which keeps a satellite in orbit.

Centrifugal (sen trif′ ye gal) **force** refers to the apparent pull away from the center when a body moves in a curve. You have had this experience when rounding a curve on a bicycle, in a bus or train. It provides many of the thrills you get on amusement park rides.

It takes a force to keep a body moving in a curved path. This pull is called **centripetal** (sen trip′ ah tal) **force**. Centripetal force acts toward the center of the curve (Figure 13-25).

Modern highways have curves of large radius. This reduces the amount of centripetal force needed for the car to travel the curve and makes it less likely for the car to go off the outside edge.

EXPERIMENT. Do this experiment out-of-doors. Attach a strong string to a ball. Swing the ball in a circle over your head. Do you pull on the string to keep it taut? How does the force on the ball change if you swing it faster or slower? What would happen to the ball if you let go of the string? In which direction would the ball travel?

Centripetal force keeps the ball in this experiment moving in a circle as long as you are holding on to the string. As Newton's first law predicts, it will fly off in a straight path if you let go of the string. The centripetal force of the road on a car's tires pushes *inward* on a car rounding a curve. Remember, it takes a force to *change* direction and speed. If the car goes around the curve too fast, inertia may cause it to fly off the road. Highways are banked on curves to increase centripetal force. Banked means the outside edge is higher than the inside edge. Banked roads increase highway safety.

Figure 13-26.

"Crack the whip" on roller skates or ice skates involves a centripetal force on each skater in the whip. If the end skater is let go when the whip "cracks" inertia causes him to fly off in a straight line.

EXPERIMENT. Draw a large circle on the floor or ground with chalk. Place a Ping-Pong ball on the circle. Provide two students with a ruler each. Push the Ping-Pong ball around the circle by using the ends of the rulers. Make a diagram of the circle and ball on a piece of paper. Draw two arrows to show the two directions the ball is pushed to make it go around the circle. Which arrow represents centripetal force on a ball swinging in a circle?

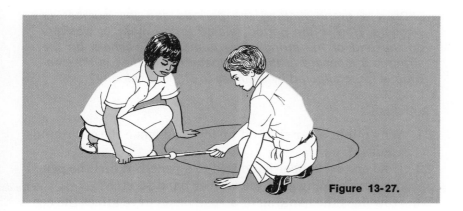

Figure 13-27.

Some automatic washing machines use circular motion. The wet clothes are spun in a circle after washing. Water flies out of the clothes through holes in the tub. The tub pushes the clothes toward the center and keeps them moving in a circle.

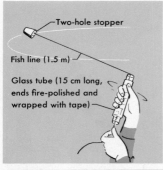

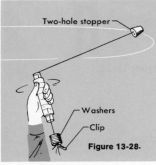

Two-hole stopper

Fish line (1.5 m)

Glass tube (15 cm long, ends fire-polished and wrapped with tape)

Two-hole stopper

Washers

Clip

Figure 13-28.

A washing machine spinning water out of clothes acts as a centrifuge. A *centrifuge* is a machine used to separate substances by spinning them. One kind of centrifuge holds test tubes containing mixtures of liquid and fine solid particles. As the test tubes spin, the solid particles sink to the bottom. Centripetal force keeps the liquid and test tube moving in a circle. When whirling a ball around your head on a string, you must pull inward to keep the ball moving. The ball tends to keep moving in a straight line due to inertia. The outward pull you feel on the string is a fictitious or imaginary force sometimes called centrifugal force. Actually, if you were to release the ball, it would travel in a straight line tangent to the circle made by the whirling stone. The inertia of the stone keeps it going in this straight line once the force is not acting on it.

EXPERIMENT. Centripetal force. (1) Arrange the apparatus shown in Figure 13–28. Hold the tube with one hand and the string with the other. Whirl the stopper over your head. (2) Repeat with six washers on the clip, but this time do not hold the string. Whirl the stopper at a rate which keeps the clip in the same position. Have a classmate measure 30 sec with a watch while you count the number of revolutions. Calculate the period of the revolutions. The time divided by the number of revolutions is the period. (3) Repeat the procedure with 3 and 9 washers. Record the periods for 3, 6, and 9 washers.

Draw a graph plotting the periods and the number of washers. How is the period related to the mass of washers on the end of the string? The number of washers on the string is a measure of the centripetal force. How is the centripetal force affected by changes in stopper velocity?

The period varies inversely as the mass of the washers. Centripetal force varies directly as the velocity.

PROBLEMS

21. Why might a car slide off an icy road when the car rounds a curve?   *See Teacher's Guide.*
22. Hold on to a rubber band tied to a pencil. Whirl the pencil in a circle. Why does the rubber band stretch? *See Teacher's Guide.*
23. How does the banking of a road on a curve affect the centripetal force which acts on a car?   *See Teacher's Guide.*

13:8   *Systems*

What is a system?

A scientific approach to understanding a system is to identify its parts and the ways in which the parts interact.

As a wristwatch ticks, a tight mainspring inside slowly unwinds. A small wheel held by a hair-thin spring rotates back and forth inside the watch. Tiny gears turn to move the hands that tell time. Potential energy stored in the wound main-spring becomes kinetic energy of the moving watch parts. Motions of moving bodies usually occur in systems. A wrist-watch is an example of a system.

A **system** is a set of related parts which we find convenient to discuss as a group. Most systems contain moving parts which make the system operate. For example, in the solar system, the planets move in orbits around the sun. Comets, asteroids, and meteors also are moving parts of the solar system. Man's circulatory system contains a heart, blood, and blood vessels. Repeated contractions of the heart pump the blood and push it through blood vessels.

Systems may be complex or simple. The solar system is a very complex system. A bicycle moving down the street is a simple system. A surfboard moving on a wave and a ball-point pen marking a piece of paper are other examples of relatively simple systems. Whenever two or more bodies interact, a system is formed. As the number of different kinds of parts in a system increases, the system becomes more complex.

Figure 13-29. A watch is a system of moving parts.

How is a complex system different from a simple system?

A bicycle is a familiar example of a system. Have students identify the parts of a bicycle (wheels, chain, gears, pedals, frame, handlebars) and explain how the parts interact.

PROBLEM

24. Name the most complex system in each of the following groups:
(a) automobile, power lawnmower, bicycle
(b) light bulb, wagon, electric vacuum cleaner
(c) wristwatch, fountain pen, box camera
(d) piano, compass, roller skates
(e) motorcycle, surfboard on wave, man-made space satellite in orbit.

EXPERIMENT. *The parts of a clock make it a system. (1) Study the parts of an old clock. Arrange them on a table in order of decreasing size and count them. How many different kinds of parts are in the clock? (2) Classify the parts into groups according to their similarities and differences; arrange each group in a separate pile. (3) Rearrange the parts, classifying them another way. Is a clock more or less complex than a pencil sharpener? Why?*   It has more parts.

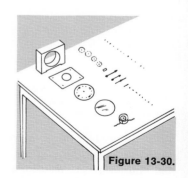

Figure 13-30.

13:9 *Momentum*

Every body in motion has **momentum** (moh men′ tum). The amount of momentum depends on mass and speed. The

How is momentum related to mass and velocity?

Figure 13-31. Huge waves give the surfer great momentum.

William Huber

more mass and speed, the greater the momentum. A baseball has more momentum than a tennis ball when they travel at the same speed. Why? The baseball has more mass. Suppose a truck and a sports car go down a freeway together at 60 mph. Which vehicle has more momentum? The truck has more momentum because it has more mass.

Why does a moving truck have more momentum than its driver?

Which has more momentum, a fast-pitch softball or a slow-pitch softball? The fast-pitch softball has more momentum

The slow pitch ball can be stopped with less force because it has the smaller momentum.

The Boeing Company

Although the pellet has a small mass its high velocity gives it a very large momentum.

Figure 13-32. A pea-sized pellet, traveling at meteoroid speeds, wrecked these sheets. The pellet punched a neat hole in the first sheet, but clouds of vaporized metal fragments tore larger holes in the next four sheets.

because of its greater speed. A bullet coming out of a rifle has more momentum than a Ping-Pong ball thrown by hand. Very high speed gives the bullet a larger momentum.

The greater the momentum of a body, the more force it takes to stop it. A body at rest has zero momentum.

A 4-ton truck moving 3 mi/hr has the same momentum as a 2-ton car moving 6 mi/hr. Doubling speed of a body doubles its momentum. If a baseball and a golf ball are both moving with the same speed, the baseball has the greater momentum because of its greater mass. To find momentum, multiply mass by velocity. Use this equation.

A pendulum illustrates the principle of momentum. The larger the mass of the pendulum the greater its momentum.

$$P = mv \qquad \begin{aligned} P &= \text{momentum} \\ m &= \text{mass} \\ v &= \text{velocity (must indicate direction)} \end{aligned}$$

An arrow above a symbol shows that it is a vector quantity (Section 12:6). Momentum is a vector quantity. It has quantity and direction.

Why is momentum a vector quantity?

Momentum is a vector quantity because it has direction and quantity.

EXAMPLE

A baseball with a mass of 0.35 kg is hit and given a forward velocity of 5 m/sec. What is its momentum?

Solution: (a) Write the equation: $P = mv$

(b) Substitute 0.35 kg for m and 5 m/sec for v

$$P = \frac{0.35 \text{ kg}}{} \left| \frac{5 \text{ m}}{\text{sec}} \right.$$

(c) Multiply 0.35 kg by 5 m

(d) Answer: $P = 1.75$ kg-m/sec forward

PROBLEMS

25. Which ball has more momentum at a forward velocity of 5 m/sec, a billiard ball or a tennis ball? Why? *The billiard ball has larger mass.*

26. A golf ball and a tennis ball of the same mass are both traveling at 10 m/sec. Compare the momentum.

The momentum of the golf ball is greater.

13:10   *Impulse*

Momentum of a body may be changed in two ways. First, the size of the force producing the motion may be increased or decreased. Second, the amount of time in which the force acts may be increased or decreased. The product of the force multiplied by the time the force acts on the body is called **impulse.** Impulse $= f \times t$.

How can the momentum of a body be increased or decreased?

Changing the size of the force or the time the force acts changes the momentum.

When you hit a tennis ball or a golf ball, you exert a large force for a short time. The size of the impulse and the momentum of the ball depend primarily upon how hard you hit the ball. A baseball batter may increase the time during which his bat exerts force on the baseball by following through with his swing. In so doing, he increases the impulse and imparts to the hit ball a higher velocity and greater momentum.

A given impulse can be produced by a large force acting for a short time or by a small force acting for a long time. For example, an ion engine for use in spacecraft can produce a large impulse with a tiny force. An ion engine is propelled by the reaction force from a stream of ions (charged atoms). The ions come from cesium metal electrically heated to 1,200°C.

In theory, an ion engine could accelerate a spacecraft to speeds close to the speed of light, 186,000 mi/sec. Tremendous speed would be produced by the small force of the ion engine acting over a long period of time. The engine would be used in outer space on a long voyage. No air friction would oppose its motion. However, a spacecraft powered by an ion engine must be lifted into space by a rocket engine. An ion engine does not produce a force large enough to overcome the gravitational attraction of the earth.

Rocket fuels are rated by their specific impulse. Fuels which burn rapidly and produce a large force (thrust) have a high specific impulse.

Figure 13-33. The two ion engines shown here are used in experimental tests. They develop power by producing a stream of charged atoms.

NASA

Specific impulse is a measure of fuel efficiency. The larger the specific impulse the greater the fuel efficiency. Specific impulse has much the same meaning for a rocket engineer as miles per gallon has for a motorist.

$$\text{specific impulse (sec)} = \frac{\text{thrust (lb)} \times \text{burning time (sec)}}{\text{weight of propellant (lb)}}$$

Table 13–1.   Specific Impulses of Selected Fuels

Fuel	Oxidizer	Specific Impulse	Temp. (°C)
Octane	Hydrogen Peroxide	230	2,200
Hydrazine	Hydrogen Peroxide	280	2,400
Liq. Hydrogen	Liq. Oxygen	375	2,300
Gasoline	Liq. Oxygen	242	2,950
Ethyl Alcohol	Liq. Oxygen	240	2,900
Octane	Liq. Oxygen	248	3,000
Hydrazine	Liq. Oxygen	259	2,400

13:11   Conservation of Momentum

A boy with 60 kg mass and a girl with 40 kg mass face each other on roller skates. The girl pushes against the boy and they roll away in opposite directions. They both have momentum. One force (the girl) produced the motion of both of them so their momentum must be equal. The girl moves faster

Figure 13-34. When two bodies interact, the change in momentum (mv) of one body is always equal and opposite to the change in momentum of the other body.

Collisions between swinging pendulums illustrate conservation of momemtum.

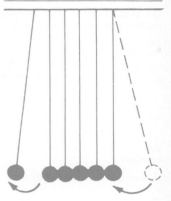

because of her lighter mass. Their momentum is found by multiplying mass times velocity. The velocity of the boy is 0.2 m/sec to the left. The velocity of the girl is 0.3 m/sec to the right. To find momentum for the boy and girl use the equation $P = mv$.

Girl: $P = mv$

$$P = \frac{40 \text{ kg} \mid 0.3 \text{ m}}{\text{sec}}$$

$$P = -12 \text{ kg-m/sec}$$

Boy: $P = mv$

$$P = \frac{60 \text{ kg} \mid 0.2 \text{ m}}{\text{sec}}$$

$$P = +12 \text{ kg-m/sec}$$

The momentum of the girl is opposite to the momentum of the boy. Therefore, a positive sign (+) is assigned to one answer. A negative sign (—) is assigned to the other answer. The sum of +12 kg-m/sec and —12 kg-m/sec is zero. There is no net increase in momentum!

When two people at rest push against each other, they move in opposite directions. The person with the larger mass will move with the smaller velocity. However, the momentum for the two persons will be equal and opposite. Thus, the net change in momentum will be zero.

A collision between two bodies is an example of a system. Scientists often use an equation to represent a system. The equation for a collision is:

$$m_1 v_1 + m_2 v_2 = 0$$

Can the total momentum of a system be increased?

Momentum may be transferred from one object to another. But total momentum is never increased.

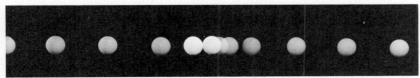

Figure 13-35. Momentum is conserved when one billiard ball strikes another.

In this equation, m_1v_1 represents the momentum of the first body. The momentum of the second body is represented by m_2v_2. Because the bodies move in opposite directions, one momentum is assigned a positive value. The other is assigned a negative value. The total momentum of the two bodies is zero.

Do billiard balls gain or lose momentum when they collide?

Both. A moving billiard ball which decreases in velocity loses in momentum. A billiard ball which gains velocity also gains momentum.

Suppose two rolling billiard balls collide. Each billiard ball has momentum before and after the collision, but the total momentum within the system does not change. The velocities of the billiard balls may change. If one speed increases, the other speed must decrease as momentum is conserved. The total momentum for the two balls before and after collision is the same. The total change in momentum as a result of the collision is zero.

Explain conservation of momentum.

When a rifle is fired the bullet is pushed out in one direction and the rifle kicks back in the other direction. The momentum of the bullet and rifle are equal and opposite.

Roller skaters and billiard balls are examples of **conservation of momentum.** This principle states that momentum cannot be created or destroyed. In a system, whenever one body gains momentum, another body loses momentum. Scientists believe that the amount of momentum in the solar system and in the universe never changes. Thus, the amount of momentum in the universe today is the same as it was a million years ago.

MAIN IDEAS

p. 264   **1.** Inertia is the tendency of a body at rest to remain at rest. It is also the tendency of a body in motion to remain in motion.

p. 265   **2.** It takes a force to start a body moving and a force to stop motion. It also takes a force to *change* the speed or direction of an object.

p. 266   **3.** Rate of acceleration and deceleration depends on the amount of force and mass of a body. $F = ma$

p. 268   **4.** For every force (action) there is an equal and opposite force (reaction).

p. 265   **5.** Newton's laws explain how forces and motion are related.

p. 272   **6.** Bodies near the earth's surface fall at a uniform rate of acceleration, 9.8 m/sec² or 32 ft/sec²; $d = \frac{1}{2} gt^2$.

p. 274   **7.** A body thrown straight up decelerates in flight at a uniform rate of 9.8 m/sec² or 32 ft/sec².

p. 275   **8.** A projectile in flight travels in a curved path. The projectile's velocity has a horizontal and a vertical component.

p. 278   **9.** Centripetal force acts inward on a body moving in a curve.

p. 278 **10.** The apparent outward force on a body moving in a curve is called centrifugal force.

p. 280 **11.** Our environment may be organized into systems. Systems range from the simple to the very complex.

p. 281 **12.** Every moving body has momentum which is equal to its mass × velocity (*mv*). Momentum within a system can neither be created nor destroyed.

p. 283 **13.** Impulse imparts momentum to an object. Impulse is found by multiplying the applied force and the time the force acts. Impulse = $F \times t$.

VOCABULARY

Write a sentence in which you correctly use each of the following words or terms.

acceleration	gravity	parabola
action force	horizontal	projectile
centripetal force	impulse	reaction force
deceleration	inertia	system
	momentum	

STUDY QUESTIONS

A. True or False   *Have students rewrite false statements to make the statements correct.*

Determine whether each of the following sentences is true or false. (Do not write in this book.)

T **1.** A force is needed to stop a moving body.

T **2.** Acceleration is always caused by a force.

F **3.** It takes ~~the same~~ force to accelerate ~~both a~~ golf ball ~~and~~ baseball from rest to a speed of 50 ft/sec.   *greater, than a*

T **4.** Reaction force is equal and opposite to the action force.

F **5.** ~~Inertia~~ makes a rotary sprinkler spin.   *Action-reaction forces*

F **6.** A hypothesis is always correct.   *not*

T **7.** A falling body accelerates at a rate of 32 ft/sec².

F **8.** To hit a distant target, a gun barrel is aimed ~~directly at~~ the target.   *above*

T **9.** Centripetal force increases as a merry-go-round increases speed.

F **10.** Two billiard balls both ~~gain~~ momentum when they strike. *change*

B.   Multiple Choice   *Some questions in part B may have more than one correct answer. Only one answer is required.*

Choose one word or phrase that correctly completes each of the following sentences. (Do not write in this book.)

1. Force is measured with a (ruler, <u>balance</u>, meter stick, graduated cylinder).

2. It takes (<u>more</u>, less, the same) force to accelerate a car as it does to keep it at constant velocity.

3. A rocket accelerates because of (<u>action-reaction</u>, inertia, centripetal) force.

4. The masses of a bowling ball and a golf ball are (<u>different</u>, the same, both 5 kg, both 5 g).

5. $d \propto t^2$ means that d is (equal to, less than, greater than, <u>proportional to</u>) t^2.

6. A hypothesis is a(n) (fact, law, <u>educated guess</u>, discarded theory).

7. When an object falls, its acceleration is (9.8 m/sec, <u>9.8 m/sec^2</u>, 32 m/sec, 9.8 ft/sec^2).

8. A projectile's path is a (circle, straight line, <u>parabola</u>).

9. According to Newton's first law, every object has (motion, velocity, acceleration, <u>inertia</u>).

C.   Completion

Complete each of the following sentences with a word or phrase that will make the sentence correct. (Do not write in this book.)

increases

1. The size of a centripetal force __?__ when the radius of the circle decreases.

newton, pound

2. A(n) __?__ is a unit of force.

gravity

3. The attractive force between two bodies is called __?__.

reaction

4. For every action force there is an equal and opposite __?__ force.

vertical

5. A projectile in flight has two motions: horizontal and __?__.

0

6. At the top of its rise, the upward velocity of a ball thrown up into the air is __?__ ft/sec.

increases

7. As a body falls, its downward velocity __?__.

acceleration

8. As a body falls, its rate of __?__ does not change.

time

9. Impulse becomes greater if there is an increase in the amount of __?__ a force acts.

D. How and Why

1. Give examples of inertia. How can inertia cause an accident? *See Teacher's Guide.*

2. Which of Newton's laws of motion applies to each case?
    (a) it takes more push to start a car moving than to keep it rolling *first*
    (b) rocket engine *third*
    (c) drag chute on a racing car *second*
    (d) a boy dives off a skateboard and each goes in an opposite direction *third*

3. An airplane loses a wheel while in flight. What is the vertical speed of the wheel after it falls for 3 sec? *29.4 m/sec or 96 ft/sec*

4. How can you use a falling stone to judge the height of a bridge? *See Teacher's Guide.*

5. A girl throws a ball upward with an initial velocity of 32 ft/sec. How long will it take for the ball to reach zero velocity? *1 sec*

6. Why is the path of a projectile a parabola? *The resultant of the horizontal and vertical motion is a parabola.*

7. In shooting an arrow, Robin Hood had to aim at a mark above his target. Explain. *Gravity causes the arrow to follow a parabolic path. Thus, an arrow aimed directly at the bullseye would strike below that mark.*

INVESTIGATION

See Teacher's Guide at the front of the book for answers and suggestions.

Investigate the use of a systems approach to solving problems such as pollution.

INTERESTING READING

Basford, Leslie, *The Science of Movement: Foundations of Mechanics and Sound.* London, Sampson, Low, Marston & Company, 1966.

Fermi, Laura, and Bernardini, Gilberto, *Galileo and the Scientific Revolution.* New York, Fawcett World Library, 1965.

Fisher, S. H., *Table Top Science: Physics for Everyone.* Garden City, New York, Natural History Press, 1972.

Helman, Hal, *Energy and Inertia.* New York, Lippincott and Co., 1970.

Valens, Evans G., *Motion.* Cleveland, World Publishing Company, 1965.

Energy

We have actually touched the borderland where matter and force seem to merge . . . the greatest scientific problems of the future will find their solution in this borderland, and even beyond . . .

William Crookes (1832-1919)

Energy exists in different forms: kinetic, heat, light, sound, electrical, chemical, and nuclear. Energy can be changed from one form to another. For example, light from an electric lamp can be changed into heat. Under special conditions, matter can be converted into energy. Energy can be converted into matter. The relationship between matter and energy is given in the equation, $E = mc^2$. Energy is equal to mass times the speed of light, squared.

Early scientists believed that heat was fluid and light was composed of particles. These theories proved inadequate. They failed to account for many properties of heat and light. Light behaves as a wave and as a particle. Modern theory proposes that light and all other forms of radiant energy consist of waves. A particle of matter in motion has an associated wave. Waves travel from one place to another. Radiant energy waves travel easily through a vacuum. For example, the sun's energy travels 93 million miles through space from the sun to the earth. A tiny fraction of the sun's energy has been stored in fuels such as oil, natural gas, and coal. All the energy on earth today originally came from the sun. What part will you play in our energy needs now and in the future?

unit
six

Heat Energy

GOAL: You will gain an understanding of kinetic energy and relationships between heat and kinetic energy.

Rub two sticks together and you can feel them become warm. Hammer a nail into wood. The nail gets so hot it may burn your fingers.

ACTIVITY. Hold a small round stick between your hands. Rotate the stick rapidly by moving your hands. Does the temperature of the stick change? Hammer a nail into a block of wood a short distance. With the claw of the hammer bend the nail back and forth a few times. Now carefully touch the nail with your finger. Is the nail cooler or warmer than before? Take a rubber band and stretch it back and forth rapidly for one minute. Does the band feel warmer or cooler than before you stretched it? Rubber becomes warmer as it is stretched repeatedly.

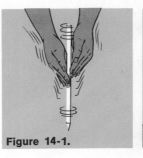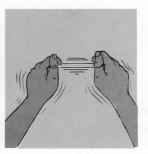

Figure 14-1.

Man gets heat from a variety of sources. The primary sources are chemical changes such as burning, nuclear reactions, electricity, and the sun. The sun's surface is about 2800°C (6000°F). Inside the center of the sun it is about 22,000,000°C (40,000,000°F). Only two-billionths of the sun's heat reaches the earth. The rest goes off into space.

Heat is used to keep us warm, cook food, produce light, and run engines. Most heated homes have a temperature about

25°C (72°F) during the winter. An automobile engine runs at about 70°C (160°F). An electric stove can cook food at 260°C (500°F). The filament in a lighted light bulb is about 1500°C (3000°F) when the bulb is "on."

14:1 *Kinetic and Potential Energy*

All moving bodies have *kinetic* (ki net′ ik) *energy*. A swinging pendulum, a soaring rocket, your beating heart, running water, and moving air are examples of bodies with kinetic energy. **Kinetic energy** is energy of motion. Mechanical energy is another name for kinetic energy.

Define kinetic energy.

PROBLEM

1. Name five other examples of bodies that have kinetic energy. *Answers will vary, motion must be involved.*

Potential energy is energy of rest or energy of position. Potential energy is sometimes called stored energy. This means that the energy is inactive at the moment but has the potential for doing work. For example, water at the top of a dam has potential energy. As the water falls over the dam, its potential energy becomes kinetic energy. Falling water has kinetic energy.

ACTIVITY.   *Place a book on a desk top. Raise the book about 20 centimeters into the air. By raising the book you increase its potential energy. Let the book drop. Does the book gain or lose potential energy? Why?* *Potential energy changed to kinetic energy.*

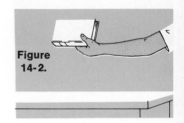

Figure 14-2.

Potential energy can be changed to kinetic energy. Kinetic energy can be changed to potential energy. Under ordinary conditions energy is never created or destroyed. What becomes of a falling book's kinetic energy? Some of it becomes the sound you hear when it strikes the desk. The rest is changed to heat energy.

Lying on the ground, a hammer does not have potential energy. However, if the hammer is raised to a height of 10 feet, energy must be added to overcome the force of gravity. The hammer gains potential energy, or energy of position. As the hammer is moved upward, its potential energy increases. The higher it is raised, the greater its potential energy. A hammer has more potential energy at 20 ft height than at

Figure 14-3. The heat energy from this fire cooks food and keeps the campers warm.

Figure 14-4. Running water in a stream has kinetic energy.

10 feet. If the hammer is dropped, it falls swiftly to the ground. Its potential energy decreases. As the hammer is raised, work is done on it and stored as potential energy. When the hammer is dropped, this work is released in the form of kinetic energy.

PROBLEM

2. Here are examples of potential energy. Explain how each changes to kinetic energy.
   (a) wound watch   *Flexed steel spring unwinds.*
   (b) stretched rubber band   *Energy used to stretch rubber band is released.*
   (c) camera shutter   *Energy stored in spring, released.*
   (d) inflated balloon   *Muscles force air into balloon.*
   (e) swimmer on a diving board   *Swimmer jumps into air, gaining height.*
   (f) kitchen match   *Chemical energy stored in bonds.*

EXPERIMENT. Is heat produced from kinetic energy? Obtain two paper drinking cups. Fill one cup one-third full of dry sand at room temperature. Place the end of a thermometer in the sand and record the temperature. Now invert the second cup over the first cup. Seal with a piece of tape. Shake the sand back and forth inside the cups for 10 minutes. Punch a hole in the top of the cup. Insert the thermometer. Record the temperature again. Why is there a change in temperature? *Kinetic energy of the shaking sand is changed to heat energy.*

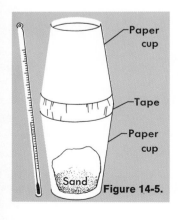

Paper cup

Tape

Paper cup

Sand   Figure 14-5.

14:2 Radiation, Conduction, and Convection

Energy can be changed from one form to another. All forms of energy can be changed to *heat energy*. **Heat** is a form of kinetic energy within a substance. Heat travels from areas of higher temperature to areas of lower temperature.

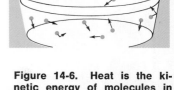

EXPERIMENT. Place some hot water in a large beaker and some cold water in a small beaker. Place a thermometer in each beaker. Record the two temperatures. Then set the small beaker inside the large beaker. Check both water temperatures after ten minutes. What is the final temperature in each beaker? Which way does the heat travel?

Heat travels from the hot to the cold water.

Figure 14-6. Heat is the kinetic energy of molecules in motion. Molecules evaporating from the liquid's surface travel fast enough to overcome the attractive forces of surrounding molecules.

Why is heat a form of kinetic energy?

Heat is the kinetic energy of molecules.

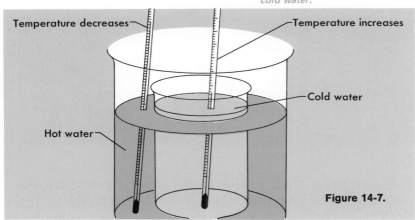

Temperature decreases

Temperature increases

Cold water

Hot water

Figure 14-7.

All molecules do not vibrate at the same rate.

Suppose you take cold lemonade from a refrigerator and want to keep it cold. If you leave the lemonade on a table, it will warm up. You can put a cold drink in a vacuum bottle and keep it cold for several hours. A vacuum bottle can also be used to keep things hot. For example, hot chocolate or soup stays hot in a vacuum bottle for several hours.

How does a vacuum bottle keep things hot or cold?

It prevents heat from easily moving in and/or out of the bottle.

Carl England

Figure 14-8. Vacuum bottles allow these students to have cold milk or hot soup for lunch.

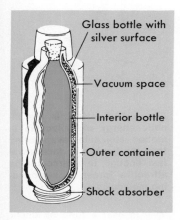

Glass bottle with silver surface

Vacuum space

Interior bottle

Outer container

Shock absorber

Figure 14-9. The vacuum in a vacuum bottle helps prevent exchange of heat between the inside and the outside of the bottle.

EXPERIMENT. Obtain a pint-size vacuum bottle and three pint-size, clear glass bottles. Cover one bottle with aluminum foil, shiny side inward. Cover the second bottle with aluminum foil, shiny side out. Leave the third bottle uncovered. Heat 3 pints of water to boiling. Fill each bottle two-thirds full with hot water. Then put a thermometer in each bottle and record the temperatures. Allow each to stand for 30 minutes. Observe the temperature of the water in the three containers every 5 minutes. Record your data in a chart or graph. Which water cools fastest? Uncovered jar cools fastest, jar with foil inward cools slowest.

Figure 14-10.

Water cools in all bottles in the experiment above. As it cools, the water loses heat. Heat is lost fastest in the clear bottle. There is little change of temperature in the vacuum bottle. The aluminum foil around the glass bottle prevents heat loss. So does the metal coating of the vacuum bottle. The vacuum between the two walls of a vacuum bottle also reduces heat loss.

Heat travels by *radiation* (rae dee ae′ shun), *conduction* (kan duck′ shun), and *convection* (kan vek′ shun). A useful model for **radiation** consists of rays which go from areas of high temperature to areas of low temperature. Heat can travel through a vacuum by radiation. Radiated heat energy is reflected by smooth surfaces such as aluminum foil and other shiny metals. The silver coating on a vacuum bottle reflects heat radiation back into the bottle. It also reflects heat rays that strike the bottle from the outside. Reflection of radiated heat energy by the metal coating reduces the movement of heat in and out of the vacuum bottle.

Figure 14-11. An electric lamp gives off radiant energy in the form of light and heat.

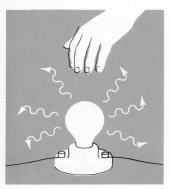

PROBLEMS

3. Name three things that emit heat by radiation.
4. In each example for Problem 3, tell how the radiation could be reduced or stopped. *Answers will vary.*

Conduction occurs when heat travels through a substance. In a vacuum, no matter is present. There is no conduction through a vacuum. Conduction can occur only through a substance—liquid, gas, or solid. The vacuum in a vacuum bottle is a partial vacuum. Partial vacuum means that most but not all of the air is removed. The partial vacuum in a vacuum bottle cuts down on heat loss by conduction. Some heat may still enter or leave the vacuum bottle. It is conducted through the remaining air. But the heat conduction is small.

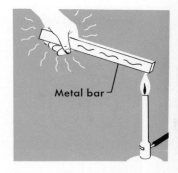

Figure 14-12. How does heat travel through the metal bar to the hand?

ACTIVITY. Push one end of a metal knitting needle into a cork. Use the cork as a handle. Place tiny pieces of wax one inch apart on the needle. Light a candle and hold the free end of the needle in the candle. Continue heating only the end of the needle until all wax pieces drop off. How long did it take for all the wax to melt? Try to repeat this experiment using a glass rod instead of a metal knitting needle. Compare the conduction in the metal needle with that of the glass rod. metal conducts heat faster

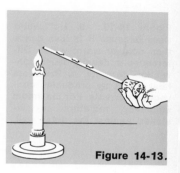

Figure 14-13.

A material through which heat passes easily is called a *conductor*. Heat travels only slowly through insulators. *Insulators* are materials used to reduce heat transfer. What is the function of the cork in this experiment?

PROBLEMS

5. What is the conductor and insulator in the activity? metal   glass
6. List 3 heat conductors and 3 heat insulators used in homes. Answers will vary.
7. Why is aluminum foil used as an insulator in many buildings? It prevents radiation of heat

ACTIVITY. Fill a beaker about two-thirds full of water. Place it on a ring stand. Add a drop of food coloring to the water. Do not stir. Be very careful not to disturb the water in the beaker. Gently heat the beaker and water. Record what you observe. Color moves by convection currents throughout water.

Convection is heat transfer in liquids and gases. When liquids or gases are heated they decrease in density. The less dense part rises in the fluid causing currents that carry heat through the material. For example, the heat from a flame can warm the bottom of a pot of water. Water at the bottom of the

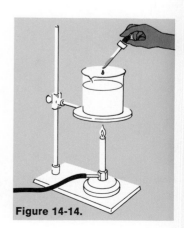

Figure 14-14.

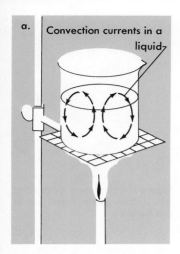

a. Convection currents in a liquid

b. Convection currents in a gas

Figure 14-15. a. Hot water rises because it is less dense than cold or warm water. Differences in density cause convection currents. b. Radiators heat rooms by producing convection currents. For maximum efficiency, radiators are installed against the outer wall.

Conduction, convection, radiation

Silver walls reflect radiation, vacuum prevents conduction, convection.

pot becomes hot and decreases in density. This lighter water floats upward through the water above and carries heat with it. Winds in the atmosphere and currents in the oceans are caused by convection.

PROBLEMS

8. Some rooms are heated by radiators. In what ways is heat transferred in warming the room?
9. Why is little heat lost by convection in a vacuum bottle?
10. Which way will convection currents flow in the equipment pictured in Figure 14–15?

(a) Hot water rises because it is less dense. (b) Warm air rises, convection current warms room.

14:3 Measuring Heat

The amount of heat energy in a body depends on both the temperature and the mass of the body. A swimming pool full of water has heat energy. So does a dishpan full of water. At the same temperature, the pool has more heat than the dishpan. This is because the water in the pool has a greater mass than the water in the dishpan. Which would lose the most heat if cooled from 30°C to 0°C?

Heat is measured in calories. One *calorie* (kal'oh ree) is the amount of heat needed to raise the temperature of one gram of water one Celsius degree. One ml of water has a mass of 1 g.

How are calories calculated?

To raise the temperature of 10 g of water 1°C, you must add 10 calories of heat to the water. To find the number of calories, multiply the change in temperature by the mass in grams. Use this equation:

$$H = (t_2 - t_1) m$$

H = heat
t_2 = final temperature
t_1 = beginning temperature
m = mass

Suppose the temperature of 4 grams of water is raised from 20°C to 25°C. The heat added is 20 calories.

$$H = (t_2 - t_1)\ m$$
$$H = (25° - 20°) \times 4\ g$$
$$H = 20\ \text{calories}$$

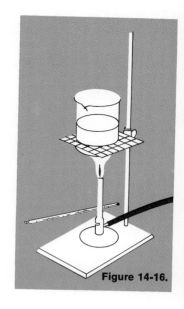

Figure 14-16.

EXPERIMENT. *How much heat is produced by a Bunsen flame in one minute? Weigh 100 g of water (room temperature) in a 250-ml beaker. Measure and record the temperature. Heat the water with a Bunsen flame for one minute. Remove the flame and measure the water temperature again. Calculate the calories of heat [H = m × (t₂ — t₁)] gained by the water. Would the calories of heat produced by the Bunsen burner be different if there were 200 g of water in the beaker?* How is the size of the Bunsen burner flame related to the calories of heat produced?

no

The larger the flame, the more calories of heat produced.

Heat energy is measured with an instrument called a *calorimeter* (kal ah rim′ et er) (Figure 14–17). For example, the heat value for a food may be found by burning it in the inner chamber of a calorimeter. Heat produced in the inner chamber is transferred to the water in the outer chamber. This heat gain causes an increase in water temperature. The amount of temperature increase is read on the thermometer. Heat gained by the water is equal to the change in tempera-

Water is used to measure heat because it is inexpensive, abundant, a good heat absorber, and its mass is easily determined. Heat = mass × temperature change. Calories = g × C°. Strictly speaking, in order for the units to be correct, the right hand side of the equation should be multiplied by the specific heat in cal/g—C°. However, since the specific heat of water is 1 cal/g—C°, this will be omitted to simplify calculations.

Specific heat is the amount of heat lost or gained by a unit mass of substance for each degree change in temperature.

Substance	Specific Heat (cal/g—C°)
water	1
aluminum	.225
copper	.0939
iron	.11

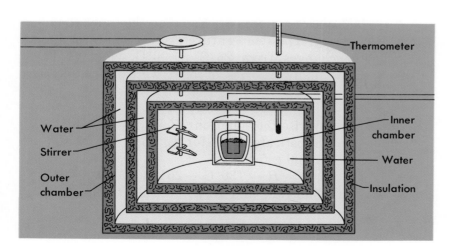

Figure 14-17. Calorimeters are used to measure the heat value of foods and fuels.

ture multiplied by the water's mass. Amount of heat gained by the water is the amount of heat produced from the food.

PROBLEM

11. Why must a calorimeter be insulated?   *So that all heat is accounted for and does not escape.*

ACTIVITY. *Make a simple calorimeter. Use two clean cans (size number 2½ and number 1). Cover the small can with rock wool or glass wool. Fit it into the large can. Make a cover for the can out of a piece of wood. Drill two holes in the center of the cover. One hole is for a piece of ¼" dowel to be used as a stirrer. The other hole is for a thermometer. Heat 100 g of water to 50°C. Place the water in the inner can. Insert the stirrer and thermometer. Wait 10 minutes then record the water temperature. Add two ice cubes to the inner can. Cover and stir until the ice cubes are melted. Record the temperature of the water again. From the weight of the water and change in water temperature, estimate the heat it took to melt the ice.* *H = 100g × temperature change*

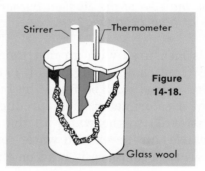

Stirrer   Thermometer

Figure 14-18.

Glass wool

EXAMPLE

A student places a piece of hot steel in the inner chamber of a calorimeter. The temperature of 1 kg of water in the calorimeter changes from 25°C to 30°C. Note: 1 kg = 1000 g. How many calories of heat were gained by the water?

Solution: (a) Write the equation: $H = (t_2 - t_1)\ m$

(b) Substitute 30°C for t_2, 25°C for t_1 and 1,000 g for m:
$$H = (30°C - 25°C)\ 1,000\ g$$

(c) Subtract and then multiply to find the answer: $H = 5C° \times 1,000\ g$

(d) Answer: 5,000 calories

PROBLEMS

12. How much heat was lost by the metal in the preceding example, excluding heat left in the inner chamber? *5000 calories*

13. A kettle containing 500 g of water is heated from 25°C to 100°C. How much heat is added to the water? *37,500 calories*

14. A baby bottle containing 20 g of water at 60°C is cooled to 40°C. How much heat is lost by the water? *400 calories*

14:4   *Joule's Experiment*

James Joule (1818-1889), an English scientist, showed that work can produce heat. Joule measured heat in British thermal units. One *British thermal unit* (B.T.U.) is the amount of heat required to raise the temperature of one pound of water one Fahrenheit degree.

Joule wound a rope on a pulley and attached the pulley to the paddles of a churn filled with water. Then he hung a weight on the rope and let the weight fall from the top of a

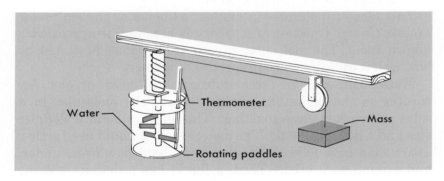

Figure 14-19. By measuring the temperature before and after the experiment, Joule proved that work produces heat.

What did Joule find out about heat?

A certain amount of work always produces a certain amount of heat.

cliff. As the weight fell, the paddles rotated rapidly and stirred the water in the churn. The kinetic energy of the moving paddles heated the water. Joule measured the temperature of the water before and after the weight fell. Knowing the mass of the water, Joule calculated the B.T.U.'s of heat gained by the water.

Joule also measured the distance the weight fell. Multiplying weight in pounds by distance in feet, he calculated the work done by the falling weight. This was the same as the work done by the paddles. Work is force exerted through a distance.

The work required to produce 1 B.T.U. of heat is called the *mechanical equivalent of heat*. Joule figured the mechanical equivalent of heat to be 778 ft-lb of work. That is, 778 ft-lb produces one B.T.U. B.T.U. is the heat unit used in engineering. It is the unit used in measuring heat loss or gain for air conditioners and heating systems.

PROBLEMS

15. Find the B.T.U. rating of your school furnace and home furnace. Compare the figures.   *Answers will vary.*
16. How many B.T.U.'s equal one calorie?   *1 cal = 0.004 B.T.U.*

14:5   *Molecular Kinetic Energy*

Explain the molecular kinetic theory.

All matter is composed of tiny particles called molecules. These molecules are in constant motion. This is true even for solids. In solids and liquids, molecules vibrate back and forth. In gases, they fly about in random motion. Since the molecules are in motion, they have kinetic energy. It is a special kind called **molecular kinetic energy.** The molecular kinetic energy in a substance is measured as heat.

This idea of molecules in motion is known as the *molecular kinetic theory.* One test of a theory is how well it agrees with known facts. The molecular kinetic theory may be tested by how well it explains some properties of matter.

How does the molecular kinetic theory explain the properties of liquids, gases, and solids?

Matter can exist in three states: *solid, liquid,* or *gas.* According to the molecular kinetic theory, the molecules in a solid are packed close together. This gives a **solid** a definite size and a definite shape. The molecules in a liquid are farther apart than in a solid. Molecules in a liquid flow over, under, and around each other. Thus, a **liquid** has a definite volume but no definite shape. A liquid takes the shape of its container. The molecules in a gas are farther apart than in a solid or liquid. They have a rapid, random motion. A **gas** has no definite volume or shape. A gas takes the size and shape of its container. It can expand or be compressed.

How does the molecular kinetic theory explain temperature and expansion?

When heat is added to a body, its temperature goes up. The heat energy becomes molecular kinetic energy within the body. As a body gains heat, its molecules vibrate faster and faster. As a body loses heat, its molecules vibrate more slowly.

For example, when a balloon is heated it expands. Why? Because the air molecules gain kinetic energy and move faster striking the sides of the balloon harder and making it expand. You may have opened a glass jar with a tight metal lid by placing the lid under hot water. Metal is a better conductor of heat than glass. The metal lid gains molecular kinetic energy and expands. The lid is loosened.

Substances contract when they cool. This is because their molecules vibrate more slowly and move closer together. Substances expand when heated. Their molecules move farther apart.

EXPERIMENT. Take a ring which just fits your finger. Place in the refrigerator for a few hours. Then try it on. Warm the ring in your hand for a few minutes. How does the ring fit your finger now? Why? When cooled the loss of heat slows down the molecules in the ring. The molecules move closer together and the ring contracts. It becomes difficult to get back on your finger.

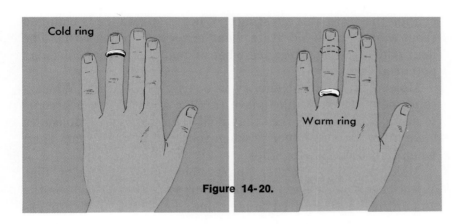

Cold ring

Warm ring

Figure 14-20.

ACTIVITY. An iron ball and ring like those in Figure 14–21 can show how solids expand. Pass the ball through the ring. Heat the ball over a flame for 10 minutes. Try to pass the heated ball through the ring. What do you observe? How did heating affect the ball? Allow the ball to cool completely. Again try to pass the ball through the ring. Explain what you observe. Heat causes expansion and ball will not fit.

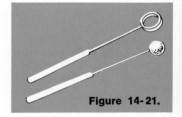

Figure 14-21.

Temperature tells how hot or cold something is compared to other things around it. Your body is warm, about 38.1°C (98.6°F), compared to room temperature. Snow is cold, 0°C (32°F) or less. According to molecular kinetic theory, temperature is the average kinetic energy of molecules in a body or substance. Each molecule has kinetic energy. But the speed of the molecules differ. Some vibrate faster than others. Therefore, the kinetic energy for each molecule in a body is not the

How is temperature different from heat?

Temperature refers to the average kinetic energy of molecules in a substance. Heat is kinetic energy of molecules. Temperature indicates the direction in which heat travels.

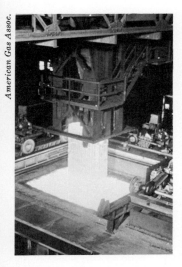

Figure 14-22. Steel is re-heated at temperatures of about 400°F to reduce brittleness.

What happens to molecules in melting and evaporation?

molecules move farther apart

Figure 14-23.   a. Water at 0°C has 80 cal/g more heat than ice has at 0°C. b. Which has the larger volume, the ice cube or the water?

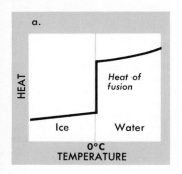

same. *Average molecular kinetic energy* is the total energy for all molecules divided by the number of molecules. If heat is added to a body, the temperature increases. Average molecular kinetic energy increases. What happens to temperature when average kinetic energy per molecule decreases?

14:6   *Melting and Vaporization*

Ice cubes melt if you leave them at room temperature. When a piece of chocolate candy is left in the sun too long, it melts. Heat energy causes substances to melt.

Melting is a change from solid to liquid. How is melting explained by the molecular kinetic theory? When a solid melts, its molecules do not gain kinetic energy. No change in temperature occurs. Then why is heat needed? It takes energy to change the state of a substance. When a substance is changed from a solid to liquid state, heat energy is added to it. The heat added to the substance when it melts becomes molecular potential energy.

Molecular potential energy is energy of position. When a solid melts, its molecules move farther apart. They overcome to some extent the forces that hold them together. Molecules have more potential energy when they are farther apart than when they are close together.

Molecules move farther apart when an object melts. The object gains molecular potential energy. *Heat of fusion* is the amount of heat required to melt one gram of a solid. For example, the heat of fusion for ice is 80 cal/g. When one gram of ice melts, the ice gains 80 calories. Yet no increase in temperature occurs. When one gram of water freezes, the water loses 80 calories. Yet no decrease in temperature occurs. In melting and *freezing*, there is a gain or loss of potential energy. There is no gain or loss of kinetic energy.

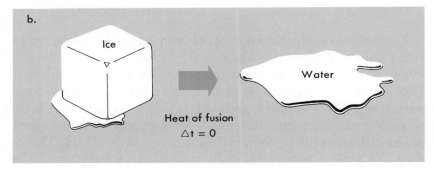

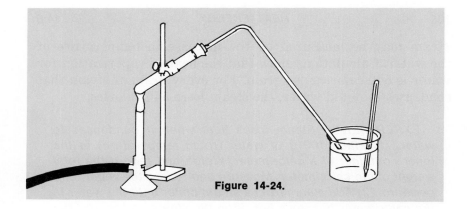

Figure 14-24.

EXPERIMENT. Fill a large test tube one-third full of water and attach a rubber stopper containing a 45-cm delivery tube. CAUTION: Follow your teacher's directions for inserting the tube into the rubber stopper. Support the test tube in a slanted position with a ring stand and test tube clamp. Set the end of the delivery tube in a small beaker full of water. Put a thermometer in the beaker and record the temperature.

Heat the water in the test tube to boiling. Keep it boiling slowly *until you get steam coming through the delivery tube for several minutes. Note any change in temperature. Then remove the delivery tube from the water. Stop heating. Does the temperature of the water change? How?* Does the amount of heat in the water change? How? *What change in your equipment would be needed if you wanted to measure the heat gained by the water?* need to find mass of water

lowers
loses heat

Vaporization (vay puhr ih zay' shun) is a change from a liquid to a gas. After reaching its boiling point, a liquid gains more heat as it vaporizes. For example, water gains 540 cal/g when it boils. A liquid's temperature does not increase when it changes to a gas. Its molecules do not gain kinetic energy. They gain potential energy. The molecules in a gas are farther apart than the molecules in a liquid. Heat added to the liquid becomes molecular potential energy of the gas molecules.

Condensation (kon den zae' shun) is a change from a gas to a liquid. When a gas condenses to form a liquid, it loses heat. But it does not decrease in temperature. The lost heat results from a decrease in the molecular potential energy of the gas as it becomes a liquid.

What happens to molecules in freezing and condensation?

molecules move closer together

The amount of heat required to change one gram of liquid to a gas is called the *heat of vaporization* (vay puhr ih zay' shun). To measure heat of vaporization, steam is passed through water in a calorimeter. Heat lost by the condensing

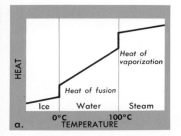

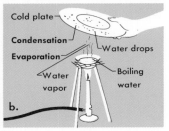

Figure 14-25. a.Steam at 100° C has 540 cal/g more heat ·than water has at 100°C. b. Water vapor is invisible; steam, which consists of condensing water vapor, is visible.

Experimental error. Some heat is lost from the calorimeter; room may change temperature; condensed water may be carried into the calorimeter from the tube.

Figure 14-27. How does heating the air in a hot air balloon cause the balloon to rise?

Brent Stockwell

steam may be measured by the increase in temperature of the water. Calculations show that the heat of vaporization for water is 540 calories per gram. For every gram of steam that condenses to liquid water, the steam loses 540 calories.

EXPERIMENT. Steam loses heat when it condenses to water. (1) Place 100 g of water (room temperature) in the inner container of a calorimeter. Weigh and record the total weight of the calorimeter. Measure and record the water temperature. (2) Add steam from a steam boiler until the water in the calorimeter becomes hot. Stop the steam and record the water temperature. (3) Weigh the calorimeter again. How many grams of steam were added? (4) Calculate the calories of heat in the room-temperature water: $cal = m \times t$. Calculate the calories of heat in the heated water, using the same equation. The difference in calories is the amount of heat added by the steam.

How many calories were gained from each gram of steam? Your answer is an experimental value for the heat of vaporization of water. Why might this value differ from the true heat of vaporization for water, 540 cal/g?

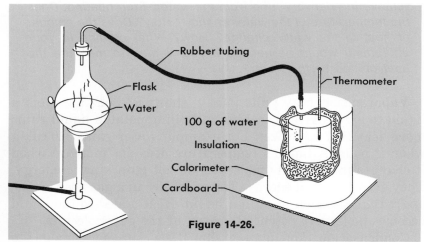

Figure 14-26.

There are two kinds of heat energy in a body: molecular kinetic energy and molecular potential energy. Changes in temperature occur when molecules lose or gain kinetic energy. Changes in state occur when molecules lose or gain potential energy. Changes in molecular potential energy occur during boiling, melting, freezing, vaporization, and condensation.

PROBLEMS

17. How does the heat of fusion of ice explain its use as a refrigerant?   *Uses heat as it melts.*

18. How does the heat of vaporization of water explain why you feel cooler after a swim?   *Takes body heat as it evaporates.*

19. Why can a steam heating system deliver more heat per hour to a room than a hot water system?   *Releases heat of vaporization as it condenses.*

MAIN IDEAS

p. 293   **1.** Potential energy is energy of position. Kinetic energy is energy of motion.

p. 294   **2.** Energy can be changed from one form to another.

p. 294   **3.** All forms of energy can be changed to heat.

pp. 296-298   **4.** Heat travels by radiation, conduction, and convection.

p. 298   **5.** Temperature is measured in degrees. Heat is measured in calories.

p. 302   **6.** Heat is the energy of molecules: molecular kinetic energy and molecular potential energy. Temperature is average molecular kinetic energy.

p. 303

p. 302   **7.** Molecular kinetic energy is the energy of molecules in motion.

p. 302   **8.** The molecular kinetic theory explains some physical properties of solids, liquids, and gases.

p. 304   **9.** Temperature is not changed by melting, boiling, or other changes in physical state.

p. 304   **10.** Heat is gained or lost during a change of physical state.

VOCABULARY

Write a sentence in which you correctly use each of the following words or terms.

B.T.U.	conductor	insulator
calorie	convection	kinetic energy
calorimeter	energy	melting
Celsius	Fahrenheit	potential energy
change of state	heat	radiation
condensation	heat of fusion	temperature
conduction	heat of vaporization	vaporization

STUDY QUESTIONS

Have students rewrite false

A.   True or False *statements to make the statements*
correct.

Determine whether each of the following sentences is true or false. (Do not write in this book.)

             F **1.** Heat is ~~not~~ a form of energy.

calories F **2.** The heat an object contains is measured in ~~degree~~s.

             T **3.** Freezing water is an example of a change in physical state.

convection F **4.** Heat is transferred through water by ~~conduction~~ currents.

potential F **5.** A wound spring is an example of ~~kinetic~~ energy.

             T **6.** A calorimeter measures calories.

             T **7.** Heat gets from the sun to earth by radiation.

             T **8.** When the temperature of a gas increases the pressure also increases, provided the volume does not change.

not F **9.** Glass is a good conductor of heat.

            T **10.** Temperature is a measure of the degree of hotness or coldness.

Some questions in part B may
have more than one correct
answer. Only one answer is
B.   Multiple Choice *required.*

Choose one word or phrase that correctly completes each of the following sentences. (Do not write in this book.)

  1. Kinetic energy is (potential energy, mass, volume, <u>energy of motion</u>).

  2. 1 kg equals (10, 100, <u>1000</u>, 10,000) grams.

  3. Heat is measured in (°C, °F, <u>calories</u>).

  4. Temperature is (calories, total kinetic energy, <u>average molecular energy</u>, heat energy).

  5. The temperature 122°F is (32, 5/9 × 32, <u>5/9 × 90</u>, 90) °C.

  6. 1 ml of water has a mass of (<u>1</u>, 10, 100, 1000) grams.

  7. 1 liter equals (10, 100, <u>1000</u>, 10,000) grams of water.

  8. Heat is measured with a (thermometer, <u>calorimeter</u>, mercury column, winch).

  9. One B.T.U. is the amount of heat required to raise the temperature of (10 ml, 453.6 g, 12 oz, <u>1 lb</u>) of water 1°F.

10. If 1 kg of water is heated from 30°C to 45°C, the heat added is (15, 150, 1,500, <u>15,000</u>) calories.

11. Two grams of water are cooled from 80°C to 60°C. The water loses (4, <u>40</u>, 20, 22) calories.

C. Completion

Complete each of the following sentences with a word or phrase that will make the sentence correct. (Do not write in this book.)

1. When 10 g of ice melts, it gains __?__ calories.
2. When substances are cooled, their molecules __?__.
3. When a solid is heated, its molecules __?__.
4. When 100 g of water boils, it gains __?__ calories.
5. __?__ is the movement of heat through a substance, from molecule to molecule.
6. __?__ is a more rapid means of heat transfer than convection and conduction.
7. Molecular kinetic energy is the energy of moving __?__.
8. When food is placed in a refrigerator, the molecular kinetic energy of the food __?__.
9. When water is heated, its molecular kinetic energy __?__.

800

lose kinetic energy

gain kinetic energy

54,000 cal

conduction

radiation

molecules

decreases

increases

D. How and Why

See Teacher's Guide at the front of this book.

1. How is heat different from temperature?
2. List 5 examples of kinetic energy and 5 examples of potential energy.
3. How is a calorimeter used to measure heat?
4. Why might the parts of an engine "freeze" if the engine overheats?
5. How is it possible for water at 0°C to melt ice at 0°C with no change in temperature?
6. A student burned some matches in a calorimeter. The temperature of 1 kg of water increased from 25°C to 26.5°C. How much heat did the matches give off?
7. A drawbridge always has a space between its moving parts. How is this fact related to the molecular kinetic theory?
8. Draw a diagram to show the difference in molecular structure of a solid, liquid, and gas. Draw three boxes 1-in. square. Use small circles for molecules.
9. The freon gas used to cool a refrigerator evaporates and condenses as it passes through coiled pipes. Explain the cooling action of the refrigerant using the molecular kinetic theory.

See Teacher's Guide at the front of this book. **INVESTIGATIONS**

1. Find out the meaning of thermal pollution. Learn what causes thermal pollution and ways to solve this problem.
2. Obtain an old thermostat such as those used on gas hot water heaters. Take it apart and learn how it works.
3. Make a collection of insulation materials such as aluminum foil, cork, and fiber glass. Obtain information on the insulating properties of each material.

INTERESTING READING

Adler, Irving, *Hot and Cold*. New York, John Day Company, 1959.

Balestrino, Philip, *Hot as an Ice Cube*. New York, Thomas Y. Crowell Company, 1972.

Keller, A. G., *Theatre of Machines*. New York, Macmillan Company, 1965.

Thompson, Paul D., *Gases and Plasmas*. Philadelphia, J. B. Lippincott Company, 1966.

Wilson, Charles Morrow, *Diesel: His Engine Changed the World*. Princeton, New Jersey, Van Nostrand Company, Inc., 1966.

This chapter further develops the concepts of heat introduced in Chapter 14 and the gas laws are developed. This information is applied to problems of refrigeration, heating systems for buildings, and heat engines. Thermal pollution and possible solutions to this problem are considered. Cryogenics and its applications are also presented.

Heat and Its Uses

GOAL: You will gain an understanding of heat energy and its practical applications.

Heat energy can be helpful or harmful to man. Buildings must be heated during cold weather for people to live and work healthfully. Cooling systems are used to take heat out of buildings during hot summer months. Heat must be removed from refrigerators and freezers or the food inside will spoil. Engines use heat to do work. They drive machines, airplanes, cars, and other vehicles. If too much heated water is dumped from factories into a river, fish and other water life may be killed. Loss of heat from a river in the winter may cause so much ice to form that the passage of ships is blocked.

15:1 Specific Heat

Heat a pot of water on a stove for a few minutes and the pot becomes too hot to touch. Yet the water may only be luke-warm. Metals and water do not increase in temperature at the same rate. It takes more heat to increase the temperature of water than to raise the temperature of an equal mass of metal.

Figure 15-1. A geothermal power plant uses heat from inside the earth to generate electricity.

Pacific Gas & Electric Co.

EXPERIMENT. Obtain a piece of three different metals. Aluminum, iron, and copper are good choices. All pieces should have the same mass. Place the metal pieces in boiling water for 5 minutes. With metal tongs, remove each piece from the water and set it on a block of paraffin. Allow the pieces of metal to stand until they are cool. Which metal melts the most paraffin? Which metal has the most heat? Explain any differences.

Specific heat is the amount of heat needed to change the temperature of one gram of a substance one Celsius degree. Specific heat is measured in calories. The **calorie** (kal'oh ree)

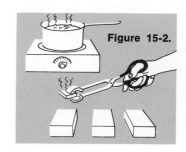

Figure 15-2.

The metal with the highest specific heat will melt the most paraffin. Aluminum should melt about twice as much paraffin as iron or copper. Water with the same mass and temperature would melt over four times more than aluminum. See Table 15-1 for specific heat values.

How does the high specific heat of water affect climate?

is a unit of heat (Section 14:3). The specific heat of water is 1 cal/g/C°. One calorie will raise the temperature of one gram of water one Celsius degree.

The specific heat of iron is 0.11. This means that it takes 0.11 calories of heat to increase the temperature of one gram of iron one Celsius degree. The higher the specific heat of a given material the more heat energy is needed to increase its temperature one Celsius degree. Table 15–1 lists specific heats for several substances. Which of the metals in the above experiment has the highest specific heat? Which metal has the lowest specific heat? *Cu*   *Al*

Table 15–1. *Specific Heats of Some Common Substances*	
Substance	*Specific Heat (cal/g/C°)*
Aluminum	0.21
Copper	0.09
Iron	0.11
Water	1.00

EXAMPLE

How much heat will increase the temperature of 10 g of water by 15 Celsius degrees. Multiply the mass by change in temperature. Then multiply by the specific heat.

temperature change × mass × specific heat = calories

$$15 \text{ C}° \times 10 \text{ g} \times 1 \text{ cal/g/C}° = 150 \text{ cal}$$

How much heat is needed to increase the temperature of 10 g of iron 15 C°? Again, multiply mass by degrees change in temperature. Then multiply by the specific heat.

$$15 \text{ C}° \times 10 \text{ g} \times 0.11 \text{ cal/g/C}° = 16.5 \text{ cal}$$

Figure 15-3.

sand

EXPERIMENT. Obtain two similar cans and two thermometers. Fill one can with sand. Fill the other with water. Put a thermometer in each can to the same depth and the same distance from the walls of each container. Record the temperature. Allow the cans to stand in the sun for one hour. Record each temperature again. Which can has the higher temperature? Allow the cans to stand in a refrigerator for one hour. Record each temperature again. Which has the higher specific heat, sand or water?   *water*

PROBLEMS

1. Compare the specific heat of water with that of sand, glass, and air.
2. Why is water used to remove heat from a car engine?
3. How do large bodies of water affect the climate of nearby land areas during winter and summer? Why?

Specific heat of water is about five times higher than that of sand, glass or air. Exact values vary with temperature and pressure.

high specific heat

Water warms land in winter and cools it in summer.

15:2 *Heating Systems*

Hot water systems are used to heat homes and other buildings. These systems include a furnace, boiler, and radiators. Radiators in rooms are connected by pipes to a boiler which is heated by a furnace. Usually the furnace and boiler are in a basement. The furnace heats the water in the boiler to about 180°F (82°C).

Convection carries the hot water up through pipes to the room radiators. Heat is released into the room from a radiator as the hot water cools. Cooler water in the radiator sinks back down again to the boiler and is replaced by rising hot water. The circulation of water from boiler to radiator is repeated over and over. In some systems a pump forces the water through the pipes and radiators. In effect, a hot water heating system transfers heat from a furnace to air inside a room.

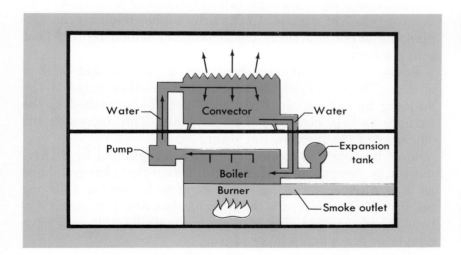

Figure 15-4. In a hot water heating system, heat is released as hot water cools.

A steam heating system is an improvement on a hot water system. In a steam heating system water is heated under pressure to boiling. Hot steam rather than water is circulated from

Why is steam heat an improvement over hot water?

A substance must absorb as much heat (without a change in temperature) when it becomes a gas as it gives up when it

becomes a liquid. As steam condenses it gives off as much heat as it absorbed on vaporizing.

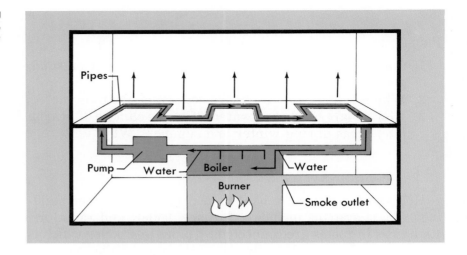

the boiler to the radiators. Inside a steam radiator, steam condenses to water which runs back down to the boiler.

When steam condenses to water it gives up 540 cal/g without a change in temperature. This figure is known as the **heat of condensation** of water (Section 14:6). If 10 g of steam condenses, 5,400 cal of heat are released. Here you see why steam radiators get hotter than hot water radiators. It takes about 50 times as much hot water to give the same heat as condensing steam.

Some heating systems use radiant heat. Radiant heat is carried into a room through radiation. In one kind of radiant heating, electric wires are heated by an electric current. Behind the wires is a shiny metal reflector which reflects heat into the room.

Some types of furnaces heat air in the furnace with a burner. The heated air is transferred to other parts of the building by convection. Frequently a fan is attached to the furnace to help circulate the warm air. This increases the efficiency of the furnace and lowers costs.

Most heating and cooling systems are regulated by a **thermostat.** A thermostat contains a thin strip that changes shape as it is warmed or cooled. This strip is *bimetallic* (bie′ me tal′ ik). Bimetallic means the strip has two different metal ribbons joined together. For example, a bimetallic strip may have a layer of brass and a layer of iron.

Metals expand when heated. Different metals expand at different rates. As a bimetallic strip is warmed, one metal expands faster than the other. This unequal expansion causes the strip to bend. When the strip cools, the metals contract. Then, the strip straightens out.

Lennox Industries

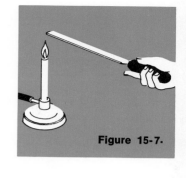

Figure 15-7.

The strip bends.

ACTIVITY. *Obtain a bimetallic strip attached to a wooden handle. Heat the free end of the strip with a Bunsen flame. What change occurs? Allow the strip to cool. Then invert the strip and heat again. Does the strip always bend in the same direction? Brass expands faster than iron when heated. Thus, a bimetallic strip bends toward the iron. Which way does a bimetallic strip bend when it is cooled?* Upon cooling the strip straightens out.

It always bends toward the iron when heated.

A bimetallic strip in a furnace thermostat acts as a switch to start and stop the system. When cool, the strip touches a contact point. This completes an electric circuit (Section 19:1) and starts the system. An electric motor pumps fuel to the furnace or an electric fan blows hot air into the area to be heated. As the thermostat warms, the bimetallic strip bends away from the contact point. The circuit is broken open and the motor stops. In effect, the bimetallic strip acts as a switch which turns the heating system on and off.

15:3   Gas Laws

Cars and bicycles move on tires inflated with air. When air is pumped into a tire, the air is compressed. It is forced into a smaller space than it occupied outside the tire. The pressure of air inside a bicycle tire may be as high as 60 lb/in.^{2}. Suppose someone rides the bicycle many miles on a hot day. An increase in tire temperature may cause the pressure to increase to 65 or 70 lb/in.^{2}.

Pressure is defined as force per unit area. Air pressure is the push of air on water or on some other substance. Pressure can be expressed in both English and metric units. In English units, pressure is pounds per in.^{2} or ft^2 of surface. The average air pressure at sea level is 14.7 lb/in.^{2}. This value is called one atmosphere of pressure. Two atmospheres of pressure would be 29.4 lb/in.^{2}. Tire pressure gauges are used to measure the difference between tire pressure and atmospheric pressure. Some automobile tires have a pressure of about 30 lb/in.^{2} above atmospheric pressure.

A *barometer* is an instrument used to measure air pressure. In a mercury barometer (Figure 15-8), a column of mercury is supported by air pressure. The mercury column rises and falls as the air pressure rises and falls. Air pressure may be recorded in inches, millimeters, or centimeters of mercury. Air pressure of one atmosphere (14.7 lb/in.^{2}) equals 76 cm or 760 mm of mercury.

13.6 x 76 cm = 10.3 m or about 34 ft

Figure 15-8. Mercury is 13.6 times as dense as water. How tall would a barometer have to be if it contained water instead of mercury?

ESSA Photo

Torricelli first measured atmospheric pressure in 1643 using a mercury barometer. To this day pressure is measured in millimeters of mercury.

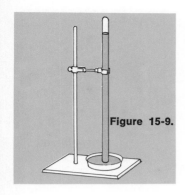

Figure 15-9.

atmospheric pressure changes with
weather conditions

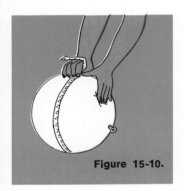

Figure 15-10.

State Boyle's law.

$P \propto V$ or $P_1 V_1 = P_2 V_2$

At constant temperatures, pressure
varies directly with volume. As
pressure increases, volume
decreases and as pressure
decreases, volume increases.

**Figure 15-11. What is the
pressure in atmospheres when
the volume in the cylinder is
reduced to ¼ liter?**

4 atmospheres

PROBLEM

4. Does your body experience more pressure at <u>sea level</u> or
at the top of a mountain? Do you experience more pressure when you swim on the surface of water or <u>under the</u>
<u>surface</u>? Why? *Pressure increases as more and
more air (or water) exerts force
on body.*

*ACTIVITY. Set up a barometer in your classroom. Fill a
long closed tube with mercury and invert the tube in a small
dish of mercury. Support the tube with a test tube clamp and
iron stand. CAUTION: Do not get any mercury on your skin.
It is poisonous.*

*Read the height of the mercury column in inches and
centimeters. Why is the height not exactly 30 in. or 76 cm?
Allow the barometer to stand in a safe place for 3 weeks.
Record the height of the column each day. Do changes
occur? Why?*

*EXPERIMENT.   Inflate a round rubber balloon. Measure its
circumference with a tape measure and determine its volume.
Warm the balloon over a heated radiator or let it sit in the
sun for ½ an hour. Calculate the volume now. Put the balloon
in a refrigerator and find its volume again when it is cold.
How does the volume of the balloon change with change in
temperature? Explain your observations.*

Volume, pressure, and *temperature* are the three main properties of a gas. These properties are explained by principles
called the gas laws. **Boyle's law** states that the volume of a gas
decreases as its pressure increases, if the temperature does
not change. Molecules of the gas are pushed closer together
when the pressure is increased. Thus, the volume decreases.

The reverse occurs when the pressure decreases. The volume of a gas increases. Remove the cap from a bottle of soda

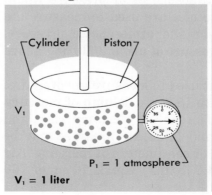

Cylinder   Piston

V_1

P_1 = 1 atmosphere

V_1 = 1 liter

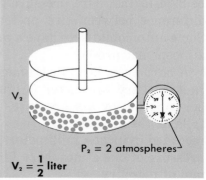

V_2

P_2 = 2 atmospheres

$V_2 = \frac{1}{2}$ liter

pop. Carbon dioxide gas rushes out because it expands with reduced pressure. Because of the spaces between molecules of a gas, a gas can be easily compressed and expanded.

Suppose a closed cylinder contains oxygen gas. A pressure gauge attached to the cylinder reads 30 lb/in.[2]. What causes this pressure? The gas molecules inside the cylinder contain kinetic energy and are in constant motion. As the molecules move about they strike each other and the walls of the container. The force of the molecules striking the walls of the container produces the pressure. If more oxygen is pumped into the tank, the pressure increases. An increase in the number of molecules striking the walls of the tank causes an increase in pressure.

Heating a gas causes it to expand (Figure 15–14). Gas molecules gain kinetic energy when they are heated. They move faster, travel farther, and strike the walls of the container more often. If the walls of the container are flexible, the gas pushes it out. There is an increase in volume. **Charles' law** states that the volume of a gas increases as its temperature increases, if the pressure is not changed. $V \propto \frac{1}{T}$ $\frac{V_1}{T_1} = \frac{V_2}{T_2}$

Figure 15-12. The carbon dioxide in soda pop expands when pressure is reduced.

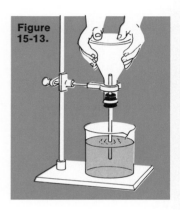

Figure 15-13.

ACTIVITY. Obtain a 500-ml flask and a one-hole rubber stopper to fit it. Moisten a glass tube. Carefully work the tube through the hole in the stopper. Insert the stopper into the flask. Invert the flask. Clamp the flask to a ring stand as shown in Figure 15–13. Place the end of the tube in a large beaker of water. Add some ink to the water. Place both hands tightly against the flask. Hold them there and watch the level of water in the tube. Record what you observe. Explain.

Figure 15-14. The balloon expands in hot water because its molecules gain kinetic energy and force themselves farther away from each other.

A kitchen pressure cooker can build up pressure to two or three atmospheres. Heating increases the pressure of water vapor inside the cooker. Increases in pressure due to high temperatures have caused accidental explosions of steam boilers. Why do tire blowouts occur most often on hot days at high speeds? Heat increases air pressure inside the tire. **Gay-Lussac's law** states that the pressure of a gas increases as the temperature increases, if the volume is not changed.

$$P \propto \frac{1}{T} \quad \frac{P_1}{T_1} = \frac{P_2}{T_2}$$

15:4 Refrigeration

Ice is used in cold drinks and picnic coolers. Ice is also used to keep food cold in some storage plants. Ice cools things because it takes on heat from its surroundings. When ice melts,

General Gas Law combines all three:

$$\frac{P_1 V_1}{T_1} = \frac{P_2 V_2}{T_2}$$

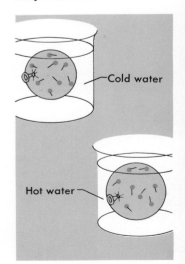

Cold water

Hot water

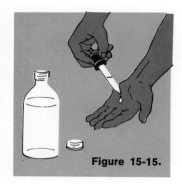

Figure 15-15.

Skin feels cool because alcohol absorbs heat as it evaporates.

each gram of ice absorbs 80 cal of heat without a change in temperature. This figure is called the **heat of fusion** for ice.

ACTIVITY. CAUTION: This experiment should be done under the direct supervision of your teacher. Wear eye protection. Place a few drops of alcohol on your skin. How does it make your skin feel? Explain. Place a mixture of water and ether in a vacuum bottle. Stir the mixture rapidly. What do you observe? Explain. Evaporating ether absorbs enough heat from the water to make it freeze.

Evaporation of a liquid is a cooling process. When ethyl alcohol evaporates it gains 204 calories of heat per gram. During evaporation ether takes heat from its surroundings and makes them cooler. A gram of ether takes on 89 calories when it evaporates. Evaporation of ether can cause the water to freeze by absorbing heat from the water.

Refrigerators, freezers, and air conditioners operate by evaporation. A gas called a *refrigerant* is circulated through pipes in the cooling unit. Ammonia (NH_3) is most often used in large freezers. Freon, an organic compound, is used in home freezers and air conditioners. Carbon dioxide (CO_2) can also be used as a refrigerant.

How does a freezer work?

The ammonia gas in a freezer is compressed by a pump called a compressor. To compress means to squeeze into a smaller space. As the ammonia gas is compressed, a fan blows cool air across the compressor. Compression and cooling causes a change in state. The ammonia gas becomes a liquid. Liquid ammonia is pumped through pipes in the freezer. As the liquid ammonia circulates, the pressure on it decreases. The ammonia evaporates. Each gram of liquid ammonia absorbs 320 calories of heat as it changes from a liquid to a gas. The freezer cabinet is cooled as it loses heat to the evaporating ammonia.

15:5   *Heat Engines*

Engines change heat energy into mechanical energy. Then they use the mechanical energy to do work. Hero's engine, steam engines, gasoline engines, and diesel engines are examples of engines that do work. Each uses the heat from a burning fuel and the pressure of hot gases. Gasoline and diesel engines are called internal combustion engines. This means the combustion or burning of fuel occurs inside the engine.

The Hero's engine shown in Figure 15–16 operates by action-reaction forces (Section 13:3). The action force of steam out of the jet causes an equal and opposite reaction force. Reaction force causes the engine to spin around in a circle.

Most gasoline engines burn gasoline vapor inside cylinders. In most automobile engines there are 4, 6, or 8 cylinders. Each cylinder has a piston that can move up and down. Burning fuel produces an explosion of hot gases inside the cylinder above the piston (Figure 15–17). These gases push against the pistons .The force of the hot gas makes the piston go up and down. Force and motion result. Work is done.

A gasoline engine has a carburetor. The carburetor supplies the gasoline-air mixture to the cylinder. Gases enter and leave the cylinder through openings called valves. Find the intake and exhaust valve in Figure 15–17. The spark plug produces an electric spark which ignites the fuel.

The piston inside a cylinder makes four strokes in its cycle:

intake stroke—piston moves downward and a mixture of
    gas and air comes into the cylinder through the intake
    valve

compression stroke—piston moves upward and compresses
    the fuel within the cylinder; at the completion of the
    compression stroke the spark plug fires and the fuel
    explodes

Figure 15-16. Hero's engine operates on the same principle as a jet engine, illustrating Newton's third law of motion.

How do engines produce power?

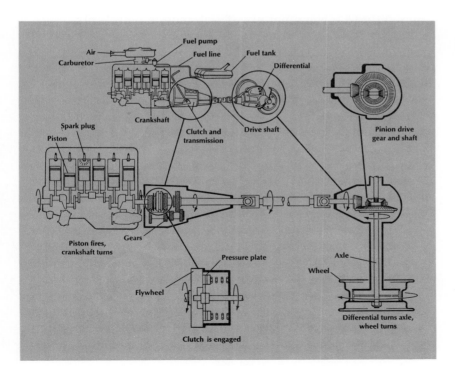

Figure 15-17. A gasoline engine uses burning gas to produce an explosion which moves the pistons up and down.

power stroke—pressure of hot gases produced by combustion forces the piston downward; this stroke gives the force that drives the car wheels

exhaust stroke—piston moves upward and expels exhaust gases through the exhaust valve

In a four-cycle engine, the four strokes in a cycle are repeated about 25 times per second. The pistons are connected to a rotating rod called a crankshaft. The crankshaft is connected to a driveshaft. As the pistons move up and down, they rotate the crankshaft which turns the driveshaft. The driveshaft extends underneath the car to the rear wheels. It turns the rear wheels. They, in turn, push against the ground and exert the action force to move the car. In front wheel drive vehicles, the engine is connected to the front wheels which drive the vehicle.

A gasoline engine has a low efficiency. Only 25 percent of the fuel it burns is changed to power. Much of the fuel goes out through the exhaust pipe in the form of unburned hydrocarbons. Also, the engine emits carbon dioxide (CO_2), carbon monoxide (CO), and oxides of nitrogen (NO, NO_2). The wastes that come out of a gasoline engine make it a source of pollution. Wastes from the engine are acted on by sunlight to form photochemical smog. Most large cities have polluted air due partly to large amounts of automobile pollutants.

How efficient is a gasoline engine?

25% efficiency — much is lost as heat and unburned fuel.

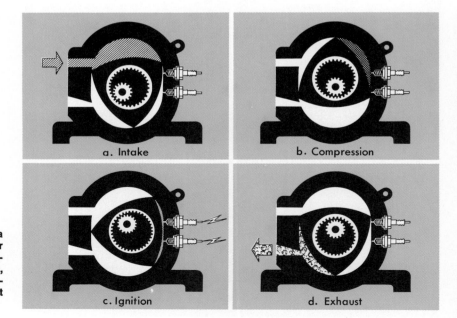

Figure 15-18. Operation of a rotary engine: (a) fuel and air mixture enters rotary, (b) turning rotary compresses mixture, (c) spark plugs ignite compressed mixture, (d) exhaust gases exit rotary.

a. Intake

b. Compression

c. Ignition

d. Exhaust

Mazda Motors of America

Figure 15-19. A Wankel engine can produce as much power as a larger piston engine.

A Wankel rotary engine is a gasoline engine that does not use pistons. At the center of the engine there is a triangular rotor. The rotor is a metal part that rotates in a chamber shaped like a figure eight. There is an intake valve, exhaust valve, and one spark plug. As the rotor rotates, gas is taken in, compressed, burned, and forced out through the exhaust valve. Explosion of the gas produces power as in a piston engine.

A small Wankel engine can produce as much power as a large piston engine. Also, it runs smoother with less vibration. The use of Wankel engines may reduce automobile pollution. Because of its smaller size, the Wankel engine can be equipped with smog control devices and not become too large and heavy for use in automobiles.

A gas turbine is more efficient than a gasoline engine. It has fewer moving parts and less vibration. Fuel and air are compressed in a turbine and burned. The pressure of hot gases against the turbine blades makes the turbine shaft rotate (Figure 15–20).

Why is the rotary engine an improvement over a piston engine?

smaller, runs smoother, easier to modify to prevent air pollution

Turbine engines may be more efficient but, in airplanes at least they still produce considerable amounts of pollution.

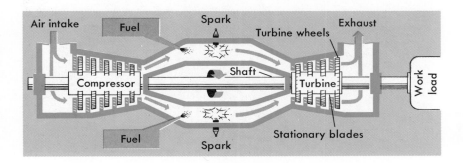

Figure 15-20. In a gas turbine, air and gas are mixed and then ignited.

15:6 *Thermal Pollution*

Engines, turbines, furnaces, electric lamps, and stoves give off heat. All the energy we use—light, electricity, chemical energy, mechanical energy—ends up as heat. Heat is the end product from the energy we use each day. Much of this heat is wasted. It goes off into the atmosphere.

What other ways can you think of to utilize "waste" heat?

How can heat be used rather than wasted? Waste heat could be used to desalinate salt water. Desalinate means to take the salt out of salt water. The salt water is distilled by heating it. Through evaporation and condensation, salt is separated from the water. Desalinated water from the ocean can be used for drinking, washing, and farming.

Waste heat from power plants could also be used to heat greenhouses for plant production. Someday the growing season on farms may be lengthened through the use of irrigation water heated by waste heat from power plants. Another idea of the future is to use waste heat to melt the ice in harbors normally closed in winter.

An increased supply of phosphates from detergents and fertilizers as well as elevated temperatures make conditions favorable for algae blooms.

Electric power plants use heat to make steam and generate electricity. Power plants and many other industries must discharge waste heat. Often this is done by using water to cool machinery and then dumping the hot water into a nearby river, lake, or ocean. Heat may increase plant growth and may cause the water to become clogged with slimy growths of green algae. The water may become so hot that fish are killed off. Most fish cannot survive drastic changes in water temperature. Brook trout, for example, can live only 30 minutes at 83°F and only 12 hours at an average 77°F.

Figure 15-21. Thermal pollution and dumping of wastes into streams and rivers can lead to large fish kills.

Vincent McGuire

Columbus & Southern Ohio Electric Co.

Figure 15-22. A turbine in an electric power plant changes heat energy (steam) into electric energy.

Dumping heated water into lakes, rivers, and oceans produces *thermal pollution.* Water temperatures in some rivers have been recorded as high as 120°F. More than 50 trillion gallons of warm water are discharged from electric power plants in the United States each year.

Cooling towers are one solution to thermal pollution. Hot water from a power plant or factory is cooled to air temperature as it flows through pipes in the tower. After the water is air cooled, it is discharged into a nearby body of water. Because the water is cooled, it does not have a harmful effect on water life. There is no thermal pollution of the water. The excess heat is released into the atmosphere.

How do cooling towers reduce thermal pollution?

Excess heat in atmosphere may be hazardous, also. Pollution abatement is very much a system of trade-offs. We should try to dump wastes where they cause the least damage at least over a short time. Much more research is necessary to even determine how pollution affects the environment.

15:7 *Cryogenics*

When matter is cooled to very low temperatures its properties change. For example, metals become better electrical conductors when they are cooled. As a substance is cooled, it loses heat. Molecules in the substance vibrate more slowly and take on a more orderly pattern. Physical and chemical properties depend on the order and arrangement of molecules. At low temperatures the arrangement of molecules change. Therefore, physical and chemical properties also change.

Cryogenics (krie' oh jen' iks) is the study of physical and chemical properties at very low temperatures. Cryogenic temperatures are usually indicated on the Kelvin temperature scale. On the Kelvin temperature scale, 0° is absolute zero.

Define cryogenics.

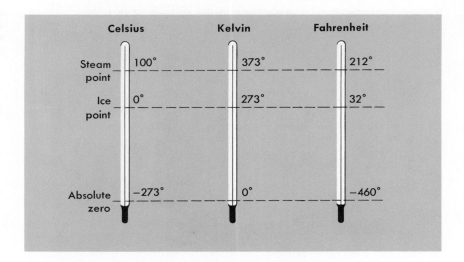

Absolute zero is the lowest temperature to which a substance can be cooled. In theory, it is the temperature at which all molecular motion stops. Zero degrees Kelvin (0°K) is equivalent to —273°C. Cryogenic temperatures are about 90°K (—183°C) or colder.

EXPERIMENT. Determine an approximate value for absolute zero. Cut a piece of 1-mm bore glass tubing, approximately 10 cm long. Seal one end in a Bunsen burner flame. While the tube is still warm, place the open end in a small dish of mercury. Allow a small globule of mercury into the open end. Let cool. Using a piece of broom straw, push the globule down to about 7 cm from the bottom. The glass tubing now contains a volume of the air under a constant pressure, the weight of the mercury. Set the tube upright. Record the room temperature. Carefully measure the distance in mm from the bottom of the inside of the tube to the bottom of the mercury. Record this measurement. With a rubber band, secure the tube to a wooden ruler. (1) Place the ruler and tube into a beaker of hot water for about a minute. Do not submerge the open end of the tube. Read the measurements through the wall of the beaker. Do not remove from the hot water bath. Record this measurement and the temperature of the hot water bath. Remove the tube and ruler. Let cool. (2) Repeat Part 1 with an ice bath. Record the measurement and the ice bath temperature. (3) Make a graph from zero to 120 mm on one axis and from 200°Celsius to—300°Celsius on the other. Plot these three points (room temperature, ice, and hot water baths). Try to connect the points with a straight line. Extend the straight line until it intersects the temperature line. What temperature is this? —273° C — absolute zero
The students if careful should be able to come quite close to the true value.

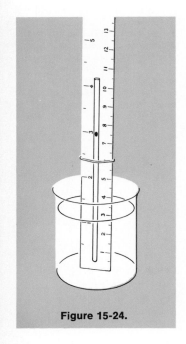

Figure 15-24.

Energy—How Much Do We Need?

During the 30 years between 1940 and 1970, the average amount of energy used by every man, woman, and child doubled. More energy was used during that period than during all the years of recorded history before 1940. Energy use is expected to double again before 1985.

Energy needs of people in the United States are tremendous. According to recent estimates, the U. S., with only 6% of the world's population, uses 33% of the world's energy.

Turn on the television set; you are using electric energy. Take a ride in a car; you are using chemical energy from petroleum. We need energy for transportation, heating and cooling homes, cooking and refrigerating food, and for most other aspects of what we have come to consider normal life.

How much energy does your family use? To some extent that depends on where you live. You could divide the total amount of energy fuels used (including water running through hydroelectric plants) by the number of households in the U. S. This gives an average of about 46 pounds of coal, 9½ gallons of oil, 7 gallons of natural gas, less than 1 pint of nuclear energy, and 1 gallon of water power per household.

Norfolk and Western Railroad

Coal—About 20% of our total energy comes from coal. Nearly half of the electricity in the United States is generated by burning coal.

El Paso Natural Gas Company

Petroleum—Oil and natural gas provide more than 77% of the total energy used in the United States.

British Columbia Government

Hydroelectricity—Of the total energy supply, 4% comes from using water spilling from dams to drive electric turbines. Because the number of suitable sites for dams is limited, hydroelectric power will provide an ever decreasing share of the total energy supply.

General Electric Research and Development Center

Nuclear energy—One pound of uranium is about the size of a golf ball, but it contains as much energy as 15 carloads of coal. The 28 nuclear power plants now in operation produce about 3% of the electricity we use. By 1980, about 20% of our electricity will be generated by nuclear energy.

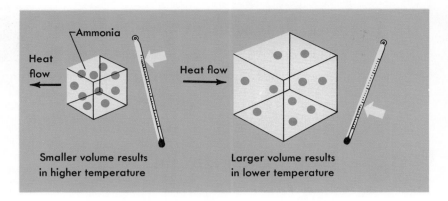

Heat flow

Ammonia

Heat flow

Smaller volume results in higher temperature

Larger volume results in lower temperature

How are very low temperatures produced?

Figure 15-26. Liquid helium is kept in a large dewar flask. Why does it remain cold?

Gardner Cryogenics Corp.

One method for producing very low temperatures is to cool and compress a gas such as helium and then allow it to expand. In expanding, the gas does not lose heat energy but cools by adiabatic cooling. *Adiabatic* (ahd' i a baht' ik) *cooling* is a decrease in temperature without loss of heat. The temperature decreases because the molecules move farther apart and thereby gain potential energy. Kinetic energy of the molecules becomes molecular potential energy. Instead of heat being lost, the molecules gain potential energy.

Helium can be compressed and cooled to form a liquid at 4°K (−267°C). The liquid helium is kept in insulated containers built like vacuum bottles. Temperatures lower than 4°K are reached by allowing the helium to evaporate. Remember, evaporation is a cooling process. In a vacuum the liquid helium cools to 0.8°K.

Liquid helium below 2.2°K conducts heat 30 times better than copper at room temperature. The viscosity or thickness of the helium liquid decreases greatly. It flows easily from place to place. The helium will flow up the sides of its container and down the outside. No force is needed to push it. It can flow through cracks less than one-millionth of an inch across. Helium in this unusual state is called a *superfluid*.

Metals lose their electrical resistance as they are cooled. This means that cooling makes the metal a better electrical conductor. At extremely low temperatures some metals lose their resistance completely. They are called *superconductors*. So far, more than 20 metals have been shown to be superconductors at very low temperatures. Mercury at very low temperatures, for example, can hold a current of electricity indefinitely. An alloy of niobium-tin is the best and most important superconductor in use today.

Superconductors are used to make "super" electromagnets. A super magnet can be made as large as an ordinary magnet.

Students might like to report on some low-temperature effects such as superconductivity and superfluidity.

326

Figure 15-27. A superconducting magnet may make use of liquid helium to produce very low temperatures.

Its advantage is that it uses ⅟₅₀ the power of an ordinary magnet. Also, once magnetized, the super magnet holds its magnetism indefinitely. A super magnet has a temperature of about —268°C. It is kept at this low temperature by a refrigeration system using liquid helium. Super magnets may someday have practical uses in electric generating plants, electron microscopes, and computers.

MAIN IDEAS

pp. 311-312 **1.** The amount of heat lost or gained by a body is equal to mass × change in temperature × specific heat.

p. 312 **2.** Water has a high specific heat ($1 \text{ cal/g/C}°$). It can absorb or release more heat than most substances.

p. 313 **3.** Water in a hot water heating system travels by convection.

p. 313 **4.** Steam heating systems supply more heat than hot water systems.

p. 314
5. The bimetallic strip in a thermostat serves as a switch in an electric circuit. Changes in temperature cause the switch to go on and off.

p. 318
6. Evaporation is a cooling process.

p. 318
7. Engines convert heat energy into mechanical energy. Engines do work.

pp. 322-323
8. Thermal pollution results from dumping heated water into a lake, river, or ocean.

p. 323
9. Physical and chemical properties of a substance change when the substance is cooled to very low temperatures.

p. 326
10. At very low temperatures some metals lose their electrical resistance and become superconductors.

VOCABULARY

Write a sentence in which you correctly use each of the following words or terms.

adiabatic cooling	Gay-Lussac's law	specific heat
barometer	heat of condensation	temperature
Boyle's law	heat of fusion	thermal pollution
Charles' law	photochemical smog	thermostat
cryogenics	pressure	volume

STUDY QUESTIONS

A. True or False   *Have students rewrite false statements to make the statements correct.*

Determine whether each of the following sentences is true or false. (Do not write in this book.)

T 1. Still air is a poor conductor of heat.

F 2. The specific heat of iron is <u>greater than 1</u> cal/g/C°. *0.11*

T 3. Evaporation is a cooling process.

F 4. The heat of fusion of water is <u>54°</u> cal/g. *80*

F 5. Cryogenics is the study of very <u>high</u> temperatures. *low*

F 6. A barometer measures <u>the specific heat of a substance.</u> *air pressure*

F 7. The most common refrigerant in household refrigerators is <u>liquid ammonia.</u> *freon*

F 8. A rotary engine has <u>only two</u> pistons. *no*

F 9. Absolute zero is <u>zero degrees</u> on the Celsius scale. *−273°*

T 10. A thermometer measures the amount of heat a substance contains.

B. Multiple Choice

Choose one word or phrase that correctly completes each of the following sentences. (Do not write in this book.)

Some questions in part B may have more than one correct answer. Only one answer is required.

1. A vacuum bottle is a good heat (<u>insulator</u>, conductor, radiator).

2. In convection, heat is moved by (conduction, <u>currents</u>, radiation).

3. If 10 g of water are heated from 15°C to 65°C, (150, 650, 800, <u>500</u>) calories are added.

4. Steam gives up (<u>540</u>, 54, 5.4, 80) calories per gram when it condenses.

5. A (<u>thermostat</u>, vacuum bottle, flask, magnet) has a bi-metallic strip.

6. If a bar of metal is heated, its length (<u>increases</u>, decreases, remains the same).

7. Heat can be converted to (temperature, pressure, <u>ft-lb</u>, evaporation).

8. Evaporation (<u>cools</u>, warms, does not change the temperature) of a substance.

9. Cooling in a refrigerator occurs by (condensation, <u>evaporation</u>, freezing, an increase in pressure).

C. Completion

Complete each of the following sentences with a word or phrase that will make the sentence correct. (Do not write in this book.)

1. A Hero's engine operates by action and __?__ forces. — *reaction*

2. Forces are produced in engines by expansion of hot __?__. — *gases*

3. A gasoline engine has __?__ efficiency. — *low*

4. CO_2, CO, NO, NO_2 and unburned hydrocarbons are found in the __?__ from gasoline engines. — *exhaust*

5. A gas turbine creates __?__ air pollution than a gasoline engine. — *less*

6. Cooling towers are used to decrease __?__ pollution. — *thermal*

7. Water may be desalinated by __?__ and condensation. — *evaporation*

8. As a substance's temperature __?__, its molecular kinetic energy decreases. — *decreases*

9. −273°C is __?__ °K. — *0*

10. Absolute zero is __?__ °K and __?__ °C. — *0, −273*

D. How and Why   *See Teacher's Guide for answers to this section.*

1. Why does a vacuum bottle keep things hot or cold?
2. How do changes in density cause convection currents?
3. Why are fruit orchards often located near large bodies of water?
4. Compare the operation of a hot water and steam heating system.
5. How does a thermostat work?
6. Explain how a gasoline engine produces power.
7. How is a Wankel rotary engine different from a piston engine?
8. Why is thermal pollution harmful?
9. What happens to substances that are cooled to temperatures near absolute zero?

INVESTIGATIONS

See Teacher's Guide at the front of the book for answers and suggestions.

1. Obtain a model kit for a Wankel engine and assemble the model.
2. Obtain information about past ice ages and theories that explain the cyclical warming and cooling of the earth.
3. Visit a local refrigeration repair shop to learn how refrigeration units operate.
4. Look up and report on some recent advances in cryogenics.
5. There are several theories on how we shall heat our homes in the future. One proposed method is drilling holes deep into the earth and using the earth's heat to generate electricity. Research and report on geothermal power.
6. Make a model of a turbine engine.

INTERESTING READING

Cole, David E., "The Wankel Engine." *Scientific American*, p. 14, August, 1972.

Rosenfeld, Sam, *Science Experiments with Air*. Irvington-on-Hudson, New York, Harvey House, 1969.

Waves

GOAL: You will gain an understanding of the properties of waves and the electromagnetic spectrum.

Drop a pebble into a pond or tub of water. What do you observe? You see tiny waves ripple away from the point of impact. Kinetic energy of the falling pebble was transferred to the water. This resulted in wave motion. Water waves carry kinetic energy from one point to another.

Light, heat, and sound, as well as other forms of energy, can move from one point to another by wave motion. Light, heat, and sound waves transmit energy from one location to another.

16:1 Waves

Have you ever watched waves in an ocean or lake? The waves travel forward as the water moves up and down. When a wave passes a point in the water, the water molecules move up and down. **Waves** are rhythmic disturbances which travel through space or matter.

Richard M. Fetters

Figure 16-1. Ripples or waves represent the kinetic energy of water.

  EXPERIMENT. Take a rope about 4.5m long and tie one end to a doorknob. Hold the other end of the rope with your hand. Shake it up and down so waves begin to form. Make a diagram of the shape of the waves produced.
  Shake the end of a long "Slinky" coil spring so waves travel the length of the spring. How are these waves different from the waves you made with the rope? —————————— *Compressional waves rather than transverse waves.*

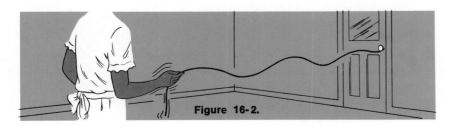

Figure 16-2.

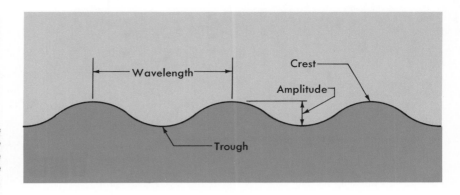

Figure 16-3. The height of water waves is determined by the size of the pebble and the speed with which the pebble hits the water.

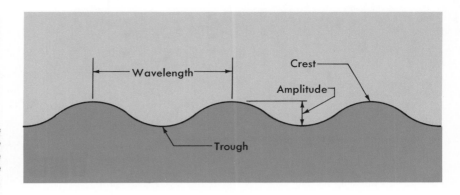

Wavelength

Crest

Amplitude

Trough

A water wave consists of a hill and a valley (Figure 16–3). The hill is called the *crest*. The valley is called the *trough* (troff). The distance between the crest of one wave and the crest of the next wave is the *wavelength*. *Amplitude* (am' pli tood) is the vertical distance through which the particles of the wave move from their rest position.

Define wave crest, trough, amplitude, frequency, wavelength.

Amplitude depends on the amount of energy which creates the wave. As the wave energy increases, the amplitude increases. For example, if you drop a large rock instead of a pebble into a pond, a bigger wave results. The amplitude is greater. How can you produce waves of large amplitude with a rope?

Increase the distance you move the end of the rope when making a wave

Waves formed by water or a rope are transverse waves. In a **transverse wave,** matter vibrates at right angles to the direction in which the wave travels. *Vibrate* means to move back and forth rapidly. In a water wave, the water molecules vibrate vertically. The wave travels horizontally. Light, heat, and radio waves are examples of transverse waves.

How is a transverse wave different from a compressional wave?

When matter vibrates in the same direction as that in which the wave is traveling, another kind of wave is formed. Waves

Vibrations produce waves in solids, liquids, and gases.

The compressional wave in a spring is similar to a sound wave.

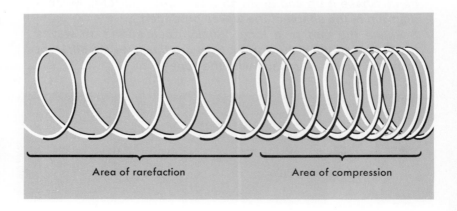

Figure 16-4. Areas of rarefaction alternate with areas of compression throughout the spring. Does the spring represent a water wave or a sound wave?

Area of rarefaction

Area of compression

can be produced in a coil spring by pinching together several of the coils and then releasing them. Parts of the spring move to and fro in a rhythm. At times, the particles of matter in the wave are compressed together. At other times, they are moved farther apart. This wave is called a *compressional* or *longitudinal wave.* In a **compressional wave,** matter vibrates in the same direction in which the wave travels. Sound waves are one type of compressional wave.

In a compressional wave in a coil spring, each area in which the coils are pushed together is an *area of compression.* When the coils are spread apart, the area is an *area of rarefaction.* Each part of the spring is alternately compressed and rarefied as a compressional wave travels through it. The spring vibrates in the same direction in which the wave travels.

The blue curve in Figure 16–5 represents a transverse wave. It can also represent a compressional wave. The upward curve

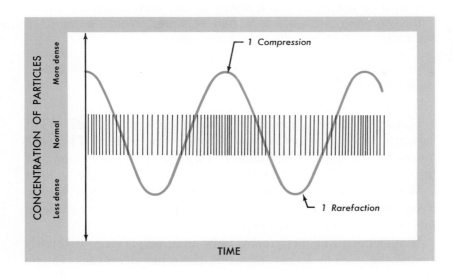

Figure 16-5. Air does not travel forward as a sound wave passes through it. As the wave passes a point, air compresses and expands.

represents one complete compression. The downward curve shows one complete rarefaction. The *wavelength* of a compressional wave is the distance from one compression to the next compression.

16:2 *Wave Frequency*

All waves have a certain frequency. *Frequency* (free′ kwan see) is the number of waves that pass a given point in a given

How is wavelength related to frequency?

$\lambda \propto \dfrac{1}{f}$, *inverse variation. As wavelength increases frequency decreases.*

unit of time. Suppose you throw a pebble into a pond. Three wave crests caused by the disturbance go by a stationary rock in 15 seconds. What is the wave frequency? The wave frequency is three waves per 15 seconds, or one wave per 5 seconds $\left(\dfrac{3 \text{ waves}}{15 \text{ sec}} = \dfrac{1 \text{ wave}}{5 \text{ sec}} \right)$. As the number of waves that pass a given point per unit of time increases, the frequency also increases.

Have you ever stood on a pier and watched water waves pass underneath? The number of waves that pass per unit of time is the wave frequency. The longer the wave, the more time it takes to pass a given point. The shorter the wave, the less time it takes to pass a given point.

> *EXPERIMENT. Hold one end of a thin strip of metal in your hand. Place the other end in a pan of water. Vibrate the metal strip so waves are produced. Obtain a tuning fork and hold it by the stem. Tap it lightly so the prongs vibrate. Dip the vibrating prongs into a pan of water. What happens? Explain your observations.* vibrations set up in water
> *You can project the waves produced if you use a flat, clear glass dish set on an overhead projector. The waves will project onto a wall or screen.*

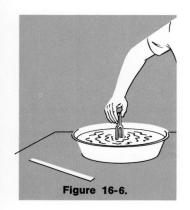

Figure 16-6.

Have you ever watched a floating cork or bottle? What happens when a wave passes through the water? The cork moves up and down. The number of up and down movements of the cork in a given unit of time is the wave frequency.

Water waves are slow compared to most energy waves. Frequencies of light waves are so large that they are difficult for the human mind to grasp.

Wavelength and frequency vary inversely. Vary inversely means that as one value increases the other decreases. If you double the wavelength, the frequency is halved. If you double the frequency, the wavelength is halved. Long waves have a low frequency. Short waves have a high frequency.

Figure 16-7. What determines the shape of a wave trace made by a tuning fork?

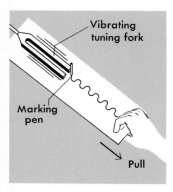

Amplitude of vibration and frequency.

PROBLEMS

1. A cork floating on water moves up and down 10 times in 30 sec. What is the frequency of the water wave? *0.3 vib/sec*
2. A tuning fork produces a sound of musical note middle C. It moves back and forth 256 times each second. What is the frequency of the tuning fork? *256 vib/sec*

16:3 *Sound Waves*

A metal disc or diaphragm inside the telephone mouthpiece vibrates when it is struck by sound waves.

When a bell or the prongs of a tuning fork vibrate, they produce sound waves. When a person speaks, vibrations of his vocal cords produce sound waves. **Sound waves** are compressional waves produced by vibrations. Sound waves move through air or other matter. They may be detected by the ear and certain sensitive electrical instruments. For example, a telephone mouthpiece can detect sound waves. The telephone converts sound waves into electrical waves which carry the message over telephone lines.

ACTIVITY. Mount an electric bell inside a bottle so that the bell can be connected to a dry cell outside. The bottle should be sealed with a one-hole stopper containing a piece of glass tubing. Attach a rubber tube to the glass tubing and connect it to a vacuum pump. Connect the bell so it rings. Then pump the air out of the bottle. Does the loudness of the sound increase, <u>decrease</u>, or remain the same?

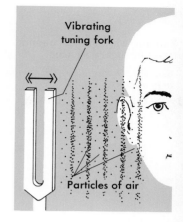

Figure 16-8. Compression is the point in a compressional wave at which particles of matter move together. Rarefaction is the point at which they move apart.

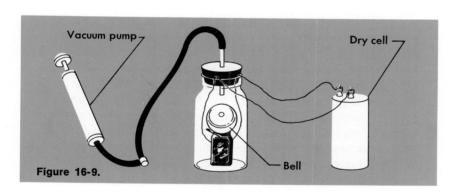

Figure 16-9.

EXPERIMENT. Obtain a test tube rack, water, medicine dropper, and 8 test tubes. Put different amounts of water in each test tube. Blow across the top of each tube to sound a musical note. Use the medicine dropper to adjust the level of water in each test tube so you can play the 8 notes of a musical scale. Make a drawing of the test tubes showing the amount of water in each test tube. Where is the sound wave produced inside the test tube, in the <u>air</u> or water?

Figure 16-10.

Sound cannot travel through empty space. It must have a substance to go through. Sound waves produced by vibrations are to-and-fro movements of particles of matter. The particles of a solid are packed closely together. It is easy to transfer

Explain why sound cannot travel through a vacuum.

Sound is transmitted by the motion of molecules.

vibrations from molecule to molecule if the molecules are close together. Therefore, sound waves move faster through solids than through liquids and gases. Do sound waves move faster through a liquid or a gas? Explain why.*The molecules are closer together.*

The speed of sound in air at 0°C and one atmosphere pressure is 335 m/sec or 1,088 ft/sec. For convenience, remember that the speed of sound in air is about 1,100 ft/sec. Sound travels through warm air faster than through cold air. The speed of sound increases about 60 cm/sec (2 ft/sec) for each Celsius degree rise in temperature. At 20°C (room temperature), sound travels through air at 344 m/sec. This speed is 1,130 ft/sec, or 765 mi/hr.

A tuning fork vibrates in only one frequency. Another tuning fork vibrating in the same frequency can cause the first tuning fork to begin vibrating spontaneously. This is called sympathetic vibration. The tuning fork vibrating and the fork which caused it to vibrate are said to be in *resonance*. That is, they vibrate at the same frequency.

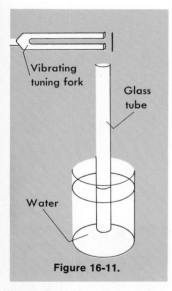

Vibrating tuning fork

Glass tube

Water

Figure 16-11.

Waves reflected back through the tube combine with and reinforce waves coming into the tube. Crest adds to crest and trough adds to trough, making the sound louder. Higher pitch sound has a shorter wavelength. Length of wave at resonance is 4X the length of the air column.

How can you find the length of a sound wave.

EXPERIMENT. Find the wavelength of a sound wave with the following method. (1) Lower a 45-cm long, 2.5-cm diameter glass tube into a jar of water. Hold a vibrating tuning fork over the end of the tube. Meanwhile, change the length of the tube by moving it up and down in the water. When the air in the tube is in resonance with the tuning fork, the sound becomes much louder. Resonance results when the air in the tube vibrates at the same frequency as the tuning fork. (2) At the resonance point, measure the length of the air column in the tube above the water. The wavelength of the sound wave produced by the tuning fork is 4 times the length of the air column at resonance. Why is the sound louder when resonance occurs? Repeat this experiment with a tuning fork of different frequency. Is the resonance column of air longer or shorter? Explain.

You can compute the wavelength of a wave with the following formula. $v = f\lambda$ or $\lambda = \dfrac{v}{f}$

$$f = \text{frequency}$$
$$v = \text{speed of sound}$$
$$\lambda = \text{wavelength}$$

To find the wavelength of a sound wave, divide the speed of sound by the frequency of the wave.

EXAMPLE

What is the wavelength of sound waves that have a frequency of 43 vib/sec in air at 20°C?

Solution: (a) Write the equation: $\lambda = \dfrac{v}{f}$

        (b) Substitute 344 m/sec for v and 43 vib/sec for f: $\lambda = \dfrac{344 \text{ m/sec}}{43 \text{ vib/sec}}$

        (c) Divide 344 by 43 to find λ

        (d) Answer: $\lambda = 8$ m/vib, or simply 8 m

PROBLEMS

3. What is the wavelength of sound waves having a frequency of 256 vib/sec at 20°C? *4.4 ft or 1.32 m*
4. What is the frequency of a sound wave with a wavelength of 1 at 0°C? *335 vib/sec*

Sound waves of different frequencies have different wavelengths. As frequency increases, wavelength decreases. When you strike the extreme right key of a piano, you produce sound waves of high frequency. Their wavelengths are about 7.7 cm (3 in.) long. Strike the extreme left key and you produce waves of low frequency. Their wavelengths are about 12.2 m (40 ft).

The human ear can detect a certain physical order in almost all the sounds considered musical. The frequencies of musical sounds have an arithmetic order and the frequencies of nonmusical sounds have no arithmetic order.

To find the frequency of a wave, use this formula: $f = \dfrac{v}{\lambda}$.

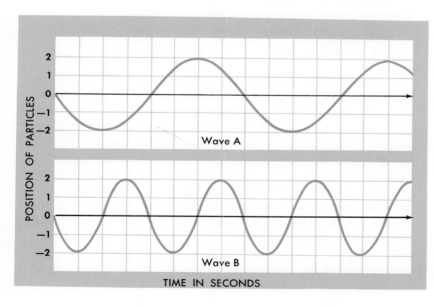

Wave A and wave B have the same amplitude.

Figure 16-12. Wave B has a wavelength ½ that of wave A. The frequency of wave B is twice the frequency of wave A.

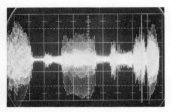

Figure 16-13. The electrical components of an oscilloscope convert invisible sound waves into visible waves on the fluorescent screen.

PROBLEMS

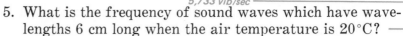

5. What is the frequency of sound waves which have wavelengths 6 cm long when the air temperature is 20°C? *5,733 vib/sec*

6. What is the frequency of sound waves which have wavelengths 12 m long when the air temperature is 20°C? *28.7 vib/sec*

7. What is the frequency of sound waves which have wavelengths 12 m long when the air temperature is 25°C? *28.9 vib/sec*

8. How long does it take sound to travel a mile? How far away is a lightning bolt if you hear the thunder 10 sec after you see the flash? *At 20°C sound travels 1 mile in 4.7 seconds — 2.1 miles*

Some sounds are so loud they hurt your ears. The *loudness* of a sound is determined by the amplitude of the sound waves. As the amplitude of the sound waves increases, the loudness of the sound increases. Do you ever shout at a basketball or football game? When you yell you produce sounds with amplitudes larger than those of normal speech.

Sound waves traveling in air from two different vibrating objects may meet and interfere with each other. This **interference** may be *destructive* or *constructive*. When the crest of one sound wave meets the trough of another sound wave, destructive interference takes place. The sound decreases in loudness and may disappear. When the crest of one sound wave meets the crest of another sound wave, constructive interference takes place. The sound increases in loudness. The same thing happens when two troughs meet.

When a crest of one wave meets a crest of another wave, the waves are said to be *in phase*. When a crest and a trough meet, the waves are said to be *out of phase*.

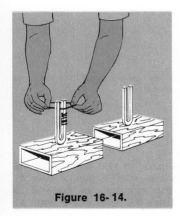

Figure 16-14.

EXPERIMENT. Have a classmate blow two whistles at the same time. How is the sound different from the sound made by one whistle? Obtain two tuning forks of the same frequency. The forks must be fastened to resonator boxes. First, sound the two forks together. Then attach several rubber bands tightly around one prong of one fork to decrease its frequency slightly. Sound the two forks again. The wavering sound is called a beat. *Count the number of beats in 15 seconds. Repeat the procedure, each time increasing the number of rubber bands. How is the frequency of beats related to the difference in frequency of two sounds? Interference causes alternating reinforcement (waves in phase) and destruction (waves out of phase) of sound waves. When is the sound volume loudest and lowest?*

The number of beats is equal to the difference in frequencies. Volume is loudest when waves are in phase *(crest adds to crest and trough adds to trough) and lowest when out of phase (crest and trough cancel).*

The *pitch* of a sound is determined by the frequency of the sound waves. Sounds of high pitch have high frequency. Sounds of low pitch have low frequency. In playing the scale on a musical instrument, a musician changes pitch. The higher the note is on the scale, the higher its frequency. There are many different kinds of musical scales. A musical scale is based on the ratios between sound frequences.

What happens to the sounds you hear? Where do they go? Sound energy is changed to heat energy. When sound moves through a substance, it causes the molecules of the substance to vibrate faster. Molecular kinetic energy of the molecules increases. Thus the substance's temperature increases a tiny amount (Section 14:5). Remember, energy can be changed from one form to another. All forms of energy can be changed to heat.

Many sound waves are around you that you cannot hear. Most people hear compressional waves if their frequency is between about 20 vib/sec and about 20,000 vib/sec. Sounds above this frequency range are said to be *ultrasonic*. Ultrasonic sounds cannot be heard by human beings. Some animals, however, can hear ultrasonic sounds. For example, a dog can hear sounds with frequencies up to 25,000 vib/sec.

Which properties of a sound wave determine loudness and pitch?

amplitude and frequency

At one time it was believed that the oceans were silent. Since the development of underwater sound detecting equipment it has been learned that all sorts of sea animals make grunts, whistles, cracks, rattles, and pops.

What is ultrasonic sound?

The development of sonar was spurred by the need to detect icebergs and submarines. One kind of sonar system emits short sound pulses (.1 sec) with a frequency ranging from 10,000 to 26,000 vib/sec.
Since the velocity of sound in seawater is 2400 km/sec the wavelengths of these sounds are from 5 to 13 centimeters.

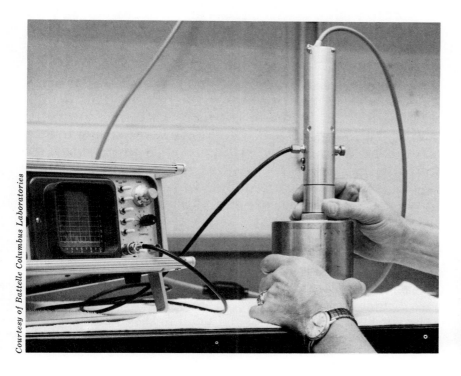

Courtesy of Battelle Columbus Laboratories

Figure 16-15. This ultrasonic instrument is being used to detect internal structural defects in metals.

PROBLEMS

9. Why can some whistles be heard by dogs and not by people? *Dogs hear the ultrasonic vibrations.*

10. How does a bat use ultrasonic sound echoes to find its way through a dark cave? *Bats emit high frequency sound which reflect off objects.*

11. How can sonar sound waves be used in naval navigation? *Sonar waves are sent out from a ship. The echo of the wave from the bottom is timed.*

16:4   *Ripple Tank*

Images of water waves in a ripple tank are produced on the screen below the glass bottom of the tank.

How is a ripple tank used to study waves?

To study waves a device known as a ripple tank is often used. A **ripple tank** is a shallow, transparent, waterproof box containing a layer of water one or two centimeters deep (Figure 16–16).

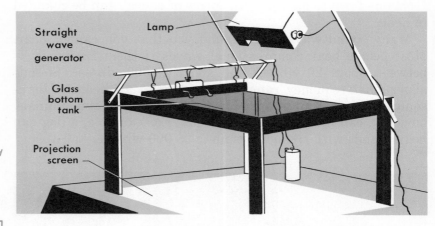

Figure 16-16. As waves move through the water, their shadows make a pattern on the screen.

These images are produced because the crest of the waves act as converging (convex) lenses and tend to focus light from the lamp. The troughs act as diverging (concave) lenses and tend to spread the light out. The crests appear as light bands and the troughs appear as bright bands.

Figure 16-17. Light waves are given off by a light bulb in all directions.

Waves produced in the ripple tank are models of sound, light, and other kinds of energy waves. Vibrations or disturbances in the center of the tank cause water waves to spread out in concentric circles. These waves are two-dimensional. Sound waves, light waves, and other energy waves are three-dimensional. Energy waves spread away from their source in a spherical pattern (Figure 16–17). The ripple tank gives us a two-dimensional idea of how a three-dimensional wave may act.

At great distances from their source, energy waves appear to straighten out. They move in straight lines parallel to each other. To illustrate, waves in the ocean or on a large lake approach the shore parallel to each other. Because these waves are distant from their source, they no longer appear circular. The ripple tank, however, is too small to show this change. A ripple tank does not permit circular waves to travel far

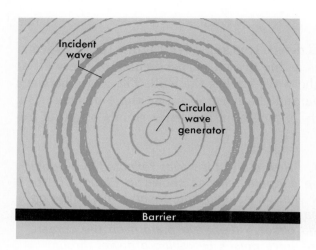
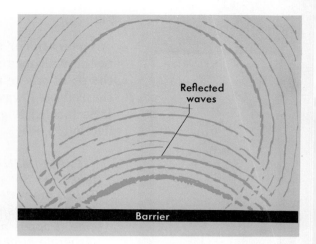

Figure 16-18. a. Vibrations at a point in the water produce circular waves. b. Circular pattern of the water waves is retained when they are reflected from a straight barrier.

enough to become parallel waves. Ripple tank waves and energy waves are not exactly alike. A model is never exactly like the real thing.

16:5 Reflection

A ripple tank can be used to investigate the reflection of waves. Wave **reflection** (ri flek′ shun) occurs when a wave strikes an object and is bounced off in a different direction. The waves that strike an object are called *incident waves*. The waves that bounce off the object are called *reflected waves* (Figure 16–18). Reflection in a ripple tank can be seen by floating a piece of wood on the water. The wood serves as a barrier parallel to the waves. When a stream of waves is generated, the waves strike the wooden barrier and bounce back in the direction from which they came (Figure 16–20). The reflecting barrier can be set at an angle to the oncoming waves. Then the waves are reflected off the barrier at an angle.

Think of a wave striking a wall at an angle. The angle between the wall and a line drawn normal to the wall is the *angle*

What is wave reflection?

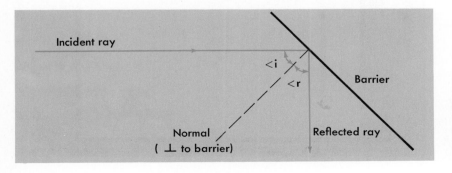

Figure 16-19. The normal is drawn perpendicular to the barrier and forms the angle of reflection and the angle of incidence with the reflected ray and the incident ray.

Figure 16-20.

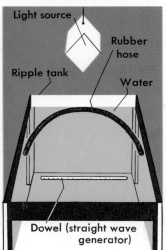

Figure 16-21. Reflection of straight waves by a parabola produces circular waves.

Angle of incidence = angle of reflection. Waves reflected off the block are parallel. Waves reflected from the hose are curved and focus at a point in front of the hose. Both the waves in the tank and electromagnetic waves can be reflected and refracted.

Figure 16-22. Waves are refracted as they pass at an angle into shallow water.

of incidence (in′ si dens). It is angle i in Figure 16–19. Normal to the wall means a line drawn perpendicular to the wall at the point where the wave strikes the wall. The angle between the reflected wave and the normal is the *angle of reflection*. It is labeled angle r. Angle of incidence equals angle of reflection: $i = r$.

EXPERIMENT. How are water waves reflected in a ripple tank? (1) Set up a ripple tank as shown in Figure 16–16. Touch the water with your finger and observe the waves on the screen. Release drops of water into the tank from a medicine dropper and observe the wave pattern on the screen. Generate straight wave pulses by rolling a dowel through a fraction of a revolution in the water. Practice until you get sharp wave images on the screen. (2) Place a wooden block in the center of the tank; then produce waves with the dowel which strike the block at 0°. Then vary the position of the block so as to reflect waves at different angles. (3) Bend a rubber tube so it forms a curve across one end of the tank (Figure 16–21). Use the tube as a reflector for the waves you generate with the dowel.

How does the angle of incidence of the waves compare with the angle of reflection? How is reflection from the parabolic hose different from the wooden block?

16:6 *Refraction*

Refraction (ri frak′ shun) is the bending of waves. You can study refraction in a ripple tank such as the one described in Section 16:4.

As water waves pass into shallow water, their wavelength becomes shorter. Their velocity decreases. What is the ex-

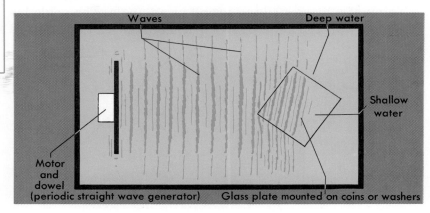

planation? Remember the equation $v = \lambda f$? Speed equals wavelength times frequency. If the frequency (f) stays the same and the wavelength (λ) becomes smaller, the speed (v) must decrease. This is what happens to water waves as they pass from deep to shallow water. In the experiment above you see the wavelength of the waves decrease over the glass plate. Therefore, you can assume the velocity of the waves decreases.

How is refraction studied in a ripple tank?

EXPERIMENT. Set up a ripple tank. Place a flat glass plate (about 12 × 18 cm) on some metal washers at one end of the tank. Adjust the plate so that its upper surface is about 1 mm below the water surface. This makes the water above the plate very shallow. The plate should be parallel to waves generated at the opposite end of the tank. Generate waves with a wooden dowel (Figure 16–23). Observe the wave path over the glass plate. Now set the plate so that its edge is at a 45° angle to the waves. Repeat the wave generation and observe the wave path over the glass plate. What change occurs?

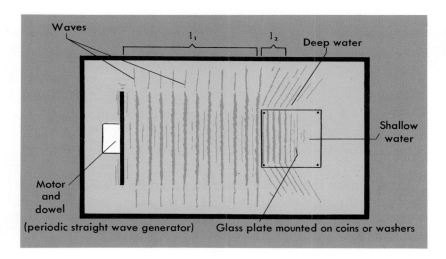

Figure 16-23. Wave speed and wavelength change when the waves pass into shallow water. How?

When waves pass into shallow water at an angle, the waves are bent, or refracted (Figure 16–22). Refraction occurs because one side of the wave passes from deep to shallow water before the rest of the wave. This side of the wave is slowed down. With one side going slow and one side going fast, the wave curves. It is refracted toward the slow side.

Refraction is always toward the area in which the velocity of a wave is decreased. This principle of refraction may be explained by an analogy. Suppose two small wheels are mounted on an axle. As they roll across a tabletop, one wheel reaches a soft velvet cloth and is slowed down by friction. The other wheel continues at its faster velocity. It is pulled toward the slower wheel. The change in velocity of the wheel on the cloth causes a change in direction of the total system. The wheels turn toward the soft cloth, the area in which velocity is decreased.

Explain how a wave is refracted.

Sound waves increase speed when passing from a solid into a gas and change speed when passing from one section of air into another section of air.

Any type of wave can be refracted. Whenever a wave passes from one substance to another substance its speed changes. If the wave approaches the boundary between two substances at an oblique angle, it is refracted. Sound waves may be refracted when they pass from a solid into a gas. Why? Sound waves also may be refracted when they pass from warm air into cold air. Or from cold air into warm air. Can you explain why?

Figure 16-24. Waves are refracted when their speed decreases.

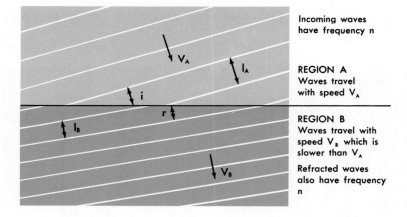

Incoming waves have frequency n

V_A

I_A

i

REGION A
Waves travel with speed V_A

r

I_B

REGION B
Waves travel with speed V_B which is slower than V_A

V_B

Refracted waves also have frequency n

Light waves that strike glass at an angle are refracted as they pass through the glass. This principle is used in lenses found in eyeglasses, cameras, telescopes, and other optical instruments.

16:7 Doppler Effect

ACTIVITY. Obtain three tuning forks. Strike each lightly to sound a tone. Why does each fork make a sound when struck? The frequency of vibrations is marked on each fork. Compare the frequency to the tone produced.

Pitch and frequency are related. The pitch of a sound is determined by its frequency. The higher the frequency, the

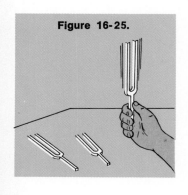

Figure 16-25.

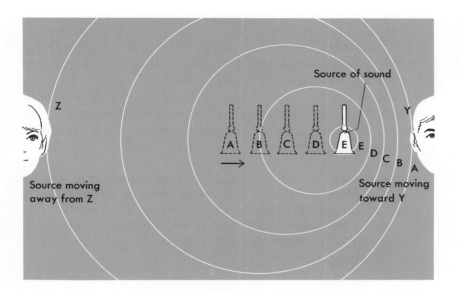

Figure 16-26. The Doppler effect shown here may also be demonstrated by swinging a toy whistle rapidly around on the end of a string.

Source of sound

Z

Source moving
away from Z

Source moving
toward Y

higher the pitch. The **Doppler effect** is an apparent change in wave frequency caused by movement of the body making the waves. A high speed racing car is a good example of the Doppler effect. As the car rapidly approaches you, the observer, the sound of the motor increases in pitch. As the car passes you and continues down the track, the pitch of the motor decreases. Why? As the high speed auto approaches you, it crowds the sound waves coming from the engine closer together causing the increase in pitch you hear. As the auto recedes, its high speed gives the effect of the sound waves from the engine spreading apart and the pitch decreases (Figure 16–27).

Have you ever heard the siren of an approaching police car? The pitch of the siren increases as the car approaches you. The Doppler effect may also be produced if the observer moves toward the source of sound. If you ride on a train moving

Explain the Doppler effect.

The Doppler effect has been used to support the theory that the universe is expanding. Light from distant stars has longer wavelengths than light from nearby stars. This phenomenon is explained by the movement of these stars away from us at tremendous speeds.

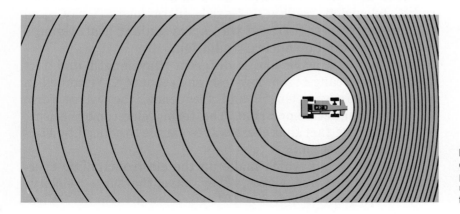

Figure 16-27. A high-speed car motor is louder as it approaches us than after it passes us because of the Doppler effect.

Figure 16-28.

toward a warning bell at a crossing, the sound of the clanging bell rises in pitch. Increasing pitch means that wave frequency is increasing and wavelength is decreasing.

As the source of a sound moves away rapidly, you hear a decrease in pitch. Decreasing pitch means that wave frequency is decreasing. What change occurs in the wavelength when frequency decreases?

EXPERIMENT. Set up a ripple tank as described in Section 16:4. Make waves with a vibrating metal strip. Move the metal strip forward slowly while it vibrates. Do you see a change in the wavelength? Repeat the procedure, but this time slowly move the strip away from the waves. How does the wavelength change?

By traveling in a small boat, you can witness an effect similar to the Doppler effect. If you travel against the waves, they strike the boat with a relatively high frequency. The ride may be very choppy. If you travel with the waves, they catch up to the boat more slowly. The frequency with which the waves strike the boat is relatively low.

One practical use of the Doppler effect is in radar speed-detecting devices. Radar waves are sent out and reflected back from a moving car to a receiver. Changes in frequency of the radar waves are caused by the car moving toward the receiver. The change in frequency is converted to speed in miles per hour by the radar receiver. In this way it is possible to detect vehicles traveling faster than legal speed limits.

Figure 16-29. Infrared photograph of a citrus orchard.

U.S. Dept. of Agriculture

16:8 *Electromagnetic Spectrum*

There are invisible waves all around you. For example: radio, television, radar, infrared, ultraviolet, X-ray, and gamma-ray waves. Infrared waves are radiant heat. Gamma rays are one kind of nuclear radiation.

Each kind of wave has a different wavelength and frequency. They range from low to high frequency. Arranged in order of their wavelength and frequency, the waves form an **electromagnetic spectrum.** The term "electromagnetism" comes from the fact that these waves can be produced by electricity or magnetism.

All of the waves which make up the electromagnetic spectrum are transverse waves. They have the same velocity: 186,282 mi/sec, or about 3×10^8 m/sec (in a vacuum). Wire-

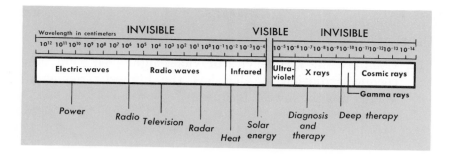

Figure 16-30. Differences in the properties of different parts of the electromagnetic spectrum are caused by differences in wavelengths.

less telegraph waves, at the long-wave end of the spectrum, have wavelengths as great as 2×10^6 centimeter. The frequency of these waves is about 15,000 vib/sec. Gamma rays, at the shortwave end of the spectrum, have wavelengths as small as 5×10^{-11} centimeter. The frequency of gamma waves is very high, up to about 5×10^{20} vib/sec. The main difference between waves in the electromagnetic spectrum is their frequency and wavelength. The higher the frequency, the greater the wave energy.

Nerve endings in your eye are sensitive to electromagnetic waves with wavelengths of about 4×10^{-5} cm (violet light) to 7×10^{-5} cm (red light). This range is known as *visible light*. Cosmic radiation comes to earth from space. It has wavelengths of about 1×10^{-11} to 1×10^{-15} cm.

What kinds of waves are in the electromagnetic spectrum?
The visible light spectrum is the part of the electromagnetic spectrum to which nerve endings (retina) in our eyes are sensitive.

How are the waves in the electromagnetic spectrum similar to, and different from each other?

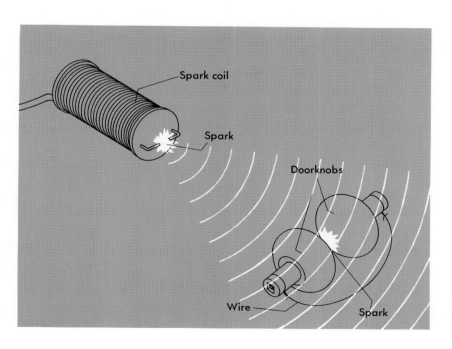

Figure 16-31. Invisible electromagnetic waves can produce an electric spark by induction.

PROBLEM

12. Compare the frequencies of violet light, red light, and cosmic radiation. Which has the highest frequency? Which has the lowest frequency? *Cosmic ray — highest frequency; red light — lowest frequency.*

MAIN IDEAS

pp. 332-334 1. Wavelength, frequency, and amplitude are three properties of a wave.

pp. 332-333 2. There are two kinds of waves: transverse and compressional.

p. 335 3. A sound wave is a kind of compressional wave which travels through matter.

p. 346 4. Electromagnetic waves are transverse waves capable of traveling in a vacuum.

p. 339 5. The pitch of a sound depends on wave frequency.

p. 341 6. Models of energy waves can be produced in a ripple tank and projected on a screen.

pp. 341-342 7. For a reflected wave, the angle of incidence equals the angle of reflection.

pp. 342-343 8. Refraction is the bending of light waves passing from one medium to another.

p. 343 9. When a light wave passes from one medium to another medium, its velocity changes.

p. 345 10. The Doppler effect is a change in wave frequency caused by the motion of the wave source.

p. 347 11. Different energy waves making up the electromagnetic spectrum differ in wavelengths and frequency.

p. 346 12. The energy waves in the electromagnetic spectrum can be produced by electric and magnetic energy.

VOCABULARY

Write a sentence in which you correctly use each of the following words or terms.

amplitude	interference	transverse
compressional wave	pitch	ultrasonic
Doppler effect	reflection	vibration
electromagnetic spectrum	refraction	wave
frequency	resonance	wavelength

STUDY QUESTIONS

Have students rewrite false statements to make the statements correct.

A. True or False

Determine whether each of the following sentences is true or false. (Do not write in this book.)

F **1.** Sound travels in ~~longitudinal~~ waves. — *compressional*

T **2.** The pitch of a sound wave depends on its frequency.

F **3.** When frequency increases, wavelength ~~increases~~. — *decreases*

T **4.** Short waves usually have a relatively high frequency.

F **5.** Sound waves travel ~~easily~~ through a vacuum. — *cannot*

T **6.** Resonance is an example of sympathetic vibration.

F **7.** ~~Frequency~~ determines the loudness of a sound wave. — *wave amplitude*

F **8.** Sound waves having a frequency ~~below 200~~ vib/sec are called ultrasonic. — *above 20,000*

F **9.** Most people can hear sound with frequencies above 20,000 vib/sec. — *not*

T **10.** The wavelength of visible light varies from 4×10^{-5} to 7×10^{-5}/cm.

Some questions in part B may have more than one correct answer. Only one answer is required.

B. Multiple Choice

Choose one word or phrase that correctly completes each of the following sentences. (Do not write in this book.)

1. Sound waves are (transverse, <u>compressional</u>, two-dimensional, visible) waves.

2. A light wave is a(n) (<u>transverse</u>, compressional, invisible, two-dimensional) wave.

3. The number of vibrations/unit time is (amplitude, wavelength, <u>frequency</u>, velocity).

4. As frequency increases, wavelength (increases, <u>decreases,</u> remains the same).

5. The loudness of a sound is a function of (<u>amplitude,</u> wavelength, frequency, velocity).

6. A sound with a frequency of 25,000 vib/sec (has a low pitch, has a long wavelength, <u>cannot be heard by human beings,</u> has a high velocity).

7. To produce a wave in a ripple tank, (turn on a lamp, put water in the tank, <u>make a vibration in the water,</u> set up a screen).

8. When a wave is reflected, its wavelength (increases, decreases, <u>remains the same</u>).

9. The law of reflection states that the angle of incidence and the angle of reflection (are equal, vary inversely, vary directly).

10. The amount that a wave is refracted depends upon the (velocity, change in velocity, amplitude, frequency).

C. Completion

Complete each of the following sentences with a word or phrase that will make the sentence correct. (Do not write in this book.)

1. The Doppler effect is caused by a change in the __?__ of a sound source. *position*

2. The use of radar speed-detecting devices is an application of the __?__. *Doppler effect*

3. The velocity of electromagnetic waves is __?__ m/sec. *3 X 10^8 m/sec*

4. __?__ waves have the highest frequency in the electromagnetic spectrum. *cosmic*

5. __?__ waves have the shortest wavelength in the electromagnetic spectrum. *electric*

6. All forms of energy can be changed to __?__ energy. *kinetic*

7. To produce refraction in a ripple tank, change the __?__ of the water waves. *speed*

8. An increase in the pitch of a sound results from an increase in the __?__ of the sound. *frequency*

D. How and Why

See Teacher's Guide for diagram. 1. A wave approaches a barrier at an angle of 25°. Draw a diagram to show the angle of incidence and the angle of reflection for the wave.

2. A ripple tank wave generator produces 15 waves in 3 seconds. What is the wave frequency? *5 waves/sec*

3. What happens to water waves traveling from shallow to deep water? *speed changes so they are refracted*

See Teacher's Guide. 4. How is a transverse wave different from a compressional wave? Name two examples of each kind of wave.

5. How can you attract the attention of a friend standing 100 yd away without using energy waves? *It cannot be done.*

See Teacher's Guide for diagram. 6. Draw a diagram of a wave and label the wavelength and amplitude. Draw a second diagram of a wave with a greater frequency than the first wave.

7. What is the electromagnetic spectrum?

8. How are infrared waves different from red light waves? How are ultraviolet waves different from violet light waves? In what ways are infrared, red, ultraviolet, and violet light waves alike?

9. How can you demonstrate the Doppler effect in a ripple tank?

10. What is the wavelength in meters of a radio wave with a frequency of 540 kilocycles (540,000 vib/sec)?

7. *See Teacher's Guide.*

8. *See Teacher's Guide.*

9. *Move the rippler.*

10. *600 m*

INVESTIGATIONS

See Teacher's Guide at the front of the book for answers and suggestions.

1. When studying the stars, scientists frequently refer to the "red shift." Do library research and report on this topic.

2. Research and report on the history of radar.

3. Obtain an 8-mm motion picture camera and make a short film of waves at the seashore. Picture different kinds of wave motion and the effects of waves. Learn about ocean waves from the book by Willard Bascom listed in Interesting Reading. Show the film and make a report to your class.

4. Obtain information on acoustics. Learn how auditoriums and other buildings are designed with sound in mind.

5. Sound travels about one mile in five seconds. During a thunderstorm, time the interval between the flash of lightning you see and the thunder you hear. Be sure to remain indoors when you make your observations. Calculate the average distance of each lightning bolt. Average your results.

INTERESTING READING

Bamberger, Richard, *Physics Through Experiments.* New York, Sterling Press, 1969.

Bascom, Willard, *Waves and Beaches: The Dynamics of the Ocean Surface.* New York, Doubleday & Company, Inc., 1964.

Stevens, S. S., and Warshofsky, Fred, *Sound and Hearing.* New York, Life Science Library, Time Inc., 1965.

Thomsen, D. E., "Rock Around the Garden." *Science News,* CII (July 15, 1972), pp. 44-45.

Optics

GOAL: You will gain an understanding of the properties of light and how to use mirrors and lenses to produce images through reflection and refraction.

Nerve endings sensitive to light are present in the retina at the rear of the eye. These nerves connect through the optic nerve to the brain.

Your sense of sight helps you to learn about the world. You see shapes and colors around you every day. However, without light your eyes would be of no use to you. Your eye contains nerve endings which sense light energy. When light reaches these nerve endings, nerve impulses travel from the eye to the brain.

To see, light must be present. The sun, stars, lamps, and even lightning bugs give off light. Light is produced in certain chemical changes such as burning. Light is also given off when solids such as steel are heated to very high temperatures. Light is also produced in neon and fluorescent lamps by passing an electric current through a gas.

17:1 *Plane Mirrors*

Optics is the branch of science which deals with the nature and properties of light. One way to study light is through the use of mirrors.

EXPERIMENT. Where does an image appear in a plane (flat surfaced) mirror? Set up a small plane mirror perpendicular to a tabletop. Place a candle taller than the mirror 10 centimeters in front of the mirror. Place a second candle of the same size behind the mirror. Look at the image of the first candle in the mirror. Move the second candle to the point at which its top portion coincides with the top portion of the image. How far is the candle beyond the mirror? 10 cm

A virtual image in a mirror can be seen although the image has no physical form.

Look at your reflection in a mirror. Your image appears to be behind the mirror. It appears the same distance behind the mirror as you are in front of the mirror. The image produced in a plane mirror is called a *virtual* (vur' teu al) *image.* Although you can see it, a virtual image does not exist in reality.

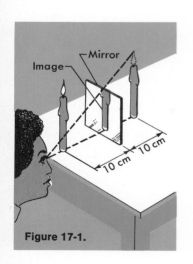

Figure 17-1.

It only appears to exist. A virtual image cannot be projected plane onto a screen.

Two physical properties of light cause a mirror to produce an image. Light travels in a straight line. The angle of incidence of a light ray is equal to the angle of reflection (Section 16:5). The smooth surface of a mirror causes nearly all light rays to be reflected in a regular pattern. If light rays are bounced off in a haphazard fashion, they are reflected in many directions. The reflected light has no pattern and produces no image. You cannot see an image in a rough surface such as a concrete floor, a grass lawn, or a brick wall. Light is reflected from these surfaces in many directions without forming a uniform pattern.

PROBLEM

1. Name 5 things in which you can see an image of yourself.

Examples are, surface of a still pond, newly-waxed car fender.

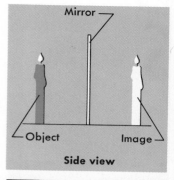

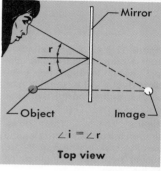

Figure 17-2. An image in a plane mirror appears to be the same distance behind the mirror as the object is in front of the mirror.

Figure 17-3. Most mirrors are pieces of smooth glass with a coating of silver on the back.

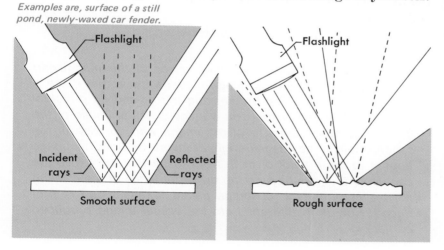

Figure 17-4. The parabolic mirror behind this lighthouse lamp focuses light into parallel rays.

17:2   *Parabolic Mirrors*

Special curved mirrors called **parabolic** (par' ah bawl' ik) **mirrors** are used as reflectors for searchlights and automobile headlights. A shaving mirror is a parabolic mirror. When a lamp is placed near a parabolic mirror, its light rays are reflected parallel to an imaginary line drawn straight out from the center of the mirror.

The surface of a parabolic mirror curves in the shape of a line called a *parabola* (Figure 17–5). A line straight out from the center of the mirror is called the **principal axis**. Light rays striking a parabolic mirror parallel to its principal axis are

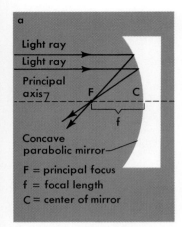

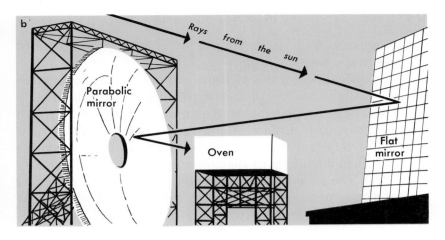

Figure 17-5 a. Light reflected from a concave parabolic mirror passes through the principal focus. The greater the curvature, the shorter the focal length.

Figure 17-5 b. This bowl-shaped mirror concentrates the parallel rays of the sun by focusing them onto a single place in the oven.

Demonstration: The principle of a parabolic mirror can be shown by arranging a half dozen small mirrors in a curve and shining a light on the mirrors.

Have the students learn the terms that apply to the parabolic mirror and lens (e.g.: principal axis, principal focus, focal length).

reflected toward a common point in front of the mirror. This point is called the *principal focus*. The distance from the center of the mirror to the principal focus is the *focal length* of the mirror. "Solar ovens" have a parabolic mirror. The parabolic shape of the reflecting mirror surface concentrates reflected heat onto a small spot for cooking.

EXPERIMENT. Use a shaving mirror of the magnifying type to produce a virtual image. Darken the room. Place a lighted candle between the shaving mirror and its principal focus. Look in the mirror. You will see a virtual image of the candle. Compare the size of the image with the size of the larger *candle itself. Is the image* upright *or inverted? Does the image appear to be* in back *of or in front of the mirror? Move the candle so that it is beyond the principal focus of the shaving mirror. Another type of image called a real image is produced. How is it different from the virtual image produced earlier?* smaller, in front of mirror, upside down

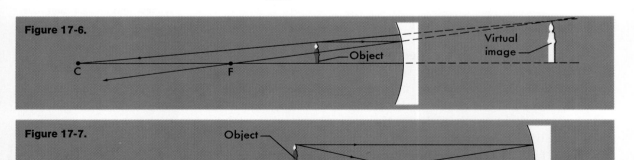

Figure 17-6.

Virtual image

Object

C   F

Figure 17-7.

P

Real image

Object

C   F

A real image formed by a parabolic mirror appears somewhere in front of the mirror. A real image can be projected onto a screen. With a real image, light rays strike the screen to form the image.

Curved mirrors are used in amusement parks to produce amusing images.

> EXPERIMENT. *Place a candle about 2 m in front of a mirror. Use a white index card or white sheet of paper to locate the image. Be careful to hold the card slightly off center from the principal axis of the mirror to allow light rays to reach the mirror and be reflected. Is the image upright or <u>inverted</u>? Is it larger or <u>smaller</u> than the candle? Is it a <u>real</u> or a virtual image?*

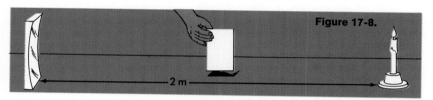

Figure 17-8.

2 m

> *Now move the candle closer to the mirror. Locate the image. How has the size changed? Move the candle toward the mirror until the candle and its real image are at the same point. Compare the size of the candle and its image.* Is the ⌐same size⌐ *image upright or <u>inverted</u>? Continue to move the candle toward the mirror until the image becomes blurred and begins to turn upright. This is the focal point of the mirror. What is the focal length of your mirror?* *Answers will vary.*

The law of reflection also applies to light reflected by a parabolic mirror. Angle of incidence equals the angle of reflection (Figure 17–9).

A parabolic mirror can produce virtual images and real images.

Its properties are similar to a convex lens, Section 17:4.

The location of the real image produced by a parabolic mirror can be calculated with the following equation:

How is mathematics used to locate the real image produced by a parabolic mirror?

$$S_i = \frac{f^2}{S_o}$$

S_i = distance from real image to principal focus

f = focal length

S_o = distance from object to principal focus

EXAMPLE

An apple is placed 50 cm from the principal focus of a parabolic mirror with a 10 cm focal length. What is the distance of the real image from the principal focus?

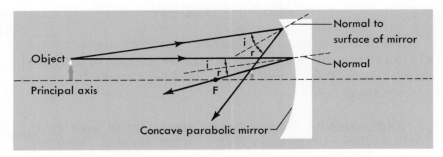

Figure 17-9. Angle of incidence for each ray is equal to the angle of reflection.

Solution: (a) Write the equation: $S_i = \dfrac{f^2}{S_o}$

(b) Substitute 10 cm for f and 50 cm for S_o

$$S_i = \frac{(10 \text{ cm})^2}{50 \text{ cm}}$$

(c) Square the 10 cm and divide by 50 cm to find S_i

$$S_i = \frac{100 \text{ cm}^2}{50 \text{ cm}} = 2 \text{ cm}$$

(d) Answer: $S_i = 2$ cm

Figure 17-10. The focal length is 10 cm and the candle is 5 cm from the principal focus. How far does the image appear to be behind the mirror?

When the object is between the focus and the mirror a virtual image is produced.

$S_i = \dfrac{(10 \text{ cm})^2}{5 \text{ cm}} = 20 \text{ cm}$

10 cm − 5 cm = 5 cm behind the mirror.

Distance of image and object from the focus vary inversely.

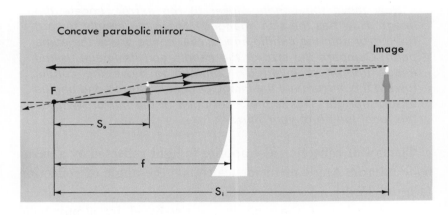

PROBLEMS

2. An object is placed 10 cm from a parabolic mirror which has a 2-cm focal length. How far is the real image from the mirror? *0.4 cm*

3. An object is 6 cm from a parabolic mirror. A real image is formed 24 cm from the mirror. What is the focal length of the mirror? *12 cm*

17:3 Index of Refraction

If you see a coin on the bottom of a swimming pool and want to dive for it, where do you aim? Not at the coin. *Refraction* (ri frak' shun) occurs as light rays are reflected off the coin and pass through the water to your eye. Refraction changes the direction of the light rays. It is hard for you to locate the coin. When you dive in for the coin, aim in front of it (Figure 17–12).

Figure 17-11.

Pencil appears bent.

> EXPERIMENT.   Hold a pencil in a glass of water so that the upper half of the pencil is above the water surface. View the pencil with your eye level to the water's surface. What do you observe? Place a coin in a teacup. Place your eye so the coin is just out of sight. Now have someone fill the teacup with water. Can you see the coin? Explain.   *Yes*

Light is refracted so image of coin reaches eye.

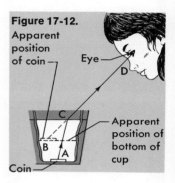

Figure 17-12. Apparent position of coin — Eye — D — Apparent position of bottom of cup — Coin

Light is refracted at an oblique angle as it passes from the water into air. Therefore, a pencil in a glass of water appears broken. Refraction of light is the bending of a light ray as it passes from one material into another (Section 16:6). Refraction is caused by an increase or decrease in the speed of light. The speed of light changes as it passes from one transparent substance to another. For example, if light passes into a glass at an angle, its speed decreases, and it is refracted.

Index of refraction is a measure of the amount that light is refracted by a substance. The greater the change in the speed of light, the larger the index of refraction.

Explain the difference between refraction and index of refraction.

Refraction changes the direction of light rays.

To be refracted, light must strike the surface of a transparent material at an angle. If light strikes perpendicular to a surface, the angle of incidence is zero. Then the light is not refracted.

Index of refraction for glass is shown by the equation below:

$$\text{index of refraction} \atop \text{(glass)} = \frac{\text{speed of light in vacuum}}{\text{speed of light in glass}}$$

Describe the procedure for measuring the index of refraction.

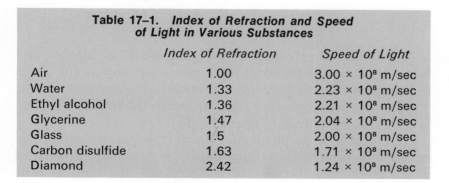

Table 17–1. *Index of Refraction and Speed of Light in Various Substances*

	Index of Refraction	Speed of Light
Air	1.00	3.00×10^8 m/sec
Water	1.33	2.23×10^8 m/sec
Ethyl alcohol	1.36	2.21×10^8 m/sec
Glycerine	1.47	2.04×10^8 m/sec
Glass	1.5	2.00×10^8 m/sec
Carbon disulfide	1.63	1.71×10^8 m/sec
Diamond	2.42	1.24×10^8 m/sec

When is light refracted? Why?

Light is refracted when it passes obliquely from one substance into another. It changes speed.

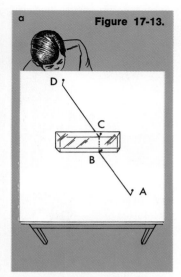

Figure 17-13.

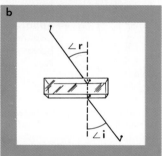

A table of trigonometric functions is needed to do this experiment. Angle i is the angle between D C and the perpendicular. Angle r is the angle between B A and the perpendicular.

The speed of light in air is very close to the speed of light in a vacuum. Therefore, index of refraction is usually found by comparing speed in a substance and air, instead of a vacuum. Measuring the speed of light is complicated. The index of refraction for a material is measured by measuring the angles formed by a refracted light ray. One such procedure is shown in the experiment below.

EXPERIMENT. Find the index of refraction for glass by tracing a light ray through a block of glass. You need a block of glass, a protractor, a piece of paper, straight pins, a pencil, and a piece of cardboard.

Place the paper on the cardboard. Lay the glass in the center of the paper and outline it with a pencil. On the side of the glass away from you, stick two pins in the paper. Place them so that the line between the two pins makes an angle of about 60° with one edge of the glass. Label the locations of the pins point A and point B. Now move your eyes to the level of the table and to the edge of the glass opposite the pins. While sighting through the glass, place two more pins so that they appear in a straight line with points A and B. Label the locations of these pins point C and point D.

Remove the glass and the pins. Draw a line to connect points A and B. Draw a line to connect points C and D. Draw another line to connect points B and C. The line ABCD traces the path of a light ray from point A through the glass. To complete the diagram, draw a line perpendicular to the edge of the glass through point B. Label angle i and angle r as in Figure 17-13b. Measure angles i and r with a protractor. The index of refraction of a transparent substance can be found by using these angles and Snell's Law of refraction.

$$\text{Snell's law: index of refraction} = \frac{\sin i}{\sin r}.$$

$$i = angle\ of\ incidence$$
$$r = angle\ of\ refraction$$

The index of refraction for liquids such as alcohol and mineral oil can be found in much the same way as for glass. Sightings are made through a thin-walled, clear plastic box. The box contains the substance for which the index of refraction is to be measured (Figure 17–14).

A line drawn perpendicular to a transparent surface is called a *normal*. When light enters a transparent surface at an angle and its velocity is decreased, the light is bent

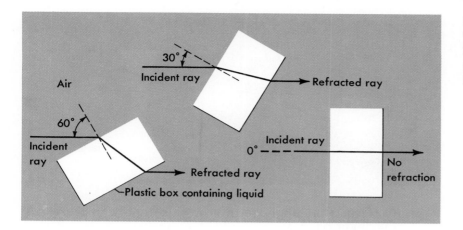

Figure 17-14. As a light ray enters the liquid its speed decreases. The ray is refracted. The slower the speed of light in a transparent material, the higher the index of refraction.

toward the normal. For example, when light passes from air into water or glass, the light is bent toward the normal. When light strikes a transparent surface at an angle and its velocity increases, it is bent away from the normal. For example, when light passes out of glass or water into air, the light is bent away from the normal.

PROBLEMS

See Teacher's Guide at the front of this book.

4. How is light bent if it passes from glass into water? To find the answer, you must know the speed of light in glass and the speed of light in water (Table 17–1). Make a drawing with a light ray to show the refraction.
5. The index of refraction for a special type of glass is 1.75. What is the speed of light in this glass? *1.7 x 10^8 m/sec*
6. The speed of light in a quartz crystal is 1.94×10^8 m/sec. What is the index of refraction for the quartz? *1.6*
7. Oleic acid has an index of refraction of 1.46. How fast does light travel when passing through oleic acid?

2.05 x 10^8 m/sec

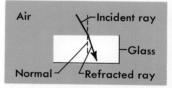

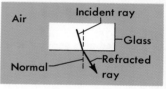

Figure 17-15. A light ray passing through a pane of glass is refracted when it enters and leaves the glass. The two refractions are in opposite directions.

Figure 17-16. To photograph the moon, a moonseeker telescope is lifted by balloon above the atmosphere.

17:4 Lenses

A **lens** is a curved transparent object, usually made of glass or clear plastic. It may have one curved and one straight surface. It may have two curved surfaces. There are two kinds of lenses: convex and concave. A *convex lens* is thicker in the middle than at the edges. Magnifying glasses are examples of convex lenses. A *concave lens* is thinner in the middle than at the edges. It is shaped like the inside of an orange peel. Figure 17–17 shows the shape of a convex lens and the shape of a concave lens.

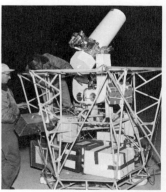

U. S. Air Force

A convex lens is used for farsightedness.

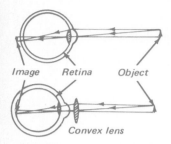

Image   Retina   Object

Convex lens

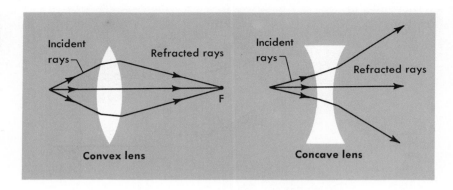

Convex lens — **Concave lens**

Many terms that apply to mirrors also apply to lenses. A convex lens brings light rays together into a principal focus. For this reason, a convex lens is also called a converging lens. Light is refracted as it passes in and out of the lens (Figure 17-17). Light is bent toward the axis of the lens, both when it enters and when it leaves the lens. Rays passing through a thick convex lens are bent more than light rays passing through a thin convex lens. The thicker the center of a convex lens, the shorter the focal length (Figure 17-18). Some light rays pass

Figure 17-18. Can this image be projected on a screen? Why is the image inverted?

It is a real image. The bending of the light rays as they pass through the lens causes them to cross.

A concave lens is used for nearsightedness.

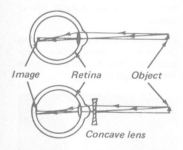

Image   Retina   Object

Concave lens

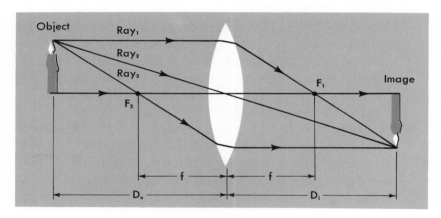

through a lens along the principal axis. Here the angle of incidence is 0°. These light rays do not bend. However, the speed of the light ray passing through the lens still changes.

EXPERIMENT. You can produce a real image with a convex lens. Place a piece of white cardboard upright on a table. Set a lighted candle about 30 cm away. Move a convex lens back and forth between the candle and the cardboard. Does an image appear on the cardboard? Is the image of the candle upright or <u>inverted</u>? The focal length of the lens is halfway between the lens and the image on the screen. Find the focal length of the lens you are using. Answers will vary.

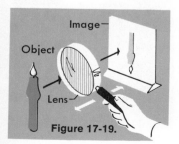

Figure 17-19.

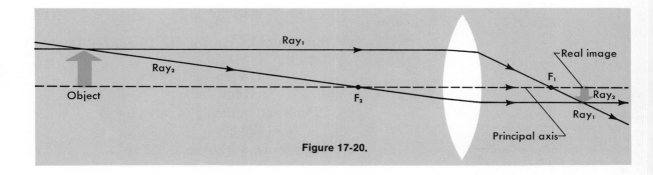

Ray₁ label as Ray_1; Ray₂ as Ray_2; Real image; F_1; F_2; Object; Principal axis

Figure 17-20.

EXPERIMENT. *You can locate a real image with a diagram. On the left side of a piece of paper, draw an upright 2 cm arrow. The arrow represents the object. 15 cm to the right of the arrow, draw a side view of a convex lens 5 cm high. With a ruler, draw a dotted line across the paper through the center of the lens to show its axis. Then measure two 5 cm focal lengths. One to the right of the lens. One to the left of the lens. Mark the principal focus to the left as F_2. Mark the principal focus to the right as F_1.*

Now draw a line parallel to the axis from the top of the arrow to the lens. This line represents a light ray. Continue the line from the lens to the principal focus F_1. Draw a second line from the top of the arrow through the principal focus F_2. Continue the line until it meets the lens. As the ray leaves the lens on the opposite side, continue the ray parallel to the principal axis. The point at which the two lines cross is the top of the real image (Figure 17–20).

As shown in Figure 17-19 when object and image are the same size the focal length is 1/2 the distance between the lens and the object.

Figure 17-20 shows the method to be used in locating a real image. The dimensions used are different from those given in the experiment.

You can use an equation to find the size of the image produced by a convex lens:

$$\frac{H_i}{H_o} = \frac{D_i}{D_o} \qquad \begin{aligned} H_i &= \text{image height} & D_i &= \text{image distance} \\ H_o &= \text{object height} & D_o &= \text{object distance} \end{aligned}$$

To use the equation, you must know three of the values. Then you can calculate the fourth, unknown value.

EXAMPLE

An object 2 cm tall is placed 10 cm from a convex lens. The real image is 24 cm tall. Find the distance of the image from the lens.

Solution: (a) Write the equation

$$\frac{H_i}{H_o} = \frac{D_i}{D_o}$$

(b) Rewrite the equation to solve for D_i

$$D_i = \frac{H_i D_o}{H_o}$$

Have students test the equation by using it for the values given and calculated in the experiment. Values for the diagram and the equation should agree.

(c) Substitute 24 cm for H_i, 10 cm for D_o, and 2 cm for H_o

$$D_i = \frac{(24 \text{ cm})}{2 \text{ cm}} \mid (10 \text{ cm})$$

(d) Divide and multiply to solve for D_i
$$D_i = 120 \text{ cm}$$

(e) Answer: $D_i = 120$ cm or 1.2 m

PROBLEMS

8. A 10-cm tall image of an object 2 cm tall is produced by a convex lens. The image is 24 cm from the lens. Find the distance of the object from the lens. *4.8 cm*

9. An image 2.5 cm tall is formed 1cm from a convex lens. How tall is the object if it is 10 cm from the lens? *0.25 cm*

An image produced by a convex lens may be larger than the object. Or it can be the same size or smaller than the object. When the image is larger than the object, the object is said to be *magnified*. Microscopes, telescopes, binoculars, and picture projectors use convex lenses to magnify objects. If the image is twice as long as the object, the magnification produced by the lens is expressed as 2 power, or 2×. *Magnification* (mag' ni fi kae' shun) is the image length divided by the object length. For example, if the image length is 12 inches and the object length is 3 inches, the magnification is 4×.

If an object is placed between a convex lens and its principal focus, the lens produces a virtual image. When you use a magnifying glass to read fine print, you see a virtual image of the print. The virtual image formed by a convex lens is larger than the object and upright. Remember, a virtual image cannot be projected on a screen. Figure 17–21 shows the virtual image produced by a convex lens.

PROBLEM

10. Close-up pictures may be made by using an extension tube between the lens and the camera. This moves the lens toward the object and away from the film. How does the image size change when the lens is extended?

image becomes larger

17:5   Telescopes

Lenses are used in telescopes to produce enlarged images of distant objects. A simple refracting telescope has two convex

When object is within the focal length distance of the point of principal focus the image is enlarged. (Draw Figure 17-18 with the candle 1/4 in. from the focal point, showing an enlarged image produced.)

Figure 17-21. An object at a distance less than one focal length from a convex lens produces a virtual, erect, enlarged image. The image is on the same side of the lens as the object.

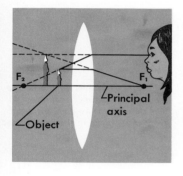

How does a convex lens magnify an object?

This question represents an inquiry or discovery situation. Have students solve the problem on a chalkboard or on paper using Figure 17-18.

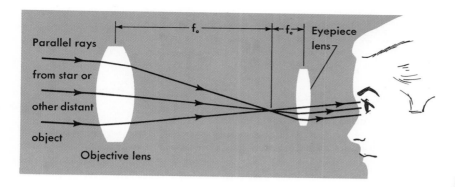

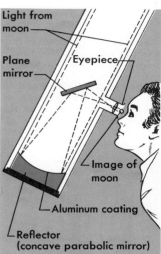

lenses. The *eyepiece lens* has a short focal length. The *objective lens* has a long focal length. Because its lenses refract light, this type of telescope is called a *refracting telescope* (Figure 17–22).

Convex lenses cannot be made much larger than about 100 cm in diameter. When a convex lens is made larger than this, the sheer weight of the lens material causes it to sag. It slowly goes out of shape. How is it possible to make astronomical telescopes with huge magnifications? The very large astronomical telescopes in observatories are parabolic mirrors (Section 17:2). Such telescopes are called *reflecting telescopes*. The Hale telescope at Mt. Palomar, California, contains a parabolic mirror 5 meters in diameter.

PROBLEM

Because the earth rotates at 15°/hr an observatory telescope is mounted so that it rotates in the opposite direction at 15°/hr and thereby continues to be aimed at the same point in the sky as time passes.

11. Does a reflecting telescope produce a real or virtual image?

Reflecting telescopes produce real images, otherwise they could not be used to photograph stars.

Figure 17-24. a. A refracting telescope uses two convex lenses to produce enlarged images. b. Reflecting telescopes are capable of much larger magnifications through the use of parabolic mirrors.

a.

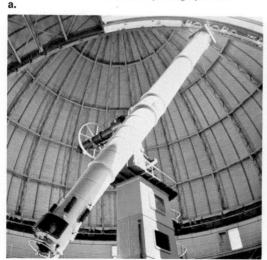

Yerkes Observatory Photo

b.

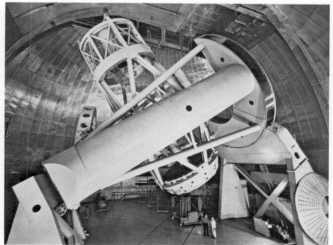

California Institute of Technology & Carnegie Institution of Washington

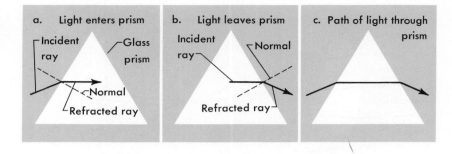

a. Light enters prism

Incident ray — Glass prism — Normal — Refracted ray

b. Light leaves prism

Incident ray — Normal — Refracted ray

c. Path of light through prism

17:6 Prisms

The direction of a light beam changes when it passes through a piece of glass with two faces at an angle to each other. The light is refracted twice. Once as it enters and once as it leaves. Both refractions are in the same direction (Figure 17-25). A transparent material with two straight faces at an angle to each other is called a **prism.**

A light beam passing through glass at an angle other than 0° is always refracted. When the sides of the glass plate are parallel, the incident and emerging light rays are also parallel. If the sides of the glass plate are not parallel, the incident and emerging light rays are not parallel.

Glass prisms can be obtained from scientific supply companies and from some "surplus" stores.

Figure 17-26. Differences in the wavelengths (colors) of light cause differences in the amount of refraction.

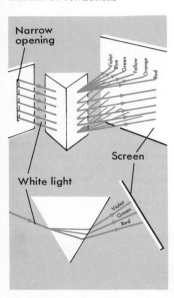

Narrow opening

Violet Blue Green Yellow Orange Red

Screen

White light

Violet Green Red

EXPERIMENT. White light may be separated into a color spectrum. Darken the room and pass a narrow beam of light through a prism. Form a spectrum on a white cardboard or screen. What colors do you see? red, orange, yellow, green, blue, violet

When a beam of white light travels through a prism, the light is spread out, or *dispersed*. The beam leaving the prism is broader than the beam entering the prism. The beam leaving the prism is also separated into the colors of the rainbow. These separated colors are red, orange, yellow, green, blue, indigo, and violet. A band of colors produced by a prism is called a *visible light spectrum*. **Dispersion** is the separation of light into its component colors.

How does a glass prism disperse light? White light is composed of the different colors of the rainbow. The refractive index of each color of light in glass is slightly different. When white light is refracted by a lens, a slight difference in refraction occurs among the various colors. In most lenses, the difference is too small to be obvious. However, the angled faces of a glass prism produce a large refraction of light. The light is refracted twice in the same direction: once as it enters and once as it leaves the prism. The light is dispersed as it enters the prism, and it is dispersed more as it leaves the prism. The refraction is so large that the various colors of light separate as they are dispersed. Red light is refracted least. Violet light is refracted most.

PROBLEMS

12. Which color in the visible light spectrum has the largest index of refraction for glass?   *violet*
13. Which color has the smallest index of refraction (Table 17–2)?   *red*
14. Which color is refracted most by a glass prism?   *violet*
15. Which color in the visible light spectrum is refracted the least?   *red*

Table 17–2.	*Index of Refraction of Glass for Spectrum Colors*
Color	*Index of Refraction*
violet	1.532
blue	1.528
green	1.519
yellow	1.517
orange	1.514
red	1.513

Spectroscopy is not restricted to visible light. Beyond the violet end of the spectrum the normal eye sees nothing, but photographic plates and fluorescent dyes show the existence of many ultraviolet lines. Invisible infrared light exists beyond the red light end of the visible spectrum.

Figure 17-27 shows how two glass prisms can recombine the colors of a visible light spectrum into white light.

Many light sources do not emit white light. Some sources emit only one color of the spectrum. For example, a sodium vapor lamp emits only yellow light. Other sources, such as a mercury vapor lamp, emit several colors of light. An important property of a chemical element is the color spectrum it

Flame tests (page 94) use colored light emitted by heated and vaporized elements to identify specific elements.

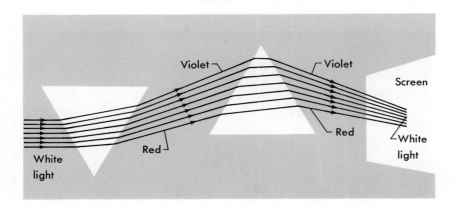

Figure 17-27. Refraction in the two prisms is equal and opposite.

Figure 17-28. A prism may be used to separate a narrow beam of white light into a spectrum of colors. Transparent colored material, called a filter, absorbs some colors and allows one or more colors to pass through. The color of the filter corresponds to the color of the light it transmits. Differences in the color of light are caused by differences in wavelength. Elements give off colored light when they are heated to a high temperature. Each element gives off a unique set of wavelengths. Rubidium, cesium, helium, and hafnium were discovered through analysis of their color spectra.

According to the Young-Helmholtz theory, the human eye has three separate color receptors sensitive to red, blue, and green light. Every color you see is the effect of the joint stimulation of these receptors in some definite proportion. Any color can be produced by mixing together the proper proportions of red, blue, and green light. Red, blue, and green are known as the primary colors of light. Mixed in equal intensities they produce white light.

Ask the students to observe the photographs and note the following: the shape of the prism used (equilateral); the angles of incidence and refraction; some of the light is reflected from the surface of the prism rather than refracted; there appears to be a second, faint spectrum produced in the last three photographs, nearly parallel to the reflected light. Have the students explain these observations.

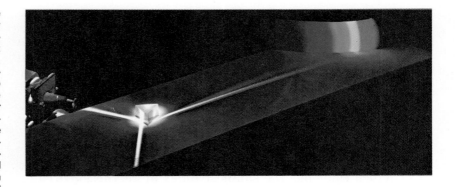

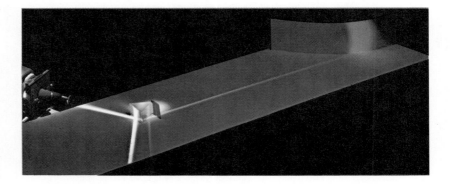

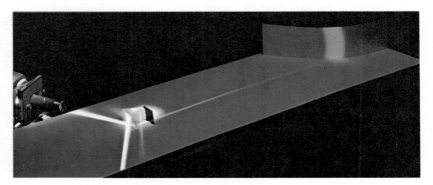

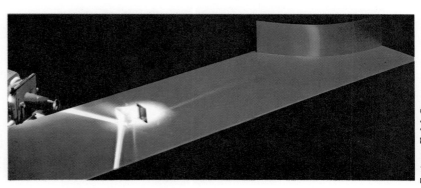

emits when heated to a high temperature. Each element has its own spectrum. An unknown substance can be identified by heating and vaporizing it. Light from the glowing vapor is then passed through a prism. From the colors in the spectrum, the substance can be identified. How might a color-blind person identify a color band in a spectrum? *The color band can be identified by its position in the spectrum.*

General Electric Co., Lamp Division

Figure 17-29. This sodium lamp emits only one color of the spectrum—yellow.

17:7   *Wavelength and Frequency*

Light waves vary in wavelength and frequency. Each color of light has a different wavelength and frequency. In this regard, the color of light is somewhat similar to the pitch of sound (Section 16:3). The frequency of a sound wave determines its pitch. The frequency of a light wave determines its color. Frequency is a physical property of a light wave. Color is what you sense with your eyes and your brain.

Light waves have very short wavelengths. The wavelength of violet light waves is 4×10^{-5} cm (0.00004 cm). The wavelength of red light waves is 7×10^{-5} cm (0.00007 cm).

How are wavelength and frequency related to color?

Paul Nesbit

PROBLEM

16. Which of the following colors has the highest and the lowest wave frequency: violet, red, or yellow?

Violet = highest wave frequency
Red = lowest wave frequency

Figure 17-30. Each of the colors in the spectrum has a different wavelength and frequency.

17:8   *Theories of Light*

Theories are based on observed facts and properties. Theories are ideas scientists develop to guide their research. New facts and experiments can prove old theories to be false.

Two theories have been developed to explain the nature of light: the wave theory and the particle theory. Sometimes light acts as waves, and sometimes light acts as particles. The **wave theory** and the **particle theory** are both worthy. Neither theory can explain all the facts known about light. Scientists are working toward fusing the wave theory and the particle theory into a single theory. How do you judge the scientific value of a theory? *How well the theory agrees with known facts. Degree to which theory can predict events. Value of theory in designing experiments.*

Many facts support the wave theory of light. For one thing, light may be refracted as its speed changes. Refraction is a characteristic of all waves (Section 16:6).

EXPERIMENT. *Hold two polarizing filters against each other. Look through them toward a lamp or window. Rotate one crystal slowly. How does the brightness change?*

Figure 17-31.

What evidence supports the particle theory of light?

Particle theory of light — photoelectric effect (p. 370) two lights together have a greater intensity than either light alone.

What evidence supports the wave theory of light?

Wave theory of light refraction, polarization, interference.

Analogy: A rope can vibrate in a vertical plane through a picket fence but we cannot make it vibrate in a horizontal plane.
If the pickets are horizontal we can make the rope vibrate in a horizontal plane but not in a vertical plane.

The "slits" in the two polarizing filters are perpendicular to each other. Light is stopped where the filters overlap. Polarized light passes out of the filters where they do not overlap.

Polarization (poh' ler i zae' shun) is another property of light that supports the wave theory. Transparent polarizing crystals can be used to demonstrate polarization. Two crystals are held together and one crystal is rotated. The light passing through the polarizing crystals changes from bright to dim and back to bright again. You may notice the same effect while wearing polarizing sunglasses. Look through the windshield of a car and move your head back and forth.

You can understand polarization if you think of light as transverse waves (Section 16:1). A polarizing crystal permits only waves vibrating in the same plane to pass through. In effect, the polarizing crystal has an infinite number of parallel "slits." Light waves vibrating in the same plane can pass through these slits. Light not vibrating in the same plane as the "slits" is reflected or absorbed. Light passing through the polarizing crystal is vibrating only in a single plane. It is called *polarized light*.

Interference is another property of light which supports the wave theory. In 1801, Thomas Young (1773-1829), an English physicist, performed an important experiment with light. He showed that two different light beams interfere with each

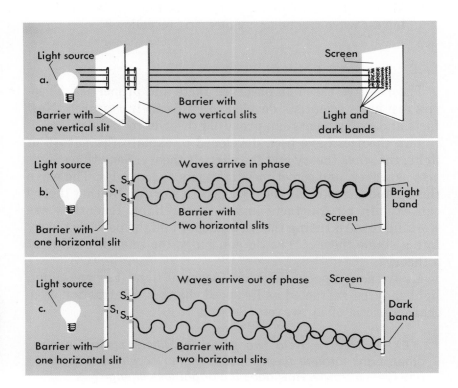

Figure 17-32. The interference pattern on the screen consists of alternate bright and dark bars of various color. If a single color light (monochromatic) source is used, all are the same color as the source.

other under certain conditions. In his experiment, Young passed light through a narrow slit in a barrier. The light passing through the slit spread out and passed through two more narrow slits side by side in another barrier. These two slits were the same distance from the first slit. The light again spread out and fell upon a screen. Young observed that the screen showed a series of light and dark bands (Figure 17–32). In the areas of the light bands, the waves were *in phase*. Here the waves reinforced each other. In the areas of the dark bands, the waves were *out of phase*. Here the waves canceled or destroyed the effect of each other. Thus there were dark bands.

If light consisted of particles, interference would not occur. Two beams of light shining together on a screen always would produce brightness. It would be somewhat like shooting two machine guns at the same target at the same time. No interference between the bullets would occur. The bullets would be traveling at the same speed, coming from two different sources.

Explain light interference.

Vocabulary: In phase *means that the crests and troughs of two or more waves coincide and reinforce each other.* Out of phase *means that wave crests are matched with troughs and cancel.*

EXPERIMENT. Construct a diffraction grating spectroscope. Use a piece of cardboard tubing or a cardboard box. Cover one end of the tube with aluminum foil containing a slit cut with a knife. Mount a 1-in.² piece of plastic diffraction grating in the opposite end. The lines in the grating must be parallel to the slit. Observe white light from a lamp through the spectroscope. Observe light from a fluorescent lamp. What colors are formed?   bands of violet and blue

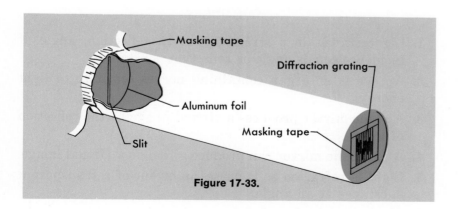

Figure 17-33.

Interference occurs when a diffraction grating is used to produce a color spectrum. A *diffraction grating* is a piece of

Figure 17-34. A light meter contains photo cells made of selenium which produce an electric current when light shines on the meter.

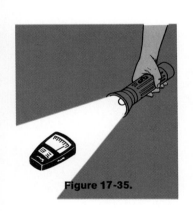

Figure 17-35.

glass containing as many as 25,000 slits per inch. The slits are produced by a machine which makes parallel scratches on the glass with a diamond stylus. When white light passes through the slits of the diffraction grating, interference occurs. This causes different wavelengths of light to reinforce or cancel each other. The net result is a spectrum of colors. Glass diffraction gratings are costly. However, plastic replicas are inexpensive. Diffraction gratings are sometimes used in place of prisms.

Many experiments support the wave theory of light. However, other evidence supports the particle theory. One such piece of evidence is the **photoelectric effect.** The photoelectric effect occurs when light shines on certain metals. The light causes electrons to be released from the atoms of the metal. The flow of the released electrons can produce an electric current.

ACTIVITY. Obtain a light meter. Open the face of the meter so that the photocell is exposed. Place a light source 10 centimeters from the opening in the light meter. Record the reading on the meter. Now move the source 20 centimeters away from the light meter. Record the reading. Keep moving the source away 10 centimeters at a time until the light meter registers near zero. CAUTION: Other sources of light in the room may affect the reading on the meter. If possible remove them. Make a graph comparing the reading on the meter to the distance from the light source. How does light intensity (read on the meter) compare to the distance of the source of light? Intensity should vary inversely as the square of the distance.

MAIN IDEAS

p. 352   1. Light travels in a straight line. In reflection, angle of incidence equals angle of reflection.

p. 352   2. An eye is an organ containing nerves sensitive to light energy.

p. 352   3. A plane mirror produces a virtual image by the reflection of light.

p. 353   4. A parabolic mirror can produce a real or a virtual image.

p. 357   5. Light is refracted as it passes in or out of a transparent substance at an angle.

p. 357   6. The index of refraction for a substance depends upon the speed of light in the substance.

p. 359   7. A convex lens can produce a real and a virtual image.

p. 363 **8.** A refracting telescope contains convex lenses.

p. 363 **9.** A reflecting telescope contains a parabolic mirror.

p. 364 **10.** A prism or a diffraction grating separates light into its various colors.

p. 364 **11.** The index of refraction is slightly different for different colors of light.

p. 367 **12.** The color of a light is determined by its frequency. Color depends on frequency of light just as pitch depends upon the frequency of a sound wave.

p. 367-370 **13.** Interference and polarization support the wave theory of light. The photoelectric effect supports the particle theory of light.

p. 367-370 **14.** Modern theory states that any particle of matter in motion has an associated wave.

VOCABULARY

Write a sentence in which you correctly use each of the following words or terms.

concave lens	magnification	plane mirror
convex lens	normal	polarized light
dispersion	optics	principal focus
focal length	parabolic mirror	prism
index of refraction	photoelectric effect	real image

STUDY QUESTIONS

A. True or False

Have students rewrite false statements to make the statements correct.

Determine whether each of the following sentences is true or false. (Do not write in this book.)

F **1.** A concave lens makes light rays ~~converge~~.   *diverge*

F **2.** The angle of reflection of a light ray is always equal to the incident angle of the ray.   *not*

F **3.** The ~~amplitude~~ of a light wave determines its color.   *frequency*

F **4.** A parabolic mirror always gives an enlarged image.   *does not*

F **5.** The image in a plane mirror is ~~always~~ inverted.   *never*

F **6.** An electron microscope ~~cannot~~ have more than 1000× magnification.

T **7.** Photon means packet of light.

T **8.** A prism disperses light rays.

T   **9.** An oblique angle is greater than 90°.

intensity F **10.** The brightness of light depends on its frequency.

B.   Multiple Choice   *Some questions in part B may   answer. Only one answer is have more than one correct   required.*

Choose one word or phrase that correctly completes each of the following sentences. (Do not write in this book.)

1. A(n) (real, virtual, inverted, erect) image can be projected on a screen.

2. The angle of incidence (equals, is greater than, is less than, is double) the angle of reflection.

3. A parabolic mirror (refracts, disperses, reflects, blends) light.

4. A parabolic mirror produces (real, virtual, erect, both real and virtual) image(s).

5. Light is refracted when (it is reflected, it is bent, its frequency increases, its frequency decreases).

6. If light changes speed, it is (refracted, reflected, unchanged).

7. The optical effects of a convex lens are most like those of a (concave lens, parabolic mirror, prism, photoelectric cell).

8. As the thickness of a convex lens increases, its focal length (increases, decreases, remains the same).

9. The equation $\dfrac{H_i}{H_o} = \dfrac{S_i}{S_o}$ may be used to predict (focal length, index of refraction, wavelength, distance of an image from a convex lens).

10. The enlarged image seen with a magnifying glass is a (real, dispersed, virtual) image.

C.   Completion

Complete each of the following sentences with a word or phrase that will make the sentence correct. (Do not write in this book.)

refracting   **1.** A(n) __?__ telescope contains convex lenses.

parabolic   **2.** The largest astronomical telescopes contain a(n) __?__ mirror.

prism   **3.** Light is dispersed by a glass __?__.

violet   **4.** When a beam of white light passes through a prism, __?__ light is refracted more than blue light.

prism, diffraction   **5.** A spectroscope contains a glass __?__ or a(n) __?__ grating.

6. A chemical element may be identified by its color __?__.

7. The color of light is similar to the __?__ of sound.

8. Visible light has a range of __?__ to __?__ centimeters.

9. Light vibrating in a single plane is __?__ light.

spectrum

pitch

4 x 10⁻⁵ cm to 7 x 10⁻⁵ cm

polarized

D. How and Why *See Teacher's Guide at the front of this book.*

1. How is the particle theory of light different from the wave theory? What evidence supports each theory?

2. How can light interference produce a color spectrum?

3. Explain the photon theory of light.

4. What is an electron microscope?

5. Why might you see a color spectrum in an aquarium tank?

6. The figure below shows the path of light traveling from air into glass. Is the glass (a) or (b)?

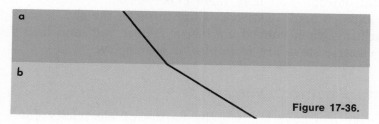

Figure 17-36.

7. Sunlight is refracted as it enters the earth's atmosphere. The sun on the horizon always looks higher in the sky than it really is. How does refraction explain this?

INVESTIGATION *See Teacher's Guide at the front of this book.*

Make a periscope out of a shoebox and two pocket mirrors. Tape the mirrors at 45° angles at opposite ends of the box. Cut a window opposite each mirror and then tape the cover on. Try it out. Use your periscope to see around corners.

INTERESTING READING

Gregg, James R., *Experiments in Visual Science: For Home and School.* New York, Ronald Press Company, 1966.

Reid, R. W., *The Spectroscope.* New York, New American Library, Inc., 1966.

Wilson, John, Jr., *Albert A. Michelson: America's First Nobel Prize Physicist.* New York, Julian Messner Publications, 1958.

GOAL: You will gain an understanding of the different kinds of electricity and the relationship between electricity and magnetism.

Chapter 18 continues the development of the concept of energy with a discussion of electricity and its effects. The objective is for the student to learn the different kinds of electricity and their effects and the relationship between electricity and magnetism.

Electricity

The word electricity comes from elektron, the Greek word for amber. The Greek philosopher Thales is said to have observed electric forces about 25 centuries ago when he rubbed amber and discovered it attracted light objects.

The effects of electricity appear in many forms. Have you ever walked across a thick wool carpet and then touched a metal object? You may have experienced an electric shock, perhaps painful. A streak of lightning in the sky, a cat's fur crackling when rubbed against a rubber rod, and heat from an electric stove are examples of electricity.

18:1 *Electric Charges*

Scientists have studied the nature of **electricity** for hundreds of years. They have determined that it is a form of energy. Electricity can do work. Tiny, invisible electrically charged particles are in all matter. These electric particles are present in atoms, the basic building blocks of all matter. The amount and kind of electric particles determine the properties of the atom. *Do this experiment as an introduction to electricity.*

EXPERIMENT. Run a comb through dry hair several times. Then try to pick up bits of paper with the comb. What happens?

Rub a glass rod with a piece of silk. Hang the rod horizontally with silk threads. Rub a second glass rod in the same way. Hang it by a silk thread and bring it near the first rod. What happens?

Using silk threads, hang two plastic rods separately. Rub the two rods with wool. Bring them close together. Do they repel or attract each other?

Now bring a suspended plastic rod rubbed with wool near a suspended glass rod rubbed with silk.

Does glass repel glass? Does plastic normally repel plastic? Does glass normally attract plastic? Explain what you observe. *Friction can produce static electricity.*

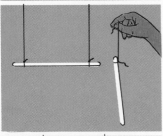

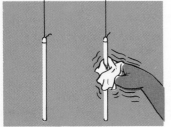

Figure 18-1.

Some materials when rubbed gain an *electric charge*. The charge can be positive (+) or negative (—). When two rods have the same charge, the rods repel each other. When two rods have different charges, the rods attract each other. For this reason, charged glass and plastic rods attract each other. The charge on the glass rod is opposite to the charge on the plastic rod. Like charges repel each other. Opposite charges attract each other.

An atom contains equal numbers of protons and electrons. For example, an oxygen atom has 8 protons and 8 electrons. A *proton* (Section 3:2) is a positively charged particle in the nucleus of an atom. An *electron* (Section 3:2) is a negatively charged particle outside the nucleus. Since the number of negative charges in an atom is equal to the number of positive charges, an atom is neutral.

If a body gains electrons, the result will be more electrons than protons. The object is then negatively charged. If an object loses electrons, the result will be more protons than electrons. Then the object is positively charged. When an atom becomes charged by losing or gaining electrons, it is called an *ion*.

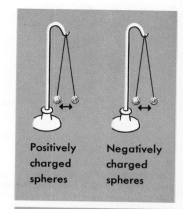

Positively charged spheres   Negatively charged spheres

Figure 18-2. When two objects have the same charge, they repel each other. When the charges are opposite, the objects attract each other.

ACTIVITY. Attach a silk thread to a glass rod. Attach a silk thread to a piece of silk cloth. Rub the rod with the silk. Suspend the rod and thread separately. Bring the silk near the rod. What do you observe?

If you rub a glass rod with silk, the glass rod loses electrons to the silk. The rod becomes positively charged. The silk becomes negatively charged. Opposite charges attract so the rod and silk attract each other.

When you rub a plastic rod with wool, the plastic rod gains electrons from the wool. Thus, the plastic rod becomes negatively charged. The wool becomes positively charged. Will the wool and the plastic rod attract each other? *yes*

Charged bodies have **static electricity**, or electricity at rest. There are two kinds of static electricity. *Positive static electricity* results when an object loses electrons and gains a positive charge. *Negative static electricity* results when an object gains electrons and a negative charge.

You see examples of static electricity when:
(a) charged clouds produce lightning
(b) someone wearing rubber-soled shoes walks over a wool rug

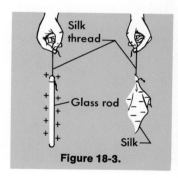

Silk thread

Glass rod

Silk

Figure 18-3.

What is static electricity?
electricity at rest

(c) a driver in a wool coat rubs against plastic car seats
(d) a nylon dress comes out of a clothes dryer
(e) a blown-up balloon is rubbed against a wool sweater

PROBLEMS

1. Name three other examples of static electricity.
2. When you comb your hair, the comb may gain a negative charge. Where do the added electrons come from? *your hair*

The electroscope is charged by conduction. When a charge of the same sign is brought near, the leaves diverge; when the opposite charge is brought near, the leaves converge.

How is an electroscope used to detect electric charges?

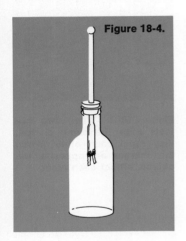

Figure 18-4.

18:2 Conduction

An **electroscope** (i lek′ trah skohp) detects an electric charge. A simple electroscope contains two thin leaves of metal hanging from the bottom of a metal rod. The rod is suspended in the neck of a glass jar (Figure 18–4). The top of the metal rod is connected to a metal knob.

ACTIVITY. You can make a simple electroscope. Take a metal curtain rod that has a ball end. Cut off the ball end in a piece 20 cm long. Obtain a bottle and a cork to fit. Make a hole in the cork and insert the rod through the hole. Flatten 5 cm of the end of the rod and attach two pieces of lightweight metal foil, ½ cm × 2 cm in size. Insert the cork into the bottle so that it fits snugly.

An electroscope can be charged positively or negatively. When charged, the leaves spread apart. Like charges in the leaves make them repel each other. When not charged, the leaves hang down.

Figure 18-5. Is the charge on the electroscope the same as or opposite to the charge on the rod?

The same. The electroscope is charged by conduction.

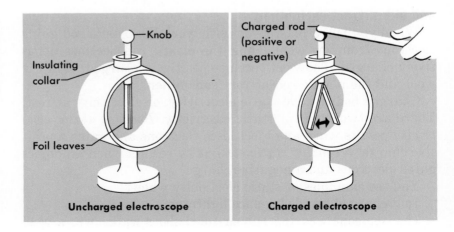

Uncharged electroscope   Charged electroscope

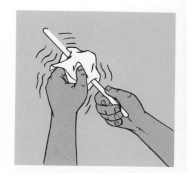

You can use a negatively charged plastic rod to give an electroscope a static charge of electricity. Touch the metal knob of the electroscope. The leaves will spring apart. Electrons from the plastic rod pass into the electroscope. This is known as *conduction* (kan duck′ shun). The electroscope thus gains electrons. It then has negative charge.

Conduction occurs when electrons are gained or lost through direct contact with a charged object. An object charged by conduction takes the same charge as the original charged object. Objects with a negative charge can produce negative charges on other objects. Objects with a positive charge can produce positive charges on other objects.

ACTIVITY. (1) Charge a plastic rod with a wool cloth. Using the charged rod, charge the electroscope by conduction. An electroscope can be discharged by conduction. Discharge means to lose charge. (2) Touch the knob of a negatively charged electroscope. What happens? (3) Repeat Part 2. This time use a piece of pencil "lead" (graphite, a form of carbon). (4) Repeat Part 2 with a metal wire. (5) Repeat Part 1 with a glass rod. (6) Repeat Parts 1, 2, 3, and 4 with a glass rod and silk cloth.

Figure 18-6.

In Part 2 of the activity the leaves fell, and the electroscope became uncharged. It loses electrons which are conducted into your hand. In Parts 3 and 4, the electroscope also is discharged. Electrons travel through the graphite or through the wire into your body. A material through which electrons can travel is a **conductor**. Graphite and metal are electrical conductors.

Some materials will not discharge an electroscope. Glass, hard rubber, porcelain, or plastic will not. Electrons do not flow well through these substances. Such materials are called *insulators* (in′ suh lay turz). An **insulator** is a substance through which electrons will not flow readily.

What is an electrical conductor?

A material through which electrons can travel.

What is an electrical insulator?

A material through which electrons cannot travel readily.

18:3   *Electrostatic Induction*

An electroscope can be charged without ever touching a charged body. This is done by *electrostatic induction* (i lek′ trah sta tik · in duck′ shun). Bring a negatively charged rod close to the knob of an uncharged electroscope. The leaves of the electroscope spring apart. Touch your finger to the side of the knob away from the charged rod. Then take your finger

Uncharged
electroscope

Leaves charged
negatively
by induction

Electrons
repelled
to earth

Positively
charged
electroscope

Figure 18-7. An electroscope can be charged by electrostatic induction.

away and remove the charged rod. The leaves continue to stand apart. The electroscope is charged.

Electrostatic induction occurs because electrons repel each other. Suppose you bring a negatively charged plastic rod near the knob of an electroscope. Some of the electrons in the knob are repelled. They flow down into the leaves and to the side of the knob opposite the rod. The leaves are now negatively charged and stand apart. Now touch the negative side of the knob with your finger. Some of the electrons are conducted out of the knob through your finger. When you remove your finger from the knob, the electrons cannot flow back into the electroscope. The electroscope now has fewer electrons than protons. The leaves stand wide apart.

The charged electroscope can be made neutral and induction repeated with a positively charged glass rod. This time the charged rod attracts electrons from the leaves and from the other side of the knob. Thus, the leaves and opposite side of the knob become positively charged. When you touch the knob, electrons flow from your body into the electroscope. The electroscope gains electrons. It becomes negatively charged. Electrons may flow from one object to another but protons never do. Why?   *Protons are in the nucleus of atom.*

The charge produced by induction is always opposite to the charge of the charging object. Through induction, positively charged objects can produce negative charges on other objects. Negatively charged objects can produce positive charges on other objects.

PROBLEMS

3. Name several electrical insulators used in home appliances.   *Glass and plastic are insulators.*
4. Sometimes a strap is attached to the frame of a truck to touch the road. Why?
5. How is a charge produced by induction different from a charge produced by conduction?
6. How is the rod in an electroscope insulated?

By its insulating collar.

By means of induction, the touch of your finger can charge an electroscope. Your finger grounds the electroscope. To *ground* means to connect an object to the earth with a conductor. Grounding allows electrons to move freely in and out of the object. Think of the earth as a huge reservoir of electrons. Electrons from the earth can be conducted into an object. Electrons from an object can be conducted into the earth. For

The charge produced by induction is opposite that of the charging object. The charge produced by conduction is the

To prevent a static electric charge from being built up on the truck.

example, lightning rods and television antennas are grounded to the earth. This is done by wires sunk into the ground. A gasoline truck may be grounded by a long chain that drags on the road. Why does a lightning rod, a television antenna, or a gasoline truck need to be grounded?

ACTIVITY. *(1) Place two metal rods end to end on two glass beakers so that they touch. Charge a plastic rod by rubbing it with wool. Bring the charged rod close to one of the metal rods. At the same time, slowly separate the rods by moving one of the beakers. Do not touch the metal rods. (2) Charge the plastic rod again. Use it to charge the electroscope. Bring each of the metal rods, separately, near the electroscope knob. What do you observe?*

Why are the beakers used in the experiment? Are the metal rods charged? Explain. Describe a way to tell if a metal rod has a positive or negative charge.

18:4   *Direct Current*

Direct current (D.C.) is the flow of electrons through a conductor. The flow may vary in rate but it is always in the same direction. When an electroscope is discharged, a tiny direct current is formed for a fraction of a second. The flow of electrons out of the electroscope through a conductor is the current. Similarly, a flash of lightning is a direct current. So is lightning traveling through a lightning rod into the ground. The electrical connection to a car battery is also a direct current.

How is a body grounded?

By connecting it to the earth through a conductor.

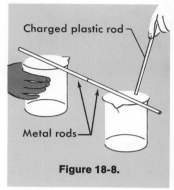

Charged plastic rod

Metal rods

Figure 18-8.

The beakers are insulators. Yes. Charge an electroscope negatively and bring the rod near without touching it. If the knob is negative the leaves will spread further apart. If the rod is positive the leaves will fall closer together.

What is direct current?

Flow of electrons through a conductor.

Figure 18-9. a and b. A lightning rod connected to a building and grounded in the earth carries the electrons from the lightning away from the building.

a.

b.

Edward Sonner

Grounding allows electrons to move in or out of the body and the earth. Thus lightning can pass through a lightning rod or T.V. antenna to the ground without *causing damage. If plastic seat covers are grounded they cannot become charged because any excess of electrons they gain will flow into the earth.*

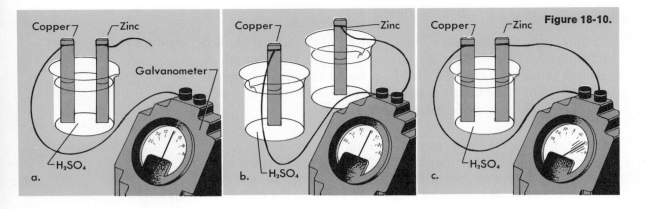

Figure 18-10.

a. Copper — Zinc — Galvanometer — H₂SO₄

b. Copper — Zinc — H₂SO₄

c. Copper — Zinc — H₂SO₄

In a the wire is not connected. In b the metals are in two different solutions. Electricity will flow only when there is a complete circuit.

An automobile storage battery has wet cells containing lead and lead oxide plates suspended in dilute sulfuric acid.

How does a wet cell generate an electric current?

It uses chemical changes to produce an electric current.

Figure 18-11. Zinc atoms will lose electrons and dissolve in the acid solution when the zinc is connected to a copper rod placed in the same solution.

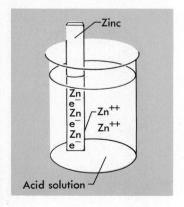

EXPERIMENT. Wet cells *make use of chemical changes to produce a direct current. You can make a wet cell. Put two different metals into a salt, basic, or acid solution. Then connect the metals with a wire. For example, a strip of zinc (Zn) and a strip of copper (Cu) placed in a solution of dilute sulfuric acid (H₂SO₄) form a wet cell (Figure 18–10). A current is produced when the two metals are connected by a wire. The wire, metals, and solution form a circuit. An electrical circuit is a closed-loop path through which an electric current is flowing.*

A *wet cell* works because of ions in a solution. When acids, bases, or salts dissolve in water, they form ions. Every ion has either a positive or negative charge. In a wet cell, the solution has an equal number of positive and negative ions.

Suppose a wet cell contains a sulfuric acid solution, a strip of zinc, and a strip of copper. The ions in the sulfuric acid solution are hydrogen (H^+)* and sulfate $(SO_4^=)$. The hydrogen ion is positively charged. What is the charge of the sulfate ion? Zinc atoms in the strip of zinc metal dissolve in the acid solution. Each atom loses two electrons. The zinc atoms (Zn) become zinc ions (Zn^{++}). The following equation shows this change:

$$Zn(s) \quad \rightarrow \quad Zn(aq)^{++} + 2\,e^-$$
$$\text{(Zinc atom)} \qquad \text{(Zinc ion)}$$

A zinc atom is uncharged. A zinc ion has a charge of $+2$. The symbol e^- represents an electron. The 2 in front of the electron symbol shows that two electrons are released when a zinc atom becomes a zinc ion. Electrons given off by the zinc move through the wire to the copper.

* In water, hydrogen ions (H^+) react with water (H_2O) to yield hydronium ions (H_3O^+).

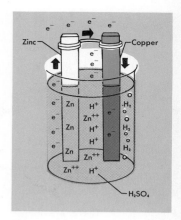

The positive charge of the zinc ions repels the positive charge of the hydrogen ions in the solution. The hydrogen ions move to the copper side of the cell. At the same time, electrons come into the copper through the wire from the zinc. The hydrogen ions gain these electrons at the copper and become hydrogen atoms. These atoms form diatomic molecules (molecules with two atoms) of hydrogen gas which bubbles out of the solution (Figure 18–12). This is the equation for the reaction:

$$2 \, H(aq)^+ + 2 \, e^- \rightarrow H_2(g)$$

In a wet cell, such as the one just described, ions move in the solution. Electrons move in the wire. Electrons flow from the zinc to the copper through the wire. This produces a direct current. However, electrons do not gather in a large number in any one spot. There is always an even distribution of electrons. The current can be stopped by opening the circuit. No point in the conductor is charged either negatively or positively. In this way a current differs from static electricity. Static electricity is a gathering or shortage of electrons in one place. A current is a flow of electrons.

Electric current produced by a wet cell results from an energy change. Chemical energy in atoms is changed into electrical energy. A dry cell and storage battery also produce direct current. They do this by converting chemical energy to electrical energy.

A "dry" cell works in much the same way as a wet cell; however, there are differences. A *dry cell* has chemicals in the form of a moist paste instead of a liquid. A dry cell is composed of a carbon rod set in the middle of a zinc can. Zinc is a metal. The rest of the can is filled with a moist paste. The paste reacts with the zinc and releases electrons. These electrons flow through a conductor to the carbon rod. The flow of electrons is direct current (Figure 18–13).

Figure 18-12. Zinc adds charged zinc atoms (+) to the solution. Copper will remove charged hydrogen atoms (+), forming hydrogen gas. Net charge on the solution remains neutral.

How does a dry cell generate an electric current?

It works like a wet cell.

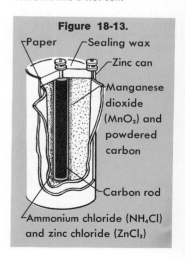

Figure 18-13.

Paper — Sealing wax — Zinc can — Manganese dioxide (MnO_2) and powdered carbon — Carbon rod — Ammonium chloride (NH_4Cl) and zinc chloride ($ZnCl_2$)

ACTIVITY. Obtain a used dry cell. With a hacksaw carefully cut the cell lengthwise down the middle. CAUTION: Do not touch the inside. The material can cause burns. Study the component parts of the cell. Was the inside of the battery moist or dry? Why? The inside of a new "dry" cell would be moist. A used cell may be dry and therefore unable to produce current.

PROBLEM

7. Why will a dry cell fail to work if it drys out completely?

The electrons cannot move.

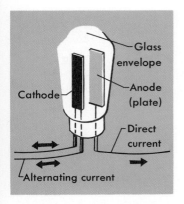

Figure 18-14. There are many different types of diodes. All have a cathode which supplies electrons and an anode which accepts electrons.

Two or more cells (wet or dry) can be connected together in a single circuit. This is called a *battery*. Electricity in a car is produced by a storage battery. The battery contains lead plates and sulfuric acid solution.

A direct current can also be produced by the *photoelectric effect* (Section 17:8). When certain metals are exposed to light, they give off electrons. These electrons can flow in a circuit and form a direct current. Photoelectric cells convert light energy into electrical energy.

18:5   Diode and Thermocouple

Flow of electrons can be produced from heat energy. A diode changes heat energy into electrical energy. A **diode** is a kind of radio tube (Figure 18–14). It is a thin, glass bulb containing a hollow metal cylinder. Inside the metal cylinder is a tungsten wire filament. There is no air inside the tube.

When a diode filament is connected to an electric current, its filament becomes hot. Electrons "boil off" and leave the hot metal filament. The electrons travel through the empty space to the metal cylinder. In effect, a direct current flows from filament to cylinder. This produces a direct current in the circuit.

Figure 18-15. Junctions of iron and copper are useful in measuring temperatures up to about 275° C. Junctions of platinum and rhodium are used to indicate temperatures up to 1000° C.

The rate at which electrons are released by a diode depends on the temperature of the filament. The higher the temperature, the faster electrons are released. Loss of electrons by heated metals is known as *thermionic emission*. There must be no air inside the diode. If air were present, the filament would react with the air and be destroyed.

A **thermocouple** is a device used to produce electric current. It has two different metals bonded or twisted together at two separate points. Copper and iron wire are sometimes used as the two metals. One point where the metals are bonded is placed in a cold substance. The other point is heated. The metals in the thermocouple produce an electric current. Differences in temperature cause an electric current to flow. The amount of current produced by a thermocouple depends on the temperature difference between the two contact points. The greater the temperature difference, the greater the current.

Thermocouples are used in a kind of thermometer called a *pyrometer* (pi rahm′ ah tur). In a pyrometer, the thermocouple is connected to a circuit containing an electric meter. The meter is scaled in degrees. The greater the current pro-

Courtesy of Battelle
Columbus Laboratories

duced by the thermocouple, the higher the temperature indicated on the meter.

Table 18–1. **Production of Direct Current (D.C.)**			
Static Discharge	*Chemical*	*Light*	*Heat*
lightning	wet cell	photo-electric cell	diode
	dry cell storage battery		thermocouple

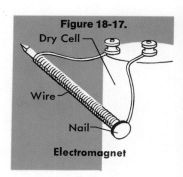

Figure 18-16. A thermocouple produces an electric current.

18:6 *Magnetism*

Magnetism is a property of matter. Magnetism can produce electricity. Electricity can produce magnetism. In an electric generator, magnets produce an electric current. In an electromagnet, an electric current produces magnetism.

How is electricity used to produce magnetism?

ACTIVITY. Obtain a long piece of copper wire. Wrap it around a large nail as shown in Figure 18–17. Attach the free ends to the poles of a dry cell. You now have an electromagnet. Try picking up paper clips or small bits of iron with it.

Wrap more wire around the nail. What happens to the strength of the magnet? Add another cell to the magnet. What happens to the strength of the magnet? In both cases, strength of magnet increases.

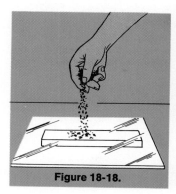

Figure 18-17.

Dry Cell

Wire

Nail

Electromagnet

Magnets are usually made of *steel, cobalt,* or *nickel.* Each of these metals has the property of being attracted to magnets. They become magnets themselves when surrounded by a coil of wire bearing an electric current. For example, a piece of steel can be magnetized by an electric current (Figure 18–17). The steel retains its magnetism after the current is removed. The magnetized piece of steel is called a *permanent* magnet.

How is electricity used to produce magnetism?

Metals become magnets when surrounded by a coil of wire bearing an electric current.

EXPERIMENT. Obtain a bar magnet. Place it on a desk top or table. Cover the magnet with a piece of thin paper or glass. Sprinkle iron filings on top of the paper where it covers the magnet. Draw the pattern formed by the filings. What do the iron filings reveal? Lines of magnetic force.

Bar magnets and horseshoe magnets are permanent magnets. Alnico, an alloy of aluminum, nickel, and cobalt, is also

Figure 18-18.

a.

b.

Figure 18-19. To suit different industrial purposes, magnets are made in a variety of shapes, such as disc-type (a) and bar-type (b).

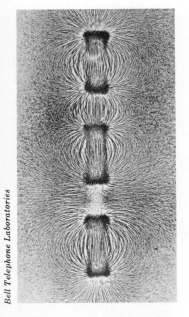

Figure 18-20. Lines of magnetic force are indicated by the pattern of iron filings.

What is alternating current?

Vibration of electrons in a circuit.

Under normal conditions, a permanent magnet retains its magnetism for a long time.

used to make permanent magnets. In time, a permanent magnet slowly loses its magnetism. A permanent magnet can also lose its magnetic properties rapidly. This happens if it is heated or hit over and over with a hard object such as a hammer.

A magnet has these properties:

(1) Two unlike poles—north and south. One pole is at each end. If a bar magnet is cut in two, two magnets are formed. Each magnet will have a north and south pole.

(2) Like poles of a magnet repel. Unlike poles of a magnet attract.

(3) Lines of force, forming a magnetic field, surround a magnet. The magnetic field can be revealed by covering the magnet with iron filings (Figure 18–20).

(4) A magnet attracts iron, cobalt, and nickel.

(5) A magnet can magnetize iron, cobalt, and nickel if a piece of one of these metals is stroked with the magnet.

(6) When a magnet is free-floating, the poles of the magnet line up with the earth's north and south magnetic poles.

(7) A magnet can cause electric currents in conductors. If a bar magnet is moved back and forth inside a coil of wire, an electric current is produced in the wire.

18:7 *Alternating Current*

Alternating current (A.C.) is the vibration of electrons in a circuit. Vibration means rapid to-and-fro movement. The circuits in your home have alternating current (A.C.). When the electricity is on, free electrons in the wires vibrate to and fro. For example, in a 60-cycle home circuit, the electrons vibrate 60 times per second.

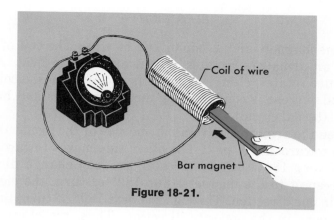

Figure 18-21.

Coil of wire

Bar magnet

Suggestion: Introduce this experiment by explaining that induction means that electrons are forced to move by means of a magnetic field. Each electron has an associated magnetic field. The presence of another magnetic field which is in motion will force the electrons to move, causing a current.

Current varies directly with the number of turns and the speed with which the magnet moves.

EXPERIMENT. Induction in a coil of wire. (1) Bend a wire to form a loop with 10 coils 5 cm in diameter. Connect the ends of the wire to a galvanometer. Hold a bar magnet and thrust it in and out of the coil. Vary the speed at which the magnet moves and observe the reading on the galvanometer. (2) Change the number of coils in the wire and repeat the procedure.

What effect does the speed at which the magnet moves have on the galvanometer reading? How is the reading changed by the number of turns in the coil? What kind of electric current is produced in the coil? Alternating current.

Alternating current is produced through electromagnetic induction. The simplest way to make an alternating current is to move a wire back and forth in a magnetic field. A weak alternating current is produced in the wire. An electric generator produces an electric current by induction. A generator

Tennessee Valley Authority

Figure 18-22. Powerhouse in the Watts Bar Dam, Tennessee. The electric generators can produce a maximum of 150,000 kilowatts of power.

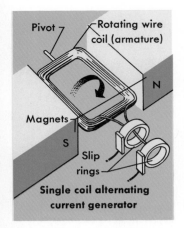

Figure 18-23. **Magnetic lines of force move electrons through the wire coil as it turns. Why is the generated current A.C. and not D.C.?**

contains magnets and a loop or coil of wire. The coil of wire, called an armature, rotates within a magnetic field. As the armature rotates, electric current is produced in the coil. The induced current is conducted by metal slip rings and brushes to an external circuit.

When the armature is rotated, one side of the armature loop moves toward the N pole. The other side moves toward the S pole. Every 180° the two sides of the loop change direction with respect to the magnets. For 180° of turn, the electrons move in one direction. Through the next 180° of turn, the electrons move in the opposite direction. Thus, the electrons vibrate to and fro with each complete turn of the armature. As the armature turns, A.C. current is produced. Figure 18–23 shows how the current is produced by a single-loop armature.

PROBLEM

8. What kind of energy change occurs in an electric generator? *Kinetic energy to electrical energy.*

18:8 *Electrical Units*

A **galvanometer** (gal vah nah′ mi tur) can detect weak electric currents. Its operation is based on the rotation of a wire coil set between two permanent magnetic poles. If an electric current is passed through the coil, it becomes magnetized. North and south poles of the magnetized coil are repelled by the nearby permanent magnetic poles. The north pole of the

How does a galvanometer detect an electric current?

A galvanometer detects weak currents as changes in magnetic strength.

Caution: Connecting a galvanometer to high voltage will cause the coil to burn out.

Relate the use of standard electric units to standard units in the metric and English systems with which the student is familiar. For example:

$1 \dfrac{volt}{sec} = 0.737 \ ft\text{-}lb$

$1 \ watt = 1 \dfrac{joule}{sec}$

Figure 18-24. **When a current flows through the coil, the forces on opposite sides of the coil cause it to rotate until it is stopped by the spring.**

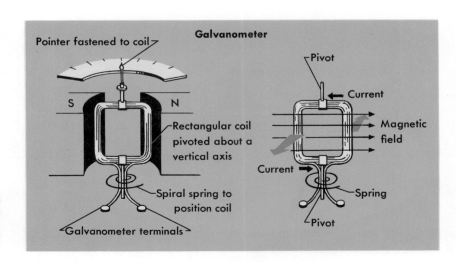

coil moves away from the north pole of the permanent magnet. The south pole of the coil moves away from the south pole of the permanent magnet. How much the coil rotates depends on the strength of the current. The greater the electric current, the greater the amount of rotation. As the coil rotates, a needle attached to the coil moves on a scale. The position of the needle indicates the size of the current.

Ampere, volt, ohm, and *watt* are standard electrical units. The ampere expresses rate of electron flow in a current. One **ampere** (am′ pere) (amp) is a current of one coulomb per second (1 coul/sec). One coulomb equals 6.25×10^{18} electrons. When a current is one ampere, 6.25×10^{18} electrons pass a given point in a circuit every second. An **ammeter** (am′ mee ter) measures current in amperes. Like a galvanometer, the ammeter is based on the rotation of a current bearing coil in a magnetic field.

Define ampere, volt, and ohm.

The ampere *expresses rate of electron flow in a current. The* volt *expresses potential difference between two points in a conductor. The* ohm *expresses electrical resistance.*

How are amperes and volts measured?

Amperes — ammeter.
Volts — voltmeter.

The charge on one electron is 1.6×10^{-19} coulomb.

Figure 18-25. The thermoelectric effect converts heat directly into electric current.

Westinghouse Photo

The **volt** (v) is a unit of potential difference. Potential difference causes the motion of electrons. It is measured in terms of the work done per unit charge in moving electrons between two points in a conductor. Potential difference is measured with a **voltmeter.**

A common "dry" cell has a potential difference of 1½ v. An automobile storage battery has a potential difference of 6 v or 12 v. The potential difference of house current is about 110-120 v. Electric transmission lines have a potential difference of thousands of volts.

Electric potential refers to electromotive force or voltage.

The international joule, a unit of electrical energy, is the work expended per second by a current of one ampere flowing through one ohm.

$$1 \text{ joule} = \frac{1 \text{ amp} \times 1 \text{ ohm}}{1 \text{ sec}}$$

$$= \frac{1 \text{ volt}}{1 \text{ sec}}$$

$$= 2.8 \times 10^{-7} \, kw/hr$$

$$= .737 \, ft\text{-}lb$$

$$= .24 \, calories$$

PROBLEM

9. Which of the following yields the most energy: dry cell, storage battery, house current?

Have students note that copper is used extensively for electric wires because of its low resistance. Silver is too expensive for most circuits. Aluminum is used in some circuits and has the advantage of being less costly than copper.

Table 18–2. *Some Common Metals and Their Electrical Resistance*

Metal (1000 ft by 0.1 in.²)	Electrical Resistance (ohms)
Copper (Cu)	1.0
Silver (Ag)	0.98
Aluminum (Al)	1.7
Tungsten (W)	3.3
Tin (Sn)	7.0
Nickel (Ni)	4.8
Gold (Au)	1.5
Iron (Fe)	6.1

This experiment is designed to derive Ohm's law as explained in the paragraph that follows the experiment.
Caution students to check the polarity of each item as it is placed in the circuit. Voltmeters and ammeters can be ruined by connecting them in the circuit backwards. Check the circuit before the cell is added. The center pole of the cell is positive and the outer pole is negative. Always connect ammeters in series with the resistance, and always connect voltmeters in parallel with the resistance. This is also for the protection of the meters.
watts = volts x amperes

Many substances, such as metals, conduct electricity. Some are better *conductors* than others. Electricity flows through some materials more easily than through others. A good **conductor** of electricity has low resistance. A poor conductor has high resistance (Table 18–2). *Resistance* (ri zis' tans) is measured in *ohms*. One **ohm** of resistance exists when there is one ampere of current in a one-volt circuit (1 v/amp).

EXPERIMENT. How are volts, amperes, and ohms related? Connect a variable resistor in series to a dry cell and ammeter. Connect the two poles of the resistor to a voltmeter. Vary the resistance by moving the slide to 3 or 4 different positions. Record in a chart the amperes and volts for each position. Resistance (ohms) increases as the length of the resistor in the circuit increases. How do the ohms of resistance (length of resistor) affect the current and voltage? Write the relationship as an equation.

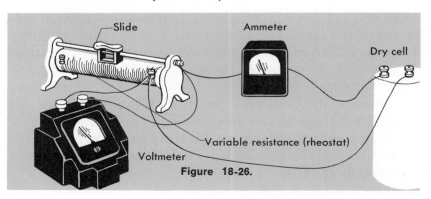

Figure 18-26.

The Laser — A Column of Light

Laser means light amplification by stimulated emission of radiation. Lasers produce a tremendously concentrated, powerful beam of light. Lasers have been used to:

1. make photographs of extremely fast-moving objects.
2. mend torn retinas in human eyes.
3. send messages for hundreds of miles.
4. produce television pictures.
5. cut and weld materials.

The light emitted from a laser is coherent light. Coherent light is light of a single frequency vibrating in a single plane. In contrast, light from an electric light bulb is inco-

This machine uses a laser to measure one type of air pollutant, nitric acid.

herent light. Incoherent light contains many frequencies vibrating in an infinite number of planes.

A ruby laser contains a ruby rod with flattened ends which are silvered to form mirrors. One end is not completely silvered, so that some light can escape. The electrons of the chromium atoms in the ruby are excited by a bright lamp and raised to higher energy levels. In effect, the lamp acts as a pump, sending light into the ruby rod. As the excited electrons drop back to lower energy states, light waves take on the emitted energy and are amplified. These parallel waves reflect back and forth between the mirrors, building up in intensity. Eventually, an intense beam of red light flashes from the end of the ruby crystal.

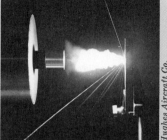

Hughes Aircraft Co.

A ruby laser beam can pierce a sheet of hard tantalum in less than 1/1000 second.

A gas laser is used to amplify infrared waves. The gas laser is a tube with mirrors in the ends. Neon gas mixed with helium fills the tube. The energy pump is a radio frequency generator. Helium atoms are used because their excited electrons, as they drop to ground state, emit energy which excites neon electrons. The excited neon electrons emit infrared radiation.

Various liquids, combinations of gases, plastics, and semi-conductors have been used as lasers. Laser beams of ultraviolet, visible, and infrared light have been produced. Solid lasers can be made with crystals of calcium tungstate ($CaWO_4$) in which small amounts of neodymium compounds are added. The neodymium atoms are used as substitutes for some calcium atoms. A mercury lamp which emits a strong white light is used as a pump for the calcium tungstate laser. This laser emits a strong infrared beam.

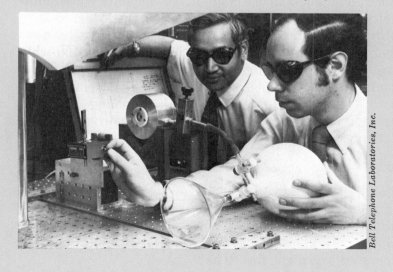

Bell Telephone Laboratories, Inc.

George Simon Ohm (1787-1854), a German physicist, discovered the relationship between volts and amperes in a circuit. This relationship is expressed in *Ohm's law:*

$$I = \frac{V}{R}$$

I = amperes
V = potential difference in volts
R = resistance in ohms

EXAMPLE

What is the current in a 3-ohm circuit connected to a 6-volt battery?

Solution: (a) Write the equation: $I = \dfrac{V}{R}$

(b) Substitute 6 v for V and 3 ohms for R:

$$I = \frac{6 \text{ volts}}{3 \text{ ohms}}$$

(c) Divide to find the current: $I = 2$ amp

(d) Answer: current $= 2$ amp

PROBLEMS

10. What is the current in a 3-ohm circuit connected to a 12-v battery?   *4 amp*
11. What is the resistance of an electric lamp using 5 amp of current in a 120-v circuit?   *24 ohms*

The power of an electric circuit is measured in *watts*. One **watt** of power exists in a circuit having a one-volt potential difference and a one-ampere current. To calculate watts, multiply volts by amperes: watts = volts × amperes.

Energy in an electric circuit can be measured in *watt-hours:* watt-hours (w-hr) = watts × hours. For example, a 100-watt light bulb burns for 10 hours. It uses 1,000 watt-hours of electricity (100 watts × 10 hours = 1,000 watt-hours). One *kilowatt-hour* (kw-hr) is 1,000 watt-hours. To change watts to kilowatts, divide by 1,000. Electric bills are figured in terms of the charge per kilowatt-hour.

1 kw/hr	$\dfrac{10^3 \ watt}{1 \ kw}$	$\dfrac{3600 \ sec}{1 \ hr}$	$\dfrac{1 \ joule/sec}{1 \ watt}$

PROBLEMS

12. How is 1 millivolt different from 1 volt?   *1 volt = 1000 millivolts*
13. If a 6-v circuit has 30 amp of current, what is the resistance?   *0.2 ohm*
14. How many kilowatt hours are used by a 500-w heater operated overnight for 10 hr?   *5 kw/hr*

MAIN IDEAS

p. 375   **1.** Objects become electrically charged by a gain or loss of electrons.

p. 375   **2.** Like charges repel and unlike charges attract.

pp. 376-378   **3.** A body may be charged by conduction or induction.

p. 379   **4.** A body may be grounded by connecting it with a conductor to the earth.

pp. 379-382   **5.** Direct current (D.C.) may be produced by static discharge, chemical change, heat, and light.

p. 385   **6.** Alternating current (A.C.) may be produced in a conductor by a magnet.

p. 386   **7.** The induction of an alternating current changes kinetic energy into electrical energy.

pp. 387-390   **8.** The quantity and properties of electricity may be measured in standard units: ampere, volt, ohm, watt, kilowatt, kilowatt-hour.

p. 377   **9.** Many substances conduct electricity. Some materials are better conductors than others.

pp. 383-384   **10.** Electricity can produce magnetism. A magnet can induce an alternating current in a conductor.

VOCABULARY

Write a sentence in which you correctly use each of the following words or terms.

alternating current	electron	magnetism
ammeter	electroscope	ohm
circuit	electrostatic induction	thermocouple
conductor	galvanometer	volt
direct current	insulator	voltmeter
dry cell	ion	watt
electric generator	ionization	wet cell
electricity		

STUDY QUESTIONS

Have students rewrite false statements to make the statements correct.

A.   True or False

Determine whether each of the following sentences is true or false. (Do not write in this book.)

1. A dry cell is a source of electricity.

T **2.** A static charge is an excess of protons or electrons on a body.

T **3.** Glass is a poor conductor of electricity.

T **4.** A charged atom is an ion.

T **5.** An electroscope can be charged by conduction by touching it with a charged rod.

T **6.** A working dry cell battery contains moisture.

light, electrical *F* **7.** Photoelectric cells convert ~~electrical~~ energy into ~~light~~ energy.

T **8.** A magnet will attract cobalt.

T **9.** Glass is a good insulator.

do not *F* **10.** All ions have a net charge of zero.

B. Multiple Choice

Choose one word or phrase that correctly completes each of the following sentences. (Do not write in this book.)

1. A glass rod rubbed with silk has (a negative charge, <u>a positive charge</u>, no charge).

2. Electrons are (uncharged, positively charged, <u>negatively charged</u>) particles.

3. When the leaves of an electroscope stand apart, the electroscope is (uncharged, neutral, <u>charged</u>, magnetized).

4. Graphite is a(n) (insulator, natural magnet, resistor, <u>conductor</u>).

5. Glass and plastic are (<u>insulators</u>, charged, resistors, conductors).

6. Two electrons (<u>repel</u>, attract, neutralize) each other.

7. A(n) (voltmeter, <u>ammeter</u>, ohmmeter, electroscope) gives a reading in amperes.

8. A galvanometer contains a(n) (electroscope, charged rod, uncharged rod, <u>magnet and coil</u>).

9. When the temperature of a conductor decreases, its resistance (increases, <u>decreases</u>, remains the same).

10. (<u>Copper</u>, Iron, Nickel, Cobalt) is *not* attracted by a magnet.

C. Completion

Complete each of the following sentences with a word or phrase that will make the sentence correct. (Do not write in this book.)

loses **1.** A body gains a positive charge when it __?__ electrons.

2. ___?___ charges repel each other.   *like*

3. The ___?___ is used to detect static electricity.   *electroscope*

4. Conductor is the opposite of ___?___.   *insulator*

5. A wet cell produces ___?___ current.   *direct*

6. An electric ___?___ changes kinetic energy into electrical energy.   *generator*

7. A.C. is produced by electromagnetic ___?___.   *induction*

8. A millivolt is ___?___ of a volt.   *1/1000*

D. How and Why

1. How is static electricity produced?   *friction*

2. What kind of energy is used to produce static electricity?   *kinetic*

3. How are chemicals in a wet cell used to produce electricity?

   Chemical reaction releases electrons to flow through an outside circuit.

4. Compare a diode with a photoelectric cell. How are they alike and different?

   4. Both are vacuum tubes and both contain a cathode and anode. In diode, heat releases electrons; in photoelectric cell, light releases electrons.

5. Compare an electric generator with a galvanometer. How are they alike and different?

   5. Both contain a wire coil and magnets. Generator produces current from motion; galvanometer produces motion from current.

6. A 12-v circuit has a resistance of 2 ohms. Calculate the amperes of current.   *6 amp*

7. Why is a Canadian nickel attracted by a magnet and a recently-minted American nickel not attracted?

   7. Canadian nickel contains nickel and American nickel does not.

See Teacher's Guide at the front of this book.

INVESTIGATIONS

1. Visit an electric power plant to learn how electricity is generated.

2. Take an old electric motor apart. Identify the commutator coil, magnets, brushes, and armature. Make a diagram showing the parts.

3. Obtain several magnets of different size. Measure the relative strength of the magnets. Strength may be measured by the number of paper clips or tacks a magnet can raise in a chain.

INTERESTING READING

Kennedy, Thomas, Jr., *Fun With Electricity*. New York, Gernsback Library, Inc., 1961.

Noll, Edward M., *Science Projects in Electricity*. New York, Howard Sams & Company, 1963.

The Way Things Work, Volume Two. New York, Simon and Schuster, 1971.

GOAL: You will gain an understanding of principles involved in electronic devices such as diodes, triodes, transistors, and cathode ray tubes.

Chapter 19 builds on the study of electricity in Chapter 18 through a discussion of principles involved in electronic devices such as diodes, triodes, rectifiers, transistors, and cathode ray tubes. Computers and other practical applications of electronics are presented and discussed.

Electronics

Sound is sent over long distances. This is done by radio, telephone, and telegraph. Pictures cross the world by means of television and artificial satellites. Recorders use electricity and magnetism to store these words and pictures for replay at a future time. High speed computers solve complex mathematical problems. These inventions affect our lives in many ways. They are made possible by **electronics.**

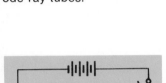

Figure 19-1.

What is a circuit?

19:1 *Circuits*

An electric **circuit** (sir′ kit) is a pathway through which electric current travels. The circuit may be connected directly to a power source such as a battery or generator. It may be connected to another circuit. For example, when a television set is "plugged into" a wall outlet, the television's circuits are connected to the house circuit. A diagram may be made to show the parts of a circuit.

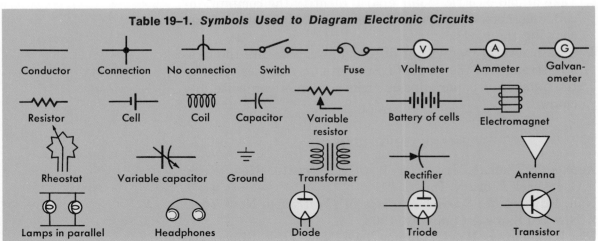

Table 19–1. *Symbols Used to Diagram Electronic Circuits*

Conductor	Connection	No connection	Switch	Fuse	Voltmeter	Ammeter	Galvanometer

Resistor	Cell	Coil	Capacitor	Variable resistor	Battery of cells	Electromagnet

Rheostat	Variable capacitor	Ground	Transformer	Rectifier	Antenna

Lamps in parallel	Headphones	Diode	Triode	Transistor

Zenith Radio Corp.

Figure 19-2. The picture on the television set travels through an electric circuit.

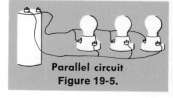

Figure 19-3.

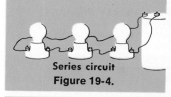

Series circuit
Figure 19-4.

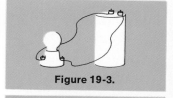

Parallel circuit
Figure 19-5.

PROBLEM

1. Using the symbols in Table 19–1, name the parts of the circuit in Figure 19–1. Straight lines represent wires.

EXPERIMENT. (1) A microlamp is a small electric bulb that can be connected to a circuit. Cut two pieces of bell wire about 30 cm long. Strip 2 cm of insulation from each end of the wires. Use the wires to connect the microlamp to a 6-volt battery. Does the lamp light? Make a diagram of the circuit. (2) Using pieces of bell wire, connect three microlamps as shown in Figure 19–4. What happens if you disconnect one of the lamps? (3) Connect the three lamps as shown in Figure 19–5. Disconnect one of the lamps. What do you observe?

In a **series** circuit, the same current flows through all parts of the circuit. If one part is disconnected, the current stops. There is no longer a circuit. A **parallel** circuit has branches. If one branch of the circuit is disconnected, current continues in the rest of the circuit. Does your home have series or parallel circuits? What kind of circuit is in a flashlight? *series*

EXPERIMENT. Connect a dry cell, bell, lamp, and switch in an electric circuit. Test your circuit to see if it works. Make a diagram of the circuit, using correct symbols. Did you make a series or parallel circuit? Draw a diagram of a circuit which would allow the bell and lamp to be operated by themselves.

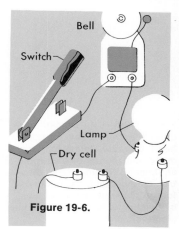

Figure 19-6.

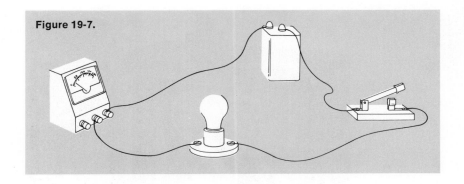

Figure 19-7.

ACTIVITY.   Connect an ammeter, lamp, and switch to a 6-volt battery. Did you make a series or parallel circuit? Why? Make a diagram of the circuit.

PROBLEM

2. Draw a diagram of a circuit with an electromagnet, voltmeter and fuse. <small>See Teacher's Guide at the front of this book.</small>

The vacuum tube was invented by Lee DeForest (1873-1961).

Most tubes used in radios and TV sets are pentodes, an improvement on the triode which gives greater amplification.

Explain the operation of a vacuum tube.

Voltage is applied to a cathode which emits electrons. The electrons travel across the vacuum to the plate which is positively charged.

19:2 *Vacuum Tubes*

Electronics deals with the release, behavior, and effects of electrons. An electron is a tiny particle of negative charge. It has a mass of 9.1×10^{-28} gram. Electrons are found in atoms. They can also be found outside atoms under certain conditions.

Radios and television sets contain *vacuum tubes*. A **vacuum tube** is a gas-tight container. It is usually made of glass. Air has been removed from the tube to form a vacuum. Inside the tube there is an electron source. It is called the *filament*. There is also an electron collector. This is called the *plate*. A vacuum tube is made so that the filament and plate can be connected to an electric circuit. The diode described in Section 18:5 is a vacuum tube.

Figure 19-8.   a. Diodes and other electron tubes form the heart of radio, television, and many other kinds of electronic equipment. Solid state electronic equipment uses transistors in place of electron tubes. b. Symbol of a diode used in electronic circuits.

a.

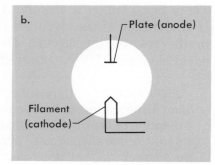

b.

Plate (anode)

Filament (cathode)

RCA

Vacuum tubes can be used to amplify (am' pli fie) voltage. Amplify means to increase the number of volts in a circuit. When a vacuum tube is used as an amplifier, the grid of the tube is connected to a circuit with small voltage. This circuit is called the *input*. The plate of the vacuum tube is connected to a circuit with high voltage. This circuit is called the *output*. The flow of electrons from the hot filament increases the voltage in the output circuit. For example, an amplifier vacuum tube can increase a 1-volt input to a 40-volt output.

Triodes are similar to diodes. They have a filament and plate. In addition, the **triode** has a *grid* of fine wire between the filament and the plate (Figure 19–9). The grid controls the flow of electrons between the filament and plate. When the filament is heated by an electric current, electrons "boil" off the filament. An electron "boils" off because heat energy overcomes forces that hold the electrons in the metal. Electrons released from the filament are attracted to the positively charged plate. They pass through the grid in their path from filament to plate.

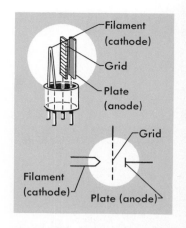

Figure 19-9. Symbols are used to show filament, grid, and plate.

Electrons are released from atoms in a hot filament.

     ACTIVITY. Obtain a used diode and triode. Very carefully break the outer covering of each tube. Dispose of the broken parts in a container provided by your instructor. Compare the structure of the tubes. Sketch the parts of each. Label important parts and tell the function of each. How does a triode differ from a diode? Find out when each is used.

A triode has a grid.

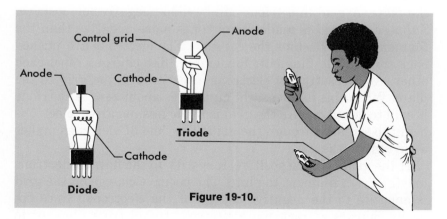

Figure 19-10.

In a circuit, the part which releases electrons is negatively charged. It is the **cathode** (—). The part of a circuit which gains electrons is positively charged. It is called the **anode** (+).

In a vacuum tube, the filament releases electrons and the plate gains electrons. Therefore, the filament is the cathode and the plate is the anode. Electrons travel through a circuit from cathode to anode. That is, from negative to positive.

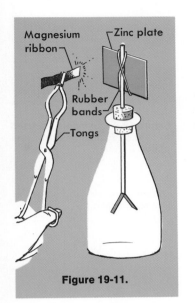

Figure 19-11.

The electroscope leaves spread apart indicating that it becomes charged by electrons released from the zinc. The zinc plate releases electrons when exposed to high intensity ultraviolet light.

EXPERIMENT. CAUTION: Do this experiment only under direct supervision of the teacher. Do not look at the burning magnesium. Can zinc metal release electrons when exposed to ultraviolet light? (1) Bend one edge of a zinc plate to form a lip. Polish the plate with sandpaper until it is very bright. Attach the plate to the knob of an electroscope, holding it with rubber bands around the lip. Charge the plate and the electroscope negatively with a charged plastic rod. (2) Hold a piece of magnesium wire with a pair of tongs 10 cm from the zinc plate. Ignite the magnesium with a match. Burning magnesium emits ultraviolet light. Observe the behavior of the electroscope leaves. (3) Repeat the procedure, holding a glass plate between the burning magnesium and the zinc. Glass filters out ultraviolet light. (4) Repeat with the electroscope charged positively.

What observation shows that the zinc loses electrons when exposed to ultraviolet light? How is the zinc plate similar to a photoelectric cell?

In a triode vacuum tube, the grid is connected to a circuit. This gives it an electric charge. The electric charge in the grid can be increased or decreased. By changing charge, the grid controls the rate at which electrons flow from the filament to the plate. A grid in a triode can be made negative or positive. Suppose the grid is made many times more negative than the filament. Then it stops the current. The electrons are pushed back toward the filament. Remember, like charges repel each other. As a result, few electrons pass through the grid to the plate. When this happens, the current is about zero. The triode is said to be cut off. As the grid is made less negative, electrons begin to stream through the grid. The flow of electrons makes a current in the plate.

If the grid is made positive, it speeds up the flow of electrons moving from filament to plate. The positive charge on the grid is opposite to the negative charge of the electrons. Since opposite charges attract, more electrons travel from filament to plate. Thus, the output voltage becomes many times greater than the input voltage. The electrons are traveling very fast. They seldom strike the grid. They fly through the openings in the grid and go directly to the plate.

The voltage of the output circuit connected to the plate can be increased or decreased. This is done by changing the voltage of the grid. A grid acts like a valve in a water pipe. It controls the flow of electrons and the voltage output. Output voltage can be increased or decreased by changing grid voltage. This causes amplification.

19:3   *Radio Receiver*

A one-tube, battery-operated radio receiver contains a triode (Figure 19–12). Radio waves passing through the air strike the radio antenna. The radio waves cause electrons in the antenna to vibrate. Vibrating electrons form a weak alternating current in the antenna and in the input coil attached to

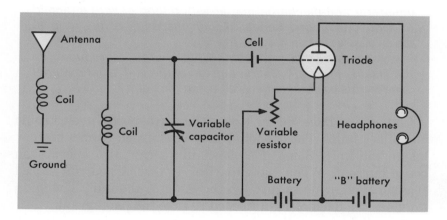

Figure 19-12. Each part of the circuit has a special function. Identify the function of each part.

the antenna. Alternating current in the input coil induces an alternating current in the circuit and capacitor. A *capacitor* (ka pas′ e ter) is a device that stores electricity. The capacitor in a radio circuit stores electrons for a short time.

Condenser is another name for capacitor.

The behavior of current in a capacitor is similar to the oscillations of a spring from which a weight is suspended. Relate this description of the operation of a simple radio to Figures 9-12 and 9-13.

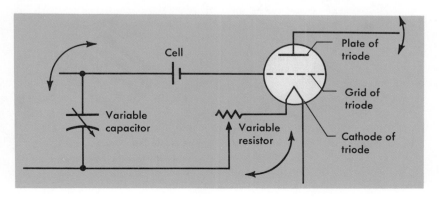

Figure 19-13. Current oscillates through the electrical circuit.

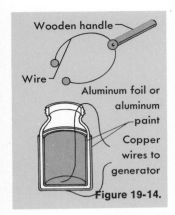

Central Scientific Co.

Wooden handle
Wire
Aluminum foil or aluminum paint
Copper wires to generator

Figure 19-14.

Alternating current flows between the capacitor and the grid of the triode vacuum tube. As the charge on the grid changes, the direct current to the speaker is changed. The headphones are operated by electricity from the triode. They produce the sound of radio. Headphones change electrical energy to sound energy. By using two triodes in a radio circuit, voltage can be amplified again. This makes the radio reception louder.

EXPERIMENT. Electric charge can be stored in a Leyden jar. (1) Line and coat a jar with aluminum foil or coat the inside and outside with aluminum paint. Stand a clean bare copper wire inside the bottle. Stand the bottle on a piece of bare copper wire. (2) Charge the Leyden jar by connecting the two wires to an electrostatic generator. (3) Disconnect the generator and discharge the jar with a loop of wire attached to a nonconducting handle. Touch the ends of the loop to the two wires connected to the jar.

Is a Leyden jar a capacitor? What charge is produced on the inside of the jar? On the outside of the jar? What material used in this experiment serves as an insulator?

Capacitors have many uses. They are used in electronic photoflash units. The capacitor may be charged from a battery inside the unit. Some photoflash units can also operate on house current. When the capacitor is discharged, its stored electric current flows through the lamp in the unit. The lamp provides the flash of light needed to take the photograph.

One kind of capacitor is used to tune a radio receiver. A tuning capacitor contains two sets of parallel metal plates. The plates of one set fit into the spaces between the plates of

Figure 19-15. The Leyden jar, one of the earliest types of condensers used to store an electric charge, is a glass jar covered with tinfoil up its sides. A brass rod connected to an electrical source is inserted through the top and charges the tinfoil when they touch.

The Leyden jar has two metal plates separated by an insulator. Opposite charges (− and +) are produced on the two plates. Glass is the insulator.

Figure 19-16. In a capacitor, thin sheets of tinfoil are separated by sheets of paraffined paper, mica, or other insulating material.

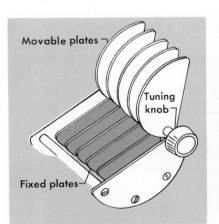

Movable plates
Tuning knob
Fixed plates

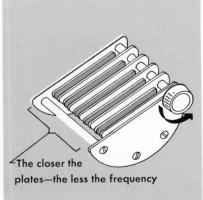

The closer the plates—the less the frequency

the other set. One set of plates is in a fixed position. The other set can be turned by hand. One set is connected to the cathode of a circuit. The other set is connected to the anode. By rotating the movable set of plates, the area of overlap is changed.

When the two sets of plates are in close alignment, the capacitor holds its greatest charge of electricity. The amount of charge decreases as the amount of overlap between the plates decreases. The electrical storing capacity of the capacitor is changed by rotating one set of plates with a knob. Frequency of the alternating current in the circuit is changed by changing the capacity of the capacitor. That is, turning the knob, changes the frequency. When the capacitor holds a large charge, the plates are close together. The frequency is low. When the capacitor holds a small charge, the plates overlap very little. The frequency is high.

To tune a radio set you adjust the capacitor with a knob until you hear the station you want. You set the capacitor plates so that the alternating current frequency is equal to the radio waves sent out by the radio station. For example, station KDKA in Pittsburgh has a broadcast frequency of 1,020 kilocycles/sec or 1,020,000 vib/sec. A radio receiver tuned to this station has an alternating current of the same frequency in its circuit. Changing a station means a shift to another radio wave frequency. When a shift is made from a high frequency to a low frequency radio station, the plates are moved farther apart. Alternating current frequency decreases. The capacitor is adjusted so that the frequency in the circuit is equal to that of the low frequency station.

Tuning means to adjust the capacitor so that its A.C. frequency is the same as the broadcast radio wave frequency of a station. When tuned the capacitor is in resonance with the radio waves.

How does a capacitor tune a radio receiver?

Different radio and TV stations broadcast at different broadcast frequencies.

19:4 *Rectifiers*

Most electrical appliances in the home use alternating current supplied by a power station. However, some electrical devices use direct current. One example is a battery charger. To recharge a battery, direct current must be sent backwards through the battery from the cathode to the anode. A battery charger contains a *rectifier*. The **rectifier** (rek′ ta fier) changes alternating current to direct current.

What does a rectifier do?
It changes A.C. to D.C.

PROBLEM

3. A battery cannot be recharged by A.C. Why not?

Many battery chargers contain a gas-filled tube called the "tungar rectifier." The tube of the tungar rectifier contains

When a battery is recharged current is pumped from cathode to anode. A.C. current would alternate cathode to anode—anode to cathode.

a filament and a plate. It is filled with a noble gas, such as argon, under low pressure. A *noble gas* does not chemically combine with other substances under ordinary conditions.

The filament of the tungar rectifier is heated by an alternating current. Because the gas is not chemically active, the filament does not burn when heated. Electrons "boil" off the filament and travel toward the positive plate. These electrons knock loose electrons which are normally attached to the gas atoms. The atoms become charged positively. A charged atom is an ion. The gas in the tube is said to be ionized because it contains many ions. An ionized gas conducts electricity.

The tungar rectifier changes the alternating current in the filament to direct current in the plate. Positive ions go to the negative filament (cathode). At the same time, electrons stream away from the filament to the positive plate (anode). From here they go into the output circuit. The current produced in the output circuit attached to the plate is direct current. In a direct current, electrons flow in one direction only.

There are many different kinds of rectifiers. For instance, both diode and triode vacuum tubes act as rectifiers. Since an X-ray tube is a diode, it acts as a rectifier.

Explain the operation of a tungar rectifier.

Electrons in the tube can flow in only one direction—filament to plate.

Figure 19-17. In rectified current (D.C.) an electron is forced constantly ahead through the circuit. It does not vibrate back to its original position as it would in A.C. current.

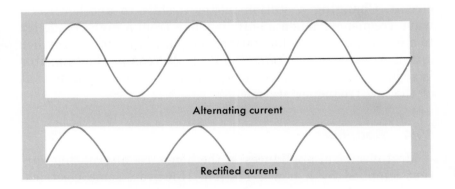

Alternating current

Rectified current

PROBLEM

　　4. Use Figure 19–17 to explain how a diode acts as a rectifier.

The principle of the transistor was discovered in 1948, a discovery for which W.H. Brattain, John Bardeen, and W.B. Shockley received the Nobel Prize in 1956.

19:5　*Transistors*

Transistors are replacing vacuum tubes for many uses. They make pocket radios, portable T.V. sets, and desk-top computers possible. The transistor has unique advantages. It is small and can operate on a very small voltage. A typical transistor is about ¼ by ¾ in. in size (Figure 19–18).

A transistor is a germanium or silicon crystal. It has an excess or lack of free electrons. A *free electron* is an electron that can drift through the crystal if a voltage is applied. *Germanium* (jur mae′ ni um) is a gray-white, brittle, crystalline metal. It is 5.4 times as dense as water. Germanium is obtained from the residues of certain zinc ores. *Silicon* is the second most plentiful element on the earth. It makes up about one fourth of the crust of the earth. It is 2.4 times as dense as water. Silicon is present in quartz and many other minerals. Pure silicon is a nonmetallic element with several forms. The crystalline form is used in transistors.

Both germanium and silicon are semiconductors. A **semiconductor** is a substance with a resistance between that of a conductor and an insulator. Pure germanium has a resistance 46,000 times that of copper! Impurities in germanium, however, greatly reduce this resistance. For example, the addition of one-millionth of one percent of arsenic to pure germanium doubles its conductivity at room temperature. Increase the impurities in a germanium crystal (or other semiconductors) and its electrical conductivity increases.

Raytheon Co.

Figure 19-18. Transistors vary in size. The transistor on the left is used in a large computer. The one on the right is used in a hearing aid.

What is a semiconductor?

Courtesy of Battelle Columbus Laboratories

Figure 19-19. Silicon crystal in a tiny circuit.

Impurities in transistor crystals are sometimes called doping agents and their addition to a crystal is called doping.

A large electronic computer may contain more than 100,000 transistors.

Control Data Corp.

Figure 19-20. Use of transistors made it possible to design smaller and more dependable computers. Shown here is a memory stack that takes information from input machines and stores information until needed.

How is an n-type transistor different from a p-type transistor?

A n-type transistor has excess free electrons. A p-type transistor is deficient in electrons.

There are two kinds of transistors. An *n-type* (negative-type) transistor has an excess of free electrons. A *p-type* (positive-type) transistor has a deficiency of free electrons.

A germanium crystal with antimony as an impurity is an n-type transistor. It has an excess of free electrons. Antimony atoms bond to germanium atoms. When this happens each antimony atom loses one of its electrons. Electrons set free from antimony atoms remain within the crystal as free electrons. These electrons drift through the crystal when it is connected to an electric circuit.

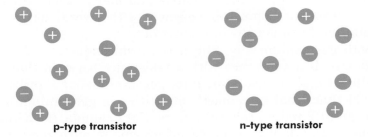

p-type transistor   n-type transistor

Figure 19-21. Differences in p-type and n-type transistors are due to differences in the number of free electrons present.

A germanium crystal which contains gallium is a p-type transistor. Gallium is a rare, grayish-white metal. It has a shortage of free electrons. Gallium atoms bond to germanium atoms. This means each gallium atom acquires one electron from the germanium atom. The captured electron leaves a "hole" behind. The electron which moves out has a —1 charge. Thus, the hole left behind is said to have a +1 charge.

Let us go back over this material. An n-type transistor has an excess of free electrons. These electrons can drift through the crystal when a voltage is applied. A p-type transistor has a shortage of free electrons. It has a large quantity of positive "holes" throughout the crystal (Figure 19–21). When current flows through a p-type transistor, electrons drift through the crystal from hole to hole.

An n-type transistor can be set face against face with a p-type transistor. Connected to a circuit, the transistors form a germanium rectifier (Section 19:4). Figure 19–22 shows the rectifier principle. The anode (+) of a battery is connected to the p-type transistor. The cathode (—) of the battery is connected to the n-type transistor. Electrons are forced through the circuit from the n-type into the p-type transistor. The flow of electrons makes a direct current in the circuit. If the anode and cathode connections are reversed, no current flows. Electrons will not flow from the p-type to the n-type transistor.

The solar cells that convert sunlight into power in satellites and other space vehicles contain transistors with p-n junctions.

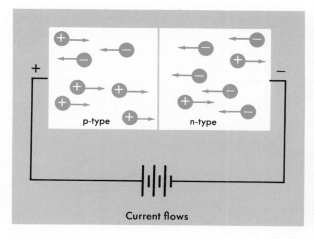

Current flows

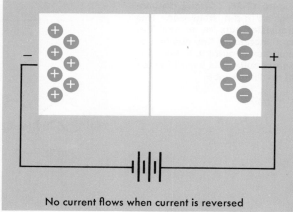

No current flows when current is reversed

Figure 19-22. When a germanium rectifier is connected to A.C. current, electrons flow only during half the A.C. cycle. Thus, A.C. is changed to D.C. current.

When an alternating current is connected to the n-type transistor, the transistors act as a rectifier. Alternating current is changed to direct current. Electrons can travel through the transistors in only one direction. The current travels from n-type to p-type transistor but not in the reverse direction. The input current is alternating current. The output current is direct current.

To amplify voltage, a point-contact transistor may be used. It operates on the same transistor principles as the germanium rectifier. The *point-contact transistor* is a small wafer of n-type germanium. It is attached to two fine bronze or tungsten wires. The wires are called "cat's whiskers." They are 0.002 to 0.005 inch in diameter. A brass disk is soldered to the germanium opposite the two "cat's whiskers." One wire attached to the germanium is the current collector. The other wire is the current emitter. The *collector* carries current into the transistor. The *emitter* carries current away from the transistor.

The collector wire of a point-contact transistor is connected to a low voltage circuit. The emitter wire is connected to another circuit (Figure 19–24). Input current is increased and comes out through the emitter circuit. It can be as much as three times greater. In effect, the transistor is an amplifier. It increases the voltage in a circuit. A transistor can be used as an amplifier in low voltage circuits in place of a vacuum tube.

Transistors operate on very low voltage. A transistor radio can operate on low voltage (3-volt to 12-volt) batteries. Yet, a transistor radio can produce sound volume equal to a vacuum tube radio connected to a 110-volt house circuit. Transistors

Figure 19-23. An n-p-n transistor may be compared to a triode. The emitter is similar to the cathode, the base to the grid, and the collector to the plate.

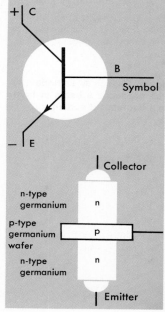

Symbol

Collector

n-type germanium

p-type germanium wafer

n-type germanium

Emitter

Both a transistor and a vacuum tube can rectify and amplify current. The left n-section of a n-p-n transistor corresponds to the cathode of a vacuum tube which emits electrons and is called an emitter; the p-layer which is called the base, acts like the control grid, and the right n-section acts like the anode and is called a collector.

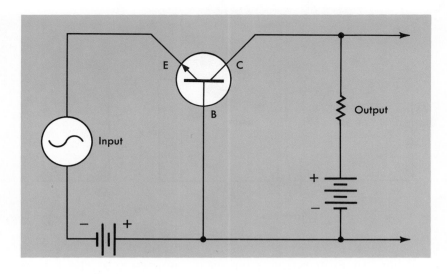

in other electronic equipment often replace vacuum tubes in their circuits.

19:6 *Cathode-Ray Tube*

Your television picture is produced on the surface of a *cathode-ray tube*. Radar sets, some computers, and various kinds of electrical testing equipment also contain cathode-ray tubes.

A **cathode-ray tube** is a special kind of vacuum tube. It contains a filament and a screen coated with fluorescent material. The cathode-ray tube takes its name from the rays of electrons. Electrons stream from the negative cathode filament

What is a cathode-ray tube?

It is a special kind of vacuum tube with a filament and a screen coated with fluorescent material.

Figure 19-25. A cathode ray tube produces a beam of light on a fluorescent screen.

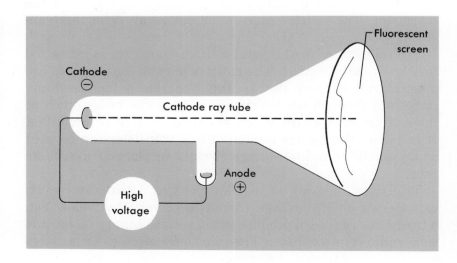

to the screen at the opposite end of the tube. Electrons in the cathode-ray are emitted from the heated filament. They form a beam directed at the screen on the face of the tube. Fluorescent material on the screen glows when it is struck by electrons. It emits visible light at each point where an electron beam strikes the fluorescent material.

The electron beam moves across the screen. In this way it produces a pattern of light which conveys information. In a radar receiver, a bright spot may appear. It is called a "pip." The pip shows the location of a moving airplane. In an electronic computer, numbers showing the solution to a problem may appear on the screen. The computer is designed to read out answers with a cathode-ray tube. The picture tube of a television set is a cathode-ray tube. The electron beam moves swiftly back and forth across the fluorescent face of the tube. This movement forms the picture.

Name three uses for a cathode-ray tube.

radar, computers, television

EXPERIMENT.   *How is a beam of electrons affected by a magnet? (1) Bring the S-pole of a bar magnet near the beam of a Crookes tube or a cathode-ray tube. Repeat with the N-pole of the magnet. (2) If a Crookes tube or cathode-ray tube is not available, try the procedure with the tube in a television set while the set is operating. (3) Repeat this experiment with magnets of different strength. Does the strength of the magnet make a difference? Why can an electromagnet control the position of a cathode ray? (Section 19:6)* Yes. Beam is deflected more by stronger magnet.

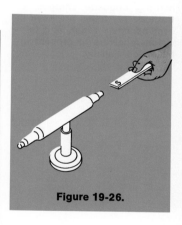

Figure 19-26.

Caution: All of these electron tubes operate on extremely high voltages. You may wish to perform this experiment as a teacher demonstration.

Either electrostatic charge or magnets control the movement of an electron beam in a cathode-ray tube. When controlled by electrostatic charge, the beam passes through charged plates. The charge on the plates varies. So the beam can be moved both horizontally and vertically as the charge is changed.

Large cathode-ray tubes contain electromagnets. An example would be the picture tube in a black and white television set. The cathode ray in the picture tube is deflected or bent from its path by the magnetic fields. By varying the strength of the electromagnets, the cathode ray can be moved both horizontally and vertically. The electron beam moves back and forth, up and down, and across the screen many times per second. The beam scans the screen.

Electromagnets in a television set are controlled by television waves coming to the antenna. Changes in the magnetic

The electromagnet can force the cathode ray into different positions, depending on the strength of the magnet.

Magnets and charged plates are used to focus electrons in beams much as glass lenses are used to focus light beams.

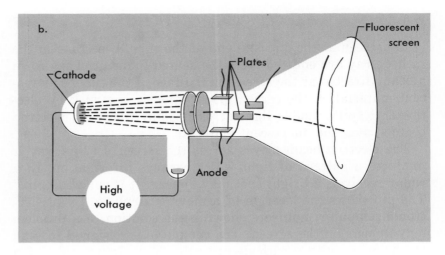

Figure 19-27. a. Movement of the electron beam is controlled by two pairs of plates, each pair bearing opposite charges. b. Cathode ray tubes are used in oscilloscopes, radar, and television receivers to present information visually.

fields regulate the path of the electron beam. The magnets regulate the number of electrons that strike the screen at different spots. Each spot hit by electrons glows for a fraction of a second. Your eye and brain blend the bright spots and the dark areas into a picture.

19:7 Digital Computers

Computers can be used to solve problems in mathematics, design airplanes and spaceships, control traffic, navigate ships, forecast weather, or compose music. The use of computers is almost endless.

Figure 19-28. Digital computers are used in many types of research.

Electronic **computers** are very complex machines. They contain electric circuits and electronic devices, such as vacuum tubes, transistors, and electromagnets. A computer can solve difficult equations with only a few numbers. In computing an answer, the computer follows known mathematical operations. A computer can add, subtract, multiply, and divide in a tiny fraction of the time it takes a person.

Computers are classified as *digital* and *analog*. A digital computer operates with numbers. It has five major units: input, output, storage, arithmetic, and control.

Input is information sent into the circuits of a computer. The *input unit* can be operated by keyboard, punched cards, punched paper tape, or magnetic tape. The input unit enters information, numbers, and problem-solving instructions into the storage unit. The *storage unit* is the computer's "memory." Information obtained from a computer's circuits is called *output*. The *output unit* records the results of the computer's computation. In other words, it gives the answer to the problem put into the computer. A computer may give out information in one or more ways. It may punch cards or paper tape, record on magnetic tape, or print words and numbers.

In a digital computer, the *arithmetic unit* performs operations needed to solve the problem. The *control unit* acts on earlier instructions put into the storage unit. It regulates the operation of the computer.

19:8   *Analog Computers*

An *analog* is something which is similar to something else. For example, a basketball is an analog of the earth. Both have a spherical shape and can be made to rotate on an axis. An analog computer works by making a model of real things or mathematical values. The model is made by electric circuits or moving parts, such as rotating wheels.

An ordinary mercury thermometer is one example of an analog device. The up-and-down movement of mercury in the thermometer is the analog of temperature change. As the temperature increases, the mercury moves up the thermometer. As the temperature decreases, the mercury moves down.

An electronic analog computer is made with electronic circuits. The equations for the circuits are the same as for the problem the computer is built to solve. For example, an analog computer can be built to calculate the thrust (force) of a

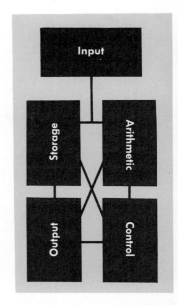

Figure 19-29. The five major units of a digital computer.

Name the five major units in a digital computer.

Input, storage, output, arithmetic, control.

Begin this section by defining analog and then having students do Problem 5 on p. 410.

What is an analog computer?

An analog computer uses electronic circuits to solve problems.

Computers can be used not only for solving mathematical problems, but also for comparing data, making predictions from data, recording complex motions, analyzing complex data, and simulating any kind of program that can be programmed. The computer seems to be limited only by the limit of the programmer's imagination.

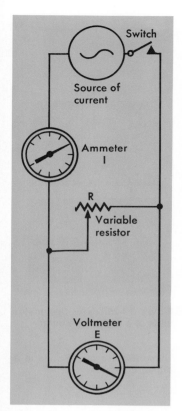

Figure 19-30. Simplified version of an analog computer circuit.

rocket. The equation for the thrust of a rocket is: thrust = mass × acceleration, or $T = ma$.

Ohm's law (Section 18:8) states that the voltage in a circuit is the product of resistance times current. The equation is: voltage = resistance × current, or $V = RI$. This equation for an electric circuit is similar to the equation for finding a rocket's thrust. Ohm's law equation is an analog of the rocket thrust equation.

Figure 19–30 shows a simplified version of an analog circuit built to solve the rocket thrust problem. Voltage (V) is the analog of thrust (T). Resistance (R) is the analog of mass (m). Current (I) is the analog of acceleration (a).

When the current (I) is turned on by closing the switch, it is multiplied by the resistance setting (R). The product IR is the voltage. It can be read on the dial of the voltmeter. The value of the computed voltage is the analog of the rocket's thrust.

PROBLEM

5. Classify the following devices into two groups: analog and digital.

a hourglass	*d* abacus	*a* ammeter
d slide rule	*d* fingers	*a* voltmeter
a clock	*d* telephone dial	*a* odometer
d Geiger counter	*a* hygrometer	*a* spring balance

MAIN IDEAS

p. 396 **1.** A vacuum tube is an electronic device.

p. 401 **2.** Rectifiers change alternating current to direct current.

p. 397 **3.** Electrons travel from cathode (—) to anode (+).

p. 398 **4.** The filament inside a vacuum tube is a cathode. The plate is an anode.

p. 398 **5.** The grid in a triode tube controls the voltage output.

p. 399 **6.** A capacitor stores electricity.

p. 403 **7.** Impurities increase the electrical conductivity of semiconductors such as silicon and germanium.

p. 403 **8.** Transistors contain semiconductors and amplify current.

p. 407 **9.** A cathode-ray tube contains a controlled beam of electrons.

p. 408 **10.** Electronic computers use electricity to solve mathematical problems.

VOCABULARY

Write a sentence in which you correctly use each of the following words or terms.

alternating current	computer	semiconductor
analog	diode	series circuit
anode	electronics	transistor
capacitor	grid	triode
cathode	parallel circuit	vacuum tube
cathode ray tube	rectifier	voltmeter

STUDY QUESTIONS

Have students rewrite false statements to make the statements correct.

A.   True or False

Determine whether each of the following sentences is true or false. (Do not write in this book.)

F **1.** Electrons flow through a circuit from ~~anode~~ to ~~cathode~~.   *cathode, anode*

F **2.** Like charges ~~attract~~ each other.   *repel*

T **3.** A rectifier changes alternating current to direct current.

F **4.** The ~~positive~~ plate of a vacuum tube is called the cathode.   *negative*

T **5.** An analog is a model of something.

T **6.** A vacuum tube can increase voltage.

F **7.** An electron is ~~positively~~ charged.   *negatively*

F **8.** Electricity is the flow of ~~protons~~ through a circuit.   *electrons*

T **9.** A capacitor can store electricity.

T **10.** A charged atom is called an ion.

B.   Multiple Choice

Some questions in part B may have more than one correct answer. Only one answer is required.

Choose one word or phrase that correctly completes each of the following sentences. (Do not write in this book.)

1. The (filament, plate, grid, vacuum) of a triode is a cathode.

2. The voltage output of a triode is controlled by the (filament, plate, grid, vacuum).

3. A (triode, diode, capacitor, transistor) is used to store electricity.

4. As the two sets of plates in a capacitor are moved farther apart, the amount of charge the capacitor can hold (increases, decreases, remains the same).

5. The symbol —⊣|ı|ı|ı|— in an electric circuit diagram is a (rectifier, battery, switch, bell).

6. Germanium and silicon are (conductors, nonconductors, insulators, <u>semiconductors</u>).

7. The electrical conductivity of pure germanium is (the same as, <u>less than</u>, greater than) that of impure germanium.

8. An n-type transistor has many (<u>free electrons</u>, holes, positive ions, free protons).

9. A cathode-ray tube is most like a(n) (rectifier, <u>triode</u>, n-type transistor, p-type transistor).

C. Completion

Complete each of the following sentences with a word or phrase that will make the sentence correct. (Do not write in this book.)

charged plates

1. The movement of the beam of electrons in a cathode-ray tube is regulated by __?__.

Answers will vary.

2. A(n) __?__ is an example of an analog device.

input, storage, arithmetic, output, control

3. The five units of a digital computer are the __?__, __?__, __?__, __?__, and __?__.

program

4. A computer __?__ is a set of instructions for computing the answer to a mathematical problem.

analog

5. Tree growth/year is the __?__ of rainfall/year.

D. How and Why   *See Teacher's Guide at the front of this book.*

1. How is a triode different from a diode vacuum tube?

2. Why must the two sets of plates in a capacitor contain opposite charges when the capacitor is connected to a battery?

3. How is an electric current in an ionized gas similar to an electric current in a solution?

4. How do a triode and a germanium rectifier change alternating current to direct current?

5. Why can't a battery be charged by alternating current?

6. Describe an experiment you could perform to show that a magnet deflects a beam of electrons.

7. Why have transistors replaced vacuum tubes in many electronic devices?

8. Explain why a thermometer, speedometer, tree, and thermostat are analog devices.

INVESTIGATIONS   *See Teacher's Guide at the front of this book.*

1. Many stores have vacuum tube testing machines. Obtain several used vacuum tubes and learn how to test them.
2. Arrange to visit a T.V. repair shop. Find out what kinds of electronic equipment are used to test and repair television sets.
3. Learn how a color television set works. A library book on television is a good starting point.
4. Build a crystal radio. The encyclopedia or book on radio will tell you how.

INTERESTING READING

Asimov, Isaac, "Happy Birthday, Transistor." *Saturday Review*, LV (October 23, 1972), pp. 45-51.

Bender, Alfred, *Let's Explore with the Electron*. New York, Sentinel Books Publishers, Inc., 1960.

Cahn, William, and Cahn, Rhoda, *The Story of Writing: Communication From Cave Art to Computer*. Irving-on-Hudson, New York, Harvey House, Inc., Publishers, 1963.

Carroll, John M., *Secrets of Electronic Espionage*. New York, E. P. Dutton & Company, Inc., 1966.

Goldman, H. L., "Nikola Tesla's Bold Adventure." *American West*, VIII (March, 1971), pp. 4-9.

Halacy, D. S., Jr., *Computers: The Machines We Think With*. New York, Dell Publishing Company, Inc., 1962.

Morgan, Alfred, *First Electrical Book for Boys*. New York, Charles Scribner's Sons, 1962.

Morgan, Alfred, *The Boy's Third Book of Radio and Electronics*. New York, Charles Scribner's Sons, 1962.

Rowland, John, *The Television Man: The Story of John L. Baird*. New York, Roy Publishers, Inc., 1966.

Nuclear Energy

Ernest Rutherford was a physicist from New Zealand whose work on radiation and atomic structure led to the field of nuclear physics. He discovered the element radon and first worked with alpha and beta rays. He is credited with being the first to change one element into another.

Anyone with imagination who has seen the trails of swift alpha particles, protons, and electrons cannot but marvel at the perfection of detail with which their short but strenuous lives are recorded.

Ernest Rutherford (1871-1937)

At the center of every atom there is a nucleus, a rich reservoir of energy. Nuclear energy is released through three kinds of reactions: transmutation, fission, and fusion. As radioactive elements (such as carbon 14) decay, they release energy as nuclear radiation. Energy from a nuclear reactor is released through the fission or splitting of uranium or plutonium atoms. In the explosion of a hydrogen bomb, nuclear energy is released through the fusion or joining of hydrogen atoms.

Nuclear energy has many uses. The list of uses is growing each year. Nuclear reactors provide energy to generate electricity and desalt water. Radioactive elements are used in the treatment of cancer and other diseases. Radioactive elements are used to learn about life processes and to investigate the composition of metals.

Someday nuclear energy from fission and fusion reactions may replace fossil fuels such as coal, oil, and gas. The "burning" of uranium 235 by fission releases an energy of 8 billion Calories per pound. This compares to only 4500 Calories per pound released by the burning of a fossil such as oil fuel. Research may eventually lead to the development of controlled fusion reactions in magnetic containers. This feat would enable man to obtain almost unlimited energy from hydrogen which is so abundant in ocean water. Will the career you choose enable man in some way to look closely at his needs and move toward solving new problems?

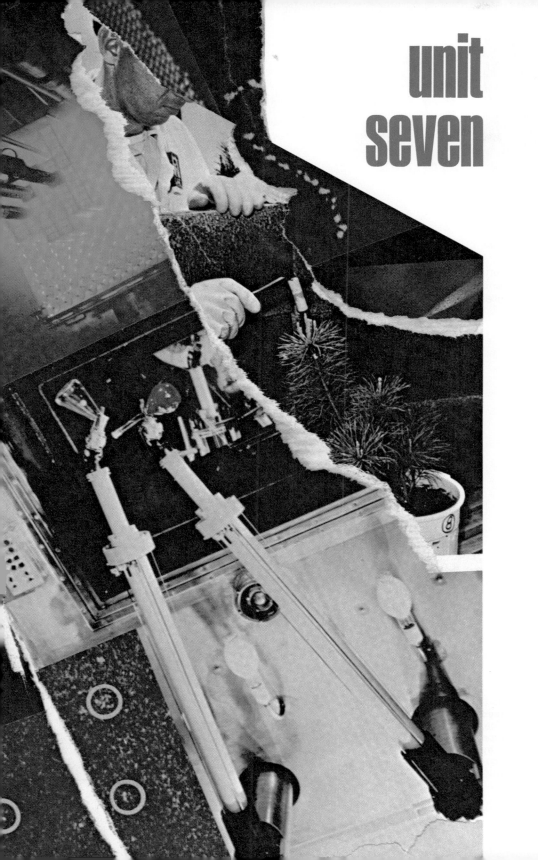

Chapter 20 discusses radiation, its detection, and measurement. The students will become acquainted with the concepts of natural radioactivity, artificial radioactivity, and half-life. Some aspects are studies within the framework of the historical development and discovery of different events in the science of nuclear physics.

Radiation

GOAL: You will gain an understanding of radiation and the detection and measurement of radiation.

In 1896 an unexpected event led to a major scientific discovery. Henri Becquerel (1852-1908), a French physicist, left some uranium salt lying on a photographic plate in a dark desk drawer. When he developed the plate, Bacquerel was surprised to find a silhouette of the uranium salt. Experimenting further, he proved that uranium releases radiant energy. This energy affects photographic film in the same way as light. The energy released by uranium is invisible. It can also penetrate opaque materials.

20:1 X rays

X rays were discovered in 1895 by W. K. Roentgen (1845-1923), a German physicist. Roentgen placed a fluorescent screen near an electric discharge tube. The discharge tube had

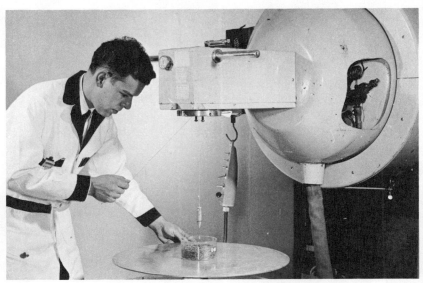

Figure 20-1. Biology department technician irradiates seed samples with an X-ray machine. Radiation increases mutation rate. Mutations produced by radiations can lead to the development of new plant varieties of economic value.

Brookhaven National Laboratory

416

Rohm and Hass Company

Figure 20-2. Each ceiling light contains three warm-white fluorescent 30-watt lamps, providing an average illumination of 85 foot-candles.

Mercury vapor inside the fluorescent lamp produces radiation when an electric current is passing through it. Radiation strikes the fluorescent coating to emit light.

a greenish glow. A *fluorescent* (floo' uh res' nt) *material* glows when exposed to radiation. **Radiation** is given off when atoms and molecules change internally. Roentgen reasoned that an unknown kind of radiation was given off by the electric discharge tube. He called the radiation **X rays.** (X often stands for unknown.) Other experiments showed that a beam of electrons produces X rays when the electrons strike a solid such as glass. The beam of electrons is called a cathode ray. We now know that X rays are a form of electromagnetic radiation. X rays have a wavelength of about 1×10^{-9} to 5×10^{-6} cm.

What are X rays?

X rays are a form of electromagnetic radiation with a wavelength of about 1×10^{-9} to 5×10^{-6} cm.

PROBLEM

1. How does the wavelength of X rays compare with the wavelength of blue light? of radio waves?

The wavelengths of blue light are longer than those of X rays; the wavelengths of radio waves are longer than those of blue light.

X rays can be produced in an X-ray tube. An X-ray tube is a high voltage cathode-ray tube. It contains a metal target and a metal filament. Voltages as high as 100,000 volts are common for an X-ray tube. The target is a dense metal, such as tungsten, set into a copper electrode. The filament in the X-ray tube is heated by the electric current in the high-voltage circuit (Section 19:1). Electrons "boil" off the hot filament. The target has a positive charge so the electrons rush toward it. Opposite charges attract. The electrons stream from the negative filament to the positive target (Figure 20–4). When the electrons strike the metal target, X rays are emitted (released) by the metal.

Why do electrons produce X rays when they strike a tungsten target? A moving electron has kinetic energy. When a high-speed electron penetrates the tungsten, it collides with a tungsten atom. Often, the electron must collide with several atoms before it is stopped. Some of the kinetic energy lost by the electron when it is stopped changes into X rays. Actually,

How are X rays produced?

Figure 20-3. These two photos show the same fluorescent rock under normal light (a) and ultra-violet light (b).

a.

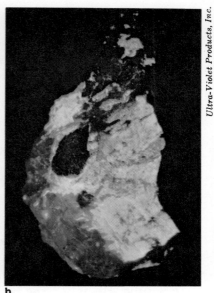

b.

List the main properties of X rays.

one percent or less of the kinetic energy is changed to X-ray radiation. The rest becomes heat energy of the target.

X rays travel at the speed of light, about 3×10^8 m/sec (186,000 mi/sec). They are emitted by an X-ray tube in tiny "bundles" of energy which are called **photons.** The energy of one photon of X rays varies directly with the wave frequency. X rays range in frequency from 3×10^{11} to 6×10^{17} vibrations per second. The higher the frequency, the greater the energy in one photon. The following equation shows how frequency, wavelength, and velocity are related:

$$f = \frac{c}{\lambda}$$

f = frequency
c = speed of light
λ = wavelength

The anode in an X-ray tube must be cooled or the heat produced will cause it to deteriorate. The wave-lengths of X rays are about 1000 times smaller than those of visible light waves.

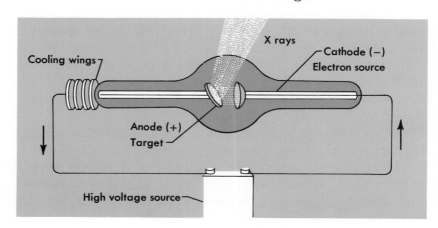

Figure 20-4. Varying the temperature of the filament controls the number of electrons striking the target which emits X rays.

EXAMPLE

Find the frequency of X rays with wavelength of 3×10^{-9} m.

Solution: (a) Write the equation: $f = \dfrac{c}{\lambda}$

(b) Substitute 3×10^8 m/sec for c and 3×10^{-9} for λ

$$f = \frac{3 \times 10^8 \quad \text{m/sec}}{3 \times 10^{-9} \text{ m}}$$

(c) Divide to find f

(d) Answer: $f = 1 \times 10^{17}$ vib/sec

PROBLEMS

2. Find the frequency of X rays with a wavelength of 1×10^{-3} m. 3×10^{11} *vib/sec*

3. What is the wavelength of X rays with a frequency of 5×10^{15} vib/sec? 6×10^{-8} *m*

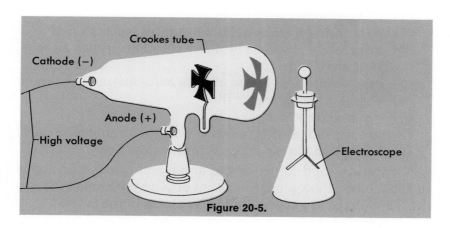

Figure 20-5.

EXPERIMENT. Can a cathode-ray tube discharge an electroscope? Charge an electroscope with a charged plastic or hard rubber rod. Aim the beam of an operating Crookes tube or cathode-ray tube at the electroscope knob. Measure the time it takes for the electroscope leaves to fall. Why do the electroscope leaves fall? How are charged particles produced by the cathode-ray tube? Why would the leaves fall less rapidly if the cathode-ray tube were covered with a lead sheet?

X rays produced by the tube ionize (remove electrons from) air molecules which are attracted to the electroscope where they neutralize its charge. Lead sheet shields the electroscope from radiation.

All substances absorb X rays to some degree. This includes gases. The amount of absorption depends upon the density of the material. For example, bone absorbs more X rays than

Figure 20-6. X-ray photographs of internal body organs are an important medical tool for the diagnosis of disease.

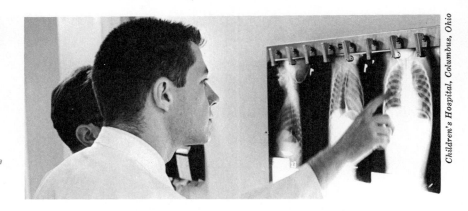

Children's Hospital, Columbus, Ohio

X-ray photographs obtained from a physician or hospital may be displayed in class by taping them to glass windowpanes.

flesh. Lead absorbs more than aluminum. You may have had X rays taken by a doctor or dentist. Why can X rays be used to make pictures of internal body parts?

Properties of X Rays

(1) travel in a straight line at the speed of light, 3×10^8 m/sec
(2) make a fluorescent screen glow
(3) pass through many solid substances, such as flesh
(4) are greatly absorbed by dense substances, such as bone, iron, and lead
(5) cast shadows of dense objects on a fluorescent screen
(6) expose a photographic film
(7) produce ions in a gas
(8) are not deflected by electric charges or magnetic fields
(9) burn flesh that is exposed to them too long

X-ray diffraction photographs are also used to probe the structure of molecules. For example, the structure of DNA, deoxyribonucleic acid (Watson-Crick model), was determined from X-ray diffraction studies. DNA is the genetic material in living cell nuclei through which hereditary traits are passed from one generation to another.

X rays are used to detect the order and spacing of atoms in substances. Pass a narrow beam of X rays through a crystal. The X rays are *diffracted* by the atoms in the crystal.

Figure 20–7 shows a diffraction pattern. These patterns are produced because rows of atoms in a crystal affect X rays. The

Figure 20-7. The big spot in the center of the diffraction pattern corresponds to the main unscattered beam. Other spots represent a scattering of the original beam through various angles.

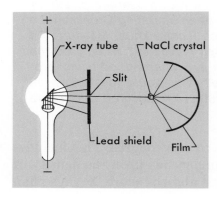

X-ray tube — NaCl crystal
— Slit
— Lead shield   Film

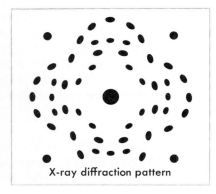

X-ray diffraction pattern

X rays change direction when they strike an atom. This is similar to the way a diffraction grating affects light (Section 17:8).

Spots form in an X-ray diffraction pattern. This occurs when waves are in phase (Section 16:3). The waves are reinforced. Spots do not form where the waves are not in phase. The waves cancel each other or destructive interference occurs. X-ray diffraction patterns help to show the arrangement of atoms in a crystal.

20:2   The Roentgen

X rays and other high-energy radiation can be harmful. Too much can cause burns, illness, and death. The standard unit to measure radiation is the *roentgen* (rent′ gun). This unit is based on the number of ions produced in a gas. One **roentgen** is the amount of radiation that will produce 2.08×10^9 pairs of negative and positive ions in one cubic centimeter of air at standard conditions. Standard conditions are 0°C and 760 millimeters of air pressure. Your chest X ray uses about 0.5 roentgen.

What is a roentgen?

A roentgen is a standard unit of radiation.

The amount and time of exposure to radiation determine its harmful effects. Large doses in a short time or small doses over a long period can be fatal. Exposure of up to 0.3 roentgen per week for the entire body is considered fairly safe. Lead absorbs most X rays. Thus, it is used to shield X-ray equipment. X-ray technicians also wear lead-coated aprons.

How are roentgens and time related to the harmful effects of radiation?

How are people protected from X rays?

Lead can be used to shield people from X rays.

PROBLEM

4. If you had one X ray per month for a year, what would be your radiation exposure in roentgens? Would this be a safe dosage of radiation?

6 roentgen/year; yes

Distinguish between X rays produced by energy changes in atomic electrons and radioactivity produced by energy changes in the nucleus.

20:3   Radioactivity

Certain atoms emit invisible high-energy radiation from their nuclei. These atoms are *radioactive*. As the radiation is released, the element decays and becomes a different element. Decay means to lose nuclear particles.

Radioactivity was discovered in uranium by Henri Becquerel in 1896. In 1898, the French chemists Marie (1867-1934) and Pierre (1859-1906) Curie discovered two new radioactive elements. These elements were named polonium and radium.

What is radioactivity?

Radioactivity is an invisible high-energy radiation emitted spontaneously from the nuclei of certain atoms.

Name three radioactive isotopes.

Three examples of radioisotopes are U 230, Po 210, and Ra 226.

The Curies extracted them from pitchblende, a uranium ore. The radioactivity of one gram of polonium or radium is greater than the radioactivity of one gram of uranium. Polonium and radium emit more radiation per minute than uranium.

Radioactivity usually occurs naturally in atoms heavier than lead. Such atoms have an atomic mass number greater than 206. However, many isotopes of lighter elements are radioactive. For example, potassium, rubidium, and carbon each have radioactive isotopes. Carbon 14 is radioactive. It has eight neutrons per atom. Carbon 12, the most common isotope, has only six neutrons per atom.

Some radioactive elements occur naturally. Others have been produced by man. Radioactive isotopes can be made by bombarding an element with high speed neutrons or charged particles. Some natural and man-made radioactive elements are listed in Table 20–1.

What elements are naturally radioactive?

The first eleven elements in Table 20-1 are naturally radioactive.

What man-made elements are radioactive?

The last eleven elements in Table 20-1 are man-made radioactive elements.

Have the students locate each of these elements in the periodic table.

Table 20–1. *Known Radioactive Elements*		
Element	At. Number (protons)	At. Mass Number (protons + neutrons)
Lead (Pb)	82	207
Bismuth (Bi)	83	209
Polonium (Po)	84	210
Astatine (At)	85	210
Radon (Rn)	86	222
Francium (Fr)	87	223
Radium (Ra)	88	226
Actinium (Ac)	89	227
Thorium (Th)	90	232
Protactinium (Pa)	91	231
Uranium (U)	92	238
Neptunium (Np)	93	237
Plutonium (Pu)	94	242
Americium (Am)	95	243
Curium (Cm)	96	245
Berkelium (Bk)	97	245
Californium (Cf)	98	249
Einsteinium (E)	99	254
Fermium (Fm)	100	252
Mendelevium (Md)	101	256
Nobelium (No)	102	251
Lawrencium (Lw)	103	257

Nuclear radiation can:

(1) "expose" a photographic plate
(2) produce ions in a gas
(3) burn flesh
(4) make a fluorescent screen glow
(5) penetrate many solid substances

When the ratio of protons to neutrons in an atom is about 1:1, the nucleus of the atom is *stable*. **Stable** means that the nucleus is not radioactive. Carbon 12 is an example of a stable atom. It has six protons and six neutrons. The ratio of protons to neutrons in carbon 12 is 1:1.

When there are more neutrons than protons in an atom, that element or its isotope may be radioactive. Carbon 14, for example, has 6 protons and 8 neutrons. Many of the common elements have radioactive isotopes (Table 20–2).

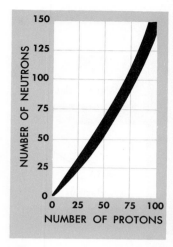

Figure 20-8.   Stable (nonradioactive) nuclei form an area of stability on this graph.

Table 20–2.   *Radioactive Isotopes of Some Common Elements*

Isotope	Protons	Neutrons
Tritium (hydrogen 3)	1	2
Helium 5	2	3
Lithium 8	3	5
Carbon 14	6	8
Nitrogen 16	7	9
Potassium 40	19	21

Most radioactive elements have more neutrons than protons. Uranium 238, for example, has 92 protons and 146 neutrons.

A radioactive element undergoes *transmutation* (tranz meu tae' shun). **Transmutation** is the process of changing from one element into another (Section 21:2). When transmutation occurs, atoms release nuclear particles. As a result, the number of protons changes and a different element forms. This continues until a stable element, such as lead, is formed.

Radioactivity is a physical property and not a chemical property.

Define transmutation.

In transmutation, the number of protons in the nucleus of an atom is changed. Thus, an atom of a different element is formed.

PROBLEMS

5. How are radioisotopes produced artificially?

Bombardment of atomic nuclei with neutrons or charged particles.

6. Why are some elements radioactive and others not?

The proton-neutron ratio in the nucleus of an atom determines nuclear stability.

20:4   *Alpha, Beta, and Gamma Rays*

During transmutation, radioactive materials emit three types of radiation. There are *alpha* (α), *beta* (β), and *gamma*

List the properties of alpha, beta, and gamma rays.

See top of next page.

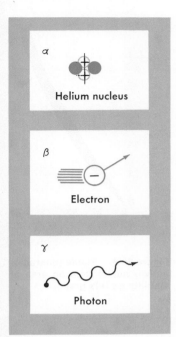

Figure 20-9. What are the main differences between alpha, beta, and gamma radiation?

Why is the path of a gamma ray unchanged by a magnetic field?

They have no electric charge.

Figure 20-10. Gamma radiation is changed to electrical energy when it strikes the cesium metal.

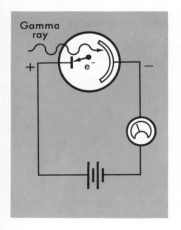

(γ) *rays.* **Alpha rays** are positively charged, high-speed *alpha particles.* They are shot out from atomic nuclei. Each **alpha particle** is a helium nucleus with two protons and two neutrons. The particle travels at a speed of 10,000 to 20,000 mile/sec. However, it does not have much penetrating power. An alpha particle can be stopped by a thin sheet of paper. Most alpha particles are absorbed after traveling through only a few centimeters of air.

Ernest Rutherford (1871-1937), an English scientist, demonstrated that alpha particles are helium nuclei. Alpha rays were passed into a glass vacuum tube. Then an electric discharge was passed through the tube. This process caused the tube to glow. A spectrum of light from the tube contained the known spectral lines of helium. The alpha particles entering the tube had collected electrons from the electric discharge. Alpha particles become helium atoms. Thus, the glowing gas in the tube was helium gas produced from alpha particles.

Beta rays are streams of fast moving *beta particles.* A **beta particle** is an electron shot out from a radioactive atomic nucleus. It has a negative charge. Beta particles travel faster and farther than alpha particles. The penetrating power of beta particles is about 100 times that of alpha particles. However, beta rays can be stopped by a sheet of aluminum one centimeter thick.

Every beta ray is a potential producer of X rays. X rays can be produced by slowing down high-speed beta-ray electrons. The kinetic energy lost by an electron as it slows down becomes X-ray radiation and heat energy. When the moving negative charge is slowed, radiation is emitted.

Gamma rays are energy waves of short wavelength and high frequency. Their wavelengths are about 10^{-10} centimeter. Gamma wavelengths are shorter than X-ray wavelengths. Most important, gamma rays are not charged particles. Gamma rays contain photons, or "bundles" of energy. They travel at the speed of light. Gamma rays are more penetrating than either alpha or beta rays. It takes several inches of lead or several feet of concrete to stop gamma rays.

Alpha rays and beta rays are deflected by a magnetic field. Gamma rays are not. This is evidence that gamma rays are not charged particles. Charged particles, such as protons and electrons, are deflected by magnetic fields. Electromagnetic rays such as light, X rays, and gamma rays are not deflected. Gamma rays can be diffracted by a crystal. This is very similar to X-ray diffraction.

Gamma rays can produce a photoelectric effect (Section 17:8). A photon from a gamma ray "kicks loose" an electron from an atom. The gamma-ray photon disappears and the electron gains kinetic energy. When atoms lose electrons, they become ions. Ionization caused by the photoelectric effect is used to detect gamma rays.

How do gamma rays produce a photoelectric effect?

Because gamma rays ionize air they can be detected with an electroscope.

PROBLEMS

7. Compare the properties of gamma rays and X rays.
8. Which has the shorter wavelength, cosmic rays or gamma rays? *Cosmic rays.*

Gamma rays have shorter wavelengths and are more penetrating than X rays. Both gamma rays and X rays are neutral.

20:5 *Half-Life*

Nuclear changes which produce radiation are completely different from chemical and physical changes. Factors in the environment, such as temperature and pressure, affect chemical and physical changes. However, the rate of nuclear change is not affected by any environmental change.

Half-life is a property of a radioactive element. **Half-life** is the time it takes for half of the atoms in a radioactive material to decay. For one isotope, half-life may be a fraction of a second. For another isotope, it may be thousands of years or more. In each succeeding half-life time interval, half the atoms left of a given radioactive element will decay. For example, barium 139 has a half-life of 86 minutes. Suppose you had 10 grams of pure barium 139 in a lead container. After 86 minutes, one-half of the atoms would have decayed. You would have only 5 grams of radioactive barium 139. After another 86 minutes, one-half of the remaining barium 139 atoms would have decayed. You would then have 2.5 grams.

Define half-life.

It is impossible to determine when a given radioactive nucleus will decay.

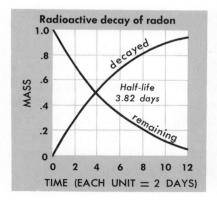

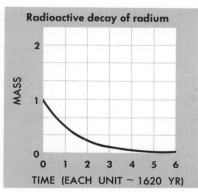

Figure 20-11. a and b. Radon is the heaviest gas known, being one hundred times as dense as hydrogen. Radioactive decay is not affected by changes in temperature or by chemical bonding. No one can predict which specific uranium nucleus will disintegrate next.

PROBLEMS

9. You have a 10-gram sample of barium 139. How much would be left after 4 hours and 18 minutes? *1.25 grams.*

10. How long would it take for all the barium 139 to decay?

Theoretically, an infinitely long period of time.

The shorter the half-life, the more radioactive the isotope. For example, radon 222 is more radioactive than radium. It is a radioactive gas produced in the decay of uranium. Its half-life is 3.82 days. The half-life of radium is 1,620 years. Radon 222 is less radioactive than polonium 214. The half-life of polonium 214 is 0.0001 second.

The half-life of uranium is 4.5 billion years. In 4.5 billion years, 1 gram of uranium 238 decays to 0.5 gram.

PROBLEM

Figure 20-12.

11. Is uranium 238 more or less radioactive than radon 222 or polonium 214? *Less.*

ACTIVITY. This is one model for radioactive decay. Obtain a square or rectangular box. Mark an X on one side of the box. Place exactly 100 kernels of corn in the box. (1) Put the lid on the box and shake. Remove the lid. Pick out all the kernels that point toward the marked side of the box (Figure 20–12). Assume that these have "decayed." Count these kernels and set them aside. How many "undecayed" kernels are still in the box? Record the number of "decayed" and "undecayed" kernels. (2) Repeat Part 1 until all kernels are removed.

20:6 *Radiation Detection*

Alpha, beta, and gamma rays cannot be seen, heard, tasted, smelled, or touched. However, it is possible to detect their presence. Alpha, beta, and gamma rays can produce three changes:

(1) ions

(2) scintillations (sin tu lae' shunz) or flashes of light

(3) tracks in photographic film

The easiest way to detect radioactivity is with an electroscope (Section 18:2). A charged electroscope loses its charge more rapidly when ionizing radiation is present than when it is absent. This loss of charge is due to the formation of ions by the radiation. Ions form in the air around the electroscope. They are attracted to the knob of the electroscope.

Cleaner "Smoke"

Dr. Meredith C. Gourdine is an engineer and an inventor. One of his inventions is Incineraid, an electrostatic precipitator for apartment buildings.

Electrostatic precipitators remove small particles such as dust from air. These devices are often used to remove pollutants from the smokestack gases of steel mills and other large factories.

As the gases pass through, the precipitator first gives each particle a positive elec-

tric charge. Then the gas and its charged particles flow through a series of charged plates. Some of the plates have a positive charge. Some have a negative charge. The positive plates repel the particles (like charges repel) toward the negative plates. The particles stick to the negative plates (opposite charges attract) until washed off with water. The cleaned gases pass out of the smokestack.

Many apartment buildings burn their garbage in incinerators. Smoke from these burners contains all sorts of particles. Unfortunately, the regular electrostatic precipitator is too large and too expensive for most apartment buildings.

Incineraid is about ⅙ the size of a normal precipitator. It costs less too. Incineraid has another advantage over the precipitator. Its plates are disposable. So no water is

used to clean its electrically charged plates.

Incineraid could help apartment dwellers get rid of their garbage without adding to air pollution.

G. Marshall Wilson, Ebony Magazine

Dr. Meredith C. Gourdine

Working on this instrument electronics assembly line requires knowledge of circuitry and careful attention to detail. Transportation, radio and television, space exploration: all these depend on electronics. People with skills in electronics are found in many industries and with many different job titles.

Bureau of Indian Affairs

Evelyn Jiu

Evelyn Jiu is training to become an aircraft instrument mechanic. Her career is one of many specialized fields in electronics.

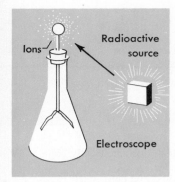

Figure 20-13. Charged particles cause an electroscope to
lose its charge and become
neutral. The leaves of the electroscope will drop as it discharges.

A positively charged electroscope attracts negative ions. A negatively charged electroscope attracts positive ions. The electroscope, depending on its charge, either gains or loses electrons. It becomes neutral. As the charge is lost, the leaves of the electroscope drop down. The rate of charge loss depends upon the number of ions formed per second by the radiation. The greater the radiation, the more ions formed per second. Thus, the rate at which the leaves drop is a measure of the strength of a radioactive material.

PROBLEM

12. How could you use an electroscope to detect radiation?

See bottom of p. 426.

20:7   Cloud Chambers and Bubble Chambers

How does a cloud chamber operate?

In 1907, C. T. R. Wilson (1869-1959), a Scottish physicist, invented the *cloud chamber*. A **cloud chamber** detects nuclear particles through the formation of *cloud tracks*. A **cloud track** is a visible line of condensed vapor formed along the path of a radioactive particle (Figure 20–14). One type of cloud chamber contains air or some other gas saturated with water vapor. It is arranged so that when a piston or bellows is released, pressure on the gas suddenly is reduced. As a result, the gas expands. Since a gas cools when it expands, the mixture of air and water vapor cools and becomes *supersaturated*. More water vapor than usual goes into solution with air. When the rays pass through air which is supersaturated with water vapor, cloud tracks are formed.

Compare the cloud chamber
tracks produced by alpha, beta,
and gamma rays.

See bottom of p. 428.

Figure 20-14. The long track
passing diagonally through the
center of the cloud chamber is
an alpha particle. The other
tracks are caused by protons.

Argonne National Laboratory

Cloud tracks in a cloud chamber form because air is ionized by radiation. For example, a beta ray traveling through the cloud chamber produces a track of ions. The ions are invisible. However, water vapor instantly forms tiny water droplets along the track of ions. The water droplets produce a cloud track which is visible. The track shows the path of the radiation. A beta ray produces a long, thin track. An alpha ray usually makes a shorter, heavier cloud track. Gamma rays can be studied by observing the cloud tracks of electrons knocked loose from atoms hit by the gamma rays. The zigzag path of the electrons show where the gamma ray passed (Figure 20–14).

A magnetic field changes the path of some rays. This can be observed with a cloud chamber. Cloud tracks show that alpha and beta rays are bent by a magnetic field. Gamma rays, however, are not deflected.

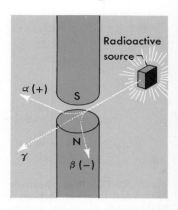

PROBLEM

13. Are alpha and beta rays in a magnetic field bent in the same or opposite directions? *Opposite*

The *diffusion cloud chamber* requires little equipment. One kind of diffusion cloud chamber is a glass jar containing a liquid. Alcohol is often used because it vaporizes easily. The jar is set on a piece of dry ice. A bright beam of light is passed through it. The dry ice cools the bottom of the jar. Warmer vapor in the upper portion of the jar descends, cools, and becomes supersaturated. Cloud tracks produced by radiation are visible in the lighted supersaturated vapor (Figure 20–16).

A *bubble chamber* is another means used to detect nuclear particles. The **bubble chamber** is based on the formation of bubbles within a *superheated liquid*. Liquid propane, hydrogen, and xenon have been used in bubble chambers. A **superheated liquid** is produced by heating the liquid under pressure and then suddenly releasing the pressure. An ionizing nuclear particle passing through a superheated liquid leaves behind a track of bubbles in its wake. Liquid is much denser than vapor. Therefore, high-energy rays which pass unnoticed through the gas of a cloud chamber show up in the denser liquid of a bubble chamber.

Figure 20-15. The extent to which alpha and beta rays are bent is proportional to the strength of the magnet. Why are the rays bent in opposite directions?
They have opposite charges.

Explain the operation of a bubble chamber.

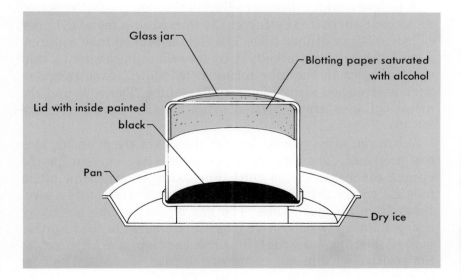

Figure 20-16. A diffusion cloud chamber is easily made by suspending a jar on a piece of dry ice.

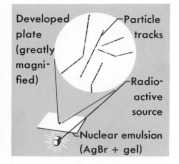

Figure 20-17. Silver bromide is reduced to silver, forming a black streak along the path of a radioactive particle.

Why is a nuclear emulsion called a "frozen cloud chamber"?

The emulsion which detects nuclear radiation is a solid, rather than a gas or liquid.

Nuclear particles expose photographic plates and thus leave a permanent record of their paths.

Geiger counter is named after its designer, Hans Geiger (1882-1945), a German physicist.

Figure 20-18. Geiger counters are sometimes used to test the effect of radiation on plant life.

20:8   *Nuclear Emulsions*

A **nuclear emulsion** (ee mawl' shun) is a thick layer of photographic emulsion. Photographic emulsion contains grains of silver bromide (AgBr) in a gelatinlike solid. It is the shiny coating on photographic film and prints. The thick layer forming a nuclear emulsion sometimes is called a "frozen cloud chamber." This is because the emulsion is a solid rather than a gas or a liquid. The emulsion can detect radiation.

Charged particles, such as alpha and beta particles and gamma rays, can be detected in a nuclear emulsion. The charged particles "expose" the grains of silver bromide in the emulsion. When placed in chemical developer, the "exposed" silver bromide is reduced to silver. The path of the nuclear particle in the developed emulsion appears as a dark track. The principle is the same as the exposure and development of photographic film. Nuclear particles travel relatively short distances. The emulsion is very dense. Therefore, nuclear tracks are a few millimeters or less in length. Because they are short, the tracks are studied with a microscope.

PROBLEM

14. How are photographic plates used in tracking nuclear particles?

20:9   *Radiation Counters*

A **Geiger counter** detects radiation through the formation of an electric current. The current is formed in a metal cylinder called a Geiger-Müller tube. The **Geiger-Müller tube** contains a gas, such as argon or helium, under reduced pressure. A thin sheet of mica in the tube forms a "window." Fine tungsten wire is stretched along the axis of the tube. The wire and the metal cylinder are connected to an electric circuit (Figure 20–19).

When radiation passes through the gas in the cylinder, ions are produced. The ions generate an electric current in the circuit connected to the tube. For example, when an alpha particle enters through the mica window, it frees a few electrons from the gas atoms. The gas atoms become positively charged ions. These positive ions are attracted to the negative wall of the tube (cathode). The free electrons are attracted to the positive wire in the center of the tube (anode). The flow of electrons to the wire produces a flash of current in the ex-

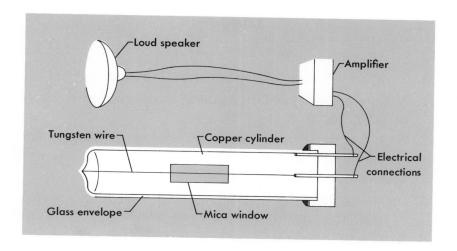

Figure 20-19. When a radioactive particle enters the gas inside the tube, ionization occurs. This causes a small, brief current in the circuit.

A pulse of current flows between the tungsten wire and copper cylinder when ions are formed in the tube.

ternal circuit. This current is amplified and fed into recording or counting devices.

A small lamp or loudspeaker is used as a counting device in a Geiger counter. A flash of the lamp or a click in the loudspeaker occurs when a radioactive particle enters the Geiger-Müller tube. The number of clicks or flashes a Geiger counter makes per unit time shows the strength of the radiation.

Explain how a Geiger counter detects nuclear radiation.

EXPERIMENT. A Geiger counter may be used to detect many types of radiation. (1) Turn on the Geiger counter. Count the number of clicks for 3 minutes and compute the average clicks per minute (clicks ÷ 3). (2) Bring a watch with a radium dial near the counter. Find the average clicks per minute. (3) Place a 2 mm-thick piece of aluminum between the Geiger tube and the watch. Again count the average clicks per minute. What do you observe? Explain. What would you observe if you put a lead plate between the watch and the Geiger counter? (4) Measure at four different distances from the radioactive source. Record distances and average number of clicks per minute. How does distance from a radioactive source affect radiation?

Watches with radium dials are no longer manufactured because of the hazards to people working with radioactive paint. Radioactive sources may be purchased from a laboratory supply house. You may wish to try using the mantle from a gas camp lantern. These mantles are made from cloth dipped in thorium and cerium salts.

Aluminum absorbs radiation and shields the Geiger counter. Lead plate shields the Geiger counter. There would only be "background" clicks.

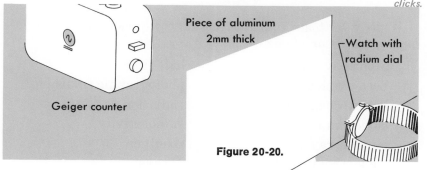

Figure 20-20.

Radiation varies inversely with the square of the distance; similar to light-distance and sound-distance relationships.

MAIN IDEAS

p. 416 **1.** X rays are a form of electromagnetic radiation.

p. 417 **2.** X rays are produced by cathode rays striking a metal target inside an X-ray tube.

p. 418 **3.** High frequency waves have more energy per photon than low energy waves.

p. 421 **4.** The roentgen is a unit of radiation.

p. 421 **5.** One large dose of radiation, or small doses over a period of time, are harmful and can cause death.

p. 421 **6.** Radioactivity results from the decay of unstable atomic nuclei.

p. 422 **7.** As the number of neutrons in the nucleus of an element increases, the stability of the element generally decreases.

p. 422 **8.** Some radioactive isotopes occur in nature. Some are made artificially.

p. 424 **9.** An alpha particle is a helium nucleus containing two protons and two neutrons. It has a $+2$ charge and a mass of 4 a.m.u.

p. 424 **10.** A beta particle is a high-speed electron emitted from an atomic nucleus. It has a -1 charge and almost no mass.

p. 424 **11.** Gamma radiation is a form of electromagnetic radiation with a wavelength of about 10^{-10} cm.

p. 425 **12.** Half-life is a measure of the radioactivity of an element.

p. 426 **13.** Radiation can be detected with an electroscope, Geiger counter, cloud chamber, bubble chamber, or nuclear emulsion.

VOCABULARY

Write a sentence in which you correctly use each of the following words or terms.

alpha ray	half-life
beta particle	photographic emulsion
bubble chamber	radiation
cloud chamber	radioactivity
gamma ray	roentgen
Geiger counter	X rays

STUDY QUESTIONS

A. True or False

Have students rewrite false statements to make the statements correct.

Determine whether each of the following sentences is true or false. (Do not write in this book.)

F **1.** A beta ray is actually a ~~hydrogen nucleus~~.   *stream of electrons*

T **2.** A beta ray has a negative charge.

F **3.** An alpha particle has ~~no~~ charge.   *a positive*

T **4.** Radiation can be detected with an electroscope.

T **5.** X rays travel at the speed of light.

T **6.** X-ray machines use small doses of X rays over a short time.

F **7.** Radioactivity was discovered by ~~Marie and Pierre Curie~~   *Becquerel*
in ~~1898.~~   *1896*

T **8.** A Geiger counter cannot detect X rays.

F **9.** Uranium 238 ~~is~~ more radioactive than radium 226.   *less*

F **10.** The half-life of uranium 238 is ~~shorter~~ than the half-life   *longer*
of uranium 235.

B. Multiple Choice

Some questions in part B may have more than one correct answer. Only one answer is required.

Choose one word or phrase that correctly completes each of the following sentences. (Do not write in this book.)

1. X rays are (positive particles, negative particles, uncharged particles, <u>part of the electromagnetic spectrum</u>).

2. The speed of X rays is (about 1,100 ft/sec, greater than the speed of light, $\underline{3 \times 10^8 \text{ m/sec}}$, 100,000 mph).

3. The energy of an X-ray photon depends on the photon's (speed, <u>frequency</u>, size, color).

4. An X-ray photon is most likely to be stopped by (oxygen, water, flesh, <u>minerals</u>).

5. (<u>Lead</u>, Paper, Aluminum, Copper) is the best shield against radiation.

6. As the number of neutrons in a nucleus increases above the number of protons, the stability of the nucleus (increases, <u>decreases</u>, remains the same).

7. A fluorescent screen glows when it is exposed to (heat, light, <u>radioactivity</u>, pressure).

8. A particle containing two protons and two neutrons is a(n) (<u>alpha</u>, beta, gamma, X-ray) particle.

9. A helium nucleus is a(n) (<u>alpha particle</u>, beta particle, proton, neutron).

C. Completion

Complete each of the following sentences with a word or phrase that will make the sentence correct. (Do not write in this book.)

negative

1. A beta particle has a(n) __?__ charge.

lost kinetic

2. When the speed of a beta particle is decreased, its __?__ energy becomes X rays and heat.

time, half

3. The half-life of a radioactive element is the amount of __?__ it takes for __?__ of the atoms in a sample to decay.

ionizes

4. A charged electroscope can detect radioactivity because radioactivity __?__ atoms in air.

supersaturated

5. The cloud tracks in a cloud chamber are produced in a __?__ mixture of liquid vapor in air.

photographic

6. Silver bromide is a chemical in the __?__ emulsion used to detect radioactivity.

Geiger counter

7. A(n) __?__ is a radiation detector in which an electric current is produced by alpha and beta particles.

gamma

8. __?__ rays are high-energy nuclear rays coming to the earth from outer space.

C 14

9. __?__ is a radioactive carbon isotope.

D. How and Why   *See Teacher's Guide at the front of the book.*

1. How are X rays produced in an X-ray tube?
2. Why must the target in an X-ray tube be cooled by air or some other cooling agent?
3. Why do X rays and radioactivity discharge a charged electroscope?
4. Why are alpha and beta particles deflected in opposite directions by a magnetic field?
5. How are a cloud chamber, bubble chamber, and nuclear emulsion used to detect radioactivity?
6. Why does a Geiger counter click when it is near radioactive material?
7. What are the properties of alpha rays, beta rays, and gamma radiation?
8. Locate the positions of X rays and gamma rays in the electromagnetic spectrum. Which of these radiations has the largest and shortest wavelength?
9. Which radiation in Question 8 has the most and the least energy per photon?

See Teacher's Guide at the front of the book for answers and suggestions.

INVESTIGATIONS

1. Find out how radiation is used to treat diseases. Make a report to your class.

2. Obtain X-ray photographs from a hospital or physician. Label the parts shown in each. Tape on classroom windows for display.

3. Read a biography of Madame Curie which describes her discovery of radium.

INTERESTING READING

Asimov, Isaac, *Inside the Atom.* New York, Abelard-Schuman, Ltd., 1961.

Hatcher, Charles, *The Atom.* London, Macmillan & Co., Ltd., 1963.

Lefort, Marc, *Nuclear Radiations.* New York, Walker and Co., 1963.

Stepp, Ann, *The Story of Radioactivity.* Irvington-on-Hudson, N.Y., Harvey House, 1971.

GOAL: You will gain an understanding of the structure of the atomic nucleus, transmutation, fission, and fusion.

Why does the nucleus contain most of an atom's mass?
Most of the volume of an atom is space and the mass of its electrons is almost zero.

Figure 21-1. Repulsion between the positive charge of a nucleus and positive charge of an alpha particle causes the alpha particle to be deflected from its path.

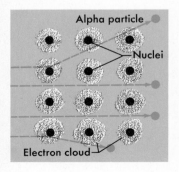

Chapter 21 describes the structure of the nucleus and three kinds of nuclear reactions: transmutation, fission, and fusion. Transmutation reactions of radioactive isotopes are explained and the practical uses of the isotopes are studied.

Nuclear Reactions

From early times, man has failed in his attempt to change metals such as iron into gold. However, with the aid of atom smashing machines, scientists today can change one element into another. For example, platinum has been changed into gold. Research in atomic physics has led to the production of new elements. One of these is plutonium. Discovery and use of nuclear energy came about by the splitting of the atom.

21:1 *Atomic Nucleus*

The basic particles of an atom are the proton, neutron, and electron. One model of an atom pictures a dense, positively charged nucleus. A cloud of negative electricity surrounds it. The cloud is produced by electrons orbiting around the nucleus. The nucleus contains positively charged protons and neutrons.

A nucleus is only a tiny fraction of an atom. Then why does it contain almost the total mass of an atom? The mass of an electron is almost nothing compared to the mass of a proton or a neutron. The mass of one proton or one neutron equals the mass of 1,837 electrons.

Protons and neutrons have about the same atomic mass. The mass of a proton or neutron is close to one a.m.u. (Section 3:2). Therefore, the mass of an atomic nucleus is nearly a whole-number multiple of one a.m.u. For example, a sodium nucleus has a mass of about 23 a.m.u. A sulfur nucleus has a mass of about 32 a.m.u. The mass of each nucleus is about equal to the sum of the atom's protons and neutrons. However, exact measurements show the actual mass of a nucleus is slightly less than its atomic mass number.

A deuterium (hydrogen isotope) nucleus contains one proton and one neutron. The total mass of a free proton and a free neutron outside a nucleus is 2.016575 a.m.u.

These two calculations are given as examples to illustrate the mass defect which exists in every nucleus.

$$1 \text{ neutron} = 1.008982 \text{ a.m.u.}$$
$$1 \text{ proton} \;\; = 1.007593 \text{ a.m.u.}$$
$$\text{Sum} = 2.016575 \text{ a.m.u.}$$

The mass of the nucleus in a deuterium atom is 2.01419 a.m.u. This mass is 0.002385 a.m.u., or about 0.0024 a.m.u. less than the sum of a free proton and neutron. The following calculation shows this difference:

$$1 \text{ proton} + 1 \text{ neutron} = 2.016575 \text{ a.m.u.}$$
$$\text{Deuterium nucleus} \;\;\;\; = 2.014190 \text{ a.m.u.}$$
$$\text{Difference} = 0.002385 \text{ a.m.u.} = \text{mass defect}$$

Mass defect is the difference between the mass of a nucleus and the total mass of its nuclear particles. The mass defect for deuterium is about 0.0024 a.m.u.

A helium nucleus has a mass defect of about 0.03 a.m.u. The helium nucleus contains two protons and two neutrons. To calculate the mass defect, add the masses of the four particles outside a nucleus:

$$2 \text{ neutrons} = 2 \times 1.008982 \quad\quad 2.017964$$
$$2 \text{ protons} \;\; = 2 \times 1.007593 \quad\quad 2.015186$$
$$\text{Sum} = 4.033150$$

The mass of a helium nucleus is 4.002775 a.m.u. Subtract the mass of a helium nucleus from the mass of the nuclear particles to find the mass defect:

$$4.033150 \text{ a.m.u.}$$
$$4.002775 \text{ a.m.u.}$$
$$\text{Difference} = 0.030375 \text{ a.m.u.} = \text{mass defect}$$

Sometimes protons and neutrons combine to form a stable nucleus. Then energy is released. This released energy is called

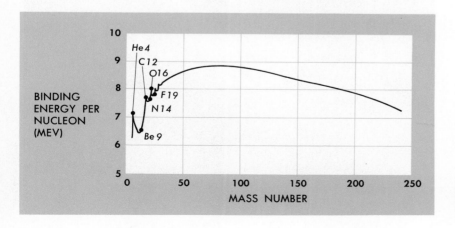

Figure 21-2. **Binding energy is the force which holds the parts of a nucleus together.**

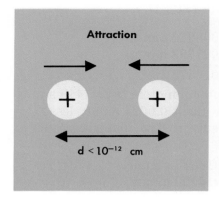
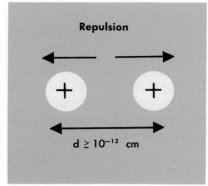

Attraction

Repulsion

$d < 10^{-12}$ cm

$d \geq 10^{-12}$ cm

Define mass defect and binding energy.

binding energy. Binding energy results from the loss of mass which creates the mass defect. The lost mass is changed into energy.

Energy equal to the binding energy can be put back into a nucleus. This causes the nuclear particles to separate. Thus, **binding energy** is the amount of energy needed to separate a nucleus into free protons and neutrons.

Mass defect and binding energy help explain one theory of the origin of atoms. This theory states that billions of years ago there was a tremendous cloud of free protons, neutrons, and electrons in space. Somehow the protons and neutrons

Figure 21-4. Nuclear forces play a role in holding the parts of this galaxy together.

Lick Observatory

combined to form atomic nuclei. The positively charged nuclei collected electrons to form atoms.

Physicists suggest that nuclear forces hold protons and neutrons together in a nucleus. Nuclear forces are not like the force of gravity or the forces between charged electrical particles. **Nuclear forces** exist only over distances shorter than the size of an atomic nucleus (10^{-12} centimeter or less). The nuclear force between two protons is greater than the repulsion between the two protons. Thus, at distances of 10^{-12} centimeter or less, protons are held together by nuclear forces. At larger distances, the positive charges of the protons cause them to repel each other. Nuclear forces also cause protons and neutrons to bind together within a nucleus.

The universe is held together by forces. Nuclear forces hold the parts of an atomic nucleus together. Atoms and molecules are held together by the ionic and magnetic forces of charged particles. The force of gravity holds the parts of the solar system together.

Figure 21-5. This sample of uranium ore is uraninite, a type of pitchblende.

Name four kinds of forces.

Nuclear forces. Nuclear force between nuclear particles is less in large atoms because the particles are further apart.

PROBLEM

1. What holds the nucleus of an atom together?

21:2 Transmutation

There are three kinds of nuclear change. These are transmutation, fission (Section 22:4), and fusion (Section 22:5). In a *transmutation*, the nuclei of a radioactive element decay at a fixed rate. They do this by emitting nuclear particles. In this process, one element is changed into a different element. For example, radioactive radium transmutes into radon, a radioactive gas.

Name three kinds of nuclear change.

This paragraph summarizes one of the main themes of this textbook.

Figure 21-6. Mass and charge of the radium atom is equal to the combined mass and charge of the radon atom and alpha particle.

A list of radioactive elements is given in Table 20-1. Nine of these elements are naturally radioactive. Those with atomic numbers greater than uranium (Z = 92) are man-made. Any element can be made radioactive by bombarding it with free alpha particles or neutrons. The element then changes into a radioactive isotope.

Nuclear equations show in simple form the changes which occur in nuclear reactions. To aid the student's learning, a word equation is given for each nuclear reaction listed in this textbook.

A nuclear change may be represented by a *nuclear equation*. The nuclear equation for the transmutation of radium is:

$$^{226}_{88}Ra \rightarrow \, ^{222}_{86}Rn + \, ^4_2He$$

The word equation for this reaction is:

one atom of radium 226 yields one atom of radon
plus one alpha particle

In a nuclear equation, the symbols for the elements are the same as in a chemical equation. In addition, the atomic mass number of each element is written to the top left of the symbol. The atomic number is written to the bottom left of the symbol.

How is a nuclear equation different from a chemical equation?

A nuclear equation must be balanced. It must follow the laws of conservation of charge and conservation of mass. The sum of the atomic mass numbers to the left of the arrow must equal the sum of the atomic mass numbers to the right of the arrow. This shows conservation of mass. Also, the sum of the atomic numbers (protons) on the left must equal the sum of the atomic numbers on the right. This shows conservation of charge.

In the radium nuclear decay reaction, the total atomic mass to the left of the arrow is 226. This number equals the sum of the atomic mass numbers to the right of the arrow $(222 + 4 = 226)$. The atomic number to the left of the arrow is 88. This represents the sum of the atomic numbers to the right of the arrow $(86 + 2 = 88)$.

PROBLEM

The symbol ^4_2He is the alpha particle because an alpha particle is a helium nucleus.

2. What symbol in the equation above is an alpha particle? Why?

How is nuclear change different from chemical change?

A nuclear change is completely different from a chemical or physical change. In a chemical change, atoms are rearranged. New compounds are formed or elements are separated from compounds. In a physical change, such as freezing or boiling, a substance changes its physical form. No new elements or compounds are produced. In a nuclear change, one element is converted to a different element. There is a change in the number of protons in the atoms.

"Radioactive" and "radiation" both come from the Latin word radius meaning ray.

Uranium 238 is a radioactive element. It decays through a series of nuclear reactions to form lead. Lead 206 is a stable isotope. It is not radioactive. The nuclear reactions through which uranium becomes lead are known as a *nuclear decay series*. In each reaction of the uranium decay series, a different radioactive element is formed.

Table 21–1. *Uranium 238 Decay Series*

Symbol	Element	Half-Life	Emitted Ray*
$^{238}_{92}$U	uranium	4.5×10^9 yr	α
$^{234}_{90}$Th	thorium	24 days	β (γ)
$^{234}_{91}$Pa	protactinium	1.14 min	β (γ)
$^{234}_{92}$U	uranium	3×10^5 yr	α
$^{230}_{90}$Th	thorium	83,000 yr	α (γ)
$^{226}_{88}$Ra	radium	1,600 yr	α (γ)
$^{222}_{86}$Rn	radon	3.8 days	α
$^{218}_{84}$Po	polonium	3.05 min	α
$^{214}_{82}$Pb	lead	26.8 min	β (γ)
$^{214}_{83}$Bi	bismuth	19.7 min	β (γ)
$^{214}_{84}$Po	polonium	10^{-5} sec	α (γ)
$^{210}_{82}$Pb	lead	22 yr	β
$^{210}_{83}$Bi	bismuth	5 days	β (γ)
$^{210}_{84}$Po	polonium	140 days	α
$^{206}_{82}$Pb	lead	stable	

* (γ) —gamma radiation may also be emitted.

Note that lead is the final element in the U 238 decay series.

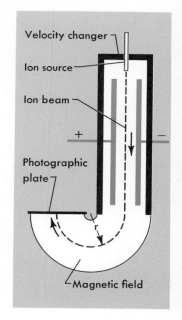

Figure 21-7. The path of an ion is bent into a circular arc in the magnetic field, ions of different masses take different paths. Using the amount of curvature, the mass of a given ion can be calculated.

Velocity changer

Ion source

Ion beam

+   −

Photographic plate

Magnetic field

Figure 21-7 is a diagram of a mass spectrograph.

PROBLEMS

3. Which of the radioactive isotopes in the uranium decay series are alpha emitters?

U 238, U 234, Th 230, Ra 226, Rn 222, Po 218, Po 214, Po 210

4. Which of the radioactive isotopes in the uranium decay series are beta emitters?

Th 234, Pa 234, Pb 214, Bi 214, Pb 210, Bi 210

21:3   *Radioactive Isotopes*

The radioactive isotopes of some elements occur in nature. For example, lead 210 and bismuth 214 are natural radioactive isotopes. In addition, man-made radioactive isotopes may be produced. These are made by bombarding elements with nuclear particles. Through bombardment with neutrons, cobalt 59 may be changed to the radioactive isotope cobalt 60:

$$^{59}_{27}\text{Co} + ^{1}_{0}n \rightarrow ^{60}_{27}\text{Co}$$

one atom of cobalt 59 plus one neutron yields
one atom of cobalt 60

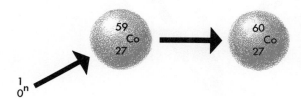

The U. S. Atomic Energy Commission is the largest supplier of radioisotopes. They are

Figure 21-8. Cobalt 59 is stable; cobalt 60 is radioactive. Cobalt 60 is the most widely used radioactive isotope in both medicine and industry.

produced in its nuclear reactor at Oak Ridge, Tennessee.

How are radioactive isotopes produced?

This equation shows that a cobalt 59 nucleus acquires a neutron. It gains one a.m.u. to become cobalt 60. As a result, its nucleus becomes unstable. Cobalt 60 decays by emitting beta particles and gamma radiation.

When sulfur is bombarded with neutrons, the radioactive isotope phosphorus 32 is produced:

$$^{32}_{16}\text{S} + ^{1}_{0}n \rightarrow ^{32}_{15}\text{P} + ^{1}_{1}\text{H}$$

one atom of sulfur 32 plus one neutron yields one atom
of phosphorus 32, plus one proton

The equation for this nuclear reaction shows that the sulfur nucleus first gains a neutron, then loses a proton. Thus, the atomic number of the atom is decreased from 16 to 15. The phosphorus 32 formed by the nuclear change decays by emitting beta particles. The symbol $^{1}_{1}\text{H}$ is used to represent a proton because a hydrogen (H) nucleus is a single proton.

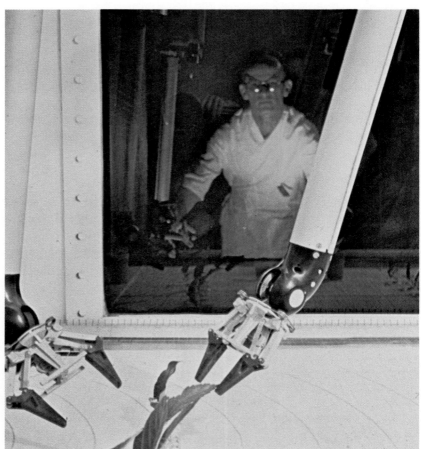

Figure 21-9. Radioactive materials must be handled with care. Here the "arms" moving a plant which has been exposed to radiation are controlled from the other side of a specially-shielded window.

U.S. Dept. of Agriculture

Man-made radioactive isotopes have many practical uses. Radiation from radioactive isotopes, such as cobalt 60, is used to treat cancer. High-energy radiation kills cancer cells. Radioactive isotopes are also used to trace the movement of an element in a plant or animal. For example, phosphorus 32 placed in the soil around a plant will be absorbed into the plant. The movement of the phosphorus 32 through the plant can be followed with a Geiger counter. Since a radioactive isotope can be traced, it is called a "tagged atom." Its radiation is a tag which allows it to be detected.

Name two uses for radioactive isotopes?

Radioactive isotopes are used as tracers in scientific studies of chemical reactions inside plants and animals.

Why are certain isotopes radioactive? The stability of a nucleus depends upon the number of protons and neutrons it contains and its binding energy (Section 21:1). The greater the *average binding energy*, the more stable the nucleus. **Average binding energy** is the total binding energy of the nucleus divided by the total number of protons and neutrons. A nucleus with a few protons and neutrons and a large binding energy is very stable. It has high binding energy per nuclear particle.

How is binding energy related to the stability of a nucleus?

The helium nucleus (alpha particle, $^4_2$He) is very stable. It has enough binding energy per nuclear particle to hold the particles together. The uranium 238 nucleus has 238 protons and neutrons. It has a low average binding energy. The uranium 238 nucleus is unstable and radioactive.

Figure 21–2 shows the average binding energy for nuclei of the most stable elements. Elements in the middle of the periodic table have the highest average binding energy. Thus, these elements are the most stable. Manganese (55 a.m.u.) and iron (56 a.m.u.), for example, have very stable nuclei. Elements with atomic mass units less than 25 have relatively low average binding energy. In the periodic table, these elements are hydrogen through magnesium.

What are "magic numbers"?

The most stable atomic nuclei follow a "magic number" sequence: 2, 8, 20, 50, 82, 126. They are called "magic" because when they were first discovered, their importance was not explained. Scientists knew that these numbers pointed out stable nuclei. But they could not explain why. Today the magic numbers are believed to be explained by the atomic orbital theory (Section 3:4).

If the number of protons or neutrons in a nucleus is a magic number, the nucleus is stable. A nucleus can have magic numbers for both protons and neutrons. Then it is called double magic. For example, the helium 4 nucleus has two protons and

Figure 21-10. In theory, "magic numbers" resemble the definite numbers of electrons needed to fill the electron shells of atoms. What is the "magic number" for this atom?

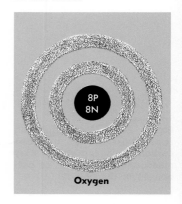

8P
8N

Oxygen

two neutrons. Oxygen has eight protons and eight neutrons. Double magic nuclei are the most stable of all.

PROBLEMS

5. Identify in the periodic table, pp. 64-65, five nuclei with magic numbers.   *He, O, Ca, Sn, Pb*
6. Why are stable nuclei more common in nature than unstable nuclei?   *Unstable nuclei naturally decay into more stable nuclei.*

A neutron or an alpha particle can be added to a nucleus. This decreases the binding energy per nuclear particle. Thus, the nucleus may become unstable and radioactive. The unstable nucleus decays by emitting a neutron, alpha particle, beta particle, or positron. A *positron* is a positively charged electron. Through the release of one or more of these particles, the nucleus decays to form a stable element. In natural radioactive elements, the binding energy is not large enough to make the nucleus stable.

Carbon 12 is an example of the change in the number of neutrons in an atom. Carbon 12 has six protons and six neutrons in its nucleus. When two neutrons are added to a carbon 12 nucleus, it changes to unstable carbon 14. Carbon 14 is a beta-emitting isotope. It has a half-life of 5,600 years. Carbon 14 decays to form nitrogen 14:

$$^{14}_{6}C \rightarrow \, ^{14}_{7}N + \, ^{0}_{-1}e$$

one atom of carbon 14 yields one atom of nitrogen 14
plus one beta particle

What is a positron?

Positrons are positively charged electrons.

Figure 21-11. A scientist can learn how old an ancient carbon-containing object is by measuring the amount of carbon 14 in the object.

U.S. Department of Interior

The amount of undecayed, natural carbon 14 in fossils and archaeological remains is a measure of the age of the material. Carbon 14 dating is so exact that some materials can be dated to within a few decades.

21:4 *Nuclear Fission*

Fission means to divide. In **nuclear fission,** a nucleus divides into two nuclei. Nuclear fission is a nuclear change. When a uranium 235 atom is bombarded with neutrons, it may split into two nuclei. The nuclei are about equal in size. For example, a uranium 235 nucleus may gain a neutron. It divides to form barium 144 and krypton 90. In this nuclear fission, two neutrons are released:

$$_{92}^{235}\mathrm{U} + _{0}^{1}n \rightarrow _{56}^{144}\mathrm{Ba} + _{36}^{90}\mathrm{Kr} + 2\,_{0}^{1}n$$

one atom of uranium 235 plus one neutron yields one
atom of barium 144, plus one atom of krypton 90,
plus two neutrons

In uranium fission, energy is released as gamma radiation. Uranium fission may result in a chain reaction. A *nuclear chain reaction* is a series of rapid nuclear fissions. First, one uranium 235 nucleus is split by a neutron. This releases two neutrons. The two neutrons released in the fission are captured by two more uranium nuclei. This causes them to split. These two nuclei each emit two neutrons. They are captured by four more nuclei, causing them to split. The fission of nuclei and emission of neutrons continue through the uranium.

A chain reaction occurs if sufficient uranium is present. Otherwise, the neutrons escape from the uranium without striking nuclei. Then there are no fissions. In this case, a chain

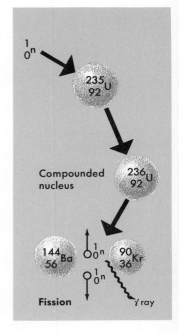

Figure 21-12. The rate of nuclear fission is constant and not affected by changes in temperature or pressure.

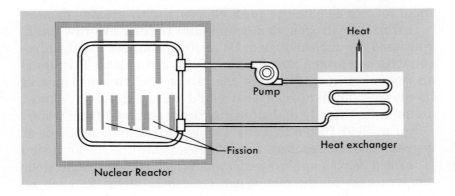

Figure 21-13. Heat produced by nuclear fission inside the reactor is carried away by liquid pumped out to the heat exchanger.

reaction does not begin. A neutron must travel at least 10 centimeters before it slows down enough to be captured by a uranium nucleus. If it escapes before it has gone this distance, the neutron will not cause an atom to split. The smallest amount of an element needed for a chain reaction is called the element's *critical mass*. The critical mass of uranium 235 is about 11 pounds.

During fission, mass is converted to energy. The energy is given off as gamma radiation. The total mass of the two nuclei and two neutrons produced in fission is less than the mass of the original uranium 235 nucleus. The energy released by nuclear fission can be calculated by the equation:

$$E = mc^2 \qquad E = \text{energy}$$
$$m = \text{mass}$$
$$c = \text{speed of light}$$

The energy released through the fission of a single uranium 235 nucleus is about 200 million electron volts. An **electron volt** is the energy gained as the charge on one electron is moved through a potential difference of one volt. For comparison, the energy in a photon of visible light is about 2.5 electron volts. The electrons hitting the screen of a television set have an energy of about 20,000 electron volts. Fantastic amounts of energy are released in nuclear fission! Energy equal to about 25 million kilowatt-hours is released through the fission of only one gram of uranium.

21:5   *Nuclear Fusion*

Nuclear fusion is the opposite of nuclear fission. To fuse means to join together. In nuclear fusion, two or more atomic nuclei unite to form a single, heavier nucleus. Elements with small masses combine to form elements with greater masses.

Ordinary hydrogen, deuterium, and tritium are raw materials used for nuclear fusion. Deuterium is an isotope of hydrogen with one proton and one neutron in its nucleus. Tritium is an isotope of hydrogen with one proton and two neutrons in its nucleus. Tritium is expensive and scarce. However, almost an unlimited supply of deuterium can be obtained from water.

For nuclear fusion to occur, temperatures in the millions of degrees must be reached. *Thermo* means heat. Nuclear fusion is termed *thermonuclear reaction*. Why? At the tremendous temperatures of thermonuclear reactions, atoms as such no longer exist. The atoms lose their electrons. This state of mat-

How is a nuclear chain reaction related to critical mass?

What quantity is represented by each letter in E = mc²?

Uranium 233, a fissionable isotope, is produced in a nuclear reaction in which thorium-232 atoms absorb neutrons. A piece of uranium no heavier than a loaf of bread and smaller than a golf ball can provide the energy of 2 x 10⁶ lb (1000 tons) of coal.

How is nuclear fusion different from nuclear fission?

What is a thermonuclear reaction?

Every minute, about 4 x 10¹⁰ tons of hydrogen atoms are fused in thermonuclear reactions occurring in the sun.

ter is known as the **plasma state.** It consists of nuclei and free electrons. The plasma state is different from the liquid, solid, and gas states.

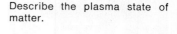

Describe the plasma state of matter.

Conditions for nuclear fusion exist in the sun and other stars. The sun has an internal temperature of about 20 million degrees Celsius. In the sun, hydrogen nuclei fuse to form a helium nucleus. Through complex series of nuclear changes, four hydrogen nuclei are fused into one helium nucleus. The equation for the overall change is:

$$4\,{}^{1}_{1}\text{H} \rightarrow {}^{4}_{2}\text{He} + 2\,{}^{0}_{+1}e$$

four hydrogen nuclei yield one helium nucleus plus
two positrons

The sun is constantly losing hydrogen and gaining helium. This occurs through nuclear fusion. About 25 million electron volts of energy are freed in the fusion of four hydrogen atoms. Energy comes from mass which is converted to energy. The helium atom has a mass almost one percent less than the mass of the original four hydrogen atoms.

Point out that the fusion occurs in a series of steps rather than all at once.

Light and heat from nuclear fusion travel 93 million miles from the sun to the earth. However, the total energy which reaches the earth is only about 1/2,000,000,000 of the total energy released by the sun into space.

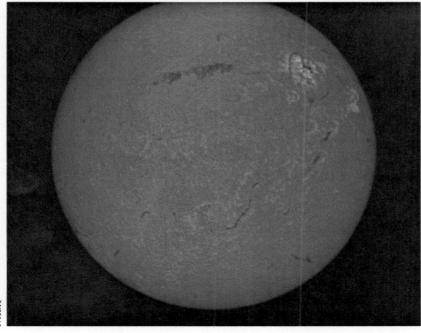

NASA

Figure 21-14. Nuclear fusion is constantly going on in the sun and in other stars.

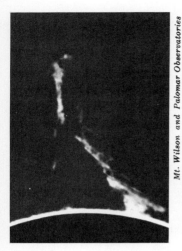

Mt. Wilson and Palomar Observatories

Figure 21-15. This solar prominence extends 570,000 miles. A solar prominence is a portion of the sun's gases which extends a great distance from the surface.

Nuclear fusion occurs in the explosion of a hydrogen bomb (Section 22:5). The reactions in a hydrogen bomb are similar to the reactions in the sun. The temperature inside an exploding hydrogen bomb is believed to be about 10 million degrees Celsius. To produce the high temperature required to start nuclear fusion, an atomic bomb is used as a fuse for a hydrogen bomb.

Deuterium and/or tritium nuclei fuse inside hydrogen bombs when they explode. The possible nuclear fusions with deuterium and tritium are shown in the following equations:

$$(1) \qquad {}_{1}^{2}D + {}_{1}^{2}D \rightarrow {}_{2}^{3}He + {}_{0}^{1}n + 3.25 \text{ Mev}$$

$$(2) \qquad {}_{1}^{2}D + {}_{1}^{2}D \rightarrow {}_{1}^{3}T + {}_{1}^{1}H + 4 \text{ Mev}$$

$$(3) \qquad {}_{1}^{2}D + {}_{1}^{3}T \rightarrow {}_{2}^{4}He + {}_{0}^{1}n + 17.6 \text{ Mev}$$

Mev is the abbreviation for million electron volts.

MAIN IDEAS

p. 438

1. An atomic nucleus contains protons and neutrons bonded together by nuclear forces. Energy must be added to a nucleus to separate its nuclear particles.

p. 439

2. Nuclear forces exist within distances of 10^{-12} cm or less.

p. 439

3. An element transmutes to form another element through the loss or gain of nuclear particles. The emission of nuclear particles is radioactivity.

p. 440

4. In a chemical change, atoms are rearranged to form different compounds. In a physical change, a compound or element is changed from one state to another. However, in a nuclear change, an element is usually changed into another element.

p. 443

5. Nuclei with magic numbers—2, 8, 20, 50, 82, 126 protons or neutrons—are most stable. Radioactive isotopes of stable elements are produced by injecting neutrons or alpha particles into the nuclei.

p. 446

6. The energy released in fission, fusion, and transmutation can be calculated by the equation $E = mc^2$.

p. 445

7. A chain reaction is a series of continuous, automatic, rapid nuclear fissions.

p. 446

8. In a thermonuclear reaction, light elements such as hydrogen are fused to form heavier elements. The fusion occurs at millions of degrees temperature.

p. 447

9. Plasma is a state of matter different from liquid, solid, and gas.

VOCABULARY

Write a sentence in which you correctly use each of the following words or terms.

binding energy	mass defect	nuclear fusion
chain reaction	nuclear decay series	plasma state
critical mass	nuclear fission	radioactive isotope
magic number	nuclear forces	transmutation

STUDY QUESTIONS

A. True or False

Have students rewrite false statements to make the statements correct.

Determine whether each of the following sentences is true or false. (Do not write in this book.)

F **1.** A uranium atom has <u>an equal number of</u> protons <u>and</u> neutrons.

fewer   *than*

T **2.** Mass defect and binding energy are the same.

F **3.** A neutron has the same mass as <u>an electron</u>.

a proton

F **4.** The changing of uranium to lead is an example of <u>atomic fusion</u>.

transmutation

T **5.** Nuclear equations represent nuclear reactions.

T **6.** In a nuclear change, a new element is usually formed.

F **7.** The mass of a helium nucleus is <u>the same as</u> the total mass of two protons plus two neutrons.

less than

F **8.** Carbon <u>14</u> has a stable nucleus.

12

F **9.** The oxygen 16 nucleus is very <u>un</u>stable because it has a double magic number of nuclear particles.

B. Multiple Choice

Some questions in part B may have more than one correct answer. Only one answer is required.

Choose one word or phrase that correctly completes each of the following sentences. (Do not write in this book.)

1. The mass of a nucleus is (greater than, ~~less than~~, the same as) the sum of the masses of the particles in the nucleus.

2. Mass defect is mass lost as (electricity, protons, neutrons, <u>energy</u>).

3. $^4_2$He is the symbol for a(n) (electron, deuterium nucleus, hydrogen atom, <u>alpha particle</u>).

4. $^{234}_{90}$Th $\rightarrow$ $^{234}_{91}$Pa $+$? To complete this equation, add a(n) (proton, alpha particle, positron, <u>beta particle</u>).

5. $\rightarrow {}^{234}_{91}\text{Pa} + {}^{0}_{-1}e$. The sum of the charges to the right of the arrow is (92, 91, 90, 234).

6. (Carbon 12, Cobalt 59, Sulfur 32, Phosphorus 32) is a radioactive isotope.

7. As the average binding energy increases, stability (decreases, increases, remains the same).

8. As the proton-neutron ratio approaches one, the stability of a nucleus (increases, decreases, remains the same).

9. The particles in a nucleus are held together by (charge, gravity, nuclear forces, glue).

10. A(n) (stable, unstable, radioactive) nucleus has a "magic number."

11. An isotope is radioactive if it (is stable, has no neutrons, has lost its electrons, emits radiation).

C. Completion

Complete each of the following sentences with a word or phrase that will make the sentence correct. (Do not write in this book.)

Carbon 14

1. __?__ is a radioactive carbon isotope.

fission

2. ${}^{235}_{92}\text{U} + {}^{1}_{0}n \rightarrow {}^{144}_{56}\text{Ba} + {}^{90}_{36}\text{Kr} + 2\,{}^{1}_{0}n$ is an example of nuclear __?__.

energy

3. $E = mc^2$ can be used to calculate __?__ converted from matter.

energy

4. A Mev is a unit of __?__.

3

5. The mass of a tritium nucleus is about __?__ a.m.u.

plasma

6. The __?__ state of matter exists at 2,000,000°C.

D. How and Why

overcome nuclear forces

1. Why must energy be added to a nucleus to separate its protons and neutrons?

2. What kinds of forces hold the universe together?

3. Write a balanced nuclear equation for a nuclear transmutation, fission, and fusion. How do these nuclear changes differ from each other?   *See Teacher's Guide.*

4. Explain how the carbon 14 dating method is used to tell the age of a fossil.   *See Teacher's Guide.*

manganese, iron, chromium
Their stability is greater than
carbon 12 and uranium 235.

5. Name three elements having high average binding energy. How does the stability of these elements compare to the stability of carbon 12 and uranium 235?

INVESTIGATIONS

1. Arrange and nail a series of mousetraps onto a wooden board to demonstrate a chain reaction. They should be linked together with string so that release of the first trap is followed in rapid order by the release of two traps, four traps, and so on.

2. Make models of the three isotopes of hydrogen. Use colored clay or styrofoam balls painted with latex paint. Parts of the models can be held together with toothpicks.

3. Look up information about recent work on the plasma state of matter. Make a report to your class.

See Teacher's Guide at the front of the book for answers and suggestions.

INTERESTING READING

Frisch, O. R., *Working With Atoms*. New York, Basic Books, Inc., 1966.

Hughes, Donald J., *The Neutron Story*. Garden City, N.Y., Doubleday Anchor Books, 1959.

Kelman, Peter, and A. Harry Stone, *Ernest Rutherford: Architect of the Atom*. New York, Prentice-Hall, 1967.

Nuclear Technology

GOAL: You will gain an understanding of the relationship between nuclear science and technology.

Man can use nuclear energy in many practical ways. For example, entire cities can be lighted by nuclear reactors using uranium fuel. Nuclear powered ships and submarines now travel the oceans. Radioactive isotopes check the wear of piston rings in engines.

The energy of atomic nuclei could someday replace coal, oil, and natural gas. These fossil fuels are being used up at a rapid rate. When they are gone, nuclear energy may become man's main source of energy.

22:1 *The Cyclotron*

How does a cyclotron split an atom?

E. O. Lawrence (1901-1958), an American physicist, invented the cyclotron in 1931. A **cyclotron** is a machine which produces high-speed beams of atomic particles. The beams are made of protons, heavy hydrogen nuclei, or alpha particles. A cyclotron is a kind of atom smasher. By firing high-speed particles into an atom's nucleus, scientists cause the nucleus to split in two. The high speed particles are called "atomic bullets." Through nuclear reactions of this kind, much has been learned about the nucleus and its structure.

Electric and magnetic forces produced by the cyclotron accelerate nuclear particles.

Name the parts of a cyclotron.

How does a cyclotron work? The main parts of a cyclotron are an electromagnet, a vacuum chamber, and two hollow, semicircular metal electrodes. The electrodes are called *dees*. Each electrode has a D shape. The dees are placed inside the vacuum chamber with their straight edges parallel and slightly separated. They look like a pillbox (Figure 22–1). The whole assembly sits between the poles of a large electromagnet. Thus, a magnetic field runs through the dees.

The dees of the cyclotron are connected to a high-voltage alternating current. The alternating current produces an elec-

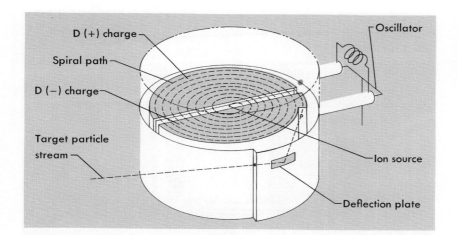

Figure 22-1. The combination of high voltage alternating current and electromagnetism cause the charged particles to take a spiral course, traveling faster each revolution.

tric field along the slit between the dees. One dee is charged negatively. The other dee is charged positively. Since alternating current is used, the electric field and the charges on the dees keep changing. First, a dee is negative. Then it is positive. The change in charge on each dee occurs many times per second.

Atomic "bullets" are injected at the center of the chamber between the dees. These bullets are charged particles or "ions" traveling at very high speeds. One method of producing atomic "bullets" is through use of a heated wire and a gas. The hot wire inside the chamber knocks electrons from the atoms of the gas. Positively charged atomic nuclei are formed from the atoms. If the gas is hydrogen, protons are produced. Heavy hydrogen gas produces deuterons. Helium gas produces alpha particles. These particles become the "bullets."

Here is what happens when atomic "bullets" are injected into the cyclotron. The particles used as "bullets" are acted on by two powerful forces. The two forces are the magnetic field and alternating electric current. Positive particles are attracted to the negative electric charge. They are deflected from a straight path into a curved path by the magnetic field. The positive particles are first drawn to the negative dee. Then the magnetic field pulls the particles in a semicircular path back to the space between the dees. At the same time, the electrical charge on the dees is reversed. The positive particles are now attracted to the negative charge of the opposite dee. Again the magnetic field pulls the particles back between the dees. And again the electric charge on the dee is reversed.

The rapid changing of the charge on the dees gives a constant acceleration to the particles. The particles soon reach a very high speed. They gain speed and kinetic energy as they

What kinds of "bullets" are used in a cyclotron?

Helium nuclei or alpha particles.

Figure 22-2. This cyclotron is releasing a beam of high-energy particles (blue in photograph).

Atomic Energy Commission

The first cyclotron was only 4 in. in diameter and accelerated protons to an energy of about 13 Kev. The first cyclotron to produce an artificial nuclear disintegration (1932) was an 11-in. model which produced 1.2 Mev protons.

The time for a complete circle is always the same. Therefore the velocity of a particle is greater in the large circles.

whirl around through the dees. The particles travel in an ever-widening circle until they are near the outer edge of the dees. Here they exit through a thin window as a beam of high-energy particles. A 150-cm diameter cyclotron can produce alpha rays with an energy of 45 Mev. Mev is an abbreviation for million electron volts. An electron volt is a measure of energy (Section 21:5). These alpha rays have 4.5 times more energy than the natural alpha particles released from a radioactive element.

A cyclotron is a tool for splitting atoms. It has been used to split the atoms of most elements. One of the first uses of the cyclotron was to split lithium atoms with protons. The experimenters observed, with a cloud chamber, alpha particles emitted from the lithium. The nuclear reaction is shown by an equation.

$$_3^7\text{Li} + {}_1^1\text{H} \rightarrow {}_2^4\text{He} + {}_2^4\text{He}$$

lithium atom plus proton yields two alpha particles

Introduce this section by directing students to Figure 22-4. Have students identify the parts of the reactor.

The first nuclear reactor was built in 1942 by Enrico Fermi (1901-1954) at the University of Chicago.

22:2 Nuclear Reactors

Fission is the splitting apart of the nucleus of an atom. Heat produced by the fission of one ounce of uranium is equal to the heat produced by burning 60 tons of coal! A **nuclear reactor** is a device for producing heat from a nuclear fuel. A nuclear reactor is sometimes called a "pile."

The parts of a nuclear reactor are:

    (1) fuel   (4) coolant
    (2) moderator   (5) heat exchanger
    (3) control rods   (6) safety shields

Locate each of these parts in Figure 22–4.

Name the main parts of a nuclear reactor.

The fuel in a nuclear reactor is uranium 235 or plutonium 239. It is enclosed in rod-shaped cans made of a magnesium alloy. Through a nuclear fission chain reaction within the fuel element, nuclear energy is released as heat. The cans holding the fuel have fins like those on the cylinder of motorcycle and lawnmower engines. These fins aid the transfer of heat out of the fuel by conduction.

What fuels are used in nuclear reactors?

The moderator is a material which slows down neutrons released through nuclear fission. To keep a fission chain reaction going, the speed of the released neutrons must be reduced. Neutrons are able to split atomic nuclei when they are moving relatively slowly.

Pure graphite, a crystalline form of carbon, is the most common type of moderator. It is placed in the reactor as blocks of graphite. The blocks surround the cans containing the uranium rods. Great care and precision go into the design and placing of graphite blocks in the pile. A reactor may have some 2,500 tons of graphite moderator arranged in 100,000 blocks or more.

Brookhaven National Laboratory

Figure 22-3. A nuclear reactor permits controlled fission of nuclear material.

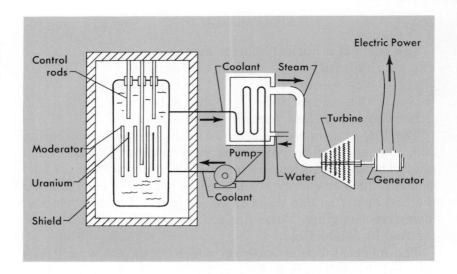

Ordinary water, heavy water, and beryllium can also be used as moderators. These substances are able to slow down speeding neutrons. Heavy water is water which contains deuterium, rather than ordinary hydrogen. A deuterium atom has a neutron as well as a proton in the nucleus. Heavy water and beryllium are expensive. Graphite has the advantage of being relatively cheap.

Explain how moderators and control rods are used in reactors.

Control rods regulate the rate of fission in the fuel element of a reactor. Control rods absorb any excess neutrons not required to keep the chain reaction going. Control rods are made of a material, such as boron and cadmium. These materials absorb neutrons. Boron or cadmium is alloyed with aluminum or steel to form the rods.

By inserting or withdrawing the control rods, the fission rate of a reactor is regulated. The farther the rods are pushed into the reactor, the more neutrons are absorbed and the slower the nuclear fission. Inserting the rods all the way stops the fission completely. In some reactors, the rods are raised and lowered with a steel cable operated by an electric motor.

What is the function of a nuclear reactor coolant and heat exchanger?

The first nuclear submarine (U.S.S. Nautilus) *uses pressurized water as a coolant, while the second nuclear powered submarine* (U.S.S. Seawolf) *uses a liquid sodium coolant.*

The coolant takes heat energy out of the reactor. Several substances have general use as nuclear reactor coolants. These substances include gases, such as helium, nitrogen, and carbon dioxide. Water, heavy water, organic liquid, and liquid metals are also used as coolants. Many reactors use carbon dioxide gas under pressure as a coolant because it is inexpensive and does not burn. Both liquid sodium metal and water have been used as reactor coolants.

The coolant is pumped through spaces in the reactor. As it contacts the cans of fuel, it absorbs heat released from fission.

The coolant carries the heat to the heat exchanger.

In the heat exchanger, the reactor coolant is allowed to flow around pipes containing circulating water. The heat from the coolant converts the water to steam. Steam carries the heat away from the reactor to a turbine.

Safety shields are necessary to protect people from the nuclear radiation produced by a reactor. Nuclear radiation can produce burns, cancer, loss of hair, vomiting, and destruction of blood cells. An overdose of radiation can cause death. Lead and concrete are used as shielding for reactors. Concrete walls seven feet thick or more are needed to protect people from the harmful radiation thrown off by a reactor.

Steam produced by a nuclear reactor is used to do work. Steam is carried from the heat exchangers to turbines. A steam turbine is a machine with a central shaft connected to large blades. Steam under pressure passes over the blades causing the shaft to rotate.

How is nuclear energy converted to mechanical or kinetic energy?

Nuclear energy is converted to heat energy in a reactor. Heat is converted to kinetic energy in a turbine. The rotating shaft of a turbine can produce power to move a ship or a submarine. Steam turbines are also used to turn electrical generators which produce electricity. A reactor generating one million watts of electric power per year uses about one gram of uranium per day.

Nuclear reactors are used to produce radioactive isotopes. Also, nuclear reactors can produce nuclear fuels such as plutonium.

22:3 *Uranium Extraction*

Uranium 235 is the main source of nuclear energy. It is a radioactive isotope that can be obtained from uranium ore. Uranium 235 is not a common isotope. Obtaining it in the large amounts needed for energy production is a complicated process. The extraction of uranium from ores is based on the application of chemical and physical principles.

Uranium has these properties:

List the main properties of uranium.

(1) dense and hard; density = 19.05 g/cm^3
(2) gray-white metal
(3) when cold, a strength near that of steel
(4) when hot, a very weak metal
(5) tarnishes in air to form an oxide film
(6) metallic luster when freshly prepared

Figure 22-5. A nuclear power plant uses a nuclear reactor to generate energy.

(7) three crystalline forms

(8) radioactive; uranium 235 has a half-life of 7.1×10^8 years and uranium 238 has a half-life of 45×10^8 years

22:4 Thermonuclear Power

What are the advantages of thermonuclear power?

The hydrogen bomb is a thermonuclear weapon. Production and control of thermonuclear energy is a scientific and engineering frontier.

Joining nuclei together to form heavier nuclei is called nuclear fusion. Power from controlled nuclear fusion may someday give man unlimited energy. With this method, heavy hydrogen (deuterium) would be tapped as a fuel. The problems connected with fossil fuels and nuclear reactors would be eliminated. There would be no poison gas wastes such as those produced through burning coal, gas, and oil. Moreover, there would be none of the dangers and safety problems that exist with uranium and radioactive wastes.

Development of controlled nuclear fusion is being investigated by scientists and engineers in many countries. The process requires a temperature of millions of degrees Celsius. The problem is how can such a high temperature be produced long enough for nuclear fusion to occur? In other words, how can a controlled, tiny sun be made in the laboratory?

At nuclear fusion temperatures, matter becomes plasma. Atoms are stripped of their electrons. Charged nuclei are formed. The nuclei have enough energy to overcome the large forces of repulsion between them. It is now possible for the nuclei to be squeezed together and fused.

Experiments with nuclear fusion aim toward fusion of heavy hydrogen nuclei in magnetic "bottles." Heavy hydrogen gas is enclosed in an aluminum tube shaped like the inner tube of an automobile tire. High-voltage alternating current is fed to the gas. The current heats the gas to a few million degrees for less than a second. Anything in contact with the hot gas would vaporize. So the gas must be kept away from the walls of the container. This is accomplished by a magnetic field from an electromagnet wound around the tube. The magnetic fields "pinch" the nuclei together inside the tube. Magnetic pinching keeps the nuclei away from the walls.

How are magnetic "bottles" used in nuclear fusion experiments?

To make a controlled thermonuclear reaction, scientists must discover how to produce a temperature of several million degrees for several seconds. Further, they must learn how to convert into electricity the heat energy produced through

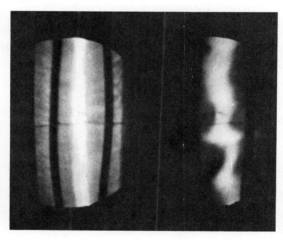

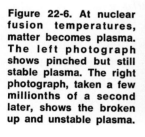
Figure 22-6. At nuclear fusion temperatures, matter becomes plasma. The left photograph shows pinched but still stable plasma. The right photograph, taken a few millionths of a second later, shows the broken up and unstable plasma.

Figure 22-7. Charged particles of plasma are contained in the magnetic 'bottle" by a magnetic field. High voltage magnetic coils create a field that keeps the plasma in the center of the tube. To cause a thermonuclear reaction, deuterium plasma would have to be heated to 100 million degrees.

fusion. The solution of these problems is a challenge to science and technology. The possible rewards certainly are worth the effort. Fusion of the nuclei in one gram of heavy hydrogen would produce the power generated by burning eight tons of coal!

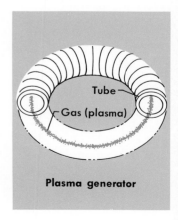
Plasma generator

MAIN IDEAS

p. 452 1. Atom smashers are machines which accelerate atomic particles to high speeds and fire them into atomic nuclei.

p. 453 2. Electric and magnetic fields exert forces on charged particles, causing them to be accelerated inside atom smashers.

p. 456   **3.** The rate of nuclear fission in the fuel of a reactor is regulated by control rods.

p. 457   **4.** Heat released from nuclear fission in a reactor is converted to kinetic energy by a steam turbine.

p. 457   **5.** Electric generators, turned by steam turbines, convert kinetic energy into electrical energy.

p. 458   **6.** Uranium 235 is the main source of nuclear energy. Uranium 235 is obtained from uranium ores through chemical and physical changes.

p. 459   **7.** At temperatures of several thousands of degrees Celsius, matter enters the plasma state. In the plasma state, electrons are set free from atoms. The bare atomic nuclei vibrate and move about at high speeds.

p. 459   **8.** Scientists and engineers experiment with plasma in magnetic "bottles" at millions of degrees temperature. They aim to produce a controlled thermonuclear fusion reaction.

VOCABULARY

Write a sentence in which you correctly use each of the following words or terms.

atomic bullets	electromagnet	nuclear reactor
Bev	heat exchanger	particle accelerator
control rod	heavy water	plasma
cyclotron	Mev	technology
"dee"	moderator	

STUDY QUESTIONS

A.   True or False

Determine whether each of the following sentences is true or false. (Do not write in this book.)

decreasing   F   **1.** The world's supply of fossil fuels is ~~increasing~~.

Alpha particles   F   **2.** ~~X rays~~ are used as atomic bullets.

helium   F   **3.** When ~~hydrogen~~ gas is ionized it becomes an alpha particle.

million   F   **4.** Mev is an abbreviation for ~~many~~ electron volts.

T   **5.** Fission is the splitting apart of the nucleus of an atom.

T   **6.** Graphite is commonly used as a moderator in a nuclear reactor.

long   F   **7.** Uranium 235 has a ~~very short~~ half-life.

T 8. A cyclotron is a tool for splitting atoms.

T 9. A beta particle is an electron traveling at high speed.

B. Multiple Choice
Some questions in part B may have more than one correct answer. Only one answer is required.

Choose one word or phrase that correctly completes each of the following sentences. (Do not write in this book.)

1. The cyclotron produces a beam of high speed (protons, neutrons, electrons, positrons).

2. Deuterons are produced from (hydrogen, helium, heavy hydrogen, beta particles).

3. Changes in the electric field of the cyclotron are caused by (electromagnets, alternating current, radioactivity, control rods).

4. Uranium 235 is a (fuel, moderator, control, coolant) in a reactor.

5. The function of plutonium 239 in a reactor is most like the function of (uranium 235, uranium 238, carbon, cobalt).

6. The moderator in a nuclear reactor (slows down, speeds up, captures) neutrons.

7. (Cobalt, Water, Carbon, Beryllium) is never used as a moderator in a reactor.

8. (Reactors, Turbines, Generators, Heat exchangers) change heat energy into kinetic energy.

9. A megawatt is (1,000, 10,000, 1,000,000, 10,000,000,000) watts.

C. Completion

Complete each of the following sentences with a word or phrase that will make the sentence correct. (Do not write in this book.)

Chapter 22 Student Questions Part C (nos. are keys)

1. __?__ and __?__ are the main nuclear fuels.

U235, Pu 239

2. Pitchblende is a uranium __?__.

ore

3. Uranium metal is __?__ and hard.

dense

4. The tarnishing of uranium in air is a(n) __?__ change.

chemical

5. Matter exists in the __?__ state at millions of degrees of temperature.

plasma

6. Nuclear __?__ occurs in a thermonuclear reaction.

fusion

7. The density of uranium is __?__ than the density of mercury.

greater

D. How and Why

to eliminate collisions of accelerating particles with contaminants

1. How does a cyclotron work? *See Teacher's Guide.*

2. Why must there be a vacuum inside a particle accelerator?

3. Why is uranium 235 used as a nuclear reactor fuel? *good breeder fuel*

A good neutron absorbing material would stop the chain reaction.

4. Why are the fuel cans in a nuclear reactor made of a substance which is a poor neutron absorber?

to resist melting at the high temperatures under which the reactor operates

5. Why must a nuclear fuel can have a high melting point?

6. A nuclear reactor is equipped with a device which automatically drops all of the control rods into the reactor. Why? *safety precaution*

See Teacher's Guide.

7. Compare the reduction of uranium with the reduction of iron from ore.

See Teacher's Guide.

8. Describe an experiment designed to produce a controlled thermonuclear reaction.

INVESTIGATIONS

See Teacher's Guide at the front of the book for answers and suggestions.

1. Obtain career information for a technical field in which you are interested. Find out the educational background needed and where you can prepare for this field.

2. Make a model of a cyclotron, nuclear power plant, or bevatron.

3. Plan a field trip to a nuclear power plant to learn about its operation. Investigate the advantages and disadvantages of nuclear power plants.

INTERESTING READING

Anderson, William R., and Pizer, Vernon, *The Useful Atom.* New York, World Publishing Co., 1966.

Hyde, Margaret, *Atoms, Today and Tomorrow* (2nd ed.). New York, Whittlesey House, McGraw-Hill Book Co., Inc., 1959.

Woodburn, John H., *Radioisotopes.* New York, J. B. Lippincott Co., 1962.

APPENDICES

APPENDIX A
Units of
Measure

TABLE A-1. Frequently Used Metric Units

LENGTH

1 centimeter (cm)	=	10 millimeters (mm)
1 meter (m)	=	100 centimeters (cm)
1 kilometer (km)	=	1000 meters (m)

VOLUME

1 liter (l)	=	1000 milliliters (ml)

MASS

1 gram (g)	=	1000 milligrams (mg)
1 kilogram (kg)	=	1000 grams (g)

TABLE A-2. Metric Unit Prefixes and Their Definitions

kilo—	1,000	= 10^3
hecto—	100	= 10^2
deka—	10	= 10^1
deci—	0.1	= 10^{-1}
centi—	0.01	= 10^{-2}
milli—	0.001	= 10^{-3}
micro—	0.000001	= 10^{-6}

TABLE A-3. Frequently Used English Units

LENGTH

1 foot (ft)	=	12 inches (in.)
1 yard (yd)	=	3 feet (ft)
1 mile (mi)	=	5280 feet (ft)

VOLUME

1 quart (qt)	=	32 ounces (oz)
1 quart (qt)	=	2 pints (pt)
1 gallon (gal)	=	4 quarts (qt)

WEIGHT

1 pound	=	16 ounces (oz)
1 ton	=	2000 pounds (lb)

Both metric units and English units are used in the United States. It is helpful to know how to convert from one system to the other. The relationships of some metric units and English units are given in Table A-4.

TABLE A-4. Equivalents

LENGTH

1 in. = 2.54 cm	1 cm = 0.3937 in.
1 ft = 0.3048 m	1 m = 39.37 in. = 3.2808 ft
1 mi = 1.609 km	1 km = 3,280 ft = 0.62137 mi

AREA

1 in.^{2} = 6.452 cm^2	1 cm^2 = 0.1550 in.^{2}
1 ft^2 = 0.09290 m^2	1 m^2 = 10.764 ft^2
1 mi^2 = 2.59 km^2	1 km^2 = 0.3861 mi^2

VOLUME

1 qt = 0.946 l	1 l = 1.06 qt
1 in.^{3} = 16.387 cm^3	1 cm^3 = 0.0610 in.^{3}
1 ft^3 = 0.02832 m^3	1 m^3 = 35.315 ft^3
1 mi^3 = 4.1681 km^3	1 km^3 = 0.2399 mi^3

MASS[1]

1 cm^3 of water = 1 g

1 atomic mass unit (a.m.u.) = 1.66 $\times$ 10^{-24} g

1 g = the mass of a 0.0022-lb or a 0.0353-oz weight

WEIGHT[2]

1 ft^3 of water = 62.4 lb

1 lb = the weight of a 453.6-g mass

1 oz = the weight of a 28.35-g mass

[1] Pounds and ounces are often used to express mass. Both, however, are English units of force (weight) not mass. For example: a mass of 3 lb means the mass of an object that weighs 3 lb. The unit of mass in the English system is the *slug*.

[2] Grams and kilograms are often used to express weight. Both, however, are metric units of mass not weight. For example: a weight of 3 kg means the weight of an object with a 3-kg mass. The unit of force in the metric system is the *newton*.

APPENDIX B

Temperature Scales

Scientists throughout the world use the Celsius (or centigrade) temperature scale. Zero degrees (0°C) is assigned to the freezing point of pure water at one atmosphere of pressure. The boiling point of pure water at one atmosphere pressure is assigned the value of one hundred degrees (100°C).

Most people in the United States commonly use the Fahrenheit scale. The freezing point of pure water at one atmosphere of pressure is thirty-two degrees (32°F). The boiling point of pure water is two hundred and twelve degrees (212°F).

The Fahrenheit scale has exactly 180 equal divisions or degrees between the freezing point and boiling point of pure water. The Celsius scale has exactly 100 equal divisions between these two points. Thus, a Fahrenheit degree is 5/9 of a Celsius degree ($\frac{100}{180} = 5/9$). A Celsius degree is 9/5 of a Fahrenheit degree ($\frac{180}{100} = 9/5$).

To change temperatures from one scale to another, these formulas can be used:

$$°F = (9/5 \times °C) + 32$$
$$°C = (°F - 32°) \times 5/9$$

Absolute temperatures are measured by the Kelvin temperature scale. This means that the scale starts from absolute zero, the temperature experimental research indicates to be the lowest that can exist. Zero degrees Kelvin (0°K), or abso-

FIGURE B-1. Comparison of temperature scales.

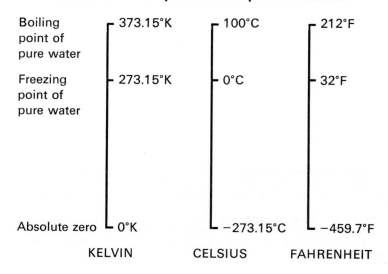

	KELVIN	CELSIUS	FAHRENHEIT
Boiling point of pure water	373.15°K	100°C	212°F
Freezing point of pure water	273.15°K	0°C	32°F
Absolute zero	0°K	−273.15°C	−459.7°F

lute zero, is equivalent to —273.15°C. A temperature on the Celsius scale is easily converted to a temperature on the Kelvin scale by adding 273.15°. For example, 22°C is 295.15°K (22°C + 273.15° = 295.15°K). One advantage of the Kelvin scale is that all temperatures are positive. There are no negative temperatures as in the Fahrenheit and Celsius temperature scales.

APPENDIX C
Working With Measurements

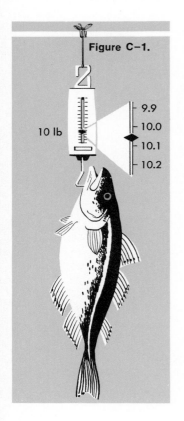

Figure C-1.

10 lb

9.9
10.0
10.1
10.2

Every measurement has some degree of error. No measuring instrument is perfect. The **accuracy** of any measurement depends on how closely the true value and the measured value agree. The difference between the true value and the measured value is called **error.**

In every measurement some values are known to be exact; others are estimated. Look at Figure C-1. We know that the fish weighs more than 10.0 lb but less than 10.1 lb. We estimate that the weight of the fish is 10.06 lb. In this measurement, the 1, the 0, and the 6 are *significant digits.*

Significant digits consist of all digits known to be true plus one estimated digit. Suppose you measure the width of a book as 11.64 cm. Your meter stick does not have 0.01 centimeter divisions so the last digit is just an estimate. Someone else might measure the book as 11.63 or 11.65 cm. Your measurement is said to have four significant digits—three known digits and one estimated digit.

Here are some rules to help you decide which digits in a measurement are significant.

(1) Most nonzero digits are significant. Examples: 356, 35.6, 3.56. All have 3 significant digits.

(2) The significance of zero depends upon its position.

　(a) Zeros which are only placeholders between significant figures and the decimal point are not significant. Examples: 4,600, 0.0046. Both have 2 significant digits.

　(b) Zeros between two digits are significant. Examples: 1002, 40.14, 3002. All have 4 significant digits.

　(c) Zeros to the right of a decimal point as the last digit in a number are significant. This is true whether the decimal point is expressed or implied. Examples: 102.00, 1020.0, and 0.010200. All have 5 significant digits.

Numbers written in scientific notation can be used to indicate the number of significant digits. The general form for scientific notation is $M \times 10^x$. The number 93,000 can be written: 9.3×10^4. For decimals the exponent of ten is the negative value of the number of places the decimal is moved to the right. The number .000354 can be written: 3.54×10^{-4}. If you include zeros in scientific notation, you are implying that the zeros are significant.

EXAMPLES

9.300×10^4 (four significant figures)
3.540×10^{-4} (four significant figures)

Precision is not the same as accuracy. **Precision** does not depend on error. It depends only on the measuring instrument used. For example, a postage scale measuring to 0.01 lb is more precise than a bathroom scale measuring to 1 lb. The postage scale counts smaller units of weight than the bathroom scale.

When working problems, the answer can be no more precise than the least precise measurement. The following are rules for the use of measurements in calculations.

RULE 1. Addition and Subtraction: Round off the answer of a problem to the same number of decimal places as in the numeral which is least precise in the problem. The least precise numeral is the one with the least number of decimal places.

EXAMPLE

Addition	*Subtraction*
12.26 cm	12.26 cm
5.8 cm	— 5.8 cm
+ 2.125 cm	6.46 cm
20.185 cm	

Round off to 20.2 cm because 5.8, the numeral which is least precise, has one decimal place.

Round off to 6.5 cm because 5.8, the numeral which is least precise, has one decimal place.

RULE 2. Multiplication and Division: Round off the answer for a problem to the same number of significant digits as in the numeral that is least precise in the problem. The least precise numeral is the one with the least number of significant digits.

EXAMPLE

Multiplication	*Division*

$$12.63 \text{ cm}$$
$$\times \ 5.1$$
$$\overline{64.413 \text{ cm}}$$

$$2.1385 \text{ m}$$
$$4.5\overline{)9.6235 \text{ m}}$$

Round off to 64 cm because 5.1, the numeral which is least precise, has two significant digits.

Round off to 2.1 m because 4.5, the numeral which is least precise, has two significant digits.

When rounding off an *answer:*

(1) Drop all digits beyond significant digits.
(2) Increase the last significant digit by 1 if the digit dropped is more than 5.
(3) If the digit dropped is exactly 5, and the last significant digit is odd, increase the last significant digit by 1.
(4) Do not change the last significant digit if the digit dropped is less than 5.

EXAMPLES

$$6.48 \text{ rounds off to } 6.5$$
$$24.75 \text{ rounds off to } 24.8$$
$$10.265 \text{ rounds off to } 10.26$$
$$8.121 \text{ rounds off to } 8.12$$

APPENDIX D
International Atomic Masses

Element	Symbol	Atomic number	Atomic mass	Element	Symbol	Atomic number	Atomic mass
Actinium	Ac	89	227*	Mercury	Hg	80	200.59
Aluminum	Al	13	26.9815	Molybdenum	Mo	42	95.94
Americium	Am	95	243*	Neodymium	Nd	60	144.24
Antimony	Sb	51	121.75	Neon	Ne	10	20.183
Argon	Ar	18	39.948	Neptunium	Np	93	237*
Arsenic	As	33	74.9216	Nickel	Ni	28	58.71
Astatine	At	85	210*	Niobium	Nb	41	92.906
Barium	Ba	56	137.34	Nitrogen	N	7	14.0067
Berkelium	Bk	97	247*	Nobelium	No	102	253*
Beryllium	Be	4	9.0122	Osmium	Os	76	190.2
Bismuth	Bi	83	208.980	Oxygen	O	8	15.9994
Boron	B	5	10.811	Palladium	Pd	46	106.4
Bromine	Br	35	79.904	Phosphorus	P	15	30.9738
Cadmium	Cd	48	112.40	Platinum	Pt	78	195.09
Calcium	Ca	20	40.08	Plutonium	Pu	94	244*
Californium	Cf	98	251*	Polonium	Po	84	209*
Carbon	C	6	12.01115	Potassium	K	19	39.102
Cerium	Ce	58	140.12	Praseodymium	Pr	59	140.907
Cesium	Cs	55	132.905	Promethium	Pm	61	145*
Chlorine	Cl	17	35.453	Protactinium	Pa	91	231*
Chromium	Cr	24	51.996	Radium	Ra	88	226.05
Cobalt	Co	27	58.9332	Radon	Rn	86	222*
Copper	Cu	29	63.546	Rhenium	Re	75	186.2
Curium	Cm	96	247*	Rhodium	Rh	45	102.905
Dysprosium	Dy	66	162.50	Rubidium	Rb	37	85.47
Einsteinium	Es	99	254*	Ruthenium	Ru	44	101.07
Erbium	Er	68	167.26	Samarium	Sm	62	150.35
Europium	Eu	63	151.96	Scandium	Sc	21	44.956
Fermium	Fm	100	253*	Selenium	Se	34	78.96
Fluorine	F	9	18.9984	Silicon	Si	14	28.086
Francium	Fr	87	223*	Silver	Ag	47	107.868
Gadolinium	Gd	64	157.25	Sodium	Na	11	22.9898
Gallium	Ga	31	69.72	Strontium	Sr	38	87.62
Germanium	Ge	32	72.59	Sulfur	S	16	32.064
Gold	Au	79	196.967	Tantalum	Ta	73	180.948
Hafnium	Hf	72	178.49	Technetium	Tc	43	97*
Helium	He	2	4.0026	Tellurium	Te	52	127.60
Holmium	Ho	67	164.930	Terbium	Tb	65	158.924
Hydrogen	H	1	1.00797	Thallium	Tl	81	204.37
Indium	In	49	114.82	Thorium	Th	90	232.038
Iodine	I	53	126.9044	Thulium	Tm	69	168.934
Iridium	Ir	77	192.2	Tin	Sn	50	118.69
Iron	Fe	26	55.847	Titanium	Ti	22	47.90
Krypton	Kr	36	83.80	Tungsten	W	74	183.85
Lanthanum	La	57	138.91	Uranium	U	92	238.03
Lead	Pb	82	207.19	Vanadium	V	23	50.942
Lawrencium	Lw	103	257*	Xenon	Xe	54	131.30
Lithium	Li	3	6.939	Ytterbium	Yb	70	173.04
Lutetium	Lu	71	174.97	Yttrium	Y	39	88.905
Magnesium	Mg	12	24.312	Zinc	Zn	30	65.37
Manganese	Mn	25	54.9380	Zirconium	Zr	40	91.22
Mendelevium	Md	101	256*				

*The mass number of the isotope with the longest known half-life.

APPENDIX E
Valences

Positive Valences	Negative Valences
+1	**−1**
Ammonium, NH_4^+	Acetate, $C_2H_3O_2^-$
Copper (I), Cu^+	Bromide, Br^-
Hydrogen, H^+	Chlorate, ClO_3^-
Lithium, Li^+	Chloride, Cl^-
Potassium, K^+	Chlorite, ClO_2^-
Silver, Ag^+	Fluoride, F^-
Sodium, Na^+	Hydroxide, OH^-
	Hypochlorite, ClO^-
+2	Iodide, I^-
Barium, Ba^{+2}	Nitrite, NO_2^-
Cadmium, $Cd^{+,2}$	Nitrate, NO_3^-
Calcium, Ca^{+2}	Perchlorate, ClO_4^-
Chromium (II), Cr^{+2}	Permanganate, MnO_4^-
Cobalt (II), Co^{+2}	
Copper (II), Cu^{+2}	**−2**
Iron (II), Fe^{+2}	Carbonate, CO_3^{-2}
Lead, Pb^{+2}	Chromate, CrO_4^{-2}
Magnesium, Mg^{+2}	Dichromate, $Cr_2O_7^{-2}$
Manganese (II), Mn^{+2}	Oxalate, $C_2O_4^{-2}$
Mercury (I), Hg_2^{+2}	Oxide, O^{-2}
Mercury (II), Hg^{+2}	Peroxide, O_2^{-2}
Tin (II), Sn^{+2}	Sulfate, SO_4^{-2}
Zinc, Zn^{+2}	Sulfide, S^{-2}
	Sulfite, SO_3^{-2}
+3	Thiosulfate, $S_2O_3^{-2}$
Aluminum, Al^{+3}	
Antimony(III), Sb^{+3}	**−3**
Chromium(III), Cr^{+3}	Phosphate, PO_4^{-3}
Iron (III), Fe^{+3}	
+4	
Tin (IV), Sn^{+4}	
+5	
Antimony(V), Sb^{+5}	

GLOSSARY

GLOSSARY

Pronunciation
Key

ae . . . bake

ah . . . father

a . . . back

ee . . . easy

e . . . less

eu . . . few

ie . . . life

i . . . trip

oh . . . flow

aw . . . soft

ah . . . odd

oo . . . food

uh . . . foot

eu . . . cube

u . . . up

y . . . yet

j . . . judge

k . . . cake

s . . . sew

th . . . thin

absolute zero: −273°C; in theory, the lowest possible temperature of a substance

acceleration (ak sel er ae′ shun): rate of increase in speed

accuracy: the relationship between a measured value and a real value

acid: substance which increases the hydronium ion concentration when added to water

acid anhydride (an hie′ dried): nonmetallic oxide which produces an acid when added to water

adiabatic (ad ee ah bat′ ik) **cooling:** decrease in temperature without loss of heat from a material

alkane (al′ kaen) **series:** series of saturated hydrocarbons having the general formula C_nH_{2n+2}

alkene (al′ keen) **series:** series of unsaturated hydrocarbons with one double bond, having the general formula C_nH_{2n}

alkyne (al kin) **series:** series of unsaturated hydrocarbons with one triple bond, having the general formula C_nH_{2n-2}

allotropes (al′ah trohps): different molecular forms of the same element

alloy: mixture of metals

alpha ray: stream of alpha particles (helium nuclei) shot out from radioactive atomic nuclei

alternating current (A.C.): movement of electrons in a conductor in a continuous back and forth vibration or cycle

ammeter (am′ mee tur): instrument used to measure the amount of electric current in a circuit

amorphous (ah mor′ fus) **solid:** material such as a glass or plastic which has no regular crystalline shape

ampere (am′ pere) **(amp):** unit for measuring the rate of flow of electricity

amplitude (am′ pli tood): vertical distance through which the particles of a wave move

analog computer: a device which solves problems by representing real things or mathematical values with electric circuits or moving parts, such as rotating wheels

angle of incidence: angle made between a wave striking a barrier and the normal to the surface

angle of reflection: angle between a reflected wave and the normal to the barrier from which it is reflected

anode (+): positive electrode in an electric circuit

antiparticle: a nuclear particle which when it combines with its opposite results in the destruction of them both

aqueous (ac′ kwee us): pertaining to water

armature (arm′ ah chur): an electromagnet that is the rotating part of a motor or generator

atom: smallest particle of an element which retains the properties of the element

atomic mass: mass of an atom relative to a carbon 12 atom

atomic mass number (A): average atomic mass rounded to the nearest whole number

atomic mass unit: 1/12 the mass of the carbon 12 atom

atomic number (Z): number of protons in the nucleus of an element

atomic weight: term referring to the average atomic masses of the isotopes of an element

average atomic mass: average of the masses of the isotopes which make up an element

barometer (ba rahm′ et er): instrument used to measure air pressure

base: substance which increases the hydroxide ion concentration when added to water

basic anhydride (an hie′ dried): metallic oxide which produces a base when added to water

battery: two or more cells connected in series

beta ray: stream of electrons shot out from radioactive nuclei

binary compounds: compounds composed of two elements

binding energy: energy needed to separate the particles in an atomic nucleus into free protons and neutrons

Bohr model: model of an atom showing the nucleus of the atom with its protons and neutrons and the arrangement of electrons outside the nucleus

boiling: rapid change from liquid to the gas state

Boyle's law: the volume of a gas decreases as the pressure on it increases, if the temperature remains constant

British thermal unit (B.T.U.): amount of heat required to raise the temperature of 1 lb of water 1°F

bubble chamber: device which detects nuclear particles through the formation of bubbles within a superheated liquid

calorie (kal' oh ree) **(cal):** standard unit of heat, the amount of heat required to raise the temperature of 1 g of water 1 C°

calorimeter (kal ah rim' et er): instrument used to measure heat in calories

capacitor (ka pas' eter): combination of conducting plates, each plate separated by an insulator, used to store an electric charge

catalyst (kat' ah list): substance which increases or decreases the rate of a chemical reaction

cathode (—): negative electrode in an electric circuit

cathode-ray tube: a kind of vacuum tube which emits a beam of electrons from the cathode to a screen at the opposite end of the tube

centimeter (cm): unit of length in the metric system; 1/100 of a meter

centrifugal (sen trif' ye gal) **force:** the apparent pull away from the center around which a body travels in a circular path

centripetal (sen trip' ah tal) **force:** a force acting toward the center around which a body travels in a circular path

Charles' law: the volume of a gas increases as its temperature increases, if the pressure remains constant

chemical activity: ease with which an element reacts with other elements

chemical change: change in which a substance becomes a different substance having different chemical properties

chemical equation: shorthand description of a chemical reaction containing symbols and formulas

chemical property: characteristic of a material which depends on the material's reaction with another material

circuit: closed-loop path of conduction through which an electric current flows

cleavage (klee' vij): tendency of a crystal to come apart or split between planes of atoms when hit a sharp blow

cloud chamber: device which detects nuclear particles through the formation of cloud tracks

coefficient (coh ih fish' nt): number placed in front of formulas to balance a chemical equation

compound: a substance containing two or more elements chemically combined

compressional (kum presh' un ul) **wave:** wave in which matter vibrates in the same direction the wave moves

concave (kahn' kaev) **lens:** a lens which is thinner in middle the than at the edges

concentration: amount of solute per unit volume of solvent

condensation: change from gaseous state to the liquid state

conduction (kan duck' shun): movement of heat through a substance from molecule to molecule; movement of electricity through a substance

conductor: a substance through which heat or electricity can flow readily

conservation of momentum: principle which states that momentum cannot be created or destroyed

control: group or activity that serves as a standard of comparison for change in an experiment

convection (kan vek' shun): transfer of heat energy by the actual movement of the heated matter

convex (kan veks') **lens:** a lens which is thicker in the middle than at the edges

cosmic rays: very high energy nuclear rays from outer space

covalent bond: bond between atoms produced by sharing electrons

crest: high point of a wave

critical mass: smallest amount of an element needed to undergo a nuclear chain reaction

Pronunciation Key

ae . . . bake

ah . . . father

a . . . back

ee . . . easy

e . . . less

eu . . . few

ie . . . life

i . . . trip

oh . . . flow

aw . . . soft

ah . . . odd

oo . . . food

uh . . . foot

eu . . . cube

u . . . up

y . . . yet

j . . . judge

k . . . cake

s . . . sew

th . . . thin

cryogenics: scientific study of physical and chemical properties at very low temperatures

crystal: solid material having a regular, geometric form characteristic of a given compound or element

cyclotron (si' klu tron): machine which produces high-speed beams of atomic particles

deceleration (de sel er a' shun): rate of decrease in speed

decomposition reaction: chemical change in which a compound breaks down or decomposes into other compounds and/or elements

deliquescent: capable of attracting and absorbing moisture from air

density: mass per unit volume

deuterium: hydrogen isotope with one proton and one neutron in its nucleus

diene (di' een) series: the unsaturated hydrocarbons with two double bonds

diffraction (di frak' shun) grating: piece of transparent or reflecting material, containing many thousands of parallel lines per inch, used to produce a light spectrum by interference

digital (dij' i tul) computer: a device using numbers to solve mathematical problems; specifically, an electronic machine which uses stored instructions and information to perform complex computations at rapid speed

diode (die' ohd): electrical vacuum tube containing a filament and a plate

dipole-dipole attraction: small attractive force between dipole molecules in which a positively charged end of one molecule is attracted to the negatively charged end of the other molecule

direct current (D.C.): flow of electrons in one direction through a circuit

discharge: loss of negative or positive electrical charge

dispersion: the separation of white light into its component wave lengths

dissociation (di soh' see ae shun): separation of the ions in an ionic compound when dissolved in water

distillation (dis ta lay' shun): physical separation of the parts of a mixture through evaporation and condensation

Doppler effect: change in wavelength by movement of the wave source

double replacement reaction: chemical change in which two ions in two different compounds replace each other, forming a precipitate, gas, or water

dry cell: device for producing a current with moist chemicals

efficiency: the ratio of the work output of a machine to its work input

efflorescent: changing to a powder from loss of water of crystallization

electrolysis: the conduction of electricity through a solution of an electrolyte together with the resulting chemical changes

electrolyte (i lek' troh liet): a substance which produces a solution capable of conducting electricity when dissolved in water

electromagnet: soft iron core surrounded by a coil of wire through which an electric current is passed, thus magnetizing the core

electromagnetic spectrum: set of invisible, transverse energy waves, ranging from low frequency to very high frequency, which can travel in a vacuum

electron: negatively charged particle in an atom

electron cloud model: model of an atom showing a cloud of negative charge surrounding the nucleus

electron microscope: a microscope in which the magnification is produced by an electron beam and magnetic field

electron shell: specific region about the nucleus of an atom in which electrons move

electron volt: the energy required to move an electron between two points that have a potential difference of one volt

electronics (i lek' tron iks): study of the release, behavior, and effects of electrons

electroscope (i lek' trah skohp): instrument used for detecting positive and negative electrical charges

electrostatic induction: charging a body with another charged body, without the two bodies touching each other

Pronunciation Key

ae . . . bake

ah . . . father

a . . . back

ee . . . easy

e . . . less

eu . . . few

ie . . . life

i . . . trip

oh . . . flow

aw . . . soft

ah . . . odd

oo . . . food

uh . . . foot

eu . . . cube

u . . . up

y . . . yet

j . . . judge

k . . . cake

s . . . sew

th . . . thin

element: a substance which cannot be broken down into simpler substances

end reaction: a reaction which does not attain equilibrium; a reaction which goes to completion by forming a gas, a precipitate, or water

endothermic (en' doh thur' mik) **reaction:** chemical reaction in which energy is taken on by the reactants

energy: ability to produce motion or change

evaporation: change from liquid state to gas state

exothermic (eks oh thur' mik) **reaction:** chemical reaction in which the energy released is greater than the energy required to start the reaction

flame test: procedure for identifying an element by observing the color of its flame

fluid: material which takes shape of its container

fluorescent (floo' uh res' nt): emitting light only when exposed to radiation such as cathode rays, X rays, and ultraviolet rays

focal length: distance between the principal focus of a lens or mirror and its optical center or vertex

force: any push or pull

formula mass: sum of the atomic masses of the atoms present in a formula of a compound

fractionation (frak' shun ae shun): a type of distillation in which compounds in petroleum are separated

frequency (free' kwan see): number of waves that pass a given point in a unit of time

friction: a force that opposes motion

fulcrum: the pivot point of a lever

galvanometer (gal vah nah' mi tur): instrument, consisting of a coil of wire pivoting between the poles of a magnet, used to detect small electric currents

gamma rays: high energy waves with a wavelength shorter than X rays

gas: a material which lacks a definite shape or volume

Gay-Lussac's law: as the temperature of a gas increases, the pressure of the gas increases, if volume remains constant

Geiger counter: instrument used to detect radioactivity through the formation of an electric current

gram (g): metric unit of mass

gravity: mutual force of attraction which exists between all bodies in the universe

ground: connection to the earth by an electrical conductor

half-life: time required for one-half the atoms in a radioactive material to decay

heat: kinetic and potential energy of molecules

heat of fusion: amount of heat required to melt one gram of a solid

heat of vaporization (vae puhr i zay' shun): amount of heat required to change one gram of a liquid to a gas

horsepower: unit of power defined as 550 ft-lb of work done in one second of time

hydrate: compound formed by the union of water with some other substance

hydrocarbon: compound containing only carbon and hydrogen

hydronium (hie drohn' ee um) **ion:** H_3O+; ion containing a proton (hydrogen ion) bonded to a water molecule

hydroxide (hi drok' sid) **ion:** OH^-; a negative ion containing one oxygen atom and one hydrogen atom

hypothesis (hie pahth' e sis): proposed or tentative solution for a problem

image: reproduction of an object formed with lenses or mirrors

immiscible (im mis' uh bl): condition in which two liquids do not dissolve each other

impulse: product of force multiplied by the time the force acts on a body

index of refraction: amount that light is refracted when it enters a substance; ratio of speed of light in vacuum to its speed in given substance

indicator: chemical used to tell by a color change the degree of acidity or alkalinity of a solution

Pronunciation Key

ae . . . bake

ah . . . father

a . . . back

ee . . . easy

e . . . less

eu . . . few

ie . . . life

i . . . trip

oh . . . flow

aw . . . soft

ah . . . odd

oo . . . food

uh . . . foot

eu . . . cube

u . . . up

y . . . yet

j . . . judge

k . . . cake

s . . . sew

th . . . thin

Pronunciation
Key

ae . . . bake

ah . . . father

a . . . back

ee . . . easy

e . . . less

eu . . . few

ie . . . life

i . . . trip

oh . . . flow

aw . . . soft

ah . . . odd

oo . . . food

uh . . . foot

eu . . . cube

u . . . up

y . . . yet

j . . . judge

k . . . cake

s . . . sew

th . . . thin

inertia (in er' shuh): tendency of matter to remain at rest or in uniform motion unless acted on by a force

insulator (in' suh lay tur): a substance through which heat or electricity cannot flow readily

interference: the mutual effect of two waves, resulting in a loss of energy in certain areas and reinforcement of energy in other areas

ion: atom or bonded atoms which have gained or lost one or more electrons

ionic bond: electrostatic bond between atoms produced through gain of electrons by one atom or group of atoms and loss by the other

ionization (ie an i zae' shun): process in which a molecular compound dissolves in water to form ions

isomers: compounds having the same number and kind of atoms, but different structures; compounds having the same molecular formula, but different structural formulas

isotopes: atoms of the same element with different numbers of neutrons

kilowatt-hour: unit used to measure electrical energy equal to 1,000 watt-hours

kinetic (ki net' ik) **energy:** energy of motion

law of conservation of mass: mass is neither gained nor lost in a chemical change

law of multiple proportions: two or more elements may unite to form different compounds

law of reflection: angle of incidence equals the angle of reflection

lens: transparent substance bounded by one curved and one straight surface or by two curved surfaces

liquid: form of matter having a definite volume but no definite shape

liter: unit of volume in metric system; volume of 1 kg of water

machine: a device which makes work easier by changing the speed, direction, or amount of force

macromolecule: giant crystal built up by bonding of atoms

magnification: image length divided by object length

mass: quantity of matter in a body

mass defect: the mass converted to energy when particles combine to form an atomic nucleus

matter: anything that has mass and takes up space

mechanical advantage: the amount by which the applied force is multiplied by a machine

melting: change from a solid to a liquid state

meson: nuclear particle having a mass about 200-270 times greater than an electron and a positive, negative, or neutral charge

metal: a substance that has a specific luster, is a good conductor of heat and electricity, and can be pounded or drawn into various shapes

metallic bonding: type of bonding typical of metals; outer electrons of atoms move throughout crystal and are shared equally by all ions

metalloid: element such as boron, having properties of both metals and nonmetals

meter (m): metric unit of length

metric system: decimal system of weights and measure based on the mass of a cubed centimeter of pure water at 3.98°C

miscible (mis' ah bl): condition in which two liquids can dissolve each other

mixture: two or more elements or compounds which are mingled, but not chemically united

molar solution: solution containing one mole of solute in enough solvent to make 1 l of solution

mole: formula mass expressed in grams

molecular formula: formula showing the number of atoms of each element in a molecule of a compound

molecular kinetic energy: energy of a molecule that results from its vibrating motion

molecular potential energy: energy of a molecule that may be released through physical or chemical change

molecule (mahl' i kewl): smallest particle of a compound; particle containing two or more atoms bonded covalently

moment: the force on a lever multiplied by the distance from the pivot point

momentum (moh men' tum): mass of a body multiplied by its velocity

neutralization: chemical reaction in which hydronium ions and hydroxide ions combine to form water

neutrino: uncharged particle having a smaller mass than a neutron

neutron: neutral particle found in the atomic nucleus, having a mass about equal to a proton

newton: unit of force required to accelerate one kilogram mass at 1 m/sec^2

Newton's first law of motion: a body continues in a state of rest unless a force causes it to move, and a body continues in motion along a straight line unless a force stops it or causes the body to change direction

Newton's law of gravitation: the gravitational attraction between two bodies is proportional to the product of their masses divided by the square of the distance between them

Newton's second law of motion: the acceleration of a body is directly proportional to the size of the force producing the acceleration and inversely proportional to the mass of the body

Newton's third law of motion: for every force there is an equal and opposite force

noble gas: members of Group VIIIA; gas that does not combine chemically under ordinary conditions; helium, argon, xenon, krypton, neon, radon

normal: a line drawn perpendicular to a line or plane

nuclear chain reaction: series of continuous rapid nuclear fissions, beginning with the splitting of an atom

nuclear emulsion (i mul' shun): thick layer of photographic emulsion, containing silver bromide dissolved in gelatinlike solid, used to detect nuclear particles

nuclear fission: nuclear change in which a nucleus is divided into two nuclei

nuclear force: force which holds together particles in an atomic nucleus

nuclear fusion: nuclear change in which two or more atomic nuclei unite to form a single, heavier nucleus

nuclear reactor: device for producing heat from a fissionable material, such as uranium or plutonium, through a controlled chain reaction

nuclear shell model: model of the atomic nucleus showing nuclear particles at different energy levels within the nucleus

octane number: unit for measuring the uniformity of burning inside a combustion engine; performance rating for gasoline

ohm: unit for measuring electrical resistance

Ohm's law: the ratio of the potential difference applied to a closed circuit and the current in the circuit is a constant; $I = V/R$

optics: science dealing with the nature and properties of light

orbital: electron path within an energy level or shell of an atom

orbital velocity: the velocity a satellite must attain to enable it to orbit

organic chemistry: study of carbon and its compounds

paper chromatography: a method of separating closely related compounds using paper and solvent

parabola: a curved line representing the path of a projectile

parabolic mirror: mirror curved in the shape of a parabola

parallel circuit: a circuit in which two or more conductors are connected across two common points in the circuit to provide separate conducting paths for the current

paramagnetic: attracted by a magnetic field

paramagnetism: magnetism produced by unpaired electrons

Pronunciation Key

ae . . . bake

ah . . . father

a . . . back

ee . . . easy

e . . . less

eu . . . few

ie . . . life

i . . . trip

oh . . . flow

aw . . . soft

ah . . . odd

oo . . . food

uh . . . foot

eu . . . cube

u . . . up

y . . . yet

j . . . judge

k . . . cake

s . . . sew

th . . . thin

Pascal's law: if pressure is applied to a liquid in a closed container, the pressure is transmitted unchanged to all surfaces of the container

perigee (per' i jee): point in orbit of satellite nearest the earth

periodic law: when atoms are arranged in order of increasing atomic number, there is a periodic repetition of similar properties

periodic table: an arrangement of the chemical elements, according to their atomic numbers, in vertical columns having similar properties and horizontal columns showing shifts in properties

permanent magnet: substance that remains magnetized for a long time after the magnetizing force has been removed

pH: measure of hydrogen ion concentration in a solution

photochemical smog: substance that forms in the atmosphere as a result of the action of sunlight on airborne pollution

photoconductor: a metal whose electrical conductivity is controlled by light

photoelectric cell: a device containing a photoelectric metal which produces an electrical current when struck by light

photoelectric effect: characteristic of certain metals, such as cesium, to give off electrons when struck by light

photon (foh' tahn): a quantum or package of light energy

physical change: change in size, shape, or form without a change in composition

physical property: characteristic of a material which may be observed without the substance interacting with another substance

pitch: tone of a sound wave, determined by the frequency of the wave, the greater frequency, the higher pitch; distance from any point on the thread of a screw to the corresponding point on an adjacent thread measured parallel to the axis

plane mirror: mirror with a flat surface

plasma: state of matter in which electrons are stripped from their atoms

plastic: material that can be shaped by moulding it when it is soft and allowing it to harden

polar: having regions of positive and negative charge

polarized light: light in which all waves are vibrating in a single plane

polyatomic ion: ion containing two or more elements

polymer: large molecule formed from the combination of smaller units or molecules

polymerization (pol' i mer i zae shun): process in which a large molecule is formed from the combination of smaller units or molecules

positron (poz' i tron): particle having the mass of an electron and a positive charge

power: amount of work done per unit time

precipitate: a solid that separates from a solution

pressure: force applied per unit area

principal axis: a line straight out from the center of a mirror or lens through the focus

principal focus: a point to which rays parallel to the principal axis converge, or from which they diverge, after reflection or refraction

prism: transparent material with two straight, nonparallel surfaces

projectile (prah jek' til): object such as a stone, ball, bullet, or rocket which is thrown or shot

program: set of instructions fed into a computer

proton: positively charged particle in the nucleus of an atom

pyrometer (pi rahm' ah tur): a thermometer, containing a thermocouple, used to measure very high temperatures

radiation (raed ee ae' shun): energy released from atoms and molecules as they undergo internal change; process of emission and transmission of radiant heat

radioactive isotope: form of an element which emits radioactive radiation

radioactivity: emitting of high-energy radiation from nuclei of radioactive atoms

rate: relationship between two quantities

Pronunciation Key

ae . . . bake

ah . . . father

a . . . back

ee . . . easy

e . . . less

eu . . . few

ie . . . life

i . . . trip

oh . . . flow

aw . . . soft

ah . . . odd

oo . . . food

uh . . . foot

eu . . . cube

u . . . up

y . . . yet

j . . . judge

k . . . cake

s . . . sew

th . . . thin

reactants: substances which react in a chemical change

real image: an image which can be projected on a surface

rectifier (rek' ta fi er): device for changing alternating current to direct current

reflecting telescope: a telescope whose magnification is produced by a parabolic mirror

reflection (ri flek' shun): wave or ray striking and bouncing off a surface

refracting telescope: a telescope whose magnification is produced by convex lenses

refraction (ri frak' shun): bending of a wave or ray, caused by a decrease in speed as it passes from one substance into another

resistance (ri zis' tans): any opposition which slows down or prevents motion; opposition to the flow of electricity

resonance (rez' oh naens): vibrations of a natural rate in matter, induced by a vibrating source having the same or a simply related frequency

resultant force: a force produced by the effects of two or more forces

ring compound: organic compound in which carbon atoms are joined in the shape of a ring

ripple tank: shallow, transparent waterproof box containing a layer of water about one centimeter deep

roentgen (rent' gun): unit of high-energy, ionizing radiation; amount of radiation that will produce 2.08×10^9 pairs of negative and positive ions

salt: ionic compound produced in a neutralization reaction; compound containing a positive ion from a base and a negative ion from an acid

satellite: a body moving in orbit around another body

saturated (sach' u raet ed): solution in which the solvent has dissolved the maximum amount of solute at a given temperature

saturated hydrocarbon: hydrocarbon in which each carbon atom is bonded to four other atoms

scale: relative dimensions of a drawing or model; instrument used to measure weight

scientific law: accepted statement of fact based on scientific evidence

scintillation (sin tu lae' shun) **counter:** instrument used to detect radioactivity through the production of flashes of light (scintillations) in a material

semiconductor: material with a resistance between that of a conductor and an insulator

series circuit: electric circuit in which the parts are connected to provide a single conducting path for the current

single replacement reaction: chemical change in which an uncombined or free element replaces an element combined in a compound

solid: form of matter having a definite volume and shape

solute (sol' oot): substance dissolved in a solvent, forming a solution

solution: mixture containing a solute dissolved in a solvent

solvent (sol' vunt): substance in which a solute is dissolved, forming a solution

sound waves: compressional waves produced by vibrations

specific heat: the quantity of heat needed to raise the temperature of a given mass of material one degree

speed: distance traveled per unit time

standard solution: solution whose concentration is known exactly

static electricity: non-moving electrical charge

structural formula: formula showing the symbols of atoms in a molecule of a compound and how they are bonded

sublimation: the change of state from a solid to a gas

substituted hydrocarbon: organic compound in which one or more hydrogen atoms in a hydrocarbon have been replaced with another kind of atom

supersaturated solution: a solution containing more solute than the amount it would normally take to saturate it at a given temperature

symmetry (sim' ah tree): similarity of form or arrangement on either side of a dividing line, plane, or point

Pronunciation
Key

ae ... bake

ah ... father

a ... back

ee ... easy

e ... less

eu ... few

ie ... life

i ... trip

oh ... flow

aw ... soft

ah ... odd

oo ... food

uh ... foot

eu ... cube

u ... up

y ... yet

j ... judge

k ... cake

s ... sew

th ... thin

synthesis reaction: chemical change in which two or more elements or compounds unite to form one compound

technology (tek nahl' i jee): application of science for practical purposes

temperature: the degree of hotness or coldness of a body, as measured by a thermometer

theory: an explanation based on available facts

thermal pollution: release of heated water into lakes and streams

thermionic emission (thurm i ahn' ik • i mish' n): loss of electrons by heated metals

thermocouple (thur' mo kup 1): two different metals twisted or bonded together at two separate points, with one point placed in a cold material and the other point heated

thermonuclear reaction: nuclear fusion reaction occurring at millions of degrees temperature

tide: periodic, rhythmic movement of matter in a body

titration (tie trae' shun): laboratory procedure in which a neutralization reaction is used to determine the concentration of acids or bases

transistor: semiconductor used as a substitute for vacuum tubes in electronic equipment

transition metals: elements located in the B columns of the periodic table

transmutation (tranz meu tae' shun): natural or artificial process in which one element changes into another element by changing its number of protons

transverse (trans' vurs) **wave**: wave in which matter vibrates at right angles to the direction in which the wave travels

triode: electric vacuum tube containing a filament, plate, and grid

trough: valley of a wave

unsaturated: solution containing less solute than the amount it would take to saturate it at a given temperature

Pronunciation
Key

ae . . . bake

ah . . . father

a . . . back

ee . . . easy

e . . . less

eu . . . few

ie . . . life

i . . . trip

oh . . . flow

aw . . . soft

ah . . . odd

oo . . . food

uh . . . foot

eu . . . cube

u . . . up

y . . . yet

j . . . judge

k . . . cake

s . . . sew

th . . . thin

unsaturated hydrocarbon: hydrocarbon in which two or more carbon atoms are joined by double or triple bonds

vacuum tube: a gas-tight envelope, usually of glass, from which air is removed to form a vacuum

valence: combining capacity of an element or an ion in forming a compound

van der Waals forces: small attractive forces between atoms caused by the attraction of the positively charged nucleus in one atom to the negatively charged electron cloud in another atom

vector: ray used to represent the quantity and direction of force

velocity (ve lahs' et ee): speed and direction of a moving body

virtual image: an image which cannot be projected on a surface

visible light spectrum: band of colors produced when white light is passed through a prism

volt (v): unit of electromotive force

voltmeter: an instrument used to measure the potential difference between two points in an electric circuit

volume: the measure of the amount of space which matter occupies

watt(w): metric unit of power; 746 watts equal 1 horsepower

watt-hour: unit used to measure electric power in a unit of time

wave: rhythmic disturbance which travels through space and matter

wavelength: distance from the crest of one wave to the crest of the next wave

weight: measurement of gravity force

wet cell: produces electric current from two metals and a chemical solution

work: product of force exerted multiplied by the distance moved

X ray: invisible electromagnetic radiation of great penetrating power

INDEX

INDEX